C'EST À TOI!

Level Three

About the Cover

First Love, the painting on the cover of the third level of *C'est à toi!*, is another original acrylic created expressly for this series by Kelly Stribling Sutherland. Reminiscent of *The Birthday* by the Russian-born French artist Marc Chagall, a man offers a bouquet of flowers to his girlfriend. Swept away with his expression of love, she floats through the air. As your class studies French art in Unit 3, you may want to have them compare this painting with the fantasy done by Chagall. Both portray a moment of celebration with unique imagery, depicting passion with a swirling, upward movement and bright blocks of pure color. The surrealism in *The Birthday* has been made even more whimsical by Ms. Sutherland's addition of two well-known nursery rhyme characters: the cat with the fiddle and the cow jumping over the moon.

C'EST À TOI!

Level Three

Annotated Teacher's Edition

Authors

Augusta DeSimone Clark

Richard Ladd

Sarah Vaillancourt

Diana Moen

EMC/Paradigm Publishing, Saint Paul, Minnesota

ISBN 0-8219-1704-8

Published by EMC/Paradigm Publishing
875 Montreal Way
St. Paul, Minnesota 55102
800-328-1452
www.emcp.com
E-mail: educate@emcp.com

Printed in the United States of America
2 3 4 5 6 7 8 9 10 XXX 04 03 02 01 00 99

Contents

SCOPE AND SEQUENCE CHART

Unité	Leçon	Fonctions	Vocabulaire
1 *La vie scolaire et les passe-temps*	A	inquiring about the past describing past events sequencing events summarizing inquiring about ability expressing inability giving examples confirming a known fact	school subjects school supplies
	B	giving orders explaining something giving examples offering something expressing astonishment and disbelief expressing enthusiasm expressing emotions expressing desire	amusement parks sports
2 *Les rapports humains*	A	asking for information expressing astonishment and disbelief expressing ridicule telling a story describing how things were telling how you were describing physical traits describing temperament	adjectives
	B	writing a letter telling a story explaining something expressing emotions expressing concern expressing suspicion apologizing expressing satisfaction	office workers reflexive verbs

3
Les arts
	A	inquiring about likes and dislikes
		expressing likes and dislikes
		listing
		stating a generalization
		stating a preference
		expressing need and necessity
		inquiring about opinions
		giving opinions
			movies
			art
			expressions dealing with:
			  Daniel Auteuil
			  Marguerite Duras
			  Céline Dion
			  Angélique Kidjo
			  Maurice Jarre
			  Camille Claudel
			  Gustave Caillebotte

	B	asking about importance and unimportance expressing importance and unimportance inquiring about agreement and disagreement giving opinions inquiring about surprise comparing inquiring about possibility and impossibility expressing possibility and impossibility expressing need and necessity telling location	movies entertainment expressions

Enquête Culturelle	Structure	Sur la bonne piste
Senegal education in Senegal education in France school supplies	present tense of regular verbs ending in *-er*, *-ir* and *re* present tense of irregular verbs interrogative pronouns direct object pronouns: *me, te, le, la, nous, vous, les* indirect object pronouns: *me, te, lui, nous, vous, leur*	writing a composition
La Ronde in Montreal cafés *le Carnaval* sports in Quebec	*passé composé* with *avoir* *passé composé* with *être* the pronoun *y* the pronoun *en* double object pronouns	review of reading strategies "La plage, c'est chouette" Sempé/Goscinny
passports travel tips *le métro*	imperfect tense present participle	narrating
international travel airports European Union French police Georges Simenon	reflexive verbs negation other negative expressions	creating mental images "Déjeuner du matin" "Le Cancre" Jacques Prévert
TV	the imperfect and the *passé composé* present tense of the irregular verb *plaire* the subjunctive of regular verbs after *il faut que*	explaining in detail
entertainment guides movies	*c'est* vs. *il/elle est* the subjunctive of irregular verbs the subjunctive after impersonal expressions	characterization *Au revoir, les enfants* Louis Malle

Unité	Leçon	Fonctions	Vocabulaire
4 *Le monde du travail*	A	writing a letter expressing desire stating want expressing hope stating a preference describing talents and abilities evaluating making requests expressing that you expect a positive response expressing appreciation	adjectives want ads business letters
	B	interviewing giving opinions expressing disagreement explaining a problem inquiring about certainty and uncertainty expressing certainty and uncertainty expressing intentions sequencing events	unemployment

5
Comment se débrouiller en voyage
	A	expressing likes and dislikes
		agreeing and disagreeing
		expressing surprise
		giving opinions
		expressing fear
		inquiring about possibility and
		   impossibility
		controlling the volume of a
		   conversation
		expressing dissatisfaction
		expressing regret
		making requests
		expressing happiness
		telling location
			hotel expressions

	B	writing postcards telling location telling a story remembering describing people you remember indicating knowing and not knowing identifying objects expressing complaint admitting expressing patience	airplane expressions train expressions

Enquête Culturelle	Structure	Sur la bonne piste
women in the work force young adults and jobs preparing for a job	*depuis* + present tense the subjunctive after expressions of wish, will or desire	writing a résumé
working conditions workers' benefits unemployment	the relative pronouns *qui* and *que* the relative pronouns *ce qui* and *ce que* the subjunctive after expressions of doubt or uncertainty	deciphering want ads
classifying hotels Saint-Martin	conditional tense the subjunctive after expressions of emotion	telling a story through pictures
Gaspé Peninsula *le Rocher Percé* *le Parc de l'Île-Bonaventure-et- du-Rocher-Percé* American vs. European trains	verbs + *de* + nouns the relative pronoun *dont*	satire *La cantatrice chauve* Eugène Ionesco

Unité	Leçon	Fonctions	Vocabulaire
6 *L'avenir: la technologie et l'environnement*	A	giving information sequencing events listing explaining something giving opinions expressing probability predicting	space technology computers
	B	asking for information giving information sequencing events giving opinions expressing enthusiasm hypothesizing predicting congratulating and commiserating expressing appreciation forgetting making requests	social problems newspaper expressions
7 *Les Français comme ils sont*	A	asking for information stating a generalization explaining something comparing requesting clarification inquiring about opinions expressing surprise inquiring about satisfaction and dissatisfaction proposing solutions	*la cité*
	B	asking about preference stating preference clarifying reporting comparing expressing importance and unimportance agreeing and disagreeing describing character expressing compassion	adjectives

8
L'histoire de France
	A	describing past events
		using links
		sequencing events
		explaining something
		having something done
		describing character
		stating a generalization
		boasting
		expressing appreciation
			expressions dealing with:
			  Vercingétorix
			  Charlemagne
			  Guillaume le Conquérant
			  Louis IX

	B	describing past events
		stating factual information
		sequencing events
		expressing obligation
		expressing incapability
		expressing criticism
		stating a preference
			expressions dealing with:
			  Catherine de Médicis
			  Louis XVI
			  le marquis de La Fayette
			  Georges Haussmann

Enquête Culturelle	Structure	Sur la bonne piste
le TGV *l'Eurostar* *l'Agence spatiale européenne* *le Minitel* computers	comparative of adjectives superlative of adjectives future tense	using computer technology
la Fondation Brigitte Bardot *Médecins Sans Frontières* *l'Équipe Cousteau*	future tense in sentences with *si* future tense after *quand*	figures of speech rhyme scheme "Comme un Arbre" Maxime LeForestier
Togo *les HLM* *les allocations familiales* immigrants in France	conditional tense in sentences with *si* the interrogative adjective *quel* the interrogative pronoun *lequel*	circumlocuting
fast-food restaurants French restaurant chains family structure *le franglais* French department stores	demonstrative adjectives demonstrative pronouns	setting *Les petits enfants du siècle* Christiane Rochefort
Jules César *Astérix* Dijon *La Chanson de Roland* *la tapisserie de Bayeux* *les croisades*	expressions with *faire* *faire* + infinitive	summarizing a literary selection

Huguenots
Nostradamus
Marie-Antoinette
the French and American
    Revolutions
Benjamin Franklin
Pierre L'Enfant
	expressions with *avoir*
	past infinitive
		research strategies
		Le Bourgeois gentilhomme
		    Molière

Unité	Leçon	Fonctions	Vocabulaire
9 *L'Afrique francophone*	A	describing past events asking what something is identifying objects telling location reminding expressing indifference expressing disappointment expressing enthusiasm boasting	African wildlife African housing
	B	writing a letter telling a story describing past events sequencing events using links giving information expressing ownership comparing	African game African landscape
10 *On s'adapte*	A	inquiring about health and welfare giving information describing character inquiring about capability asking for help expressing displeasure agreeing and disagreeing comparing accepting and refusing an invitation expressing gratitude terminating a conversation	hospital expressions injuries pharmacy expressions
	B	describing past events asking for permission expressing confirmation admitting asking for a price estimating hypothesizing agreeing and disagreeing expressing emotions expressing disappointment making suggestions	shopping electronic equipment

Enquête Culturelle	Structure	Sur la bonne piste
Niger *le musée national de Niamey*	expressions with *être* pluperfect tense	comparing and contrasting
Mali Oumou Sangaré	possessive adjectives possessive pronouns	cultural inferences *Trois Prétendants, un Mari* Guillaume Oyônô-Mbia
Fontainebleau soccer *le SAMU* the Good Samaritan law pharmacies	expressions of quantity indefinite adjectives indefinite pronouns	persuading
le Midi Avignon	past conditional tense past conditional tense in sentences with *si*	reading instructions

Introduction

C'est à toi! is a totally new three-level French program that has been developed in response to needs expressed by teachers throughout the country who are looking for the latest in a communication-based, functional approach to teaching French language and culture. Based on detailed surveys involving hundreds of experienced educators and information gleaned from focus groups conducted in various parts of the country, *C'est à toi!* offers an innovative, creative approach to meeting the needs of students in the twenty-first century.

C'est à toi! was designed to address the goals expressed in the National Foreign Language Standards:

Communication — Engaging in both oral and written communication, students ask for and give information, express their feelings, and present their ideas on a variety of topics.
Culture — Students develop a sensitivity to, understanding of, and appreciation for the daily activities of a variety of culture groups in the francophone world.
Connections — As a result of cross-curricular activities and references, students learn more about other disciplines and how they relate to the French language and culture.
Comparisons — Through critical thinking activities, students learn more about the nature of language and culture as they explore the relationship between French and their native language and discover similarities and differences between francophone culture and their own.
Communities — Students use French both in the school environment and in their personal lives for enjoyment and enrichment.

C'est à toi! features a fresh approach to function-based communication. Written by four experienced high school French teachers, the *C'est à toi!* program provides a realistic balance among all five skill areas that will develop proficiency in each one. Paired, small group, and cooperative group activities are at the heart of today's student-centered classroom. In the *C'est à toi!* program, students assume a more active role in their learning, working with each other to accomplish linguistic tasks, with teachers serving primarily as facilitators.

The comprehensive *C'est à toi!* program, composed of the textbook and its fully integrated set of additional components, offers instructors and students the most complete materials possible to teach and learn French. The accompanying ancillaries may be used as enrichment, additional practice, or reinforcement. These tailor-made materials, which fit individual students' needs and learning styles, include the annotated teacher's edition, workbook, assessment program (with quizzes, tests, and portfolio assessment), audiocassette/CD program, teacher's resource kit, video program, and overhead transparencies. One of the greatest challenges that teachers face today is reaching students with varying abilities, backgrounds, interests, and learning styles. The extensive instructional program of *C'est à toi!* recognizes, anticipates, and provides for these differences.

About This Annotated Teacher's Edition

The front section of this Annotated Teacher's Edition contains:

- a Scope and Sequence Chart that gives a complete overview of each unit in *C'est à toi!*
- a description of each section of the textbook along with a list of the other *C'est à toi!* components
- relevant information about the program's authors
- philosophy of proficiency, culture, structure, and reading
- the *C'est à toi!* program's philosophy and learning strategies that are incorporated in the textbook
- a list of practical classroom expressions (**Expressions de communication**)
- a list of all the communicative functions covered in *C'est à toi! Level Three* and the units in which they are practiced
- a unit-by-unit list of all the active French vocabulary (with English equivalents) introduced in the third-level textbook

The annotated version of the expanded student textbook contains:

- correlations of ancillary materials to the textbook

    a. **Workbook Activity**

    b. **Audiocassette/CD Activity**

    c. **Transparency**

    d. **Listening Activity**

    e. **Quiz**

    f. **Advanced Placement**

- answers to both oral and written activities (except where answers are personalized)
- cultural notes (information that may be useful to teachers and interesting to students)
- additional background information
- linguistic and pronunciation notes
- teaching suggestions
  a. paired activities
  b. cooperative group practice
  c. TPR
  d. critical thinking skills
  e. cross-curricular activities
  f. games
  g. activities for students with multiple intelligences
  h. ideas for modifying and expanding activities

Components

C'est à toi! is a comprehensive three-level French language program written to meet the needs of French students as they enter the twenty-first century. The third-level program includes the following components:

- Textbook
- Annotated Teacher's Edition
- Workbook
- Workbook Teacher's Edition
- Teacher's Resource Kit
    - Additional Listening Activities
    - Additional Listening Activities Teacher's Edition
    - Audiocassettes/CDs with Additional Listening Activities
    - Workbook Teacher's Edition
    - Audiocassette/CD Program Manual
- Audiocassette/CD Program
    - Audiocassettes/CDs
    - Audiocassette/CD Program Manual
- Assessment Program
    - Lesson Quizzes
    - Lesson Quizzes Teacher's Edition
    - Unit Tests Booklet
    - Unit Tests Booklet Teacher's Edition
    - Unit Tests Audiocassettes/CDs
    - Portfolio Assessment with Proficiency Tests
- Video Program
    - Videos
    - Video Manual
- Overhead Transparencies

Textbook

This totally new textbook contains 10 **unités**. Each **unité** is composed of two **leçons**, labeled **A** and **B**. At the end of the textbook you will find a grammar summary, an end vocabulary section (French/English and English/French), and a grammar index. All the **unités** have been designed in a similar manner so that students will be familiar with the format and know exactly what to expect. Each lesson gives students the communicative functions, vocabulary, structures, and cultural information necessary to communicate in authentic French about a variety of everyday situations that interest teenagers. The entire textbook's active vocabulary is less than 900 words, and grammatical structures are recycled systematically to help students bridge from the known to the unknown.

Unit Opener — The unit begins with a list of communicative functions. This provides a preview of the tasks that students will be able to accomplish when they complete the unit. Functions are continually recycled from one unit to the next, with functions repeated only when a different way of expressing that specific function is introduced. A two-page photo or collage visually prepares students for one of the main cultural components of the unit.

Lesson Opener — Each lesson begins with a list of the communicative functions that pertain to that lesson. Colorful illustrations introduce all the new vocabulary groups and expressions in the lesson in a meaningful context. Students should be told that illustrations in the lesson opener are part of the basic textbook material, visually explaining words and expressions that students are expected to know.

Tes empreintes ici — This section, new in the third-level textbook, follows the list of communicative functions in **Leçon A**. It offers introductory, personalized questions intended to motivate students and connect them with the unit's topic(s). This section encourages students to compare and contrast their experiences with those they will read about.

Dossier ouvert — Also new in the third-level textbook, this section presents a cultural "teaser" to challenge students to interact and problem solve in an authentic cultural situation in the francophone world. Students answer a multiple-choice question about how they would react in the given situation. (Its answer and explanation are given in the **Dossier fermé** section at the end of the unit.)

Dialogue — Next comes a dialogue, letter, postcard, journal entry or reading that follows a natural format and dramatizes a situation typical of everyday life in francophone regions. Speakers represent a cross section of age groups, although the emphasis is on activities of teenagers. The dialogue is introduced with a colorful illustration that reinforces the cultural content and makes each situation more meaningful. The dialogue contains an example of how each one of the lesson's communicative functions is expressed. (This is summarized for students in the **Communication active** section in the **C'est à moi!** review section at the end of every unit.) Each dialogue has been carefully designed not only to present authentic speech but also to contain at least one instance in which each of the new structures in the lesson is used. All words in the dialogue are active vocabulary; that is, students are expected to produce the words in **Pratique** and **Communication** activities and use them again in following units. To understand the lesson's new vocabulary words, students can look back at the introductory illustrations or photos, refer to the glossary following the exposition, or infer meaning from the context. Previously learned words and structures are regularly recycled.

Activités — Following the exposition is a series of activities that checks comprehension of its content and new vocabulary that has been presented either visually or in context. Following the comprehension activities, students are challenged to answer personalized questions dealing with the exposition's theme in the **C'est à toi!** activity. All of these activities may be done orally, in writing, or both.

Enquête culturelle — Directly after the *Activités*, a group of notes highlights certain cultural subtleties or presents more detailed information about the French-speaking world. These notes are not related to each other; they refer to various sentences in the exposition and expand upon the information presented there. These comments are intended to heighten students' interest in, appreciation for, and understanding of certain aspects of francophone culture and to provide insight into the daily activities of French speakers. Accompanying photos help to expand students' cultural horizons. Comprehension questions and realia-based activities help students apply what they have learned.

Journal personnel — This is another new section in the third-level textbook. Students record their observations about specific aspects of francophone culture, note similarities and differences between it and their own, and reflectively compare them, writing either in French or English.

Structure — This section presents the lesson's main grammatical topics in a concise, clear manner. Examples in French are presented along with their English equivalents to help students' comprehension. Colorful charts provide reinforcement as do photo captions that illustrate how the specific structures are used in context.

Pratique — Following the presentation of each grammar topic is the **Pratique** section, composed of contextualized activities that allow students to practice both oral and written skills. Realistic situations as a basis for the activities make students' communication more relevant. You may choose whether students respond orally, in writing, or both. The more mechanical activities precede those that allow students more creativity or are open-ended. The type of activities in the **Pratique** section varies—those

based on visual cues and realia, dehydrated sentences, paired activities, and sentence completion. The **Modèle**, in the side margin, demonstrates a correct response to help students succeed immediately.

Communication — A group of proficiency-based activities appears at the end of each lesson following the last **Structure** and **Pratique** sections. These activities provide opportunities for students to develop oral and written proficiency using the functions that are presented in each lesson. Task-based paired and cooperative learning activities as well as activities that encourage the development of multiple intelligences foster the creative use of French to practice using the lesson's vocabulary and structures to express specific functions. For example, students may be asked to write lists, design invitations and menus, order at a restaurant, conduct surveys and interviews, label photos, do role-plays, write postcards and faxes, make posters and drawings, give directions, or review films.

Sur la bonne piste — There are two **Sur la bonne piste** sections in each unit of the third-level textbook. They highlight various reading, writing, and oral communication strategies in French. Techniques for successfully completing tasks associated with college placement exams are also included. The section in **Leçon A** focuses on strategies for successful function-based oral and written communication. For example, students learn how to write compositions and résumés, circumlocute, and tell stories using visual cues. The section in **Leçon B** features specific strategies appropriate to third-level reading selections. Each unit focuses on a different literary technique to help students experience success as they read in French. Students are carefully guided before and as they read authentic French texts (stories, poems, excerpts from plays, screenplays, and novels) so that they can apply the strategies presented in each unit. Various activities follow, some calling for specific answers and others calling for critical thinking and interpretation. The Annotated Teacher's Edition gives suggestions on how to holistically grade these answers.

Dossier fermé — Students "uncover" the answer and explanation to the cultural "teaser" presented earlier in the **Dossier ouvert** section.

C'est à moi! — The first of the four-part review section at the end of each unit, **C'est à moi!** consists of a personalized checklist of all the functions that have been introduced in the unit. If students are unsure of how to express a certain function, they should look for an example of it in the following **Communication active** section. **C'est à moi!** also has a true-false quiz on the cultural information presented in the unit's **Enquêtes culturelles**.

Communication orale — This cumulative oral proficiency activity usually takes the form of a paired role-play. Students are carefully guided as to what each partner should include in the conversation. The activity combines all the elements in the unit — functions, topics, vocabulary, and structures — into one final, contextualized situation.

Communication écrite — This cumulative proficiency-based writing activity is the written equivalent of the **Communication orale**. Again, students are carefully guided as to what they should include in their postcards, journal entries, reports, letters, and newspaper articles.

Communication active — The final part of the review section summarizes all of the unit's communicative functions. Along with each function are the phrases used in the unit to express each language task. English equivalents are also given for easy reference. The words in boldface type are the invariable elements; those not in bold may change depending on the specific information that students want to express.

Grammar Summary — This useful reference section summarizes for students' convenience the structures introduced in all three levels of *C'est à toi!* Present tense forms of all irregular verbs are also included.

Vocabulary — All words and expressions introduced as active vocabulary in all three levels of *C'est à toi!* appear in this end vocabulary. The number following the meaning of each word or expression indicates the unit in which it appears for the first time in this book. For convenient and flexible use, both French-English and English-French vocabularies are included. Passive vocabulary found in the direction lines to activities and in authentic readings is not included.

Grammar Index — A complete index of all the grammar points covered in the third level of *C'est à toi!* is provided for easy reference and location.

Annotated Teacher's Edition

This Annotated Teacher's Edition contains a front section and an annotated version of the student textbook.

Front Section:
- Scope and Sequence Chart
- description of all the program's components
- information about the authors
- philosophy of proficiency, culture, structure, and reading
- program philosophy and learning strategies
- classroom expressions
- communicative functions
- unit-by-unit active vocabulary

Annotated Version of the Student Textbook:
- correlations of ancillary materials to the textbook
- answers to both oral and written activities
- cultural notes
- additional background information
- linguistic and pronunciation notes
- teaching suggestions (paired activities, cooperative group practice, TPR, critical thinking skills, cross-curricular activities, activities to engage students' multiple intelligences, games)

Workbook

The workbook reviews and expands upon the material covered in the textbook with additional written exercises that reinforce students' language skills and cultural awareness. These innovative activities help students become proficient in written French as they further practice the functions, vocabulary, and structures in each unit. The workbook also recombines previously learned language concepts to broaden students' understanding. Again, many of these activities are written situationally to make them more realistic and relevant to students. Realia-based activities prepare students to use French in authentic situations. Exercises in the workbook are carefully coordinated with the textbook. The Annotated Teacher's Edition contains icons that tell where each workbook activity best fits in.

Workbook Teacher's Edition

An answer key for all exercises contained in the workbook is available.

Teacher's Resource Kit

The Teacher's Resource Kit contains a variety of useful and practical tools to help teachers make their daily lesson plans. The following components are included in the Teacher's Resource Kit:

- **Additional Listening Activities (on blackline duplicating masters)**

  There are three additional listening comprehension activities in each unit, one for each lesson and a cumulative activity. They check students' ability to understand authentic French speech in the form of narratives or dialogues. Students have an answer sheet on which they respond in writing either by completing a checklist or by answering true-false, multiple-choice, or matching questions. These activities help to prepare students for the listening comprehension sections of the Unit Tests in the Assessment Program. The Annotated Teacher's Edition contains icons that tell where each listening activity best fits in.

- **Additional Listening Activities Teacher's Edition**

  The complete text for the recorded additional listening activities as well as an answer key is available.

- **Audiocassettes/CDs with Additional Listening Activities**

  These audiocassettes/CDs contain the additional listening activities for each unit.

- **Workbook Teacher's Edition**

  An answer key for all exercises contained in the workbook is available.

- **Audiocassette/CD Program Manual**

  This manual contains the complete script of the recorded material (introduction of new words and expressions, **Dialogue**, **Pratique**, and **Sur la bonne piste** sections) for each lesson in the textbook.

Audiocassette/CD Program

The various components included in the Audiocassette/CD Program are:

- **Audiocassettes/CDs**

  The Audiocassette/CD Program is an integral part of *C'est à toi!* Appropriate icons in the Annotated Teacher's Edition designate which material in the textbook has been recorded on cassettes or CDs by native speakers of all ages from a variety of francophone countries. Recorded material in each unit includes:

  Introduction of new words and expressions (for student repetition)
  Dialogue (recorded as a listening experience)
  Pratique (selected activities for student response)
  Sur la bonne piste (recorded as a listening experience)

- **Audiocassette/CD Program Manual**

  This manual contains the complete script of the recorded material (introduction of new words and expressions, **Dialogue**, **Pratique**, and **Sur la bonne piste** sections) for each lesson in the textbook.

Assessment Program

The *C'est à toi!* Assessment Program contains the following components:

- **Lesson Quizzes**

  There are two quizzes for each unit, one at the end of every lesson. Each quiz consists of four sections: speaking (role-playing activities or personalized questions), vocabulary, grammar (both mastery and proficiency activities), and culture. These quizzes provide students with excellent practice before they take the unit test. Appropriate icons in the Annotated Teacher's Edition designate at what point in the lesson the quiz may be given.

- **Lesson Quizzes Teacher's Edition**

  A complete answer key for the Lesson Quizzes is available.

- **Unit Tests Booklet**

  The Unit Tests in the *C'est à toi!* program evaluate to what degree students are attaining the program's goals and objectives. A unique format in assessment allows teachers to design tests that evaluate what they have taught in the way they have taught it. Teachers may choose to use whatever sections reflect their students' learning styles and their teaching style: vocabulary, structure, proficiency writing, culture, listening, speaking, and reading. For example, to evaluate students' speaking ability, teachers can choose a paired activity or a teacher/student interview.

- **Unit Tests Booklet Teacher's Edition**

  The Teacher's Edition of the Unit Tests Booklet contains the text of the material recorded for the listening comprehension section and answer keys to the listening comprehension section and written sections (vocabulary, structure, proficiency writing, culture, speaking, and reading) of each Unit Test.

- **Unit Tests Audiocassettes/CDs**

  The Unit Tests Audiocassettes/CDs evaluate students' listening comprehension. Students hear authentic French in conversations or narratives and respond by choosing the best answer or continuation to the conversation. They may also see a visual and respond by choosing the best answer to a related question.

- **Portfolio Assessment with Proficiency Tests**

  The first section of the *C'est à toi!* Portfolio Assessment is a rationale for using portfolios in the French class and tips on how to implement this form of evaluation. Next comes a variety of forms for both students and teachers to complete, such as a learner profile, peer evaluation sheet, communicative functions checklist, and suggested rubrics for evaluating oral and written production. The final section contains a proficiency-based exam evaluating all five skills for use at the end of the first semester, and another for use at the end of the year.

Video Program

The various components included in the Video Program are:

- **Videos**

  As its name suggests, "Trois minutes, s'il vous plaît," the new video program coordinated with the third-level textbook, contains 20 short episodes each about three minutes long. Using professional actors and a clever, amusing concept, the video series helps students expand upon and review basic vocabulary, structures, and functions as they see and hear situations related to themes in the textbook. A subtitled version in French follows each episode. The segments include:

  - *La famille* — A young woman who is about to be married has a father who paints family portraits. She shows them to her fiancé, who is not impressed.
  - *Bonjour* — A man and woman, both strangers waiting for a bus, communicate by cell phone.
  - *Au café* — A man and woman meet by chance at a café, and she leaves without paying her bill.
  - *Les vêtements* — As a girl gets ready to go to a party, her father and boyfriend comment on what she is wearing.
  - *En boîte* — Two young adults meet at a disco and start dancing together.
  - *Rendez-vous* — A young man is looking at the personal ads on the Minitel. He arranges to meet a girl, but is she really the one who placed the ad?
  - *À l'hôtel* — The night desk clerk at a hotel has a famous, unexpected guest. Is he dreaming?
  - *Entre amis* — A man starts up a conversation with a woman about the guests at the party they are at. But he doesn't know that she's the hostess.
  - *Ça ne va pas?* — A boy is sick, must stay in bed, and can't go out with his girlfriend. He doesn't know that she is sick as well.
  - *Au boulot* — When a father returns home from work, he tells his family that he has just been laid off. His son comes home with news, too.
  - *En vacances* — On vacation in Normandy, a girl complains to her father about the bad weather. But the arrival of a new boy changes her mind.
  - *En voyage* — A briefcase mix-up at a hotel leads to unexpected consequences.
  - *À la télé* — A young couple discusses TV programs and has differing opinions on what to watch.
  - *Le protagoniste* — A TV performer talks to his makeup artist as she gets him ready for his show.
  - *C'est où?* — A participant in the Tour de France has lost his way. Spectators try to help by giving him directions.
  - *À la campagne* — A Parisian can't cope with life in the country when he goes to visit relatives.
  - *Quelle vie!* — An exhausted wife comes home to find her husband glued to the TV and not about to help her with the housework. Upon waking from a nap, she wonders if her dream has come true.
  - *Le gros lot* — A store owner is notified that his shop has sold the winning lotto ticket. But who bought the ticket?
  - *Le bal masqué* — Because her husband has to work, a woman goes to an elegant dance alone and meets a charming gentleman.
  - *Aux voleurs!* — Two thieves think they have been successful in their attempt at robbery, but they are interrupted by a surprise phone call.

- **Video Manual**

  The Video Manual is included in the Video Program. It contains transcripts of the video units as well as a variety of innovative viewing and post-viewing activities, some based on additional authentic materials.

Overhead Transparencies

A set of 32 full-color transparencies offers illustrations of scenes (as a stimulus for conversation), objects (with identifying overlays), realia, fine art, and maps. These transparencies provide an outstanding method of teaching, visually reinforcing, or reviewing the lesson's content in a creative, communicative manner. Students can apply their knowledge of vocabulary and culture using different visual stimuli. The Annotated Teacher's Edition contains icons that tell where each transparency best fits in.

About the Authors

Augusta DeSimone Clark has been an instructor for 20 years. She teaches French I through French Advanced Placement Language at Saint Mary's Hall in San Antonio, Texas. Clark received her M.A. degree in French Literature from the University of California, Davis. She was selected to be included in *Who's Who Among America's Teachers*, was the recipient of a Holt-DuPont Foundation grant to study and travel in France, and received the Outstanding Teacher Award from the University of Chicago. A reader for the College Board, she has also been vice president of the Alliance Française in San Antonio. Clark has served as a mentor to local teachers working to establish French language or AP programs in their schools and has led many student groups on trips to France.

Richard Ladd is an instructor of French and Spanish at Ipswich High School in Ipswich, Massachusetts, where he is department director. He has also taught at various secondary schools and colleges in Massachusetts. Ladd earned his M.A. degree in French from l'École Française, Middlebury College, and a Doctor of Arts in Foreign Language Education from the State University of New York at Stony Brook. A past president of the Massachusetts Foreign Language Association, he has given presentations at local, state, regional, and national conferences on a variety of topics, including teaching advanced placement classes, adapting lessons to the long block schedule, using children's literature in the secondary classroom, and teaching multilevel classes. Ladd has written video activities booklets and assessment programs for the French classroom. Ladd coauthored *AP French: Preparing for the Language Examination*.

Sarah Vaillancourt is French Editor at EMC/Paradigm Publishing. She is a graduate of Macalester College and the recipient of two NDEA Foreign Language Institute grants, studying in Paris, Tours, and Grenoble. She taught French I-V at East High School in Madison, Wisconsin, for 22 years where she received the Bassett Award for Excellence in Teaching. As a program administrator for various student travel organizations, she has taken high school students on more than 20 study-travel tours to Europe, Africa and Canada. Vaillancourt authored the textbooks in the series *Perspectives françaises*, and has been the editor of the textbooks and ancillary materials in the series *Le français vivant* and *C'est à toi!* She has spoken at many state, regional, and national foreign language conventions and workshops on topics such as using paired activities for proficiency, engaging students' multiple intelligences, and weaving culture through the French curriculum.

Diana Moen is Associate French Editor at EMC/Paradigm Publishing. She received her M.Ed. degree in Second Languages and Cultures from the University of Minnesota. Moen has taught French and English for 15 years in Minnesota high schools and has led student groups to France and Switzerland. She is listed in *Who's Who in the Midwest* and *Who's Who Among America's Teachers*. Moen has been awarded scholarships to study French language and francophone culture in Avignon through the American Association of Teachers of French and in Quebec through the French-Canadian Institute for Language and Culture. She has also received a Rockefeller Fellowship. As a presenter at various regional foreign language conferences, she has shared strategies for teaching the culture of French business that she developed after having completed a seminar at the École Supérieure de Commerce de Lyon.

Foreign Language Proficiency
by Toni Theisen

Proficiency as an organizing concept and as a thoughtful philosophy for second language acquisition has given our content area new life and meaning since its realization in the 1980s with the advent of the ACTFL Proficiency Guidelines. We as language instructors and facilitators are becoming more and more aware of the power, meaning, and relevancy of knowing a second language. It is an exciting time to be a part of the profession as we begin to see enrollments increase steadily. We are also encouraged by the growing number of people who value communication skills in our global society. Therefore, the *C'est à toi!* program provides a series of proficiency activities in which students can experience situations in a range of contexts that they would most likely encounter in the francophone culture. Language learners actually use French to solve language tasks.

The ACTFL Proficiency Guidelines

The ACTFL Proficiency Guidelines have given us a clearer definition of the manner and degree in which language is acquired at different levels. We now know the appropriate language tasks and the level of accuracy we can expect from our students in all language skills, ranging from novice-low to superior levels. Proficiency activities involve all language modalities—from listening and reading to speaking and writing, with culture naturally integrated into each language task. We expect novice-mid language learners to function only with limited accuracy in simple survival situations using vocabulary that deals with high-frequency phrases. For example, novice-mid students can successfully order in a café or listen to a set of directions to arrive at a given place. Language learners at the advanced level are able to function at a higher degree of accuracy in situations with a problem or twist, often using circumlocution to negotiate meaning. For example, advanced students are able to write a narrative describing a situation that occurred in the past, such as retelling the events of an accident that they might have witnessed and then relating their reaction to the situation. These guidelines help us design realistic and attainable goals for our language learners.

The Rationale for Proficiency Activities

In order for students to truly own a language, they need to be able to interact with it on successful terms. Proficiency activities act as a catalyst for authentic language use, and students begin to identify with the real purpose of language learning. This ability to interact with others using any of the skills of listening, speaking, reading, and writing, all integrated with culture, gives language learners a true sense of accomplishment in French.

Research shows that the optimum scenario for learning is actually doing or experiencing. Through lecture and passive reception, students retain only about 10 percent of the material, whereas with experiential, active learning, students can achieve a 90 percent retention rate. Learning through experience involves students in such a way that vocabulary, structures, and functions are put into long-term memory.

Responsibilities of the Learner and Teacher

When incorporating proficiency activities into a lesson, the instructor or facilitator turns over the responsibility of the cognitive learning process to the language learners. It is this opportunity to create with the language that motivates students not only to successfully complete the task, but also to do it with a certain amount of risk involved. As teachers, it is then a part of our job to encourage and effectively praise our students for taking that risk with their acquired language skills and cultural knowledge. In this process, students will discover more ways to negotiate meaning in French. They will arrive at a clear understanding of the linguistic task and all its variables.

Using Many New Strategies

Proficiency is a philosophy and not a strategy. Using proficiency as an organizing principle opens the doors to many new learning strategies. This is a great forum for the use of cooperative learning activities that encourage language learners to work together to complete a given task and to depend on and trust each other in order for the group to be successful. The use of pairs and cooperative groups has proved to be tremendously effective in foreign language classrooms. Proficiency also encourages student-centered activities in which the teacher becomes the facilitator of the language. Many instructors integrate authentic materials into their lesson plans as ways to more easily negotiate meaning. Using authentic materials, teachers have learned to change the task rather than change the text.

Proficiency links the learner with language. This real-world use of language framed in real-life situations makes learning French even more relevant. As students strive for higher and higher levels of proficiency, our country will feel more a part of the whole world. In the words of the French Canadian singer Michel Rivard, "C'est la langue de mon cœur et le cœur de ma vie." Hopefully, our students will also feel this way about French.

The Teaching of Culture
by Karla Winther Fawbush

It is impossible to understand another culture thoroughly without speaking its language. Language and culture are directly linked to each other. Words themselves have cultural connotations. For example, the word **marché** evokes an image of a bustling marketplace, the scent of flowers and spices in the air, people bumping into one another as they shop for the freshest produce, and the shouts of vendors advertising their wares. What does this say about the value of fresh food in French-speaking households? How do the colors, smells, and animation of the marketplace compare to the efficient, sterile atmosphere of the contemporary supermarkets that are springing up in many francophone countries? In what ways does the visual image of the word **marché** help students to understand the deeper aspects of both traditional and contemporary francophone culture?

Ask most students what picture comes to mind when they think of Paris, and they will usually respond "the Eiffel Tower." Built for the World's Fair in 1889, this famous landmark certainly represents the traditional view of French culture: Paris as the center for the best in art, literature, music, and architecture. Although historically valid to a point, this definition of culture must be expanded. Culture is more than the great masterpieces of one city; it is how a variety of francophone people speak and behave in everyday situations.

Communicative competency includes both linguistic and cultural proficiency. Therefore, the teaching of culture must extend to every aspect of instruction in a proficiency-based classroom. Certainly there remains a place for the formal, "big C" study of the fine arts in French civilization. Students of all levels of French can appreciate the paintings of Monet, the poems of Prévert, the music of Debussy, and the stained glass windows and flying buttresses of Chartres Cathedral. However, the definition of culture needs to extend to a more anthropological view of daily life and language in the francophone world. Why is it inappropriate to bring chrysanthemums as a gift to a dinner party in France? Why should the expression **je suis pleine** be avoided when you have had enough to eat? Why might a young person in Cameroon refer to an adult as Mama Renée or Papa Jean?

Cultural instruction should: (1) expand the study of isolated facts to include a deeper understanding of the various values, beliefs, and behavior of French speakers; (2) recognize similarities, as well as differences, among cultures; (3) help students to develop critical thinking skills so that they learn to notice details and work toward independence in novel social situations; and (4) be entwined with the language as a means of communication.

French teachers cannot be expected to be the authority on every aspect of francophone culture. Native guest speakers or teaching assistants, radio and television programs, magazines, newspapers, computer networks, videos, and other forms of realia are helpful sources of cultural information.

Moving from the identification of the various components of a cultural program to its implementation in the classroom can be done in several ways. In order to integrate culture into the study of the French language, students should be encouraged to: (1) keep a cultural notebook and make culture a component of their language portfolio; (2) reflect on their own cultural background; and (3) practice questioning and hypothesizing in order to recognize patterns that will help them interact successfully in the francophone culture. Culture engages the heart, and students are most motivated to learn French when it is taught through relevant, meaningful content.

From their first day of French, students should learn to integrate cultural information with the study of the language. By maintaining a cultural notebook, students can explore their own cultural self-awareness as they expand their appreciation of other cultures, learn to express what they have observed, examine their attitudes, and enhance their ability to make choices.

As they become exposed to various aspects of francophone culture, students need to examine their own background. For example, students can form groups to select ten items for a time capsule that would represent American culture. Or, students can compare French and American TV commercials to identify the methods used to sell various products in the two cultures. What do these methods say about the subjective values, beliefs, and behavior of these two groups? To what extent are the goals (i.e., the need for food, shelter, clothing, and education) the same in both cultures?

Students also need to utilize critical thinking skills in order to identify patterns and act appropriately in novel situations. For example, after listening to a foreign exchange student from France, American students may observe that French teenagers seem to rely on automobiles less than they do. Why? At what age do young people in various countries get their driver's license? Is gas more expensive in French-speaking countries than in the United States? Do French-speaking high school students have part-time jobs that would help them pay for the expenses of driving a car? What is public transportation like in francophone countries? Do people often walk or bike to their destination? Finding out the answers to these questions will help students learn to understand francophone culture, while realizing how much of their personal behavior stems from their own geographical and socioeconomic background.

In *C'est à toi!* culture is integrated into the study of French. Dialogues are placed in a variety of francophone settings, as a backdrop for the language itself. Cultural information corresponds to the topics and vocabulary introduced in each unit. Realia engages students to use both inductive and deductive reasoning. Teacher's notes offer supplementary cultural information and suggestions on how to make culture an integral part of each day's activities. For example, in the critical thinking activities, questions are provided that students might think about and answer in their cultural journals. Organized on the premise that awakening student interest in the diverse aspects of the francophone world can only enhance linguistic growth, *C'est à toi!* encourages students to widen their cultural horizons as they develop their proficiency in French.

Structural Practice

by Dianne Hopen

> ## Achievement = Personal Experience and Ability + Practice

Each student is the sum of his or her previous learning through a variety of educationally and noneducationally oriented situations, plus his or her ability to process new learning. Student achievement depends on the *amount of practice* available to the student in order to compensate for differing amounts of previous learning and the student's natural ability to learn.

Each of our students enters the language learning setting with a unique set of personal experiences and a differing ability to participate successfully in each new learning situation. As teachers we cannot change our students' previous experience, nor can we alter their ability to learn. What we can do is provide adequate practice.

Research on cognitive learning style preferences has validated foreign language educators' long-held belief that a variety of learning activities is necessary for students to realize their objectives in language learning. Activities that provide contextually meaningful practice are appropriate for all students. Those students with a structured approach to learning benefit the most from structured practice, but all students increase their level of confidence with such practice.

Controlled structural practice or the practice of the mechanics of a language in a contextually meaningful activity allows students to master communicative patterns that lead to the development of free-flowing speech. Students are not logically capable of responding appropriately or accurately in all language settings until they have had the opportunity to practice the functions and vocabulary relating to each particular setting.

Each time a student miscommunicates, it reinforces the importance of accuracy and serves to motivate the student to practice the structure of the language. In a learning setting where both the teacher and the student seek quality control of French for accurate communication, mechanical practice serves as one of the building blocks to success.

Identifying appropriate language components and providing varied and sufficient practice with each one is the goal of the **Structure** sections in the *C'est à toi!* program. Once students have had the opportunity to experience authentic French in realistic situations, structured practice becomes meaningful by providing increasingly more thoughtful practice with manageable portions of communication. This is how students work toward achieving their goal of communicating in French.

Reading

by Linda Klohs

Reasons for Reading

We read for two basic reasons: (1) for pleasure, and (2) for information. In order to read for pleasure, we must first understand what we are reading, that is, read for information. There are various strategies that our students can use to efficiently glean appropriate information from what they read. Unfortunately, these strategies do not come easily to many of them. It is part of our job as educators to find and teach these methods, techniques, or strategies.

Learning to Infer: Part of the Reading Act

Many students believe that they must understand each word of every sentence in order to proceed to the next one. In many real-life reading acts, this need to understand each word is not necessary. Furthermore, such dependence is self-defeating, culminating in students' reluctance or refusal to continue when they encounter new or forgotten information or structures. Students need to be encouraged to read for the main idea and to infer meaning from previous sentences or paragraphs or ones that follow.

The Role of the Student and Teacher in the Reading Process

At one time, reading was called a "passive" skill. Many still refer to it as a "receptive" skill. But it is important for students to know that reading is, in fact, an "active" skill. Students must take an active part in the reading process, constantly inferring, deducing, anticipating, guessing, predicting, checking, and asking themselves questions about the text. How we, as teachers, encourage them in this process requires us to ask a broader range of questions and accept a wider range of responses than those required by traditional multiple-choice or fill-in-the-blank tests.

Reading Progression in *C'est à toi!*

Readings in the third level of *C'est à toi!* come from original texts that are followed by achievable tasks, such as responding to content questions about an article or recognizing literary devices and interpreting poetry. The difficulty of a reading passage in authentic French depends greatly on what is required of the student after reading the text.

Assessment of the Reading Process

Students bring various personal experiences from life and past reading, both in English and in French, to the reading task. The temptation to lead students toward a single interpretation may curtail thought and enjoyment of a reading passage. If they believe that there is only one answer or way to perceive the reading, many will be discouraged from developing idiosyncratic thought or offering well-thought-out answers. Depending on their level of reading proficiency, students may arrive at various acceptable answers to the activities that follow some of the readings in *C'est à toi!* If students believe that delving deeper into a reading will result in a superior score, many will take the risk to do so. Assessment of students' answers or responses should be judged on a holistic basis, with superior scores given to students

who produce more creative or thought-provoking answers. While holistic grading is new to some teachers, suggestions on how to implement this means of assessment are made in the Annotated Teacher's Edition.

Some students depend entirely on teachers for assessment and approval of their work. It becomes increasingly important that as students become more proficient in French, they must be able to diagnose both their own learning process and achievement in the language in order to become independent learners. Teachers can decide when students are ready to self-assess, and will find techniques in the Annotated Teacher's Edition of *C'est à toi!* that will help them in the process.

Philosophy and Learning Strategies

C'est à toi! is a function-based textbook series that uses a communicative approach to teach students the French language within the context of the francophone world. Students acquire proficiency in listening to, speaking, reading, and writing French while developing cultural sensitivity to the everyday activities of French-speaking people throughout the world. Since the focus of the classroom is student interaction, from day one students practice communicating easily and confidently with their peers in paired or cooperative learning groups. A balance of activities, both in the textbook and in the comprehensive ancillary program, allows students with a variety of learning styles to be successful in French as they progress from carefully structured practice to more creative expression. The five "C's" addressed by the National Foreign Language Standards are artfully interwoven throughout each section of the textbook, integrating the principles of COMMUNICATION, CULTURE, CONNECTIONS, COMPARISONS, and COMMUNITIES to help prepare students for an active, informed role as world citizens in the twenty-first century.

Many activities in the student textbook, as well as additional activities suggested in the color-coded sections of the Annotated Teacher's Edition, incorporate the following learning strategies and techniques to make learning more actively student centered and relevant to those with diverse learning styles.

- **Paired Activities**

As the teacher-centered classroom moves toward the student-centered classroom where students are directly involved in and responsible for their own learning, teachers find that paired activities (in which one student is paired with a partner):

1. give students markedly increased practice time in using French
2. promote cooperation with others to achieve clearly stated goals
3. instill in students greater self-confidence in their language abilities by placing them with their peers in less-threatening situations
4. place students in more realistic, communicative settings
5. lead to increased student involvement and motivation
6. provide for a variation in classroom routine
7. allow the teacher to assume a facilitating role, circulating throughout the room to answer questions and assist those who can benefit from individual help

In order to assure students' success in a paired activity, teachers should make certain that the activity's goal is clearly communicated to students, tell them how to proceed in order to achieve their goal (provide a model), announce how much time they have to finish their task, and inform them how their learning will be evaluated at the end of the activity. Paired activities appear in the **Pratique**, **Communication**, and **C'est à moi!** sections of the textbook as well as in the color-coded Paired Practice section of the Annotated Teacher's Edition.

- **Cooperative Group Activities**

Cooperative learning involves students working together to access, share, and process knowledge, increase academic competencies, and develop interpersonal and small group social skills. Putting students in cooperative learning groups makes them individually accountable for the outcome of their learning. Each member of a cooperative group must assume some responsibility for completing his or her task in order for the group to attain the stated goal. Students practice positive

interdependence as they interact face-to-face with each other. Usually cooperative learning groups consist of four students who are grouped heterogeneously. As with paired activities, the teacher's role is to clearly communicate the activity's goal, tell how to proceed, set time limits, and clarify evaluation procedures. When assigning group roles, the teacher should divide up responsibilities to ensure students' interdependence and cooperation. Each group should have a leader or facilitator, recorder, and reporter. The final step in a cooperative group activity is to share the group's product with the rest of the class, who, along with the teacher, should assess the quality of the group's production. Cooperative learning activities are provided in the **Communication** and **C'est à moi!** sections of the textbook as well as in the color-coded Cooperative Group Practice section of the Annotated Teacher's Edition.

- **TPR Activities**

  In the TPR (Total Physical Response) approach to second language acquisition, students are actively engaged in listening comprehension activities while limiting their responses to physical rather than to verbal demonstrations of comprehension. The teacher initially gives commands or verbal cues that elicit specific student behavior. Students may respond, for example, by pointing, gesturing, moving around the classroom, or manipulating objects. This is an effective method of introducing new vocabulary words and expressions as well as new structures. This physical response to verbal stimuli aids students' comprehension of new elements and helps students to internalize and remember them longer. A list of practical classroom commands (**Expressions de communication**) that are useful in doing TPR activities is located on page TE32 of the Annotated Teacher's Edition. There are TPR activities in the color-coded TPR and Games sections of the Annotated Teacher's Edition.

- **Cross-curricular Activities**

  The French language and francophone culture are artfully interwoven into other areas of the secondary school curriculum so that students form connections to additional bodies of knowledge that may be unavailable to the monolingual English speaker. For example, students use their knowledge of French language and francophone culture as a stepping stone to a deeper understanding of geography, history, mathematics, art, music, and science. Cross-curricular activities help to expand students' global thinking and understanding as enlightened world citizens. Cross-curricular activities are found in the **Pratique** and **Communication** sections of the textbook as well as in the color-coded Cross-curricular section of the Annotated Teacher's Edition.

- **Critical Thinking Activities**

  It is essential to emphasize the development of critical thinking skills, or higher order thinking skills, if our students are to succeed in school and later in life. There are many activities in *C'est à toi!* in which students practice critical thinking. The cognitive abilities and their associated critical thinking skills included in the program are: knowledge acquisition (locate, describe, identify, list, match, name); comprehension (summarize, rewrite, rearrange, paraphrase); analysis (compare and contrast, order, categorize, distinguish); evaluation (conclude, justify); synthesis (associate, combine, compile, plan, generalize); and application (compose, create, design, produce). Critical thinking activities appear in both the **Pratique** and **Communication** sections of the textbook and in the color-coded Critical Thinking section of the Annotated Teacher's Edition.

- **Activities for Students with Multiple Intelligences**

Recent explorations in brain research and human intelligence have provided a wealth of valuable information that is changing the perspectives of learning and teaching. The Multiple Intelligences Theory proposes a pluralized way of understanding the intellect. This theory states that our brain processes and uses information either separately or together in concert through these seven intelligences:

1. verbal-linguistic or "word smart," a type of intelligence related to words and languages
2. logical-mathematical or "logic smart," a type of intelligence that emphasizes logic, order, inductive reasoning, and abstract concepts
3. visual-spatial or "picture smart," a type of intelligence in which the learner relies on the sense of sight to create internal mental pictures
4. bodily-kinesthetic or "body smart," a type of intelligence that thrives in an environment where movement is incorporated into learning by doing
5. musical-rhythmic or "music smart," a type of intelligence that has a powerful connection to changing the consciousness of learning by using and creating with music
6. interpersonal or "people smart," a type of intelligence identified by person-to-person contact and team-building relationships
7. intrapersonal or "self-smart," a type of intelligence that acknowledges an understanding of oneself, including self-reflection

It is important to understand that these intelligences exist in everyone in different degrees and in different combinations. These intelligences do not relate specifically to content areas, but rather to the ability to process information. Additional intelligences may also exist, for Multiple Intelligences research is just beginning. Therefore, weaving the magic of the diversity of learning with the intent of "intelligence fair" strategies challenges all teachers to explore new possibilities to honor the human potential. There are activities for students with multiple intelligences in the **Communication** and **C'est à moi!** sections of the textbook as well as in the color-coded Teacher's Notes and Cross-curricular sections of the Annotated Teacher's Edition.

- **Games**

Games in French are excellent motivational tools that give students the opportunity to learn in a context that varies from the daily routine. During this "learning pause," students review and reinforce previously introduced material as they expand upon their language skills. Appropriate French songs are also presented in the color-coded Games section of the Annotated Teacher's Edition.

EXPRESSIONS DE COMMUNICATION

À demain.	*See you tomorrow.*
Allez au laboratoire.	*Go to the laboratory.*
Allez au tableau.	*Go to the board.*
Attention.	*Be careful.*
Bon appétit.	*Have a good meal.*
Bonne journée.	*Have a good day.*
Bon weekend.	*Have a good weekend.*
C'est bien.	*That's good.*
Comment dit-on...?	*How do you say . . . ?*
Comment s'appelle-t-il?	*What's his name?*
Comment s'appelle-t-elle?	*What's her name?*
Continuons.	*Let's continue.*
Écoutez.	*Listen.*
Écrivez.	*Write.*
Encore.	*Again.*
Épelez.	*Spell.*
Fermez la porte.	*Close the door.*
Fermez le livre.	*Close your books.*
Je ne comprends pas.	*I don't understand.*
Lisez.	*Read.*
Maintenant, une dictée.	*And now a dictation.*
Montre-moi....	*Show me . . . .*
Ouvrez la porte.	*Open the door.*
Ouvrez le livre à la page....	*Open your book to page . . . .*
Prenez votre (vos) livre(s).	*Take out your book(s).*
Présente-moi....	*Introduce me . . . .*
Présentez-nous....	*Introduce us . . . .*
Répétez.	*Repeat.*
Répondez.	*Answer.*
Tous ensemble.	*All together.*

Functions

in C'est à toi!

The number indicates in what unit a specific way to express that function is presented for the first time.

accept and refuse an invitation 10
admit 5, 10
agree and disagree 5, 10
apologize 2
ask about importance and unimportance 3
ask about preference 7
ask for a price 10
ask for help 10
ask for information 2, 6, 7
ask for permission 10
ask what something is 9

boast 8, 9

clarify 7
compare 3, 7, 9, 10
confirm a known fact 1
congratulate and commiserate 6
control the volume of a conversation 5

describe character 7, 8, 10
describe how things were 2
describe past events 1, 8, 9, 10
describe people you remember 5
describe physical traits 2
describe talents and abilities 4
describe temperament 2

estimate 10
evaluate 4
explain a problem 4
explain something 1, 2, 6, 7, 8
express agreement and disagreement 7
express appreciation 4, 6, 8
express astonishment and disbelief 1, 2
express certainty and uncertainty 4
express compassion 7
express complaints 5
express concern 2
express confirmation 10
express criticism 8
express desire 1, 4
express disagreement 4
express disappointment 9, 10
express displeasure 10
express dissatisfaction 5
express emotions 1, 2, 10
express enthusiasm 1, 6, 9
express fear 5
express gratitude 10
express happiness 5
express hope 4
express importance and unimportance 3, 7
express inability 1
express incapability 8
express indifference 9
express intentions 4
express likes and dislikes 3, 5
express need and necessity 3

Vocabulary

Unité 1

une **agrafeuse** stapler
l' **algèbre (f.)** algebra
une **arcade** arcade
auto: une auto tamponneuse bumper car
avoir de la chance to be lucky

un **bloc-notes** notepad
un **bureau** office

le **calcul** calculus
un **carnet** notebook
un **censeur** assistant principal, dean
comprendre to understand
une **conférence** lecture
une **consultation** séance, session

un **directeur, une directrice** principal
une **dissertation** research paper

l' **enseignement (m.)** education
ensuite next
s' **entraîner** to train, to work out
essayer to try
un **examen** test, exam
un **exposé** report

faire de la luge to go tobogganing
faire de la planche à neige to go snowboarding
faire de la planche à roulettes to go skateboarding
faire du ski de fond to go cross-country skiing
faire un tour de grande roue to go on the Ferris wheel
faire un tour de manège to go on the merry-go-round
faire un tour de montagnes russes to go on the roller coaster
un **feutre** felt-tip pen
une **fiche d'inscription** registration form
la **fin** end
une **fois** once
un **fou, une folle** crazy person

gagner to win
la **galerie des miroirs déformants** fun house
la **géométrie** geometry
une **gomme** eraser
le **grec** Greek

Hein? Huh? What?
heurter to hit, to run into

jamais ever
des **jeux d'adresse (m.)** games of skill

un **labo (laboratoire)** laboratory
la **lecture** reading
une **liste** list
la **littérature** literature
une **luge** toboggan
un **lycéen, une lycéenne** high school student

un **manège** merry-go-round
un **manuel** textbook
un **miroir** mirror
des **montagnes russes (f.)** roller coaster

la **neige** snow
une **note** note

oral(e) oral

un **parc d'attractions** amusement park
passer to take (a test)
un **passe-temps** pastime
une **piste** trail, run, track
une **planche à neige** snowboard
une **planche à roulettes** skateboard
po: les sciences po (f.) political science

rater to fail
la **recherche** research
une **rédaction** composition
la **rentrée** first day of school
une **responsabilité** responsibility
revenir: Je n'en reviens pas. I can't get over it.
rigoler to laugh
rigoler comme des fous to laugh like crazy
une **roue** wheel
une grande roue Ferris wheel
le **russe** Russian

une **salle de conférences** lecture hall
les **sciences po (f.)** political science
sécher to skip (a class)
le **ski de fond** cross-country skiing

un **ticket** ticket
un **trombone** paper clip

un(e) **voyant(e)** fortuneteller, clairvoyant

Unité 2

un **accent** accent
accueillant(e) hospitable, friendly
l' **air** (m.) appearance
une **ambassade** embassy
s' **approcher (de)** to approach, to come up (to)
s' **attendre à** to expect
aucun(e)... ne (n') not one, no
avoir l'air to look

calme calm
un **car** tour bus
un **chef** boss
un **commissariat** police station

le **début** beginning
une **déclaration** report
déprimé(e) depressed
un **document** document

effrayé(e) frightened
un(e) **employé(e)** employee, clerk
en while, upon
un **endroit** place
s' **entendre** to get along
épuisé(e) exhausted
exigeant(e) demanding
expliquer to explain

fâché(e) angry
se **fâcher** to get angry
faire attention to pay attention
fatigant(e) tiring
fouiller to search, to go through

un **grand-parent** grandparent

habillé(e) dressed
humain(e) human

un(e) **imbécile** idiot
important(e) important
incroyable unbelievable
inutile useless

se **méfier de** to distrust

ne (n')... aucun(e) no, not any
ne (n')... ni... ni... neither . . . nor
ne (n')... que only
ni... ni... ne (n') neither . . . nor
un **nom de jeune fille** maiden name

se **passer** to happen
payer to pay
pendant que while
personne ne (n') nobody, no one
plutôt rather
la **police** police
poser to ask (a question)
puisque since

une **question** question

se **rappeler** to remember
des **rapports** (m.) relations, relationship
rassurant(e) reassuring
un **récépissé** receipt
regretter to regret
répéter to repeat
répondre to answer
une **réponse** answer
se **reposer** to rest
rien ne (n') nothing

satisfait(e) (de) satisfied (with)
se **sentir** to feel
souriant(e) smiling
surprenant(e) surprising

se **taire** to be quiet
tout à coup all of a sudden

un **vol** theft
voler to steal (from), to rob

une **abréviation** abbreviation
un **album** album
un **arrondissement** district
un(e) **assistant(e)** assistant
un **atelier** studio
autobiographique autobiographical

un **ballet** ballet
une **bande originale** sound track
bas: en bas at the bottom
le **Bénin** Benin
un **bureau de location** box office

chanter to sing
un **chef d'orchestre** conductor
un **chef-d'œuvre** masterpiece
un **cinéma** movie theater
une **collection** collection
composer to compose
un **compositeur, une compositrice** composer
controversé(e) controversial

descendre to get off
une **description** description
une **distraction** entertainment
une **durée** length

en bas at the bottom
en général in general
enregistrer to record
essentiel, essentielle essential

le **fon** Fon (African language)

général(e) general
un **genre** kind, type
un **guide** guidebook

impossible impossible
une **impression** impression, feeling
un **indice** rating
indispensable indispensable
l' **Indochine (f.)** Indochina
interdit(e) prohibited
une **intrigue** plot

un(e) **jeune** young person
jouer to act, to play (a part)

un **kiosque à journaux** newsstand

une **langue** language
une **location: un bureau de location** box office
lorsque when

même same
la **nature** nature
une **nature morte** still life
nécessaire necessary

un **orchestre** orchestra

partout everywhere
un **paysage** landscape
peindre to paint
un(e) **peintre** painter
une **pièce (de théâtre)** play
une **place** seat
plaire to please
plusieurs several
populaire popular
un **prix** price

reconnaître to recognize
réduit(e) reduced
des **renseignements (m.)** information
un **rôle** role

un **scénario** script
un(e) **scénariste** scriptwriter
un **sculpteur** sculptor
un **signe** sign
un **spectacle** show
le **succès** success

un **tarif** rate, price
tourner to shoot (a movie)
se **trouver** to be (located)

utile useful

valable valid
valoir mieux to be better
une **variété** variety
vaut: il vaut mieux it is better
vécu(e) real-life
une **vedette** (movie) star
une **version** version

à plein temps full-time
administratif, administrative administrative
agréer to accept
  Je vous prie d'agréer, Monsieur (ou Madame), mes salutations distinguées. yours truly
une **annonce** advertisement
  des petites annonces (f.) want ads
annoncer to announce
s' **appeler** to be named
apprécier to appreciate
assez enough
l' **assurance (f.)** insurance

un **besoin** need
bilingue bilingual

le **cadre** sector
ce que what
ce qui what
certain(e) certain
une **chaîne** channel
un **chef** head
ci-joint enclosed
une **clientèle** customers, clientele
une **compagnie** company
compter to intend
un **contrat** contract
contre against
créer to create
un **CV** curriculum vitae

diplômé(e) possessing a diploma
direct: en direct live
distingué(e) distinguished
  Je vous prie d'agréer, Monsieur (ou Madame), mes salutations distinguées. yours truly
douter to doubt

école: les grandes écoles elite, specialized universities
élevé(e) high
embaucher to hire
un **emploi** job
en direct live
enthousiaste enthusiastic
évident(e) evident, obvious
exiger to require
une **expérience** experience

faire des études to study
flexible flexible
un **formulaire** form

garanti(e) guaranteed
un **gouvernement** government
les **grandes écoles (f.)** elite, specialized universities

inférieur(e) less, lower

un(e) **manifestant(e)** demonstrator
une **manifestation** demonstration
manifester to demonstrate
le **maximum** maximum
le **mécontentement** dissatisfaction
minimum minimum
un **moyen** way

un **numéro** issue

organisé(e) organized

un **parti** (political) party
participer à to take part in
le **personnel** personnel, staff
plein: à plein temps full-time
un **poste** job, position
un **pourcentage** percentage
pousser to push
préparatoire preparatory
se **présenter** to come, to appear
prier to beg
  Je vous prie d'agréer, Monsieur (ou Madame), mes salutations distinguées. yours truly
un **projet** project

une **qualification** qualification
le **Québec** Quebec (Province)

une **raison** reason
reconnaissant(e) grateful
un **reportage** report

un **salaire** salary
une **salutation** greeting
  Je vous prie d'agréer, Monsieur (ou Madame), mes salutations distinguées. yours truly
un **service** service
le **SMIC** minimum wage
souhaiter to wish, to hope
se **spécialiser** to specialize
suffisamment enough
sûr(e) sure

un **taux** rate
temps: à plein temps full-time
se **terminer** to end

la **vente** sales

à ta place if I were you
accompagner to accompany
une **activité** activity

la **beauté** beauty
un **bisou** kiss

cela that
un **chef de train** conductor
Chut! Sh!
la **clim (climatisation)** air conditioning
croire: Je crois que oui. I think so.

d'accord: être d'accord to agree
se **débrouiller** to manage
disponible available
dont of which/whom, about which/
    whom, whose
    la façon dont the way in which

embêter to bother
en plus in addition
des **ennuis (m.)** problems
s' **ennuyer** to get bored, to be bored
étonné(e) surprised
être d'accord to agree

une **façon** way
    la façon dont the way in which
faire les touristes to act like tourists
faire un somme to take a nap
faire un voyage to take a trip
un **fax** fax

un **garde forestier** park ranger
un **gars** guy
un(e) **gérant(e)** manager
un **groupe** group
un **gymnase** gym

une **hôtesse de l'air** flight attendant

s' **installer** to move

longtemps (for) a long time

Madame une telle Mrs. So-and-so
marcher to work
le **meilleur, la meilleure** best
un **mètre** meter
mettre to turn on
Monsieur un tel Mr. So-and-so

une **nuit** night

s' **occuper de** to take care of

panoramique panoramic
parcourir to travel through, to cover
parler: Tu parles! You're not kidding!
se **passer** to go
la **patience** patience
un **paysage** scenery
percé(e) pierced
place: à ta place if I were you
se **plaindre** to complain
plus: en plus in addition
un **porte-bagages** overhead compartment
proposer to propose
propre own
une **province** province

rendre un service to help
    se **rendre compte** to realize
retourner to return
un **rocher** rock

le **sable** sand
un **satellite** satellite
sauvage wildlife
service: rendre un service to help
servir to serve
    se **servir de** to use
situé(e) situated
un **somme** nap
    faire un somme to take a nap
sonner to ring
se **souvenir** to remember
un **steward** flight attendant
surprendre to surprise

tellement so much
un(e) **touriste** tourist
traiter to treat
se **tromper (de)** to be mistaken, to be
    wrong
un **truc** thing

un **ventilateur** fan

accéder to access
appuyer to press
un article article
avancé(e) advanced
l' avenir (m.) future

un bébé baby
se brancher to connect
Bravo! Well done!

ce qui that
un clavier keyboard
cliquer to click
le commerce trade
commercial(e) commercial
la connaissance knowledge
construire to build

la défense defense
dénoncer to denounce, to expose
dépenser to spend
dès que as soon as
développer to develop
un domaine field, area

écologique ecological
un écran screen
électronique electronic
l' e-mail (m.) e-mail
en ligne online
engagé(e) committed
entendre parler de to hear about
entier, entière whole
une équipe team
l' espace (m.) space
établir to establish
excellent(e) excellent

une famine famine
une fondation foundation
la fourrure fur
une frontière border, boundary
une fusée rocket

grâce thanks

humanitaire humanitarian

une imprimante printer
l' inforoute (f.) information superhighway
un intérêt interest
l' Irak (m.) Iraq

lancer to launch
un lanceur de satellites satellite launcher
une ligne line
en ligne online
une lutte fight

maltraité(e) mistreated
meilleur(e) better
un milliard billion
une mission mission
mondial(e) world-wide
un moniteur monitor

l' océanographie (f.) oceanography
oublier to forget
un outil de recherche search engine

parmi among
une partie part
passionnant(e) exciting, fascinating
la pauvreté poverty
permettre to permit, to allow
le progrès progress
la protection protection
protéger to protect

quant à as for

recherche: un outil de recherche search
engine
un refuge shelter
rendre to hand in, to return
la République Démocratique du Congo
Democratic Republic of the Congo
le Ruanda Rwanda

sauvegarder to save
une souris mouse
spatial(e) space
une stratégie strategy
un sujet subject

la technologie technology
la télématique communication by computer
la terre earth
un titre title
une touche key (on keyboard)
un traitement treatment

le web Web

agresser to attack
Ah bon? Really?
les **allocations (f.)** benefits, allowance
une **ambiance** atmosphere
une **apparence** appearance
appeler to call
l' **avenir (m.)** future

bon: Ah bon? Really?
un **budget** budget

une **cage** cage
    une cage à lapins rabbit hutch
car because
celui, celle; ceux, celles this one, that one, the one; these, those, the ones
un **chômeur, une chômeuse** unemployed person
circonspect(e) cautious, reserved
une **cité** housing development
un **climat** climate
un **coin** corner
compter to count, to rely
considérer to consider
culturel, culturelle cultural

d'habitude usual
dépendre (de) to depend (on)
déprimant(e) depressing
différent(e) different
diffuser to broadcast
une **discothèque** discotheque
se **disputer** to argue
se **distraire** to enjoy oneself, to have a good time
une **diversité** diversity
un **divorce** divorce
divorcer to get divorced

un **étranger, une étrangère** foreigner

familial(e) family
le **franglais** franglais (English words used in French)

génial(e) great, terrific, fantastic
des **graffiti (m.)** graffiti

une **HLM (habitation à loyer modéré)** public housing

un(e) **immigré(e)** immigrant
indépendant(e) independent
une **influence** influence

s' **intégrer** to become integrated

un **journal** journal

lequel, laquelle; lesquels, lesquelles which one; which ones
le **logement** housing
une **loi** law

maghrébin(e) inhabitant of/from the Maghreb
se **marier** to get married
une **marque** brand
monoparental(e) single-parent
un **mot** word
un **mur** wall

nombreux, nombreuse numerous
non-traditionnel, non-traditionnelle nontraditional
une **note** grade

optimiste optimistic
une **origine** origin
ouvert(e) frank

un(e) **passant(e)** passerby
passer to play (on the radio)
perdre son temps to waste one's time
la **plupart (de)** most
pressé(e) in a hurry
propre clean

une **radio** radio
une **relation** relation(ship)
rencontrer to meet
un(e) **résident(e)** resident

simple simple
social(e) social
une **société** society
sujet: au sujet de about

tendu(e) strained
le **Togo** Togo
toucher to get

universitaire university

le **vocabulaire** vocabulary

une administration administration
des affaires (f.) business
ambitieux, ambitieuse ambitious
améliorer to improve
assassiner to assassinate
l' Autriche (f.) Austria
avoir beau (to do something) in vain
avoir lieu to take place

une bataille battle
beau: avoir beau (to do something) in vain

un(e) catholique Catholic
la chasse hunting
un chef chief
le christianisme Christianity
complexe complicated
un(e) conquérant(e) conqueror
un conseil (piece of) advice
la construction building
contre for
copier to copy
une cour court
critiquer to criticize
une croisade crusade

défendre to defend
démolir to demolish
Dieu (m.) God
diviser to divide
un duc duke
durer to last

un empereur emperor
un empire empire
envers towards
un événement event

faire prisonnier/prisonnière to take prisoner
fier, fière proud

la Gaule Gaul
un(e) Gaulois(e) inhabitant of/from Gaul
un général general
gouverner to govern
guillotiner to guillotine

illuminé(e) illuminated
un impôt tax
l' indépendance (f.) independence

la justice justice

large wide
libéral(e) liberal
un lieu place
avoir lieu to take place
la loyauté loyalty

maintenir to maintain
un(e) marquis(e) marquis, marchioness
un massacre massacre
un moine monk
une monarchie monarchy
monétaire monetary

négocier to negotiate
un(e) Normand(e) inhabitant of/from Normandy

l' Occident (m.) West
s' occuper de to deal with
ordonner to order

la paix peace
par conséquent consequently
le passé past
le peuple people
pieux, pieuse pious
le présent present
un prisonnier, une prisonnière prisoner
un(e) protestant(e) Protestant
province: en province in the provinces

un règne reign
la religion religion
une relique relic
réunir to reunite, to bring together
une révolution revolution
un(e) Romain(e) Roman
rusé(e) crafty, sly

survivre to survive
un système system

une terre land
tomber to fall
transformer to transform
une tribu tribe
troublé(e) disrupted
tuer to kill

vaincre to defeat, to conquer
la violence violence
des vitraux (m.) stained glass windows

abondant(e) plentiful
ainsi que as well as
une antilope antelope
un appareil-photo camera
un artisan craftsperson
un atelier workshop
autrefois formerly
une autruche ostrich

le banco adobe
un baobab baobab tree
Bof! What can I say?

une case hut
chasser to hunt
une concession African housing area
un contraste contrast
contre: par contre on the other hand
coranique of the Islamic religion
côté: de l'autre côté on the other side

de l'autre côté on the other side
de nos jours these days
de sorte que so that
un dinosaure dinosaur

emprunter (à) to borrow (from)
une époque time
être à to belong to

faire partie de to be a part of
fantastique fantastic
la faune animal life
fin(e) intricate

une gazelle gazelle
le gibier game
un gratte-ciel skyscraper

une habitude habit
une hyène hyena

informer to inform
un instrument instrument
s' intéresser à to be interested in

jour: de nos jours these days

le leur, la leur theirs

malheureusement unfortunately
le Mali Mali
la maroquinerie leather goods
le mien, la mienne mine
le mil millet
modèle model
le moyen means

le Niger Niger
le nôtre, la nôtre ours
des nouvelles (f.) news

une occasion opportunity

un pagne African skirt
une paire pair
par: par contre on the other hand
partager to share
un pavillon pavilion, hall
un paysan, une paysanne peasant
une peau skin
la pluie rain
pourri(e) spoiled
pourtant however
pousser to grow
prêter to lend
un projet plan

Qu'est-ce que c'est que...? What is . . . ?

rappeler to remind
religieux, religieuse religious
se rencontrer to meet
une réussite success

le Sahara Sahara
le sien, la sienne his, hers, its, one's
un snack-bar snack bar
une sorte: de sorte que so that
un squelette skeleton

temps: au bon vieux temps in the good
  old days
le tien, la tienne yours
traditionnel, traditionnelle traditional

se vanter to boast
le vôtre, la vôtre yours

Unité 10

un accident accident
un achat purchase
s' adapter to adapt
un antibiotique antibiotic
un appareil appliance
arriver to happen
une aspirine aspirin
une attente: une salle d'attente waiting room
autant de as much, as many
avoir raison to be right

un ballon (inflated) ball
un bandage bandage
une béquille crutch
une blague joke
Sans blague! No kidding!
une blessure wound
une boîte box
un bon de réduction coupon

c'est: C'est à vous de voir. It's up to you.
une canette can
cassé(e) broken
se casser to break
une cheville ankle
un(e) client(e) customer
compliqué(e) complicated
un coup: jeter un coup d'œil to take a quick look

déçu(e) disappointed
devoir to owe
un dico dictionary
droit(e) right

élevé(e) raised
embêtant(e) annoying
entouré(e) wrapped
environ about
éviter to avoid
une expression expression

se faire mal to hurt oneself
fauteuil: un fauteuil roulant wheelchair
se fouler to sprain
frustré(e) frustrated

gauche left
gêner to bother
gratuitement free

un hôpital hospital

jeter un coup d'œil to take a quick look

justement exactly

laisser: laissez-moi let me

le Midi the south of France
le mode d'emploi instructions
moi-même myself

n'importe quel, n'importe quelle just any
n'importe qui anyone
neuf, neuve new

œil: jeter un coup d'œil to take a quick look
une ordonnance prescription

une pastille lozenge
une pharmacie pharmacy, drugstore
une phrase phrase, sentence
une pile battery
un plâtre cast
un poignet wrist

une radiographie X ray
raison: avoir raison to be right
rapporter to bring back
rattraper to trap
un rayon (store) department
une réduction reduction
rembourser to reimburse
rendre (+ adjective) to make
réparer to repair
un résultat result
se retrouver to meet
revoir to see again
rien nothing
roulant(e): un fauteuil roulant wheelchair

une salle d'attente waiting room
une salle des urgences emergency room
le SAMU (service d'assistance médicale d'urgence) emergency medical service
si what if

un tel, une telle such a
un ticket de caisse receipt
le tracas trouble

l' un(e)... l'autre (the) one . . . the other
une urgence: la salle des urgences emergency room

C'EST À TOI!

Level Three

Authors

Augusta DeSimone Clark

Richard Ladd

Sarah Vaillancourt

Diana Moen

Contributing Writer

Christine Gensmer

EMC/Paradigm Publishing, Saint Paul, Minnesota

Credits

Editor
Sarah Vaillancourt

Associate Editor
Diana Moen

Desktop Production Specialist
Chris Vern Johnson

Design
The Nancekivell Group

Illustrator
Hetty Mitchell

Chief Consultants

Karla Winther Fawbush
Brooklyn Center High School
Brooklyn Center, Minnesota

Nathalie Gaillot
Language Specialist
Lyon, France

Christine Gensmer
Language Specialist
Minneapolis, Minnesota

Consultants

Lynn Heyman-Hogue
La Costa Canyon High School
Carlsbad, California

Michael Nettleton
Smoky Hill High School
Aurora, Colorado

Ann J. Sorrell
South Burlington High School
South Burlington, Vermont

Caroline Durand
Language Specialist
Perpignan, France

ISBN 0-8219-1703-X
© 1999 by EMC Corporation

Published by EMC/Paradigm Publishing
875 Montreal Way
St. Paul, Minnesota 55102
800-328-1452
www.emcp.com
E-mail: educate@emcp.com

Printed in the United States of America
2 3 4 5 6 7 8 9 10 XXX 04 03 02 01 00 99

Bienvenue au troisième niveau de français!

Welcome back to *C'est à toi!* You should feel a great sense of accomplishment having successfully completed the first two levels of this program. Congratulations on your decision to continue! What are you able to do by studying French? Communicating with others is probably your most important goal in learning French, but you benefit in other ways as well. You are developing cultural understandings about how people in French-speaking regions live, act, and think, as well as what they value. In addition, you are learning skills that will help you act independently and successfully in new cultural situations. You are expanding your knowledge of other subject areas through your study of French, finding many connections to French history, geography, art, music, literature, science, etc. You are also learning about your own language and culture as you explore the relationship between them and French. And finally, you are using French to enrich your life and to connect to the world around you, skills that will serve you both now and in the future.

In the third level of *C'est à toi!*, you will expand upon the communicative tasks and skills you have already practiced. For example, you will be able to explain problems you encounter when traveling or buying something; express feelings like happiness, anger, fear, and disappointment; give your opinions; discuss contemporary social and political problems in France; apply for a job; and use computer technology. Your ability to read and write French will improve as you learn how to write compositions and job résumés, give detailed explanations, tell stories using pictures, compare and contrast, decipher want ads, and read instructions. You will become acquainted with French speakers, both past and present, who have become famous for their contributions to history, art, science, music, movies, and the environment. You will learn more about interesting cities and regions in France. You will also heighten your awareness of other areas in the world where French is spoken: from Saint-Martin to Senegal, from Montreal to Mali.

The format of this textbook is similar to the first and second levels of *C'est à toi!* In the first **Unité** you will review specific verbs and structures from the previous textbooks in order to have a firm foundation for the new material you are about to encounter. In **Unités 2-10**

you will learn new vocabulary, structures, and functions as well as recycle those that you have already learned. There are several new or expanded sections in each unit of this book, designed to enrich your learning:

- **Tes empreintes ici** and **Dossier ouvert**
  These new sections begin each unit. In **Tes empreintes ici**, you will find introductory questions to connect you with the topic of the opening dialogue or reading. **Dossier ouvert** presents a cultural "teaser," challenging you to interact and problem solve in a situation that might happen if you are in a francophone environment. By the end of the unit, you will "uncover" the answer and check it in the **Dossier fermé** section.

- **Enquête culturelle**
  Two expanded sections have been designed to broaden your understanding of authentic, contemporary francophone culture. Following each reading are accompanying realia-based activities to help you apply what you have learned in real-life situations.

- **Journal personnel**
  In the past, your teacher may have suggested that you keep a cultural journal to record your observations about specific aspects of francophone culture and reflectively compare it with your own. In this book, a specific journal activity has been included in each lesson.

- **Sur la bonne piste**
  This section has been expanded to accompany each lesson in the unit. The new section in **Leçon A** focuses on strategies for communicating successfully in French. Techniques for preparing for college placement exams are also included.

Once again you will have the opportunity to interact with your classmates either in pairs or in small groups as you apply your knowledge in different situations typical of those that you might encounter as you communicate with French speakers. As you complete your journey with us in the francophone world, we wish you many interesting, enjoyable, and rewarding experiences that will enrich your life for years to come.

Table of Contents

Unité 1 La vie scolaire et les passe-temps 1

Unité 2 Les rapports humains 51

Unité 3 Les arts 95

Unité 4 Le monde du travail 141

Unité 5 Comment se débrouiller en voyage 179

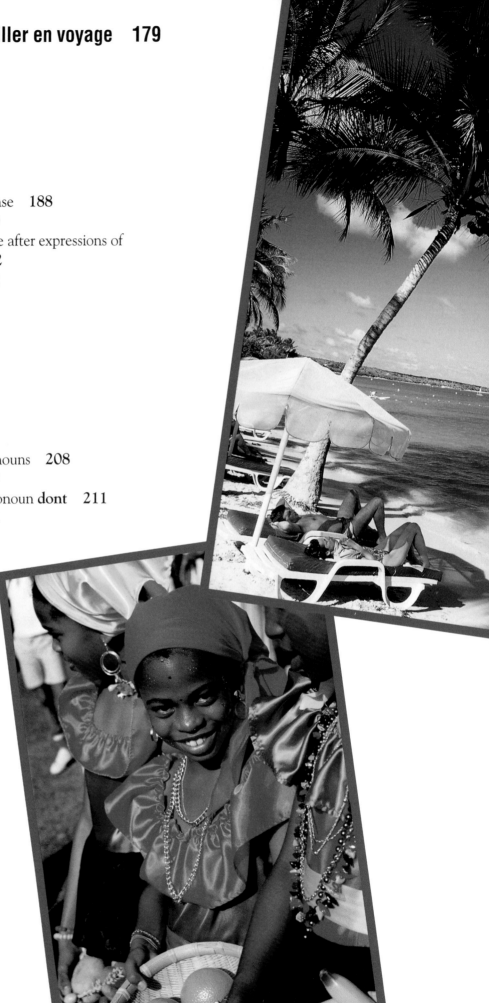

Unité 6 L'avenir: la technologie et l'environnement 225

Unité 7 Les Français comme ils sont 263

Unité 8 L'histoire de France 305

Unité 10 On s'adapte 383

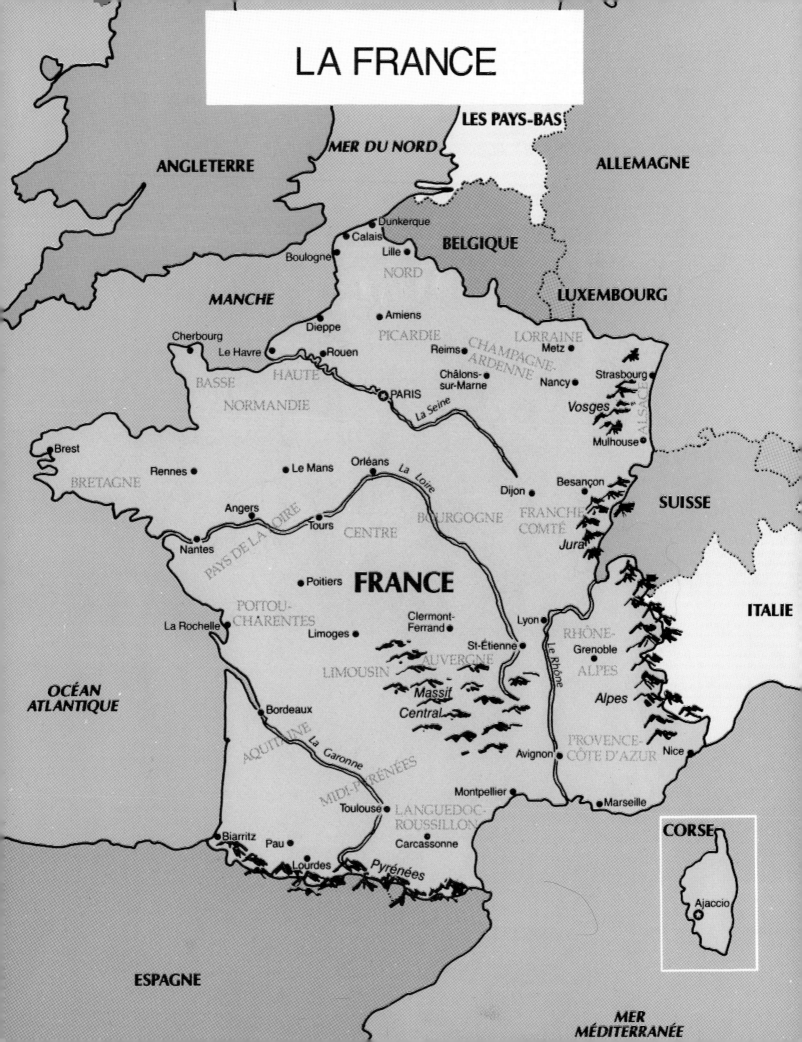

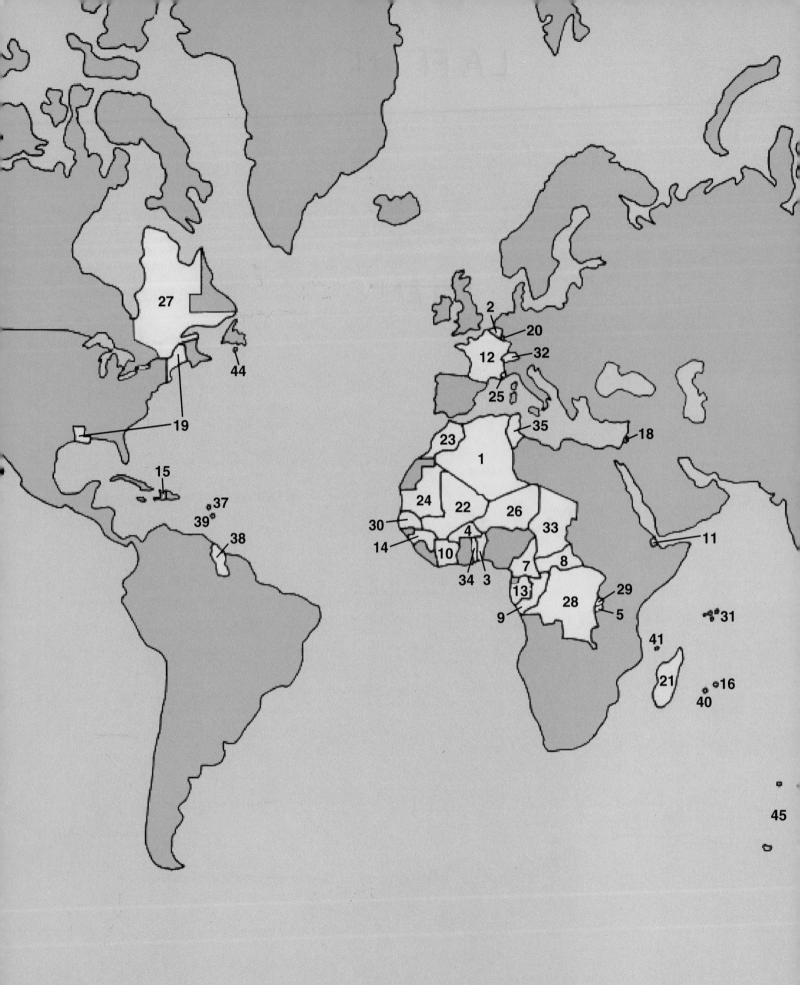

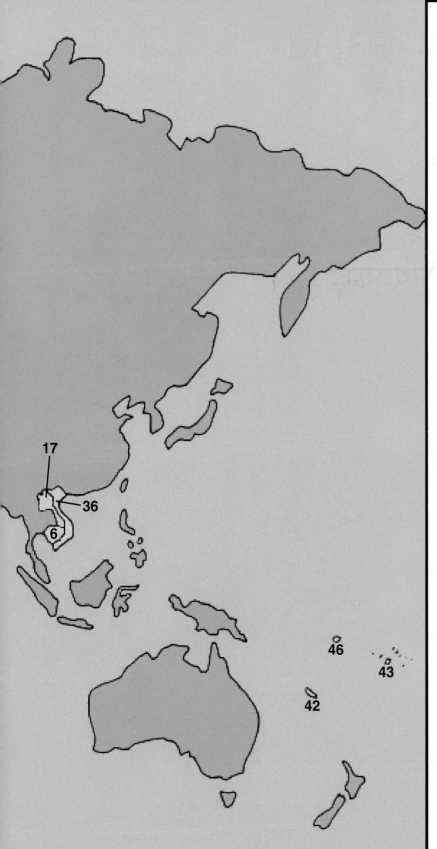

Les pays francophones

It's not only in France that people speak French. In more than 30 countries of the world, there are about 200 million people who speak French either as their mother tongue or as an unofficial second language. These countries are called *les pays francophones* (French-speaking countries). They are very different. There are European countries, of course, like France and Switzerland, and there is Canada, but there are also African countries and tropical islands.

1. l'Algérie
2. la Belgique
3. le Bénin
4. le Burkina-Faso
   (*la république du...*)
5. le Burundi
   (*la république du...*)
6. le Cambodge
7. le Cameroun
   (*la république du...*)
8. Centrafricaine
   (*la république...*)
9. le Congo
   (*la république du...*)
10. la Côte-d'Ivoire
11. Djibouti
    (*la république de...*)
12. la France
13. le Gabon
    (*la république du...*)
14. la Guinée
15. Haïti
    (*la république d'...*)
16. l'île Maurice
17. le Laos
18. le Liban
19. la Louisiane,
    la Nouvelle-Angleterre
20. le Luxembourg
21. Madagascar
    (*la république de...*)
22. le Mali
    (*la république du...*)
23. le Maroc
24. la Mauritanie
    (*la république de...*)
25. Monaco
26. le Niger
27. le Québec
28. la République
    Démocratique du
    Congo
29. le Ruanda
30. le Sénégal
    (*la république du...*)
31. les Seychelles
32. la Suisse
33. le Tchad
34. le Togo
35. la Tunisie
36. le Vietnam

La France d'outre-mer

Did you know that the islands of *Martinique* and *Guadeloupe* (more than 6,000 kilometers from Paris) are, in fact, French? They are overseas departments or *départements d'outre-mer* (*les DOM*). There are four in all. The others are *la Guyane française* and *la Réunion*.

The inhabitants of these islands have the same rights as the mainland French. They have the same government with the same president and the same system of education, and they often take trips to France.

There are also overseas territories or *territoires d'outre-mer* (*les TOM*), which are more independent and have their own system of government.

les départements
37. la Guadeloupe
38. la Guyane française
39. la Martinique
40. la Réunion

les territoires
41. l'île Mayotte
42. la Nouvelle-Calédonie
43. la Polynésie française
44. Saint-Pierre-et-
    Miquelon
45. les Terres australes et
    antarctiques françaises
46. Wallis-et-Futuna

Unité 1

La vie scolaire et les passe-temps

In this unit you will be able to:

➤ inquire about the past

➤ describe past events

➤ sequence events

➤ confirm a known fact

➤ explain something

➤ give examples

➤ summarize

➤ inquire about ability

➤ express inability

➤ give orders

➤ offer something

➤ express astonishment and disbelief

➤ express enthusiasm

➤ express emotions

➤ express desire

1. The communicative functions provide a preview of the tasks that students will be able to accomplish when they complete the unit. Functions are continually recycled from one unit to the next in the *C'est à toi!* program, and they are repeated only when a different way of expressing that specific function is introduced. Communicative functions that are recycled in this lesson are "greeting someone," "expressing astonishment," "expressing need" and "asking for information." 2. In **Tes empreintes ici** students are asked to respond to questions designed to connect them with the subject of the lesson. No new vocabulary is introduced in this section. 3. The **Dossier ouvert** is a cultural "teaser" intended to make students think about how they would react to a typical situation in the francophone world that differs from their own culture in some respect. Tell students to look for the answer, which is hinted at somewhere in the unit. In the **Dossier fermé** at the end of the unit, the "teaser" is reviewed and the answer is provided and explained. Some new vocabulary is introduced in these **Dossiers**; however, the words are easily recognizable cognates.

Leçon A

In this lesson you will be able to:

➤ inquire about the past

➤ describe past events

➤ sequence events

➤ summarize

➤ inquire about ability

➤ express inability

➤ give examples

➤ confirm a known fact

Tes empreintes ici

Tu viens de rentrer au lycée après les vacances d'été. Tu penses aux copains, aux profs, aux cours, à la nourriture et au travail. Toi, es-tu prêt(e) à commencer la nouvelle année scolaire?

- Quelle était la date du premier jour de classes à ton lycée?
- Comment est-ce que tu t'es préparé(e)?
- Qu'est-ce que tu as été obligé(e) d'acheter? Tu es allé(e) à une librairie?
- Quels cours sont difficiles? Faciles?
- Quels profs sont sympa?
- Comment est la nourriture à la cantine?
- Est-il difficile de faire des amis dans ton lycée?
- Es-tu content(e) de rentrer au lycée? Pourquoi ou pourquoi pas?

Les élèves sont contents de rentrer au lycée après les grandes vacances. (Calais)

Dossier ouvert

Imagine que tu étudies dans un lycée français et c'est le jour de ton premier examen. Tu regardes l'examen et tu vois qu'il consiste seulement en questions à longue réponse. Quelle est ta réaction?

   A. Tu demandes au professeur de te donner l'examen avec des questions à choix multiples.
   B. Tu demandes au professeur si c'est un examen à livre ouvert.
   C. Tu continues parce que c'est le style d'un examen français.

Journal personnel

If students are keeping a cultural journal, you might ask them to reflect on what makes a good school. Have them record how they would rate their school on the attractiveness of the building and campus, its accessibility for the handicapped, its variety of facilities and courses, and the attitude of the teachers, administrators and support staff.

le grec

le russe

le calcul

Bloc perforé "Idea".
80 feuilles, petits ou
grands carreaux au choix.
21 x 32 cm.
9F

VELLEDA
Ardoise + feutre + effacette,
18 x 26 cm.

Agrafeuse, corps translucide,
pour agrafes n°10.
19F

un labo

un bloc-notes

un manuel

Chimie

l'histoire de la chimie

une agrafeuse

un carnet

un feutre

un trombone

un examen

une rédaction

une gomme

■ **Workbook Activity 1**

🎙 **Audiocassette/CD Classroom Expressions**

📽 **Transparencies 1-2**

Teacher's Notes

1. **Un carnet** is smaller than **un cahier**. 2. **Un bloc-notes**, sometimes referred to simply as **un bloc**, is a notepad that opens from the top rather than from the side. 3. While many French students now use disposable pens, such as **un feutre**, fountain pens with replaceable cartridges, **des stylos à cartouche**, are still very popular. 4. Other school-related terms and expressions include **une chemise** (*folder*), **une agrafe** (*staple*), **une salle d'étude** (*study hall*), **une heure d'étude** (*study hall period*), **une révision** (*review*), **un amphithéâtre** (*lecture hall*), **un pupitre** (*student desk*), **un laboratoire de langues** (*language lab*) and **un(e) remplaçant(e)** (*substitute teacher*).

Cooperative Group Practice

Vocabulary Identification

Put students in small groups of four or five. Give each group a set of flash cards of French terms for school supplies from this lesson and any you wish to review from Unit 4 in the first level of *C'est à toi!* Place the cards face down in a pile. The first student takes a card and gives a clue about the term, for example, **On écrit avec ça.** The student who first guesses the correct term (**C'est un feutre**) gets the card and places it on his or her desk. Then the second student takes a card and gives a clue about the next term, and so on. The student with the most cards at the end of the activity wins.

Game

La vieille fille

Make five sets of identical cards with illustrations of school-related vocabulary from this lesson and any you wish to review from Unit 4 in the first level of *C'est à toi!* Divide the class into five small groups and give each group two sets of cards. Shuffle and deal the cards until none are left. The first student tries to find a match for one of the cards in his or her hand by asking another student a question with **avoir**, for example, **As-tu un manuel de calcul?** The student questioned answers affirmatively (**Oui, j'ai un manuel de calcul**) or negatively (**Non, je n'ai pas de manuel de calcul**). If the response is **oui**, the student relinquishes his or her card to the student who asked for it. When a student gets a pair, he or she sets it down and takes another turn. Students ask and answer questions until all pairs of cards are displayed. The student with the most pairs of cards wins.

Workbook
Activity 2

Audiocassette/CD
Dialogue

1. French secondary schools were discussed in Unit 4 in the first level of *C'est à toi!* and again in Unit 9 in the second level. 2. Often seen in advertisements, **la mode de la rentrée** and **les affaires de la rentrée** mean "autumn fashions" and "back-to-school bargains." **La rentrée** also refers to the general time period of the return to classes after **les grandes vacances**. However, the French also use the expression to refer to the return to classes after other holidays, for example, **la rentrée de Noël**. 3. Like **le lycée Henri IV**, many schools in France are named for famous historical figures, such as Saint-Louis, Louis le Grand and Charlemagne. Other schools bear the names of famous authors. 4. Remind students that **je suis** is the present tense form of both **être** and **suivre** and may mean "I am," "I follow" or "I take (a class)," depending on the context. 5. The **passé composé** will be reviewed in **Leçon B**. 6. The word **bureau**, meaning "desk," was introduced in Unit 4 in the first level of *C'est à toi!* 7. French teenagers often use shortened forms of words when discussing school-related topics. For example, **sciences po** is the abbreviated form of **sciences politiques**. The abbreviated form of **dissertation (dissert)** refers to a composition rather than a research paper. 8. Glossed vocabulary follows the exposition in the third level of *C'est à toi!* Cognates and illustrated words are not glossed.

Le lycée Henri IV, situé sur la rive gauche, est près du Panthéon et de la Sorbonne. (Paris)

Aujourd'hui c'est la rentrée.° Amadou, qui vient de déménager de Dakar, et sa nouvelle copine Gilberte sont assis dans la salle de conférences° du lycée Henri IV à Paris. Ils attendent la prof d'histoire avec beaucoup d'autres lycéens.°

Amadou: Salut, Gilberte. Ça va?

Gilberte: Ça va bien, mais je suis fatiguée. Et toi?

Amadou: Oh là là! Crois-moi! Les cours vont être si difficiles pour moi. À Dakar j'ai souvent séché° le cours d'algèbre. Alors, je l'ai raté° et j'ai dû passer° un examen. Enfin, j'ai réussi.

Gilberte: L'enseignement° qu'on offre ici est vraiment extra. Comment est-ce que tu trouves les profs et les copains?

Amadou: Je les trouve sympa.

Gilberte: Tu as rempli la fiche d'inscription° ce matin?

Amadou: Oui. D'abord, j'ai eu rendez-vous avec le directeur° dans son bureau.° Après, le censeur° m'a donné mon emploi du temps. Puis, j'ai assisté à mon cours de sciences po.°

Gilberte: Le prof de littérature nous a donné une liste de responsabilités—un exposé° oral chaque semaine, une rédaction deux fois par semaine, une dissertation° à la fin° du cours et des interros. Et bien sûr, la lecture,° c'est du boulot.

Amadou: Voilà un cours difficile. C'est comme ça dans mon cours de philosophie et aussi en géométrie. Qu'est-ce qui t'inquiète?

la rentrée le premier jour de l'année scolaire; **une salle de conférences** *lecture hall;* **un lycéen** un élève au lycée; **sécher** ne pas aller (en cours); **rater** ne pas réussir; **passer** *to take;* **l'enseignement** (m.) *education;* **une fiche d'inscription** *registration form;* **un directeur** *principal;* **un bureau** où travaille le directeur; **un censeur** *dean;* **po** politique; **un exposé** *report;* **une dissertation** *research paper;* **la fin** *end;* **la lecture** *reading*

Cross-curricular

Geography

Have each of your students make a map of Senegal to familiarize themselves with the country Amadou comes from. On the map have students identify principal cities, rivers, neighboring countries, **l'océan Atlantique**, **la savane** in the center, **le Sahara** in the north and **la forêt tropicale** in the southwest. The next day play a game with the class to practice identifying these geographical features. At the front of the class, display a large unlabeled map of Senegal and its surroundings. Then divide the class in half. As one student from each team goes to the map at the same time, name one of these geographical features. The student who locates it first on the map earns one point for his or her team. Continue the game until you have named all the features that you want students to identify. The team with the most points wins the game.

Gilberte:	C'est le calcul. Réussir, ce n'est pas facile. Je prends beaucoup de notes dans mon cahier. Après, je les mets dans mon sac à dos parce que je les perds toujours.
Amadou:	J'écris beaucoup dans le labo de chimie. Je ne peux pas dormir dans ce cours—il est trop difficile à comprendre.°
Gilberte:	Tu parles! Dis, je dois aller à la librairie après les cours. Est-ce que tu peux venir avec moi?
Amadou:	Oui, à 5h00. Je suis arrivé il y a une semaine, et alors je n'ai pas eu le temps de tout acheter.
Gilberte:	Bon ben, j'ai une autre conférence,° puis je vais aller au Centre de recherches° et ensuite° je peux aller avec toi à la librairie. De quoi as-tu besoin?
Amadou:	Qu'est-ce qui est sur ta liste? Qu'as-tu acheté?
Gilberte:	Oh, j'ai déjà acheté des trombones, un feutre, une gomme, un bloc-notes, un carnet, le manuel de calcul, une agrafeuse et une belle trousse.
Amadou:	Tout ça?
Gilberte:	Bien sûr. Dis donc, Amadou, tu choisis le russe ou le grec cette année?
Amadou:	Je suis le cours de russe.
Gilberte:	Et moi, de grec. Alors, il faut chercher ces livres aussi.
Amadou:	Bon, d'accord. Oh, attention! Voilà la prof.

Qu'est-ce qu'on peut acheter à la librairie? (Paris)

---

comprendre *to understand*; **une conférence** *lecture*; **la recherche** *research*; **ensuite** *puis*

Complétez chaque phrase avec l'expression convenable (appropriate) de la liste suivante d'après le dialogue.

comprendre	russe	censeur	rentrée	séchée
enseignement	notes	trombones	dissertation	

1. Aujourd'hui Amadou et Gilberte sont au lycée Henri IV parce que c'est la....
2. Au Sénégal, Amadou n'a pas réussi tout de suite en algèbre parce qu'il l'a souvent....
3. Le lycée Henri IV est bien connu; l'... qu'on y offre est superbe.
4. Le... a donné à Amadou son emploi du temps.
5. Les lycéens qui suivent la littérature doivent écrire une... à la fin du cours.
6. Gilberte écrit beaucoup de... dans son cahier.
7. Pour Amadou, le cours de chimie est difficile à....
8. Gilberte a déjà acheté des... à la librairie.
9. Amadou a choisi de suivre le....

Pierre écrit sa dissertation de littérature sur ordinateur.

Cooperative Group Practice

Un plan de Paris

Put students in small groups, and give each group a map of Paris and a map of the **métro**. First, have students locate **le lycée Henri IV** on the Left Bank. Next, have them make a list of activities that Gilberte and Amadou can easily do after school, getting to the appropriate location either on foot or by **métro**. If students have Gilberte and Amadou walk to a park, store or museum, ask them to write the directions Gilberte and Amadou take to get to their destination. If they have Gilberte and Amadou take the **métro**, have them write the name of the **métro** lines they take, listing all **correspondances**.

**Audiocassette/CD
Activity 3**

Answers

2 1. la salle de classe
2. la librairie
3. la librairie
4. le bureau du directeur
5. la salle de classe
6. chez moi
7. chez moi
8. la librairie
9. le bureau du directeur
10. la salle de classe
11. chez moi

3 Answers will vary.

2 | *Où êtes-vous quand vous faites les activités suivantes? Mettez un* ✓ *dans le blanc approprié.*

	la salle de classe	la librairie	chez moi	le bureau du directeur
1. prendre des notes				
2. choisir de nouveaux feutres				
3. acheter des manuels				
4. recevoir un emploi du temps				
5. assister à une conférence				
6. sécher un cours				
7. finir la lecture				
8. chercher un bloc-notes				
9. remplir une fiche d'inscription				
10. passer un examen				
11. parler du calcul au téléphone				

3 | *C'est à toi!*

1. Est-ce que tu as séché un cours l'année dernière? Si oui, quel cours?
2. La rentrée cette année, c'était quand?
3. Tu as un bon emploi du temps? Pourquoi ou pourquoi pas?
4. Quels cours vont être difficiles pour toi cette année?
5. Quel cours t'inquiète?
6. Dans quel cours est-ce qu'il n'est pas possible de dormir?
7. Dans ton cours de littérature, est-ce que tu as une liste de responsabilités comme Gilberte?
8. Qu'est-ce que tu as besoin d'acheter à la librairie?

Enquête culturelle

Comme vous savez déjà, le Sénégal est une république depuis 1960 quand il a reçu son indépendance de la France. Aujourd'hui, comme beaucoup de pays africains, le Sénégal a des problèmes avec l'environnement. Le nombre d'animaux et de poissons au Sénégal diminue, et le pays, qui se développe, contribue à la déforestation et aussi à la désertification de l'Afrique. Dakar est la capitale du Sénégal. Située au bord de la mer, la ville est sur le point le plus à l'ouest de toute l'Afrique.

Amadou est de Dakar, la plus grande ville du Sénégal.

À Dakar il est facile de trouver l'influence de la colonisation des Français. Par exemple, le système d'enseignement reflète le système français. Même au Sénégal on donne une grande importance au bac. Seulement 70 à 80 pour cent des lycéens francophones y réussissent. À l'école les cours sont en français, mais au C.E.S. et au lycée, on étudie aussi l'anglais. Pour les élèves qui vont quitter leurs villages, il est important d'apprendre le français aussi bien que l'ouolof, la langue nationale du Sénégal.

Les étudiants sénégalais qui ont réussi au bac suivent des cours à l'Université de Dakar.

Les écoles françaises insistent sur la compétence de l'élève. On demande souvent aux élèves d'écrire des rédactions et des dissertations. Les examens avec des questions à choix multiples n'existent pratiquement pas.

Une célèbre librairie-papeterie parisienne est Gibert Jeune.

En France on a souvent des cours dans une salle de conférences ou dans un amphithéâtre où le professeur donne une conférence à peut-être 200 élèves.

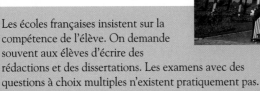

Jacqueline écrit une rédaction pour son cours de philosophie.

C'est la responsabilité des lycéens d'acheter les livres et les autres nécessités pour les cours. On achète les livres et les manuels pour les cours dans une librairie, et on trouve les cahiers, les stylos et le papier dans une papeterie. On trouve souvent une librairie-papeterie où on vend toutes ces choses.

Critical Thinking

Le Sénégal

If students made a map of Senegal as described in the cross-curricular activity on page 4, ask them to determine why Senegal's proximity to the ocean and the presence of a savanna have contributed to the country's economic prosperity. Students should point out that the fishing industry and international trade are a direct result of the country's location on the Atlantic, and the savanna is an arable region conducive to the growing of crops.

Teacher's Notes

1. The **Enquête culturelle** section contains a number of words that are not active vocabulary, but they are all easily recognizable cognates. Cognates in this reading include **république, indépendance, nombre, diminue, se développe, contribue, déforestation, désertification, située, point, influence, colonisation, système, reflète, importance, pour cent, important, ouolof, langue, insistent, compétence, questions, multiples, existent, pratiquement, amphithéâtre, nécessités, papier** and **papeterie**. These passive vocabulary words will be used again only in activities that specifically check comprehension of the **Enquête culturelle**. Before beginning this section, you may want to review reading strategies relating to cognates in the **Sur la bonne piste** section of Units 2, 3 and 11 in the first level of *C'est à toi!* 2. Senegal was discussed on page 359 in the first level of *C'est à toi!* and on page 376 in the second level. 3. Since its independence, Senegal has been a multiparty democracy. Thanks largely to Senegal's first president, Léopold Senghor, the country achieved economic and political stability. Abdou Diouf, Senghor's prime minister, succeeded the first president of the country in 1981 when Senghor retired. In the 1990s there have been mounting protests over government corruption, unemployment and poverty. 4. Another ecological problem in Senegal is soil damage in certain regions due to an overcultivation of peanuts. Consequently, there has been an effort to plant other crops. Senegal is primarily an agricultural country, with peanuts and peanut products making up 20 percent of its exports.

Answers

4 1. Le numéro d'animaux et de poissons diminue au Sénégal.
2. Le Sahara devient plus grand aujourd'hui.
3. Dakar est situé au bord de la mer, sur le point le plus à l'ouest de l'Afrique.
4. Le système d'enseignement sénégalais ressemble au système français.
5. Vingt à 30 pour cent des élèves francophones ne réussissent pas au bac chaque année.
6. Le grand débat maintenant est : Doit-on donner les cours en français ou en ouolof?
7. En général, les élèves français écrivent plus que les élèves américains.
8. Deux cents élèves peuvent assister à une conférence dans un lycée français.
9. Non, les élèves français doivent acheter les manuels pour les cours.
10. On achète toutes les nécessités pour l'école dans une librairie-papeterie.

Teacher's Notes

1. In the first and second levels of *C'est à toi!*, you may have asked your students to keep a cultural journal. In the third level of *C'est à toi!*, students are asked to record their cultural reflections and understandings about a key topic in each unit in a **Journal personnel**. Additional questions for this cultural journal will be presented in critical thinking activities throughout the third-level book. You may want students to write in French or in English, depending on the difficulty of each topic and their ability. 2. All structure in Unit 1 is recycled from the first and second levels of *C'est à toi!* 3. Regular **-er** verbs, presented on page 25 in the first level of *C'est à toi!* and re-

La désertification est un problème pour le Sénégal parce que le Sahara devient de plus en plus grand.

Arabéa et Paul travaillent dans le labo de chimie.

4 | *Répondez aux questions suivantes.*

1. Qu'est-ce qui diminue au Sénégal?
2. Est-ce que le Sahara devient plus grand ou plus petit aujourd'hui?
3. Où est situé Dakar?
4. Le système d'enseignement sénégalais ressemble au système de quel autre pays?
5. Combien d'élèves francophones ne réussissent pas au bac chaque année?
6. Quel est maintenant le grand débat dans les écoles sénégalaises?
7. En général, est-ce que les élèves français écrivent plus ou moins que les élèves américains?
8. Combien d'élèves peuvent assister à une conférence dans un lycée français?
9. Est-ce que les lycées donnent les manuels pour les cours aux élèves en France?
10. Où achète-t-on toutes les nécessités pour l'école?

Journal personnel

In first- and second-year French, you may have kept a cultural journal in which you recorded your observations about francophone cultures, similarities and differences between francophone and American cultures, and personal reflections. In this unit you have learned that French students are evaluated on their written and oral work with little testing of specific data as found on multiple-choice or fill-in-the-blank exams. Instead, teachers in France require students to synthesize their knowledge by writing compositions, major papers and essay tests, as well as by reciting in class and giving oral reports. How do you think this type of evaluation helps a student? Compare the French method with your own experiences. How are they the same? How are they different? Which do you prefer? Now begin a cultural journal for third-year French and record your responses to these questions and comments.

Structure

Present tense of regular verbs ending in *-er, -ir* and *-re*

To form the present tense of a regular **-er** verb, add the endings **-e**, **-es**, **-e**, **-ons**, **-ez** and **-ent** to the stem of the verb depending on the corresponding subject pronouns.

regarder			
je	**regarde**	Je **regarde** l'heure.	*I look at the time.*
tu	**regardes**	**Regardes**-tu le tableau?	*Are you looking at the board?*
il/elle/on	**regarde**	Elle **regarde** son emploi du temps.	*She's looking at her schedule.*
nous	**regardons**	Que **regardons**-nous à la télé?	*What are we watching on TV?*
vous	**regardez**	Vous ne **regardez** pas vos notes.	*You don't look at your notes.*
ils/elles	**regardent**	Ils **regardent** le directeur.	*They're looking at the principal.*

viewed on page 4 in the second level, are recycled here. 4. You might choose to review orthographically changing **-er** verbs at this time. Infinitives that end in **-cer**, such as **commencer** and **recommencer**, have a **nous** form ending in **-çons**. Infinitives that end in **-ger**, like **changer**, **déménager**, **manger**, **nager**, **plonger**, **ranger** and **voyager**, have a **nous** form ending in **-eons**.

Infinitives that end in **-yer**, such as **envoyer** and **nettoyer**, change the y to an i in the **je, tu, il/elle/on** and **ils/elles** forms. Infinitives that end in **-eter**, such as **acheter**, change the e to an è when the following vowel is not pronounced. Infinitives that end in **-ener**, **-eser** or **-ever**, such as **emmener**, **peser**, **enlever** and **se lever**, also change the e to an è when the following vowel is not pronounced. Infini-

tives that end in **-écher**, **-érer** or **-éter**, such as **sécher**, **espérer**, **préférer** and **s'inquiéter**, also change the é to an è when the following vowel is not pronounced.

To form the present tense of a regular **-ir** verb, add the endings **-is, -is, -it, -issons, -issez** and **-issent** to the stem of the verb depending on the corresponding subject pronouns.

choisir

je	**choisis**	Je **choisis** un cours d'algèbre.	*I choose an algebra course.*
tu	**choisis**	Tu **choisis** tes cours?	*Are you choosing your classes?*
il/elle/on	**choisit**	Il ne **choisit** pas le bac S.	*He doesn't choose the bac S.*
nous	**choisissons**	Nous **choisissons** nos profs.	*We choose our teachers.*
vous	**choisissez**	Ne **choisissez**-vous pas le russe?	*Don't you choose Russian?*
ils/elles	**choisissent**	Elles **choisissent** leurs manuels.	*They're choosing their textbooks.*

M. Aknouch finit le journal chaque soir. (La Rochelle)

Pour téléphoner, choisissez votre heure.

Télécarte 50　France Telecom

To form the present tense of a regular **-re** verb, add the endings **-s, -s, —, -ons, -ez** and **-ent** to the stem of the verb depending on the corresponding subject pronouns.

perdre

je	**perds**	Je **perds** souvent mes notes.	*I often lose my notes.*
tu	**perds**	Quand **perds**-tu ton chemin?	*When do you lose your way?*
il/elle/on	**perd**	Elle ne **perd** jamais aux échecs.	*She never loses at chess.*
nous	**perdons**	Nous ne **perdons** pas notre temps.	*We don't waste our time.*
vous	**perdez**	Vous **perdez** toujours quelque chose.	*You're always losing something.*
ils/elles	**perdent**	Ils **perdent** quelquefois leurs billets.	*Sometimes they do lose their tickets.*

Perdez vite tous vos kilos en trop

OBJECTIF BAC
GUIDE SECONDE
Cours, Méthodes, Corrigés-types
○ Français
○ Histoire
○ Géographie
○ Économie
○ Anglais
○ Mathématiques
○ Physique
○ Biologie
HACHETTE Éducation

Vous attendez le bus?

Oui, nous l'attendons depuis cinq minutes.

Teacher's Notes

1. Regular **-ir** verbs, introduced on page 104 in the first level of *C'est à toi!* and reviewed on page 5 in the second level, are recycled here. 2. Here are the other regular **-ir** verbs that students learned in the first and second levels of *C'est à toi!*: **atterrir, choisir, finir, nourrir, remplir** and **réussir**. 3. Regular **-re** verbs, introduced on pages 231-32 in the first level of *C'est à toi!* and reviewed on page 5 in the second level, are recycled here. 4. Here are the other regular **-re** verbs that students learned in the first and second levels of *C'est à toi!*: **descendre, entendre, perdre, rendre** and **vendre**.

TPR

Verbs Ending in -re

To practice listening for the distinction made between the third person singular and plural forms of regular **-re** verbs, you may choose to have students do this activity. Ask each student to make two cards, one with one person pictured and the other with two people pictured. Read pairs of sentences using pronouns and **-re** verbs, for example, **Il perd le carnet** and **Ils perdent le carnet**. Students should raise the card picturing one person if they hear a singular verb; they should raise the card with two people pictured if they hear a sentence with a plural verb.

Paired Practice

Verb Review

You may want to put your students in pairs to review regular verbs ending in **-er, -ir** and **-re**. Have students make subject cards with various noun or pronoun subjects, for example, **je, tu, le directeur, Suzanne, Marc et moi, Chantal et toi, les profs**. One student holds up a subject card and names an infinitive from Unit 1 in the third level of *C'est à toi!* or the first or second level of the series. The other student combines the two orally to form a complete sentence, for example, **Le directeur déjeune**. Students earn a point for each accurate sentence that they form. (You may also want to award points to students who detect incorrect sentences.) Students take turns until all the verbs assigned for review are covered.

Audiocassette/CD
Activity 5

Answers

5 1. Sabrina parle pendant la leçon.
2. Angélique pense avant de parler en classe.
3. Sabrina joue avec les trombones en classe.
4. Angélique finit le travail.
5. Sabrina vend ses devoirs.
6. Sabrina sèche le cours de littérature.
7. Sabrina perd le manuel de chimie.
8. Sabrina rate le cours de russe.
9. Angélique accepte ses responsabilités.

Teacher's Notes

1. To practice the third person singular and plural forms of regular **-er**, **-ir** and **-re** verbs, follow up Activity 6 with questions about the survey, for example, **Quand est-ce que Jean nage?** **Qui finit les devoirs à l'école?** 2. You might choose to further review regular **-er**, **-ir** and **-re** verbs by making a list of locations other than school. For each location, such as **la banque**, **le grand magasin** or **l'hôtel**, give a noun or pronoun subject. Then ask the class to brainstorm sentences using **-er**, **-ir** and **-re** verbs that express actions that occur there. For example, students might say **M. Duval touche ses chèques de voyage à la banque**, **Les vendeurs vendent des gants au grand magasin** and **Nous remplissons nos fiches de commande à l'hôtel.**

Pratique

Modèles:

écouter le professeur en classe
Angélique écoute le professeur en classe.

manger en classe
Sabrina mange en classe.

5 *Dites si c'est Angélique, la bonne élève, ou Sabrina, la mauvaise élève, qui fait les choses suivantes.*

1. parler pendant la leçon
2. penser avant de parler en classe
3. jouer avec les trombones en classe
4. finir le travail
5. vendre ses devoirs
6. sécher le cours de littérature
7. perdre le manuel de chimie
8. rater le cours de russe
9. accepter ses responsabilités

6 *Faites une enquête où vous demandez à cinq élèves s'ils ou elles font les choses suivantes à l'école ou après l'école. Copiez la grille suivante. Demandez à chaque élève s'il ou elle fait chaque chose. Puis mettez "à" ou "après" dans l'espace blanc, selon sa réponse.*

Modèle:

Anne: Est-ce que tu prépares un exposé oral à l'école ou après l'école?

Patrick: Je prépare un exposé oral après l'école.

	Patrick	**Éric**	**Katia**	**Sophie**	**Jean**
préparer un exposé oral	*après*				
attendre les profs					
étudier					
aider tes amis					
échanger des notes					
finir les devoirs					
montrer des photos aux amis					
nager					
recycler les boîtes					
téléphoner					

Est-ce que Marie-France finit ses devoirs à l'école ou après l'école?

Cooperative Group Practice

Regular Verbs

Put students in small groups of four or five. Give each student several blank note cards. The first student in each group writes an **-er**, **-ir** or **-re** infinitive on his or her card, for example, **finir**, and holds it up for the group to see. He or she then says a sentence using that verb in the present tense, for example, **Je finis mes devoirs.** Then the next student in the group gives a new sentence using a different subject and changing the end of the sentence, for example, **Jean-Paul finit le petit déjeuner.** When each student has given a sentence with the first verb, the second student begins with a new verb.

Avec un(e) partenaire, jouez les rôles d'un(e) élève de votre lycée et d'un(e) élève d'un échange international qui veut connaître la vie dans cette école. L'élève d'un échange international pose les questions et l'autre élève y répond.

1. porter des jeans
2. choisir les cours
3. acheter les manuels
4. rendre visite au directeur ou à la directrice chaque jour
5. entrer dans la salle de classe en retard
6. travailler dur
7. utiliser les ordinateurs

Present tense of irregular verbs

Many French verbs are called irregular because their forms follow an unpredictable pattern. Here are the present tense forms of four important irregular verbs, **aller**, **être**, **avoir** and **faire**. These "building block" verbs are also used to form many expressions.

aller

je	**vais**	Je **vais** au bureau de la directrice.	*I'm going to the principal's office.*
tu	**vas**	Où **vas**-tu?	*Where do you go?*
il/elle/on	**va**	Ça **va**?	*How are things going?*
nous	**allons**	Nous **allons** acheter ces manuels.	*We're going to buy these textbooks.*
vous	**allez**	Vous n'**allez** pas bien?	*Aren't you feeling well?*
ils/elles	**vont**	Ils **vont** toujours en cours.	*They always go to class.*

être

je	**suis**	Je ne **suis** pas chez moi.	*I am not at home.*
tu	**es**	**Es**-tu lycéenne?	*Are you a (high school) student?*
il/elle/on	**est**	C'**est** la rentrée.	*It's the first day of school.*
nous	**sommes**	Nous **sommes** diligents.	*We are hardworking.*
vous	**êtes**	Vous **êtes** russe?	*Are you Russian?*
ils/elles	**sont**	Ces cours **sont** difficiles.	*These courses are hard.*

Jim Carrey
"Je suis un vrai clown !"

Modèles:

parler anglais dans le cours de français
Élève A: Est-ce que vous parlez anglais dans le cours de français?
Élève B: Non, nous ne parlons pas anglais dans le cours de français.

déjeuner à la cantine
Élève A: Est-ce que vous déjeunez à la cantine?
Élève B: Oui, nous déjeunons à la cantine.

Grattez-vite la case dorée ci-dessous pour savoir si vous allez recevoir cette superbe peluche !

Grattez vite!

Votre cadeau !

FAMILLE
et avec votre belle-soeur ça va comment ?

Nous sommes en terminale cette année.

Answers

7 Possible answers:

1. Est-ce que vous portez des jeans?
   Oui, nous portons des jeans.
2. Est-ce que vous choisissez les cours?
   Oui, nous choisissons les cours.
3. Est-ce que vous achetez les manuels?
   Non, nous n'achetons pas les manuels.
4. Est-ce que vous rendez visite au directeur chaque jour?
   Non, nous ne rendons pas visite au directeur chaque jour.
5. Est-ce que vous entrez dans la salle de classe en retard?
   Non, nous n'entrons pas dans la salle de classe en retard.
6. Est-ce que vous travaillez dur?
   Oui, nous travaillons dur.
7. Est-ce que vous utilisez les ordinateurs?
   Oui, nous utilisons les ordinateurs.

Teacher's Notes

1. **Aller**, introduced on page 58 in the first level of *C'est à toi!* and reviewed on page 18 in the second level, is recycled here. 2. Remind students that liaison is optional between the **je**, **tu**, **nous**, **vous** and **ils/elles** present tense forms of **aller** and a word beginning with a vowel sound. 3. **Être**, introduced on page 140 in the first level of *C'est à toi!* and reviewed on page 18 in the second level, is recycled here. 4. You might remind students that liaison is optional with **être** when words that follow it begin with a vowel sound, but is usually made after the third person singular form. 5. Remind students that when giving a person's profession with **être**, the indefinite article is omitted in French, for example, **M. Fajour est directeur.**

Game

On y va!

You might want to create game boards to help students review forms of **aller** in the present tense. On pieces of poster board or card stock, make an upside down "U" and divide it into 15 even squares. In each square paste a picture of a location that students know, such as **l'aéroport, la librairie, la montagne** and **le parc**. Make sets of cards with pronoun and noun subjects (**je, Danielle, les médecins,** etc.). Put students in small groups and give each group a board, a set of cards and a die. The first student in each group rolls the die and advances the number of squares indicated by the roll. Then he or she takes a card from the pile and states where the person on the card is going, according to what is pictured on the square. If the student gives a correct sentence, for example, **Ahmed va à la librairie**, he or she gets to stay on the square; if the student gives an incorrect sentence, he or she goes back to the beginning of the board. The first student to reach the end of the board wins. You may choose to have students play the game again, this time giving sentences in the near future, for example, **Ahmed va aller à la librairie.**

Teacher's Notes

1. **Avoir**, introduced on page 95 in the first level of *C'est à toi!* and reviewed on page 34 in the second level, is recycled here. 2. **Faire**, introduced on page 192 in the first level of *C'est à toi!* and reviewed on page 34 in the second level, is recycled here. 3. You may want to remind students that **ai** in the **je**, **tu**, **il/elle/on** and **vous** forms of **faire** is pronounced [ɛ], and **ai** in the **nous** form is pronounced [ə]. 4. You may want to review reflexive pronouns with your students as you go over the forms of **s'asseoir**. Reflexive verbs were introduced in Unit 4 in the second level of *C'est à toi!* Reflexive verbs will be reviewed in Unit 2. 5. You may want to remind students that **î** is used only in the infinitive and the third person singular of **connaître**, or when **t** follows **i**. 6. Remind students that **devenir** and **revenir** both belong to the **venir** verb family. 7. Remind students that **falloir** has only one present tense form: **il faut**.

Cooperative Group Practice

Survey

To practice the forms of **avoir**, have students each make a grid. Across the top have them write the names of five of their classmates; from top to bottom, have them write the names of ten items that could be found in a house or garage. Each student interviews the five classmates listed on his or her grid, asking each one if his or her family has each object, for example, **Jérôme, vous avez une tondeuse?** The interviewee responds affirmatively or negatively. (**Oui, nous avons une tondeuse./Non, nous n'avons pas de tondeuse.**) Each student records the answers on the grid and summarizes the results. When all the surveys are completed, put students in small groups and have them share their findings.

Qu'est-ce que Floriane porte quand il fait froid?

Qu'est-ce que Véronique conduit au lycée?

Bis « La Cage aux Folles » devient «The Birdcage»

Elle a envie de lire

avoir

j'	ai	J'**ai** un cours de sciences po à 11h00.	*I have a political science course at 11:00.*
tu	as	**As**-tu rendez-vous avec le prof?	*Do you have an appointment with the teacher?*
il/elle/on	a	Il **a** quel âge?	*How old is he?*
nous	avons	Nous **avons** un autre exposé.	*We have another report.*
vous	avez	Vous **avez** besoin d'une gomme?	*Do you need an eraser?*
ils/elles	ont	Ils n'**ont** pas faim.	*They're not hungry.*

faire

je	fais	Je **fais** la connaissance du censeur.	*I'm meeting the dean.*
tu	fais	**Fais**-tu du sport?	*Do you play sports?*
il/elle/on	fait	Il **fait** du soleil.	*It's sunny.*
nous	faisons	Nous ne **faisons** rien.	*We're not doing anything.*
vous	faites	Que **faites**-vous?	*What are you doing?*
ils/elles	font	Ils **font** du vélo.	*They go biking.*

Here is the **je** form of the other irregular verbs that you have already learned. Beside it is a sentence containing one of the other forms of the verb. To review all the present tense forms of these verbs, see the Grammar Summary at the end of this book.

s'asseoir	je m'assieds	Nous **nous asseyons** dans la salle de conférences.	*We're sitting in the lecture hall.*
boire	je bois	Que **buvez**-vous?	*What are you drinking?*
conduire	je conduis	Ils **conduisent** trop vite.	*They drive too fast.*
connaître	je connais	Elle **connaît** le nouvel élève.	*She knows the new student.*
courir	je cours	Il ne **court** plus.	*He doesn't run anymore.*
croire	je crois	Nous ne te **croyons** pas.	*We don't believe you.*
devenir	je deviens	Elle **devient** comptable.	*She's becoming an accountant.*
devoir	je dois	Ils **doivent** réussir.	*They have to succeed.*
dire	je dis	Que **dites**-vous?	*What are you saying?*
dormir	je dors	Vous **dormez** en cours?	*Do you sleep in class?*
écrire	j'écris	Ils **écrivent** une dissertation.	*They write a research paper.*
falloir	il faut	Il ne **faut** pas sécher les cours.	*You must not skip class.*
lire	je lis	**Lisez**-vous la lecture?	*Are you reading the reading?*

Critical Thinking

Irregular Verbs

When students ask why there are so many irregular verbs in French, you might offer the theory that verbs become irregular as forms and usage change due to frequent use. Challenge students to find examples of this in English ads. For example, "Got milk?" deviates from the standard question "Do you have milk?"

TPR

Connaître ou savoir?

Remind students that **connaître** is used to express knowing in the sense of being familiar or acquainted with people, places and things, while **savoir** is used to express knowing factual information or how to do something. To give students practice differentiating between these two verbs, play a tape or sing excerpts from famous songs that have the verb "to know" in them, for example, "Do you know the way to San José?" or "To know, know, know you is to love, love, love you." Have students hold up a card with "C" if they think the lyrics of the song would be expressed in French by **connaître** or a card with "S" if they think the lyrics would be expressed by **savoir**.

mettre	je **mets**	Où **mettez**-vous mes manuels?	*Where are you putting my textbooks?*
offrir	j'**offre**	Qu'est-ce que tu m'**offres**?	*What are you giving me?*
ouvrir	j'**ouvre**	Vous **ouvrez** à quelle heure?	*At what time do you open?*
partir	je **pars**	Ils **partent** tout de suite.	*They're leaving right away.*
pouvoir	je **peux**	Nous ne **pouvons** pas comprendre.	*We can't understand.*
prendre	je **prends**	Vous **prenez** l'agrafeuse?	*Are you taking the stapler?*
recevoir	je **reçois**	Nous **recevons** nos emplois du temps.	*We get our schedules.*
revenir	je **reviens**	D'où **revenez**-vous?	*Where are you coming back from?*
savoir	je **sais**	**Savez**-vous le grec?	*Do you know Greek?*
sortir	je **sors**	Ils ne **sortent** plus ensemble.	*They don't go out together anymore.*
suivre	je **suis**	Quel cours **suis**-tu?	*What class are you taking?*
venir	je **viens**	Il **vient** de Chine.	*He comes from China.*
vivre	je **vis**	Nous **vivons** à Montréal.	*We live in Montreal.*
voir	je **vois**	Vous **voyez** mon carnet?	*Do you see my notebook?*
vouloir	je **veux**	Elle ne **veut** pas passer cet examen.	*She doesn't want to take this test.*

L'enseignement qu'on offre au lycée est extra.

Pratique

Dites qui a besoin de chaque objet illustré.

1. je

3. tu

2. Joanne et toi

4. Nathalie et moi

Modèle:

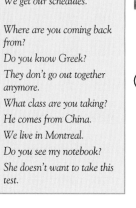

Françoise
Françoise a besoin d'un roman.

Tu viens au match avec moi ce soir?

Audiocassette/CD Activity 8

Answers

8 1. J'ai besoin d'un carnet.
2. Joanne et toi, vous avez besoin d'une gomme.
3. Tu as besoin d'un bloc-notes.
4. Nathalie et moi, nous avons besoin d'une agrafeuse.
5. La prof a besoin d'un trombone.
6. Laurent et Céline ont besoin d'un manuel de russe.

Teacher's Notes

1. You might tell students that **pouvoir** is usually followed by an infinitive. 2. You may want to remind students that **prendre** can also mean "to have something to eat or drink." 3. Point out that **recevoir** can also mean "to receive (guests)." 4. Remind students that to express an event that has just taken place, they should use **venir de** followed by an infinitive, for example, **Je viens de préparer mon exposé oral**. 5. **Venir de** is also used to express "coming from" a location, for example, **Élisabeth vient d'Italie**. To say that someone is from a country with a masculine name, you use **du**. To express that someone comes from a country with a feminine name, you use **de** or **d'**. To say that someone is from a large island with a feminine name, you use **de la**. 6. **Vouloir** can be followed by either a noun or an infinitive. The conditional forms of **vouloir** are used to express politeness, for example, **Nous voudrions une omelette**.

Games

Mon sac à dos

To practice the present tense forms of **prendre** and vocabulary from this lesson, divide the class into two teams. Students take turns naming an item they take from their **sac à dos**. For example, the first student on the first team begins by saying **Je prends un bloc-notes de mon sac à dos.** The second student on the same team then says **Je prends un bloc-notes et un feutre de mon sac à dos.** Students on the first team continue adding items to the original sentence until one of them gets the order wrong or forgets an object. Then the second team begins. The team that finishes with the longest sentence wins.

Verb *Tic Tac Toe*

To practice irregularly formed verbs, have students work in pairs. Each student plays with a different colored pen. Pass out a copy of the *Tic Tac Toe* worksheet to each pair. The heading of the worksheet is the infinitive of the verb to be conjugated. In the grid each of the nine boxes contains one subject pronoun (**je, tu, il, elle, on, nous, vous, ils, elles**). Students proceed as in the English game and write the correct verb form in each box to match the given pronoun. If a student makes a mistake, his or her opponent can correct the mistake, steal the square and proceed with his or her regular turn. Three squares in a row wins the game. Two evenly matched students will have no winner, only a draw.

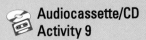

Audiocassette/CD
Activity 9

Answers

9 Possible answers:

1. Jean-Luc et Louis suivent un cours de calcul. Ils vont dans la salle de classe.
2. Tu suis un cours de biologie. Tu vas au labo.
3. Assane et Nora suivent un cours d'algèbre. Ils vont dans la salle de classe.
4. Martine et toi, vous suivez un cours de physique. Vous allez au labo.
5. Je suis un cours de sciences po. Je vais dans la salle de conférences.
6. Olivier suit un cours de philosophie. Il va dans la salle de conférences.
7. Marielle et moi, nous suivons un cours de géométrie. Nous allons dans la salle de classe.
8. Benjamin et Patricia suivent un cours de littérature. Ils vont dans la salle de conférences.

10 Possible answers:

1. Nadia lit un livre.
2. Jean-Marc et Lucien parlent.
3. Babette et moi, nous faisons les devoirs.
4. Gisèle écrit.
5. Robert boit.
6. Julie va au tableau.
7. Thierry ouvre la fenêtre.
8. Tu sors.

Paired Practice

Forming Sentences

Put students in pairs. Have one partner write ten original sentences using irregular verbs from the list on page 12. Have the other partner write ten original sentences using irregular verbs from the list on page 13. After they have finished, have each student read his or her sentences aloud. Partners repeat each sentence, changing singular verbs to plural ones and vice versa, for example, **Tu reçois des copains vendredi soir./Vous recevez des copains vendredi soir.**

5. la prof   6. Laurent et Céline

Modèle:

Gérard/la chimie
Gérard suit un cours de chimie.
Il va au labo.

Modèle:

Raphaël dort.

9 *Dites que vous et vos copains suivez les cours indiqués. Puis dites où vous allez pour ces cours avec l'expression convenable de la liste suivante.*

au labo	dans la salle de classe	dans la salle de conférences

1. Jean-Luc et Louis/le calcul
2. tu/la biologie
3. Assane et Nora/l'algèbre
4. Martine et toi/la physique
5. je/les sciences po
6. Olivier/la philosophie
7. Marielle et moi/la géométrie
8. Benjamin et Patricia/la littérature

VACANCES
Suivez le bon guide !

10 *Utilisez l'illustration pour dire ce que (what) fait chaque élève avant la classe.*

Game

Le cuirassé

To further review irregular verbs, have pairs of students play a modified version of "Battleship." Across the top of a sheet of paper, students list six pronoun subjects (**je, tu, il, nous, vous, elles**). In a column on the left, they list ten infinitives. (Both partners list the same infinitives.) Next, students create and fill in their own grid, choosing 15 combinations from the various possibilities. For example, if the student chooses the square where **il** and **revenir** meet, he or she writes **Il revient** there. Students then take turns calling out subject/verb combinations to see if they can sink their opponent's ships by guessing which subject/verb combinations he or she chose. If the opponent's ship is not hit, the opponent says **non**. If the opponent's ship is hit, the opponent says **oui** and the caller wins another turn. If the caller conjugates the verb incorrectly, the opponent challenges the target by conjugating the verb correctly, thus voiding the hit. Each student marks on his or her paper the number of hits received. At the end of the allotted time, the student who has sunk the most verb ships wins.

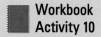

Amadou a écrit une lettre à ses parents à Dakar. Avant de l'envoyer, il veut vérifier les verbes. Aidez-le et écrivez le présent des verbes indiqués.

> Mes chers parents,
>
> Je (être) à Paris chez les Morot depuis huit jours. Ils (habiter) dans un appartement assez loin de mon lycée. Mme Morot (travailler) comme médecin, et son mari (faire) le ménage pour le moment.
>
> Je (aller) au lycée tous les jours. Mes amis et moi, nous (prendre) le métro au lycée.
>
> Mon professeur de sciences po n'(être) pas un très bon prof. Par exemple, quand il (donner) une conférence, il (lire) ses notes d'un livre, puis il (sortir) sans nous dire le travail pour demain.
>
> Pour mon cours de français nous (préparer) un exposé oral deux fois par semaine. Nous (étudier) beaucoup et nous (écrire) une rédaction chaque jour. Tous les élèves (vouloir) suivre ce cours parce que la prof (être) dynamique. Mlle Nguyen (vivre) à Paris depuis quelques semaines. Là, on (savoir) qu'on (aller) apprendre quelque chose!
>
> À la fin de la journée, je (mettre) tout dans mon sac à dos, et je (partir) pour le café où je (voir) mes amis. Nous (boire) un café, un jus de fruit ou un coca.
>
> (Envoyer)-moi une lettre bientôt!
>
>   Ton fils,
>
>   Amadou

Chaque jour Amadou prend le métro au lycée. (Paris)

ÉTUDES
QUAND "LES NULS" REPASSENT LE BAC

Interrogative pronouns

To ask for information, use interrogative pronouns. The pronoun you use depends on whether you are referring to a person or a thing and on whether the pronoun is the subject, direct object or object of a preposition.

	Subject	Direct Object	Object of Preposition
People	qui qui est-ce qui	qui qui est-ce que	qui
Things	qu'est-ce qui	que qu'est-ce que	quoi

Use **qui**, **qui est-ce qui** or **qu'est-ce qui** as the subject of the verb.

Qui te donne ton emploi du temps?   *Who gives you your schedule?*

Qu'est-ce qui t'inquiète?   *What worries you?*

Workbook Activity 10

Answers

11 suis, habitent, travaille, fait, vais, prenons, est, donne, lit, sort, préparons, étudions, écrivons, veulent, est, vit, sait, va, mets, pars, vois, buvons, Envoyez

Teacher's Notes

1. Interrogative pronouns, introduced on page 327 in the second level of *C'est à toi!*, are recycled here. 2. **Qui est-ce qui** is used less frequently than **qui** when the subject of a verb refers to a person. You might tell students that they can also ask the question in the first example by saying **Qui est-ce qui te donne ton emploi du temps**? 3. You may want to tell students that **qui** as a subject pronoun is always followed by a singular verb.

Cooperative Group Practice

Group Story

Put students in small groups of four or five. Give each group a set of ten cards; each card has a regular or an irregular verb on it. Have each group write a creative story in the present tense, built around the verb cards that they received. Tell students to add the nouns, adjectives and adverbs they need to make their story interesting. Next, have them practice telling their story to another group. Finally, you may wish to have each group present its story to the entire class, with each group member saying a sentence or two. (You might also choose to have each student write a short summary of what happens in other groups' stories to check listening comprehension.)

Cooperative Group Practice

Sentence Construction

To practice the present tense of **venir** and the expression **venir de** followed by an infinitive, put students in small groups of four or five. Give each group two sets of note cards. The first set contains different subjects (nouns or pronouns); the second set contains ten different noun phrases and infinitive phrases, for example, **la campagne** and **prendre des notes**. (Write different noun and infinitive phrases for each group.) The first student takes one card from each set and forms a sentence orally, for example, **Nous venons à la campagne** or **Nous venons de prendre des notes**. After all the cards have been used, groups exchange cards and students begin the activity again.

Answers

12 1. Que
2. Qu'est-ce que
3. Qu'est-ce que
4. À quoi
5. Qu'est-ce qui
6. Qui
7. Qui est-ce que
8. De qui
9. De quoi
10. Que

13 Possible answers:

1. Qu'est-ce que Salima porte sur la photo?
2. Avec qui Salima habite-t-elle?
3. Qui est allé la chercher à l'aéroport?
4. Qu'est-ce que Thomas lui a offert?
5. Qui conduit Salima à l'école tous les jours?
6. Qu'est-ce que Salima a préparé pour la famille Johnson?
7. Qu'est-ce qui est le plat national en Tunisie?
8. De quoi avait-elle besoin pour le couscous?
9. Avec qui a-t-elle assisté à un concert le weekend dernier?

Teacher's Notes

1. When **qui** and **que** are used as the direct object of a verb, the subject and verb are inverted. 2. If a noun subject is used with the object **que**, this noun subject follows the verb, for example, **Que lit Sabrina**? 3. For the two examples of an object of a preposition, you could also ask **Pour qui les cours vont-ils être difficiles**? and **De quoi est-ce que tu as besoin**? 4. You may want to point out to students that in French, interrogative pronouns always come directly after a preposition.

De quoi Thérèse a -t-elle besoin? (Les Antilles)

Modèle:

Qu'est-ce que tu aimes à l'école?
les cours

Qui est-ce que tu attends?

J'attends le censeur. J'ai besoin de mon emploi du temps.

Qu'est-ce que tu prends?

Moi, je prends le steak-frites.

Use **qui**, **qui est-ce que**, **que** or **qu'est-ce que** as the direct object of the verb.

Qui est-ce que Gilberte et Amadou attendent?	*For whom are Gilberte and Amadou waiting?*
Qu'est-ce que tu as acheté?	*What did you buy?*
Que remplit-on?	*What are they filling out?*

Use **qui** or **quoi** as the object of a preposition.

Pour qui est-ce que les cours vont être difficiles?	*For whom are classes going to be hard?*
De quoi as-tu besoin?	*What do you need?*

Pratique

12 *Sandrine est reporter pour le journal du lycée. Elle a fait une enquête sur ce que ses copains pensent de leur école, mais elle a perdu la première partie des questions de l'enquête de Khadim. Elle a toujours ses réponses à droite. Aidez Sandrine à compléter chaque question avec l'expression interrogative convenable.*

Questions	Réponses
1. ... suis-tu cette année?	français, grec, maths
2. ... tu aimes écrire?	des rédactions
3. ... tu n'aimes pas?	les dissertations
4. ... est-ce que tu réussis?	à des examens
5. ... t'inquiète?	le bac
6. ... est ton professeur favori?	Mlle Jourlait
7. ... tu n'aimes pas beaucoup?	le prof de maths
8. ... parles-tu avec tes amis?	du directeur
9. ... as-tu souvent besoin?	d'un ordinateur
10. ... viens-tu d'acheter à la librairie?	des carnets

13 *Sandrine vient d'écrire un article pour le journal sur Salima, une élève qui vient de Tunisie. Sandrine n'est pas certaine si tous les détails sont corrects. Quelles questions doit-elle poser pour vérifier les expressions en italique?*

1. Sur la photo Salima porte *un tee-shirt de Westbury High School*.
2. Salima habite *avec les Johnson*.
3. *Toute la famille* est allée la chercher à l'aéroport.
4. Thomas lui a offert *des fleurs*.
5. *Mme Johnson* conduit Salima à l'école tous les jours.
6. Salima a préparé *le couscous* pour la famille Johnson.
7. En Tunisie *le couscous* est le plat national.
8. Elle avait besoin *de poulet et de légumes* pour le couscous.
9. Le weekend dernier elle a assisté à un concert *avec Brandon et Sherry*.

Paired Practice

Sentence Reconstruction

Put students in pairs. Prepare eight questions using interrogative pronouns. Cut each question into three segments, making sure that there is only one possibility for recombining each question, for example, **Qui est-ce/qui a une/agrafeuse?** and **Que choisis-/tu à la/librairie?** Place the pieces for all eight sentences in an envelope and give a similar envelope to each pair of students. As each pair finishes combining the eight sentences, check the students' accuracy. You might choose to award a point for each question that is correctly recombined.

Les bandes dessinées

Put students in pairs. Select an American comic strip with a story that lends itself to asking questions using interrogative pronouns. Then take correction fluid and eliminate the words. Give a copy of the modified comic strip to each pair of students. Have the pairs write the dialogue in French, creating their own story. You may want to share each pair's cartoon with the entire class by making transparencies or posting the cartoons for all to see.

Direct object pronouns: *me, te, le, la, nous, vous, les*

Direct object pronouns answer the question "who" or "what" and replace direct objects. **Le**, **la** and **les** may refer to either people or things; **me**, **te**, **nous** and **vous** refer only to people.

	Masculine	Feminine	Before a Vowel Sound
Singular	me te le	me te la	m' t' l'
Plural	nous vous les	nous vous les	nous vous les

"Pourquoi ce mariage? C'est tout simple... Je l'aime"

These pronouns come right before the verb of which they are the object. The sentence may be affirmative, interrogative, negative or have an infinitive.

La tour Eiffel? Nous l'avons déjà vue.

Marie-Claire, tu m'entends?
Non, je ne t'entends pas, papa.

Marie-Claire, do you hear me?
No, I don't hear you, Dad.

Votre dissertation? Où la mettez-vous?
Je vais la mettre dans mon cahier, Monsieur.

Your research paper? Where are you putting it?
I'm going to put it in my notebook, Sir.

Le censeur nous attend dans son bureau?
Non, il vous attend dans le couloir.

Is the dean waiting for us in his office?
No, he's waiting for you in the hall.

Tes cours? Tu les as ratés?
Non, mais le bac, je l'ai raté.

Your classes? Did you fail them?
No, but the bac, I failed it.

Note that in the final pair of examples, the past participle of **rater** agrees in number and in gender with the preceding direct object pronoun.

IL (ou elle) **VOUS A QUITTÉ...**
Comment RETROUVER son amour ?
Ne restez pas dans la peine.
Vite ! Renseignez-vous sans engagement de votre part.
Appelez moi de suite (ou écrivez) à :
R. DE FREVILLE (TVmag) B.P. 316 · 55007 BAR-LE-DUC Cedex
29 79 28 24
Je peux vous aider à rétablir votre bonheur.

Game

Pronoun Relay Race

To practice using direct object pronouns in the **passé composé**, you might have students play this game. Divide the class into two teams. Prepare two sets of construction paper cards of subject pronouns, direct object pronouns, **avoir** forms, past participles, **e** and **s**. (It is a good idea to use a different color for each category.) Place one set of each category on the floor in front of each team. Make a list of about 20 sentences that each contain a preceding direct object in the **passé composé**. Have one student from each team go to the front of the room. Read the English version of a sentence from your list, for example, *The composition? I wrote it.* Instruct students to construct **Je l'ai écrite** by placing the correct cards on the ledge of the board. Then have two other students come to the board and set up the second sentence that you say, and so on. The team with the most correct sentences wins the game.

Workbook Activities 11-12

Teacher's Notes

1. Direct object pronouns, introduced on pages 183 and 191 in the second level of *C'est à toi!*, are recycled here. Before reviewing direct object pronouns with your students, you might ask them to find all the examples of direct object pronouns in the **Dialogue**. 2. You might want to review with students a list of other verbs that take direct objects, for example, **acheter, admirer, adorer, aider, aimer, apprendre, boire, chercher, choisir, comprendre, connaître, croire, demander, écouter, emmener, intéresser, inviter, lire, mettre, prendre, recevoir, regarder, remercier, remplir, suivre, trouver, utiliser, vendre** and **voir**. 3. You may want to review the difference between **nous** and **vous** as subject pronouns and direct object pronouns. 4. Remind students that **le, la, l'** and **les** can be used as both definite articles and direct object pronouns. 5. You may want to explain that direct object pronouns may precede **voici** and **voilà**, for example **Me voici.** (*Here I am.*) 6. Point out liaison after **nous, vous** and **les** before a verb beginning with a vowel sound. 7. Explain that when a pronoun is the direct object of an infinitive, it comes right before the infinitive and not before the conjugated verb. 8. You may want to point out verbs such as **attendre, chercher, demander, écouter** and **regarder** that do not take **à** or **pour** before a direct object in French because these prepositions are considered part of the infinitive. 9. Point out to students that in the **passé composé** the direct object pronoun in a negative sentence immediately precedes the form of **avoir**. 10. You may want to model the use of direct object pronouns by frequently peppering your French with statements that use them, for example **Je le sais** and **Je vous comprends**. Students will get used to hearing direct object pronouns and will find it more natural to produce them in classroom communication.

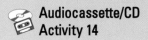
Pratique

Answers

14 1. Il le met dans son sac à dos.
2. Il la met dans sa trousse.
3. Il les met dans sa trousse.
4. Il le met dans son sac à dos.
5. Il les met dans sa trousse.
6. Il le met dans son sac à dos.
7. Il la met dans son sac à dos.
8. Il le met dans son sac à dos.

14 | *Est-ce qu'Amadou met les objets illustrés dans sa trousse ou dans son sac à dos?*

Modèles:

Il le met dans sa trousse.

1.

5.

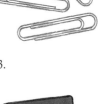

2.

6.

Il la met dans son sac à dos.

> Ce roman, tu le lis pour ton cours de littérature?

> Oui, je dois le finir ce soir.

3.

7.

4.

8.

Guy va à la maison tout de suite après les cours, et il veut prendre l'autobus avec ses amis. Lisez la liste suivante qui dit où vont les autres élèves après les cours. Puis dites si Guy attend ou n'attend pas ces personnes.

Sandrine	à la maison
Paul	chez lui
Delphine	au Centre de recherches
Julien	au fast-food
moi	chez moi
Marc	au stade
Éric	en ville
Mélanie	chez elle
Gisèle	à la librairie
toi	au travail
Élise	à la maison

1. Gisèle
2. je
3. Sandrine et Mélanie
4. Éric
5. Delphine et toi
6. Paul
7. Julien et Marc
8. Élise et moi

Modèles:

Sandrine
Il l'attend.

tu
Il ne t'attend pas.

Avec un(e) partenaire, demandez si les personnes indiquées écoutent les personnes qui les suivent. Dites qu'elles les écoutent, mais qu'elles ne les comprennent pas. Alternez les questions et les réponses avec votre partenaire. Suivez le modèle et l'ordre indiqué par le cercle.

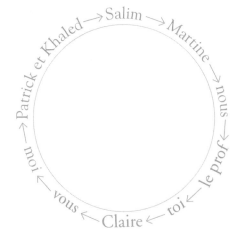

Modèle:

Élève A: Est-ce que Salim écoute Martine?

Élève B: Oui, il l'écoute, mais il ne la comprend pas. Est-ce que Martine nous écoute?

Élève A: Oui, elle vous écoute, mais elle ne vous comprend pas. Est-ce que nous…?

Mon ami Bernard? Je l'écoute toujours.

Mais il ne me comprend pas. Il est trop jeune.

Audiocassette/CD Activity 15

Answers

15 1. Il ne l'attend pas.
2. Il m'attend.
3. Il les attend.
4. Il ne l'attend pas.
5. Il ne vous attend pas.
6. Il l'attend.
7. Il ne les attend pas.
8. Il nous attend.

16 Est-ce que nous écoutons le prof?

Oui, vous l'écoutez, mais vous ne le comprenez pas. Est-ce que le prof t'écoute?

Oui, il m'écoute, mais il ne me comprend pas. Est-ce que tu écoutes Claire?

Oui, je l'écoute, mais je ne la comprends pas. Est-ce que Claire vous écoute?

Oui, elle nous écoute, mais elle ne nous comprend pas. Est-ce que vous m'écoutez?

Oui, nous t'écoutons, mais nous ne te comprenons pas. Est-ce que j'écoute Patrick et Khaled?

Oui, tu les écoutes, mais tu ne les comprends pas. Est-ce que Patrick et Khaled écoute Salim?

Oui, ils l'écoutent, mais ils ne le comprennent pas.

Cooperative Group Practice

Matching Cards

For additional practice with direct object pronouns, make a note card for each student in your class. On half of the cards write questions that take direct object pronouns, and on the other half write an answer for each question, for example, **Tu m'aides au labo**? **Oui, je t'aide au labo.** Shuffle the cards and distribute one card to each student. Tell students to memorize their question or answer. Then, have them circulate around the room, asking their question or stating their answer when asked by other students. When all the matches have been found, have each pair of students say its sentences to the class.

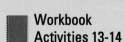

Workbook Activities 13–14

Answers

17 1. nous
2. vous
3. l'
4. la
5. la
6. la
7. les
8. l'
9. te
10. me

Teacher's Notes

1. Indirect object pronouns, introduced on pages 229 and 240 in the second level of *C'est à toi!*, are recycled here. Before reviewing indirect object pronouns with students, you might ask them to locate the two examples of indirect object pronouns in the **Dialogue.** Tell them that both examples are in the **passé composé** and use the same verb. 2. You might want to review with students a list of other verbs that take indirect objects, such as **demander, dire, écrire, lire, montrer, parler, présenter, raconter, rendre visite (à), ressembler** and **vendre.** 3. You may want to point out that some verbs take both a direct object and an indirect object, for example, **demander, dire, donner, écrire, lire** and **montrer.** 4. Point out that **me, te, nous** and **vous** are also used as direct object pronouns. 5. Explain the difference between **nous** and **vous** as subject pronouns, direct object pronouns and indirect object pronouns. 6. Point out liaison with **nous** and **vous** before a verb beginning with a vowel sound. 7. Remind students that the indirect object pronoun **leur** resembles the singular possessive adjective. 8. The past participle in the **passé composé** agrees in neither gender nor number with a preceding indirect object, for example, **Jamila? Nous lui avons vendu notre ordinateur.** 9. Point out that when a pronoun is the indirect object of an infinitive, it comes right before the infinitive and not before the conjugated verb.

Modèle:

— Tu entends la voix du censeur?
— Oui, je l'entends.

Tu me montres une photo de ta fiancée?

Oui, je te montre une photo de Fatima.

17 | *Complétez les petits dialogues avec* **me, te, le, la, nous, vous** *et* **les.**

1. — Est-ce que le censeur vous a vus?
   — Eh ben, non! Il ne... a pas vus.
2. — Dis, Aurélie, c'est nous, Leïla et Julien.
   — Comment? Je ne... connais pas.
3. — Marie, où as-tu acheté ce manuel de français?
   — Je... ai acheté à la librairie, bien sûr.
4. — Tu vas montrer cette dissertation à la prof?
   — Oui, et je vais... montrer à Mme Auteuil aussi.
5. — Tu n'as pas de problèmes avec cette rédaction?
   — Non, et je vais... terminer avant toi!
6. — Vas-tu faire la lecture pour demain maintenant?
   — Non, je vais... faire ce soir.
7. — J'ai mis tous mes devoirs dans mon sac à dos.
   — Pardon? Où... as-tu mis?
8. — Vas-tu montrer ton problème au prof?
   — Non, je dois partir tout de suite. Je ne peux pas... attendre.
9. — Jean-Marie, est-ce que tu me cherches?
   — Oui, je... cherche depuis deux heures. Où étais-tu?
10. — Pourquoi est-ce que tu parles à Francine?
    — Parce qu'elle... comprend bien.

Indirect object pronouns: *me, te, lui, nous, vous, leur*

Indirect object pronouns answer the question "to whom" and replace indirect objects. Note that the preposition **à** is considered part of the indirect object pronouns.

	Masculine or Feminine	Before a Vowel Sound
Singular	me te lui	m' t' lui
Plural	nous vous leur	nous vous leur

These pronouns come right before the verb of which they are the object. The sentence may be affirmative, interrogative, negative or have an infinitive.

Qui **t'**a donné la rédaction? Le prof de littérature. Il va **me** donner une interro aussi.	*Who gave you the composition? The literature teacher. He is going to give me a quiz, too.*
Vous donne-t-elle son numéro de téléphone? Oui, elle **nous** donne son nouveau numéro de téléphone.	*Does she give you her telephone number? Yes, she gives us her new telephone number.*

Critical Thinking

Indirect Object Pronouns in English

Students may sometimes have difficulty recognizing indirect object pronouns in English because often they are positioned to look like direct object pronouns, for example, *I bought you the ticket.* Ask students if this can be restated another way. (They should say, *I bought the ticket for you.*) Tell students that this test of replacing a pronoun with a prepositional phrase sometimes helps to identify indirect object pronouns in English.

Distinguishing between Direct and Indirect Object Pronouns

Write the sentence **Marc téléphone à Yves** on the board. Ask students whether or not the verb "to phone" takes an indirect object in both French and English. Students should answer that it takes an indirect object in French but a direct object in English. Ask students to think of other verbs that work this way, such as **demander** and **ressembler.**

Tu offres un cadeau à Annick ou à ses parents?
Je **leur** offre un cadeau, mais je ne **lui** offre rien.

Do you give a gift to Annick or to her parents?
I give them a gift, but I don't give her anything.

Pratique

8 *Mme Vernaud travaille à la librairie. Dites ce qu'elle vend aux personnes indiquées.*

Modèle: Jeanne

Modèle:

Jeanne
Elle lui vend des feutres.

9 *Avant de partir en vacances, Abdel-Cader a fait une liste des personnes à qui il doit envoyer une carte postale. Ce matin il a mis un "X" devant les noms des personnes à qui il écrit aujourd'hui. Avec un(e) partenaire, demandez s'il écrit aux personnes indiquées. Alternez les questions et les réponses avec votre partenaire.*

> X　Thomas
> 　　Geneviève et Mireille
> X　Mohamed et Abdou
> X　mes parents
> X　Saleh
> 　　M. Laye
> 　　mes cousins
> X　ma sœur
> 　　Moustapha
> 　　les Diouf

Modèle:

Élève A: Est-ce qu'Abdel-Cader écrit à Thomas aujourd'hui?
Élève B: Oui, il lui écrit aujourd'hui. Est-ce qu'il écrit à Geneviève et Mireille aujourd'hui?
Élève A: Non, il ne leur écrit pas aujourd'hui. Est-ce qu'il écrit à...?

Audiocassette/CD Activity 18

Answers

18 Elle lui vend un carnet.
Elle nous vend des bloc-notes.
Elle lui vend des trombones.
Elle leur vend des manuels de grec.
Elle te vend une gomme.
Elle me vend un roman.
Elle vous vend des crayons.
Elle lui vend une agrafeuse.

19 Est-ce qu'il écrit à Mohamed et Abdou aujourd'hui?
Oui, il leur écrit aujourd'hui.
Est-ce qu'il écrit à ses parents aujourd'hui?
Oui, il leur écrit aujourd'hui.
Est-ce qu'il écrit à Saleh aujourd'hui?
Oui, il lui écrit aujourd'hui.
Est-ce qu'il écrit à M. Laye aujourd'hui?
Non, il ne lui écrit pas aujourd'hui. Est-ce qu'il écrit à ses cousins aujourd'hui?
Non, il ne leur écrit pas aujourd'hui. Est-ce qu'il écrit à sa sœur aujourd'hui?
Oui, il lui écrit aujourd'hui. Est-ce qu'il écrit à Moustapha aujourd'hui?
Non, il ne lui écrit pas aujourd'hui. Est-ce qu'il écrit aux Diouf aujourd'hui?
Non, il ne leur écrit pas aujourd'hui.

Teacher's Note

You may want to have students do Activity 18 again, this time using the near future.

TPR

Direct or Indirect?

To practice distinguishing between direct and indirect object pronouns, prepare a list of ten sentences that use them, for example, **Michel va m'inviter à sa boum** and **Nadine m'a donné son feutre.** Have each student make two cards, one with "D" for "Direct" and one with "I" for "Indirect." Read the sentences you have prepared. Have students raise the "D" card if they hear a sentence using a direct object pronoun; have them raise the "I" card if they hear a sentence using an indirect object pronoun.

Cooperative Group Practice

Classroom Objects

To practice using indirect object pronouns in the **passé composé,** put students in small groups of four or five. Give each student a classroom object introduced in this lesson or in Unit 4 in the first level of *C'est à toi!* First, tell each student to give the object to another student in the group. Next, have the first student in each group ask the person on the right where he or she got the object, for example, **Qui t'a donné le carnet?** The student on the right responds, for example, **Jean m'a donné le carnet.** The activity continues until everyone in the group has asked and answered a question.

Audiocassette/CD
Activity 20

Listening
Activity 1

Quiz
Leçon A

Answers

20 1. Est-ce que ton professeur d'histoire vous montre des films? Et toi, est-ce que ton professeur d'histoire vous montre des films?

2. Est-ce que ton professeur d'anglais vous raconte des histoires? Et toi, est-ce que ton professeur d'anglais vous raconte des histoires?

3. Est-ce que ton professeur de géométrie vous demande de penser? Et toi, est-ce que ton professeur de géométrie vous demande de penser?

4. Est-ce que ton professeur de maths vous donne beaucoup de devoirs? Et toi, est-ce que ton professeur de maths vous donne beaucoup de devoirs?

5. Est-ce que ton professeur de sciences vous dit de sécher son cours? Et toi, est-ce que ton professeur de sciences vous dit de sécher son cours?

6. Est-ce que ton professeur de biologie vous téléphone à la maison? Et toi, est-ce que ton professeur de biologie vous téléphone à la maison?
Students' responses to these questions will vary.

Modèle:

ton professeur de littérature/lire des livres en classe
Élève A: Est-ce que ton professeur de littérature vous lit des livres en classe?
Élève B: Non, il ne nous lit pas de livres en classe. Et toi, est-ce que ton professeur de littérature vous lit des livres en classe?
Élève A: Oui, il nous lit des livres en classe.

Modèle:

aller au centre commercial
Élève A: Est-ce que tu vas au centre commercial?
Élève B: Oui, je vais au centre commercial.

Christiane et Simone ne s'inquiètent pas avant la rentrée.

---

20 Avec un(e) partenaire, posez des questions sur ce que les professeurs à votre école font pour vous. Puis répondez aux questions. Suivez le modèle.

1. ton professeur d'histoire/montrer des films
2. ton professeur d'anglais/raconter des histoires
3. ton professeur de géométrie/ demander de penser
4. ton professeur de maths/donner beaucoup de devoirs
5. ton professeur de sciences/dire de sécher son cours
6. ton professeur de biologie/téléphoner à la maison

DÉTENDEZ-VOUS LES CLUBS MOVING VOUS OFFREN 3 JOURS GRATUITS DE REMISE EN FORM

Communication

21 Qu'est-ce que vous faites pour vous préparer pour la rentrée? Copiez la grille suivante. Puis complétez-la selon les réponses de votre partenaire. Demandez-lui s'il ou elle fait les actions indiquées. Mettez un ✓ dans l'espace blanc convenable. Puis changez de rôles.

Actions	Oui	Non
aller au centre commercial	✓	
écrire ton emploi du temps dans un carnet		
s'inquiéter		
chercher les amis de l'année dernière		
recevoir ton emploi du temps		
parler avec le censeur		
acheter des stylos et des cahiers		
choisir les cours		
remplir la fiche d'inscription		
acheter de nouveaux vêtements		
décider de réussir		
avoir rendez-vous avec le directeur		
trouver ton sac à dos		
aller à la librairie		
faire une liste de choses à faire		

22 Mettez les réponses de votre partenaire de l'enquête dans l'Activité 21 en ordre chronologique. Puis utilisez ces réponses pour écrire un paragraphe où vous décrivez ce que votre partenaire fait pour se préparer pour la rentrée. Pour vous aider à faire les transitions entre les phrases, utilisez les expressions comme **d'abord**, **ensuite**, etc.

Game

Pronoun Relay Race

For additional practice using indirect object pronouns in the present tense, you may want students to play this game. Divide the class into two teams. Prepare two sets of construction paper cards of subject pronouns, indirect object pronouns and verb stems, such as **ressembl-** and **vend-**. (It is a good idea to use a different color for each category.) Place one set of each category on the floor in front of each team. Make a list of about 20 sentences that contain an indirect object. Have one student from each team go to the front of the room. Read the English version of a sentence from your list, for example, *My aunt? I look like her.* Instruct students to construct **Je lui ressemble** by placing the correct cards on the ledge of the board. Have them write the verb ending on the board. The student who first forms the correct sentence wins a point for his or her team. Then have two other students come to the board and set up the second sentence that you say, and so on. The team with the most correct sentences wins the game.

Writing a Composition

Sur la bonne piste

A typical, well-organized composition contains an introduction, a body and a conclusion. The introduction and the conclusion normally consist of one paragraph each. The number of paragraphs in the body varies, depending on how much you develop your topic and on how many separate subtopics you have.

An effective introduction attracts and holds your readers' attention. The introduction usually begins with a *thesis statement* that gives the main idea of your composition. The thesis statement can often by presented in one tightly focused sentence. The type of thesis statement you choose depends on the type of composition you are writing. For example, if you plan to report other people's ideas in your composition, you summarize what these ideas are. Or if you plan to develop your personal opinion about an experience, you state that opinion. After writing your thesis statement, you need to indicate to your readers what they are going to read about in the body of your composition. You might provide an overview of the main points, describe a situation using an unusual or amusing anecdote about your topic, ask a question or use a quotation. The last sentence of the introduction should lead smoothly into the body of the composition.

Each of the paragraphs in the body supports or gives examples of the main idea of the composition, as expressed in the thesis statement. Each paragraph needs a *topic sentence* to tell what the topic is and what your paragraph will say about it. Like the thesis statement, the topic sentence may appear anywhere in the paragraph, but it is often the first sentence. The rest of the paragraph contains supporting details that prove, clarify or expand on your main idea. Supporting details can be concrete examples, incidents, facts, statistics or reasons. To make each paragraph in the body of your composition flow smoothly into the next one, connect the paragraphs by means of a *transition*. Some transition phrases used to indicate time include **d'abord** (*first*), **puis** (*then*), **ensuite** (*next*) and **enfin** (*finally*). If you are writing about a cause-and-effect relationship, you might choose phrases such as **en conséquence** (*consequently*), **parce que** (*because*) or **pour cette raison** (*for that reason*). To compare, you might use **comme** (*like*) or **de la même manière** (*in the same way*). Or if you need to contrast, the expressions **mais** (*but*), **cependant** (*however*) and **au contraire** (*on the contrary*) are effective.

Finally, write a conclusion that pulls together all your paragraphs and alerts the readers that you are ending your composition. As with an introduction, a conclusion can be written in many different ways. If you are trying to prove a position, you might summarize the main points that you developed in the body of your composition. Or if you are writing from personal experience, you might build a conclusion that expresses your thoughts and feelings about the main idea.

Now write a composition in French using what you have just learned. Your topic is **Pourquoi étudier le français**. You will find many reasons to support the study of French in this textbook series. Others may come to mind from your personal experiences and from talking to friends, parents, guidance counselors and teachers.

Workbook Activity 15

Advanced Placement

Teacher's Notes

1. You will notice that there are two **Sur la bonne piste** sections in each unit. The **Sur la bonne piste** section in **Leçon A** is designed to teach various strategies for communication that reinforce the listed communicative functions in each unit. In addition, **Sur la bonne piste**, **Leçon A**, is designed to develop skills that will help students prepare to take the Advanced Placement Exam in French Language. In this section students practice such skills as writing a composition, explaining in detail, narrating a picture sequence and circumlocuting in order to develop the ability to express themselves with reasonable fluency and accuracy in both written and spoken French. The **Sur la bonne piste** section in this lesson develops writing proficiency. The **Sur la bonne piste** section in **Leçon B** resembles the **Sur la bonne piste** section in the first and second levels of *C'est à toi!*, where specific reading strategies were introduced. 2. Other useful transition phrases include **après** (*afterward*), **contrairement à** (*unlike*), **d'un part** (*on one hand*), **d'autre part** (*on the other hand*), **en attendant** (*meanwhile*), **le dernier point** (*the last point*), **par opposition à** (*in contrast to*), **principalement** (*primarily*) and **semblablement** (*similarly*).

Teacher's Note

You may choose to have students use the writing process for writing their composition. Have them begin with an outline. (To review with students how to write an outline, refer to pages 280-81 in the second level of *C'est à toi!*) Then have students compose a first draft, making sure that paragraphs connect ideas smoothly.

Remind students that effectively placed transitions will help the reader follow the ideas expressed. You may choose to have students work with a peer reviewer when they have finished their first draft. The peer reviewer should focus on the ideas expressed. Is the composition interesting? Is it easy to follow? How can it be improved? Comments like "I don't think this sentence belongs here"

and "I would like to see an example" will help the writer revise. The peer reviewer can mark his or her comments directly on the composition or on an evaluation form that you prepare. As students revise their first draft, they should make sure that their topic sentences are clear and that all their supporting sentences help to prove the main idea. Finally, students need to edit their

composition for errors in grammar, usage, mechanics and spelling. You may choose to share one or two of the best compositions with the class to model effective writing.

Workbook Activity 16

 Audiocassette/CD
Le parc d'attractions,
Les sports

Transparencies 5-8

Teacher's Notes

1. A merry-go-round is also called **un manège de chevaux de bois**. 2. You may want to tell students that a synonym for **le ski de fond** is **le ski de randonnée**. 3. Other related terms and expressions include **une boule de cristal** (*crystal ball*), **un télésiège** (*chairlift*), **un moniteur/une monitrice** (*ski instructor*), **une chaussure de ski** (*ski boot*), **des vêtements de ski** (*skiwear*), **une station de ski** (*ski resort*), **un saut à skis** (*ski jump*), **faire une promenade en traîneau** (*to go for a sleigh ride*), **faire de la motoneige** (*to go snowmobiling*), **faire du ski de piste** (*to go downhill skiing*), **faire du patin à roulettes** (*to go roller skating*) and **une patinoire** (*skating rink*). 4. Communicative functions that are recycled in this lesson are "describing past events," "sequencing events," "explaining something," "inviting," "accepting an invitation" and "expressing intentions."

Leçon B

In this lesson you will be able to:

➤ give orders

➤ explain something

➤ give examples

➤ offer something

➤ express astonishment and disbelief

➤ express enthusiasm

➤ express emotions

➤ express desire

un parc d'attractions

Denise fait un tour de montagnes russes.

les autos tamponneuses (f.)

Jacques et Lamine font un tour de grande roue.

des jeux d'adresse (m.)

Jérémy fait un tour de manège.

la galerie des miroirs déformants

une voyante

Yves fait de la planche à neige.

Caro et Anne font de la luge.

Marc et Martine font du ski de fond.

une piste

Sports Vocabulary

You may choose to introduce the new sports vocabulary with books closed. As you perform an action, for example, sitting in two chairs that are facing each other as if you are tobogganing, say what sport you are practicing (**Je fais de la luge**). Perform a similar action for each of the three sports and any sports you wish to review. Then call on individual students to go to the front of the room to act out each sport as you say your sentences without actions.

Faire de vs. *jouer à*

Ask students if they can come up with a rule for when to use **faire de** and when to use **jouer à** with a sport. Students should tell you that **faire de** is usually used with sports that can be practiced individually, whereas **jouer à** is usually used with sports that require two or more players.

Véro fait de la planche à roulettes.

**Workbook
Activity 17**

Audiocassette/CD
Dialogue

On a rigolé dans les autos tamponneuses.

Lucien, Francine, Robert et Annette ont passé le weekend après la rentrée à La Ronde, le grand parc d'attractions à Montréal. Maintenant ils sont au café pour déjeuner et pour parler de leurs aventures.

Lucien: Oh là là! Que je suis fana de ce parc! J'ai presque tout fait ce matin. Annette, où as-tu commencé?

Annette: D'abord, André et moi, nous sommes entrés dans la galerie des miroirs déformants pour nous regarder. Après, nous sommes montés dans les autos tamponneuses et nous avons heurté° tout le monde. Nous avons rigolé comme des fous!° Je n'en reviens pas.° Qu'as-tu fait, Francine? Dis-le-moi!

heurter *to run into*; rigoler comme des fous *to laugh one's head off*; Je n'en reviens pas. *Vous ne pouvez pas imaginer.*

Teacher's Notes

1. La Ronde is located on the northeast end of the île Sainte-Hélène. Also on the island are the Hélène-de-Champlain Park, the Lévis Tower (a water reservoir), the Biosphere (a geodesic dome that housed the U.S. pavilion at Expo 67) and Alexander Calder's sculpture "Man." The island is also home to the Théâtre de la Poudrerie, the David M. Stewart Museum in the Old Fort and the Hélène-de-Champlain and Festin du Gouverneur restaurants. To get to La Ronde by métro, get off at the Île Sainte-Hélène station. Visitors to La Ronde can easily get to the nearby man-made île Notre-Dame, an island built for Expo 67, for dances, car races, swimming and gambling. 2. Montreal was introduced in Unit 7 in the first level of *C'est à toi!* and was presented again in Unit 8 in the second level. 3. **Une folle**, the feminine form of **un fou**, is irregular.

Teacher's Notes

1. Up until now students have seen **jamais** used only as part of the negative expression **ne... jamais**.
2. You may want to point out that **essayer** is an orthographically changing verb ending in **-aie, -aies, -aie** and **-aient** for the **je, tu, il/elle/on** and **ils/elles** forms.
3. **Le Carnaval de Québec** was introduced on page 16 in the second level of *C'est à toi!* This annual event started in 1894 when city officials conceived of a celebration "to enliven the monotony of our dull season." During the "Mardi Gras of the North," the population of Quebec nearly doubles. One popular event is ice canoe racing, which attracts both professional and amateur participants. Teams of five push their canoes up the river's icy shore to open water. Then they hop in their canoes and paddle furiously until they reach an ice floe, when they jump out and carry or push the canoe to the next open water. Teams continue in this fashion until one crosses the finish line. For those who prefer less challenging activities, there is tobogganing down a 1,400-foot runway ending near **le château Frontenac** or ice skating to recorded music. **Le Bonhomme Carnaval** is a seven-foot snowman dressed in a red cap and flowing sash. On the first day of the celebration, he parades through the city until he reaches his palace, which officially starts the festivities.
4. **Le snowboarding** is the French equivalent of the Canadian expression **la planche à neige**. While Canadians would say **Je fais de la planche à neige**, the French would say **Je fais du snow-**boarding. 5. Although **un ticket** and **un billet** are sometimes used interchangeably, **un ticket** is usually a small ticket obtained from a machine or torn off from a roll for the movies, the subway, the bus or parking. **Un billet** is any other kind of ticket that someone might buy for the theater, a concert, a plane trip or a train trip.

Francine: Je vous y ai vus avant de flâner dans l'arcade. J'y ai parlé avec une voyante qui m'a dit que je vais avoir de la chance° en amour.

Annette: Hein?° Tu l'as crue?

Francine: Pourquoi pas? Tu as jamais° eu une consultation?°

Annette: Non, mais je veux bien en avoir une. Je voudrais y aller avec toi une fois.° Je peux?

Francine: Bien sûr.

Robert: Dis, Francine, tu as essayé° des jeux d'adresse?

Francine: Naturellement. J'en ai beaucoup essayé, mais je n'ai rien gagné.°

Robert: Dites, vous avez jamais assisté au Carnaval de Québec? C'est ma fête favorite. J'y ai assisté cette année. On a pu aussi profiter de la saison pour faire des sports d'hiver, par exemple, faire de la planche à neige, faire du ski de fond et faire de la luge sur de belles pistes. Enfin, on a pu faire un peu de tout.

Annette: Tu as fait de la planche à neige? Quelle chance! J'en fais souvent en hiver parce qu'en été je fais de la planche à roulettes et j'aime continuer à m'entraîner.°

Francine: Tiens! On a fini de déjeuner? On y va ensemble? Il faut se dépêcher de faire un tour de manège, de montagnes russes et de grande roue.

Robert: Ben, j'en ai un peu peur mais je vais essayer. Lucien, tu as acheté assez de tickets° au guichet?

Lucien: Oui, j'y en ai beaucoup acheté. Je te les donne, si tu veux.

Annette: Alors, on y va?

Francine: D'accord.

Robert a fait de la planche à neige.

avoir de la chance *to be lucky;* Hein? Comment?; jamais *ever;* une consultation *séance;* une fois *once;* essayer *to try;* gagner ne pas perdre; s'entraîner *to work out;* un ticket un billet

1 | *Mettez les aventures dans le dialogue en ordre chronologique. Écrivez "1" pour la première phrase, "2" pour la deuxième phrase, etc.*

1. Francine a eu une consultation.
2. Les copains sont allés au parc d'attractions.
3. Robert a parlé de sa fête favorite.
4. On a fini de manger.
5. Annette et André ont rigolé comme des fous.
6. Lucien, Francine, Robert et Annette sont arrivés à Montréal.
7. On est parti pour faire un tour de manège.
8. Les amis ont commencé à déjeuner au café.

Cooperative Group Practice

Labeling Pictures

You might ask a talented art student in one of your classes to draw all eight scenes depicted in Activity 1. Divide your students into small groups. Then give each group a copy of the drawings and an envelope with the matching labels, the eight sentences in Activity 1. Have each group match the labels with the pictures and then place them in the correct order, based on the dialogue. When all groups have correctly arranged and labeled the pictures, tell them to put the pictures away and do Activity 1 orally from memory. The first student in each group gives the first sentence, the second student gives the first and second sentences, and so on, until students have summarized all the main events of the dialogue.

Qu'est-ce que c'est?

1.

4.

7.

Modèle:

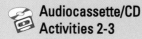

C'est une planche à roulettes.

2.

5.

3.

6.

Qui fait de la luge au Québec? Marie, Thérèse, Michel et Robert en font.

Un champion de la planche à roulettes, Hervé s'entraîne quatre fois par semaine.

C'est à toi!

1. Est-ce que tu es déjà allé(e) à Montréal?
2. Est-ce que tu habites près d'un parc d'attractions? Si oui, quel est son nom?
3. Est-ce que tu préfères faire un tour de manège, de montagnes russes ou de grande roue?
4. Est-ce que tu as essayé des jeux d'adresse? Si oui, est-ce que tu as gagné?
5. Est-ce que tu crois aux voyants? Tu as jamais eu une consultation?
6. Tu t'entraînes chaque semaine? Chaque jour?
7. Tu fais de la planche à roulettes? Si oui, où?
8. Quel sport d'hiver fais-tu?

Audiocassette/CD
Activities 2-3

Answers

2 1. C'est une luge.
   2. C'est un manège.
   3. Ce sont des jeux d'adresse.
   4. Ce sont des montagnes russes.
   5. C'est la galerie des miroirs déformants.
   6. Ce sont des autos tamponneuses.
   7. C'est une grande roue.

3 Answers will vary.

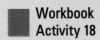

**Workbook
Activity 18**

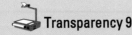

Transparency 9

À la Ronde, il y a des attractions pour les petits enfants. (Montréal)

 Enquête culturelle

La Ronde est le plus grand parc d'attractions du Québec. Elle est située sur l'île Sainte-Hélène sur le fleuve Saint-Laurent qui traverse Montréal. Ouverte entre mai et septembre, La Ronde offre 35 attractions. À La Ronde il y a "Le Monstre," la plus grande des montagnes russes du Canada et la plus rapide à 90 kilomètres à l'heure. D'autres attractions sont "Le Cobra," "Le Boomerang" et "Le Bateau Pirate." On y trouve aussi des jeux d'adresse et un spectacle de ski nautique. Un mini-parc offre dix attractions uniquement pour les petits enfants, et le soir on peut voir le grand spectacle de feu d'artifice. Votre ticket offre accès à toutes les attractions du parc. On vend aussi des billets de saison valides pendant tous les 98 jours de l'été.

Quand il fait beau, les Montréalais aiment être servis à la terrasse d'un café.

Le café français ou canadien est le centre de la vie des jeunes gens. On s'y rejoint souvent pour acheter une boisson, s'asseoir et y passer du temps. Au printemps et en été, on préfère s'asseoir à une table dehors.

Le Carnaval est une fête d'hiver à Québec en février. Les fanas des sports d'hiver peuvent y faire de la planche à neige ou du ski de fond. Le Carnaval offre des compétitions comme le mini-golf et le volleyball sur neige et la course de motocyclettes sur le fleuve Saint-Laurent. Les gens qui n'aiment pas les sports d'hiver peuvent admirer les jolies sculptures d'hiver à la Place Desjardins et sur les Plaines d'Abraham ou voir les spectacles et les jeux devant le Parlement de Québec sur la Place Loto-Québec. Le soir on peut assister aux défilés ou aller danser. Le Bonhomme, symbole du Carnaval, vous invite à participer au Carnaval. Il vous assure des "Wow!" et des "Ho!"

Le Québec est idéal pour pratiquer des sports d'hiver parce qu'il y neige souvent entre novembre et avril. Avec ses pistes de ski, la région est superbe pour skier. On fait du ski de fond même dans le centre-ville sur les plaines d'Abraham, site historique d'une victoire anglaise au XVIIIᵉ siècle qui a décidé de l'histoire du Canada.

Au Canada comme en France, il n'est pas rare de voir des jeunes gens qui font de la planche à roulettes pour aller ici et là. C'est un sport, oui, mais c'est aussi un transport.

Les Québécois font de la luge sur une longue piste qui se termine près du château Frontenac.

Répondez aux questions suivantes.

1. Est-ce que La Ronde est située dans la ville de Montréal ou dans la ville de Québec?
2. À quelle saison est-ce que La Ronde est ouverte?
3. Quelle est une des grandes attractions à La Ronde?
4. Qu'est-ce que La Ronde offre aux petits enfants?
5. Pourquoi va-t-on à un café?
6. Quand est-ce la fête du Carnaval à Québec?
7. Quelles attractions a le Carnaval pour les personnes qui n'aiment pas les sports d'hiver?
8. Qui nous invite au Carnaval?
9. Peut-on skier dans la ville de Québec?
10. Où à Québec est le site d'une victoire qui a décidé de l'histoire du Canada?

Regardez l'horaire des activités pour le Carnaval de Québec. Puis répondez aux questions.

En 1759, sur les plaines d'Abraham, le général Wolfe a gagné la bataille qui a donné le Québec aux Anglais. (Québec)

Carnaval de Québec Événements		
SAMEDI 1ᵉʳ FÉVRIER		
10h00	Ouverture officielle de la Place	Place Desjardins
10h00	Match de volleyball sur neige	Stade McDonald's
13h30	Championnat provincial de course de traîneaux à chiens	Place Desjardins
18h00	Grand prix auto	Pointes-aux-Lièvres
20h00	Bal au palais	Place Loto-Québec
24h00	La nuit des longs couteaux (sculpture)	Place Desjardins
DIMANCHE 2 FÉVRIER		
10h00	Vote du public (sculpture)	Place Desjardins
10h00	Journée familiale de ski de fond	Place Desjardins
10h00	Match de soccer sur neige	Stade McDonald's
10h00	Course de motos sur rivière	Rivière Saint-Charles
SAMEDI 8 FÉVRIER		
10h00	Petit déjeuner western de Calgary	Place Loto-Québec
15h00	Bain de neige	Place Loto-Québec
19h00	Défilé de Charlesbourg	Charlesbourg
20h00	Bal au palais	Place Loto-Québec
24h00	La nuit des longs couteaux (sculpture)	Place Desjardins

Tout le monde s'amuse à créer des sculptures de glace. (Québec)

Answers

4 Possible answers:

1. La Ronde est située à Montréal.
2. La Ronde est ouverte pendant l'été.
3. "Le Monstre" est une grande attraction à La Ronde.
4. Pour les petits enfants il y a un mini-parc avec dix attractions.
5. On va à un café pour voir des amis, acheter une boisson, s'asseoir et y passer du temps.
6. Le Carnaval à Québec est en février.
7. Il y a de jolies sculptures d'hiver, des spectacles, des jeux, des défilés et des bals pour les personnes qui n'aiment pas les sports d'hiver.
8. Le Bonhomme nous invite au Carnaval.
9. Oui, on peut faire du ski de fond sur les plaines d'Abraham.
10. Les plaines d'Abraham sont le site d'une victoire qui a décidé de l'histoire du Canada.

Teacher's Note

You may want to use the Internet to find out about events being held at **le Carnaval** this year. The web address is www.carnaval.qc.ca., or just type **Carnaval de Québec** using the search engine of the program.

Answers

5 1. Les activités du Carnaval sont le samedi et le dimanche.
2. On peut assister à la première activité officielle du Carnaval à la Place Desjardins.
3. McDonald's participe aux activités du Carnaval.
4. Au Carnaval on danse à la Place Loto-Québec.
5. Le match de soccer sur neige est à 10h00 au Stade McDonald's.
6. On peut assister à la course de motos sur rivière à 10h00 à la Rivière Saint-Charles.
7. Le petit déjeuner western de Calgary et le brunch de Bonhomme font partie du Carnaval.
8. Les deux défilés sont à Charlesbourg et à Haute-Ville.
9. La dernière activité du Carnaval est le départ de Bonhomme.

Entrez dans la grande famille de Bonhomme Carnaval et vivez, à Québec, la plus grande fête de l'hiver au monde!

DIMANCHE 9 FÉVRIER		
10h00	Vote du public (sculpture)	Place Desjardins
13h30	Course en canot (finales)	Port de Québec
15h00	Parade des drapeaux	Place Loto-Québec

SAMEDI 15 FÉVRIER		
10h00	Compétition de planche à neige	Place Desjardins
11h00 14h00	Fantaisies sur glace	Galeries de la Capitale
12h00 14h00	Spectacle de Ronald McDonald	Stade McDonald's
19h00	Défilé de la Haute-Ville	Haute-Ville

DIMANCHE 16 FÉVRIER		
10h30	Brunch de Bonhomme	Radisson des Gouverneurs
11h00	Spectacle de Ronald McDonald	Stade McDonald's
13h00	Les Carnavaleries	Stade McDonald's
14h00	Spectacle de clôture et départ de Bonhomme	Place Loto-Québec

Pour plus de détails, procurez-vous le programme officiel disponible un peu partout dans la grande région de Québec.

Le Château de Bonhomme promet encore cette année des "Wow!" et des "Ho!"

Place Desjardins
Les Plaines d'Abraham deviennent un immense terrain de jeu hivernal pour toute la famille

1. Quels jours de la semaine sont les activités du Carnaval?
2. Où est-ce qu'on peut assister à la première activité officielle du Carnaval?
3. Quelle compagnie internationale participe aux activités du Carnaval?
4. Où danse-t-on au Carnaval?
5. Où et à quelle heure est le match de soccer sur neige?
6. Où et à quelle heure peut-on assister à la course de motos sur rivière?
7. Quels repas font partie du Carnaval?
8. Où sont les deux défilés?
9. Quelle est la dernière activité du Carnaval?

Journal personnel

In this unit you learned about life in Senegal and Canada. What impact do you think climate has on teenagers' activities and pastimes in both countries? For instance, what activities might you expect to see young Canadians participating in that you wouldn't see in Senegal, and vice versa? How does the climate of the region where you live control the types of activities that you enjoy? Write your responses to these questions in your cultural journal.

Structure

Passé composé with *avoir*

The **passé composé** is used to tell what happened in the past. For most verbs the **passé composé** consists of the appropriate present tense form of **avoir** and the past participle of the main verb.

> Lucien a acheté assez de tickets.   *Lucien bought enough tickets.*

To form the past participle of **-er** verbs, add an **é** to the stem of the infinitive. For most **-ir** verbs, add an **i**, and for most **-re** verbs, add a **u**. Here are the verbs you've already studied that have irregular past participles in the **passé composé** formed with **avoir**. Note the position of negative expressions in the **passé composé** and how to form questions using inversion. Remember that the past participle agrees in number and in gender with a preceding direct object pronoun.

Verb	Past Participle	*Passé Composé*
avoir	eu	Tu **as** jamais **eu** une consultation?
boire	bu	Ils **ont bu** de la limonade au café.
conduire	conduit	Patrick **a conduit** comme un fou.
connaître	connu	Les **avez**-vous déjà **connus**?
courir	couru	Pour s'entraîner, il **a couru**.
croire	cru	La voyante? Tu l'**as crue**?
devoir	dû	Nous **avons dû** partir.
dire	dit	Qu'est-ce qu'ils **ont dit**?
écrire	écrit	Christelle ne m'**a** rien **écrit**.
être	été	Elle **a été** obligée de venir.
faire	fait	Qu'**as**-tu **fait**, Francine?
falloir	fallu	Il n'**a** pas **fallu** se dépêcher.
lire	lu	Tout le monde **a lu** mes notes.
mettre	mis	Je les **ai mises** sur mon bureau.
offrir	offert	Le prof les **a offertes** à Magali.
ouvrir	ouvert	Jérôme **a ouvert** son carnet.
pouvoir	pu	On **a pu** profiter de la neige.
prendre	pris	Nous **avons pris** la première piste.
recevoir	reçu	Élise **a reçu** son bac en 1998.
savoir	su	L'**as**-tu **su**?
suivre	suivi	Guy **a suivi** un cours de russe.
vivre	vécu	Ses parents **ont vécu** à Toronto.
voir	vu	Je vous y **ai vus** hier.
vouloir	voulu	Les amis **ont voulu** partir.

M. et Mme Charbonneau ont fait du ski de fond à Mont Tremblant dans les Laurentides. (Québec)

Workbook Activities 19-20

Teacher's Notes

1. The **passé composé** with the helping verb **avoir**, introduced on page 390 in the first level of *C'est à toi!* and reviewed on page 55 in the second level, is recycled here.
2. Remind students that to form a negative sentence in the **passé composé**, ne (n') is placed before the form of **avoir**, and pas is placed after it, for example, **Nous n'avons pas gagné le match**. 3. To ask a question using inversion in the **passé composé**, put the subject pronoun after the form of **avoir**, for example, **Avez-vous rigolé comme des fous?** For a negative question using inversion, put ne (n') in front of the form of **avoir** and pas after the pronoun, for example, **N'as-tu pas fait de planche à roulettes?** 4. The direct object pronouns me, te, nous, vous, le, la, l' and les precede the form of **avoir** in the **passé composé**. The past participle agrees in gender and in number with the preceding direct object pronoun, for example, **La planche à neige, tu l'as essayée?** Past participles that end in -s do not change in the masculine plural, for example, **Où as-tu mis les tickets? Je les ai mis dans mon portefeuille.** If the past participle ends in -s or -t, this consonant is pronounced in the feminine form, for example, **La bouteille? Je l'ai ouverte.** When que is used as a direct object, the past participle must agree in gender and in number with the word that que refers to, for example, **Les sculptures qu'on a vues étaient superbes.** 5. You may want to review with students the use of adverbs in the **passé composé**. Most short, common adverbs, such as **beaucoup, bien, déjà, enfin, mal, même, peut-être, souvent, toujours, trop, un peu** and **vite**, come before the past participle, for example, **Nadia a vite compris la lecture.** Adverbial expressions of time, such as **ce matin, hier soir** and **le lendemain**, come either at the beginning or end of a sentence in the **passé composé**.

Paired Practice

Time Line

Tell students to prepare six sentences about their life using the **passé composé** with **avoir**. Then have them illustrate their sentences with drawings or photos. They may use regular and irregular verbs. Then put students in pairs. The first student in each pair describes the six events in his or her life using visuals to help the partner understand, for example, **À l'âge de sept ans, j'ai reçu mon premier vélo.** The second student listens, making a time line in the third person for the first student's sentences. Then the roles are reversed, and the second student tells his or her sentences while the first student makes a time line. For practice changing the **je** to the **il/elle** form of the verbs used, you may choose to put students in new pairs. Students use the time lines and illustrations to tell a new partner about their original partner's life. Finally, you may choose to have students place their original partner's visuals on the time lines they wrote and display them for the entire class to see.

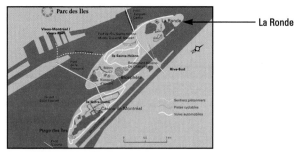

La Ronde

Answers

6 1. a acheté
2. ont attendu
3. a flâné
4. ont fini
5. avez essayé
6. a gagné
7. as perdu
8. avons heurté
9. ai rigolé

Cooperative Group Practice

Interview

To practice regular verbs that take **avoir** in the **passé composé**, write four infinitives or infinitive expressions on the board, such as **acheter, gagner, rendre visite à** and **choisir**. Have students count off 1, 2, 3, 4, 1, 2, 3, 4, etc. and form groups. The first four students form the first group, the second four students form the second group, and so on. The first student in each group asks a question using the first verb, for example, **Qu'est-ce que vous avez acheté pour la rentrée?** The other students in the group answer the question, for example, **J'ai acheté trois nouveaux feutres pour la rentrée.** Then the second student interviews the other three students, asking a question that uses the second verb. When each student has asked his or her interview question, ask the groups to report to the class on the findings of the interviews. Each student says what question he or she asked and reports on the answers of the other members of the group, for example, **J'ai demandé "Qu'est-ce que vous avez acheté pour la rentrée?" Marie a acheté trois nouveaux feutres. Paul a acheté....**

Pratique

6 | *Dites ce que tout le monde a fait pendant le weekend dernier à La Ronde à Montréal. Pour chaque phrase utilisez le verbe convenable de la liste suivante.*

| acheter | gagner | passer | attendre | rigoler |
| heurter | finir | perdre | flâner | essayer |

Modèle:

Robert et ses amis ont passé le weekend à La Ronde.

1. Jean-Luc... des tickets au guichet.

3. On... dans le parc.

2. Françoise et Claire... les garçons devant la galerie des miroirs déformants.

4. Ils... de déjeuner à une heure et demie.

Game

Le baseball

On an overhead transparency, write a list of sentences that show the different meanings of the **passé composé** in English, for example, "I won," "They did sell" and "She has chosen." Divide the class into two teams, for example, **les tigres** and **les couguars.** Then draw two baseball diamonds on the board, one for each team. The first student on the first team orally translates the first sentence into French, for example, **J'ai gagné.** If the student changes the sentence correctly, he or she advances to first base, designated by marking a stick figure along the side of the base, and the next player on that team takes a turn. If the student incorrectly changes the sentence, he or she stays at home plate and the first player from the second team takes a turn. A run is scored after a team gets four correct answers, thus arriving at home plate. The team having the largest number of runs wins.

5. Renée et toi, vous... des jeux d'adresse.

8. Laure et moi, nous... tout le monde.

6. Renée... l'animal de son choix.

9. J'... comme un fou.

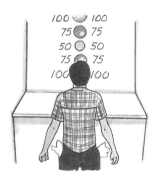

Qu'est-ce que Chantal a gagné aux jeux d'adresse?

7. Tu... tout ton argent.

Answers

7 1. avez ouvert
 2. ai offert
 3. avons été
 4. a fait
 5. a vécu
 6. a dit
 7. a... cru
 8. a suivi, a... su
 9. ont voulu
 10. as... dû

8 1. Est-ce que tu as pris l'auto-bus pour aller au parc d'attractions?
 2. Est-ce que tu as eu une consultation avec une voyante?
 3. Est-ce que tu as fait un tour de montagnes russes?
 4. Est-ce que tu as conduit les autos tamponneuses?
 5. Est-ce que tu as bu beaucoup de boissons froides?
 6. Est-ce que tu as vu un beau feu d'artifice?
 7. Est-ce que tu as écrit des cartes postales?
 8. Est-ce que tu as fait de la planche à roulettes?
 9. Est-ce que tu as pu faire un peu de tout?
 Students' responses to these questions will vary.

7 | *Pour savoir ce qui (what) a eu lieu au parc d'attractions, complétez les phrases avec les formes convenables des verbes indiqués au passé composé.*

 1. Au parc d'attractions, Sandrine et toi, vous... vos portefeuilles pour nous acheter des cocas et des hot-dogs. (ouvrir)
 2. Après le déjeuner, j'... des tickets à tout le monde pour faire un tour de grande roue. (offrir)
 3. Oh là là! Après ça, nous... malades. (être)
 4. Cécile... la connaissance d'un garçon timide, Patrick, devant l'arcade. (faire)
 5. L'année dernière Patrick... à Rome. (vivre)
 6. Dans l'arcade le voyant lui... qu'il aurait de la chance en amour. (dire)
 7. Mais Patrick ne l'... pas.... (croire)
 8. Il... Cécile pendant une heure sans lui parler parce qu'il n'... pas... quoi dire. (suivre, savoir)
 9. Mes amis... partir à vingt-deux heures. (vouloir)
 10. Quand...-tu... partir? (devoir)

JAMAIS PHOTOCOPIER N'A ÉTÉ AUSSI SIMPLE.

Modèle:

visiter un parc d'attractions

Robert: Est-ce que tu as visité un parc d'attractions pendant les vacances?

Michèle: Oui, j'ai visité un parc d'attractions pendant les vacances.

8 | *Trouvez une personne qui.... Interviewez des élèves de votre classe pour déterminer s'ils ou elles ont jamais fait les choses indiquées pendant les vacances d'été. Sur une feuille de papier copiez les expressions indiquées. Formez des questions avec ces expressions pour poser aux élèves. Quand vous trouvez une personne qui répond par "oui," dites à cette personne de signer votre feuille de papier à côté de l'activité convenable. Trouvez une personne différente pour chaque activité.*

 1. prendre l'autobus pour aller au parc d'attractions
 2. avoir une consultation avec une voyante
 3. faire un tour de montagnes russes
 4. conduire les autos tamponneuses
 5. boire beaucoup de boissons froides
 6. voir un beau feu d'artifice
 7. écrire des cartes postales
 8. faire de la planche à roulettes
 9. pouvoir faire un peu de tout

Est-ce que tu as pu faire un peu de tout pendant les vacances?

Oui, j'ai fait de la planche à roulettes avec de nouveaux copains.

Teacher's Note

You may choose to do this activity to provide students with additional practice using the **passé composé** with **avoir**. Write the following paragraph on an overhead transparency, and have students supply the **passé composé** of the regular and irregular verbs indicated.

Le matin de la rentrée, Chloé (mettre) son nouvel ensemble. Elle (prendre) une tartine et un jus d'orange. Puis, elle (chercher) son cahier et ses manuels. Elle (attendre) Joëlle devant l'appartement. Mais Joëlle (être) en retard. Elles (devoir) courir ensemble au lycée. Le censeur leur (dire), "Allez vite." En cours Chloé (ne pas pouvoir) prendre des notes parce qu'elle (laisser) son stylo chez elle. La rentrée (commencer mal)! (Answers: a mis, a pris, a cherché, a attendu, a été, ont dû, a dit, n'a pas pu, a laissé, a mal commencé)

Avec un(e) partenaire, posez des questions sur ce que vous avez fait l'hiver dernier. Puis répondez aux questions. Suivez le modèle.

1. skier
2. mettre un nouvel anorak
3. faire de la planche à neige
4. jouer au volley sur neige
5. courir tous les jours
6. recevoir de bons cadeaux de Noël
7. lire des romans intéressants
8. profiter de la neige
9. voyager dans un pays chaud

Passé composé with être

Certain verbs form their **passé composé** with the helping verb **être**. Most verbs that use **être** in the **passé composé** *express motion or movement* of the subject from one place to another. Note that the ending of the past participle of the verb agrees in gender and in number with the subject.

Nous sommes montés dans les autos tamponneuses.	*We got in the bumper cars.*

Here are the verbs you've already learned that use the helping verb **être**, along with their past participles. In addition to the agreement of the past participles, note the position of negative expressions and how to form questions using inversion.

Verb	Past Participle	Passé Composé
aller	**allé**	Gilberte **est-elle allée** à la librairie?
arriver	**arrivé**	Amadou y **est arrivé** il y a une heure.
descendre	**descendu**	Les filles ne **sont** pas **descendues** pour prendre le petit déjeuner.
devenir	**devenu**	M. Poux **est-il devenu** censeur?
entrer	**entré**	Nous **sommes entrés** dans la galerie des miroirs déformants.
monter	**monté**	Les copains **sont montés** dans le métro.
mourir	**mort**	Jeanne d'Arc **est morte** en 1431.
naître	**né**	Vous **êtes née** à Québec, Mme Vaillancourt?
partir	**parti**	Nous **somme parties** pour l'Europe.
rentrer	**rentré**	René, tu **es rentré** à quelle heure?
rester	**resté**	Maman **est restée** au lit.
revenir	**revenu**	Je n'en **suis** jamais **revenu**.
sortir	**sorti**	Avec qui **es-tu sortie**, Mireille?
venir	**venu**	Ils ne **sont** plus **venus** en retard.

Modèle:

assister au Carnaval de Québec

Élève A: Est-ce que tu as assisté au Carnaval de Québec?

Élève B: Non, je n'ai pas assisté au Carnaval de Québec. Et toi, est-ce que tu as assisté au Carnaval de Québec?

Élève A: Oui, j'ai assisté au Carnaval de Québec.

M. et Mme Olivier sont partis du café montréalais à 14h00.

UN NOUVEAU N° 5 EST NÉ

Workbook Activities 21-22

Audiocassette/CD Activity 9

Answers

9 1. Est-ce que tu as skié? Et toi, est-ce que tu as skié?

2. Est-ce que tu as mis un nouvel anorak? Et toi, est-ce que tu as mis un nouvel anorak?

3. Est-ce que tu as fait de la planche à neige? Et toi, est-ce que tu as fait de la planche à neige?

4. Est-ce que tu as joué au volley sur neige? Et toi, est-ce que tu as joué au volley sur neige?

5. Est-ce que tu as couru tous les jours? Et toi, est-ce que tu as couru tous les jours?

6. Est-ce que tu as reçu de bons cadeaux de Noël? Et toi, est-ce que tu as reçu de bons cadeaux de Noël?

7. Est-ce que tu as lu des romans intéressants? Et toi, est-ce que tu as lu des romans intéressants?

8. Est-ce que tu as profité de la neige? Et toi, est-ce que tu as profité de la neige?

9. Est-ce que tu as voyagé dans un pays chaud? Et toi, est-ce que tu as voyagé dans un pays chaud?

Students' responses to these questions will vary.

Teacher's Notes

1. The **passé composé** with the helping verb **être**, introduced on page 350 in the first level of *C'est à toi!* and reviewed on page 99 in the second level, is recycled here.
2. In current French you may find agreement between the past participle and the implied gender and number of the subject pronoun **on**, for example, **On est descendus des autos**

tamponneuses. 3. In this lesson we list only those 14 **être** verbs that have been previously introduced. You may want to introduce the verbs **retourner** (*to return*) and **tomber** (*to fall*) that also take **être** as a helping verb in the **passé composé**. 4. Remind students that to form a negative sentence in the **passé composé**, **ne (n')** is placed before the form of **être**, and **pas** is placed after it.

5. To ask a question using inversion in the **passé composé**, put the subject pronoun after the form of **être**, for example, **Pourquoi Martine est-elle arrivée en retard?** For a negative question using inversion, put **ne (n')** in front of the form of **être** and **pas** after the pronoun, for example, **N'êtes-vous pas allés au parc d'attractions?** 6. You way want to review with students the use of

adverbs in the **passé composé**. Most short, common adverbs, such as **beaucoup, bien, déjà, enfin, mal, même, peut-être, souvent, toujours, trop, un peu** and **vite**, come before the past participle, for example, **Djamel est souvent allé à l'arcade.** Adverbial expressions of time, such as **ce matin, hier soir** and **le lendemain**, come either at the beginning or end of a sentence in the **passé composé**.

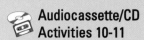

Audiocassette/CD Activities 10-11

Answers

10 1. Luc est devenu malade.
2. Tu es descendu(e) en ville.
3. Chantal et Hélène sont revenues trop tard hier soir.
4. Frédéric et moi, nous sommes allés au cinéma.
5. Vincent est arrivé en retard.
6. Gisèle et toi, vous êtes descendu(e)s en ville.
7. Christian est resté au lit.
8. Karine est sortie avec sa correspondante.
9. Je suis allé(e) au cinéma.
10. Guillaume et Marcel sont rentrés de l'école avec trop de devoirs.

11 1. Quel jour es-tu arrivé(e) à Québec?
2. Où es-tu resté(e)?
3. Avec qui es-tu sorti(e)?
4. À quelle heure es-tu parti(e) le soir?
5. Dans quel restaurant es-tu entré(e)?
6. Pourquoi es-tu devenu(e) fatigué(e)?
7. Quand es-tu revenu(e) aux États-Unis?
Students' responses to these questions will vary.

Paired Practice

On est resté?

Put students in pairs, and give each pair a stack of ten note cards. On each card write a sentence in the **passé composé** using a different pronoun or noun subject. Half the cards should describe activities that take place in the home and half activities that take place away from home, for example, **Tu as fait un tour de grande roue** and **Luc et Simone ont fait la vaisselle.** The first student takes a card and reads the sentence. He or she says whether or not the person or persons in the sentence stayed at home, for example, **Tu n'es pas resté(e) chez toi** or **Luc et Simone sont restés chez eux.** Then the

Pratique

10 | *Pauvre Sébastien! Il n'a trouvé personne pour l'accompagner au parc d'attractions aujourd'hui. Selon la liste suivante, faites les excuses de tout le monde.*

Modèle:

Jeanne
Jeanne est partie à la montagne.

> Dommage, Sébastien! Nous sommes sorties pour faire du shopping en ville.

Chantal	revenir trop tard hier soir
Christian	rester au lit
Gisèle	descendre en ville
Guillaume	rentrer de l'école avec trop de devoirs
moi	aller au cinéma
Jeanne	partir à la montagne
Luc	devenir malade
Vincent	arriver en retard
toi	descendre en ville
Karine	sortir avec sa correspondante
Frédéric	aller au cinéma
Marcel	rentrer de l'école avec trop de devoirs
Hélène	revenir trop tard hier soir

1. Luc
2. tu
3. Chantal et Hélène
4. Frédéric et moi
5. Vincent
6. Gisèle et toi
7. Christian
8. Karine
9. je
10. Guillaume et Marcel

Modèle:

pourquoi/aller au Canada
Élève A: Pourquoi es-tu allé(e) au Canada?
Élève B: Je suis allé(e) au Canada pour voir le Carnaval de Québec.

11 | *Avec un(e) partenaire, jouez les rôles d'un(e) élève de votre lycée et d'un(e) autre élève qui vient de rentrer d'un voyage au Canada. L'élève qui a voyagé répond logiquement aux questions que l'autre élève lui pose.*

1. quel jour/arriver à Québec
2. où/rester
3. avec qui/sortir
4. à quelle heure/partir le soir
5. dans quel restaurant/ entrer
6. pourquoi/devenir fatigué(e)
7. quand/revenir aux États-Unis

Restaurant au Parmesan

Spécialités italien et françaises
◆
Pâtes maison, ve fruits de mer

38, rue Saint-Lo Vieux-Québec
692-0341

Vos hôtes, Luigi et Cesare

Stationnement gratuit ave À un coin de rue d Château Frontena

«L'ENDROIT OÙ TOUT EST SPÉCIAL»
Accordéoniste à tous les soirs

second student takes the next card and gives both sentences. Students continue taking turns until all the cards have been used.

Critical Thinking

Le passé composé with être

Draw a house and use it to tell the story of Jacques' life with sentences using **être** verbs in the **passé composé**, for example, **Jacques est né dans cette maison en 1920** and **Il est parti en 1938 pour aller à l'université.** Ask students what all the **être** verbs have in common. They should tell you that, as seen in the sentences you gave as examples, verbs that use **être** express movement as well as a change of condition. This activity will help students remember which verbs take **être** in the **passé composé.**

TPR

Aller

Display a map of Quebec at the front of the room. Read sentences to the class that tell where certain people went in Quebec and when they arrived there. Then call on a student to show the location on the map and have the student use a clock with movable hands to indicate the time.

Francine et sa classe de physique ont fait une excursion à La Ronde. Complétez sa description de la journée au passé composé avec les formes convenables des verbes indiqués.

Hier mes camarades de classe et moi, nous (aller) à La Ronde. M. Tremblay, notre prof de physique, (dire) que nous allions faire des devoirs scientifiques au parc, mais nous, on voulait s'amuser. Mon amie Aurélie n'(venir) pas parce qu'elle (rester) au lycée pour passer un examen d'anglais.

M. Tremblay (acheter) les tickets au guichet, et nous (entrer) dans le parc. J'(courir) et tous les autres élèves m'(suivre). Claudette et moi, nous (monter) dans les autos tamponneuses. Comme d'habitude Julien (arriver) en retard, mais, lui aussi, il (venir) aux autos pour nous rejoindre. Nous (heurter) tout le monde.

Puis Yasmine et moi, nous (aller) faire un tour de grande roue. Pauvre Yasmine! Chaque fois que nous (descendre), elle (devenir) malade!

Ensuite tout le monde (entrer) dans la galerie des miroirs déformants. Nous (rigoler) comme des fous. Enfin nous (sortir) de la galerie des miroirs déformants, et nous (aller) faire un autre tour de grande roue. Mais pas Yasmine!

Après deux heures au parc, tout le monde (avoir) très faim. Alors nous (manger) au café. Mais Yasmine (boire) seulement une limonade. Nous autres, nous (prendre) des sandwichs.

Après le déjeuner, nous (faire) la queue pour faire un tour de montagnes russes. Formidable! Cette fois, c'était Jérémy qui (devenir) malade, et nous (devoir) l'aider quand il (descendre).

Nous (partir) à une heure et demie, et nous (rentrer) au lycée pour le cours de physique. Comme vous pouvez imaginer, on n'(faire) pas de devoirs scientifiques au parc!

Francine et ses camarades de classe ont-ils fait un tour de montagnes russes à La Ronde? (Montréal)

The pronoun *y*

The pronoun **y** (*there*) replaces a preposition plus the name of a previously mentioned place. It can also mean "(about) it" and replaces **à** plus the name of a thing. Note its position right before the verb of which it is the object in sentences that are affirmative, interrogative, negative and have an infinitive.

Karine était en Suisse? **Y** est-elle restée chez sa correspondante?	*Karine was in Switzerland? Did she stay there at her host sister's house?*
Bien sûr, elle **y** est restée chez Nathalie.	*Of course, she stayed there at Nathalie's house.*
Tu as assisté au Carnaval de Québec?	*Did you attend the Quebec Winter Carnival?*
Non, je n'**y** ai pas assisté cette année, mais je vais **y** assister l'année prochaine.	*No, I didn't attend it this year, but I'm going to attend it next year.*

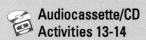

Audiocassette/CD Activities 13-14

Answers

13 1. Il n'y va pas.
2. Nous n'y allons pas.
3. Tu n'y vas pas.
4. Elles y vont.
5. Ils y vont.
6. Elle y va.
7. Vous n'y allez pas.
8. J'y vais.

14 1. Est-ce que tu achètes des manuels pour les cours à la librairie? Et toi, est-ce que tu achètes des manuels pour les cours à la librairie?
2. Est-ce que tu conduis pour aller au lycée? Et toi, est-ce que tu conduis pour aller au lycée?
3. Est-ce que tu déjeunes souvent au fast-food? Et toi, est-ce que tu déjeunes souvent au fast-food?
4. Est-ce que tu étudies à la bibliothèque? Et toi, est-ce que tu étudies à la bibliothèque?
5. Est-ce que tu passes des heures au café? Et toi, est-ce que tu passes des heures au café?

Students' responses to these questions will vary.

Teacher's Note

You may want to have students do Activity 13 again, this time in the **passé composé**.

Paired Practice

Answering Questions

In order to practice using the pronoun **y**, put students in pairs. Each student writes six questions that can be answered using **y**, for example, **As-tu joué au foot hier?** Then partners exchange questions, and each student writes answers to the questions prepared by his or her partner. (This activity may also be done orally.)

Es-tu jamais allé(e) à Los Angeles?

Put students in pairs to practice **y** with the **passé composé**. Tell students to make a list of five cities in the United States that they want to find out if their partner has gone to. At the top of the list they make a **oui** and a **non** column. Then the first student asks the second student if he or she has ever gone to the first city on the list, for example, **Es-tu jamais allé(e) à Los Angeles?** The partner answers **Oui, j'y suis allé(e)** or **Non, je n'y suis jamais allé(e)**. After the first student asks all five of his or her questions, the roles are reversed and the respondent now becomes the interviewer. You may choose to display a map of the United States and do a follow-up activity, asking students at random if they've been to a city that you name. When a student answers affirmatively, have that student place a pin on the map on that city.

Tu veux parler à Thierry? Alors, vas-y!

In an affirmative command, **y** follows the verb. But in a negative command, it precedes the verb.

Tu vas au marché? Alors, achètes-**y** des tomates! Mais n'**y** achète pas d'oignons! — *Are you going to the market? Then buy some tomatoes there! But don't buy any onions there!*

Pratique

13 *Tout le monde va faire quelque chose de différent. Si on peut faire l'activité indiquée à l'endroit (place) entre parenthèses, dites qu'on y va. Si non, dites qu'on n'y va pas.*

Modèles:
Jacqueline va skier. (à la montagne)
Elle y va.

Raoul va acheter des manuels pour les cours. (à la boucherie)
Il n'y va pas.

1. Jérôme va faire de la planche à neige. (à la plage)
2. Nous allons assister au Carnaval. (à Montréal)
3. Tu vas faire du ski de fond. (à la salle de conférences)
4. Claire et Juliette vont acheter des billets. (au guichet)
5. Guy et Sylvie vont faire un tour de montagnes russes. (à La Ronde)
6. Véronique va faire un tour de grande roue. (au parc d'attractions)
7. Vous allez faire de la planche à roulettes. (au Carnaval)
8. Je vais prendre un coca. (au café)

Au Carnaval de Québec? Tout le monde y va en février.

14 *Avec un(e) partenaire, jouez les rôles d'un(e) élève de votre lycée et d'un(e) élève qui vient de France et qui va assister aux cours dans votre lycée cette année. Pour mieux connaître l'autre élève, posez des questions sur ce que vous faites pendant l'année scolaire. Puis répondez aux questions. Suivez le modèle.*

Modèle:
aller en cours le samedi
Élève A: Est-ce que tu vas en cours le samedi?
Élève B: Oui, j'y vais. Et toi, est-ce que tu vas en cours le samedi?
Élève A: Non, je n'y vais pas.

1. acheter des manuels pour les cours à la librairie
2. conduire pour aller au lycée
3. déjeuner souvent au fast-food
4. étudier à la bibliothèque
5. passer des heures au café

The pronoun *en*

The pronoun **en** (*some, any, of it/them, about it/them, from it/them*) refers to and replaces a previously mentioned expression containing **de**. Note its position right before the verb of which it is the object in sentences that are affirmative, interrogative, negative and have an infinitive.

Qui a essayé des jeux d'adresse?	*Who has tried (some) games of skill?*
Marc **en** a beaucoup essayé.	*Marc has tried a lot (of them).*
Vous faites des sports d'hiver? Non, je n'**en** fais pas, mais je voudrais **en** faire. **En** faites-vous? Non, j'**en** ai peur.	*Do you play winter sports? No, I don't (play any), but I'd like to (play some). Do you (play any)? No, I'm afraid to (play any).*
Tu as jamais eu une consultation? Oui, j'**en** ai eu une.	*Have you ever had a séance? Yes, I've had one (of them).*

In an affirmative command, **en** follows the verb. But in a negative command, it precedes the verb.

Manges-**en**, mais n'**en** mange pas trop!	*Eat some (of them), but don't eat too many (of them)!*

Tu voudrais de l'aide avec tes valises?

Non, merci, je n'en ai pas besoin.

Pratique

Imaginez que vous faites une excursion au parc d'attractions avec vos amis. Répondez aux questions basées sur l'illustration. Utilisez en *dans vos réponses.*

André et Philippe
Cécile
VOYANTE
Michel
Amélie
René et moi
Robert
Denis et Julie

Modèles:
Est-ce que Cécile prend des photos?
Oui, elle en prend.

Est-ce que Denis et Julie mangent des sandwichs?
Non, ils n'en mangent pas.

•Comment elles en parlent.
•Ce qu'elles en pensent.

1. Est-ce que Robert choisit des cadeaux?
2. Est-ce que René et toi, vous buvez de l'eau minérale?
3. Est-ce que Michel essaie des jeux d'adresse?
4. Est-ce que Julie et Denis prennent de la pizza?
5. Est-ce qu'Amélie a une consultation?
6. Est-ce que tu bois un coca?
7. Est-ce qu'André et Philippe font de la planche à roulettes?
8. Est-ce que tout le monde profite de la journée?

Game

Le frigo

Put your students in pairs to practice replacing **de** plus a noun. Give each student a diagram of an empty open refrigerator. Tell them to draw eight items to fill it up. (These should be items that they know how to express in French.) The questioner asks his or her partner if there is a certain item in the refrigerator, for example, **Il y a de la moutarde dans ton frigo?** If the partner has that item, he or she responds affirmatively (**Oui, il y en a dans mon frigo**) and the questioner gets another turn. If the partner does not have that item, he or she responds negatively (**Non, il n'y en a pas dans mon frigo**) and then becomes the questioner. Respondents cross off items in their refrigerators as they are guessed by their partners. The student who first guesses all the contents of his or her partner's refrigerator is the winner.

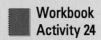

Workbook Activity 24

Answers

15 1. Non, il n'en choisit pas.
2. Non, nous n'en buvons pas.
3. Oui, il en essaie.
4. Oui, ils en prennent.
5. Oui, elle en a une.
6. Oui, j'en bois un.
7. Non, ils n'en font pas.
8. Oui, tout le monde en profite.

Teacher's Notes

1. The pronoun **en**, introduced on page 383 in the second level of *C'est à toi!*, is recycled here. 2. You may want to review the four uses of **en** with your students. **En** replaces a form of **de** plus a noun, for example, **Gabriel fait de la planche à roulettes? Non, il n'en fait pas.** (When **de** is followed by a person, however, stress pronouns are used, for example, **Mme Morisot parle de son fils. Elle parle de lui.**) **En** replaces **de** plus an infinitive, for example, **Tu as envie de faire un tour de grande roue? Oui, j'en ai envie.** **En** replaces **de** plus a noun after **assez, beaucoup, combien, (un) peu** or **trop**, for example, **Vous prenez beaucoup de notes? Non, je n'en prends pas beaucoup. Assez, beaucoup, (un) peu** and **trop** are repeated in the answer. **En** replaces a noun after a number, for example, **Tu as de nouveaux carnets? Oui, j'en ai deux.** 3. Note that the number is repeated in the answer to the question, for example, **Tu as jamais eu une consultation? Oui, j'en ai eu une.** The number **un(e)** is not repeated in a negative response, for example, **Noëlle a un bloc-notes? Non, elle n'en a pas.** 4. You may want to remind students that **en** comes before the helping verb in the **passé composé**. 5. Note that the **s** is retained in affirmative commands in the **tu** form of **-er** verbs. In a negative command the **tu** form does not end in **-s**. 6. Students may be interested to learn idiomatic expressions that use the pronoun **en**, such as **J'en ai marre** and **J'en ai ras le bol** (*I'm fed up*).

Workbook Activity 25

Audiocassette/CD Activity 16

Answers

16 1. Est-ce qu'Amélie a acheté des casquettes?
Non, elle n'en a pas acheté.

2. Est-ce que Bruno et Amélie ont acheté des hot-dogs?
Non, ils n'en ont pas acheté.

3. Est-ce que Serge a acheté des tee-shirts?
Oui, il en a acheté un.

4. Est-ce que Fred et Serge ont acheté des casquettes?
Non, ils n'en ont pas acheté.

5. Est-ce qu'Amélie a acheté des limonades?
Oui, elle en a acheté une.

6. Est-ce que Bruno a acheté des tee-shirts?
Non, il n'en a pas acheté.

7. Est-ce que Fred a acheté des hot-dogs?
Oui, il en a acheté deux.

8. Est-ce que Diane a acheté des tee-shirts?
Oui, elle en a acheté trois.

Teacher's Notes

1. Double object pronouns, introduced on page 254 in the second level of *C'est à toi!*, are recycled here. 2. You may want to review with students that **me**, **te**, **le** and **la** become **m'**, **t'** and **l'** before a word beginning with a vowel sound. 3. Remind students that there is no agreement when **lui**, **leur**, **y** and **en** precede the helping verb in the **passé composé**. 4. Point out that object pronouns precede the infinitive. 5. In a negative command, direct and indirect object pronouns precede the verb. 6. **Me** and **te** become **moi** and **toi** in an affirmative command, for example, **Donnez-les-moi!** 7. Object pronouns precede the verb in a question with inversion, for example, **Les y as-tu vus?**

Modèles:

Fred/limonades
Élève A: Est-ce que Fred a acheté des limonades?
Élève B: Oui, il en a acheté une.

Diane/casquettes
Élève B: Est-ce que Diane a acheté des casquettes?
Élève A: Non, elle n'en a pas acheté.

> *Tu vas acheter des pêches au marché?*
>
> *Oui, je vais y en acheter.*

> Vous avez envie de savoir ce que vous achetez. On vous le dit.
>
> **E.LECLERC**

16 *Les ados ont acheté certaines choses au parc d'attractions. Avec un(e) partenaire, demandez si les personnes suivantes ont acheté ce qui est indiqué. Alternez les questions et les réponses avec votre partenaire. Suivez les modèles.*

	tee-shirts	casquettes	limonades	hot-dogs
Diane	3			
Bruno		2	1	
Serge	1			
Amélie			1	
Fred			1	2

1. Amélie/casquettes
2. Bruno et Amélie/hot-dogs
3. Serge/tee-shirts
4. Fred et Serge/casquettes
5. Amélie/limonades
6. Bruno/tee-shirts
7. Fred/hot-dogs
8. Diane/tee-shirts

Double object pronouns

When there are two pronouns in one sentence, their order before the verb in a declarative sentence is:

subject +	me te nous vous	+	le la les	+	lui leur	+ y + en + verb

These pronouns come right before the verb of which they are the object in sentences that are affirmative, negative, interrogative and have an infinitive. They also precede the verb in a negative command.

Quand nous as-tu vus au parc d'attractions?
Je vous y ai vus hier.

When did you see us at the amusement park?
I saw you there yesterday.

Où sont les tickets?
Il va me les donner demain.

Where are the tickets?
He's going to give them to me tomorrow.

Comment Paul a-t-il trouvé ce nouveau film?
Ne lui en parle pas!

What did Paul think about this new movie?
Don't talk to him about it!

TPR

Double Object Pronouns

To give students practice with double object pronouns, have them make a card for each pronoun in the chart and spread all the cards out on their desk. Prepare a list of questions requiring a response with double object pronouns, for example, **Est-ce que le censeur donne l'emploi du** temps au lycéen? Students hold up two pronoun cards in the correct order of the response, for example, **le lui**. This activity will make students more comfortable with double object pronouns and prepare them for making verbal responses.

In an affirmative command, their order is:

verb	+	le la les	+	lui leur	+	moi toi nous vous	+	y	+	en

Tu veux aller à La Ronde?	*Do you want to go to La Ronde?*
Oui, emmène-m'y!	*Yes, take me (along) there!*
Je lis des histoires aux enfants?	*Shall I read some stories to the children?*
Bien sûr. Lis-leur-en!	*Of course. Read them some!*

Pratique

Avec un(e) partenaire, demandez si les personnes indiquées ont acheté quelque chose pour les personnes qui suivent. Dites que oui. Alternez les questions et les réponses avec votre partenaire. Suivez le modèle et l'ordre indiqué par le cercle.

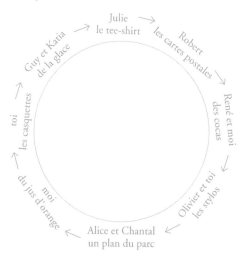

Modèle:

Élève A: Est-ce que Julie achète le tee-shirt pour Robert?

Élève B: Oui, elle le lui achète. Est-ce que Robert achète les cartes postales pour René et moi?

Élève A: Oui, il vous les achète. Est-ce que René et moi, nous...?

Te voilà! Qui t'a indiqué le chemin?

Bruno me l'a indiqué.

Avec un(e) partenaire, posez et répondez aux questions au passé composé. Suivez le modèle.

1. conduire les autos tamponneuses au parc d'attractions
2. emmener ton ami(e) au centre commercial
3. acheter des cadeaux d'anniversaire pour tes amis
4. montrer ton emploi du temps à tes parents
5. parler au censeur de tes problèmes

Modèle:

rendre visite à des amis à Montréal

Élève A: Est-ce que tu as rendu visite à des amis à Montréal?

Élève B: Oui, je leur y ai rendu visite. Et toi, est-ce que tu as rendu visite à des amis à Montréal?

Élève A: Non, je ne leur y ai pas rendu visite.

 Audiocassette/CD
Activity 18

Answers

17 Est-ce que René et moi, nous achetons des cocas pour Olivier et toi?
Oui, vous nous en achetez.
Est-ce qu'Olivier et toi, vous achetez les stylos pour Alice et Chantal?
Oui, nous les leur achetons.
Est-ce qu'Alice et Chantal m'achètent un plan du parc?
Oui, elles t'en achètent un.
Est-ce que je t'achète du jus d'orange?
Oui, tu m'en achètes.
Est-ce que tu achètes les casquettes pour Guy et Katia?
Oui, je les leur achète.
Est-ce que Guy et Katia achètent de la glace pour Julie?
Oui, ils lui en achètent.

18 1. Est-ce que tu as conduit les autos tamponneuses au parc d'attractions? Et toi, est-ce que tu as conduit les autos tamponneuses au parc d'attractions?
2. Est-ce que tu as emmené ton ami(e) au centre commercial? Et toi, est-ce que tu as emmené ton ami(e) au centre commercial?
3. Est-ce que tu as acheté des cadeaux d'anniversaire pour tes amis? Et toi, est-ce que tu as acheté des cadeaux d'anniversaire pour tes amis?
4. Est-ce que tu as montré ton emploi du temps à tes parents? Et toi, est-ce que tu as montré ton emploi du temps à tes parents?
5. Est-ce que tu as parlé au censeur de tes problèmes? Et toi, est-ce que tu as parlé au censeur de tes problèmes?
Students' responses to these questions will vary.

Cooperative Group Practice

Le cambrioleur

To practice double object pronouns in the **passé composé**, put your students in small groups of four or five. Prepare a worksheet with pictures of objects a burglar might steal from a home. Designate a leader in each group. The leader passes out the worksheet picturing objects that were reported stolen by M. Brochet when a burglar broke into his home. The leader questions other group members about what M. Brochet had to give the burglar, for example, **Il lui a donné la télé?** Group members give an affirmative response if the item is pictured (**Oui, il la lui a donnée**) or a negative response if the item is not pictured (**Non, il ne la lui a pas donnée**).

Teacher's Note

Before students begin Activity 18, you may want to read each phrase to them, asking what parts of the phrase will be replaced with pronouns and which pronouns will replace them.

Listening
Activity 2

Quiz
Leçon B

Communication

19   *Avec un(e) partenaire, jouez les rôles d'un reporter d'un journal québécois et d'un(e) élève qui sont à La Ronde. Le reporter va écrire un article qui décrit les expériences d'un(e) élève typique qui y passe la journée. Pendant votre conversation le reporter demande à l'élève:*

    1.   s'il ou elle s'y est bien amusé(e)
    2.   comment il ou elle a trouvé les attractions
    3.   quelle attraction il ou elle a préférée et pourquoi
    4.   quand il ou elle a rigolé le plus
    5.   s'il ou elle a gagné quelque chose
    6.   s'il ou elle a goûté les spécialités du parc
    7.   s'il ou elle a acheté des souvenirs

À la fin de votre conversation, le reporter demande à l'élève s'il ou elle a des tickets qui restent, et l'élève lui en offre.

20   *Imaginez que vous avez passé la journée à un parc d'attractions. Avant de sortir, on vous demande de compléter une évaluation du parc. À côté de chaque attraction, écrivez un chiffre (number) entre "1" et "10" qui donne votre opinion sur chacune (each one). ("10" est le maximum.) Puis écrivez une phrase qui explique votre évaluation. Par exemple,* **des jeux d'adresse—10—J'y ai gagné un grand gorille**.

Attractions	Évaluation	Commentaire
la galerie des miroirs déformants		
les autos tamponneuses		
l'arcade		
le/la voyant(e)		
les jeux d'adresse		
le manège		
des montagnes russes		
la grande roue		
les cafés		
les boutiques		
le cinéma		

21   *Vous travaillez pour un parc d'attractions américain où vous êtes responsable de la publicité. Vous devez dessiner un dépliant (leaflet) pour encourager les touristes francophones à le visiter. Dans votre dépliant nommez toutes les attractions du parc en français. Puis dessinez un plan qui montre où on peut trouver chaque attraction, les cafés et les toilettes. Mentionnez aussi quand le parc est ouvert et combien coûte un billet d'entrée.*

Sur la bonne piste

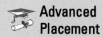
In the first and second levels of C'est à toi! you practiced numerous strategies to help you read successfully in French. Now you are going to read a story by Sempé/Goscinny from a popular series about a young boy, Nicolas, and his misadventures on vacation with his parents. Before you begin, it is useful to establish a "mind-set" to help you understand the story. Here are some reading techniques to keep in mind:

1. Read the title. It can give you a preliminary idea of what the story is about.
2. Look at the illustrations. They can help you identify the characters and understand what happens in the story.
3. Become familiar with new vocabulary words.
   - Look for cognates. For example, the adjective **tranquille**, meaning "peaceful" or "tranquil," is a cognate that you can easily recognize because it looks like a word you know in English.
   - Watch out for false cognates—French words that resemble English words but have a different meaning. For example, the verb **crier** looks like "to cry" but means "to shout."
   - Pay attention to words you think you already know; they may have new meanings. For example, as you read about Nicolas' father applying **l'huile** at the seaside, you may realize that "oil (for a car)," the meaning you already know, does not fit the context. The word must also mean "suntan oil."
   - Try to make educated guesses about the meaning of a new word by looking for a root word that you can recognize and by identifying the prefix or suffix to understand the longer word. For example, look at the word **reboucher** in the expression **reboucher le trou**. You already know that the word **bouche** means "mouth," that the suffix **-er** often indicates the infinitive of a verb and that the prefix **re-** means "again." These clues can lead you to guess that **reboucher le trou** means "to fill in (the mouth of) the hole again."
4. Ask yourself the five "W" questions: *Who* are the characters? *What* adventures does Nicolas have? *Where* is Nicolas spending his vacation? *When* does the story take place? *Why* does Nicolas have a good day but his father have a bad day?
5. If there are still words that you can't understand, use your dictionary skills. Although you shouldn't get into the habit of looking up every unknown word in the dictionary, sometimes you will not be able to guess the meaning of a new word, even after considering the context of the story and applying what you know about cognates and false cognates. If a new word causes a gap in your comprehension of the story, look it up in the dictionary. First try to identify its part of speech, and then choose the definition that makes the most sense for the story.
6. Think about the point of view from which the story is written. Why is this story more enjoyable seen through the eyes of a young boy? How would it be different if Nicolas' father told the story? How does the author's use of language imitate a child's speech?

Avant de lire la lecture, répondez aux questions suivantes.

1. Avec qui est-ce que tu vas à la plage? Qu'est-ce que tu y fais?
2. Qu'est-ce que tu faisais à la plage quand tu étais petit(e)?

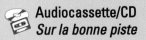

Teacher's Notes

1. To help students analyze what makes this story amusing, begin by making a list of its funny moments. Then make categories for each example. For example, Nicolas' father's getting hit on the head with a soccer ball is an example of physical comedy. You might make comparisons to slapstick comedy in films. Another example occurs when Nicolas' father is digging a new hole after being told to fill it up. The incident is humorous because there is a misunderstanding on the part of **le monsieur à la casquette blanche**, who is angry at not having his directive followed, not knowing yet that the father is looking for his son's pail. The conclusion where Nicolas' father repeats in a different tone **quand je pense aux copains qui sont restés au bureau** is an example of irony. Irony is a difference between appearance and reality. In appearance the father had a vacation day at the beach, but his day was disappointing because of his son's mischief. 2. Sempé and Goscinny cowrote the *Petit Nicolas* series. Jean-Jacques Sempé (1932-), born in Bordeaux, was an average student known for causing problems at school. At 19 he began drawing cartoons, and over a long, successful career has contributed to many magazines, including *Paris-Match*, *Punch* and *l'Express*. In 1954, inspired by his son Nicolas, he launched the *Petit Nicolas* series with his friend René Goscinny. René Goscinny (1926-77), born in Paris, spent his childhood in Buenos Aires where he passed his **bac** with high marks at a French school. Goscinny tried many careers before becoming a successful illustrator and journalist. Besides collaborating on the *Petit Nicolas* books, Goscinny is famous for creating the celebrated *Astérix* series.

La plage, c'est chouette

À la plage, on rigole bien. Je me suis fait des tas de copains, il y a Blaise, et puis Fructueux, et Mamert; qu'il est bête celui-là! Et Irénée et Fabrice et Côme et puis Yves, qui n'est pas en vacances parce qu'il est du pays et on joue ensemble, on se dispute, on ne se parle plus et c'est drôlement chouette.

"Va jouer gentiment avec tes petits camarades, m'a dit papa ce matin, moi je vais me reposer et prendre un bain de soleil." Et puis, il a commencé à se mettre de l'huile partout et il rigolait en disant: "Ah! quand je pense aux copains qui sont restés au bureau!"

Nous, on a commencé à jouer avec le ballon d'Irénée. "Allez jouer plus loin", a dit papa, qui avait fini de se huiler, et bing! le ballon est tombé sur la tête de papa. Ça, ça ne lui a pas plu à papa. Il s'est fâché tout plein et il a donné un gros coup de pied dans le ballon, qui est allé tomber dans l'eau, très loin. Un shoot terrible....

—Écoutez, les enfants, je veux me reposer tranquille. Alors, au lieu de jouer au ballon, pourquoi ne jouez-vous pas à autre chose?

—Ben, à quoi par exemple, hein, dites? a demandé Mamert. Qu'il est bête celui-là!

—Je ne sais pas, moi, a répondu papa, faites des trous, c'est amusant de faire des trous dans le sable. Nous, on a trouvé que c'était une idée terrible et on a pris nos pelles....

On a commencé à faire un trou. Un drôle de trou, gros et profond comme tout. Quand papa est revenu avec sa bouteille d'huile, je l'ai appelé et je lui ai dit:

—T'as vu notre trou, papa?

—Il est très joli, mon chéri, a dit papa.... Et puis, est venu un monsieur avec une casquette blanche et il nous a demandé qui nous avait permis de faire ce trou dans sa plage. "C'est lui, m'sieur!" ont dit tous mes copains en montrant papa. Moi j'étais très fier, parce que je croyais que le monsieur à la casquette allait féliciter papa. Mais le monsieur n'avait pas l'air content.

—Vous n'êtes pas un peu fou, non, de donner des idées comme ça aux gosses? a demandé le monsieur. Papa... a dit: "Et alors?" Et alors, le monsieur à la casquette s'est mis à crier que c'était incroyable ce que les gens étaient inconscients, qu'on pouvait se casser une jambe en tombant dans le trou, et qu'à marée haute, les gens qui ne savaient pas nager perdraient pied et se noieraient dans le trou, et que le sable pouvait s'écrouler et qu'un de nous risquait de rester dans le trou, et qu'il pouvait se passer des tas de choses terribles dans le trou et qu'il fallait absolument reboucher le trou.

—Bon, a dit papa, rebouchez le trou, les enfants. Mais les copains ne voulaient pas reboucher le trou.

—Un trou, a dit Côme, c'est amusant à creuser, mais c'est embêtant à reboucher.

—Allez, on va se baigner! a dit Fabrice. Et ils sont tous partis en courant. Moi je suis resté, parce que j'ai vu que papa avait l'air d'avoir des ennuis.

Critical Thinking

Point of View

You might ask students to brainstorm about what types of features they would expect to find in a story told from a child's point of view. They should list features such as heavy use of dialogue and reporting, run-on sentences and the use of idiomatic language. Instruct students to make a list of examples of each feature as they read.

—Les enfants! Les enfants! il a crié papa, mais le monsieur à la casquette a dit:

—Laissez les enfants tranquilles et rebouchez-moi ce trou en vitesse! Et il est parti.

Papa a poussé un gros soupir et il m'a aidé à reboucher le trou. Comme on n'avait qu'une seule petite pelle, ça a pris du temps et on avait à peine fini que maman a dit qu'il était l'heure de rentrer à l'hôtel pour déjeuner, et qu'il fallait se dépêcher, parce que, quand on est en retard, on ne vous sert pas, à l'hôtel. "Ramasse tes affaires, ta pelle, ton seau et viens", m'a dit maman. Moi j'ai pris mes affaires, mais je n'ai pas trouvé mon seau. "Ça ne fait rien, rentrons", a dit papa. Mais moi, je me suis mis à pleurer plus fort.

Un chouette seau, jaune et rouge, et qui faisait des pâtés terribles. "Ne nous énervons pas, a dit papa, où l'as-tu mis, ce seau?" J'ai dit qu'il était peut-être au fond du trou, celui qu'on venait de boucher. Papa m'a regardé comme s'il voulait me donner une fessée, alors je me suis mis à pleurer plus fort et papa a dit que bon, qu'il allait le chercher le seau, mais que je ne lui casse plus les oreilles. Mon papa, c'est le plus gentil de tous les papas! Comme nous n'avions toujours que la petite pelle pour les deux, je n'ai pas pu aider papa et je le regardais faire quand on a entendu une grosse voix derrière nous: "Est-ce que vous vous fichez de moi?" Papa a poussé un cri, nous nous sommes retournés et nous avons vu le monsieur à la casquette blanche. "Je crois me souvenir que je vous avais interdit de faire des trous", a dit le monsieur. Papa lui a expliqué qu'il cherchait mon seau. Alors, le monsieur lui a dit que d'accord, mais à condition qu'il rebouche le trou après. Et il est resté là pour surveiller papa.

"Écoute, a dit maman à papa, je rentre à l'hôtel avec Nicolas. Tu nous rejoindras dès que tu auras retrouvé le seau." Et nous sommes partis. Papa est arrivé très tard à l'hôtel, il était fatigué, il n'avait pas faim et il est allé se coucher. Le seau, il ne l'avait pas trouvé, mais ce n'est pas grave, parce que je me suis aperçu que je l'avais laissé dans ma chambre. L'après-midi, il a fallu appeler un docteur, à cause des brûlures de papa. Le docteur a dit à papa qu'il devait rester couché pendant deux jours.

—On n'a pas idée de s'exposer comme ça au soleil, a dit le docteur, sans se mettre de l'huile sur le corps.

—Ah! a dit papa, quand je pense aux copains qui sont restés au bureau!

Mais il ne rigolait plus du tout en disant ça.

Teacher's Note

To assess students' comprehension of the story, prepare a list of quotes, ask who said them and invite students to explain the importance of each one, for example: A. "Un trou... c'est amusant à creuser, mais c'est embêtant à reboucher." (Côme) Les copains de Nicolas décident de se baigner et de ne pas aider le père de Nicolas à reboucher le trou. B. "On n'a pas idée de s'exposer comme ça au soleil...." (le docteur) Le père de Nicolas a des brûlures, et il doit rester couché pendant deux jours. C. "Qu'il est bête celui-là!" (Nicolas) Nicolas parle de Mamert, un de ses nouveaux copains, quand son père dit aux garçons de creuser un trou dans le sable. D. "Je crois me souvenir que je vous avais interdit de faire des trous." (le monsieur à la casquette blanche) Le père de Nicolas vient de reboucher le trou, mais il le creuse encore parce que Nicolas a perdu son seau. E. "... je vais me reposer et prendre un bain de soleil." (papa) Le père de Nicolas est content de passer ses vacances à la plage. Bientôt il demande aux enfants de jouer à autre chose quand le ballon tombe sur sa tête.

Answers

23 Possible answers:

1. La plage est chouette parce qu'on y rigole bien avec des tas de copains.
2. Le père de Nicolas veut se reposer et prendre un bain de soleil à la plage.
3. Le père de Nicolas n'est pas content parce que le ballon est tombé sur sa tête.
4. Le père de Nicolas dit aux garçons de faire des trous dans le sable au lieu de jouer au ballon.
5. Le monsieur à la casquette blanche a dit qu'on pouvait se casser une jambe en tombant dans le trou et qu'on pouvait perdre pied et se noyer dans le trou.
6. Les copains de Nicolas ne rebouchent pas le trou parce que c'est embêtant à reboucher un trou, et qu'ils préfèrent se baigner.
7. Le trou est difficile à reboucher parce qu'il est gros et profond, et qu'il y a seulement une petite pelle.
8. Nicolas commence à pleurer parce qu'il pense qu'il a perdu son chouette seau jaune et rouge.
9. Pour trouver le seau de son fils, le père de Nicolas creuse au fond du trou qu'ils viennent de boucher.
10. Quand il rentre à l'hôtel, le père de Nicolas est fatigué et il n'a pas faim; donc, il se couche.
11. Selon le docteur, le père de Nicolas doit rester couché pendant deux jours.
12. Le père de Nicolas ne rigole pas cette fois quand il dit "... quand je pense aux copains qui sont restés au bureau" parce qu'il ne peut pas se reposer et il a des brûlures.

23 *Répondez aux questions suivantes.*

1. Selon Nicolas, pourquoi est-ce que la plage est chouette?
2. Qu'est-ce que le père de Nicolas veut faire à la plage?
3. Pourquoi le père de Nicolas n'est-il pas content?
4. Qu'est-ce que le père de Nicolas dit aux garçons de faire au lieu de jouer au ballon?
5. Le monsieur à la casquette blanche dit que le trou est une mauvaise idée. Pourquoi?
6. Pourquoi les copains de Nicolas ne rebouchent-ils pas le trou?
7. Le trou est-il facile ou difficile à reboucher? Pourquoi?
8. Pourquoi Nicolas commence-t-il à pleurer?
9. Que fait le père de Nicolas pour trouver le seau de son fils?
10. Comment est le père de Nicolas quand il rentre à l'hôtel? Que fait-il?
11. Selon le docteur, qu'est-ce que le père de Nicolas doit faire?
12. Pourquoi le père de Nicolas ne rigole-t-il pas cette fois quand il dit "... quand je pense aux copains qui sont restés au bureau"?

24 *Imaginez que le père de Nicolas rentre au bureau et parle avec ses collègues de ses vacances au bord de la mer. Racontez l'histoire que vous venez de lire du point de vue (point of view) du père de Nicolas. Commencez avec le jeu de ballon. Puis continuez avec l'arrivée du monsieur à la casquette, la recherche (search) du seau et la visite du docteur à l'hôtel.*

25 *Avec trois autres élèves, faites un sketch (skit) où vous jouez les rôles de Nicolas, de son père, de sa mère et du docteur à l'hôtel. Nicolas raconte au docteur ses aventures à la plage, la mère lui pose des questions sur la santé de son mari, le père se plaint (complains) et le docteur répond à chaque membre de la famille.*

Dossier fermé

Imagine que tu étudies dans un lycée français, et c'est le jour de ton premier examen. Tu regardes l'examen et tu vois qu'il consiste seulement en questions à longue réponse. Quelle est ta réaction?

C. Tu continues parce que c'est le style d'un examen français.

Peut-être que tu es surpris(e) parce qu'il n'y a pas de questions à choix multiples, de questions "vrai-faux" ou de questions où tu remplis l'espace blanc d'une phrase. Ces sortes d'examens sont pratiquement inexistantes en France. Tu as vu dans cette unité que les professeurs et les examens français demandent à l'élève un bon travail où il ou elle doit beaucoup penser. La sorte de question que tu trouves dans un examen français fait justement ça.

Le jour de son examen d'histoire, Bénédicte doit beaucoup penser.

Teacher's Notes

1. Words used in the story that are not in the end vocabulary of *C'est à toi!* are used to ask questions in Activity 23. 2. You may want students to work in pairs or small groups as they answer the questions. 2. Optional activity. To further explore the point of view of characters in the story, ask students to make lists of adjectives to describe how the children view **le monsieur à la casquette blanche,** how the latter views Nicolas and the other children, and how Nicolas' father and **le monsieur à la casquette blanche** view each other. 3. Optional activity. You might want to have students brainstorm about other situations where Nicolas might have misadventures, such as at school, at a zoo or on a farm. Then put students in pairs and have them write a new Nicolas story, imitating the authors' style and sense of humor. They could also illustrate the story. 4. You might provide interested students with additional stories recounting the misadventures of Nicolas from *Les vacances du petit Nicolas* or one of the other books in the series.

C'est à moi!

Now that you have completed this unit, take a look at what you should be able to do in French. Can you do all of these tasks?

➤ I can ask questions about what happened in the past.

➤ I can talk about what happened in the past.

➤ I can talk about things sequentially.

➤ I can confirm specific information.

➤ I can explain why.

➤ I can give examples.

➤ I can summarize what has been said.

➤ I can ask if someone is able to do something.

➤ I can say that someone is not able to do something.

➤ I can tell someone to do something.

➤ I can offer something to someone.

➤ I can express astonishment.

➤ I can express enthusiasm.

➤ I can express emotions.

➤ I can express what I want.

Pour voir si vous avez bien compris la culture francophone, décidez si chaque phrase est vraie ou fausse.

1. Dakar est une ville située sur la côte est de l'Afrique.
2. Le système d'enseignement sénégalais a comme modèle les écoles françaises.
3. Les professeurs français forcent les élèves à travailler, à penser et à apprendre avec des examens à choix multiples.
4. En France il n'est pas rare d'avoir un cours de 200 élèves dans une salle de conférences.
5. Il faut que les élèves français achètent leurs manuels pour les cours.
6. La Ronde est un parc d'attractions à Québec qui reste ouvert pendant l'hiver pour profiter du Carnaval.
7. "Le Monstre" est une attraction spectaculaire à La Ronde.
8. Au Carnaval il y a des compétitions comme la course de motocyclettes sur le Saint-Laurent.
9. Un autre sport d'hiver qu'on pratique au Carnaval est la planche à roulettes sur le Saint-Laurent.
10. Si l'on achète une boisson à un café français, on peut s'asseoir et y passer des heures.

Pendant le Carnaval les défilés du soir illuminent les rues de Québec.

Answers

1. fausse
2. vraie
3. fausse
4. vraie
5. vraie
6. fausse
7. vraie
8. vraie
9. fausse
10. vraie

Teacher's Notes

1. Dakar, also the largest city in Senegal, with approximately 1,489,000 people, is the most important seaport in West Africa. It is located on Cape Verde on the Atlantic coast. In this city of contrasts, you can find business-men in European suits, tourists and people dressed in traditional costumes, as well as colonial-style villas, modern buildings, supermarkets and open-air markets. 2. Currently, Wolof is taught in teacher-training schools. Despite advances made in the educational system and the increasing enrollment in institutions of higher learning, the dropout rate in Senegal remains extremely high, with about 35 percent of Senegalese children attending elementary and secondary schools. French, taught in schools and used in the media, is spoken only by the educated minority of the population.

Communication orale

Imaginez qu'Ibrahim, un nouvel élève sénégalais, assiste aux cours dans votre lycée cette année. Avec un(e) partenaire, jouez les rôles d'Ibrahim et d'un(e) élève américain(e) du lycée. Pendant votre conversation l'élève américain(e) demande à Ibrahim:

1. *comment il trouve votre lycée, votre ville et les États-Unis en général*
2. *de lui dire les sports qu'il pratique et s'il s'entraîne souvent*
3. *de décrire son emploi du temps*
4. *de lui dire les cours et les profs qu'il aime et n'aime pas et pourquoi*
5. *de comparer les devoirs et les examens américains aux devoirs et aux examens sénégalais*
6. *de lui décrire l'enseignement dans son pays et de le comparer à l'enseignement aux États-Unis*

Communication écrite

Maintenant jouez le rôle d'Ibrahim, l'élève sénégalais. Écrivez un article que vous allez faxer au journal de votre lycée au Sénégal. Dans cet article parlez de vos impressions du lycée américain; faites votre nouvel emploi du temps; dites si vous aimez vos cours et vos professeurs; et comparez la difficulté des cours, des devoirs et des examens américains et sénégalais. Enfin parlez de vos passe-temps favoris aux États-Unis.

Communication active

Qu'as-tu acheté comme souvenir du parc?

Cette casquette. Tu l'aimes?

To inquire about the past, use:

Tu as rempli la fiche d'inscription ce matin?	*Did you fill out the registration form this morning?*
Qu'as-tu acheté?	*What did you buy?*

To describe past events, use:

J'ai souvent **séché** le cours d'algèbre.	*I often skipped algebra class.*
J'ai dû passer un examen.	*I had to take a test.*

To sequence events, use:

Après, le censeur m'a donné mon emploi du temps.	*After that, the dean gave me my schedule.*
Je suis arrivé **il y a une semaine**.	*I arrived a week ago.*
Ensuite je peux aller avec toi à la librairie.	*Next I can go with you to the bookstore.*

To confirm a known fact, use:

C'est ça.	*That's right.*
Bien sûr.	*Of course.*

Teacher's Note

Dictation

To provide additional written practice, you might want to give this dictation. Read each sentence twice, once at a natural speed and once more slowly. Have students write what you say. As a group correction activity, either put the paragraph on a transparency in advance or have volunteers write the sentences on the board.

Vendredi matin Guy et Claire ne sont pas allés à la salle de conférences. Pourquoi? Ils ont séché le cours d'histoire. Ils ont pris le métro pour aller au parc d'attractions. D'abord, ils ont fait un tour de grande roue. Puis, ils ont essayé des jeux d'adresse dans l'arcade, mais ils n'y ont rien gagné. Ensuite, ils ont eu une consultation avec la voyante qui leur a dit, "Vous n'allez pas avoir de la chance aujourd'hui." À 14h00, quand ils sont rentrés au lycée, le censeur les a vus, et ils ont dû entrer dans son bureau.

To explain something, use:

Ils se sont assis au café **pour** déjeuner et **pour** parler.

They sat down at the café (in order) to have lunch and (in order) to talk.

To give examples, use:

Voilà un cours difficile.
C'est le calcul.
On a pu aussi profiter de la saison pour faire des sports d'hiver, **par exemple**, faire de la planche à neige.

There's a difficult course.
It's calculus.
One could also take advantage of the season to do winter sports, for example, snow-boarding.

To summarize, use:

Alors, je l'ai raté.
Enfin, j'ai réussi.
Tout ça?
Donc, il faut chercher ces livres aussi.

So then, I failed it.
Finally, I passed.
All that?
So, I have to get these books too.

To inquire about ability, use:

Est-ce que tu peux venir avec moi?

Can you come with me?

To express inability, use:

Je l'ai raté.
Réussir, ce n'est pas facile.
Je ne peux pas dormir dans ce cours.
Il est difficile à comprendre.
Je n'ai pas eu le temps de tout acheter.

I failed it.
Passing isn't easy.
I can't sleep in this class.

It's hard to understand.
I didn't have time to buy everything.

To give orders, use:

Dis-le-moi!

Tell (it to) me!

To offer something, use:

Je te les donne, si tu veux.

I'll give them to you, if you want.

To express astonishment, use:

Je n'en reviens pas.
Hein?

I can't get over it.
Huh?

To express enthusiasm, use:

Que je suis fana de ce parc!
C'est ma fête **favorite.**

I'm really a fan of this park!
It's my favorite festival.

To express emotions, use:

Nous avons rigolé comme des fous.

We laughed our heads off.

To express desire, use:

Je voudrais y **aller** avec toi une fois. **Je peux?**

I'd like to go (there) with you once. May I?

Teacher's Note

Here are the regular **-er** verbs that students learned in the first and second levels of *C'est à toi!*: accélérer, accepter, admirer, adorer, aider, aimer, allumer, s'amuser, (s')arrêter, arriver, arroser, assister, baisser, se brosser, brûler, chercher, collectionner, composter, consommer, continuer, contrôler, se coucher, coûter, danser, décider, déclarer, décoller, se déguiser, déjeuner, délivrer, demander, démarrer, déménager, dépasser, se dépêcher, se déshabiller, désirer, donner, doubler, échanger, écouter, entrer, étudier, faxer, fermer, fêter, flâner, garder, gâter, goûter, s'habiller, habiter, imaginer, indiquer, intéresser, inviter, jouer, laisser, se laver, louer, se maquiller, marcher, monter, montrer, parier, parler, passer, se peigner, penser, se perfectionner, piqueniquer, porter, (se) préparer, présenter, préserver, profiter, quitter, raconter, se raser, recommander, recycler, regarder, régler, regretter, remercier, rentrer, repasser, réserver, ressembler, rester, se réveiller, rêver, rouler, sembler, signer, skier, sympathiser, téléphoner, terminer, tomber, toucher, tourner, travailler, traverser, trouver, utiliser, vérifier and visiter.

Unité 2

Les rapports humains

In this unit you will be able to:

➤ **ask for information**

➤ **express astonishment and disbelief**

➤ **express suspicion**

➤ **express emotions**

➤ **express concern**

➤ **express ridicule**

➤ **apologize**

➤ **express satisfaction**

➤ **write a letter**

➤ **tell a story**

➤ **describe how things were**

➤ **explain something**

➤ **describe physical traits**

➤ **describe temperament**

➤ **tell how you were**

Tes empreintes ici

As-tu jamais perdu quelque chose de spécial? Bien sûr, tu étais triste ou au moins tu n'étais pas content(e).

Est-ce que quelqu'un a jamais été méchant ou pas du tout gentil dans un magasin, à la banque, où tu travailles ou pendant un voyage? Qu'as-tu fai

As-tu jamais voyagé où on ne parle pas anglais? Il est toujours plus facile d voyager avec un(e) ami(e) qui peut t'aider à résoudre un problème. Si tu avais la chance de voyager avec un(e) ami(e) favori(te), qui est-ce que tu choisirais? Pourquoi?

Leçon A

In this lesson you will be able to:

➤ ask for information

➤ express astonishment and disbelief

➤ express ridicule

➤ tell a story

➤ describe how things were

➤ tell how you were

➤ describe physical traits

➤ describe temperament

J'ai la chance de voyager avec mes amis favoris.

Dossier ouvert

Imagine que tu voyages en Europe avec tes copains français Bénédicte et Sébastien. En Italie Sébastien perd son passeport, mais il ne s'en inquiète pas. Pour rentrer en France, il n'a même pas de problèmes quand il passe au contrôle des passeports. Comment est-ce que c'est possible?

    A. Sébastien a un autre passeport dans sa valise.
    B. Il est sympa et semble innocent. On lui permet de passer.
    C. Il n'a pas besoin de passeport pour aller d'Italie en France.

un récépissé

une ambassade

un commissariat

Salim est souriant.

Il est fâché.

Il est déprimé.

Il est effrayé.

Il est épuisé.

**Workbook
Activity 1**

**Audiocassette/CD
Adjectives**

Teacher's Notes

1. **Un reçu** is another word for a receipt. 2. **Un poste de police**, another word for a police station, is smaller than **un commissariat**. In the countryside and in small towns, a police station is called **une gendarmerie**. 3. **Avoir peur (de)**, a synonym for **effrayé(e)**, and **fatigué(e)**, a synonym for **épuisé(e)**, were introduced in Unit 10 in the first level of *C'est à toi!* 4. Other related terms include **un ambassadeur/une ambassadrice** (*ambassador*), **un sourire** (*smile*), **la dépression** (*depression*), **la colère** (*anger*), **l'épuisement** (*exhaustion*) and **la crainte, la peur** (*fear*).

**Workbook
Activity 2**

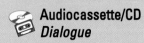

Audiocassette/CD
Dialogue

Suzanne entre dans sa chambre d'hôtel à Paris. Sa copine Ellen est en train de changer ses vêtements pour sortir parce que c'est son dernier jour à Paris. Demain on rentre aux États-Unis après dix jours passés en France. Suzanne n'est pas souriante. Elle a l'air° épuisé et déprimé.

Ellen:	Mais, dis donc, Suzanne, qu'est-ce que tu as?
Suzanne:	Quelle histoire! On m'a volée° dans le métro.
Ellen:	Zut! Qu'est-ce qui s'est passé?°
Suzanne:	Assieds-toi! Je vais tout te raconter. Angie, Jim et moi, nous rentrions en métro. Il y avait beaucoup de monde. Tout à coup° un mec m'a demandé l'heure. Son copain était à côté de lui. Je lui ai dit qu'il était 16h00. Je ne sais pas s'il m'a comprise ou pas mais il continuait à répéter la question. Pendant que° le premier mec me demandait l'heure, son copain fouillait° dans mon sac à dos. Il a tout pris.
Ellen:	C'est pas vrai! Mais c'est incroyable!°
Suzanne:	Attends. Alors, en° sortant du métro, nous avons décidé d'acheter une crêpe. Mais quand j'ai essayé de trouver mon portefeuille dans mon sac à dos, j'ai vu qu'il n'y avait rien, zéro. On a tout pris—mon argent français et américain, mon passeport, mes cartes de crédit, mes chèques de voyage. Alors, en étant effrayée et fâchée, je suis rentrée tout de suite à l'hôtel. J'ai tout raconté à la réceptionniste qui a

avoir l'air to look; **voler** *prendre quelque chose d'une autre personne;* **se passer** *to happen;* **tout à coup** *suddenly;* **pendant que** *while;* **fouiller** *chercher;* **incroyable** *pas possible à croire;* **en** *while*

---

1. In the expression **avoir l'air**, the adjective that follows is masculine to agree with **l'air**. 2. **Volée** agrees with the person who is the direct object, i.e., Suzanne. 3. From now on, past participles, such as **passés**, may be used as adjectives. They will not be listed separately in the end vocabulary. 4. **Qu'est-ce qui est arrivé** is another way to ask **Qu'est-ce qui s'est passé?** 5. "Pickpocketing" is called **le vol à la tire**. 6. **Les crêperies** were introduced on page 66 in the first level of *C'est à toi!* A recipe for **crêpes** is found on page 308 in the second-level Annotated Teacher's Edition of *C'est à toi!*

Critical Thinking

Journal personnel

Before beginning the **Dialogue**, you might ask students how they would help a friend if he or she were robbed here in the United States. How would they comfort their friend and help him or her regain the lost property? Ask students to explain how this situation would be complicated if the friend were robbed while traveling in France, what steps they would take to report the crime and how they might try to get the stolen property back.

téléphoné à l'ambassade. On lui a dit qu'il était inutile° de venir à 17h00 samedi après-midi, mais qu'il fallait aller au commissariat faire une déclaration de vol.° Heureusement, Mme Taylor était dans sa chambre, et nous sommes allées ensemble au commissariat. J'étais contente d'avoir la prof avec moi. Nous y sommes entrées, et Mme Taylor est allée au comptoir pour tout expliquer à l'agent de police. Après quelques minutes un autre agent de police est arrivé. Il nous a invitées à venir nous asseoir dans son petit bureau. Il posait° beaucoup de questions— mon nom, mon adresse, mon anniversaire. L'agent de police m'a aussi demandé comment étaient les deux mecs, leur taille, leur âge et s'ils parlaient avec un accent. Cet agent de police était exigeant,° tu vois. Alors, j'ai répondu qu'ils étaient un peu moches, de taille plutôt° petite que grande, qu'ils avaient les cheveux noirs et les yeux marron, qu'ils n'avaient pas de barbe et qu'ils ne portaient pas de lunettes. Oh, et ils étaient bien habillés.° Le mec qui m'a parlé avait au moins 15 ans. Son français était facile à comprendre. Enfin, l'agent nous a dit qu'on chercherait mes documents et qu'il fallait montrer le récépissé à l'immigration aux États-Unis. L'agent de police était accueillant° et rassurant,° et je me sentais° un peu mieux. Mme Taylor et moi, nous avons remercié l'agent et avons quitté le commissariat. Et me voilà! Quelle imbécile!° Je ne faisais pas attention° dans le métro.

Si on vous vole en France, il faut faire une déclaration de vol au commissariat.

Ellen: Pauvre Suzanne! Je t'offre quelque chose à boire. Tu veux?

Suzanne: Oui, s'il te plaît. Tu sais, je vais devoir tout expliquer deux ou trois fois à l'aéroport. C'est si fatigant.°

Ellen: Ne t'inquiète pas! Tu vas avoir Mme Taylor pour t'aider.

inutile *useless;* **un vol** l'action de voler quelque chose; **poser** *demander;* **exigeant(e)** *demanding;* **plutôt** *rather;* **habillé(e)** *dressed;* **accueillant(e)** *aimable;* **rassurant(e)** *reassuring;* **se sentir** *to feel;* **un(e) imbécile** *idiot;* **faire attention** *to pay attention;* **fatigant(e)** *tiring*

Les agents de police parisiens sont-ils accueillants?

Choisissez l'expression qui complète chaque phrase d'après le dialogue.

1. Quand Suzanne rentre à l'hôtel, elle a l'air....
   a. souriant   b. rassurant   c. déprimé
2. Dans le métro un mec lui a demandé....
   a. son nom   b. l'heure   c. son adresse

Teacher's Notes

1. Another word for a police officer is **un gardien de la paix**. 2. You may want to point out that the adjective **habillé(e)** comes from the past participle of the reflexive verb **s'habiller**, which was introduced on page 138 in the second level of *C'est à toi!* 3. **Les papiers** is another term for **les documents**.

Teacher's Note

So that students can simulate responding to the imaginary situation of having their passport stolen while traveling in France, prepare a message on your answering machine at home, pretending to be the American Embassy in Paris. Before you do this, tell students their passport has been stolen and they are to call the embassy at the number you give them. Have students identify themselves, explain their problem and ask for a return phone call at their hotel. If you aren't comfortable giving out your home phone number, you can substitute two cassette recorders for the answering machine. Students turn on the first cassette recorder to hear the embassy message. Then they use the second cassette recorder to leave their message. You may want to grade student messages based on enunciation, politeness and appropriate completion of the three oral tasks.

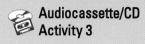

**Audiocassette/CD
Activity 3**

Answers

2 1. h
2. d
3. g
4. a
5. f
6. c
7. b
8. e

3 Answers will vary.

Paired Practice

Crossword Puzzles

After they have completed Activities 1 and 2, have students work in pairs. Instruct each pair to create an original crossword puzzle in French and a separate answer key. You may want to specify a minimum number of horizontal and vertical expressions or give extra credit to the pair whose puzzle contains the most expressions. Ask students to focus on new vocabulary that describes the events in the **Dialogue** and to write their clues in sentence form, for example, **Suzanne va au... faire une déclaration de vol.** Check each pair's puzzle for accuracy and have students correct any errors. Then have pairs exchange puzzles and solve them.

---

3. Suzanne avait... dans son sac à dos.
    a. ses vêtements   b. son récépissé   c. son portefeuille

4. Il était inutile d'aller....
    a. au commissariat   b. à l'hôtel   c. à l'ambassade

5. L'agent a invité Mme Taylor et Suzanne à venir s'asseoir....
    a. dehors   b. dans son bureau   c. à côté du comptoir

6. L'agent a posé beaucoup de questions; il était....
    a. épuisé   b. accueillant   c. exigeant

7. Les mecs avaient....
    a. des lunettes   b. les yeux marron   c. un accent

8. Il fallait montrer... à l'immigration.
    a. des documents   b. le récépissé   c. la déclaration de vol

9. Suzanne... dans le métro.
    a. faisait de la musculation
    b. faisait la queue
    c. ne faisait pas attention

Jean-Paul est épuisé parce qu'il vient de s'entraîner.

---

2 | *Choisissez la phrase à droite qui suit logiquement chaque phrase à gauche.*

1. On répond aux questions et on écoute le prof.
2. On est de Marseille. On ne parle pas comme quelqu'un qui est de Paris.
3. On dit "Bienvenue!"
4. On dit quelque chose deux fois.
5. On a peur des lions.
6. On a un passeport, un récépissé et un permis de conduire.
7. On fait ses devoirs depuis cinq heures.
8. On fait une déclaration de vol.

   a. On répète.
   b. On est épuisé.
   c. On a ses documents.
   d. On a un accent.
   e. On est au commissariat.
   f. On est effrayé.
   g. On est accueillant.
   h. On fait attention.

3 | *C'est à toi!*

1. Ton professeur de français, il a l'air comment aujourd'hui?
2. Est-ce que tu fais bien attention aux gens dans la rue? Peux-tu les décrire?
3. Est-ce qu'on t'a jamais volé(e)? Si oui, où? Quoi?
4. Est-ce que tu as jamais perdu quelque chose qu'il fallait avoir? Si oui, qu'est-ce que tu as fait?
5. Si tu as jamais voyagé, quels sont les documents que tu avais sur toi?
6. Si tu avais un problème pendant un voyage, à qui est-ce que tu demanderais de l'aide? Pourquoi?
7. Est-ce que tu as jamais voyagé en France? Si oui, où?
8. Si tu as déjà voyagé dans un autre pays, comment étaient les gens? Ils étaient accueillants?

Solange a l'air déprimé parce qu'elle ne peut pas sortir ce soir.

Quand vous voyagez, votre passeport est très important parce qu'il aide à vous identifier quand vous passez à la douane, quand vous arrivez à l'hôtel et quand vous touchez vos chèques de voyage. Ne le perdez pas! Mettez votre passeport et vos autres papiers importants (chèques de voyage, argent, cartes de crédit) où ils ne sont pas visibles. Vous devez contacter l'ambassade ou le consulat américain tout de suite si vous perdez ou si on vous vole un passeport américain. L'ambassade américaine à Paris est à 2, avenue Gabriel, près de la place de la Concorde. Vous devez aussi faire une déclaration de vol à la police.

Enquête culturelle

Workbook Activity 3

Teacher's Notes

1. Cognates in this reading include **important**, **identifier**, **papiers**, **visibles**, **contacter**, **consulat**, **remboursement**, **compagnie**, **lignes**, **système**, **transport**, **intérieur**, **direction**, **certainement**, **valide**, **accès**, **commun**, **certaines**, **zones** and **simple**. 2. Located next to the Crillon Hotel and the French Navy headquarters, the American Embassy stands on the site where a wealthy agriculturalist built a luxurious home in the 18th century. In 1816 the building became provisions headquarters for the Duke of Wellington. When the building became the property of the U.S. government in 1928, the original house was torn down and replaced with a structure similar to the current building. The cornerstone ceremony took place on May 2, 1932. No French officials attended the ceremony, as French President Loumer had just died. Constructed of stone and brick, the embassy contains about 190 rooms. The interior is inspired by American Colonial architecture. 3. The American Consulate in Paris is located at 2, rue St.-Florentin. 4. The American Express office in Paris is located at 11, rue Scribe. 5. **Les chèques de voyage** are often called **les traveller's** in conversational French. 6. Exchange rates are most favorable for credit card withdrawals, followed by traveler's checks and then cash. A web address for international exchange rates is http://www.ita.doc.gov/import_admin/records/exchange/exchange.html. To find the exchange rate for France, click on "France." 7. The **métro** was presented on pages 387-88 in the first level of *C'est à toi!* and on page 50 in the second level. 8. You may want to reuse Transparency 64 (**Le plan de métro**) from the Level One transparencies.

C'est une bonne idée aussi d'avoir des chèques de voyage. Si vous les perdez ou si on vous les vole, vous pouvez chercher un remboursement au bureau de la compagnie ou à la banque.

TRAVELLERS CHEQUES THOMAS COOK UNE SÉRÉNITÉ DE TOUS LES INSTANTS

Il est toujours important de savoir le nom et l'adresse de votre hôtel. Beaucoup d'hôtels offrent une petite carte avec le nom, l'adresse et le numéro de téléphone de l'hôtel. Vous pouvez montrer cette carte à un chauffeur de taxi pour rentrer à votre hôtel.

HÔTEL REGINA
★★★★

2, PLACE DES PYRAMIDES - 75001 PARIS
TÉL. : 01 42 60 31 10 - FAX : 01 40 15 95 16

À l'extérieur de la bouche de métro, il y a un plan qui montre la ligne qu'il vous faut. (Paris)

Il y a 13 lignes de métro qui traversent la ville de Paris et offrent aux voyageurs un système de transport très rapide et bon marché. Avec 319 stations de métro à l'intérieur de Paris, on n'est jamais loin d'une "bouche de métro." Vous prenez le train qui va en direction de la station à la fin de la ligne. Vous pouvez changer de

Teacher's Note

To get an American passport, applicants over the age of 13 should apply in person at the courthouse or post office. Applicants must demonstrate proof of citizenship by submitting a certified copy of their birth record or their certificate of naturalization. (To renew a passport, a previous passport provides proof of citizenship.) Applicants must show proof of identity (a valid driver's license or military identification card), supply their social security number and submit two identical passport photos. Passports cost $40.00 for minors under the age of 18 and $65.00 for adults age 18 and over. Currently, passports are valid for ten years. If your students need passports for an upcoming trip to France, encourage them to apply early. Passports can take six weeks or more to process. For additional information on applying for a U.S. passport, access the U.S. Department of State web site on the Internet. The web address is http://www.state.gov/test.html. First click on "Site Index." Then click on "Services." Under "Travel," click on "Passports."

train et changer de ligne pour sortir à la station près de votre destination. À beaucoup de stations de métro, il y a deux ou trois lignes qui se rejoignent. En ce cas, cherchez le panneau "Correspondance" qui indique les autres lignes qui sortent de la station.

Teacher's Notes

1. The web address for a map of the **métro** is http://www.paris.org/Metro/. 2. To provide practice using a **métro** map, you may want to have students research five museums in Paris they would like to visit and explain what lines they would take to get there. A list of Paris museums is available on the Internet. The web address is http://www.paris.org/Musees/.

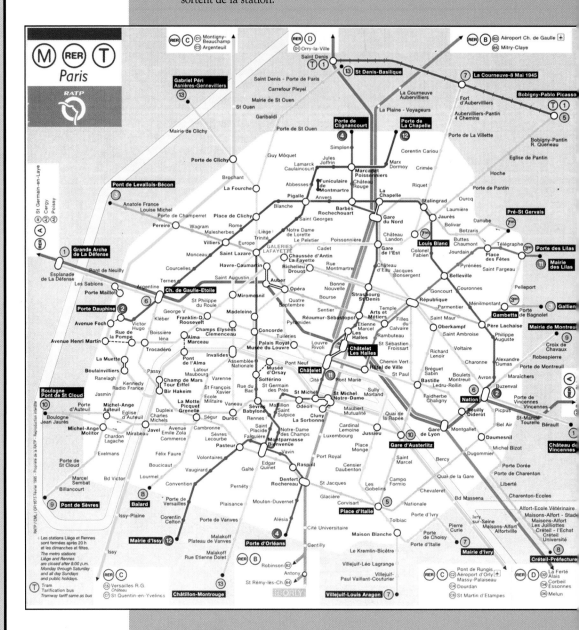

Critical Thinking

Analyzing Subway Maps

Divide your class into small groups. Give each group a Paris **métro** map and a map of a subway in another city, such as New York, Boston, Washington, D.C., London, Madrid or Moscow. Have students begin by comparing the Paris map with the map from the other city. Are the subway lines on the maps organized by color, name or number? How many lines serve each city? What's the average number of stations on a line? After making these preliminary comparisons, have each group research in the library the average distance between subway stops, the price of a ticket and the hours the subway is open in Paris and the other city. Then have students make a chart comparing the features of both subway systems. Finally, tell students to assess which of the two cities has the better subway system.

Si vous allez passer quelques jours à Paris, vous voudrez certainement acheter un ticket spécial pour le métro. La carte "Paris Visite" est valide pour un, trois ou cinq jours. Elle vous donne accès à tous les transports en commun: métro, R.E.R., train, bus. Vous pouvez acheter la "Carte Orange" pour une semaine ou pour un mois de voyages en métro. Ces tickets sont aussi valides pour l'autobus et le R.E.R. dans certaines zones. Bien sûr, vous pouvez toujours acheter un ticket simple ou un carnet (dix tickets).

Les nouvelles voitures de métro sont plus ouvertes, et on peut passer d'une voiture à l'autre. (Paris)

Les cartes "Paris Visite" et "Carte Orange" sont aussi valides pour le bus.

Teacher's Note

Tourists in Paris should determine approximately how many times a day they are going to use the **métro** before deciding on the "Paris Visite" card or the "Carte Orange." Sometimes buying a **carnet** or two is less expensive.

Answers

4 Possible answers:

1. Votre passeport est très important quand vous passez à la douane, quand vous arrivez à l'hôtel et quand vous touchez vos chèques de voyage.
2. On doit mettre le passeport où il n'est pas visible.
3. Si on perd le passeport, on doit contacter l'ambassade ou le consulat américain.
4. Si on lui vole ses chèques de voyage, on peut chercher un remboursement au bureau de la compagnie ou à la banque.
5. Les clients peuvent demander une carte avec le nom, l'adresse et le numéro de téléphone de l'hôtel.
6. Il y en a 319.
7. Pour changer de ligne dans le métro, il faut suivre le panneau "Correspondance."
8. La carte "Paris Visite" reste valide pour un, trois ou cinq jours.
9. Les Parisiens qui voyagent souvent en métro achètent généralement la "Carte Orange."
10. Il y en a dix.

4 | *Répondez aux questions suivantes.*

1. Pourquoi est-ce que votre passeport est très important quand vous voyagez?
2. Où doit-on mettre le passeport?
3. Qu'est-ce qu'on doit faire si on perd le passeport?
4. Qu'est-ce qu'on peut faire si on lui vole ses chèques de voyage?
5. Qu'est-ce que les clients peuvent demander à la réception de leur hôtel pour savoir tous les détails importants?
6. Combien de stations de métro y a-t-il à Paris?
7. Quel panneau faut-il suivre pour changer de ligne dans le métro?
8. Pour combien de jours est-ce que la carte "Paris Visite" reste valide?
9. Les Parisiens qui voyagent souvent en métro, quelle carte est-ce qu'ils achètent généralement?
10. Combien de tickets y a-t-il dans un carnet?

L'ambassade américaine aide les Américains qui ont perdu leurs passeports. (Paris)

Comme vous savez déjà, Suzanne a dû aller au commissariat faire une déclaration de vol après qu'on l'a volée dans le métro. Regardez la déclaration que l'agent de police a remplie. Puis répondez aux questions.

MINISTÈRE DE L'INTÉRIEUR ET DE LA SÉCURITÉ PUBLIQUE

DIRECTION GÉNÉRALE DE LA POLICE NATIONALE

RÉPUBLIQUE FRANÇAISE
Liberté Égalité Fraternité

Commissariat de Voie Publique

9, Rue Fabert
75007 PARIS
Tél.: 44 18 69 07
Fax: 44 18 33 87

CODE INSEE DU SERVICE	Dept	Commune	N° du Service
	75		

1 RÉCÉPISSÉ DE DÉCLARATION DE

- ☒ **VOL À LA TIRE**
- ☐ **VOL À L'ÉTALAGE OU DANS UN TIROIR-CAISSE**
- ☐ **VOL DANS UN APPAREIL AUTOMATIQUE**
- ☐ **AUTRE VOL SIMPLE**
- ☐ **FILOUTERIE**

2 L'an mil neuf cent quatre-vingt <u>dix-huit</u>
le <u>Vingt-cinq mars</u> à <u>Dix-sept</u> heures <u>quinze</u>
Nous <u>CRAVEAU Éric, Gardien de la Paix</u>
__Officier <u>X</u> Agent de police Judiciaire, en fonction à <u>Paris 7ᵉ</u>
dressons procès-verbal de la plainte ci-dessous

3 PLAINTE (L'ÉTAT-CIVIL DU PLAIGNANT DOIT ÊTRE RÉLEVÉ SUR UNE PIÈCE D'IDENTITÉ OFFICIELLE)

SERVICE DE RÉCEPTION DE LA PLAINTE / DATE ET HEURE
<u>7ᵉ Arrdt</u>   <u>17 heures 15</u>
PRÉNOM, NOM, GRADE DU RÉDACTEUR
<u>CRAVEAU Éric, Gardien de la Paix</u>
(ÉVENTUELLEMENT NOM DE JEUNE FILLE SUIVI DU NOM D'ÉPOUSE ET PRÉNOMS)
Je soussigné(e) <u>WEILER Suzanne</u>
né(e) le <u>14/11/81</u> à <u>HOUSTON (Texas)</u>
nationalité <u>Américaine</u> profession <u>Étudiante</u>
demeurant <u>P.O. Box 1235 BROOKSHIRE, TEXAS 77423 USA</u>
DÉPOSE PLAINTE CONTRE INCONNU POUR LES FAITS RELATES (REMPLIR LA RUBRIQUE VICTIME SI LE PLAIGNANT AGIT POUR LE COMPTE D'AUTRUI)

VICTIME	NOM ET PRÉNOMS (OU RAISON SOCIALE) **WEILER Suzanne**	
DATE ET LIEU DE NAISSANCE	**14/11/81 HOUSTON TEXAS** NATIONALITÉ **Américaine**	
ADRESSE	**P.O. Box 1235 BROOKSHIRE TEXAS 77423 USA**	
CODE POSTAL ET COMMUNE	TÉLÉPHONE	
DATE EXACTE OU PRÉSUMÉE	JOUR, MOIS, AN, HEURE OU MOMENT **25/03/98 vers 16 heures**	
NATURE DU JOUR	L M W J V **X**D ln ☐ VEILLE DE FÊTE LÉGALE OU CONGÉS SCOLAIRES ☐ PÉRIODE DE FÊTE LÉGALE OU CONGÉS SCOLAIRES ☐ JOUR DE FÊTE OU DE MANIFESTATION LOCALE	
LIEU INFRACTION	**75 PARIS 7ᵉ Métro La Tour Maubourg** NATURE DU LIEU **Métro** (EX. AUTOBUS, BUREAU DE POSTE, MARCHÉ...)	
OBJETS VOLÉS	DIFFERENCIER LES OBJETS PAR VICTIME: NATURE, MARQUE, NUMÉRO(S), CARACTÉRISTIQUES, ÉTAT-CIVIL COMPLET DE TOUTES LES VICTIMES **Un passeport de nationalité américaine au nom de WEILER Suzanne N° 131082315, une somme de 18 dollars américains, 180 dollars en chèques de voyage, et 200 francs français, une MasterCard Gold et un permis de conduire de Texas avec photographie.**	
MODE OPÉRATOIRE PRÉCISIONS COMPLÉMENTAIRES	**Deux individus de type méditérranéen d'environ une quinzaine d'années. L'un demande l'heure pendant que l'autre fouille dans le sac à dos.**	

---

1. Quelle est l'adresse du commissariat où Suzanne est allée?
2. Quelle est la date du vol?
3. À quelle heure est-ce qu'on l'a volée, et à quelle heure a-t-elle fait sa déclaration au commissariat?
4. Comment s'appelle l'agent de police qui a rempli la déclaration?
5. Quel est le nom de famille de Suzanne?
6. Où et quand est-elle née?
7. Quelle est son adresse aux États-Unis?
8. À quelle station de métro est-ce qu'on l'a volée?
9. Quels sont les six choses spécifiques qu'on a volées à Suzanne?
10. Selon la description physique que Suzanne a donnée, comment l'agent a-t-il décrit les deux hommes?

Teacher's Notes

1. The **Structure** section in Unit 2 contains both new and recycled grammatical concepts. 2. The imperfect tense, introduced on page 298 in the second level of *C'est à toi!*, is recycled here. 3. The differences between the imperfect and the **passé composé** will be reviewed in Unit 3. 4. You may want to have students give all the imperfect forms for a regular -**er**, -**ir** and -**re** verb as well as for some irregular verbs. You may want to remind them that the stem of -**ir** verbs ends in -**iss** in the imperfect, for example, **nous choisissions**. 5. **Être**, the only verb with an irregular stem in the imperfect, has regular endings. 6. Verbs that end in -**cer** have a cedilla under the final **c** when it precedes an **a**, for example, **elle recommençait**. 7. Verbs that end in -**ger** have an **e** after the **g** before the endings in all forms except **nous** and **vous**, for example, **on voyageait**. 8. Other verbs with spelling changes in the present tense form the imperfect regularly, for example, **je préférais**, **j'achetais** and **j'envoyais**. 9. Verbs ending in -**ier**, such as **étudier**, have a double **i** for the imperfect ending of the **nous** and **vous** forms, for example, **vous étudiiez**. 10. **Falloir**, **neiger** and **pleuvoir** have only one form in the imperfect: **il fallait**, **il neigeait** and **il pleuvait**. 11. Age, time and feelings, when described in the past, are usually expressed in the imperfect.

Journal personnel

Many people say that our modern society is based on numbers and papers. For example, we carry driver's licenses, passports, credit cards, traveler's checks, social security numbers and personal identification numbers. How important are these identification papers to you? What happens if you lose one of them? The French also carry a **carte d'identité**, a sort of national identity card that contains the same information found on a passport. Why do you think the French government issues such a card? Have you read any stories or seen any movies in which this card plays a crucial part? How important is this card to its owner? How important is it to the police or other agents of the government (immigration, customs, military)? Do you think United States citizens should be required to carry a national identity card? What are the advantages and disadvantages of having a national identity card? Write your responses to these questions in your cultural journal.

Structure

Imperfect tense

The **imparfait** (*imperfect*) is another tense used to talk about the past. You use the imperfect to describe how people or things were and to describe repeated or habitual actions in the past.

Ce mec parlait avec un accent.	*This guy spoke with an accent.*

To form the imperfect, add the endings -**ais**, -**ais**, -**ait**, -**ions**, -**iez** and -**aient** to the stem of the present tense **nous** form. The verb **être** has an irregular stem: **ét-**.

Ils ne portaient pas de lunettes, et ils étaient bien habillés.	*They didn't wear glasses, and they were well dressed.*

The imperfect is used to describe:

* people or things as they were or used to be

Cet agent de police était exigeant.	*This police officer was demanding.*
Je me sentais un peu mieux.	*I felt a little better.*

Critical Thinking

Meanings in the Imperfect

You may want to ask your students how to say "I wrote," "I was writing," "I used to write" and "I did write." Tell them that you are looking for one French sentence that would work for all the English sentences. Students should say that the French expression is **J'écrivais**. This activity helps students remember the four ways that the imperfect can be expressed in English.

- conditions as they were or used to be

Il **fallait** montrer le récépissé à l'immigration.
It was necessary to show the receipt at immigration.

Il n'y **avait** rien.
There was nothing there.

- actions that took place repeatedly or regularly in the past

Son copain **fouillait** dans mon sac à dos.
His friend was going through my backpack.

Il **continuait** à répéter la question.
He continued to repeat the question.

Pratique

Était-on une victime facile? Dites ce que tout le monde faisait dans le métro quand des hommes suspects y sont arrivés. Pour chaque phrase utilisez le verbe convenable de la liste suivante.

fouiller	rigoler	regarder	boire	lire
se maquiller	dormir	manger	ouvrir	

Tous les matins Xavier achetait deux baguettes à la boulangerie. (Bayonne)

Modèle:

Malick et Pierre regardaient un plan de métro.

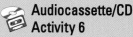

Audiocassette/CD Activity 6

Answers

6 Hélène mangeait un sandwich.
Tu dormais.
Paul fouillait dans son sac à dos.
Mme Claret ouvrait son sac à main.
M. Yuen lisait un journal.
Anne et Denise se maquillaient.
Cédric et moi, nous rigolions.
Nicolas buvait du jus d'orange.

Teacher's Notes

1. Mental activity in the past, expressed by verbs like **adorer, aimer, avoir, connaître, croire, espérer, être, penser, pouvoir, savoir** and **vouloir**, also takes the imperfect, for example, **Suzanne ne connaissait pas les deux mecs dans le métro**. 2. Remind students that the imperfect is often used with time expressions like **toujours, tous les matins, chaque soir, souvent** and **quelquefois**. 3. To prepare students for practicing the imperfect, you may want to do a **vous/nous** present tense drill with **-er, -ir** and **-re** verbs so that they can practice identifying the stems used in the imperfect, for example, **Est-ce que vous finissez vos devoirs chaque jour?** (**Oui, nous les finissons chaque jour.**)

Game

La tempête

Divide the class into two teams. Tell students that there was a power outage yesterday due to a severe storm and they are to tell whether everyone was able to do certain activities or not. Have the first student from each team go to the board. Then read the first activity from a list that you have prepared, for example, **tu/jouer du violon** or **Diane/travailler sur ordinateur**. The first student to write **Tu jouais du violon** or **Diane ne travaillait pas sur ordinateur** wins a point for his or her team. The team with the most points wins.

Cooperative Group Practice

Identifying Dialogue Characters

So that students can identify main characters in the **Dialogue** by describing them in the **imparfait**, put them in small groups of five or six. Prepare one card for each member of the group, listing the name of a character in the **Dialogue**. Give a set of cards to each group and tell each student to pick one. Each student prepares two sentences describing his or her character or stating what the character was doing, for example, **Cette personne demandait le nom, l'adresse et l'anniversaire de Suzanne. Cette personne était accueillante.** Then the first student says his or her sentences, and the other group members try to guess the identity of the character, for example, **C'est le deuxième agent de police.** Group members take turns until everyone has had a chance to say their sentences and all the characters have been identified. (Characters to include on the cards are **Suzanne, Ellen, le premier mec, le deuxième mec, Mme Taylor** and **le deuxième agent de police**).

Answers

7 1. Pourquoi est-ce que Sophie et Martine cherchaient un restaurant?
Elles avaient faim.

2. Pourquoi est-ce que Julianne et toi, vous buviez du café?
Nous avions soif.

3. Pourquoi est-ce que tu prenais l'addition?
Je finissais de manger.

4. Pourquoi est-ce que les filles entraient dans la pâtisserie?
Elles désiraient des tartes aux cerises.

5. Pourquoi est-ce que Laurent achetait des timbres?
Il envoyait des cartes postales.

6. Pourquoi est-ce que la vieille dame regardait la circulation?
Elle traversait la rue.

7. Pourquoi est-ce que les trois mecs faisaient la queue devant le guichet?
Ils allaient voir une comédie au cinéma.

8. Pourquoi est-ce que Mme Javel téléphonait à son mari?
Elle était en retard.

8 Possible answer:

D'abord, il y avait un ado de 16 ans. Il était petit, et il portait un anorak, un jean et des bottes. Il avait les cheveux courts et noirs. Le deuxième ado était très grand et très mince. Il avait les cheveux longs et roux et une barbe. Il portait un pantalon vert, un tee-shirt blanc et des baskets. Il y avait aussi un garçon de 15 ans. Il était de taille moyenne. Il avait les cheveux courts et noirs, et il portait une chemise violette, un pantalon noir et des chaussures noires. Enfin, il y avait un homme moche de taille moyenne. Il n'avait pas de cheveux. Il avait 60 ans et portait un blouson gris, une chemise bleue, un jean et des tennis.

Modèle:

Raoul/attendre devant la librairie

L'agent de police: Pourquoi est-ce que Raoul attendait devant la librairie?

Le témoin: Il voulait acheter une agrafeuse.

Modèle:

D'abord, il y avait un ado de 16 ans. Il était petit, et il portait un anorak....

---

7 *Avec un(e) partenaire, jouez les rôles d'un agent de police et d'un témoin (witness) d'un crime. L'agent de police pose des questions au témoin, et le témoin choisit une réponse logique de la liste suivante. Suivez le modèle.*

vouloir acheter une agrafeuse	avoir faim
envoyer des cartes postales	traverser la rue
aller voir une comédie au cinéma	être en retard
désirer des tartes aux cerises	avoir soif
finir de manger	

1. Sophie et Martine/chercher un restaurant
2. Julianne et toi/boire du café
3. tu/prendre l'addition
4. les filles/entrer dans la pâtisserie
5. Laurent/acheter des timbres
6. la vieille dame/regarder la circulation
7. les trois mecs/faire la queue devant le guichet
8. Mme Javel/téléphoner à son mari

---

8 *Il y avait quatre personnes qui vous ont volé(e) hier soir. D'après vos souvenirs (recollections), décrivez chaque personne à la police.*

Game

Imparfait **Relay Race**

To practice all the uses of the imperfect, divide the class into two teams. On two sides of the board, write different sentences with blanks where the imperfect will go. Give the infinitive of the verb to be used. For example, the first sentence for Team 1 might read: **(fouiller) Malick ___ dans son** sac à dos. The first sentence for Team 2 might read: **(se sentir) Zakia ___ fâchée.** One student from each team goes to his or her side of the board and writes the imperfect for the first sentence. When the first students return to their seats, the second student from each team goes up to the board to complete the second sentence, and so on. As the teams finish, circle any mistakes and allow team members to continue going, one at a time, to the board to make corrections. The first team to finish with no mistakes wins.

Present participle

The present participle is a verb form that ends in **-ant**. This ending corresponds to the suffix *-ing* in English. To form the present participle, add **-ant** to the stem of the present tense **nous** form of the verb.

Verb	Present Participle
entrer	**entrant**
aller	**allant**
offrir	**offrant**
sortir	**sortant**
répondre	**répondant**
dire	**disant**

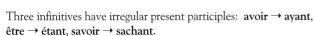

Three infinitives have irregular present participles: **avoir** → **ayant**, **être** → **étant**, **savoir** → **sachant**.

The preposition **en** usually precedes the present participle. **En** means "while," "upon," "in" or "on" if the two actions in the sentence take place at the same time.

En sortant du métro, nous avons décidé d'acheter une crêpe.   *Upon getting off the subway, we decided to buy a crêpe.*

Workbook Activity 6

Teacher's Notes

1. Verbs ending in **-cer** take a **ç** before the **-ant** ending, for example, **en commençant**. 2. Verbs ending in **-ger** take an **e** after the **g** before the **-ant** ending, for example, **en mangeant**. 3. Note that **ayant** is pronounced [ɛjã]. 4. Reflexive pronouns, when used with a present participle, refer to the verb's subject, for example, **Quel dentifrice utilises-tu en te brossant les dents?** 5. The present participle may also be used as an adjective. In this case it usually follows the word it describes and agrees with it in gender and in number, for example, **L'agent de police était accueillant et rassurant.** In this example, the adjective **accueillant** comes from the verb **accueillir**, and the adjective **rassurant** comes from the verb **rassurer**. 6. You may want to point out that the present participle can be used with object pronouns, for example, **(le dîner à la cuisine) En l'y préparant, Raoul regardait la télé.** (*While preparing it there, Raoul watched TV.*) 7. **Tout** is sometimes added for emphasis when a present participle is used, for example, **Mon camarade de classe prend des notes tout en écoutant le prof.** (*My classmate takes notes while listening to the teacher.*)

TPR

Matching Pictures

To give students practice identifying present participles, display six numbered pictures in front of the class that lend themselves to the use of the present participle. Have students make six cards, numbered one to six. Out of order, say a sentence to describe each picture, for example, **M. Blondel parle au marchand de fruits en achetant des bananes.** Students raise the card with the correct number to identify which picture is being described.

Paired Practice

Combining Sentences

To practice forming sentences using present participles, put students in pairs. Have each pair of students prepare a list of six pairs of sentences that can be combined using present participles, for example, **M. Lannion se rase. Il se regarde dans la glace.** Tell students to write each pair of sentences on a piece of construction paper. Then have them cut the two sentences in half and mix them up. Each pair gives the 12 sentences to another pair of students, who match and then combine them using a present participle, for example, **M. Lannion se rase en se regardant dans la glace.** When each pair has written their six combined sentences, they give them to the pair who wrote them for correction. To bring closure to this activity, you might ask each pair to write a sentence that they combined on the board.

Answers

9 1. posant
2. sachant
3. travaillant
4. étant
5. donnant
6. ayant
7. profitant
8. flânant, courant

Cooperative Group Practice

Sentence Completion

To practice forming present participles, put students in small groups of four or five. Give each group a worksheet that you have prepared with six incomplete sentences, for example, **Amine fait ses devoirs....** Each group writes as many logical completions as they can that use present participles, for example, **Amine fait ses devoirs (en téléphonant, en mangeant une pizza, en prenant le bus au lycée, en regardant les dessins animés).** Here are five other incomplete sentences that you might use:
1. **Je fête mon anniversaire....**
2. **Anne et ses copines apprennent l'anglais....** 3. **Tu écoutes de la musique....** 4. **Nous prenons des photos....** 5. **Vous voyagez en train....** After each group finishes, you may want to compile a list of all the present participle phrases that the groups came up with to complete each sentence.

Forming Sentences

Put students in small groups of four or five. Prepare a set of note cards for each group. Each card should have a vocabulary word on it from **Leçon A**. The first student in each group takes a card and forms a sentence with a present participle that incorporates the word on the card, for example, **une déclaration de vol: En faisant une déclaration de vol, Pierre parlait à l'agent de police.** Students take turns until a sentence using a present participle has been formed for each card.

En rentrant à l'hôtel, Suzanne avait l'air épuisé. *On returning to the hotel, Suzanne looked exhausted.*

En means "by" if a cause-and-effect relationship is expressed.

En essayant des jeux d'adresse, j'ai gagné 100 francs. *By trying some games of skill, I won 100 francs.*

En travaillant sur ordinateur, Chloé buvait du café.

Pratique

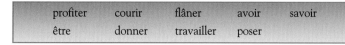

9 | Votre grand-père fait toujours des remarques très sages (wise). Complétez chaque phrase en utilisant le verbe convenable de la liste suivante.

profiter	courir	flâner	avoir	savoir
être	donner	travailler	poser	

1. En... des questions, on comprend.
2. En... lire, on connaît beaucoup de choses.
3. En... dur, on réussit.
4. En... égoïste, on n'a pas beaucoup d'amis.
5. En... un coup de main à quelqu'un qui n'a rien, on reçoit beaucoup.
6. En... envie d'être riche, on devient pauvre.
7. En... de la vie au maximum, on n'est jamais déprimé.
8. En..., on voit tout; en..., on ne voit rien.

En parlant, on n'apprend rien; en écoutant, on apprend beaucoup.

THÉÂTRE
DU ROND-POINT
CHAMPS-ÉLYSÉES
MARCEL MARÉCHAL

5 novembre · 25 janvier

Pierre Arditi, Jean-Michel Dupuis
Robert Hirsch, Marcel Maréchal

en attendant godot

de Samuel Beckett
mise en scène **Patrice Kerbrat**

Game

Sentence Match

Divide the class into two teams. Call two students from the first team to the front of the room. On a set of note cards, write sentences that need to be completed with a present participle, for example, **J'aide mes parents ___.** Student A selects a card and writes in the blank the response that he or she thinks Student B will make, for example, **... en faisant la vaisselle.** Student A returns the card to you. Read the sentence without the completion for Student B, who has ten seconds to complete the sentence with a phrase using a present participle. If Student B guesses what Student A wrote, their team earns ten points. If not, Student B gets another turn. If he or she makes an accurate guess on the second try, their team earns five points. If Student B does not guess the correct answer after two attempts, the other team gets a turn. Teams alternate until all the cards are used or the allotted time is up. The team with the highest score at the end of the game wins.

Quelle mauvaise journée! Julianne a perdu beaucoup de choses hier. Dites ce qu'elle a perdu pendant qu'elle faisait ce qui est illustré. Suivez le modèle.

Modèle:

1.

3.

5.

En quittant la maison,
Julianne a perdu ses gants.

2.

4.

6.

7.

🎧 **Audiocassette/CD
Activities 10-11**

Answers

10 Possible answers:

1. En parlant à une copine, Julianne a perdu de l'argent.
2. En fouillant dans son sac à dos, Julianne a perdu son feutre.
3. En montant dans l'autobus, Julianne a perdu sa trousse.
4. En se lavant les mains, Julianne a perdu sa bague.
5. En jouant au tennis, Julianne a perdu son verre de contact.
6. En faisant du vélo, Julianne a perdu sa casquette.
7. En rentrant à la maison, Julianne a perdu son chat.

Avec un(e) partenaire, posez des questions sur ce que vous faites pendant que vous faites d'autres choses. Puis répondez aux questions. Suivez le modèle.

1. finir tes devoirs/regarder la télé
2. se regarder dans la glace/se brosser les cheveux
3. dire à tes parents où tu vas/ sortir
4. faire attention/conduire
5. faire de l'aérobic/écouter de la musique
6. téléphoner à des amis/faire du baby-sitting
7. prendre des photos/fêter l'anniversaire d'un(e) ami(e)
8. s'amuser/visiter un parc d'attractions

Modèle:
manger/parler au téléphone
Élève A: Est-ce que tu manges en parlant au téléphone?
Élève B: Non, je ne mange pas en parlant au téléphone. Et toi, est-ce que tu manges en parlant au téléphone?
Élève A: Oui, je mange en parlant au téléphone.

Est-ce que tu fais
la bise à ta mère en
rentrant du lycée?

11 1. Est-ce que tu finis tes devoirs en regardant la télé? Et toi, est-ce que tu finis tes devoirs en regardant la télé?
2. Est-ce que tu te regardes dans la glace en te brossant les cheveux? Et toi, est-ce que tu te regardes dans la glace en te brossant les cheveux?
3. Est-ce que tu dis à tes parents où tu vas en sortant? Et toi, est-ce que tu dis à tes parents où tu vas en sortant?
4. Est-ce que tu fais attention en conduisant? Et toi, est-ce que tu fais attention en conduisant?
5. Est-ce que tu fais de l'aérobic en écoutant de la musique? Et toi, est-ce que tu fais de l'aérobic en écoutant de la musique?
6. Est-ce que tu téléphones à des amis en faisant du baby-sitting? Et toi, est-ce que tu téléphones à des amis en faisant du baby-sitting?
7. Est-ce que tu prends des photos en fêtant l'anniversaire d'un(e) ami(e)? Et toi, est-ce que tu prends des photos en fêtant l'anniversaire d'un(e) ami(e)?
8. Est-ce que tu t'amuses en visitant un parc d'attractions? Et toi, est-ce que tu t'amuses en visitant un parc d'attractions?
Students' responses to these questions will vary.

En recyclant les bouteilles, Fabrice aidait l'environnement.
Seven other pairs of sentences that you might use are: 1. J'ai fait du baby-sitting. J'ai reçu 100 francs. 2. Tu as pris un taxi. Tu as été en avance. 3. Nous avons fait le ménage. Nous avons aidé nos parents. 4. Vous avez visité un musée. Vous avez beaucoup appris sur l'art. 5. Sylvie et Bruno ont étudié. Ils ont réussi à l'examen.

6. Suzanne parlait à l'agent de police. Elle se sentait un peu mieux. 7. Nous sommes restés dans une auberge de jeunesse. Nous avons fait la connaissance de beaucoup de jeunes gens.

Communication

12 *Avec un(e) partenaire, jouez les rôles de deux personnes au commissariat. L'Élève A joue le rôle d'un témoin d'un vol. L'Élève B joue le rôle d'un agent de police. Pendant votre conversation, l'agent de police demande au témoin de décrire le suspect. L'agent de police veut savoir des détails sur:*

1. sa taille
2. son âge
3. la couleur de ses cheveux
4. la couleur de ses yeux
5. sa voix
6. s'il parlait avec un accent
7. s'il avait une barbe
8. s'il portait des lunettes
9. comment il était habillé
10. quel air il avait
11. si quelqu'un était avec lui

À la fin de votre conversation, l'agent de police remercie le témoin de son aide.

Et il n'y avait personne avec lui.

Merci, Monsieur.

13 *Imaginez que vous êtes un écrivain célèbre et que vous êtes prêt(e) à commencer votre prochain roman policier. Le sujet de cette intrigue policière est le vol d'un objet d'art. Vous vous préparez à écrire en pensant aux circonstances du vol. Faites une liste des détails du crime en utilisant les questions suivantes comme guide.*

1. Quel objet d'art est-ce qu'on a volé?
2. Comment s'appelle la personne qui l'a pris?
3. Cette personne, était-elle petite ou grande? Jeune ou âgée? Grosse ou mince?
4. Avait-elle les cheveux blonds, bruns, noirs ou roux?
5. Que portait-elle?
6. Comment a-t-elle volé l'objet d'art?
7. Avait-elle quelque chose à la main?
8. D'où ou de qui est-ce qu'elle l'a pris?
9. Quand l'a-t-elle pris?
10. Est-ce que quelqu'un l'a vue?

Paired Practice

Police Artist

After they have completed Activity 13, you may want to put students in pairs to play the roles of a police artist and a witness to a crime. (Witnesses saw the criminal they described in Activity 13.) The police artist asks detailed questions about the robber's description (size, shape, age, hair and eye color, clothing), and the witness describes the criminal with as much detail as possible. After the artist has completed the criminal's portrait, students switch roles.

*Maintenant utilisez votre liste des détails du crime dans l'Activité 13 pour écrire le premier paragraphe de votre roman policier. Pour vous aider à faire les transitions entre les phrases, utilisez les expressions comme d'abord, **puis**, **ensuite**, **alors**, **de plus**, **enfin**, etc.*

**Workbook
Activity 7**

 **Listening
Activity 1**

 **Quiz
*Leçon A***

 **Advanced
Placement**

Narrating

Sur la bonne piste

When Suzanne relates her misadventure in **le métro**, she is narrating. Narrating is simply telling a story. Narrating can take the form of fiction, like a short story or novel, or nonfiction, like a biography or a news report. Both types of narrative writing have similar features. We learn whom the story is about and where it takes place, a complication or problem is introduced and events are described that lead to its eventual resolution or solution.

Suzanne's narrative provides a model for how you would go about writing your own narrative. First, make the character and the setting interesting. Why do you care about what happens to Suzanne? She is someone approximately your age to whom you can relate. This makes you want to find out what happens to her. The primary setting of Suzanne's story is the hotel room where she tells her story to her friend Ellen. By introducing other locations, such as **le métro** and **le commissariat**, the city of Paris becomes more real. The fact that the story takes place in an exciting foreign city makes it more interesting than if the theft took place in Suzanne's hometown, for example. Second, introduce a complication. In this case, Suzanne tells how she reacted to being robbed. You are probably interested in finding out how someone copes with a theft in another culture. Third, describe events that lead to a resolution of the complication. Suzanne first told her story to the receptionist at her hotel. Then she asked Mme Taylor for help, and together they went to **le commissariat** to report the theft. These events and the interactions with **les agents de police** develop the complication with specific, realistic details that make Suzanne's story more believable. Finally, resolve the complication. Suzanne learns **le récépissé** will allow her to reenter the United States when she flies home the next day.

Teacher's Note

Sur la bonne piste, Leçon A, is designed to develop skills that will help students prepare to take the Advanced Placement Exam in French Language. In this lesson **Sur la bonne piste** focuses on written narration, which builds on the lesson functions of "describing past events" and "sequencing events." Oral narration (telling a story based on a picture sequence) will be covered in Unit 5.

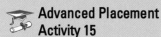

Advanced Placement Activity 15

1. You may want students to use the writing process when they write a fictional narrative of their own in Activity 15. Students begin by writing an outline of their story. After completing their first draft, students work with a peer reviewer who makes non-threatening, constructive comments like "As a reader, I would like to know what the character looks like." You may want to model the peer reviewer's role by making comments for the class about one of the student's stories and provide a peer reviewer's evaluation form to guide peer reviewers with their comments. Then, students make revisions based on the peer reviewer's comments and their own ideas for improvement. At this point ask students to check that they have incorporated all the elements of the Narrative Plan on this page. Next, students edit their fictional narratives, correcting them for errors in grammar, usage, mechanics and spelling. Finally, they prepare their final draft and hand it in to you for a grade. You may want to assess students on how well they completed the writing process rather than on the finished product.

2. Optional activity. Rather than do Activity 15, students could write a personal narrative that comes directly from their own experience. Have students chart or map a visit they made to a person or a place that interested them. As part of the pre-writing process, have students state what they wanted to discover, and list the events that occurred during their visit. After students write the first draft of their personal narrative, have them follow the rest of the steps of the writing process as described in the preceding teacher's note. Advise peer reviewers to look for a chronological development of events, a first person point of view and a conclusion that explains what the experience meant to the writer.

Here are some tips for writing a fictional narrative. Review how choices were made in Suzanne's story to develop a realistic and interesting narrative.

Narrative Plan

Introduce a main character	Suzanne, American student
Describe the setting	l'hôtel, le métro and le commissariat in Paris
Introduce a complication	Suzanne's money, passport, credit cards and traveler's checks are stolen. How will she be able to reenter the U.S. without a passport?
List events in chronological order that advance the plot	Event 1 - encounter with two boys in le métro Event 2 - discovery of theft while trying to buy une crêpe Event 3 - help sought from receptionist and l'ambassade Event 4 - help sought from Mme Taylor and les agents de police
Suggest the resolution	le récépissé will allow Suzanne to reenter the U.S.

In Suzanne's story, dialogue brings her character to life and advances the plot. Dialogue is written from a first person point of view that allows you to hear the thoughts of the character. This is often an effective tool for describing a person's emotional state. When Suzanne says "Quelle imbécile!" we learn how angry she is at herself for not being more alert in **le métro**. Also keep in mind the character's age, personality and educational background when you create dialogue. After placing quotation marks around a line of dialogue, write a tag line, or the words that identify the speaker, such as "a dit l'agent de police." If you use a pronoun subject like **il** or **elle**, invert this pronoun subject and the verb and separate them with **-t-**, for example, " 'Pauvre Suzanne,' a-t-elle dit."

15 Now it's your turn to write a fictional narrative. Relate the plot of a film or TV program that you watched or a book or story that you read. If you prefer, invent your own story. Be sure to follow the narrative plan on this page so that you remember to include the necessary features of an interesting, realistic fictional narrative.

La littérature française

Put your students in five small groups. Pass out to each group a different French short story or novella with which you are familiar. Ask each group to determine the main character, setting and complication for their story. Then have the groups report to the class on their findings. You may want to write the three elements for each group's story on a chart on the board to help students compare the different authors' narrative plans. (You might consider using titles from EMC's *Easy Reader* series.) This activity will help students write a more effective story opener for Activity 15.

un chef

un employé

Nicolas Ferrié
CHEF

une employée

Suzanne s'approche du car.

Elle se tait.

Elle se fâche.

Elle se repose.

Leçon B

In this lesson you will be able to:

➤ write a letter

➤ tell a story

➤ explain something

➤ express emotions

➤ express concern

➤ express suspicion

➤ apologize

➤ express satisfaction

**Workbook
Activity 8**

**Audiocassette/CD
Office Workers, Reflexive
Verbs**

Teacher's Notes

1. Communicative functions that are recycled in this lesson are "describing past events," "sequencing events," "describing physical traits," "giving examples" and "expressing need and necessity." 2. **Chef**, meaning "cook," was introduced on page 322 in the second level of C'*est à toi!* 3. The adjective **fâché(e)** was introduced in **Leçon A** of this unit. 4. You may want to introduce the present tense forms of the irregular verb **se taire: je me tais, tu te tais, il/elle/on se tait, nous nous taisons, vous vous taisez** and **ils/elles se taisent.** 5. Other related terms include **un(e) gérant(e)** (*manager*), **un(e) assistant(e)** (*assistant*) and **un P.D.G.** (CEO).

**Workbook
Activity 9**

Audiocassette/CD
La lettre

Transparency 10

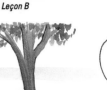

"Je n'avais aucune idée que mon passeport était si important."

Une fois rentrée aux États-Unis, Suzanne écrit une lettre à ses grands-parents au Canada pour leur raconter le drame à l'aéroport.

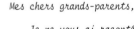

le 30 mars

Mes chers grands-parents,

Je ne vous ai raconté au téléphone que° le début° de mes problèmes en rentrant aux États-Unis. Voilà la fin de l'histoire. Le jour après le vol dans le métro, mes copains et moi, nous sommes descendus à la réception, et le car° est arrivé à l'heure. En allant à l'aéroport, nous nous sommes bien amusés à nous rappeler° tous les endroits° que nous avons aimés. Aucun° de nous ne voulait rentrer aux États-Unis.

À l'aéroport tout le monde a fait la queue au comptoir d'Air France. D'abord il fallait montrer nos passeports et nos billets. Quand l'employé s'est approché de moi, j'ai commencé à m'inquiéter. Mme Taylor restait à côté de moi. Quand j'ai dit à l'employé que je n'avais plus mon passeport, il nous a emmenées, Mme Taylor et moi, au bureau de son chef. Elle avait l'air occupé. Je ne sais pas pourquoi, mais je me méfiais° d'elle. Mme Taylor lui a raconté

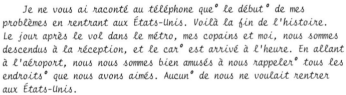

ne (n')... que seulement; **le début** pas la fin; **un car** un bus pour les touristes; **se rappeler** *to remember*; **un endroit** *place*; **aucun(e)... ne (n')** *not one*; **se méfier de** *to distrust*

l'histoire, puis le chef a téléphoné à l'ambassade. On m'a posé beaucoup de questions, par exemple, le nom de jeune fille° de ma mère. Personne ne° pouvait m'aider à répondre à des questions comme ça... même pas Mme Taylor. Heureusement, on était satisfait de mes réponses. Ensuite le chef a regardé le récépissé. Puisque° je ne suis pas allée à l'ambassade, je vais être obligée de payer une amende de 100 dollars à l'immigration aux États-Unis. Mme Taylor s'est fâchée et a expliqué que je n'avais ni argent français ni° argent américain. Moi, je me suis tue. Ce problème de l'immigration, je n'y ai rien compris.

Finalement, une employée nous a aidées à faire enregistrer nos bagages. Puis c'était le moment de passer à la police française. Mme Taylor a dû expliquer l'histoire une deuxième fois. Bien sûr, rien n'était surprenant° pour l'agent de police. Après, nous avons trouvé les autres. On s'est reposé un peu, puis on est allé à la porte d'embarquement. Et voilà un autre contrôle de sécurité ! Pauvre Mme Taylor! Ni° elle ni moi n'étions calmes. J'ai dit que je regrettais tous ces problèmes. Enfin nous sommes montées dans l'avion et il a décollé.

Quand nous sommes arrivées à l'immigration aux États-Unis, nous avons raconté l'histoire et avons montré le récépissé une quatrième fois. L'agent a expliqué que je pouvais payer l'amende par courrier. Je n'avais aucune° idée que mon passeport était si important.

Alors, la fin de l'histoire? Tout est bien qui finit bien. Ellen et moi, nous nous sommes si bien entendues° que nous allons être camarades de chambre à l'université l'année prochaine. Et la police de Paris m'a envoyé mon passeport, mes cartes de crédit et mes chèques de voyage. Quelle chance ! Je ne m'attendais° pas à une fin si heureuse. À bientôt!

Grosses bises,
Suzanne

Teacher's Notes

1. **Aidées** agrees with the direct object **nous**, which refers to Suzanne and Mme Taylor. 2. You may want to point out that the adjective **surprenant(e)** is related to the noun **surprise**, introduced on page 105 in the second level of *C'est à toi!* 3. **Tout est bien qui finit bien** is the French version of the proverb "All's well that ends well."

le nom de jeune fille le nom d'une femme avant son mariage; **personne ne (n')** *no one;* **puisque** *since;* **ne (n')... ni... ni...** *neither . . . nor;* **surprenant(e)** quelque chose qui est une surprise; **ni... ni... ne (n')...** *neither . . . nor;* **ne (n')... aucun(e)** *no;* **s'entendre** *to get along;* **s'attendre à** *to expect*

En attendant leurs vols, où les passagers se reposent-ils? (Roissy-Charles de Gaulle)

Audiocassette/CD
Activities 1, 3

Answers

1 1. faux
  2. faux
  3. vrai
  4. faux
  5. vrai
  6. faux
  7. vrai
  8. faux
  9. vrai

2 1. g
  2. d
  3. i
  4. c
  5. f
  6. a
  7. j
  8. e
  9. b
  10. h

3 Answers will vary.

1 | *Répondez par "vrai" ou "faux" d'après la lettre de Suzanne.*

  1. Les élèves ont pris un taxi pour aller de l'hôtel à l'aéroport.
  2. Tous les élèves voulaient rentrer aux États-Unis.
  3. À l'ambassade on était satisfait des réponses de Suzanne.
  4. Suzanne doit payer une amende parce qu'elle est allée à l'ambassade.
  5. Suzanne n'avait ni argent américain ni argent français pour payer l'amende.
  6. Mme Taylor s'est tue parce qu'elle n'y a rien compris.
  7. Mme Taylor a expliqué l'histoire quatre fois.
  8. Suzanne ne pouvait pas payer l'amende par courrier.
  9. La police de Paris a tout envoyé à Suzanne sauf ses dollars et ses francs.

Arianne et Katia se taisent en lisant.

2 | *Choisissez l'expression à droite qui est le contaire de l'expression à gauche.*

  1. le début   a. demander
  2. tout le monde   b. s'approcher (de)
  3. un(e) employé(e) c. se fâcher
  4. être calme   d. personne ne (n')
  5. parler beaucoup   e. une réponse
  6. répondre   f. se taire
  7. rien ne (n')   g. la fin
  8. une question   h. satisfait(e) de
  9. quitter   i. un chef
  10. pas content(e) avec j. quelque chose

3 | *C'est à toi!*

Les collègues du bureau s'entendent bien.

  1. Est-ce que tu as jamais eu un problème à l'aéroport? Si oui, quel problème? À qui as-tu demandé de l'aide? Comment te sentais-tu?
  2. Est-ce que tu as jamais payé une amende? Si oui, pourquoi?
  3. Quel endroit aux États-Unis aimes-tu le mieux?
  4. Est-ce que tu écris souvent des lettres? Si oui, à qui écris-tu?
  5. Est-ce que tu t'entends bien avec ton frère ou ta sœur? Pourquoi ou pourquoi pas?
  6. Est-ce que tu te fâches souvent? Si oui, quand?
  7. Est-ce que tu te méfies de quelqu'un? Si oui, de qui? Pourquoi?
  8. Qu'est-ce qui est très important dans ta vie?

Game

Faites le match

For additional practice reviewing the content of the letter on pages 72-73, divide the class into two teams. Prepare ten questions about the letter on construction paper and ten answers on a set of note cards. For example, one match might be: **À qui est-ce que Suzanne écrit? Elle écrit à ses** grands-parents. Tape the questions in random order on the board. Call the first player from each team to the front of the room. Take an answer card and read it to the two players. The player who first removes the matching question from the board wins a point for his or her team. Then the first two players take their seats, and the next two players take their turn. The game continues until there is only one match left to be made. The team with the most points wins.

Quand vous partez en voyage international, ne mettez pas votre passeport dans votre valise! Vous allez en avoir besoin pendant le voyage. Il vous faut montrer le passeport au comptoir quand vous présentez votre billet. À la douane aussi vous devez le montrer au douanier ou à la douanière.

Enquête culturelle

Workbook Activity 10

Transparency 11

Chaque aéroport a un contrôle de sécurité qui vérifie que l'on n'a ni armes ni autre contrebande. Les contrôleurs regardent dans les valises, les sacs à dos et les sacs à main à l'aide des rayons X. Les rayons X ne sont pas dangereux pour les films ou les disquettes. Les passagers passent par une porte spéciale qui détermine si on a des objets en métal, par exemple, un revolver ou un couteau.

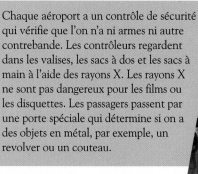

La Police de l'Air et des Frontières vérifient que les voyageurs n'ont pas d'armes. (Paris)

Dans les aéroports européens il y a deux portes d'entrée: une porte pour les habitants des pays de l'Union européenne et une autre porte pour les voyageurs qui ne viennent pas d'un pays membre. Presque tous les pays de l'Europe participent à l'Union européenne. Les habitants des pays membres n'ont pas besoin de passeport pour aller d'un pays à l'autre. Entre les pays membres il y a aussi moins de taxes sur les importations et les exportations. L'Union européenne va commencer un système d'argent commun avec "l'euro."

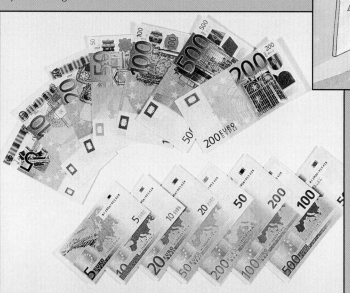

Les pays membres de l'Union européenne ont introduit de nouveaux billets.

Teacher's Notes

1. In 1992 the 12 member states signed the Treaty on European Union in Maastricht. Beginning in 1993, the integration process reached a new stage with the completion of the internal market for 345 million citizens. Persons, goods, services and capital are now able to move freely within the community, unobstructed by frontier controls. 2. This treaty established a future European currency, rights for European citizens, new powers for the European community, increased powers for the European Parliament and the introduction of a common foreign and security policy. 3. The "euro" is the single European currency that will replace national coins and banknotes in the member states. The euro will be launched Jan. 1, 1999; euro banknotes and coins will begin circulation two years later. 4. Primarily an economic power up to now, the European community's common foreign and security policy will eventually include defense. 5. For up-to-date information on the European Union, you may want to access its web site on the Internet. The web address is http://www.eurunion.org.

Teacher's Notes

1. Cognates in this reading include **international, présentez, armes, contrebande, rayons X, dangereux, films, détermine, objets, métal, revolver, habitants, Union, participent, taxes, importations, exportations, système, commun, ordre, public, assuré, municipale, fonctions, différentes, s'occupe, criminalité, sécurité, locale, véhicules, identités, administratives, généralement, Compagnie, Républicaine, chargée, présents, démonstrations, inspecteur, intrigues, crimes, existent, non** and **langues.** 2. The 12 original members of the European Union (formerly called the European Economic Community) and the dates they joined are France (1952), Germany (1952), Italy (1952), Belgium (1952), the Netherlands (1952), Luxembourg (1952), Denmark (1973), Ireland (1973), the United Kingdom (1973), Greece (1981), Spain (1986) and Portugal (1986). In 1995 Austria, Finland and Sweden also became members. Countries that have subsequently applied for membership include Estonia, Poland, the Czech Republic, Hungary, Cyprus, Slovenia, Turkey, Romania, Latvia, Lithuania and Bulgaria. 3. The main institutions of the European Union are the European Parliament, the European Commission, the European Court of Justice, the Council of Ministers and the Court of Auditors.

Answers

4 1. Quand on part en voyage international, il faut montrer son passeport au comptoir quand on présente son billet et aussi à la douane.

2. Au contrôle de sécurité on vérifie qu'on n'a ni armes ni autre contrebande.

3. Les contrôleurs de sécurité regardent dans les valises, les sacs à dos et les sacs à main à l'aide des rayons X.

4. Presque tous les pays de l'Europe participent à l'Union européenne.

5. Les habitants des pays qui participent à l'Union européenne n'ont pas besoin de passeport.

6. La monnaie qu'on va employer dans les pays membres de l'Union européenne est l'euro.

7. On trouve la police nationale à l'aéroport.

8. La station de police est un commissariat.

9. Non, M. Maigret est un inspecteur dans les romans policiers de Simenon.

10. On peut lire les romans policiers de Simenon en plus de 30 langues.

L'ordre public est assuré par la police nationale et la police municipale, qui ont des fonctions différentes. La police nationale s'occupe de la criminalité, de la circulation sur les grandes routes, de la sécurité dans les villes et de l'entrée en France. La police municipale contrôle la circulation locale des véhicules, vérifie les identités et remplit d'autres fonctions administratives et locales. Généralement il y a un commissariat de police municipale dans les villes. Enfin, la C.R.S. (Compagnie Républicaine de Sécurité) est chargée de la sécurité du pays et de l'ordre public. Ses agents sont souvent présents à des démonstrations publiques.

La police nationale en France porte un uniforme bleu. (Antony)

Le policier le plus célèbre du monde n'est pas un vrai policier du tout! C'est l'inspecteur Maigret dans les romans policiers de l'écrivain belge Georges Simenon (1903-89). Simenon a écrit plus de 200 intrigues policières où Maigret essaie de résoudre des crimes à Paris. Les livres de Simenon existent non seulement en français mais en plus de 30 autres langues.

M. Schneider, membre de la police nationale, travaille pour un commissariat franco-allemand à Strasbourg.

4 | *Répondez aux questions suivantes.*

1. Où faut-il montrer son passeport quand on part en voyage international?
2. Qu'est-ce qu'on vérifie au contrôle de sécurité?
3. Comment est-ce que les contrôleurs de sécurité regardent dans les valises, les sacs à dos et les sacs à main?
4. Qui participe à l'Union européenne?
5. Qui n'a pas besoin de passeport?
6. Comment s'appelle la monnaie qu'on va employer dans les pays membres de l'Union européenne?
7. Est-ce qu'on trouve la police municipale ou nationale à l'aéroport?
8. Comment s'appelle la station de police?
9. M. Maigret, est-ce un écrivain belge?
10. En combien de langues peut-on lire les romans policiers de Simenon?

TELEFILM **20.50**
LES VACANCES DE MAIGRET
Mansuy (Ronny Coutteure) et **Maigret** (Bruno Cremer)

Teacher's Notes

1. The number of municipal police officers in France has doubled since 1984. Thirty-six percent of municipal police officers carry firearms. Some young men fulfilling their military service choose to work for the police.

2. Georges Simenon, who sometimes used the pen name Georges Sim, earned a living as a writer from the age of 21. Only the Bible and the works of Lenin and Mao Tse-tung have been published in greater numbers than his novels. His first Maigret mystery, *Pietr le letton*, appeared in 1930. Simenon is credited with endowing the mystery genre with a human dimension. At the age of 33, he abandoned mystery novels to devote himself to writing more "personal works." The Simenon myth, a wealthy man with a pipe, subject to frequent withdrawals and his work's "instinctive development," emerged in the 1940s.

Journal personnel

Traveler's checks, credit cards, security checks, X rays, passport control, customs, immigration, embassies and police of every kind! Travelers seem to need a variety of ways to protect themselves from other people. Why is this? Are travelers more prone to crime than others? Would you stand the same chance of being robbed in your hometown as in a very large American city? As in a very large French-speaking city? What protective measures can you take as a traveler to avoid robbery and other crimes? Should you take the same steps when you are at home? Write your responses to these questions in your cultural journal.

Structure

Reflexive verbs

Reflexive verbs describe actions that the subject performs on or for itself. Reflexive pronouns (**me, te, se, nous, vous**) are used with reflexive verbs and represent the same person or thing as the subject.

Vous **vous reposez** avant votre vol?	*Are you resting before your flight?*
Oui, nous **nous asseyons** près de la porte d'embarquement.	*Yes, we're sitting down near the departure gate.*
Tu **t'inquiètes**?	*Are you worried?*
Non, je **me sens** beaucoup mieux maintenant.	*No, I'm feeling much better now.*

In an affirmative, negative or interrogative sentence, the reflexive pronoun comes directly before the verb. In an affirmative command, the reflexive pronoun follows the verb. But in a negative command, it precedes the verb.

Te méfies-tu de cette fille?	*Do you distrust this girl?*
Oui, un peu. Nous ne **nous entendons** pas très bien.	*Yes, a little. We aren't getting along very well.*
Geneviève, **tais-toi**!	*Geneviève, be quiet!*

The **passé composé** of reflexive verbs is formed with **être**. The past participle usually agrees in gender and in number with the subject.

En allant à l'aéroport, les copains **se sont** bien **amusés**.	*While going to the airport, the friends really had a good time.*
Nous **nous sommes tues** parce que nous n'avons pas compris.	*We were quiet because we didn't understand.*

Que s'est-il passé l'année de votre naissance ?

Pourquoi est-ce que Dominique se fâche?

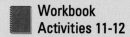

En forme, L'ÉCUREUIL s'engage dans l'action sociale

Offrez-vous Femme Actuelle

Bertrand et Latifa se sont rejoints à leur café favori.

Teacher's Notes

1. Reflexive verbs, introduced in Unit 4 in the second level of *C'est à toi!*, are recycled here. 2. Here are the other reflexive verbs that students have learned up to this lesson: **s'appeler, s'arrêter, se brosser, se coucher, se déguiser, se dépêcher, se déshabiller, s'entraîner, s'habiller, se laver, se lever, se maquiller, se peigner, se perfectionner, se préparer, se raser, se regarder, se rejoindre** and **se réveiller**. 3. When reflexive verbs are used to express the action of doing something to a part of one's own body, the definite article is used instead of the possessive adjective, for example, **Annick se lave les cheveux**. 4. Some verbs may be either reflexive or non-reflexive; that is, the subject may perform an action on itself or on someone or something else, for example, **Jean amuse les enfants** but **Jean s'amuse au parc d'attractions**. 5. Note that **te** changes to **toi** in an affirmative command when the reflexive pronoun follows the verb. 6. The reflexive verbs **s'asseoir, se rejoindre** and **se taire** have irregular past participles: **assis, rejoint** and **tu**. 7. You may want to tell students that the past participle agrees in gender and in number with the reflexive pronoun only if this pronoun is a direct object.

Critical Thinking

Reflexive Pronouns

Write a sentence with a reflexive verb and a sentence with a related non-reflexive verb on the board, for example, **Mireille se regarde** and **Mireille regarde la télé**. Ask students to explain what the direct object is in each sentence. They should say that in the first sentence the reflexive pronoun **se** is the direct object and refers to Mireille, but in the second sentence **la télé** is the direct object. This activity will help students remember the function of reflexive pronouns and when to use them.

Cooperative Group Practice

Daily Routine

Put students in small groups. Prepare a set of note cards with reflexive verbs describing students' daily routines, and give the time for each activity. Write a different noun or pronoun subject on each card, for example, **Jérémy/7h30/se brosser les dents**. The first student in each group forms a sentence in the present tense, for example, **À 7h30 Jérémy se brosse les dents**. The second student then forms a sentence using a reflexive or non-reflexive verb representing an activity that might logically take place after the first activity, for example, **À 7h45 Jérémy se dépêche pour aller au lycée**. After each student in the group has contributed a sentence to describe the first character's routine, the first student takes another card and begins again, for example, **À 4h00 tu te prépares pour le travail**.

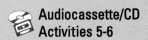

Answers

5 1. Je me dépêche.
2. David et Abdou se rasent.
3. Denise et moi, nous nous regardons dans la glace.
4. Daniel et toi, vous vous brossez les dents et les cheveux.
5. Sylvie et Christiane se rappellent la dernière fois.
6. Tu te reposes un peu.
7. Sabine s'attend à un soir extra.

6 Quand est-ce que tu te fâches?
De qui est-ce que tu te méfies?
Avec qui est-ce que tu t'entends bien?
Qu'est-ce que tu te rappelles?
Où est-ce que tu t'amuses bien?
Students' responses to these questions will vary.

Teacher's Notes

1. In the sentence **Suzanne s'est rappelé tous les endroits qu'elle a aimés**, the reflexive pronoun is an indirect object, so the past participle does not agree. 2. If a part of the body follows the verb in the **passé composé**, the past participle does not agree with the subject, for example, **Claudine s'est brossé les dents**. 3. To ask a question in the **passé composé** using inversion, put the subject pronoun after the form of **être**. 4. You may want to point out that, as with other verbs in the **passé composé**, most short, common adverbs used with reflexive verbs come before the past participle, for example, **Je me suis bien amusé(e)**. 5. Reflexive verbs may also express a reciprocal action, that is, something that people perform for or to each other, for example, **Hélène et Jacques se regardent en cours**. In this case use a plural verb form and the reflexive pronoun **nous, vous** or **se**.

However, if a direct object follows the verb, there is no agreement between the past participle and the subject.

> Suzanne s'est **rappelé** tous les endroits qu'elle a aimés.   *Suzanne remembered all the places that she liked.*

In an affirmative, negative or interrogative sentence in the **passé composé**, the reflexive pronoun comes directly before the form of **être**.

> Pourquoi t'es-tu fâchée, Marie?   *Why did you get angry, Marie?*
> Parce que je ne **me** suis pas réveillée à l'heure.   *Because I didn't wake up on time.*

Pratique

5 | *Dites ce que vous et vos amis faites pour vous préparer pour aller en boîte ce soir.*

1. je/se dépêcher
2. David et Abdou/se raser
3. Denise et moi, nous/se regarder dans la glace
4. Daniel et toi, vous/se brosser les dents et les cheveux
5. Sylvie et Christiane/se rappeler la dernière fois
6. tu/se reposer un peu
7. Sabine/s'attendre à un soir extra

Modèle:
Jean-Marc/se peigner
Jean-Marc se peigne.

Les grandes s'habillent en Kookaï.

6 | *Faites une enquête où vous posez des questions à trois élèves sur leurs émotions. Copiez la grille suivante. Posez les questions indiquées à chaque élève. Puis écrivez sa réponse dans l'espace blanc convenable.*

Modèle:
Sara: Quand est-ce que tu t'inquiètes?
Fabienne: Je m'inquiète quand je pense au bac.

	Fabienne	Charles	Ahmed
quand/s'inquiéter	*quand elle pense au bac*		
quand/se fâcher			
de qui/se méfier			
avec qui/s'entendre bien			
qu'est-ce que/se rappeler			
où/s'amuser bien			

Bénédicte et Olivier s'amusent bien au travail.

Paired Practice

Ordering Sentences

To practice forming reflexive and non-reflexive verbs in the present tense, put students in pairs. Prepare a set of note cards for each pair with two related activities and a noun or pronoun subject, for example, **aller chez Claudette/se préparer pour la boum (nous)**. The first student in each pair takes a card and reads the two phrases to his or her partner. The partner then changes the phrases into complete sentences and orders them logically using **d'abord** and **ensuite**, for example, **D'abord, nous nous préparons pour la boum** and **Ensuite, nous allons chez Claudette**. Students take turns until they have made pairs of sentences for each card in the stack.

TPR

Une histoire

Read the class a story in the **passé composé** that uses reflexive and non-reflexive verbs. Ask a student to act out the verbs as you read. Then say a series of true and false statements. Have students make a "V" card to hold up if a statement about the story is true and an "F" card to hold up if a statement about the story is false.

Les Roget sont à l'aéroport, prêts à partir en vacances. Dites si les membres de la famille ont fait les choses suivantes avant d'arriver à l'aéroport.

1. Delphine/se réveiller
2. Chloé et Michèle/se laver la figure
3. M. Roget et Philippe/se raser
4. Chloé et Michèle/s'habiller bien
5. Mme Roget/se peigner
6. Philippe/bien se reposer
7. M. Roget/se brosser les cheveux
8. M. et Mme Roget/s'habiller bien

Modèle:

Mme Roget/se maquiller
Mme Roget s'est maquillée.

On annonce le vol des Roget à la porte d'embarquement. Dites aux membres de la famille de faire ou de ne pas faire ce qui est indiqué avant de monter dans l'avion.

1. Michèle/se laver la figure
2. M. Roget/se brosser les cheveux
3. Chloé et Michèle/s'approcher du restaurant
4. Philippe/s'asseoir
5. M. et Mme Roget/se lever
6. Chloé/s'inquiéter
7. M. Roget/se dépêcher
8. les Roget/se préparer pour le vol

Habillez-vous promo!

Modèle:

Delphine/se réveiller
Delphine, réveille-toi!

Ne vous inquiétez pas!

Cooperative Group Practice

Reflexive and Non-reflexive Commands

To practice forming commands with both reflexive and non-reflexive verbs, put students in small groups. Prepare a set of note cards with infinitives of both reflexive and non-reflexive verbs and subject pronouns for each group, for example, **se lever/tu**, **ouvrir le manuel de français/vous** and **se brosser les dents/nous**. The first student in each group takes a card from the stack and gives a command to a specific student or students of his or her choice, for example, **Pierre, lève-toi!** or **Anne et Guillaume, ouvrez vos manuels de français!** For commands using **nous**, the student indicates everyone in the group, for example, **Tout le monde, brossons-nous les** dents! The student or students called upon act out the command. Then the second student takes a card and gives a command to the student(s) of his or her choice, and so on. (New and review non-reflexive verbs that you might practice with students before beginning the activity include **fermer**, **tourner**, **indiquer**, **enlever**, **jeter**, **mettre**, **prendre**, **toucher**, **plier** and **sauter**.)

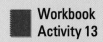

**Workbook
Activity 13**

**Audiocassette/CD
Activity 9**

Answers

9 1. Je n'ai jamais séché un cours.

2. Je n'ai jamais raté un examen.

3. Je ne me suis jamais inquiété(e).

4. Je n'ai jamais fait de planche à neige.

5. Je n'ai jamais goûté la cuisine martiniquaise.

6. Je ne me suis jamais rappelé l'anniversaire de ma grand-mère.

7. Je n'ai jamais perdu mon chemin.

8. Je n'ai jamais déménagé.

9. Je n'ai jamais voyagé en avion.

10. Je ne suis jamais allé(e) en Europe.

Teacher's Notes

1. **Ne (n')... pas**, introduced on page 44 in the first level of *C'est à toi!* and reviewed on page 37 in the second level, is recycled here. **Ne (n')... jamais, ne (n')... personne, ne (n')... plus** and **ne (n')... rien**, introduced on page 326 in the first level of *C'est à toi!* and reviewed on page 37 in the second level, are also recycled here. 2. Indefinite articles and partitive articles become **de** or **d'** in a negative sentence, for example, **Suzanne n'a pas de carte de crédit**. However, the indefinite and partitive articles do not change to **de** or **d'** after a form of the verb **être** in a negative sentence, for example, **Ce n'est plus un chef.** 3. In a sentence with both a conjugated verb form and an infinitive, **personne** follows the infinitive, for example, **L'ambassade ne peut aider personne le week-end. Personne** may also be used after a preposition, for example, **Tu ne crois à personne.** 4. **Jamais, rien** and **personne** can stand alone as one-word answers to questions. 5. The use of negation with the **passé composé**, introduced on

pages 351 and 390 in the first level of *C'est à toi!* and reviewed on pages 55 and 99 in the second level, is also recycled here. 6. When **ne (n')... personne** and **ne (n')... rien** act as the subject of a sentence, object pronouns precede the verb or helping verb, for example, **Personne ne l'a expliqué.** 7. You may want to introduce the negative expression **ne (n')... pas encore** (*not yet*).

Critical Thinking

Negative Expressions

Write the affirmative expressions **souvent, toujours, quelqu'un** and **quelque chose** on the board or on an overhead transparency. Ask students to name the negative expressions that are the opposite of the affirmative expressions. Students should name **ne (n')... jamais, ne (n')... plus, ne (n')...**

personne and **ne (n')... rien.** This activity will help students remember when to use these negative expressions.

Saxo

LA VOITURE DE CEUX QUI NE VEULENT PLUS JOUER AUX PETITES VOITURES.

« Personne ne parle des amours tardives. »

Negation

To make a verb negative, put **ne (n')** before the verb and **pas, plus, jamais, rien** or **personne** after it.

Suzanne **n**'est **pas** souriante.   *Suzanne isn't smiling.*

Elle **n**'a **plus** son passeport.   *She no longer has her passport.*

C'est Anne-Marie qui s'approche?

Ben... je ne vois personne.

In the **passé composé, ne (n')** precedes the helping verb and **pas, plus, jamais** or **rien** follows it. **Personne**, however, follows the past participle.

Suzanne **n**'a parlé à **personne** dans le bureau du chef parce qu'elle **n**'a **rien** compris.   *Suzanne spoke to no one in the boss's office because she understood nothing.*

The expressions **ne (n')... personne** and **ne (n')... rien** may also be used as subjects. In this case, **personne** or **rien** begins the sentence and **ne (n')** is in its usual position.

Qu'est-ce qui s'est passé au commissariat?   *What happened at the police station?*

Rien ne s'est passé. **Personne ne** pouvait m'aider.   *Nothing happened. No one could help me.*

Pratique

9   *Dites que vous n'avez jamais fait les choses suivantes quand vous étiez petit(e).*

1. sécher un cours
2. rater un examen
3. s'inquiéter
4. faire de la planche à neige
5. goûter la cuisine martiniquaise
6. se rappeler l'anniversaire de ma grand-mère
7. perdre mon chemin
8. déménager
9. voyager en avion
10. aller en Europe

Modèle:

visiter un parc d'attractions
Je n'ai jamais visité un parc d'attractions.

Je n'ai jamais séché un cours de sciences po.

Comparez les deux illustrations. Puis répondez aux questions en suivant le modèle.

Modèle:

Il y avait un train sur la voie numéro quatre?

À onze heures il y avait un train sur la voie numéro quatre, mais à minuit il n'y avait plus de train.

1. Qui compostait son billet?
2. Il y avait quelque chose dans la poubelle?
3. Une femme lisait le journal?
4. Qui dormait?
5. Il y avait deux personnes qui s'entendaient bien?
6. Qu'est-ce qu'il y avait sur le quai?

Avec un(e) partenaire, jouez les rôles de deux personnes au commissariat. L'Élève A joue le rôle d'un inspecteur de police, et l'Élève B joue le rôle d'un suspect d'un vol. L'inspecteur de police pose des questions au suspect, et, naturellement, le suspect répond négativement.

1. qu'est-ce qui/se passer hier soir
2. qu'est-ce qui/vous inquiéter hier soir
3. qui/être avec vous hier soir
4. qui/ouvrir la porte de la maison des Curielli
5. qui/allumer la lampe dans le salon
6. qu'est-ce qui/vous intéresser dans leur maison
7. qu'est-ce qui/faire un bruit dans le jardin
8. qui/pouvoir dire où vous étiez hier soir

Modèle:

qui/entrer dans la maison des Curielli
L'inspecteur: Qui est entré dans la maison des Curielli?
Le suspect: Personne n'y est entré.

Other negative expressions

The expression **ne (n')... que** (*only*) is often used instead of the adverb **seulement**. This expression restricts or limits choices. **Ne (n')** precedes the verb, or the helping verb in the **passé composé**, and **que** comes before the word or expression it describes.

Suzanne **ne** devait payer **que** 100 dollars.

Suzanne had to pay only 100 dollars.

Elle **ne** leur a raconté au téléphone **que** le début de ses problèmes.

On the phone she told them only the beginning of her problems.

« On n'a qu'une maman. »

ARTEL 6 CINÉMAS

On ne passe que les films américains dans ce cinéma. (Créteil)

Workbook Activities 14-15

Answers

10 Possible answers:

1. À onze heures un homme compostait son billet, mais à minuit il n'y avait personne qui compostait son billet.
2. À onze heures il y avait beaucoup de choses dans la poubelle, mais à minuit il n'y avait rien dans la poubelle.
3. À onze heures une femme lisait le journal, mais à minuit elle ne lisait plus le journal.
4. À onze heures un sans-abri dormait, mais à minuit il n'y avait personne qui dormait.
5. À onze heures il y avait deux personnes qui s'entendaient bien, mais à minuit ces deux personnes ne s'entendaient plus bien.
6. À onze heures il y avait des bagages sur le quai, mais à minuit il n'y avait rien sur le quai.

11 Possible answers:

1. Qu'est-ce qui s'est passé hier soir? Rien ne s'est passé hier soir.
2. Qu'est-ce qui vous inquiétait hier soir? Rien ne m'inquiétait hier soir.
3. Qui était avec vous hier soir? Personne n'était avec moi hier soir.
4. Qui a ouvert la porte de la maison des Curielli? Personne ne l'a ouverte.
5. Qui a allumé la lampe dans le salon? Personne ne l'a allumée.
6. Qu'est-ce qui vous intéressait dans leur maison? Rien ne m'y intéressait.
7. Qu'est-ce qui a fait un bruit dans le jardin? Rien n'y a fait de bruit.
8. Qui peut dire où vous étiez hier soir? Personne ne peut le dire.

Teacher's Notes

1. **Ne (n')... que** does not have a negative meaning, even though it resembles other negative expressions. 2. Since **ne (n')... que** is not a negative expression, the partitive and indefinite articles do not change after it, for example, **Jean Valjean n'a volé que du pain** and **Suzanne ne remplit qu'une déclaration de vol**.

Game

Une mauvaise journée

To practice negative expressions with the **passé composé**, divide your class into two teams. Prepare a list of questions that can be answered using **ne (n')... jamais, ne (n')... pas, ne (n')... personne, ne (n')... plus** and **ne (n')... rien**. Tell the players that they have had a bad day and are to answer every question negatively. The first player from each team comes to the board. Ask a question, for example, **Qu'est-ce que vous avez acheté au magasin?** The first player to write a logical negative response, for example, **Je n'ai rien acheté au magasin**, earns a point for his or her team. Then the next two players come to the board. At the end of the allotted time, the team with the most points wins the game.

1. With the negative expression **ne (n')... ni... ni...**, partitive and indefinite articles are dropped when each **ni** precedes a noun, for example, **Ce car n'a ni passagers ni chauffeur**. However, definite articles and possessive adjectives are kept, for example, **Mlle Cousseman n'aime ni le chef ni les employés**.
2. In the **passé composé** each **ni** precedes the past participle, for example, **Suzanne n'a ni vu ni arrêté le vol**. 3. In the example **Ni Mme Taylor ni moi n'étions calmes**, **étions** agrees in number with the combined plural subject, **nous**. In the example **Ni l'employé ni son chef ne pouvait nous aider**, **pouvait** agrees in number with **l'employé** and **son chef**, since the subjects are both singular.
4. **Aucun(e)** has no plural form.
5. **Nul(le)** has the same meaning as **aucun(e)**.

The negative expression **ne (n')... ni... ni...** means "neither . . . nor." **Ne (n')** precedes the verb, or the helping verb in the **passé composé**, and each **ni** comes directly before the word or expression it describes.

> Suzanne **ne** pouvait trouver **ni** son passeport **ni** ses chèques de voyage. — *Suzanne could find neither her passport nor her traveler's checks.*

> Elle n'avait **ni** argent français **ni** argent américain. — *She had neither French nor American money.*

Ni... ni... ne (n') may begin a sentence. In this case, each **ni** precedes the word or expression it describes and **ne (n')** is in its usual position.

> **Ni** Mme Taylor **ni** moi n'étions calmes. — *Neither Mme Taylor nor I was calm.*

> **Ni** l'employé **ni** son chef **ne** pouvait nous aider. — *Neither the employee nor his boss could help us.*

The negative expression **ne (n')... aucun(e)** may be used as an adjective or a pronoun and means "no," "not any" or "not one." As an adjective, **aucun(e)** agrees in gender with the noun following it. **Ne (n')** precedes the verb, or the helping verb in the **passé composé**, and **aucun(e)** comes after the verb, or the past participle in the **passé composé**, and before the noun it describes.

> Il n'y avait **aucun** employé au comptoir. — *There was no clerk at the counter.*

> Je n'en ai vu **aucun**. — *I didn't see any.*

Aucun(e) may also begin a sentence. In this case, it precedes the word or expression it describes and **ne (n')** is in its usual position.

> **Aucun** passager **ne** faisait la queue. — *No passenger was standing in line.*

> **Aucun** de nous **ne** voulait rentrer. — *Not one of us wanted to return home.*

To practice using negative expressions from this lesson in the context of Suzanne's story, write the questions that follow on an overhead transparency, indicating in parentheses which negative expression to use in formulating an answer. Students may answer the questions orally or in writing.

1. Suzanne est-elle heureuse? (ne... plus) 2. Suzanne a-t-elle un portefeuille? (ne... pas) 3. Suzanne a-t-elle son argent et ses chèques de voyage? (ne... ni... ni...) 4. Suzanne a-t-elle arrêté les deux mecs dans le métro? (ne... personne) 5. Qui a aidé Suzanne dans le métro? (personne... ne) 6. Suzanne est-elle allée à l'ambassade? (ne... jamais) 7. Qu'est-ce que l'ambassade a fait pour elle? (ne... rien) 8. Les élèves veulent-ils rentrer aux États-Unis? (aucun... ne) 9. Suzanne et Mme Taylor sont-elles calmes à l'aéroport? (ni... ni... ne...) 10. Suzanne va-t-elle payer cent dollars à l'immigration? (ne... que) (Answers: 1. Non, elle n'est plus heureuse. 2. Non, elle n'a pas de portefeuille. 3. Non, elle n'a ni son argent ni ses chèques de voyage. 4. Non, elle n'y a arrêté personne. 5. Personne ne l'y a aidée. 6. Non, elle n'y est jamais allée. 7. L'ambassade n'a rien fait pour elle. 8. Non, aucun élève ne veut rentrer aux États-Unis. 9. Non, ni Suzanne ni Mme Taylor n'est calme à l'aéroport. 10. Suzanne ne va payer que cent dollars à l'immigration.)

Pratique

Gisèle est très difficile. Elle n'aime que certaines choses à manger et à boire. Dites que Gisèle n'aime ni la première chose ni la deuxième chose. Puis faites une généralisation en disant ce qui ne lui plaît pas (she doesn't like). Suivez le modèle.

Modèle:

Gisèle n'aime ni les cerises ni les bananes. Aucun fruit ne lui plaît.

1.

2.

3.

4.

5.

6.

7.

8.

Aurélie et Leïla n'achètent ni camembert ni brie. Aucun fromage ne leur plaît. (La Rochelle)

Answers

12 Possible answers:

1. Gisèle n'aime ni les crevettes ni les moules. Aucun fruit de mer ne lui plaît.
2. Gisèle n'aime ni les petits pois ni les carottes. Aucun légume ne lui plaît.
3. Gisèle n'aime ni les hamburgers ni les hot-dogs. Aucun sandwich ne lui plaît.
4. Gisèle n'aime ni la crème caramel ni la tarte aux fraises. Aucun dessert ne lui plaît.
5. Gisèle n'aime ni la glace à la vanille ni la glace au chocolat. Aucune glace ne lui plaît.
6. Gisèle n'aime ni le jus de pomme ni le jus d'orange. Aucun jus de fruit ne lui plaît.
7. Gisèle n'aime ni le vin rouge ni le vin blanc. Aucun vin ne lui plaît.
8. Gisèle n'aime ni le café au lait ni le thé au citron. Aucune boisson chaude ne lui plaît.

Teacher's Note

Remind students to pay attention to the gender of the nouns in Activity 12. **Aucune** will be used with a feminine noun.

Paired Practice

Sentence Reconstruction

So that students can practice using new negative expressions, put them in pairs. Have each pair prepare five negative sentences using **ne (n')... que, ne (n')... ni... ni..., ni... ni... ne (n'), ne (n')... aucun(e)** and **aucun(e)... ne**. Tell pairs to write each sentence on a piece of construction paper. Have them cut each sentence into three logical parts and mix up the order, for example, **ne voulait/aucun élève/préparer son exposé oral**. Tell students to make sure that there is only one possibility for recombining each sentence and to vary the tenses used. Students exchange their sentences with those of another pair. Each pair works together to reorder the sentences. Finally, when all the sentences have been recombined, the pair that wrote the sentences checks the recombinations for accuracy.

**Audiocassette/CD
Activities 13-14**

Answers

13 1. Non, il n'y avait que trois ados américains qui rentraient en métro.
2. Non, il n'y avait que deux mecs qui se sont approchés de Suzanne dans le métro.
3. Non, il n'était que seize heures.
4. Non, il n'a fouillé que dans son sac à dos.
5. Non, à l'aéroport l'employé d'Air France n'a emmené que Suzanne et Mme Taylor au bureau de son chef.
6. Non, elle n'a dû payer que cent dollars.
7. Non, elle n'a montré le récépissé qu'une fois à l'immigration aux États-Unis.
8. Non, elle ne va avoir qu'une camarade de chambre à l'université.

14 1. Est-ce que tu loues des films d'amour et des films d'aventures? Et toi, est-ce que tu loues des films d'amour et des films d'aventures?
2. Est-ce que tu fais de la musculation et de l'aérobic? Et toi, est-ce que tu fais de la musculation et de l'aérobic?
3. Est-ce que tu joues au golf et au tennis? Et toi, est-ce que tu joues au golf et au tennis?
4. Est-ce que tu fais du camping et de l'escalade? Et toi, est-ce que tu fais du camping et de l'escalade?
5. Est-ce que tu joues du piano et de la guitare? Et toi, est-ce que tu joues du piano et de la guitare?
6. Est-ce que tu écoutes le rock et le jazz? Et toi, est-ce que tu écoutes le rock et le jazz?
Students' responses to these questions will vary.

Modèle:

Suzanne et Ellen ont passé deux semaines en France. (dix jours)
Non, elles n'ont passé que dix jours en France.

Modèle:

regarder les feuilletons et les jeux télévisés
Élève A: Est-ce que tu regardes les feuilletons et les jeux télévisés?
Élève B: Non, je ne regarde ni les feuilletons ni les jeux télévisés. Et toi, est-ce que tu regardes les feuilletons et les jeux télévisés?
Élève A: Je ne regarde que les feuilletons.

**GOLF
DE VALGARDE**

UNE BONNE ADRESSE
POUR HANDICAPS
ÉLEVÉS

13 *Quand votre ami Luc raconte l'histoire de Suzanne et son expérience avec les deux mecs dans le métro, il exagère toujours. Corrigez (correct) ses phrases selon les réponses indiquées.*

1. Il y avait quatre ados américains qui rentraient en métro. (trois ados américains)
2. Il y avait trois mecs qui se sont approchés de Suzanne dans le métro. (deux mecs)
3. Il était dix-sept heures. (seize heures)
4. Un mec a fouillé dans le sac à dos et le sac à main de Suzanne. (dans son sac à dos)
5. À l'aéroport l'employé d'Air France a emmené Suzanne, Mme Taylor et les autres élèves au bureau de son chef. (Suzanne et Mme Taylor)
6. Suzanne a dû payer deux cents dollars. (cent dollars)
7. Suzanne a montré le récépissé six fois à l'immigration aux États-Unis. (une fois)
8. Suzanne va avoir deux camarades de chambre à l'université. (une camarade de chambre)

14 *Avec un(e) partenaire, posez des questions sur vos sports et loisirs préférés. Puis répondez aux questions. Suivez le modèle.*

1. louer des films d'amour et des films d'aventures
2. faire de la musculation et de l'aérobic
3. jouer au golf et au tennis
4. faire du camping et de l'escalade
5. jouer du piano et de la guitare
6. écouter le rock et le jazz

Cooperative Group Practice

Matching Cards

To practice using negative expressions in a question-answer format, prepare a note card for each student in your class. On half of the note cards write questions that can be answered with a negative expression. On the other half, write an answer for each question, for example, **Est-ce que les élèves se sont tus? Non, aucun élève ne s'est tu.** Shuffle the cards, and distribute one card to each student. Tell students to memorize their question or answer. Then, have them circulate around the room asking their question or stating their answer when asked. When all the matches have been found, have each pair of students say its matching sentences to the class. You might prepare a worksheet listing all the questions and have students write the answers as they hear them from the pairs at the end of the activity.

Écrivez le contraire de chaque phrase. Faites attention aux expressions en italique.

1. *Un mec un peu moche* regardait Jérôme.
2. *Thomas et Rogatien* ont suivi ce mec jusqu'au quai.
3. Jérôme a parlé à *ses deux copains*.
4. Il avait *une bonne* idée que ce mec allait le voler.
5. *Quelque chose* lui a dit de faire attention.
6. Ce mec a pris *cent francs* de son sac à dos.
7. Jérôme a cherché *un* agent de police dans le métro.
8. En sortant du métro, Jérôme savait qu'il avait son passeport *et* son portefeuille.
9. Il avait *toujours* son argent français.

Communication

Avec un(e) partenaire, comparez vos derniers voyages. Copiez la grille suivante. Puis posez les questions indiquées à votre partenaire, et complétez la grille selon ses réponses. Enfin changez de rôles.

Destination	le Canada
Date du départ	
Moyen de transport	
Autres voyageurs	
Logement	
Activités	
Réactions	
Problèmes	
Satisfaction	

1. où/aller
2. quand/partir
3. comment/voyager
4. avec qui/voyager
5. où/rester
6. qu'est-ce que/faire
7. comment/se sentir
8. quels problèmes/avoir
9. de quoi/être satisfait(e)

Modèle:

Jérôme a vu *quelqu'un* dans le métro.
Jérôme n'a vu personne dans le métro.

Modèle:

Élève A: Où es-tu allé(e)?
Élève B: Je suis allé(e) au Canada.

De quoi est-ce que tu étais satisfaite?

J'étais satisfaite du camping et du parc d'attractions.

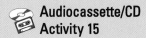

Answers

15 1. Personne ne regardait Jérôme.
2. Ni Thomas ni Rogatien n'a suivi ce mec jusqu'au quai.
3. Jérôme n'a parlé à personne.
4. Il n'avait aucune idée que ce mec allait le voler.
5. Rien ne lui a dit de faire attention.
6. Ce mec n'a rien pris de son sac à dos.
7. Jérôme n'a cherché aucun agent de police dans le métro.
8. En sortant du métro, Jérôme savait qu'il n'avait ni son passeport ni son portefeuille.
9. Il n'avait plus son argent français.

Paired Practice

Les sketches

For additional practice using negative expressions, put students in pairs. Give each student a role either as a principal or a student, a police officer or a tourist, a store security guard or a customer. The students, tourists and customers have all been robbed. They report the robbery to the principals, police officers or security guards, who ask a series of questions to try to solve the crime. Students should use at least two negative expressions in their skits. Then have each pair present its skit to the class. During the presentations, have students write one sentence using a negative expression for each skit they see. You may choose to have students vote on the most creative robbery skit and award a yellow construction paper "Oscar" to the winning pair.

Game

Mémoire

To practice the new and review negative expressions in this lesson, put students in small groups of four or five. Give each group a blank grid with 12 squares the size of small adhesive notes. Tell each group to prepare six questions that require answers with negative expressions. Each question should have only one possible response, for example, **Éric, qui t'a attendu devant le commissariat? Personne ne m'y a attendu.** Have each group write the questions and answers at random on the grid and place adhesive notes over each square. When all the groups have prepared a grid, have them exchange grids with another group. The first student in each group removes two of the adhesive notes from the new grid. If they are a match, he or she earns a point and takes another turn. If not, the adhesive notes are replaced and the second student gets a turn. Students in each group keep taking turns until all the matches on the grid have been made. The student with the most matches at the end of the game is the winner.

Audiocassette/CD
Sur la bonne piste

Listening
Activity 2

Quiz
Leçon B

Advanced
Placement

Teacher's Notes

1. **Sur la bonne piste, Leçon B**, is designed to develop skills that will help students prepare to take the Advanced Placement Exam in French Literature. In this section, students read a variety of prose, poetry and drama from different periods; answer content questions; and demonstrate their critical understanding of literary techniques, such as character development, setting, point of view, satire, figures of speech and inference. In this **Sur la bonne piste** section, students practice visualizing the setting, characters and events in two poems by Jacques Prévert. 2. Take this opportunity to discuss with students the hazards of smoking. You may wish to contact a school counselor for suggestions. You could also choose to tell students that when "Déjeuner du matin" was written, people weren't as aware of the health risks of smoking as we are today. 3. You may want students to do this pre-reading activity which will help them prepare to write their own poem after reading "Déjeuner du matin." Remove the past participles and some of the nouns from the poem. Distribute a copy to students, who fill in the blanks as they wish to create their own interpretation based on the remaining elements. 4. Another idea for a pre-reading activity for "Déjeuner du matin" is to ask students to draw a scene depicting an emotional event in their life or in the life of a fictional character. Underneath their drawing, students should make an outline of verbs that tell its story. Then, using only their verb outlines and drawings, students tell their story to a partner. This activity will help students focus on the past tense structures used in the poem and appreciate the simplicity of Prévert's narration. 5. You might ask students if the illustration accompanying "Déjeuner du matin" describes the beginning, middle or end of the poem. 6. Poetry by Jacques Prévert (1900-77) is as popular now as it was during his lifetime. Translated in-to 80 languages, Jacques Prévert's simple, poignant, often humorous verse has an unerring feel for the quality of everyday life. A member of the surrealist group until ousted by André Breton in 1928, Prévert incorporated surrealist notions in his earliest writings. His commercial success came with the realistic, poetic screenplays that he wrote for directors such as Jean Renoir and Marcel Carné. *Les Enfants du paradis* (1945) has become a film classic. Prévert's first collection of poetry, *Paroles* (1946), was followed by *Spectacle* (1951), *La Pluie et le Beau Temps* (1955) and *Fatras* (1965). Filled with word games and satire, Prévert's poetry reveals concerns about the social order, an unrelenting affirmation of love and respect for the underdog.

17 | *Utilisez les réponses de l'enquête dans l'Activité 16 pour écrire un paragraphe où vous décrivez les bonnes expériences et les mauvaises expériences de votre partenaire pendant son dernier voyage. Rappelez-vous les expressions comme **d'abord**, **ensuite**, etc., qui vous aident à faire les transitions entre les phrases.*

Sur la bonne piste

When you read a poem or story in French, it is important to visualize the setting, characters and events. The writer counts on his or her descriptions to evoke feelings as you read and to help you "see" what is taking place. For example, what feelings and images come to mind when you read "cotton candy at the fair," "a mysterious man with a revolver" and "The runner raised her arms high above her head, a smile of triumph on her face"? The two poems that follow, written by the popular 20th century French poet Jacques Prévert, are made up of a series of images that tell a story. As you read them, try to create mental pictures and get in touch with what the setting, characters and events make you feel.

18 | *Avant de lire le premier poème de Prévert, répondez aux questions suivantes.*

1. Qu'est-ce que tu prends comme petit déjeuner?
2. Le matin parles-tu beaucoup?
3. Est-ce que tu es triste quand il pleut?
4. Quand est-ce que tu as pleuré (*cried*)?

Déjeuner du matin

1 Il a mis le café
2 Dans la tasse
3 Il a mis le lait
4 Dans la tasse de café
5 Il a mis le sucre
6 Dans le café au lait
7 Avec la petite cuiller
8 Il a tourné
9 Il a bu le café au lait
10 Et il a reposé la tasse
11 Sans me parler
12 Il a allumé
13 Une cigarette
14 Il a fait des ronds
15 Avec la fumée
16 Il a mis les cendres
17 Dans le cendrier
18 Sans me parler
19 Sans me regarder

20 Il s'est levé
21 Il a mis
22 Son chapeau sur sa tête
23 Il a mis
24 Son manteau de pluie
25 Parce qu'il pleuvait
26 Et il est parti
27 Sous la pluie
28 Sans une parole
29 Sans me regarder
30 Et moi j'ai pris
31 Ma tête dans ma main
32 Et j'ai pleuré.

Répondez aux questions suivantes.

1. Qu'est-ce que l'homme a pris au petit déjeuner?
2. Est-ce qu'on sait si ces deux personnes étaient à la maison ou au café?
3. Qu'est-ce que l'homme a mis avant de sortir?
4. Quel temps faisait-il?
5. Combien d'actions l'homme a-t-il faites?
6. Quelles deux expressions sont répétées deux fois pour montrer que l'homme n'était pas content?
7. Selon toi, est-ce que la deuxième personne est un homme ou une femme? Explique.
8. La scène est très simple mais aussi très forte. Quels sont les détails que tu imagines ou que tu "vois"? Qui sont ces deux personnes? Pourquoi n'ont-elles pas de noms? Qu'est-ce qui s'est passé avant?

Faites un dessin original de la scène dans le poème "Déjeuner du matin." Mettez-y les deux personnes et tous les objets du poème. Indiquez aussi le temps qu'il fait et les sentiments (feelings) des deux personnes.

Imaginez l'homme et la femme cinq minutes avant la scène dans le poème. Écrivez le dialogue entre ces deux personnes. Cette conversation devrait expliquer pourquoi la femme est triste et pourquoi l'homme part sans lui parler, sans la regarder.

Answers

19 Possible answers:

1. L'homme a pris du café au lait.
2. Non, on ne sait pas si ces deux personnes étaient à la maison ou au café.
3. Il a mis son chapeau et son manteau de pluie avant de sortir.
4. Il pleuvait.
5. L'homme a fait 13 actions.
6. Les expressions "sans me parler" et "sans me regarder" sont répétées deux fois pour montrer que l'homme n'était pas content.
7. Answers will vary.
8. Answers will vary.

Teacher's Notes

1. Cognates not found in the end vocabulary of *C'est à toi!* are used to ask questions about the poem "Déjeuner du matin" in Activity 19.
2. To holistically grade Activities 19 and 23, either you or the students can give a check (✓) to an answer that comes directly from the reading passage, a plus (+) to an answer that requires thinking that goes beyond the text's answer and a minus (-) to an answer that is not at all related to the text. You or the students can give a zero (0) for no answer at all, which may encourage some reticent students to make an effort at answering. If students understand the assessment process and know how their performance will be rated, they will perform the activities differently than if they think they are not graded.

Critical Thinking

Original Poem

As a post-reading activity, ask students to write a poem in the **passé composé** that depicts an emotional scene. Students can expand on the picture they drew in the pre-reading activity described in the teacher's note on page 86 or select an emotion such as anger, love, jealousy, hate, happiness or unhappiness to depict. Have students describe at least ten actions that imitate Prévert's narrative style of actions building upon one another in succession. While students may feel more comfortable imitating the third person narration of "Déjeuner du matin," they should consider whether their own poem might be more convincing if written in the first person.

TPR

Class Poem

If your students write an original poem based on the previous critical thinking suggestion, select one student's poem told in the first person to act out in front of the class. As you describe and act out each successive action in the first person, students write a corresponding poem in the third person in the **passé composé**.

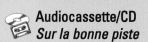

Audiocassette/CD
Sur la bonne piste

22   *Avant de lire le deuxième poème de Prévert, répondez aux questions suivantes.*

1. Quels sentiments est-ce que tu as quand tu vois ou penses à ton école? Fais-en une liste, et donne une situation spécifique pour chaque sentiment.
2. Est-ce que tu es souvent heureux ou heureuse quand tu es en cours? Pourquoi ou pourquoi pas?
3. Connais-tu des élèves qui ne sont pas comme les autres élèves? Ont-ils des idées différentes? Comment sont ces élèves? Sont-ils heureux?

Le Cancre

1   Il dit non avec la tête
2   Mais il dit oui avec le cœur
3   Il dit oui à ce qu'il aime
4   Il dit non au professeur
5   Il est debout
6   On le questionne
7   Et tous les problèmes sont posés
8   Soudain le fou rire le prend
9   Et il efface tout
10   Les chiffres et les mots
11   Les dates et les noms
12   Les phrases et les pièges
13   Et malgré les menaces du maître
14   Sous les huées des enfants prodiges
15   Avec des craies de toutes les couleurs
16   Sur le tableau noir du malheur
17   Il dessine le visage du bonheur.

Répondez aux questions suivantes.

1. Où est l'élève?
2. Qui lui pose des questions?
3. Est-ce qu'il sait les réponses à ces questions?
4. Quelle est la réaction de l'élève quand "tous les problèmes sont posés"?
5. "Les chiffres" et "Les dates et les noms" indiquent quels deux cours?
6. Quel mot (*word*) est le contraire du "bonheur"?
7. Dans quelles deux lignes est-ce qu'on comprend que le cancre est heureux?
8. Selon Prévert, faut-il être intelligent pour être heureux?

Faites un dessin original de la scène dans le poème "Le Cancre." Quelles autres personnes est-ce que vous voyez? Quels objets est-ce qu'il y a dans la salle de classe?

Prévert explique que le cancre "dit oui à ce qu'il aime." Imaginez que vous êtes le cancre. Faites une liste des choses que vous aimez et une autre liste des choses que vous détestez.

---

*Pensez aux cours que vous suivez cette année, et puis écrivez une expression qui est associée à chaque cours. Par exemple, **la chimie—le carnet, le français—les verbes***.

Dossier fermé

Imagine que tu voyages en Europe avec tes copains français Bénédicte et Sébastien. En Italie Sébastien perd son passeport, mais il ne s'en inquiète pas. Pour rentrer en France, il n'a même pas de problèmes quand il passe au contrôle des passeports. Comment est-ce que c'est possible?

    C. Il n'a pas besoin de passeport pour aller d'Italie en France.

Les habitants de France sont membres de l'Union européenne et n'ont pas besoin de passeport pour aller de pays en pays en Europe.

Critical Thinking

Original Poem

As a post-reading activity, have students write an original poem about what school means to them. You may choose to have them make a poem in the shape of a diamond, using a noun, two adjectives, three verbs, a complete sentence and a final noun which sums up the meaning of the poem.

C'est à moi!

Now that you have completed this unit, take a look at what you should be able to do in French. Can you do all of these tasks?

➤ I can ask for information about what's happening.
➤ I can express astonishment and disbelief.
➤ I can say whom I'm suspicious of.
➤ I can express emotions.
➤ I can express concern.
➤ I can make fun of myself.
➤ I can apologize for what I've done.
➤ I can say that I'm satisfied with something.
➤ I can write a letter.
➤ I can tell a story.
➤ I can describe how things were in the past.
➤ I can explain why.
➤ I can describe someone's physical traits.
➤ I can describe someone's temperament.
➤ I can tell how I was.

Pour voir si vous avez bien compris la culture francophone, décidez si chaque phrase est vraie ou fausse.

1. C'est une bonne idée de mettre son passeport et ses chèques de voyage dans sa valise où personne ne peut les trouver.
2. Il faut avoir son passeport quand on touche des chèques de voyage.
3. Si vous perdez votre passeport, il faut simplement aller au commissariat de police.
4. Puisqu'il y a 13 stations de métro à l'intérieur de Paris, on n'est jamais loin d'une "bouche de métro."
5. Vous pouvez changer de ligne de métro là où le panneau indique "Correspondance."
6. À l'aéroport les rayons X ne sont pas dangereux pour le film.
7. Tous les pays d'Europe sont membres de l'Union européenne.
8. Les habitants de l'Union européenne n'ont pas besoin de passeport pour visiter les États-Unis.
9. Il y a différents groupes de police qui remplissent des fonctions différentes.
10. L'inspecteur Maigret est un policier dans les romans de Georges Simenon.

Answers

1. fausse
2. vraie
3. fausse
4. fausse
5. vraie
6. vraie
7. fausse
8. fausse
9. vraie
10. vraie

Teacher's Notes

1. The Treaty on European Union, signed in Maastricht in 1992, bestows certain rights of European citizenship, including the right to vote and to be a candidate in municipal elections and the right to reside in any member state. The single market that it established allows all European citizens to move freely from one member state to another; customs controls on the community's internal borders have been abolished. 2. The powers of the European Parliament have been increased to make the European community more democratic, shifting more decisions and responsibility from the member states and their national parliaments to the community. Major international agreements with important implications for the budgetary situation or the legislation of the community now require the consent of parliament. 3. The community has been given further powers so that more and more matters directly affecting everyday life can be dealt with by the member states working together. These new areas include health and consumer and environmental protection. The community will also contribute to the establishment of trans-European transport, telecommunications and energy networks to bring the member states closer together. Other areas in which the community's powers have been extended include relations with developing countries, education and culture. The member states have also agreed to step up cooperation in the fields of justice and home affairs.

Communication orale

Avant de partir en vacances avec quelqu'un, il faut savoir si on va bien s'entendre. Pour le déterminer, travaillez avec un(e) partenaire. Faites une enquête pour voir si vous vous entendez bien. Copiez la grille suivante. Mais avant de parler à votre partenaire, mettez un ✓ dans l'espace blanc qui décrit votre personnalité. Ensuite posez les questions indiquées à votre partenaire, et mettez un ✗ dans l'espace blanc qui correspond à ses réponses. Enfin changez de rôles.

Modèle:
Élève A:　Es-tu content(e)?
Élève B:　Je suis souvent content(e).

	toujours	souvent	jamais
Es-tu... ?			
1.　souriant(e)	✓	✗	
2.　triste			
3.　bavard(e)			
4.　drôle			
5.　honnête			
6.　timide			
7.　calme			
8.　déprimé(e)			
9.　effrayé(e)			
10.　exigeant(e)			
Est-ce que tu... ?			
1.　te réveilles tôt			
2.　aimes faire du shopping			
3.　aimes visiter les musées			
4.　te fâches			
5.　te méfies de tout le monde			

Combien de vos réponses ressemblent aux réponses de votre partenaire?

1. *Si vous avez 11-15 réponses identiques, vos personnalités sont presque similaires. Vous pouvez voyager ensemble sans problèmes. Bon voyage!*
2. *Si vous avez 6-10 réponses identiques, il y a des différences entre vos deux personnalités. Pouvez-vous voyager ensemble? Il faut voir.*
3. *Si vous avez 0-5 réponses identiques, vos personnalités s'opposent. Il faut beaucoup réfléchir avant de partir en vacances ensemble. Le voyage peut être un désastre!*

Communication écrite

Quand on part en vacances, on entend souvent l'expression "Bon voyage." Mais les voyages sont-ils toujours bons? Selon les réponses que vous avez notées dans l'enquête sur les personnalités de vous et votre partenaire dans l'activité précédente, remplissez les cercles suivants.

Mon partenaire
souvent souriant(e)

Mon partenaire
et moi

Moi
toujours souriant(e)

Maintenant imaginez que vous êtes parti(e) en vacances avec votre partenaire. En retournant, écrivez une lettre à vos grands-parents où vous leur décrivez tous les détails de ce voyage. Dites où vous et votre partenaire êtes allé(e)s et ce que vous avez fait. Puis dites si vous vous êtes bien entendu(e)s, et expliquez pourquoi ou pourquoi pas, selon les cercles que vous avez remplis. Enfin dites si c'était un bon voyage ou un désastre.

Communication active

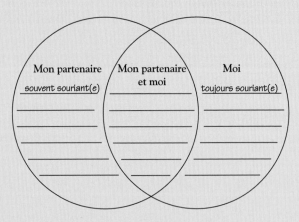

To ask for information, use:

Qu'est-ce qui s'est passé?   *What happened?*

To express astonishment or disbelief, use:

Quelle histoire!   *What a story!*

C'est pas vrai!   *It's not true!*

Mais c'est incroyable!   *But that's unbelievable!*

To express suspicion, use:

Je me méfiais d'elle.   *I distrusted her.*

To express emotions, use:

Aucun de nous ne voulait rentrer.   *Not one of us wanted to return.*

Elle s'est fâchée.   *She got angry.*

Ni elle ni moi n'étions calmes.   *Neither she nor I was calm.*

To express concern, use:

J'ai commencé à m'inquiéter.   *I was beginning to worry.*

To express ridicule, use:

Quelle imbécile!

What an idiot!

To apologize, use:

J'ai dit que **je regrettais** tous les problèmes.

I said that I regretted all the problems.

To express satisfaction, use:

On était satisfait de mes réponses.

They were satisfied with my answers.

Il y avait beaucoup de monde à la Fête du Vin et du Fromage. (Antony)

To write a letter, use:

Mes chers grands-parents

My dear grandparents

To tell a story, use:

Je vais tout te raconter.
Alors, la fin de l'histoire?

I'm going to tell you everything.
So, the end of the story?

To describe how things were, use:

Il y avait beaucoup de monde.
Il était inutile de venir à 17h00 samedi après-midi.
Il fallait montrer le récépissé à l'immigration aux États-Unis.

There were a lot of people.
It was useless to come at 5:00 Saturday afternoon.
It was necessary to show the receipt to U.S. immigration.

To explain something, use:

Elle a expliqué que je n'avais ni argent français ni argent américain.

She explained that I had neither French nor American money.

To describe physical traits, use:

Elle a l'air épuisé et déprimé.

She looks exhausted and depressed.

Ils étaient un peu moches, de taille plutôt petite que grande.

They were somewhat un-attractive, short rather than tall.

Ils avaient les cheveux noirs et les yeux marron.
Ils ne portaient pas de lunettes.

They had black hair and brown eyes.
They didn't wear glasses.

To describe temperament, use:

Cet agent de police **était** exigeant.

This police officer was demanding.

To tell how you were, use:

En étant effrayée et fâchée, je suis rentrée tout de suite à l'hôtel.
J'étais contente d'avoir la prof avec moi.
Je me sentais un peu mieux.

Being frightened and angry, I returned to the hotel right away.
I was happy to have the teacher with me.
I felt a little better.

Unité 3

Les arts

 THÉÂTRE FRANÇAIS

COMÉDIE FRANÇAISE 1680

L'IMPROMPTU DE VERSAILLES
LES PRÉCIEUSES RIDICULES

27 JUILLET 1998   cat.3   65 F
LUNDI   20H30   **CO 133**

0712CF1000001MH   FAUT. CORBEILLE

IMPORTANT : Voir au Dos

FILM 20.40

CAMILLE
CLAUDEL

Drame. De Bruno Nuytten.
1988. Fra. Durée : 2h45.
Avec **Isabelle Adjani** (Camille Claudel), **Gérard Depardieu** (Auguste Rodin).
Le sujet : l'histoire pas-
sionnelle de Camille Claudel et d'Auguste Rodin. -
Le début : 1885, à Paris.
Camille Claudel, la sœur
de l'écrivain Paul Claudel,
issue d'une famille bour-
geoise, se voue jour et nuit
à la sculpture...
*Notre avis : sans doute
trop classique, mais le sujet est passionnant et l'interprétation d'Isabelle Adjani époustouflante.   B. T.*
**Adultes et
adolescents.** 57 454 100♦

In this unit you will be able to:

➤ ask about importance
   and unimportance

➤ express importance and
   unimportance

➤ inquire about likes and
   dislikes

➤ express likes and dislikes

➤ list

➤ state a preference

➤ state a generalization

➤ inquire about opinions

➤ give opinions

➤ inquire about agreement
   and disagreement

➤ inquire about surprise

➤ compare

➤ inquire about possibility
   and impossibility

➤ express possibility and
   impossibility

➤ express need and necessity

➤ tell location

Tes empreintes ici

Quand tu as du temps libre, qu'est-ce que tu aimes faire?

J'écoute mes CDs quand j'ai du temps libre.

- Tu écoutes de la musique? Tu peux acheter de la musique américaine, canadienne, française, anglaise ou africaine.
- Tu aimes aller au cinéma? Tu as un grand choix. Il y a des films d'amour, des films d'aventures, des comédies, des drames, des films d'épouvante et des documentaires. Qu'est-ce que tu préfères?

- Est-ce que tu aimes lire? Tu peux acheter des magazines, des journaux ou des romans.
- Est-ce que le théâtre t'intéresse? As-tu envie de devenir acteur ou actrice?
- Tu aimes visiter un musée? Tu peux regarder la sculpture, les tableaux ou même les photos.

L'art te parle....

Leçon A

In this lesson you will be able to:

➤ inquire about likes and dislikes

➤ express likes and dislikes

➤ list

➤ state a generalization

➤ state a preference

➤ express need and necessity

➤ inquire about opinions

➤ give opinions

Teacher's Note

Communicative functions that are recycled in this lesson are "making suggestions," "describing past events," "explaining something," "identifying professions" and "giving examples."

AIR PLAY HIT-PARADE FRANCOPHONE STATIONS FM	
1 Billy Ze Kick	"Mangez-moi, mangez-moi"
2 Tonton David	"Sûr et certain"
3 Alain Souchon	"Les Regrets"
4 Goldman/Fredericks/Jones	"Des vies"
5 Francis Cabrel	"La Cabane du pêcheur"
6 Francis Cabrel	"Je t'aimais, je t'aime..."
7 Native	"Tu planes sur moi"
8 Florent Pagny	"Si tu veux m'essayer"
9 MC Solaar	"Obsolète"
10 MC Solaar	"Séquelles"
11 Renaud Hantson	"Apprendre à vivre sans toi"
12 Véronique Sanson	"Bahia"
13 Alain Bashung	"Ma Petite Entreprise"
14 Liane Foly	"Les Yeux doux"
15 IAM	"Je danse le mia"
16 Axelle Red	"Elle danse seule"
17 Bernard Lavilliers	"Troisième Couteau"
18 Eddy Mitchell	"Te perdre"
19 Jean-Louis Aubert	"Moments"
20 Nilda Fernandez	"Marie-Madeleine"

Dossier ouvert

Imagine que tu passes une semaine à Paris. Comment décider quoi faire dans cette grande ville? Par exemple, à quels concerts, films et spectacles peux-tu aller? Quelles sont les dates et les heures de ces spectacles? Où sont-ils? Est-ce que tu peux acheter quelque chose qui te dit tous ces détails? Mais oui! Tu dois acheter:

 A. *Pariscope*
 B. un journal quotidien
 C. le *Guide Michelin Vert*

les vedettes inattendues de cette grande soirée

Si tous les petits peintres du monde...

Teacher's Notes

1. **Vedette** is always feminine, even when it refers to a masculine star. **Star**, also always feminine, is a synonym for **vedette**. 2. **Un metteur en scène** was introduced on page 322 in the second level of *C'est à toi!* 3. **Un(e) scénariste** will be introduced in **Leçon B**. 4. You may want to give your students the forms of the irregular verb **peindre**: **peins, peins, peint, peignons, peignez, peignent**. 5. Other related terms and expressions include **interpréter** (*to perform*), **réaliser** (*to produce*), **un écran** (*screen*), **le grand écran** (*movies*), **le petit écran** (*television*), **les sous-titres** (*subtitles*), **le public** (*audience*), **un navet** (*third-rate film*), **un portrait** (*portrait*), **un autoportrait** (*self-portrait*), **une esquisse** (*sketch*), **une toile** (*canvas*), **dessiner** (*to draw*), **à l'arrière-plan** (*in the background*), **au premier plan** (*in the foreground*), **la poterie** (*pottery*), **la céramique** (*ceramics*), **les beaux-arts** (*fine art*) and **une école des Beaux-Arts** (*art college*).

Critical Thinking

Journal personnel

If students are keeping a cultural journal, you might ask them to write about a famous artist they admire. Why do they admire this person? What do they know about his or her life? What impact has this person made on their life? Do they feel that he or she is a good role model? Why or why not?

**Workbook
Activity 2**

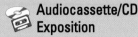

**Audiocassette/CD
Exposition**

Teacher's Notes

1. The **César** is a French film award similar to the Oscar. 2. *Jean de Florette* and *Manon des Sources* are films based on the novels of Marcel Pagnol (1895-1974). Both novels take place in Pagnol's native Provence. 3. Daniel Auteuil shared the Best Actor award at Cannes in 1996 with his costar of *Le huitième jour*, Pascal Duquenne. 4. *Lucie Aubrac* tells the true story of a French woman who rescued her husband, a key leader in the French Resistance, from the Nazis during World War II. 5. Other recent films starring Daniel Auteuil include *Le Bossu*, *L'Enfant de la Nuit* and *The Lost Son* (filmed in English). 6. Marguerite Duras, née Donnadieu, was the youngest child of two teachers. As an adolescent she attended boarding school in Saigon, which provides the autobiographical background for *L'Amant*. After passing the **bac** at the Lycée de Saigon, Duras studied law, political science and mathematics at the Sorbonne, later taking a job at the Ministère des Colonies. 7. Duras belongs to the group of modern "neorealist" writers. In the **nouveau roman**, or antinovel, there are few characters, the plot is simple, the time period covered is short and the description limited. The author says little to guide the reader in understanding the characters or the story. 8. Duras' 1958 novel *Moderato Cantabile* is composed of a series of conversations between Anne, the wife of a wealthy businessman, and Chauvin, a man who works for her husband, in which they speculate about the murder they have both witnessed. 9. In 1959 Duras was asked by film director Alain Resnais to write the screenplay for *Hiroshima mon amour*, which became a worldwide success. It tells the story of a French actress working in Tokyo whose affair with a Japanese architect recalls her wartime affair in France

with a Nazi officer. 10. *L'Amant*, which won Duras the Prix Goncourt in 1984, focuses on the memory of a 60-year-old woman recalling her adolescent love affair with a wealthy Chinese planter. 11. Of her novels Duras has said, "Even when my books are completely invented, even when I think they have come from elsewhere, they are always personal."

Est-ce que les arts vous plaisent?° À quoi pensez-vous lorsque° vous pensez à la culture des pays francophones? À la nourriture, aux vêtements, aux sports? Naturellement. Mais il faut que vous pensiez aussi aux films, à la musique, à la littérature, à la sculpture et aux tableaux. Faisons la connaissance de quelques artistes du monde francophone.

Daniel Auteuil

Une des vedettes du cinéma français la plus populaire, c'est Daniel Auteuil. À 17 ans il étudiait pour devenir acteur quand on l'a choisi pour son premier rôle. Ces premiers rôles étaient petits, mais très vite ils sont devenus plus importants. Il a reçu un César pour les films *Jean de Florette* et *Manon des Sources*. Ses autres films très connus sont *Ma saison préférée*, *La Reine Margot*, *Un cœur en hiver*, *Le huitième jour* et *Lucie Aubrac*. On passe souvent ses films à la télé.

Daniel Auteuil

Marguerite Duras

Née au Vietnam en 1914 et morte à Paris en 1996, Marguerite Duras est venue en France après son bac. Elle a écrit des pièces de théâtre,° des scénarios et des romans. Elle reste populaire parce que ses idées sont toujours controversées. Deux de ses romans les plus connus sont *Moderato Cantabile* et *L'Amant*. Ce dernier, roman autobiographique, décrit l'Indochine des années 30. Ses films les plus populaires sont *Hiroshima mon amour* et *L'Amant* (du roman).

Marguerite Duras

plaire faire plaisir à, aimer; **lorsque** quand; **une pièce de théâtre** *play*

Cross-curricular

The Modern French Novel

You may want to have students read some of Marguerite Duras' prose to acquaint them with the modern French novel. Students could read the first few pages of *Moderato Cantabile*, looking for the sounds she describes that mark time in the opening episode of the novel.

Céline Dion

La plus jeune de 14 enfants, Céline Dion est née en 1968 près de Montréal. Céline a toujours voulu devenir chanteuse. Très jeune, elle travaillait et chantait° dans le restaurant de ses parents. De plus, toute sa famille passait son temps libre à faire de la musique et à chanter. C'est une musicienne diligente qui n'arrête pas de travailler. On peut acheter ses cassettes et CDs en version anglaise et française. Peut-être que vous l'avez vue chanter à la télé. Ses chansons sont souvent premières au hit-parade. Céline Dion a reçu un Grammy pour la chanson principale du film *La Belle et la Bête* de Disney. Elle a aussi enregistré° la chanson "My Heart Will Go On" pour le film *Titanic*.

Céline Dion

Angélique Kidjo

Angélique Kidjo est née au Bénin en Afrique en 1960. Comme Céline Dion, elle vient d'une famille de musiciens. Elle chantait déjà à l'âge de six ans, d'abord avec sa mère et puis avec ses frères. Elle a déménagé en France pendant les années 80. Elle a eu beaucoup de succès avec son troisième album *Logozo*, qui était au hit-parade dans beaucoup de pays. Dans son quatrième album elle chante en fon, la langue° qu'on parle au Bénin. Kidjo a aussi composé la musique des bandes originales° de plusieurs° films. Elle donne des concerts un peu partout° dans le monde. Il faut qu'on assiste à un de ses concerts pour profiter de sa musique dynamique qui plaît à tous. Cette musique est si pleine d'énergie qu'on a envie de danser.

Angélique Kidjo

Maurice Jarre

On chante lorsqu'on pense à Maurice Jarre. C'est l'un des compositeurs français modernes qu'on écoute le plus. Aux États-Unis il a composé la musique de plusieurs films, par exemple, *Doctor Zhivago*, *Lawrence of Arabia*, *Gorillas in the Mist*, *Witness* et *Fatal Attraction*. Pour lui la bande originale est aussi importante que l'intrigue. Jarre a composé la musique des ballets et a été le chef d'orchestre° du London Philharmonic Orchestra et du Los Angeles Philharmonic Orchestra.

Maurice Jarre

chanter *to sing*; **enregistrer** *to record*; **une langue** *language*; **une bande originale** *sound track*; **plusieurs** *quelques*; **partout** *everywhere*; **un chef d'orchestre** *conductor*

Teacher's Notes

1. **Un chanteur, une chanteuse** and **une chanson** were introduced in Unit 9 in the second level of *C'est à toi!* Point out that **chanter** belongs to the same word family as these nouns. 2. In 1996 Céline Dion was named a Chevalier de l'Ordre des Arts et des Lettres. The French minister congratulated her for being the best ambassador of the French language today. 3. Dion has also produced some of her songs in German and Spanish. 4. Her album *D'eux* is the best-selling French language album of all time. 5. *La Belle et la Bête* is based on the fairy tale by Charles Perrault (1628-1703). 6. **Une bande originale** refers to the songs on a sound track, while **une bande sonore** refers to the entire sound track, including the words. 7. Angélique Kidjo's albums, in order, are *Pretty*, *Parakou*, *Logozo*, *Ayé*, *Fifa* and *Soundtracks*. Using rhythms from reggae, samba, funk, gospel, zouk and traditional African music, Kidjo shapes her music into her own unique sound. 8. One of Kidjo's goals as an artist is to share the culture of her native Benin, a small, developing, agricultural country in French-speaking West Africa, with her listeners. 9. **Chef d'orchestre** is pronounced [ʃefdɔrkɛstr(ə)]. 10. The plural of **chef-d'œuvre** is **chefs-d'œuvre**. **Chef-d'œuvre** is pronounced [ʃɛdœvR(ə)]. 11. Born in 1924 in Lyon, Maurice Jarre served as director of music at the Théâtre national populaire before writing scores for films. His music for *Lawrence of Arabia* (1963) and "Lara's Song" from *Doctor Zhivago* (1965) won him Oscars.

Camille Claudel du bonnet (Auguste Rodin)

Teacher's Notes

1. **Sculpteur** is pronounced [skyltœR]. 2. **Une sculpture** was introduced on page 58 in the second level of *C'est à toi!* 3. Camille Claudel (1864-1943) destroyed much of her own work, disheartened at neither being successful nor being accepted as an artist in her own right. She spent the last 30 years of her life in a psychiatric clinic. 4. Some of her work can be seen at the **musée Rodin** in Paris. Her early sculptures, such as *L'Abandon* (1888), *La Valse* (1893) and *L'Âge mûr* (1899), show the influence of Auguste Rodin. Her later work is more classical. 5. The poet and playwright Paul Claudel (1868-1955) was Camille's brother. 6. You may want to show the film *Camille Claudel*, in which Gérard Depardieu plays the role of Rodin and Isabelle Adjani stars as the troubled Claudel. 7. During a trip to Italy, Auguste Rodin (1840-1917) was inspired by the works of Donatello and Michelangelo. In 1879, with *Saint Jean Baptiste*, his talent was unanimously recognized. In his later career Rodin achieved critical and commercial success as a portrait sculptor of famous dignitaries, such as Victor Hugo and Georges Clemenceau, capturing their inner conflicts and emotions almost psychoanalytically. The *Bourgeois de Calais*, considered his masterpiece, aroused controversy for depicting the pathos rather than the stoic heroism of a group of medieval political martyrs. Other famous sculptures by Rodin include *Le Penseur*, *Porte de l'Enfer* (unfinished), *Balzac* and *Le Baiser*. Fiercely independent, Rodin is impossible to classify with one particular art movement. His energetic expression recalls romanticism, while his attention to precise anatomical detail suggests naturalism. His importance as France's most distinguished sculptor rests on the role he played in releasing artistic expression from the dictates of academic classicism, which mandated that sculpture provide an ideal image of man. Rodin left his art collection, including his own works, to the French government. 8. French painting and Paris art museums were introduced in the second level of *C'est à toi!* on pages 71-73. 9. Gustave Caillebotte (1848-94) combined aspects of the academic and impressionist styles in a unique synthesis. Initially influenced by Gustave Courbet's realism, he came under the spell of the impressionists, especially Frédéric Bazille, Claude Monet and Pierre Auguste Renoir. He showed his works at the impres-sionist exhibitions beginning in 1876 and acted as the chief organizer, promoter and financial backer of the exhibitions for the next six years. His paintings, such as *Le Pont de l'Europe*, demonstrate his interest in the modern urban environment. Having amassed a considerable fortune, Caillebotte generously aided other painters in need, particularly Monet and Renoir. He bequeathed 67 paintings to the state. His reputation languished after his death until the second half of the 20th century because most of his paintings were kept by his family.

Camille Claudel

En général on n'acceptait pas les femmes dans beaucoup de professions au 19e siècle. Il était même difficile pour une femme de devenir sculpteur. Camille Claudel faisait ses études à Paris quand elle est devenue l'assistante du sculpteur Auguste Rodin. Pendant 15 ans elle a travaillé dans son atelier et l'a aidé avec ses plus grandes sculptures. Quand Claudel a quitté l'atelier de Rodin, elle a continué à faire des sculptures, mais elle n'a pas réussi à être acceptée pendant sa vie. Elle est morte en 1943.

Gustave Caillebotte

Gustave Caillebotte est devenu l'un des plus importants peintres impressionnistes. Il a préféré peindre sa maison, la vie et les rues de Paris, et la nature. Même les fleurs et les fruits de ses natures mortes plaisent aux yeux. Ses paysages donnent une jolie vue de la campagne. En ce temps, peindre dehors était une nouvelle idée. On a l'impression que la lumière danse dans tous ses tableaux. Caillebotte a aidé ses amis impressionnistes en achetant beaucoup de leurs tableaux. Il a décidé de donner toute sa collection à la France. Aujourd'hui la collection Caillebotte est une des plus importantes du musée d'Orsay. Et si vous allez à Chicago, il faut que vous passiez par le Art Institute pour voir son chef-d'œuvre,° *Rue de Paris; Temps de pluie*.

un chef-d'œuvre *masterpiece*

Rue de Paris; Temps de pluie (Gustave Caillebotte)

Répondez aux questions d'après les descriptions des personnes célèbres.

1. Qui a reçu un César pour les films *Jean de Florette* et *Manon des Sources*?
2. Pourquoi est-ce que Marguerite Duras reste populaire aujourd'hui?
3. Avec qui est-ce que Céline Dion passait son temps libre à faire de la musique et à chanter?
4. En quelles langues peut-on acheter les cassettes et les CDs de Céline Dion?
5. Quelle chanteuse africaine a eu du succès avec *Logozo*, enregistré en fon?
6. Selon Maurice Jarre, qu'est-ce qui est aussi important que l'intrigue d'un film?
7. Quand est-ce que Camille Claudel est devenue l'assistante d'Auguste Rodin?
8. Comment est-ce que Gustave Caillebotte a aidé ses amis impressionnistes?

Indiquez quelles expressions vous associez à chaque artiste. Il y a plus d'une réponse pour chaque personne.

1. Daniel Auteuil
2. Marguerite Duras
3. Céline Dion
4. Angélique Kidjo
5. Maurice Jarre
6. Camille Claudel
7. Gustave Caillebotte

a. chante en plusieurs langues
b. des tableaux
c. enregistre des albums
d. des bandes originales
e. une vedette
f. la musique
g. joue des rôles
h. un atelier
i. célèbre
j. des scénarios
k. un sculpteur
l. le Bénin
m. des idées controversées

20.35   *Cinéma*
UN CŒUR EN HIVER
De Claude Sautet.
Avec Daniel Auteuil,
Emmanuelle Béart,
André Dussollier.

C'est à toi!

1. Est-ce que tu peux voir des films français dans ta ville?
2. Est-ce que tu as jamais vu un film français en cours? Si oui, quel(s) film(s)?
3. Quel acteur ou quelle actrice est-ce que tu aimes le mieux? Pourquoi?
4. Est-ce que tu aimes lire? Qu'est-ce que tu lis souvent?
5. Quelle musique est-ce que tu aimes? Quel chanteur ou quelle chanteuse préfères-tu?
6. Est-ce que la sculpture te plaît? Connais-tu les sculptures de Rodin? Est-ce que tu aimes la sculpture moderne?
7. Est-ce que tu as jamais visité un musée d'art?
8. Est-ce que tu aimes mieux les peintres impressionnistes ou les peintres modernes? Pourquoi?

**Audiocassette/CD
Activities 1, 3**

Answers

1 1. Daniel Auteuil a reçu un César pour les films *Jean de Florette* et *Manon des Sources.*
2. Marguerite Duras reste populaire aujourd'hui parce que ses idées sont toujours controversées.
3. Céline Dion passait son temps libre à faire de la musique et à chanter avec toute sa famille.
4. On peut acheter les cassettes et les CDs de Céline Dion en version française et anglaise.
5. Angélique Kidjo a eu du succès avec *Logozo*, enregistré en fon.
6. Selon Maurice Jarre, la bande originale est aussi importante que l'intrigue d'un film.
7. Camille Claudel faisait ses études à Paris quand elle est devenue l'assistante d'Auguste Rodin.
8. Gustave Caillebotte a aidé ses amis impressionnistes en achetant beaucoup de leurs tableaux.

2 1. e, g, i
2. i, j, m
3. a, c, d, f, i
4. a, c, d, f, i, l
5. d, f, i
6. h, i, k
7. b, i

3 Answers will vary.

Cross-curricular

Visit to an Art Museum

You may want to plan a field trip with your students to a nearby art museum to see sculptures and paintings by French artists and to have a guided tour. In preparation introduce your students to the characteristics of some of the major art movements, such as neoclassicism, romanticism, impressionism and expressionism.

Game

Loto

To practice vocabulary introduced in this lesson, students might play this game. Have them make a small grid containing nine squares on a sheet of paper and write the English equivalent of nine new vocabulary words in the grid. Start reading off French words that you have selected from the lesson.

Whenever students have a match, they cross the English word off their square. The first student to complete a vertical, horizontal or diagonal line of three squares is the winner. You may choose to award extra credit points if the student can correctly pronounce the French equivalent for the English word listed on each of his or her winning squares.

Workbook Activity 3

Teacher's Notes

1. Cognates in this reading include **variété, chaînes, téléspectateurs, câble, réception, satellite, programmation, fiction, publicités, divers, récente, déterminé, programmes, télécommande, zapping, noter, consacrent, télévisées, diminuer, probablement, vidéo, adultes** and **multimédia**. 2. Students may be interested to learn the French titles for some American programs shown in France: "La vie à cinq" ("Party of Five"), "Star Trek: La Nouvelle Génération" ("Star Trek: The Next Generation"), "Urgences" ("ER") and "Dingue de toi" ("Mad About You"). 3. You may want to reuse Transparency 36 (**La télé**) from the Level Two transparencies to show French TV listings. 4. You might find a similar graph showing U.S. viewing percentages for different categories of TV programs. For each category, call on students to give you the percentages in French, for example, **En France seulement cinq pour cent des téléspectateurs regardent les émissions sportives, mais aux États-Unis 20 pour cent des téléspectateurs les regardent.** Bring closure to the activity by discussing what cultural values the graphs seem to underline in both countries.

Enquête culturelle

Presque toutes les familles en France (95 pour cent) ont la télévision. En général, les Français passent au moins cinq heures par jour devant la télé à regarder une grande variété d'émissions sur 30 chaînes. Presque 20 pour cent des téléspectateurs paient pour la chaîne Canal+, 7 pour cent ont la télévision par câble et 6 pour cent ont la réception par satellite. En France on reçoit aussi les émissions en français de la Belgique et de la Suisse. De plus, la programmation en d'autres langues vient d'Angleterre, d'Allemagne, d'autres pays européens et des États-Unis.

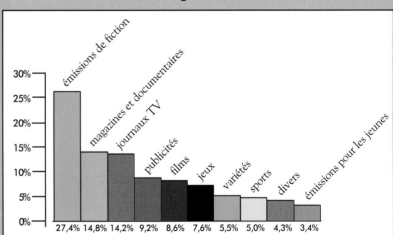

M. et Mme Labrosse choisissent de regarder "Star Trek: La Nouvelle Génération" à la télé.

Que regarde-t-on?

émissions de fiction	magazines et documentaires	journaux TV	publicités	films	jeux	variétés	sports	divers	émissions pour les jeunes
27,4%	14,8%	14,2%	9,2%	8,6%	7,6%	5,5%	5,0%	4,3%	3,4%

Une enquête récente a déterminé que les Français ne sont pas satisfaits des programmes offerts, mais ils continuent à regarder la télévision. Presque tous les Français (91 pour cent) ont une télécommande pour changer rapidement entre chaînes. Avec la télécommande, les Français font beaucoup plus de zapping qu'avant.

Il est intéressant de noter que les heures que les jeunes consacrent aux émissions télévisées commencent à diminuer. C'est probablement parce qu'ils passent plus de temps à regarder des films vidéo avec leurs magnétoscopes ou à jouer aux jeux vidéo. Les adultes, eux aussi, commencent à passer moins de temps devant la télé depuis l'arrivée des multimédia qu'ils regardent sur l'ordinateur. Il y a 21 pour cent des familles qui ont l'ordinateur à la maison. Bon ou mauvais, les Français, comme les Américains, sont des fanas de la télévision.

Répondez aux questions suivantes.

1. Combien de familles françaises ont la télévision?
2. Combien d'heures par jour les Français passent-ils devant la télévision?
3. Pour quelle chaîne française est-ce qu'on paie?
4. Est-ce qu'il y a beaucoup d'émissions qui viennent des États-Unis?
5. Quelles émissions sont les plus populaires en France?
6. Est-ce que les sports ou les documentaires sont plus populaires?
7. Combien de Français ont une télécommande?
8. Est-ce que les jeunes d'aujourd'hui passent plus de temps ou moins de temps à regarder la télé? Pourquoi?
9. Qu'est-ce qui commence à occuper le temps des adultes?
10. Combien de Français ont l'ordinateur à la maison?

Même les enfants savent changer la chaîne avec une télécommande.

CANAL JIMMY

20.00 Seinfeld
Série américaine.

Le rendez-vous. George confie à Jerry qu'il n'existe que peu d'endroits propices à rencontrer l'élue de son cœur. Cynthia se plaint à Elaine de ne pas trouver d'hommes à sa pointure. Jerry et Elaine décident alors de se transformer en joyeux entremetteurs... Avec : Jerry Seinfeld, Jason Alexander, Michael Richards. [14801217]

RTL 9

20.30 La vie à cinq
Série américaine.

Secrets de famille. Bailey se fait du souci au sujet des absences répétées de Charlie... Avec : Matthew Fox, Scott Wolf. [4130867]

Answers

4
1. Presque toutes les familles françaises (95 pour cent) ont la télévision.
2. En général les Français passent au moins cinq heures par jour devant la télévision.
3. On paie pour la chaîne Canal+.
4. Oui, il y a beaucoup d'emissions qui viennent des États-Unis.
5. Les émissions de fiction sont les plus populaires en France.
6. Les documentaires sont plus populaires.
7. Presque tous les Français (91 pour cent) ont une télécommande.
8. Les jeunes d'aujourd'hui passent moins de temps à regarder la télé parce qu'ils regardent les films vidéo avec leurs magnétoscopes ou jouent aux jeux vidéo.
9. Les multimédia commencent à occuper le temps des adultes.
10. Il y a 21 pour cent des familles françaises qui ont l'ordinateur à la maison.

Teacher's Note

Another word for **une télécommande** is **un zappeur**.

Workbook Activities 4-5

Answers

5 1. Six chaînes sont représentées dans cette liste.

2. France 2 offre l'émission américaine "Friends."

3. On peut regarder "La petite maison dans la prairie" deux fois le 19 septembre.

4. "The Price is Right" est "Le juste prix" en français.

5. On peut regarder *Tirez sur le pianiste*, un film de François Truffaut, sur Arte.

6. Arte et M6 offrent deux films chaque jour.

7. On peut regarder des informations trois fois par jour sur la chaîne TF1.

8. France 3 offre un programme sur le sport à 20h35.

9. Answers will vary.

Teacher's Notes

1. The **Structure** section in Unit 3 contains both new and recycled grammatical concepts. 2. The imperfect and the **passé composé** were first compared on page 336 in the second level of *C'est à toi!* 3. You might point out that, unlike the **passé composé**, the imperfect is a simple tense composed of only one word. 4. Remind students that the imperfect is often expressed in English by "was" or "were" plus a verb ending in "-ing." 5. You may want to remind students that in a sentence with both the imperfect and the **passé composé**, the imperfect describes the action that was not completed. Students may benefit from seeing sample sentences illustrated by symbols to help them visualize which part of the sentence is ongoing and which is a completed action. Draw a spiral to indicate the imperfect and a straight line with two end points to indicate the **passé composé**. 6. You might give students a list of common expressions that often indicate when to use the imperfect or the **passé composé**. For example, expressions such as **d'abord, enfin,**

---

160 - TÉLÉVISION

VENDREDI 19 SEPTEMBRE

TF1
12h15: Le juste prix.— 13h: Journal.— 13h50: Les feux de l'amour.— 14h40: Arabesque.— 15h40: Côte Ouest.— 16h35: TF1 jeunesse.— 17h05: 21 Jump Street.— 18h: Pour être libre.— 18h30: Mokshû Patamû.— 19h: Tous en jeu.— 20h: Journal.— 20h45 : Et si ça vous arrivait.— 23h05 : Sans aucun doute.— 0h55: Journal.

FRANCE 2
12h20: Pyramide.— 13h: Journal.— 13h50: Rex.— 14h40: Dans la chaleur de la nuit.— 15h40: La chance aux chansons.— 16h35: Des chiffres et des lettres.— 17h10: Un poisson dans la cafetière.— 17h40: Qui est qui.— 18h15: Friends.— 18h45: C'est l'heure.— 19h25: C'est toujours l'heure.— 20h: Journal.— 20h55: P.J.— 23h20: Bouillon de culture.— 24h: Journal.— 0h20: Ciné-Club « Journal d'une femme de chambre », film de Luis Bunuel avec Jeanne Moreau, Michel Piccoli, Françoise Lugagne, Georges Géret.

FRANCE 3
12h30: Journal.— 13h40: Parole d'expert.— 14h35: « Une lueur au crépuscule », téléfilm de David Jones avec Olympia Dukaris, Lindsay Wagner, Jean Stapleton.— 16h10: Côté jardins.— 16h40: Minikeums.— 17h45: Je passe à la télé.— 18h20: Questions pour un champion.— 18h55: Le 19/20.— 20h05: Fa si la chanter.— 20h35: Tout le sport.— 20h50: Thalassa.— 22h10: Faut pas rêver.— 23h20: Journal.— 23h35: Les dossiers de l'histoire : la sécurité sociale, 30 ans d'indécision.— 0h20: Libre court.

LA 5ᵉ
12h: Fête des bébés.— 12h30: À tout savoir.— 13h: Une heure pour l'emploi.— 14h : Caravanes du désert.— 14h30: Jean XXIII: le bon pape Jean.— 15h30: La jeune fille et la glace.— 16h30: La France aux 1000 villages.— 17h: Cellulo.— 17h30: Allô la terre.— 17h45: Quest-ce qu'on mange: le chocolat.— 18h: La course pour la lune.— 18h30: L'île aux oiseaux.

ARTE
19h: Tracks.— 19h30: 7 1/2.— 20h: Brut.— 20h30: Journal.— 20h45 : « Les allumettes suédoises », téléfilm de Jacques Ertaud avec Naël Marandin, Anne Jacquemin, Dora Doll, Martine Guillaud, Philippe Clay, 3/4.— 22h30 : Grand format.— 23h50: « Tirez sur le pianiste », film de François Truffaut avec Charles Aznavour, Marie Dubois, Nicole Berger, Michèle Mercier.

M6
12h: Madame est servie.— 12h30: La petite maison dans la prairie.— 13h25 : La petite maison dans la prairie.— 15h20: Wolf.— 16h10: Hit machine.— 17h30: Les piègeurs.— 18h: Highlander.— 19h: Los Angeles heat.— 20h: Mister biz.— 20h45: « Armen et Bullik », téléfilm de Alan Cooke avec Mike Connors, Roch Voisine, Marushka Detmers.— 22h35: Two.— 23h30 : « Piège pour un flic », téléfilm de Frank Harris avec Richard Lynch, Chris De Rose, Chuck Jeffreys.

"Mon grand-père était à la fois mon aïeul, mon père, mon guide, mon modèle. Il m'appartenait."

---

5 Voici une page de L'Officiel des Spectacles, *un des magazines qui offrent la liste des émissions à la télé française. Lisez la page et puis répondez aux questions.*

1. Combien de chaînes sont représentées dans cette liste?

2. Quelle chaîne offre l'émission américaine "Friends"?

3. Quelle émission américaine peut-on regarder deux fois le 19 septembre?

4. Quel est le nom en français du jeu télévisé américain "The Price is Right"?

5. Sur quelle chaîne peut-on regarder un film de François Truffaut? Quel film est-ce?

6. Quelles deux chaînes offrent deux films chaque jour?

7. Combien de fois par jour peut-on regarder des informations sur la chaîne TF1?

8. À quelle heure est-ce que France 3 offre un programme sur le sport?

9. Notez que la liste des programmes est faite par chaîne et pas en ordre chronologique comme dans les journaux et magazines américains. Qu'est-ce que ça vous dit des téléspectateurs français?

Journal personnel

In this unit you are introduced to a variety of francophone artists including actors, writers, composers, singers, sculptors and painters, all representative of the culture shared by French speakers. Can you add to this list any other French or French-speaking artists with whom you are familiar? If so, what categories do they represent? What accomplishments make them worth including in your list?

Now imagine that you are writing to tell a French friend about actors, writers, composers, singers, sculptors and painters in American culture. Choose five of these American artists that exemplify our culture. Whom would you pick and why? What categories would be represented in your selection? Write your responses to both sets of questions in your cultural journal.

Structure

The imperfect and the *passé composé*

You have learned two past tenses in French, the imperfect and the **passé composé**. These two tenses are not used in the same way.

The imperfect describes how people or things were in the past, what happened regularly or a condition that existed at some time in the past.

Céline Dion travaillait dans le restaurant de ses parents.	*Céline Dion used to work in her parents' restaurant.*
La famille de Céline passait son temps libre à chanter.	*Céline's family spent their free time singing.*

---

ensuite and finalement often suggest the **passé composé**, whereas expressions like **chaque année, quelquefois, tous les soirs** and **toujours** often suggest the imperfect.

Critical Thinking

Imperfect vs. *Passé Composé*

You might want to illustrate the difference between the two past tenses by telling a story. Tell students **Danielle a l'air déprimé. Pourquoi?** Then on the board write the following three imperfect sentences that describe Danielle's normal routine: **Tous les soirs Danielle conduisait au travail en voiture. Elle accélérait doucement. Elle faisait attention.** Underneath write five sentences that explain how that scenario

changed one day: **Un soir Danielle a été en retard. Elle a accéléré très vite. Elle n'a pas fait attention. Elle n'a pas vu le chien dans la rue. Le chien est mort.** Ask students why the first three sentences of the story are in the imperfect and the last five are in the **passé composé**. Students should be able to explain that the first three sentences are in the imperfect because they express

Parce qu'il faisait beau sur la côte d'Azur, le peintre peignait dehors. (Saint-Tropez)

The **passé composé** indicates a single, completed action.

Dion est née en 1968 près de Montréal.	*Dion was born in 1968 near Montréal.*
Elle a enregistré la chanson "When I Fall in Love."	*She recorded the song "When I Fall in Love."*

To tell a story, use the imperfect to give background information and to describe circumstances in the past. The imperfect answers the question "How were things?" Use the **passé composé** to express what events took place only once in the past. The **passé composé** answers the question "What happened?"

Angélique Kidjo chantait déjà à l'âge de six ans avec sa mère et ses frères.	*Angélique Kidjo was already singing at the age of six with her mother and her brothers.*
Elle a déménagé en France pendant les années 80.	*She moved to France during the 80s.*

The imperfect and the **passé composé** are often used in the same sentence to describe an ongoing action that was interrupted by another action. Use the imperfect to express the background condition or ongoing action and the **passé composé** to describe the completed action.

Kidjo a eu beaucoup de succès avec son troisième album qui était au hit-parade dans beaucoup de pays.	*Kidjo had a lot of success with her third album, which was on the charts in many countries.*
Camille Claudel faisait ses études à Paris quand elle est devenue l'assistante de Rodin.	*Camille Claudel was studying in Paris when she became Rodin's assistant.*

J'ai traversé Paris à pied

Je jouais au golf avec Christelle quand tu m'as téléphoné.

Game

Qui suis-je?

To review vocabulary and the lives of the famous francophone people introduced in this lesson, you might have students play this game. Put them in small groups. Have each student draw a name from these choices: Daniel Auteuil, Marguerite Duras, Céline Dion, Angélique Kidjo, Maurice Jarre, Camille Claudel and Gustave Caillebotte. Then each student in turn goes in front of the rest of the group to answer imperfect and **passé composé** questions from members who try to discover his or her assumed identity. A questioner may ask, for example, **Êtes-vous née au Vietnam**? or **Travailliez-vous dans le restaurant de vos parents**? The student in front of the group answers each question with a complete sentence, using the imperfect or the **passé composé**. After the assumed identity of the first student is guessed, the second student goes in front of the group to answer questions, and so on.

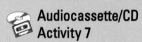

Audiocassette/CD Activity 7

Answers

6 1. avait, a joué
2. a enregistré, était
3. avait, a commencé
4. habitait, est devenu
5. étudiait, a invitée
6. adorait, a donné
7. est née, a déménagé

7 Possible answer:

Mon grand-père est né au Canada en 1938. Sa famille et lui ont déménagé aux États-Unis quand il avait dix ans. Il voulait être acteur, et il passait tout son temps libre au cinéma. Ses vedettes favorites étaient John Wayne et Katharine Hepburn. En 1955 mon grand-père a commencé ses études de théâtre. Trois ans plus tard un metteur en scène très important l'a choisi pour son premier rôle. En 1959 il a fait la connaissance de ma grand-mère. Elle avait 18 ans et était très jolie. Il l'aimait beaucoup. Elle ne voulait pas être la femme d'un acteur, donc il a décidé de quitter le théâtre et de trouver un autre métier. Il a suivi des cours de littérature à l'université. En 1966 il a écrit son premier roman qui a été très populaire. Mon grand-père est devenu un écrivain célèbre.

Quand elle était à New York pour les "Grammy Awards" en 1997, Céline Dion a reçu une statuette pour son album "Falling Into You."

Pratique

6 | *Complétez chaque phrase avec l'imparfait ou le passé composé des verbes indiqués.*

1. Quand Daniel Auteuil... 17 ans, il... dans son premier film. (avoir/jouer)
2. Céline Dion, la chanteuse canadienne qui... "Because You Love Me,"... la plus jeune de 14 enfants. (enregistrer/être)
3. Il y... beaucoup de musiciens dans la famille d'Angélique Kidjo, qui... à chanter à l'âge de six ans. (avoir/commencer)
4. Pendant qu'il... aux États-Unis, Maurice Jarre... le chef d'orchestre du Los Angeles Philharmonic Orchestra. (habiter/devenir)
5. Camille Claudel... à Paris quand Auguste Rodin l'... à devenir son assistante. (étudier/inviter)
6. Gustave Caillebotte, le peintre qui... peindre dehors,... toute sa collection de tableaux à la France. (adorer/donner)
7. Marguerite Duras... au Vietnam, mais elle... en France après son bac. (naître/déménager)

7 | *Vous avez décidé d'écrire l'histoire de la vie de votre grand-père. Avant de commencer, vous l'avez interviewé. Selon les notes que vous avez prises, écrivez des phrases complètes pour raconter les événements les plus importants de sa vie.*

Quand j'avais 28 ans, j'ai écrit mon premier roman.

> 1938: · mon grand-père/naître au Canada
> 1948: · sa famille et lui/déménager aux États-Unis
>   · il/vouloir être acteur
>   · il/passer tout son temps libre au cinéma
>   · ses vedettes favorites/être John Wayne et Katharine Hepburn
> 1955: · il/commencer ses études de théâtre
> 1958: · un metteur en scène très important/le choisir pour son premier rôle
> 1959: · il/faire la connaissance de ma grand-mère
>   · ma grand-mère/avoir 18 ans
>   · elle/être très jolie
>   · il/l'aimer beaucoup
>   · elle/ne pas vouloir être la femme d'un acteur
>   · il/décider de quitter le théâtre et de trouver un autre métier
>   · il/suivre des cours de littérature à l'université
> 1966: · il/écrire son premier roman
>   · le roman/être très populaire
>   · mon grand-père/devenir un écrivain célèbre

« Jacques Martin m'a donné ma première chance... »

Cooperative Group Practice

Quand papa est rentré....

To practice using the imperfect and the **passé composé** when one action is interrupted by another, write four infinitive expressions on the board, for example, **chanter, choisir une émission à la télé, tondre la pelouse** and **faire la lessive.** Have students count off: 1, 2, 3, 4, 1, 2, 3, 4, etc. The first four students form the first group, the second four students form the second group, and so on. Students take turns expressing what they were doing when Dad came home. The first student in each group forms a sentence using **chanter,** the second forms a sentence using **choisir une émission à la télé,** and so on. Students use both the imperfect and the **passé composé** in their sentence, for example, **Je** chantais quand papa est rentré. When all the groups have finished, change the situation and the verbs again, for example, **Quand la prof est entrée.... (parler à mon copain, finir les devoirs, écouter de la musique, écrire au tableau).**

Vous savez que Lucie Aubrac est un des films très connus de Daniel Auteuil. Voici l'histoire de cette femme. Complétez-la en utilisant les verbes entre parenthèses à l'imparfait ou au passé composé.

C'(être) en 1943 pendant la guerre que l'histoire de Lucie Aubrac (se passer). Elle (habiter) à Lyon avec sa famille. Lucie (être) très contente parce qu'elle (avoir) un bon mari et un fils adorable qui (avoir) deux ans. De plus, Lucie et son mari, Raymond, (attendre) leur deuxième enfant. Elle (travailler) dans un lycée où elle (être) professeur d'histoire. Son mari (être) très actif dans la Résistance.

Le 13 mai les Allemands (entrer) dans une maison à Lyon où ils (trouver) six membres de la Résistance. L'un de ces Résistants (être) Raymond Aubrac. Les agents allemands (emmener) Raymond à leur bureau où leur chef, Klaus Barbie, lui (poser) beaucoup de questions. Mais Raymond ne (répondre) pas. Barbie (se fâcher) et le (mettre) en prison. Barbie (déclarer) "Aubrac doit mourir."

Naturellement, Lucie (vouloir) aider son mari. Elle (être) intelligente et douée, et elle (penser) à une idée pour délivrer son mari des Allemands. Lucie (prendre) rendez-vous avec Barbie. Personne ne (savoir) que Raymond (être) le mari de Lucie. Elle (dire) à Barbie que Raymond (être) le père de son enfant. Elle lui (expliquer) que sa famille exigeante (vouloir) un mariage entre les deux avant l'exécution de Raymond. Barbie (croire) l'histoire de Lucie, et les Allemands (emmener) Raymond à la mairie pour le mariage. En route des Résistants (délivrer) Raymond des mains des Allemands.

Avec leur fils, Lucie et Raymond (déménager) en Angleterre où ils (avoir) leur deuxième enfant. Quand enfin Lucie (revenir) en France pour recommencer sa vie, elle (avoir) 30 ans.

Present tense of the irregular verb *plaire*

The verb **plaire** (*to please*) is irregular. Only two of its present tense forms are frequently used, **il/elle/on plaît** and **ils/elles plaisent**. To express likes or dislikes, **plaire** is often used instead of **aimer**. **Plaire** takes an indirect object, using the pronoun **à** with a person or an indirect object pronoun.

La musique dynamique d'Angélique Kidjo **plaît** à tous.	*The dynamic music of Angélique Kidjo pleases everyone.*
Est-ce que les arts vous **plaisent**?	*Do you like the arts?*
Oui, la sculpture me **plaît** beaucoup.	*Yes, I like sculpture a lot.*

The irregular past participle of **plaire** is **plu**.

Est-ce que le roman de Marguerite Duras t'a **plu**?	*Did you like Marguerite Duras' novel?*

TEST
Est-ce que vous lui plaisez ?
36 70 21 03

Est-ce que la fondue plaît à Simone?

CLAUDE SARRAUTE
Mademoiselle, s'il vous plaît !

Workbook Activity 6

Answers

8 était, s'est passée, habitait, était, avait, avait, attendaient, travaillait, était, était, sont entrés, ont trouvé, était, ont emmené, a posé, n'a pas répondu, s'est fâché, l'a mis, a déclaré, voulait, était, a pensé, a pris, savait, était, a dit, était, a expliqué, voulait, a cru, ont emmené, ont délivré, ont déménagé, ont eu, est revenue, avait

Teacher's Notes

1. The story in Activity 8 that recounts Lucie Aubrac's life comes from her autobiography. 2. Klaus Barbie was known as the "Butcher of Lyon." In 1987 he was sentenced to life imprisonment for war crimes. He died in prison in 1991. 3. Cognates used in this story include **adorable**, **Résistance**, **Résistants**, **prison** and **exécution**. 4. Point out to students that they have already seen the verb **plaire** in the expression **s'il vous (te) plaît**. 5. You may want to give students the other present tense forms of **plaire** for recognition: **je plais**, **tu plais**, **nous plaisons** and **vous plaisez**. 6. When **plaire** is used instead of **aimer**, the direct object of **aimer** becomes the subject of **plaire**, for example, **Est-ce que tu aimes ces paysages? Non, ils ne me plaisent pas.**

Teacher's Note

If you have the videocassette series that accompanies the first and second levels of *C'est à toi!*, you might want to do this activity. Select one of the episodes. Push the "pause" button on action scenes, such as Aurélie and Leïla studying. Ask your students, **Qu'est-ce qu'Aurélie et Leïla faisaient quand j'ai arrêté la** vidéocassette? Have students respond with a sentence using both the imperfect and the **passé composé**, for example, **Elles étudiaient quand vous avez arrêté la vidéocassette.**

Paired Practice

Les sketches

For additional practice using the imperfect and the **passé composé** together, put students in pairs. Student A says that he or she saw one of the famous French-speaking people introduced in this lesson. Student B asks a series of questions in French to find out more information: 1. Où étais-tu? 2. Que faisait (la personne célèbre)? 3. Qu'est-ce que tu as fait quand tu as vu (la personne célèbre)? Have each pair present its skit to the class. Then, orally or in writing, have the other students summarize Student A's responses, for example, **Marc était à Montréal dans un café. Céline Dion y mangeait un sandwich. Marc l'a prise en photo.**

Audiocassette/CD
Activities 9-10

Answers

9 1. La nature morte plaît beaucoup à Madeleine.
2. Les sculptures ne plaisent pas aux élèves de Mme Chapelle.
3. Le paysage ne plaît pas à M. Roland.
4. Les vases plaisent beaucoup à M. et Mme Deslauriers.
5. Les sculptures plaisent beaucoup à Mme Chapelle.
6. La nature morte ne plaît pas à Pierre-Jean.

10 1. Est-ce que les romans autobiographiques te plaisent? Et toi, est-ce que les romans autobiographiques te plaisent?
2. Est-ce que le cinéma français te plaît? Et toi, est-ce que le cinéma français te plaît?
3. Est-ce que le théâtre te plaît? Et toi, est-ce que le théâtre te plaît?
4. Est-ce que le ballet te plaît? Et toi, est-ce le ballet te plaît?
5. Est-ce que les chansons de Céline Dion te plaisent? Et toi, est-ce que les chansons de Céline Dion te plaisent?
6. Est-ce que la musique africaine te plaît? Et toi, est-ce que la musique africaine te plaît?
7. Est-ce que les tableaux impressionnistes te plaisent? Et toi, est-ce que les tableaux impressionnistes te plaisent?
8. Est-ce que les sculptures de Rodin te plaisent? Et toi, est-ce que les sculptures de Rodin te plaisent?
Students' responses to these questions will vary.

Cooperative Group Practice

Les blasons

Put students in small groups of four or five to make a coat of arms. Have them divide it into four sections, illustrating items that they like, such as foods, sports, pastimes and courses. The first student holds up his or her coat of arms and says sentences using **plaire** in the affirmative, for example, **La glace me plaît**, **Le football me plaît**, **Les jeux vidéo me plaisent** and **Le français me plaît**.

Paired Practice

Le musée des beaux-arts

Put students in pairs. Post reproductions of French art at the front of the room, for example, Monet's water lilies, two still lifes by Caillebotte, a landscape by Pissarro and two sculptures by Rodin. Have students pretend they are in an art museum. The students should ask each other if they like the art works exhibited. For example, Student A asks, **Est-ce que la collection de Monet te plaît?** Student B responds, **Oui, elle me plaît** or **Non, elle ne me plaît pas**. Then Student B asks Student A's opinion about the same art. When each pair has finished giving opinions about all the art, you may want to have the pair make intersecting circles in order to list the art they both admire. Then ask students to share with the class which art pleases both of them, for example, **Les natures mortes de Caillebotte nous plaisent.**

Pratique

9 *Dites si ce que ces personnes regardent au musée leur plaît beaucoup ou ne leur plaît pas, selon les illustrations.*

Modèles:

Claire et Dominique
Le paysage plaît beaucoup à Claire et Dominique.

Didier
Les vases ne plaisent pas à Didier.

1. Madeleine
2. les élèves de Mme Chapelle
3. M. Roland
4. M. et Mme Deslauriers
5. Mme Chapelle
6. Pierre-Jean

Modèle:

la littérature
Élève A: Est-ce que la littérature te plaît?
Élève B: Oui, elle me plaît beaucoup. Et toi, est-ce que la littérature te plaît?
Élève A: Non, elle ne me plaît pas du tout.

10 *Avec un(e) partenaire, posez des questions sur ce qui vous plaît. Puis répondez aux questions. Suivez le modèle.*

1. les romans autobiographiques
2. le cinéma français
3. le théâtre
4. le ballet
5. les chansons de Céline Dion
6. la musique africaine
7. les tableaux impressionnistes
8. les sculptures de Rodin

Est-ce que les films Spielberg te plaisent?

Oui, ils me plaisent beaucoup.

The subjunctive of regular verbs after *il faut que*

Verb forms in both English and French depend on the tense (time of the action) and the mood (attitude of the speaker) they reflect. You already know two moods in French: the indicative, used to state certainty or fact; and the imperative, used to give a command. A third mood is called the subjunctive. This mood is used to express necessity, doubt, uncertainty, possibility, wish, feeling or emotion.

In French the subjunctive usually appears after **que (qu')** *(that)* in a dependent clause. What comes before **que** is one of several expressions. The first of the expressions that you will learn is the expression of necessity **il faut**. You already know that to express necessity or obligation in general, you use **il faut** plus an infinitive. However, to say who specifically needs to do something, you use **il faut que** plus a verb in the subjunctive.

Il faut **travailler**.	*It is necessary to work.*
Il faut que Malick **travaille**.	*Malick must work. (It is necessary for Malick to work.)*

To form the subjunctive of most verbs, drop the **-ent** of the present tense **ils/elles** form and add the ending **-e, -es, -e, -ions, -iez** or **-ent**, depending on the corresponding subject. Here are the subjunctive forms of regular **-er, -ir** and **-re** verbs.

	chanter	*choisir*	*vendre*
que je (j')	chante	choisisse	vende
que tu	chantes	choisisses	vendes
qu'il/elle/on	chante	choisisse	vende
que nous	chantions	choisissions	vendions
que vous	chantiez	choisissiez	vendiez
qu'ils/elles	chantent	choisissent	vendent

Note that the **nous** and **vous** subjunctive forms are exactly like those for the imperfect. The subjunctive in French can be expressed by the present, future, conditional or an infinitive in English.

Il faut qu'on **assiste** aux concerts d'Angélique Kidjo pour profiter de sa musique dynamique.	*It's necessary to attend (that one attends) Angélique Kidjo's concerts to benefit from her dynamic music.*
Il faut que vous **regardiez** le chef-d'œuvre de Caillebotte à Chicago.	*You'll have to look at Caillebotte's masterpiece in Chicago.*
Il faut que vous **pensiez** aux films et à la musique.	*You should think about movies and music.*

Il faut que ça change

C'EST MAINTENANT QU'IL FAUT TENTER VOTRE CHANCE !

Pourquoi faut-il que tu t'entraînes?

Ben, je vais courir le marathon dans quinze jours.

Workbook Activities 7-8

Teacher's Notes

1. The subjunctive of irregular verbs will be presented in **Leçon B**. 2. You may want to tell students that the indicative describes a definite action that took place in the past, is taking place now or will take place in the future. The subjunctive describes an action that may or may not take place. 3. The mnemonic device WEDDINGS (**w**ish, **e**motion, **d**esire, **d**emands, **i**mpersonal, **n**egation, **g**eneral, **s**uperlative) may help your students remember when to use the subjunctive. Examples of these categories include: (wish) **Je souhaite que vous finissiez vos devoirs.** (emotion) **Je suis heureux que vous m'écoutiez.** (desire) **Je désire que vous chantiez en français.** (demands) **J'exige que vous vous brossiez les dents.** (impersonal expressions) **Il est bon que vous y attendiez.** (negation) **Je ne crois pas que vous réussissiez à l'examen.** (general) **Est-ce qu'il y a quelqu'un qui puisse m'aider?** (superlative) **C'est le plus beau film que je connaisse.** 4. The subjunctive appears in the dependent or subordinate clause, and the expression of necessity is in the independent or main clause. When the subjects of the dependent and independent clauses are the same, an infinitive is used. But if they are different, the subjunctive must be used. 5. Except for **aller**, every **-er** verb, including orthographically changing verbs, follows the regular pattern. Therefore, the **je, tu, il/elle/on** and **ils/elles** subjunctive forms of **-er** verbs are the same as those in the present tense. 6. Remind students that verbs ending in **-ier** have **-ii** in the **nous** and **vous** forms of the subjunctive, for example, **Il faut que nous étudiions.**

Teacher's Note

You might want to have students prepare a report card for themselves to assess their progress in each course at this point in the school year. You could use the report card on page 109 in the first level of *C'est à toi!* as a model. In the left-hand column students list their courses in French. In the middle column they give themselves the grade they think they have earned in each course thus far. In the right-hand column they write a comment they think each teacher would make to suggest improvement, for example, **Il faut que tu... travailles plus, parles moins, finisses tes devoirs chaque jour.**

Critical Thinking

The Subjunctive in English

Write the sentence "It is necessary that you be on time" on the board. Ask students to identify what form of "to be" is usually used in English with the pronoun "you" ("are"). Explain that this is an example of the subjunctive in English. Ask students to think of other examples of the subjective in English.

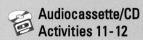

Audiocassette/CD Activities 11-12

Answers

11 Il faut que papa et Serge nettoient le garage.
Il faut que Sylvie et moi, nous rangions le séjour.
Il faut que papa tonde la pelouse.
Il faut que je mette la table.
Il faut que Daniel sorte la poubelle.
Il faut que Sophie et Sylvie finissent leurs devoirs.

12 1. Alors, il faut que je m'arrête au musée Rodin.
2. Alors, il faut que Sabrina visite le musée Picasso.
3. Alors, il faut que Marie-France achète des CDs de Céline Dion.
4. Alors, il faut que Mireille écoute l'album *Logozo*.
5. Alors, il faut que tes parents entendent la bande originale de *Doctor Zhivago*.
6. Alors, il faut que tu assistes à *Manon des Sources*.
7. Alors, il faut que Jean-Jacques loue *Jean de Florette*.
8. Alors, il faut que nous lisions *L'Amant* de Marguerite Duras.

Teacher's Notes

1. After students have completed Activity 11, you might consider having them write a paragraph describing what chores their family members are responsible for. Other possible chores to include are **arroser les plantes, passer l'aspirateur, repasser les vête-ments, enlever la poussière** and **préparer les repas.** 2. Before beginning Activity 12, you may want to introduce the expression **Chacun son goût.** (*Every person to his or her own taste.*)

Pratique

11 *Dites quelles corvées les membres de la famille Vannier doivent faire.*

Modèle:
Il faut que maman nourrisse Médor.

Il faut que Clarisse aide sa mère au jardin.

maman: nourrir Médor

papa: tondre la pelouse

papa et Serge: nettoyer le garage

moi: mettre la table

Daniel: sortir la poubelle

Sylvie et moi: ranger le séjour

Sophie et Sylvie: finir leurs devoirs

Modèle:
Nous aimons les tableaux impressionnistes de Caillebotte. (passer par le musée d'art à Chicago pour voir son chef-d'œuvre)
Alors, il faut que vous passiez par le musée d'art à Chicago pour voir son chef-d'œuvre.

12 *Naturellement, chaque personne a des goûts (tastes) différents. Faites une recommandation fondée sur les préférences des personnes suivantes. Suivez le modèle.*

1. Tu trouves *Le Penseur* formidable. (s'arrêter au musée Rodin)
2. L'art du 20ᵉᵐᵉ siècle plaît à Sabrina. (visiter le musée Picasso)
3. Marie-France adore la chanson "My Heart Will Go On." (acheter des CDs de Céline Dion)
4. Les cassettes d'Angélique Kidjo intéressent Mireille. (écouter l'album *Logozo*)
5. La musique de Maurice Jarre plaît à mes parents. (entendre la bande originale de *Doctor Zhivago*)
6. Les films de Daniel Auteuil me plaisent. (assister à *Manon des Sources*)
7. Jean-Jacques préfère les films de Gérard Depardieu. (louer *Jean de Florette*)
8. Vous aimez les romans auto-biographiques. (lire *L'Amant* de Marguerite Duras)

Si vous êtes à Paris, il faut que vous le musée Rodin.

Game

Career Advice

Put your students in small groups of four or five. Prepare two sets of note cards for each group. In the first set write six different noun and pronoun subjects, for example, **je, tu, on, Clarisse et moi, Amine et toi** and **les élèves.** In the second set write professions in which students in your class have expressed an interest. The first student in each group takes a card from both stacks, for example, **je/ingénieur.** Within a ten-second time frame, the student gives a logical piece of advice on what the indicated person must do to reach his or her stated career goal, for example, **Pour être ingénieur, il faut que j'étudie les maths.** If the student thinks up appropriate advice within the allotted time frame, he or she earns a point. Students alternate drawing cards until all the professions have been used. The student with the most points at the end of the game wins.

Est-ce qu'une profession dans les arts vous intéresse? Avec un(e) partenaire, demandez s'il faut faire certaines choses pour y réussir. Puis répondez aux questions. Alternez les questions et les réponses avec votre partenaire. Suivez le modèle.

1. sculpteur/travailler dur
2. vedette/choisir de bons rôles
3. metteur en scène/s'entendre avec tout le monde
4. acteur ou actrice/se perfectionner en théâtre
5. chanteur ou chanteuse/donner des concerts
6. compositeur/suivre beaucoup de cours de musique
7. chef d'orchestre/étudier la musique du 17ème siècle
8. écrivain/écrire chaque jour

Modèle:

peintre/montrer ses tableaux à des expositions

Élève A: Pour devenir peintre, est-ce qu'il faut que je montre mes tableaux à des expositions?

Élève B: Oui, pour devenir peintre, il faut que tu montres tes tableaux à des expositions.

Pour devenir écrivain, est-ce qu'il faut que je lise des romans d'auteurs célèbres?

Oui, pour devenir écrivain, il faut que tu lises des romans d'auteurs célèbres.

Communication

Quels arts vous plaisent? Interviewez un(e) partenaire. Copiez la grille suivante. Demandez à votre partenaire si chaque art indiqué lui plaît. Mettez un ✓ dans l'espace blanc convenable. Si la réponse est "oui," demandez un exemple. Puis demandez l'impression de votre partenaire. Écrivez l'exemple et l'impression dans les espaces indiqués. Puis changez de rôles.

art	non	oui	exemple	impression
1. les films d'épouvante		✓	*Scream*	formidable
2. les comédies				
3. les émissions de télé				
4. les pièces de théâtre				
5. les tableaux				
6. les sculptures				
7. les chansons				
8. les romans autobiographiques				

Modèle:

les films d'épouvante
Élève A: Est-ce que les films d'épouvante te plaisent?
Élève B: Oui, ils me plaisent beaucoup.
Élève A: Alors, quel est ton film d'épouvante favori?
Élève B: C'est *Scream*.
Élève A: Et comment tu trouves ce film?
Élève B: Il est formidable.

 Audiocassette/CD Activity 13

Answers

13 Possible answers:

1. Pour devenir sculpteur, est-ce qu'il faut que je travaille dur? Oui, pour devenir sculpteur, il faut que tu travailles dur.
2. Pour devenir vedette, est-ce qu'il faut que je choisisse de bons rôles? Oui, pour devenir vedette, il faut que tu choisisses de bons rôles.
3. Pour devenir metteur en scène, est-ce qu'il faut que je m'entende avec tout le monde? Oui, pour devenir metteur en scène, il faut que tu t'entendes avec tout le monde.
4. Pour devenir acteur, est-ce qu'il faut que je me perfectionne en théâtre? Oui, pour devenir acteur, il faut que tu te perfectionnes en théâtre.
5. Pour devenir chanteur, est-ce qu'il faut que je donne des concerts? Oui, pour devenir chanteur, il faut que tu donnes des concerts.
6. Pour devenir compositeur, est-ce qu'il faut que je suive beaucoup de cours de musique? Oui, pour devenir compositeur, il faut que tu suives beaucoup de cours de musique.
7. Pour devenir chef d'orchestre, est-ce qu'il faut que j'étudie la musique du 17ème siècle? Oui, pour devenir chef d'orchestre, il faut que tu étudies la musique du 17ème siècle.
8. Pour devenir écrivain, est-ce qu'il faut que j'écrive chaque jour? Oui, pour devenir écrivain, il faut que tu écrives chaque jour.

Cooperative Group Practice

Il faut qu'on....

Divide students into small groups. Write four topics on the board, such as **un bon conducteur, un bon élève, un bon ami** and **un bon père**. Each group writes as many sentences as possible using **Il faut qu'on...** that express what it takes to be a good driver, student, friend or father, for example, **Il faut qu'on (accélère doucement, regarde à droite et à gauche, s'arrête au feu rouge) pour être un bon conducteur.** When each group has completed its list for each topic, compile a classroom list to see how many different sentences students could come up with that use the subjunctive of regular verbs.

Paired Practice

Les directions

Put students in pairs. Have each pair write directions on how to get to a location in your school from the French classroom. Then students exchange their directions with those of another pair. Students read their new set of directions and guess the destination described.

Workbook Activity 9

Listening Activity 1

Quiz *Leçon A*

Advanced Placement

Teacher's Note

Sur la bonne piste, Leçon A, is designed to develop skills that will help students prepare to take the Advanced Placement Exam in French Language. In this lesson **Sur la bonne piste** develops writing proficiency. Students focus on explaining in detail when narrating in the past tense.

15 *Groupez-vous avec deux autres paires d'élèves. Avec vos grilles de l'Activité 14, discutez les résultats des interviews sur les arts qui vous plaisent. Puis préparez une affiche qui annonce votre "hit-parade," la liste des exemples favoris de votre groupe dans chaque catégorie, et montrez-la à la classe.*

16 *Imaginez que vous avez un petit frère ou une petite sœur de six ans et que c'est la rentrée. Faites une liste de dix choses qu'il faut faire et qu'il ne faut pas faire quand il/elle va à l'école pour la première fois. Utilisez **il (ne) faut (pas) que tu....***

Modèle:
En allant à l'école, il ne faut pas que tu montes dans la voiture d'une personne que tu ne connais pas.

 ## *Sur la bonne piste*

Explaining in Detail

To tell an interesting story, you need to explain in detail. As you narrate, keep two things in mind: background description and events. In French, descriptions are generally in the **imparfait** and listed events take the **passé composé**.

Think of narration as a simple listing of events in chronological order:

Pierre *est arrivé* chez Gabrielle.
Il *est sorti* de sa voiture.
Il *s'est approché* de la porte.
Gabrielle *a répondu* à la porte.

The preceding narration of events is bland and tells us nothing other than the general sequence of events, for we do not know who these characters are or why they are meeting. Background description can set the stage for these events, making the location, time and occasion more realistic and interesting. Suppose the narration had begun like this:

C'était lundi après-midi.
Il *faisait* du soleil, mais Gabrielle *était* déprimée.
C'était son anniversaire, et elle *voulait* le fêter avec des amis.

Now the story begins to take shape, and our interest in the characters and events is heightened. To enhance and add to the narration, combine and weave the events and the descriptions together by mentioning the characters' actions and feelings, as well as places and objects in the story.

Pierre est arrivé chez Gabrielle.
Il est sorti de sa voiture. *Il avait dans la main un cadeau.*
Il s'est approché de la porte *pendant qu'il chantait "Joyeux anniversaire."*
Gabrielle a répondu à la porte *avec anticipation.*

To add detail to any description, use:

• adjectives
Il est sorti de sa *nouvelle* voiture *de sport rouge.*
Il avait dans la main un cadeau *énorme couvert* de papier *jaune* et *rose.*

- adverbs

    Pierre est arrivé *un peu en retard.*
    Il est *vite* sorti de sa voiture.

- relative clauses

    Pierre, *qui était un ami du frère de Gabrielle,* est arrivé.
    Il avait dans la main un cadeau énorme *qu'il venait d'acheter dans la boutique préférée de Gabrielle.*

- appositives (expressions after a noun, usually set off by commas, that help explain in detail):

    Pierre, *un grand garçon marocain,* est arrivé.
    Gabrielle, *une petite fille timide,* a répondu à la porte.

By now you are probably curious about Gabrielle's gift and her relationship with Pierre. Putting all these elements together makes any story come alive and motivates the reader to find out what happens next.

Now read the basic events that take place in the two paragraphs that follow. For each one, enhance the narration by adding interesting elements to create an original, more fully developed paragraph.

1. Claire a entendu quelque chose. Elle s'est réveillée. Elle est allée à la fenêtre. Elle l'a ouverte. Elle a vu un chat dans l'arbre.

2. Bernard est entré dans le parc d'attractions. Il a eu une consultation avec une voyante. Il a mangé. Il a essayé des jeux d'adresse.

M. et Mme Bonnaffé, qui sont en vacances, voyagent en bateau sur un canal français.

Teacher's Notes

1. To prepare for Activity 17, you may want to do this activity with students. Choose a children's story in French that is told in the imperfect and the **passé composé**. Use correction fluid to delete each verb, putting an infinitive in each blank space. Then call on students to read the story aloud, replacing each infinitive with the appropriate imperfect or **passé composé** verb form. You might also discuss how the adjectives, adverbs, relative clauses and appositives make the story more interesting. 2. You might consider selecting an interesting news article in a French magazine. Make a copy for students and have them highlight with a marker the adjectives, adverbs, relative clauses and appositives the reporter uses to create a fully developed story. 3. After students have completed Activity 17, you might ask them to write a short autobiography in the imperfect and the **passé composé**. When completed, pair each student with a peer editor who can suggest where additional detail could be added to make the autobiography more interesting. You may want to model the types of comments peer reviewers might make by using one student's autobiography as an example. Comments should be constructive and nonthreatening, for example, "As a reader, I would like to know what kind of house you moved to. Can you add some adjectives here?"

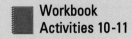

Workbook
Activities 10-11

Audiocassette/CD
Exposition

Transparency 13

Teacher's Note

Communicative functions that
are recycled in this lesson are
"sequencing events," "stating a
warning," "asking for information"
and "pointing out something."

Leçon B

In this lesson you will be
able to:

➤ ask about importance and
unimportance

➤ express importance and
unimportance

➤ inquire about agreement
and disagreement

➤ give opinions

➤ inquire about surprise

➤ compare

➤ inquire about possibility
and impossibility

➤ express possibility and
impossibility

➤ express need and
necessity

➤ tell location

guide

prix

Qu'est-ce que vous achèteriez au kiosque à journa

Quand vous êtes à Paris, il
y a une grande variété de
distractions. Mais comment
choisir? Ce n'est pas difficile.
D'abord, pour tout savoir sur
les spectacles, il faut que vous
alliez au kiosque à journaux°
pour acheter un guide. Le
prix? Ce n'est pas cher. Les
renseignements° sont
valables° pour une semaine.

un kiosque à journaux où vous achetez des journaux, des guides et des magazines; **des
renseignements** *information*; **valable** *valid*

genre

films en exclusivité

EXPLICATION — GENRE DES SIGNES — DES FILMS

○ Films classés X
☐ Interdits aux moins de 16 ans.
△ Interdits aux moins de 12 ans.
◆ Recommandés aux très jeunes.
(vo) : version originale
(va) : version anglaise

A Aventure
B Biographie
C Comédie
D Drame

E Epouvante Horreur
F Fantastique Science-Fiction
G Guerre
H Historique
J Dessin animé Vie animaux
K Karaté

M Film musical
O Comédie dramatique
P Policier Espionnage
S Erotisme
W Western
X Divers

Est-il possible que vous sachiez l'indice° d'un film en avance? Mais oui! Vous n'avez qu'à regarder les signes. Attention! Il est possible qu'un film soit interdit.° Il est aussi utile° que vous ayez une idée du genre de film que vous préférez.

description {

C ◆ **ZAZIE DANS LE MÉTRO** - Franç., coul. (60 - 1h28). Comédie, de Louis Malle: Le séjour mouvementé d'une petite provinciale délurée à Paris. D'après le roman de Raymond Queneau. Avec Catherine Demongeot, Philippe Noiret, Jacques Dufilho, Hubert Deschamps, Vittorio Caprioli, Annie Fratellini, Carla Marlier, Yvonne Clech, Antoine Roblot, Nicolas Bataille. **Denfert 14ᵉ**.

Pour tout savoir sur un film, il est indispensable que vous fassiez attention à la description dans le guide. Où a-t-on tourné° le film? C'est un film en noir et blanc ou en couleur? Est-il surprenant que vous reconnaissiez° le nom du metteur en scène? C'est Louis Malle. Est-ce qu'on recommande le film aux jeunes?°

durée ——→

cinéma ——→

O ◆ **JOUR ET LA NUIT (LE)** - Franç., coul. (96 - 1h52). Comédie dramatique, de Bernard-Henri Levy: Au Mexique, dans l'étrange climat d'une hacienda délabrée, la malédiction d'un premier roman poursuivant un écrivain vieillissant et une femme mystérieuse fait d'une jeune actrice une nouvelle victime. Avec Alain Delon, Lauren Bacall, Xavier Beauvois, Marianne Denicourt, Arielle Dombasle, Julie Du Page, Jean-Pierre Kalfon, Francisco Rabal, Karl Zéro. **Saint-Lambert 15ᵉ**.

Est-il important que vous ne preniez pas le métro trop tard? Voilà la durée du film. Où passe-t-on le film? Pouvez-vous trouver le nom du cinéma? Il est en bas.°

un indice *rating;* **interdit(e)** *prohibited;* **utile** *useful;* **tourner** *to shoot (a movie);*
reconnaître *to recognize;* **des jeunes** *des jeunes gens;* **en bas** *at the bottom*

Teacher's Notes

1. Point out that this guide also indicates whether a film is shown in the **version originale** (vo) or in the **version anglaise** (va). Make students aware of the abbreviations used in the guides, for example, **Franc.** for a film in French and **coul.** for en couleur. 2. Most movie theaters in Paris offer reduced prices to students, as well as a general price reduction to all ticket holders on Monday. 3. Louis Malle (1932-95), a French filmmaker who married actress Candice Bergen in 1980, began his career as a cameraman and codirector with Jacques Cousteau, filming an undersea documentary *Le Monde du Silence* (1956). He is considered the most wide-ranging of the **auteurs** who comprised the French **nouvelle vague** in the late 1950s, using the camera innovatively, broaching controversial subjects and exerting complete creative control of all aspects of his films. In 1957 he directed his first nondocumentary feature film, *Ascenseur pour l'Échafaud*, a psychological thriller starring Jeanne Moreau. *Zazie dans le métro* (1960), a zany, dadaistic comedy, was followed by *Vie Privée*, loosely based on Brigitte Bardot's life, and *Viva Maria!* (1965), a lampoon of action pictures starring Moreau and Bardot. Malle often explored themes of social alienation and isolation, perhaps most effectively in the grim tragedy *Le Feu Follet* (1963). In *Le Souffle au Cœur* (1971) Malle tells the touchingly comic story of a young boy's coming of age in the early 1950s. After moving to the U.S. in 1975, Malle made films in English, such as *Pretty Baby* (1978), *My Dinner with André* (1981) and *Uncle Vanya on 42nd Street* (1994). An excerpt from his screenplay for *Au revoir, les enfants* is included in the **Sur la bonne piste** section of this lesson. 4. Point out that **reconnaître** belongs to the **connaître** verb family.

Le cinéma 14 Juillet Odéon se trouve dans le 6ᵉ arrondissement. (Paris)

O ◆ **HIROSHIMA MON AMOUR** - Franco-japonais, noir et blanc (59 - 1h30). Comédie dramatique, de Alain Resnais: Dans Hiroshima détruite, les amours éphémères d'une Française venue tourner un film au Japon et d'un architecte nippon. Scénario et dialogues de Marguerite Duras. Un film-clé de la Nouvelle Vague. Avec Emmanuelle Riva, Eiji Okada, Bernard Fresson, Stella Dassas. **Accatone 5ᵉ**

→ **arrondissement**

Il est essentiel que vous sachiez dans quel arrondissement° se trouve° le cinéma. Voilà l'abréviation du cinquième arrondissement. Il est impossible que vous ne voyiez pas le nom de Marguerite Duras. C'est la scénariste° du film. C'est aussi elle qui a écrit le roman du même nom.

drame vécu →

D ◆ **LUCIE AUBRAC** - Franç., coul. (96 - 1h55). Drame vécu, de Claude Berri: Grande figure de la Résistance, l'amour pousse Lucie aux plus téméraires actions pour arracher, à Klaus Barbie et à la Gestapo, son mari, Raymond, arrêté à Caluire avec Jean Moulin. D'après "Ils partiront dans l'ivresse" de Lucie Aubrac. Avec Carole Bouquet, Daniel Auteuil, Jean-Roger Milo, Éric Boucher, Patrice Chéreau, Heino Ferch, Bernard Verley, Jean Martin, Hubert Saint-Macary, Andrzej Seweryn, Pascal Greggory, Jean-Louis Richard, Jacques Bonnaffé, Alain Sachs. **UGC Ciné Cité Les Halles 1ᵉʳ, Gaumont Opéra Premier 2ᵉ, UGC Danton 6ᵉ, UGC Rotonde 6ᵉ, Gaumont Ambassade 8ᵉ, UGC Triomphe 8ᵉ, UGC Opéra 9ᵉ, UGC Lyon Bastille 12ᵉ, Gaumont Gobelins Fauvette 13ᵉ, Gaumont Alésia 14ᵉ, Gaumont Parnasse 14ᵉ, Gaumont Convention 15ᵉ, Pathé Wepler 18ᵉ, Gambetta 20ᵉ.**

Les Français trouvent que le cinéma est un passe-temps extra. À combien de cinémas passe-t-on ce film? Ce film n'est pas le même° genre que les autres films de Daniel Auteuil. C'est un drame vécu,° une histoire vraie.

→ **bureau de location**

On peut aussi voir beaucoup de spectacles formidables à Paris. Vous ne trouvez pas? Pour réserver une place,° il vaut mieux° que vous veniez au bureau de location.° Il est bon qu'il y en ait plusieurs.

---

un arrondissement *district;* **se trouver** être situé(e); **un(e) scénariste** la personne qui écrit un scénario; **même** *same;* **vécu(e)** *real-life;* **une place** *seat;* **il vaut mieux** *it is better;* **un bureau de location** où vous achetez des billets

HUCHETTE, **TP** 23, rue de la Huchette, Pl. St-Michel (5ᵉ), Mᵒ St-Michel. (H). Loc. 01 43 26 38 99 (sf dim) de 17h à 21h.

tarif ⟶ **À 19h (sauf dim), pl. 100F, étud. (sauf sam) 80F:**

D'Eugène Ionesco, mise en scène de Nicolas Bataille, avec LES COMÉDIENS DU THÉÂTRE DE LA HUCHETTE:

LA CANTATRICE CHAUVE

Une autopsie de la société contemporaine par le truchement de propos ridicules par leur banalité et que tiennent deux couples au coin du feu.

D'Eugène Ionesco, mise en scène de M. Cuvelier par LES COMÉDIENS DU THÉÂTRE DE LA HUCHETTE

LA LEÇON

Un professeur timide, une élève insolente. Mais les rôles vont changer, la situation se renverser. Lui tyrannique, elle soumise, ce nouveau rapport de force aboutira au crime.

Peut-être que les pièces de théâtre vous plaisent. En général les étudiants paient un tarif réduit° aux théâtres. Si vous y allez, il est nécessaire que vous regardiez l'abréviation Mᵒ dans le guide qui vous dit où descendre° du métro.

À la Comédie-Française on peut voir des pièces de théâtre classiques. (Paris)

réduit(e) moins cher/chère; **descendre** ne pas monter

Répondez aux questions d'après les renseignements sur les distractions à Paris.

1. Où faut-il aller pour acheter un guide sur les spectacles à Paris?
2. Qu'est-ce qu'il faut faire pour savoir l'indice d'un film avant de le voir?
3. Qui est le metteur en scène du film *Zazie dans le métro*?
4. Quel est le nom du cinéma où on passe le film *Le Jour et La Nuit*?
5. Quelle est la durée de ce film?
6. Quand est-ce qu'on a tourné le film *Hiroshima mon amour*?
7. Quel est le genre du film *Lucie Aubrac*?
8. À combien de cinémas passe-t-on ce film?
9. Quels sont trois endroits où on peut acheter des billets pour le spectacle "Holiday on Ice"?
10. Combien paient les étudiants au Théâtre de la Huchette?

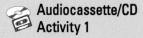

Audiocassette/CD Activity 1

Answers

1 Possible answers:

1. Pour acheter un guide sur les spectacles à Paris il faut aller au kiosque à journaux.
2. Pour savoir l'indice d'un film avant de le voir il faut regarder les signes.
3. Le metteur en scène du film *Zazie dans le métro* est Louis Malle.
4. On passe le film *Le Jour et La Nuit* au cinéma Saint-Lambert.
5. La durée de ce film est une heure 52 minutes.
6. On a tourné le film *Hiroshima mon amour* en 1959.
7. *Lucie Aubrac* est un drame vécu.
8. On passe ce film à 14 cinémas.
9. On peut acheter des billets pour le spectacle "Holiday on Ice" au Palais des Sports, au Virgin Megastore et aux Galeries Lafayette.
10. Au Théâtre de la Huchette les étudiants paient 80 francs.

Teacher's Notes

1. You may want to reuse Transparency 64 (**Le plan de métro**) from the Level One transparencies to show students the Saint-Michel metro station. 2. An excerpt from *La cantatrice chauve* will be presented in Unit 5 in **Sur la bonne piste**. 3. Three loud knocks, called **les trois coups**, are heard backstage to signal that a play is about to begin. 4. **Descendre**, meaning "to go down," was introduced in Unit 8 in the second level of *C'est à toi!*

Answers

2 Possible answers:

1. le genre
2. le film
3. la durée
4. le metteur en scène
5. la description
6. les vedettes
7. les cinémas
8. le théâtre
9. le métro
10. l'arrondissement
11. le prix des places
12. le tarif réduit
13. les pièces

3 Answers will vary.

2 | *Choisissez l'expression convenable de la liste suivante qui correspond à chaque expression indiquée dans le guide.*

l'arrondissement	les cinémas	la description
les vedettes	la durée	le genre
les pièces	le prix des places	le metteur en scène
le tarif réduit	le théâtre	le métro
le film		

D CHACUN CHERCHE SON CHAT Franç., coul. (95 1h35) Comédie de Cédric Klapisch. À la veille de partir en vacances, Chloé cherche quelqu'un pour garder son chat noir. Une occasion pour elle d'apprendre à connaître les gens de son quartier proche de la Bastille. Avec Garance Clavel, Olivier Py, Zinedine Soualem, Renée Le Calm, Romain Duris, Estelle Larrivaz, Nicolas Koretzky. **14 Juillet Parnasse 6ᵉ, Denfert 14ᵉ, Grand Pavois 15ᵉ, Saint-Lambert 15ᵉ.**

COMÉDIE-FRANÇAISE RICHELIEU NA Pl. du Théâtre Français (2ᵉ), Mᵒ Palais-Royal. Loc. uniquement 2 semaines à l'avance jour pour jour, par tél: 01 44 58 15 15 ou aux guichets. Pl. de 30F à 185F. TJ dernière minute: 65F (- 25 ans, étud. - 27 ans) 3/4 d'h. avant le début de la représentation. **Voir aussi rubrique "Spectacles musicaux".**

À 20h30 les 19, 31 mars, 4, 9, 18, 23 avril et 2 mai.

À 14h30 les 22, 30 mars, 5, 13, 19 avril et 3 mai (dernière):

De Marivaux, mise en scène de Jean-Pierre Miguel, avec Catherine SAMIE, Gérard GIROUDON, Andrzej SEWERYN, Cécile BRUNE, Florence VIALA, Michel ROBIN, Laurent d'OLCE, Nicolas LORMEAU, Jean-Pascal ABRIBAT, Roch-Antoine ALBALADEJO:

LES FAUSSES CONFIDENCES

Une peinture exacte et une critique acérée de la société monarchique et mondaine du temps de Marivaux.

À 20h30 les 20, 24, 26, 30 mars, 1ᵉʳ, 3, 7, 10, 17, 21, 24 avril. À 14hh30 dim 23 mars, les 6, 12, 20 avril:

De Molière, avec C. FERRAN, J. DAUTREMAY, A. KESSLER, P. TORRETON, I. TYCZKA, C. BRUNE, N. NERVAL, C. BLANC, O. DAUTREY, E. RUF, B. RAFFAELLI:

TARTUFFE ou L'imposteur

La traversée des illusions est rude dans "Tartuffe": elle secoue une famille aux prises avec le plus malfaisant des hypocrites, si malfaisant que son nom est devenu commun.

Est-ce que tu aimes les drames vécus?

Non, moi, je préfère les films d'épouvante.

3 | *C'est à toi!*

1. Quel est le dernier film que tu as vu? Est-ce que tu le recommanderais?
2. As-tu jamais vu un film en version française? Si oui, quel film?
3. Où est-ce que tu peux trouver la description d'un nouveau film?
4. Quels genres de films est-ce que tu préfères?
5. Qu'est-ce qui est important quand tu choisis un film à voir? L'indice? Les vedettes? Le metteur en scène?
6. Est-ce que tu paies un tarif réduit aux cinémas ou aux théâtres?
7. As-tu jamais vu une pièce de théâtre? Si oui, quelle pièce?
8. Si tu as envie d'assister à un spectacle dans ta ville, où vas-tu pour réserver une place?

Cooperative Group Practice

Vocabulary Cards

To practice the vocabulary in this lesson, put students in small groups of four or five. Write the new vocabulary words and expressions on note cards, and give each group a set. (It is a good idea to write "**+ subjonctif**" on the cards listing an impersonal expression.) Also prepare a list of all the new words and expressions in this lesson, and give each student a copy. (You may want to make copies of this unit's new words that can be found in the front section of this Annotated Teacher's Edition.) The first student in each group selects a card from the stack and forms a sentence using the word or expression on the card and a different word or expression from the vocabulary list, for example, (**Il est utile/un kiosque à journaux**) **Il est utile que nous achetions un guide au kiosque à journaux.** After saying the sentence, the student places the card in the discard stack. Students take turns forming sentences until all the cards in the stack have been used. (Vocabulary words on the list may be reused, but the cards in the stack are used only once.)

Pour tout savoir sur les spectacles à Paris, achetez *Pariscope* ou *L'Officiel des Spectacles*, deux guides qui offrent des listes de toutes les attractions et les distractions dans la région parisienne. Tout est là avec l'adresse, la station de métro, le numéro de téléphone du bureau de location, les heures, les dates et les tarifs. Et pour deux ou trois francs, c'est pas mal! Dans ces deux guides vous pouvez trouver tous les renseignements sur:

le cinéma
le théâtre (classique, moderne)
les concerts
les cabarets
les discothèques
le sport
les musées
les parcs d'attractions
les jardins
les monuments
les spectacles "Son et lumières"
les zoos
les marionnettes
les variétés
les expositions pour les jeunes
les fêtes populaires
la musique (classique, rock, jazz)
l'opéra
le ballet
la danse
les cafés et les restaurants

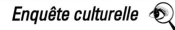

Enquête culturelle

Selon *Pariscope*, il faut qu'on descende du métro à Austerlitz ou Jussieu pour visiter le Jardin des Plantes.

Workbook Activity 12

Transparency 13

Teacher's Notes

1. Cognates in this reading include **attractions, région, parisienne, classique, cabarets, discothèques, marionnettes, opéra, danse, activités, culturelles, participé, historique, public, peinture, folklorique, récentes, approximativement, inventé, cinématographe, spectateurs, commencement, modeste, attribue, popularité, diversification, programmation, permet, limité, fréquente, pratiquement, occasion, groupe, proportion, diminuer, origine, préférences, personnelles, nombre** and **violence**. 2. The web address for *Pariscope* is http://www.pariscope.fr.

1. Louis and Auguste Lumière grew up in Lyon where the family owned a profitable photography business. In 1880 the two brothers invented an improved dry plate. In 1894 they borrowed some ideas from Edison's kinetoscope and developed a combined camera, printing machine and projector, which they patented in 1895 as the **cinématographe**. In their motion picture camera the frames of film were pulled down at a rate of 16 per second, while a semicircular shutter cut off the light between the lens and the film. Louis made 100 short 35-mm films. By 1895 2,000 people a night were coming to view them at a café in Paris. Auguste subsequently became well known for his medical research, but Louis continued in photography, inventing the photorama for panoramic photography in 1899 and a color photography process in 1907. In 1920 he made improvements in stereoscopic photography and in 1935 he produced a three-dimensional film. 2. The **complexes multisalles** in Paris are predominantly owned by UGC and Gaumont, with Pathé and a certain number of independent owners comprising the rest of the market. There are approximately 300 movie theaters in Paris. 3. In Paris 90-minute films are normally shown every two hours from 2:00 P.M. to 10:00 P.M.

À quelles activités culturelles les Français ont-ils participé dans la dernière année?

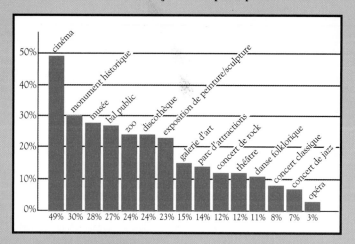

cinéma 49% | monument historique 30% | musée 28% | bal public 27% | zoo 24% | discothèque 24% | exposition de peinture/sculpture 23% | galerie d'art 15% | parc d'attractions 14% | concert de rock 12% | théâtre 12% | danse folklorique 11% | concert classique 8% | concert de jazz 7% | opéra 3%

Comme vous le voyez, la visite au cinéma est la première attraction sur la liste des passe-temps culturels pour les Français, surtout dans les années récentes. Il y a approximativement 100 ans les frères Louis et Auguste Lumière ont inventé le cinématographe. On a montré le premier film en public à Paris en 1895. Trente-trois spectateurs ont payé un franc pour y assister. Depuis ce commencement modeste, on voit aujourd'hui 130 millions de spectateurs qui vont au cinéma chaque année. On attribue la popularité récente du cinéma à la diversification de programmation, aux tarifs moins chers et aux cinémas plus accueillants. Maintenant on va au cinéma dans un complexe multisalle qui permet aux spectateurs un plus grand choix de films.

La visite au cinéma est donc devenue l'activité culturelle la plus populaire, mais avec un public limité. Un Français sur deux ne fréquente pratiquement jamais le cinéma. Et pour chaque 1.000 heures qu'on passe devant la télé, les Français passent quatre heures au cinéma. Il y a des fanas du cinéma qui assistent aux films au moins une fois par mois; ce sont souvent les jeunes. Les enfants demandent à leurs parents de les emmener au cinéma pour y voir des dessins animés ou des films avec des animaux. Les ados y vont parce que ça leur offre l'occasion de sortir avec des amis, en groupe ou en couple.

Y a-t-il un tarif réduit pour les étudiants?

On voit plus de films américains que de films français dans les cinémas en France, mais la proportion commence à diminuer. Il y a deux films d'origine américaine pour chaque film français. Bien sûr, comme tout le monde, les Français ont leurs préférences personnelles: le plus grand nombre des Français aime assister à des comédies.

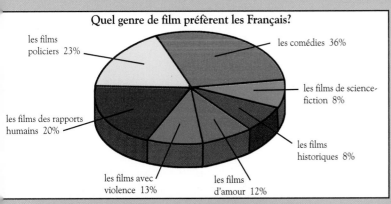

Quel genre de film préfèrent les Français?

- les films policiers 23%
- les comédies 36%
- les films de science-fiction 8%
- les films des rapports humains 20%
- les films historiques 8%
- les films avec violence 13%
- les films d'amour 12%

Combien de films américains passe-t-on ici?

Workbook Activities 13-14

Answers

4 1. *Pariscope* est un guide qui offre des listes de toutes les attractions et les distractions dans la région parisienne.

2. On peut y trouver l'adresse, la station de métro, le numéro de téléphone du bureau de location, les heures, les dates et les tarifs des spectacles à Paris.

3. Le passe-temps le plus populaire en France est le cinéma.

4. Les Français vont plus souvent aux musées qu'aux parcs d'attractions.

5. Les frères Louis et Auguste Lumière ont inventé le cinématographe.

6. Chaque année 130 millions de spectateurs vont au cinéma en France.

7. Le complexe multisalle permet aux spectateurs un plus grand choix de films.

8. Le cinéma est le plus populaire avec les jeunes.

9. On passe plus de films américains que de films français en France.

10. La comédie est le genre de film le plus populaire.

Teacher's Notes

1. **C'est** vs. **il/elle est** was introduced on page 180 in the first level of *C'est à toi!* 2. Modified nouns of profession and nationality use **c'est**, for example, **C'est le caissier de Monoprix** and **C'est un Français**. 3. A noun of nationality is capitalized, but an adjective of nationality is not, for example, **une Française** but **une voiture française**. 4. In conversation **c'est** is often used instead of **il/elle est** to introduce the main idea of a sentence. 5. The corresponding plural forms of **c'est** and **il/elle est** are **ce sont** and **ils/elles sont**.

FRANCE GALL AU ZENITH

Sophie Marceau "Anna Karénine c'est moi"

Être jeune et indépendant, c'est normal.

4 | *Répondez aux questions suivantes.*

1. *Pariscope*, qu'est-ce que c'est?
2. Qu'est-ce qu'on peut y trouver?
3. Quel est le passe-temps le plus populaire en France?
4. Est-ce que les Français vont plus souvent aux musées ou aux parcs d'attractions?
5. Qui a inventé le cinématographe?
6. Combien de spectateurs vont au cinéma chaque année en France?
7. Que permet le complexe multisalle?
8. Avec les personnes de quel âge est-ce que le cinéma est le plus populaire?
9. Est-ce qu'on passe plus de films français ou de films américains aux cinémas en France?
10. Quel genre de film est le plus populaire?

Journal personnel

We have seen that the French participate in a wide variety of activities in their free time based on their personal choices, influences of family and friends, opportunity, availability and advertising. What influences determine the pastimes you choose? Why do you become involved in certain activities and not in others? How do you select your forms of entertainment, such as films, concerts and exhibits? Write your responses to these questions in your cultural journal.

Structure

C'est vs. il/elle est

Both **c'est** and **il/elle est** can mean "it is" as well as "he/she is." The expression that you use depends on what follows the verb **être**.

Use **c'est**:

- before a noun modified by an article, an adjective or both.

Marguerite Duras? C'est la scénariste du film.	*Marguerite Duras? She's the movie's scriptwriter.*
C'est un drame vécu.	*It's a real-life drama.*
Céline Dion? C'est une musicienne diligente. C'est une Canadienne.	*Céline Dion? She's a hardworking musician. She's Canadian.*

- before a proper noun.

C'est Louis Malle.	*It's Louis Malle.*

- before a stress pronoun.

C'est elle qui a écrit le roman du même nom.	*It's she who wrote the novel by the same name.*

- before an adjective that refers to a preceding idea.

Mais comment choisir? Ce n'est pas difficile.	*But how to choose? It's not difficult.*

Paired Practice

Answering Questions

To practice using **c'est** and **il/elle est,** put your students in pairs. Prepare a worksheet for Student A of each pair using the following questions: 1. *Lucie Aubrac,* qu'est-ce que c'est? 2. Quelle est la nationalité de Marguerite Duras? 3. C'est elle qui a écrit le scénario de *Zazie dans le métro*? 4. Comment est la musique d'Angélique Kidjo? For Student B, prepare a worksheet with these questions: 1. Qui est la vedette de *Lucie Aubrac*? 2. Céline Dion, c'est une chanteuse française? 3. C'est Rodin qui compose la musique des films? 4. Quelle est la profession d'Angélique Kidjo? Student A asks Student B four questions that Student B answers using **c'est** or **il/elle est**. Then students switch roles. (Possible answers: (A) 1. C'est un drame vécu. 2. Elle est française. 3. Non, ce n'est pas elle. 4. Elle est dynamique. (B) 1. C'est Daniel Auteuil. 2. Non, c'est une chanteuse canadienne. 3. Non, ce n'est pas lui. 4. Elle est chanteuse.)

Use **il/elle est**:

- before an adjective or before an unmodified noun that functions
  as an adjective (for example, the name of an occupation or a
  nationality).

Il n'est pas cher.	*It's not expensive.*
Il est metteur en scène.	*He's a director.*
Elle est canadienne.	*She's Canadian.*

C'est Marcel Ponty.
Il est employé au
supermarché.

- to refer to a previously mentioned person or thing.

Pouvez-vous trouver le nom	*Can you find the name of the*
du cinéma? Il est en bas.	*movie theater? It's at the bottom.*

Où se trouve la poste?

Elle est là-bas, à côté
du café. Tu vois?

- to introduce the main idea of a sentence. **Il est** is usually followed by an adjective and either **de** plus an infinitive or **que**
  plus the subjunctive.

Il est nécessaire de regarder	*It's necessary to look at the*
le guide.	*guidebook.*
Il est utile que vous sachiez le	*It's useful that you know the*
genre de film.	*type of movie.*

Audiocassette/CD Activity 5

Answers

5 Possible answers:

1. C'est Céline Dion. C'est une chanteuse populaire. Elle est canadienne.
2. C'est la tour Eiffel. C'est un monument à Paris. Elle est très grande.
3. C'est *Pariscope*. C'est un guide. Il est utile.
4. C'est Angélique Kidjo. C'est une chanteuse africaine. Elle est dynamique.
5. C'est le Bonhomme Carnaval. C'est un Québécois. Il est drôle.
6. C'est le Louvre. C'est un musée d'art. Il est célèbre.
7. C'est Daniel Auteuil. C'est une vedette. Il est très doué.
8. C'est *Le Penseur*. C'est une sculpture. Il est au musée Rodin.

Pratique

5 *Identifiez la personne ou la chose dans l'illustration. Puis donnez deux ou trois phrases d'explication (explanation) ou de description sur la personne ou la chose. Suivez le modèle.*

Modèle:

C'est Marie-José Pérec. C'est une athlète. Elle est très forte.

Tour Eiffel, Champ-de-Mars, M° Bir-Hakeim, RER Champ-de-Mars, 44 11 23 23. T.l.j. sans exception de 9h30 à 23h. Ascenseur: 3ᵉ étage: 55F. 2ᵉ étage: 38F. 1ᵉʳ étage: 20F TR. Pour - 12 ans. Escalier: 1ᵉʳ et 2ᵉ étages: 12F. Au 1ᵉʳ étage: "Observatoire des mouvements du sommet". Ciné-musée audiovisuel. Bureau de poste ouvert t.l.j. de 10h à 19h30.

1.

5.

2.

6.

3.

7.

4.

8.

Cooperative Group Practice

Identification and Description

For practice choosing between **c'est, ce sont, il/elle est** and **ils/elles sont,** put students in groups of four or five. On note cards write the names of famous people or objects that can be categorized, for example, *Logozo,* **Kidjo et Dion, Caillebotte et Monet, La Ronde,** *Rue de Paris*;

Temps de pluie, **Notre-Dame et l'arc de triomphe, le ski de fond** and **une bague en or et des boucles d'oreille en argent.** Give a similar set of cards to each group. The first student takes a card, identifies the category and describes the person or object, for example, (*Logozo*) **C'est un album d'Angéligue Kidjo. Il est intéressant.** Students take turns until all the cards in the stack

have been identified and described.

Qui est-ce? Choisissez une personne célèbre. Votre partenaire va vous poser des questions pour déterminer l'identité de cette personne. Vous pouvez répondre à ses questions seulement avec "oui" ou "non." Quand votre partenaire devine (guesses) l'identité de la personne, changez de rôles. Suivez le modèle.

Complétez les petits dialogues avec ce, c', il ou elle.

1. — Tu connais Daniel Auteuil? ... est ma vedette favorite. ... est lui qui est dans ce nouveau drame vécu. Pouvons-nous le voir ce soir?
   — Oui, mais pour savoir où aller, ... est nécessaire d'acheter un guide.
2. — Tu as vu *Zazie dans le métro*? ... est super! ... est un film en noir et blanc. Le metteur en scène, ... est Louis Malle.
   — Non, je ne l'ai pas encore vu. Est-... un film américain ou français?
   — ... est français, bien sûr.
3. — Oh là là! ... est difficile de choisir un film à voir ce soir!
   — Mais non, ... est facile. Voilà le nom d'un bon film. ... est en bas.
4. — Qui est Marguerite Duras? ... est chanteuse?
   — Non, ... est un écrivain. Elle a écrit *Hiroshima mon amour*. ... est née au Vietnam.
   — Ah bon. Et ... est aussi scénariste?
5. — Tiens! Tu vois? ... est Angélique Kidjo. ... est une musicienne extra.
   — ... est elle qui a enregistré *Logozo*?
   — Oui, ... est nécessaire que tu l'écoutes. ... est un CD formidable.

Modèle:
Élève A: C'est une femme?
Élève B: Non, ce n'est pas une femme.
Élève A: Alors, c'est un homme. Il est acteur?
Élève B: Oui, il est acteur.
Élève A: C'est un acteur américain?
Élève B: Oui, c'est un acteur américain.
Élève A: Il est beau?
Élève B: Oui, il est beau.
Élève A: C'est Brad Pitt?
Élève B: Oui, c'est lui!

Je viens de voir *Le huitième jour*. C'est un film avec Daniel Auteuil.

Ah oui? Il est bien?

Structure

The subjunctive of irregular verbs

You learned how to form the subjunctive of regular verbs by dropping the **-ent** of the present tense **ils/elles** form and adding the endings **-e, -es, -e, -ions, -iez** and **-ent**. However, there are certain groups of verbs that have irregular forms in the subjunctive.

Workbook Activities 15-17

Answers

7 1. C', C', il
2. Il, C', c', ce, Il
3. Il, c', Il
4. Elle, c', Elle, elle
5. C', C', C', il, C'

TPR

Classroom Directives

To provide listening and writing practice for the subjunctive of regular and irregular verbs, you may want to do this activity. On a slip of paper have each student write a statement using **il faut que** about an action that another student in the class must perform, for example, **Il faut que Jeanne écrive son nom au tableau** and **Il faut qu'Éric aille à la porte**. Collect all the slips and place them in a bag. Select a slip at random from the bag and read the directive, which the named student performs. When that student has completed the directive, select another slip from the bag and read the directive for the new student. The activity continues until all the directives have been performed. After doing this activity, students will be more comfortable using the subjunctive of regular and irregular verbs in classroom communication.

Cooperative Group Practice

Après les cours

To practice regular and irregular verbs that take the subjunctive after **il faut que**, put students in small groups of four. Prepare two sets of note cards for each group. On the first set write six different noun and pronoun subjects, for example, **je, tu, mon frère, Alice et moi, Normand et toi** and **mes sœurs**. On the second set write

eight activities that students might do after school using regular and irregular verbs, for example, **faire les courses, finir les devoirs, passer l'aspirateur, aller à la bibliothèque, recevoir des amis, voir un film, jouer du piano** and **prendre le bus**. The first student in each group takes a card from both piles and forms a sentence using the subjunctive, for example, **(je/faire les courses) Il faut que je fasse les courses**. Students take

turns until each verb card has been used.

La boum

For additional practice, reuse the noun and pronoun subject cards from the preceding activity. This time, on the second set of note cards, write tasks that students might do to prepare for a party using regular and irregular verbs, for example, **faire un gâteau, choisir la musique, inviter des**

copains, **aller au supermarché, faire le ménage, repasser la nappe, mettre la table** and **nettoyer la cuisine**. The first student in each group takes a card from both stacks and forms a sentence using **il faut que** and the subjunctive, for example, **(je/faire un gâteau) Il faut que je fasse un gâteau**. Students take turns until each verb card has been used.

1. The **nous** and **vous** forms of **aller** and **vouloir** are the same in the subjunctive and the imperfect. 2. The sound of **aille**, **ailles** and **aillent** is the same as the sound of **-aille** in **travaille**. 3. The imperative forms of **savoir** are derived from the subjunctive stem. However, the **tu** form has no final **s** in the imperative. 4. The **nous** and **vous** forms of **boire**, **croire**, **devoir**, **prendre**, **recevoir**, **venir** and **voir** are the same in both the subjunctive and the imperfect. 5. **Apprendre** and **comprendre** in the subjunctive follow the pattern of **prendre**. **Devenir** and **revenir** in the subjunctive follow the pattern of **venir**. 6. The **nous** and **vous** subjunctive forms of orthographically changing verbs resemble the imperfect, for example, **que nous achetions** and **que vous pesiez**. 7. The imperatives of **avoir** and **être** are derived from the subjunctive stem. However, the **tu** form of **avoir** has no final **s** in the imperative. 8. The irregular forms of **falloir** and **pleuvoir** in the subjunctive are **qu'il faille** and **qu'il pleuve**. 9. The irregular forms of **mourir** in the subjunctive are **meure**, **meures**, **meure**, **mourions**, **mouriez** and **meurent**.

Game

Seven in One

Divide your class into two teams. Write seven pronouns spread out across the board in any order, for example, **vous, il, elles, tu, je, on** and **nous**. Call the first seven students from Team A to the board, asking each student to stand under a pronoun. Call out an irregular verb, such as **savoir**, at which point the seven students begin writing a subjunctive sentence beginning with **il est essentiel que** that incorporates their pronoun, for example, (**vous**) **Il est essentiel que vous sachiez dans quel arrondissement se trouve le cinéma.** For each correct sentence, Team A earns a point. If all the

Il faut que vous fassiez un tour à la campagne.

Il est indispensable que vous compreniez le subjonctif!

Verbs such as **aller**, **faire**, **pouvoir**, **savoir** and **vouloir** have irregular stems but regular endings in the subjunctive. Note that the **nous** and **vous** forms of **aller** and **vouloir** use the infinitive stem.

	aller	*faire*	*pouvoir*	*savoir*	*vouloir*
que je (j')	aille	fasse	puisse	sache	veuille
que tu	ailles	fasses	puisses	saches	veuilles
qu'il/elle/on	aille	fasse	puisse	sache	veuille
que nous	allions	fassions	puissions	sachions	voulions
que vous	alliez	fassiez	puissiez	sachiez	vouliez
qu'ils/elles	aillent	fassent	puissent	sachent	veuillent

Il faut que vous **alliez** au kiosque à journaux pour acheter un guide.   *You must go to the newsstand to buy a guidebook.*

Verbs such as **boire**, **croire**, **devoir**, **prendre**, **recevoir**, **venir** and **voir** have regular endings in the subjunctive but irregular stems in the **nous** and **vous** forms.

	boire	*croire*	*devoir*	*prendre*	*recevoir*
que je	boive	croie	doive	prenne	reçoive
que tu	boives	croies	doives	prennes	reçoives
qu'il/elle/on	boive	croie	doive	prenne	reçoive
que nous	buvions	croyions	devions	prenions	recevions
que vous	buviez	croyiez	deviez	preniez	receviez
qu'ils/elles	boivent	croient	doivent	prennent	reçoivent

	venir	*voir*
que je	vienne	voie
que tu	viennes	voies
qu'il/elle/on	vienne	voie
que nous	venions	voyions
que vous	veniez	voyiez
qu'ils/elles	viennent	voient

The verbs **avoir** and **être** have both irregular stems and endings in the subjunctive.

	avoir	*être*
que je (j')	aie	sois
que tu	aies	sois
qu'il/elle/on	ait	soit
que nous	ayons	soyons
que vous	ayez	soyez
qu'ils/elles	aient	soient

members of Team A write a perfect sentence, that team wins another turn. If not, call seven members from Team B to the board and call out a new verb. When the allotted time is over, the team with the highest score wins. (You may choose to award additional points to team members who write sentences using vocabulary from this lesson.)

Cooperative Group Practice

Les charades

To provide additional practice forming sentences using the subjunctive of irregular verbs, put students in small groups of four or five. Make a set of note cards on which you write infinitive expressions that use irregular verbs, such as **aller au marché**, **faire la lessive, savoir l'heure, boire du jus d'orange, prendre le**

petit déjeuner, **voir un film** and **être à l'heure**. Give each group a stack of cards. The first student in each group draws a card and silently acts out the activity until another student in the group makes a correct identification by saying a sentence in the subjunctive, for example, **Il faut que tu ailles au marché.** The student who accurately identifies the activity selects the next card.

Pratique

Avec les élèves de votre cours de français, vous faites une excursion au musée d'art. Mais tout le monde ne suit pas la liste d'instructions que le prof a faite. Dites ce qu'il faut que certains élèves fassent pour les suivre. Suivez le modèle.

Modèle:

Raoul/#7
Il faut que Raoul fasse toujours attention.

Instructions pour la visite au musée

1. ne pas venir en retard
2. avoir un ticket
3. prendre un plan du musée
4. être toujours avec le professeur
5. ne pas faire beaucoup de bruit
6. voir les tableaux les plus importants
7. faire toujours attention
8. aller à la cantine avec les autres
9. ne rien boire dans le musée
10. savoir l'heure du départ

1. Céleste et moi/#4
2. Damien/#1
3. toi/#3
4. Bernard et Clément/#9
5. Ahmed et Katia/#10
6. Sabrina et toi/#8
7. Zakia/#2
8. moi/#5
9. Bénédicte et Lucien/#6

Il faut que vous voyiez les tableaux de Van Gogh. (Paris)

---

*Pendant votre visite à Paris, votre partenaire et vous ne vous entendez pas très bien. De plus, vous voulez faire le contraire de ce que votre partenaire veut faire. Dites-lui ce qu'on doit faire en faisant des phrases avec **il faut que**. Suivez le modèle.*

1. avoir des chèques de voyage/avoir de l'argent français
2. croire le guide/croire le commerçant
3. prendre le métro/prendre un taxi
4. voir les monuments importants/voir les boutiques célèbres
5. faire le tour du Louvre/faire les magasins
6. boire quelque chose au café/boire quelque chose au fast-food
7. vouloir aller au ballet/vouloir aller au match de foot
8. essayer de s'entendre/essayer de s'amuser

Modèle:

aller au théâtre/aller en boîte
Élève A: Il faut qu'on aille au théâtre.
Élève B: Mais non, il faut qu'on aille en boîte.

 Audiocassette/CD Activities 8-9

Answers

8 1. Il faut que Céleste et moi, nous soyons toujours avec le professeur.
2. Il faut que Damien ne vienne pas en retard.
3. Il faut que tu prennes un plan du musée.
4. Il faut que Bernard et Clément ne boivent rien dans le musée.
5. Il faut qu'Ahmed et Katia sachent l'heure du départ.
6. Il faut que Sabrina et toi, vous alliez à la cantine avec les autres.
7. Il faut que Zakia ait un ticket.
8. Il faut que je ne fasse pas beaucoup de bruit.
9. Il faut que Bénédicte et Lucien voient les tableaux les plus importants.

9 1. Il faut qu'on ait des chèques de voyage. Mais non, il faut qu'on ait de l'argent français.
2. Il faut qu'on croie le guide. Mais non, il faut qu'on croie le commerçant.
3. Il faut qu'on prenne le métro. Mais non, il faut qu'on prenne un taxi.
4. Il faut qu'on voie les monuments importants. Mais non, il faut qu'on voie les boutiques célèbres.
5. Il faut qu'on fasse le tour du Louvre. Mais non, il faut qu'on fasse les magasins.
6. Il faut qu'on boive quelque chose au café. Mais non, il faut qu'on boive quelque chose au fast-food.
7. Il faut qu'on veuille aller au ballet. Mais non, il faut qu'on veuille aller au match de foot.
8. Il faut qu'on essaie de s'entendre. Mais non, il faut qu'on essaie de s'amuser.

Cooperative Group Practice

Les règles

After completing Activity 8, put students in small groups of four or five. Tell each group to write rules for the French classroom, the cafeteria, the computer lab and the library. Rules may begin with either **il faut que** or **il ne faut pas que**. When each group has finished, you may want to post the combined rules for the French classroom.

Game

Le cuirassé

So that students can practice irregular verbs in the subjunctive, have pairs of students play a modified version of "Battleship." Across the top of a sheet of paper, students list six pronoun subjects. In a column on the left, students list ten verbs that are irregular in the subjunctive. (Both partners list the same infinitives.) Next, students create and fill in their own grid, choosing 15 combinations from the various possibilities. For example, if a student chooses the square where **elles** and **avoir** meet, he or she writes **elles aient** there. For the remaining directions for the game, refer to page 14 in this Annotated Teacher's Edition.

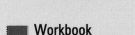

Workbook
Activities 18-19

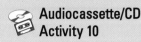

Audiocassette/CD
Activity 10

Answers

10 1. Il faut que Fayçal et toi, vous alliez au kiosque à journaux.
  2. Il faut que tu achètes un guide.
  3. Il faut que le prof fasse attention à la description du film.
  4. Il faut que la famille de Sandrine sache l'indice du film.
  5. Il faut que Fabienne et Yvonne soient au bureau de location à 21h00.
  6. Il faut qu'on paie un tarif réduit.
  7. Il faut que nous ne prenions pas le métro trop tard.
  8. Il faut que tout le monde descende du métro à Montparnasse.

Teacher's Notes

1. Other impersonal expressions followed by the subjunctive include **il est absurde, il est bien, il est dommage, il est étonnant, il est étrange, il est juste, il est naturel, il est normal, il est peu probable, il est préférable, il est rare, il est souhaitable, il est temps, il importe, il se peut, il semble** and **il suffit.** 2. Impersonal expressions used in a general sense are followed by **de** and an infinitive, for example, **Il est nécessaire de réserver une place au bureau de location.** 3. These impersonal expressions are also followed by the subjunctive when the sentence is negative or interrogative, for example, **Il n'est pas surprenant que nous soyons en retard. Est-il nécessaire qu'on fasse la queue au théâtre?**

Modèle:

je/lire tout sur le film
Il faut que je lise tout sur le film.

10 *On passe le nouveau film de Gérard Depardieu pendant que vous êtes en France, et tout le monde s'intéresse à le voir. Dites ce qu'il faut que tout le monde fasse.*

  1. Fayçal et toi/aller au kiosque à journaux
  2. tu/acheter un guide
  3. le prof/faire attention à la description du film
  4. la famille de Sandrine/savoir l'indice du film
  5. Fabienne et Yvonne/être au bureau de location à 21h00
  6. on/payer un tarif réduit
  7. nous/ne pas prendre le métro trop tard
  8. tout le monde/descendre du métro à Montparnasse

The subjunctive after impersonal expressions

You know that the subjunctive is used after the expression of necessity **il faut que**. There are other impersonal expressions that are followed by the subjunctive. These expressions give an opinion about someone or something specific. Here are some of these impersonal expressions.

il est nécessaire que	*it is necessary that*
il est important que	*it is important that*
il est indispensable que	*it is indispensable that*
il est essentiel que	*it is essential that*
il est possible que	*it is possible that*
il est impossible que	*it is impossible that*
il vaut mieux que	*it is better that*
il est bon que	*it is good that*
il est surprenant que	*it is surprising that*
il est utile que	*it is useful that*

Il est essentiel que vous sachiez où se trouve le cinéma. — *It's essential that you know where the movie theater is located.*

Il est nécessaire que vous regardiez l'abréviation. — *It's necessary that you look at the abbreviation.*

Il est possible qu'un film **soit** interdit. — *It's possible that a movie is prohibited.*

Il est bon qu'il y en **ait** plusieurs. — *It's good that there are several (of them).*

Il n'est pas surprenant que tu sois en mauvaise forme après ton accident de voiture.

Cooperative Group Practice

La chasse au trésor

To practice the subjunctive of regular and irregular verbs after impersonal expressions, put students in small groups of four or five. Each group writes five clues that eventually lead to the location of their treasure, for example, **Il est nécessaire que vous lisiez un livre sur le bureau du prof** or **Il vaut** mieux que vous voyiez une vidéocassette. Each group hides their last four clues and gives their first clue to another group. (It is a good idea for each group to use paper of a different color for their clues so that clues from different groups won't be mixed up.) Then each group hunts for the successive clues until it locates the hidden treasure. The treasure may be a drawing of a treasure chest that groups exchange for a small prize once they have located it.

Pratique

À votre avis, est-ce que les choses suivantes sont possibles ou impossibles? Faites des phrases avec il est possible que ou il est impossible que.

1. Ton frère sort avec Céline Dion.
2. Tes parents veulent préserver l'environnement.
3. Ta sœur reçoit du courrier de Tom Cruise.
4. Ton prof connaît Gérard Depardieu.
5. Tous les élèves dans ton cours de français réussissent.
6. Tu continues tes études à l'université.
7. Les jeunes ont des idées controversées.
8. Tes copains et toi, vous pouvez aller à Paris.
9. Tu ne te rappelles pas ton adresse.

Est-il possible que M. Svobada fasse un vase?

Modèles:

Le nouveau film de Disney est interdit.
Il est impossible que le nouveau film de Disney soit interdit.

Ta grand-mère te rend visite ce soir.
Il est possible que ma grand-mère me rende visite ce soir.

Vos amis et vous allez sortir ce soir. Formez sept phrases logiques sur votre décision d'aller au cinéma. Choisissez un élément des colonnes A, B et C pour chaque phrase. Suivez le modèle.

A	B	C
vaut mieux	prendre	au guichet
utile	avoir	assez d'argent
essentiel	savoir	un guide
surprenant	se taire	aller au cinéma à pied
bon	arriver	le nom du film
indispensable	choisir	pendant le film
nécessaire	pouvoir	à l'heure
important	aller	un film en noir et blanc

Modèle:

Il vaut mieux que nous puissions aller au cinéma à pied.

Il est essentiel que Claude arrive à l'heure.

Answers

11 Possible answers:

1. Il est impossible que mon frère sorte avec Céline Dion.
2. Il est possible que mes parents veuillent préserver l'environnement.
3. Il est impossible que ma sœur reçoive du courrier de Tom Cruise.
4. Il est impossible que mon prof connaisse Gérard Depardieu.
5. Il est possible que tous les élèves dans mon cours de français réussissent.
6. Il est possible que je continue mes études à l'université.
7. Il est possible que les jeunes aient des idées controversées.
8. Il est possible que mes copains et moi, nous puissions aller à Paris.
9. Il est impossible que je ne me rappelle pas mon adresse.

12 Possible answers:

Il est utile que nous ayons un guide.
Il est essentiel que nous sachions le nom du film.
Il est surprenant que nous choisissions un film en noir et blanc.
Il est bon que nous prenions assez d'argent.
Il est indispensable que nous arrivions à l'heure.
Il est nécessaire que nous allions au guichet.
Il est important que nous nous taisions pendant le film.

Cooperative Group Practice

Pour changer l'école

For additional practice forming sentences in the subjunctive after impersonal expressions, put students in small groups of four or five. Each group writes six changes its members would make to improve their school. Each desired change is introduced by an impersonal expression followed by

the subjunctive, for example, **Il vaut mieux que nous commencions à 9h00.** When each group has completed its list, you may want to have students share one of their suggested changes with the class and make a class list. Students could then vote on their top three desired changes for the school.

Game

Subjunctive Relay Race

To practice using impersonal expressions with the subjunctive, divide your class into two teams. Prepare a list of sentences with impersonal expressions. Call the first player from each team up to the board. Then say the sentence that you want changed, for example, **Il est possible que nous**

sachions l'indice d'un film. (tu) Both students write out the new French sentence using the **tu** form of **savoir** in the subjunctive. The first student to correctly write **Il est possible que tu saches l'indice d'un film** wins a point for his or her team. The team with the most points wins.

Modèle:

réussir à l'école

Élève A: Pour réussir à l'école, il faut que je fasse attention au prof.

Élève B: Pour réussir à l'école, il est important que je finisse mes devoirs.

Élève C: Pour réussir à l'école, il est nécessaire que je prenne de bonnes notes.

13 *Avec deux autres camarades de classe, parlez de vos ambitions pour l'avenir (future). Dites ce qu'il faut faire, à votre avis, pour réaliser ces ambitions. Alternez les phrases avec vos partenaires en utilisant les expressions de la liste suivante.*

il est nécessaire que	il faut que	il est indispensable que
il est important que	il est essentiel que	

1. avoir de bons amis
2. trouver un boulot intéressant
3. avoir assez d'argent
4. aider les gens pauvres
5. devenir célèbre
6. contrôler la pollution
7. être heureux/heureuse

Communication

14 *Interviewez cinq élèves de votre classe pour tout savoir sur le dernier film qu'ils ont vu. Sur une feuille de papier, copiez la grille suivante. Demandez à chaque élève le nom du film, son genre et ses vedettes. Puis demandez-lui s'il ou elle l'a aimé et s'il ou elle recommande le film à d'autres (par exemple, **Oui**, il m'a beaucoup plu. **Il faut que tu le voies!**). Écrivez ses réponses dans l'espace blanc approprié.*

	Élève	Film	Genre	Vedettes	Recommandation
1.					
2.					
3.					
4.					
5.					

Quel est le dernier film que tu as vu?

C'est *Le Mariage de mon meilleur ami*, une comédie avec Julia Roberts.

15 *Maintenant écrivez un sommaire de l'enquête que vous avez faite dans l'Activité 14 sur les films que vos camarades de classe ont vus. Dites quel film chaque élève a vu, son genre, ses vedettes, s'il ou elle l'a aimé et s'il ou elle le recommande. Puis, pour chaque film, dites si vous l'avez vu aussi. Si oui, donnez votre opinion du film et dites si vous le recommandez.*

Choisissez le film qui vous intéresse le plus de votre sommaire dans l'Activité 15 et dessinez (design) une affiche qui fait de la publicité pour ce film. Sur votre affiche il faut donner les renseignements suivants:

1. le nom du film
2. les vedettes
3. le genre
4. l'indice
5. la durée
6. le nom du cinéma
7. l'adresse du cinéma
8. le tarif
9. les jours et les heures du film

Enfin écrivez une phrase persuasive qui dit pourquoi il faut que tout le monde voie ce film.

Sur la bonne piste

In this unit you will read an excerpt from *Au revoir, les enfants*, a movie script written by the film's director, Louis Malle. The story revolves around two students at a Catholic boarding school during the German occupation of France in World War II. Julien and his older brother, François, have been sent away from Paris by their parents to keep them safe. Joseph, a boy with a physical disability who works for the demanding Mme Perrin in the school's kitchen, has found a creative but questionable way to make money. In the excerpt that follows, the headmaster, Père Jean, deals with Joseph and the students who have been caught trading supplies with him. In order to fully understand the characters, picture in your mind what they look and sound like as you read this selection. Then determine their motivations and decide what kinds of people they are. As you prepare to analyze the character of Père Jean, it is important to consider how the writer develops it.

A *flat character* exhibits a single dominant quality or character trait; a *rounded character* exhibits a complexity of traits, more like a real human being.

Authors create their characters in one of two ways. In *direct characterization* the writer comments on a character's traits explicitly, telling about such matters as the character's appearance, habits, dress, background, personality and motivations. For example, the author may write "John is stingy." In *indirect characterization* the author reveals a character by means of what he or she says and does and by means of the reactions of other people that shed light on the character's beliefs, actions and motivations. When using indirect characterization, the writer allows the reader to draw his or her own conclusions based on clues to determine a character's traits.

When Malle says "Le Père Jean [a] le visage dur," you must decide if this is a permanent characteristic of the headmaster or simply a reaction to the event at hand. What kind of a man is the headmaster? Is he a flat or rounded character? Does Malle decide to reveal his character directly or indirectly? Does Père Jean ignore or confront the conflict that erupts in his school over the stolen goods that Joseph sells on the black market? How do you imagine that his role as a priest affects the decision he makes? Does Père Jean see things in black and white, or is it difficult for him to punish Joseph? Is Père Jean strict or lenient, compassionate or unfeeling, fair or unfair, decisive or wavering, materialistic or unworldly, idealistic or realistic? Does he exhibit a combination of these traits?

Listening Activity 2

Quiz
Leçon B

Advanced Placement

Teacher's Notes

1. You may want to display the posters that students make for Activity 16 around the classroom or in the school hallways for all to see. 2. **Sur la bonne piste, Leçon B**, is designed to develop skills that will help students prepare to take the Advanced Placement Exam in French Literature. In this section students read a variety of prose, poetry and drama from different periods; answer content questions; and demonstrate their critical understanding of literary techniques, such as character development, setting, point of view, satire, figures of speech and inference. In this **Sur la bonne piste** section, students learn to differentiate between flat and rounded characters and between direct and indirect characterization. 3. To help students understand the difference between a flat character and a rounded character, you may want to use examples from television. Generally, half-hour sitcoms use flat characters, while one-hour dramas depict more fully rounded characters. 4. *Au Revoir les enfants* (1987) is based on Malle's autobiographical experiences in a Catholic boarding school during the Resistance. "The monks," Malle has recounted, "were in the Resistance, and were sheltering some young Jewish boys. One day a cook got fired and he informed to the Gestapo, and the head monk and the boys were arrested and died in camps." In his fictional *Lacombe, Lucien* (1974) Malle also dealt with the subject of the Nazi occupation, raising the question of the collaborationist guilt of ordinary French citizens.

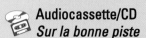

Audiocassette/CD
Sur la bonne piste

1. To help students with new vocabulary words in *Au revoir, les enfants*, you might want to read the beginning of the script with them and point out various strategies. First, remind students to rely on cognates. You might point out an example, such as **volumineuse**, asking students what English word it looks like. Second, remind students to guess the meaning of new words in context. What does the expression **avoir un verre dans le nez** imply about Mme Perrin's drinking habits? You might suggest that students visualize this expression to figure out its meaning. Finally, tell students to use the dictionary as a last resort for words, such as **saindoux**, that they cannot guess in context. Remind students to figure out the part of speech for each new word they need to look up. Review with them the abbreviations in the dictionary after the word and before its definition(s), for example, *nf, nm, adj, vi, vt, adv*, etc. 2. You may want to place *Au revoir, les enfants* in a historical context for your students. The Germans invaded France from Belgium in 1940, entering Paris on June 14. On June 22 France signed an armistice with the Germans, who subsequently occupied the northern two-thirds of France. Southern France, governed from Vichy by Marshal Henri Philippe Pétain, remained under French control, although Pétain cooperated with the Germans. After France fell, General Charles de Gaulle fled to London, where he encouraged all French patriots to resist the Germans and join Free France. De Gaulle formed a provisional government after the Allies landed in Normandy and liberated Paris.

17 | *Avant de lire les scènes suivantes, répondez aux questions.*

1. Pour vivre qu'est-ce que tu es préparé(e) à faire?
2. Quelle décision difficile as-tu prise (*made*) dans ta vie? As-tu eu des regrets après?

Au revoir, les enfants

On entend des hurlements. La volumineuse Mme Perrin surgit de la cuisine, poursuivant Joseph qu'elle frappe avec un torchon.... la cuisinière est vraiment furieuse. Elle a un verre dans le nez, elle titube et manque de tomber. Elle aperçoit le Père Michel parmi les joueurs d'échasses.

Mme Perrin: Père Michel, Père Michel! Je l'ai attrapé en train de voler du saindoux. Il le mettait dans son sac pour aller le vendre. Je vous l'avais bien dit qu'il volait... Voleur, voleur,...!

Tout en parlant, elle continue à taper sur Joseph, acculé contre un mur. Il lève les bras pour se protéger et semble terrifié.

Joseph: C'est pas vrai, elle ment! C'est elle qui vole!

Les jeux se sont arrêtés, tout le monde regarde. Le Père Michel prend Joseph par le bras et l'entraîne vers la cuisine.

Le Père Michel: Pas devant les enfants, madame Perrin. Rentrez dans votre cuisine et calmez-vous.

François: (*à Julien*) Je lui avais dit à ce crétin qu'il allait se faire piquer.

Ils lèvent la tête et aperçoivent le Père Jean, qui observe la scène de la fenêtre de son bureau....

Sept élèves de différentes classes sont alignés dans le bureau du Père Jean. Parmi eux, François et Julien.

Le Père Jean: Joseph volait les provisions du collège et les revendait au marché noir. Mme Perrin aurait dû nous prévenir plus tôt et je ne crois pas qu'elle soit innocente. Mais il y a plus.

Il montre sur sa table des boîtes de pâté, des bonbons, des pots de confiture.

Le Père Jean: Voilà ce qu'on a trouvé dans son placard. Ce sont des provisions personnelles. Il vous a nommés tous les sept.

Il prend une boîte de pâté.

Le Père Jean: Auquel d'entre vous appartient ce pâté?
Un élève: À moi.
Le Père Jean: Et ces confitures?
Julien: À moi.
Le Père Jean: Vous savez ce que vous êtes? Un voleur, tout autant que Joseph.
Julien: C'est pas du vol. Elles m'appartiennent, ces confitures.
Le Père Jean: Vous en privez vos camarades. (*À tous:*) Pour moi, l'éducation, la vraie, consiste à vous apprendre à faire bon usage de votre liberté.

Et voilà le résultat! Vous me dégoûtez. Il n'y a rien que je trouve plus ignoble que le marché noir. L'argent, toujours l'argent.

François: On ne faisait pas d'argent. On échangeait, c'est tout.

Le Père Jean s'avance vers lui, le visage dur.

Le Père Jean: Contre quoi?

François: (*après une hésitation*) Des cigarettes.

Le Père Jean: Quentin, si je ne savais pas tous les problèmes que cela poserait à vos parents, je vous mettrais à la porte tout de suite, vous et votre frère. Je suis obligé de renvoyer Joseph, mais je commets une injustice. Vous êtes tous privés de sortie jusqu'à Pâques. Vous pouvez retourner à l'étude.

Les élèves sortent.... Dans le couloir, ils se trouvent en face de Joseph qui attend avec le Père Michel, le dos au mur. Il pleurniche comme un gosse.

Joseph: Et où je vais aller, moi? J'ai même pas où coucher.

Les élèves sont très gênés. Julien lui met une main sur l'épaule.

Le Père Michel: Allez en classe.

Ils s'éloignent. À l'extrémité du couloir, Julien se retourne et voit le Père Jean qui apparaît à la porte de son bureau.

Le Père Jean: (*à Joseph*) Allez voir l'économe. Il vous paiera votre mois.

Joseph: Y a que moi qui trinque. C'est pas juste.

Le Père Michel: Allez, viens, Joseph.

Il l'entraîne, sous le regard du Père Jean, qui semble regretter la décision qu'il a prise.

Répondez aux questions suivantes.

1. Qui accuse Joseph d'un vol dans la cuisine?
2. Pourquoi Joseph lève-t-il les bras?
3. Selon Joseph, est-ce que Mme Perrin est innocente?
4. Quelle est la réaction des élèves quand ils voient cette scène?
5. Qui observe la scène de son bureau?
6. Où est-ce que Joseph revendait les provisions du collège?
7. Comment le Père Jean sait-il que les provisions dans le placard de Joseph appartenaient aux sept élèves?
8. Pourquoi le Père Jean accuse-t-il Julien d'être un voleur comme Joseph?
9. Quelle est la défense de Julien devant cette accusation?
10. Selon le Père Jean, en quoi consiste la vraie éducation?
11. Le Père Jean, est-il fâché? Si oui, pourquoi?
12. Comment est le visage du Père Jean quand il s'avance vers François?
13. Les sept élèves échangeaient leurs provisions contre quoi?
14. Pourquoi le Père Jean dit-il qu'il commet une injustice quand il renvoie Joseph?
15. De quelle liberté les sept élèves sont-ils privés? Jusqu'à quand?
16. Que fait Julien pour montrer sa compassion pour Joseph?
17. Quelles deux phrases du scénario montrent que le Père Jean regrette sa décision de renvoyer Joseph?

Answers

18 Possible answers:

1. Mme Perrin l'accuse d'un vol dans la cuisine.
2. Joseph lève les bras pour se protéger de Mme Perrin qui tape sur lui.
3. Non, selon Joseph, c'est elle qui vole et pas lui.
4. Ils s'arrêtent de jouer et regardent.
5. Le Père Jean observe la scène de son bureau.
6. Joseph les revendait au marché noir.
7. Le Père Jean le sait parce que Joseph a nommé les sept élèves.
8. Le Père Jean pense que Julien prive ses camarades de ses confitures.
9. Julien dit que les confitures lui appartiennent.
10. Selon le Père Jean, la vraie éducation consiste à apprendre aux élèves à faire bon usage de leur liberté.
11. Oui, il est fâché parce qu'il n'y a rien qu'il trouve plus ignoble que le marché noir.
12. Il a le visage dur.
13. Les sept élèves échangeaient leurs provisions contre des cigarettes.
14. Le Père Jean dit qu'il commet une injustice parce que les élèves, et peut-être Mme Perrin, ne sont pas innocents.
15. Les sept élèves sont privés de sortie jusqu'à Pâques.
16. Julien montre sa compassion pour Joseph quand il lui met une main sur l'épaule.
17. Les deux phrases sont "... je commets une injustice" et "... [le] Père Jean,... semble regretter la décision qu'il a prise."

Teacher's Notes

1. You may want to point out the danger of smoking to your students. You might also choose to tell students that during World War II, people weren't as aware of the health risks that smoking poses as we are today. 2. Some new words used in the screenplay and cognates not found in the end vocabulary of *C'est à toi!* are used to ask questions about *Au revoir, les enfants* in Activity 18.

1. You may want to have students demonstrate their understanding of at least five new words by writing sentences that use them. 2. Optional activity. Divide your class into groups of seven to produce a radio play from the script. Assign the roles of **Mme Perrin, Joseph, Père Michel, Père Jean, un élève, Julien** and **François.** (For a group of six, one student could play the roles of both **un élève** and **François.**) Students should be encouraged to read their parts with appropriate emotion. Students might even add sound effects as indicated by the narration. After practicing their parts several times, have students record their interpretation of the script. Finally, select the best version to play for the class as students silently read the script again. 3. Optional activity. You might have students write a section of a film script, imagining their best friend in the major role. Have them begin by assessing characteristics of their friend by selecting his or her dominant traits from pairs of adjectives. Students place each of the following pairs of adjectives at either end of a continuum numbered 1 through 10: **extroverti(e), introverti(e); avare, généreux/ généreuse; bavard(e), tranquille; gentil(le), méchant(e); idéaliste, réaliste; matérialiste, spirituel(le); sérieux/sérieuse, gai(e).** After assigning a number to each pair of traits, students pick one or two traits that they want to depict in their film script. Instruct students to use indirect characterization to reveal their friend's nature, showing what their friend is like rather than summarizing him or her for the reader. Using *Au revoir, les enfants* as a model, students' scripts should use narrative descriptions and dialogue to draw a full portrait of their friend. Some students may want to depict a scene from real life, while others may want to create a completely fictitious scenario. 4. You may want to show the movie *Au revoir, les enfants* to students

after they have read this excerpt from the screenplay.

Modèle:

Le Père Jean est très strict. Il renvoie Joseph parce qu'il a volé du collège et a vendu des provisions au marché noir.

19 Écrivez le scénario qui a lieu (*takes place*) quand le Père Jean accuse Joseph du vol. Où la scène a-t-elle lieu? Le Père Jean et Joseph, sont-ils assis ou debout (*standing*)? Comment sont les visages des deux personnes? Que dit le Père Jean quand il accuse Joseph? Que dit Joseph pour se défendre?

20 Faites un sketch qui a lieu dans un lycée moderne. Avec un(e) partenaire, jouez les rôles d'un(e) élève qui a volé quelque chose du lycée et du directeur qui lui pose des questions. Si vous jouez le rôle de l'élève, donnez une explication ou une défense de vos actions. Si vous jouez le rôle du directeur, décidez comment vous allez punir (*to punish*) l'élève.

21 Pour analyser le caractère du Père Jean, faites une grille (*grid*) comme la suivante. Pour chaque adjectif, choisissez le numéro qui exprime (*expresses*) le caractère du Père Jean (5 indique qu'il montre le maximum de cette qualité). Mettez un ✓ dans l'espace blanc approprié. Puis écrivez deux phrases. Dans la première phrase, faites une généralisation fondée sur la grille que vous avez remplie. Dans la deuxième phrase, défendez votre généralisation avec un exemple du scénario.

	1	2	3	4	5
strict					✓
compatissant (*compassionate*)					
juste (*fair*)					
décisif					
matérialiste					
idéaliste					

22 Écrivez un paragraphe où vous décrivez le caractère du Père Jean. Est-ce que c'est un bon directeur? Quelle est sa philosophie? Comment est-ce qu'il est influencé par son rôle de prêtre (*priest*) quand il prend une décision? Est-il difficile pour lui de renvoyer Joseph? Pourquoi ne punit-il pas sévèrement les sept élèves et Mme Perrin? Utilisez votre grille et vos phrases de l'Activité 21 pour développer un portrait précis du Père Jean.

Dossier fermé

Imagine que tu passes une semaine à Paris. Comment décider quoi faire dans cette grande ville? Par exemple, à quels concerts, films et spectacles peux-tu aller? Quelles sont les dates et les heures de ces spectacles? Où sont-ils? Est-ce que tu peux acheter quelque chose qui te dit tous ces détails? Mais oui! Tu dois acheter:

A. *Pariscope*

Tu peux trouver des renseignements dans tous les trois: *Pariscope*, un journal quotidien et le *Guide Michelin Vert*. Certains journaux donnent les heures de films et d'expositions. Le *Guide Michelin Vert* offre des informations historiques et les heures générales des musées et des monuments. Mais il vaut mieux acheter *Pariscope* pour vous informer sur toutes les attractions et les distractions à Paris.

C'est à moi!

Now that you have completed this unit, take a look at what you should be able to do in French. Can you do all of these tasks?

➤ I can ask whether or not something is important.

➤ I can say what is important.

➤ I can ask what someone likes.

➤ I can tell what someone likes.

➤ I can list things.

➤ I can state someone's preference.

➤ I can make a generalization.

➤ I can ask someone's opinion about something.

➤ I can give my opinion by saying what I think.

➤ I can ask whether or not someone agrees with me.

➤ I can ask whether or not something surprises someone.

➤ I can say what is better.

➤ I can ask whether or not something is possible.

➤ I can say what is possible and impossible.

➤ I can say what someone needs to do.

➤ I can say what it is necessary to do.

➤ I can tell location.

Pour voir si vous avez bien compris la culture française, décidez si chaque phrase est vraie ou fausse.

1. Presque tout le monde en France a la télévision.
2. Il n'y a pas beaucoup de Français qui ont le câble ou le satellite.
3. Les émissions de sports sont les plus populaires à la télévision française.
4. Le Français typique est content de son choix d'émissions à la télé.
5. Le magnétoscope, les jeux vidéo et l'ordinateur commencent à prendre la place de la télévision.
6. Le *Guide Michelin Vert* offre les renseignements sur les films et les spectacles à Paris.
7. Les deux guides qui offrent des listes de toutes les attractions parisiennes coûtent 25 francs.
8. Les frères Lumière ont inventé la caméra vidéo.
9. Les Français vont plus souvent au cinéma qu'au théâtre.
10. Les Français aiment surtout les drames historiques.

Answers

1. vraie
2. vraie
3. fausse
4. fausse
5. vraie
6. fausse
7. fausse
8. fausse
9. vraie
10. fausse

Communication orale

Qu'est-ce qu'on peut faire dans votre ville pour s'informer et pour s'amuser? Avec un(e) partenaire, parlez des attractions et des distractions dans votre ville. Regardez la liste suivante et demandez à votre partenaire de nommer une attraction dans chaque catégorie et de vous en donner son opinion.

- musées
- expositions
- librairies
- théâtres
- cinémas
- concerts
- spectacles
- fêtes
- restaurants et cafés
- boutiques, magasins et centres commerciaux
- stades et équipes (*teams*) de sport

Puis discutez avec votre partenaire lesquelles (which ones) de ces attractions et ces distractions sont les plus populaires et les plus intéressantes. Est-il important que les ados fréquentent toutes ces attractions? Enfin est-il possible que votre ville ait de nouvelles attractions et distractions à l'avenir?

Communication écrite

Pour aider les touristes francophones qui vont visiter votre ville, préparez un guide des attractions et des distractions que vous venez de discuter avec votre partenaire. Choisissez les attractions qui intéresseraient le plus aux visiteurs. Pour chaque attraction que vous discutez dans ce guide, écrivez une phrase de description et les renseignements nécessaires, par exemple, l'adresse, le numéro de téléphone, le tarif ou les prix, les dates et les heures d'ouverture. Si vous voulez, vous pouvez mettre une photo ou une illustration de l'attraction à côté de chacune.

Communication active

To ask about importance, use:

Est-il important que vous ne preniez pas le métro trop tard?

Is it important for you not to take the subway too late?

To express importance, use:

Il est essentiel que vous sachiez dans quel arrondissement se trouve le cinéma.

It's essential that you know in which district the movie theater is located.

To ask what someone likes, use:

Est-ce que les arts **vous plaisent**?

Do you like the arts?

Est-ce que la musique d'Angélique Kidjo **te plaît**?

Do you like Angélique Kidjo's music?

Est-ce que les paysages te plaisent?

To say what someone likes, use:

Même les fleurs et les fruits de ses natures mortes **plaisent** aux yeux.

Even the flowers and fruit in his still lifes are pleasing to the eyes.

Sa musique dynamique **plaît** à tous.

Everyone likes her dynamic music.

To list, use:

Ses autres films très connus **sont** *Ma saison préférée, La Reine Margot, Un cœur en hiver, Le huitième jour* et *Lucie Aubrac*.

His other well-known movies are Ma saison préférée, La Reine Margot, Un cœur en hiver, Le huitième jour and Lucie Aubrac.

To state a preference, use:

Il a préféré peindre sa maison, la vie et les rues de Paris, et la nature.

He preferred painting his house, Parisian life and streets, and nature.

To state a generalization, use:

En général on n'acceptait pas les femmes dans beaucoup de professions au 19ᵉ siècle.

In general women weren't accepted in many professions in the 19th century.

To inquire about opinions, use:

À quoi pensez-vous lorsque vous pensez à la culture des pays francophones?

What do you think about when you think of the culture of French-speaking countries?

To give opinions, use:

Cette musique **est si** pleine d'énérgie **qu'**on a envie de danser.

This music is so full of energy that you want to dance.

On a l'impression que la lumière danse dans tous ses tableaux.

You have the impression that light dances in all his paintings.

Aujourd'hui la collection Caillebotte **est une des plus importantes du** musée d'Orsay.

Today the Caillebotte collection is one of the most important in the Orsay Museum.

Il est bon qu'il y en ait plusieurs.

It's good that there are several (of them).

Il est bon que tu m'aides avec ma rédaction.

To inquire about agreement, use:

Vous ne trouvez pas?

Don't you think so?

To inquire about surprise, use:

Est-il surprenant que vous reconnaissiez le nom du metteur en scène?

Is it surprising that you recognize the director's name?

To compare, use:

Pour réserver une place, **il vaut mieux que** vous veniez au bureau de location.

To reserve a seat, it's better that you come to the box office.

To inquire about possibility, use:

Est-il possible que vous sachiez l'indice d'un film en avance?

Is it possible for you to know a movie's rating in advance?

To express possibility, use:

Il est possible qu'un film soit interdit.   *It's possible that a movie is prohibited.*

To express impossibility, use:

Il est impossible que vous ne voyiez pas le nom de la scénariste du film.   *It's impossible for you not to see the name of the movie's scriptwriter.*

To express need and necessity, use:

Il faut que vous pensiez aussi aux films, à la musique, à la littérature, à la sculpture et aux tableaux.   *You must also think about movies, music, literature, sculpture and paintings.*

Il faut qu'on assiste à un de ses concerts.   *You have to attend one of her concerts.*

Il est indispensable que vous fassiez attention à la description dans le guide.   *It's indispensable for you to pay attention to the description in the guidebook.*

Il est nécessaire que vous regardiez l'abréviation dans le guide.   *It's necessary that you look at the abbreviation in the guidebook.*

To tell location, use:

Le nom du cinéma est **en bas**.   *The movie theater's name is at the bottom.*

Il est essentiel que vous sachiez dans quel arrondissement **se trouve** le cinéma.   *It's essential that you know in which district the movie theater is located.*

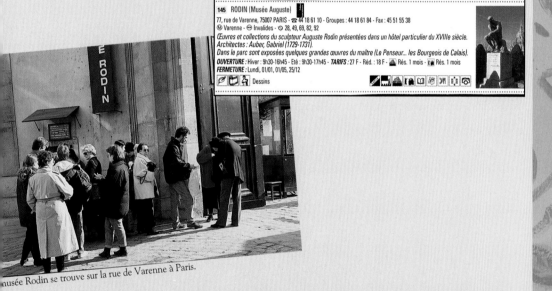

Le musée Rodin se trouve sur la rue de Varenne à Paris.

Listening Activity 3

Unité 4

Le monde du travail

In this unit you will be able to:

➤ write a letter
➤ express intentions
➤ express desire
➤ state want
➤ express hope
➤ state a preference
➤ give opinions
➤ express disagreement
➤ inquire about certainty and uncertainty
➤ express certainty and uncertainty
➤ describe talents and abilities
➤ sequence events
➤ evaluate
➤ make requests
➤ explain a problem
➤ interview
➤ express that you expect a positive response
➤ express appreciation

Tes empreintes ici

Est-ce que tu travailles? Si oui, tu dois savoir qu'il est difficile de travailler et d'être lycéen(ne) à la même fois, et d'avoir assez de temps pour étudier et pour t'amuser.

Il n'est pas toujours facile de trouver le boulot parfait. Tu peux chercher un travail dans les journaux. Tu peux demander aux fast-foods, aux supermarchés, aux grands magasins ou aux stations-service. Si tu as un(e) ami(e) qui travaille, tu peux toujours demander là où il ou elle travaille pour savoir si on a besoin de quelqu'un. Tu as déjà quelque chose à offrir comme employé(e). Par exemple:

- si tu es doué(e) en maths, travaille à la caisse.
- si tu es fort(e) en informatique, travaille sur un ordinateur.
- si tu aimes parler avec les gens, deviens vendeur ou vendeuse.
- si tu parles bien une autre langue, travaille dans un hôtel ou dans un camping où tu peux parler cette langue.
- si tu aimes les enfants, fais du baby-sitting.

Bonne chance dans le monde du travail!

Je travaille comme vendeuse parce que j'aime parler avec les gens.

Leçon A

In this lesson you will be able to:

➤ write a letter

➤ express desire

➤ state want

➤ express hope

➤ state a preference

➤ describe talents and abilities

➤ evaluate

➤ make requests

➤ express that you expect a positive response

➤ express appreciation

Teacher's Note

Communicative functions that are recycled in this lesson are "introducing yourself," "asking for information," "giving information," and "pointing out something."

Dossier ouvert

Imagine que tu passes l'été à Paris. À la fin de ton séjour, tu trouves qu'il y a beaucoup de restaurants et de boutiques qui sont fermés. Qu'est-ce qui se passe?

A. On célèbre la fête de l'Assomption (le 15 août).
B. Tout le monde va en vacances au mois d'août.
C. C'est le résultat d'une crise économique.

Francine est diplômée.   *Elle est organisée.*   *Elle est enthousiaste.*   *Elle est bilingue.*

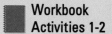
Workbook Activities 1-2

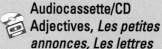
Audiocassette/CD Adjectives, *Les petites annonces, Les lettres*

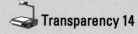
Transparency 14

Je m'appelle° Jean-Guy Letourneau. J'ai 25 ans, et j'habite à Saint-Lazare au Québec. Je travaille avec Assurance° Canada depuis deux ans. On m'a embauché° à plein temps° après mes études à l'université. J'ai un contrat de deux ans. Alors, maintenant je cherche un poste dans une autre compagnie. Depuis quand est-ce que je cherche un nouveau poste? Je regarde les petites annonces depuis le début du mois de juin, et j'ai enfin trouvé une annonce qui m'intéresse. J'ai les qualifications qu'on cherche: je suis bilingue, diligent et fort en informatique. Avec mon expérience je souhaite° qu'on m'offre un gros salaire. Voici l'annonce que j'ai lue, la lettre que j'ai écrite et la réponse que j'ai reçue.

Quelles sont vos qualifications?

Je suis bilingue et très forte dans le service à la clientèle.

je m'appelle mon nom est; **l'assurance (f.)** *insurance*; **embaucher** *to hire*; **à plein temps** huit heures par jour; **souhaiter** espérer

Teacher's Notes

1. Other related terms and expressions include **un diplôme** (*diploma*), **l'organisation (f.)** (*organization*), **l'enthousiasme (m.)** (*enthusiasm*), **avec enthousiasme** (*enthusiastically*), **s'enthousiasmer** (*to be enthusiastic*), **le bilinguisme** (*bilingualism*), **une carrière** (*career*), **une demande d'emploi** (*job application*), **pendant le travail** (*on the job*), **une description de poste** (*job description*), **la chasse à l'emploi** (*job hunting*), **la satisfaction au travail** (*job satisfaction*), **la garantie de l'unité de l'emploi** (*job security*), **poser sa candidature à** (*to apply for*), **un entretien, une entrevue** (*interview*), **avoir une entrevue avec** (*to interview*) and **les références** (*references*). 2. Job ads are found in the **Emplois** or **Carrières et emplois** section of **Les petites annonces**. 3. The leading French-language newspapers in Montreal are *Le Journal de Montréal* and *La Presse*. 4. Another term for **un CV (curriculum vitae)** is **un résumé**. 5. **Un boulot**, synonym for **un poste**, was introduced in Unit 9 in the second level of *C'est à toi!* **Un emploi** will be introduced in **Leçon B**. 6. Synonyms for **une compagnie** include **une entreprise, une firme** and **une société**. 7. You may want to review the singular forms of the orthographically changing verb **s'appeler** and introduce the plural forms: **je m'appelle, tu t'appelles, il/elle s'appelle, nous nous appelons, vous vous appelez, ils/elles s'appellent**. 8. Saint-Lazare is a small town 45 minutes southwest of Montreal. 9. "Part-time" is **à mi-temps** or **à temps partiel**.

M. Dombasle a cinq années d'expérience avec sa compagnie. (Paris)

ASSURANCE LACERTE

Depuis combien de temps cherchez-vous le poste parfait? Si vous le cherchez depuis des mois, venez chez nous. Nous sommes la compagnie d'assurance numéro un et nous devenons encore plus importants. Nous cherchons du personnel très fort dans le service à la clientèle.

Vous devez être bilingue et doué(e) pour la vente.° Nous préférons que vous soyez enthousiaste. De plus nous aimerions que vous soyez flexible et organisé(e). Nous désirons aussi que vous soyez fort(e) en informatique.

Nous voudrions que vous soyez diplômé(e), et nous exigeons° que vous ayez au moins deux années d'expérience.

Envoyez votre CV le plus vite possible à:

ASSURANCE LACERTE
Paul Bagnal
Chef° du Personnel
1800, rue Victoria
Montréal, Québec H3A 3J6
Faxer au 555-9235

Teacher's Notes

1. Students learned how to format and write a French business letter on pages 129-31 in the second level of *C'est à toi!* 2. You will notice that **Vous trouverez** is in the future tense, which will be presented in Unit 6. 3. You may want to remind students that they have already seen the verb **prier** in the expression **Je vous en prie**, introduced on page 77 in the first level of *C'est à toi!* 4. Other closings used in French business letters include **Je vous prie de croire à l'expression de mes sentiments les meilleurs** and **Je vous prie d'agréer l'expression de mes sincères salutations.**

Jean-Guy Letourneau
12, avenue Laval
Saint-Lazare, Québec J7T ZA1

Saint-Lazare, le 26 juillet 1998

Monsieur Paul Bagnal
Chef du Personnel
Assurance Lacerte
1800, rue Victoria
Montréal, Québec H3A 3J6

Monsieur,

Votre annonce dans le numéro du 26 juillet du *Courrier de Montréal* m'a beaucoup intéressé. Mon contrat avec Assurance Canada va bientôt se terminer. Je pense avoir l'expérience et les qualifications que vous cherchez. Vous trouverez ci-joint° mon CV avec photo.

En attendant une réponse favorable, je vous prie° d'agréer,° Monsieur, mes salutations° distinguées.°

Jean-Guy Letourneau

---

la vente *sales;* exiger *to require;* un chef *head;* ci-joint *enclosed;* prier *to beg;* agréer *accepter;* des salutations (f.) *greetings;* Je vous prie d'agréer, Monsieur, mes salutations distinguées. *yours truly*

Assurance Lacerte
1800, rue Victoria
Montréal, Québec H3A 3J6

Montréal, le 31 juillet 1998

Monsieur Jean-Guy Letourneau
12, avenue Laval
Saint-Lazare, Québec J7T ZA1

Monsieur,

En réponse à votre lettre du 26 juillet, nous avons le plaisir de vous annoncer que vos qualifications répondent à nos besoins.° Nous vous serions très reconnaissants° de bien vouloir vous présenter° vendredi, le 8 août, à 10h00. Remplissez, s'il vous plaît, le formulaire° de travail ci-joint avant votre arrivée.

En attendant de vous voir, je vous prie d'agréer, Monsieur, mes salutations distinguées.

Paul Bagnal
Chef du Personnel

un besoin *need*; **reconnaissant(e)** *grateful*; **se présenter** venir; **un formulaire** une fiche

Teacher's Notes

1. Point out that the adjective **reconnaissant** comes from the present participle of **reconnaître**.
2. In France it is not against the law to ask personal questions during an interview. For example, French job seekers might be asked if they are married and if they have children.

Au
44.35.80.00
je vous
accueille
à bras
ouverts
pour passer
votre
annonce

*Les
Petites Annonces
du Figaro*

1 *Dans chaque phrase corrigez la faute (mistake) en italique d'après la description de Jean-Guy, l'annonce de la compagnie Assurance Lacerte, la lettre de Jean-Guy et la réponse qu'il a reçue.*

1. Jean-Guy Letourneau cherche *une annonce* dans une autre compagnie.
2. Quelles sont les qualifications de Jean-Guy? Il est *distingué*, diligent et fort en informatique.
3. Avec *sa clientèle* Jean-Guy souhaite qu'on lui offre un gros salaire.
4. Assurance Lacerte veut avoir un(e) employé(e) doué(e) pour *la recherche*.
5. Cet(te) employé(e) doit être *exigeant(e)* et organisé(e).
6. *La salutation* dans le numéro du 26 juillet a beaucoup intéressé Jean-Guy.
7. M. Bagnal peut vérifier les qualifications de Jean-Guy en regardant *son contrat*.
8. M. Bagnal serait très *enthousiaste* si Jean-Guy voulait bien se présenter vendredi, le 8 août.

Jérôme lit une annonce dans *Le Figaro*. (Angers)

2 *Qu'est-ce qu'on peut trouver dans l'annonce pour la compagnie Assurance Lacerte? Indiquez si on peut ou ne peut pas trouver les choses suivantes dans leur annonce en mettant un ✓ dans l'espace blanc convenable.*

	Oui	Non
1. l'âge qu'il faut avoir		
2. le salaire		
3. si c'est une compagnie importante		
4. si le service à la clientèle est important		
5. un formulaire à remplir		
6. les qualifications qu'on voudrait		
7. où on envoie son CV		
8. si on doit envoyer sa photo		
9. si on travaille à plein temps		
10. combien d'années d'expérience il faut avoir		

**Audiocassette/CD
Activities 1-2**

Answers

1 1. Jean-Guy Letourneau cherche un poste dans une autre compagnie.
2. Quelles sont les qualifications de Jean-Guy? Il est bilingue, diligent et fort en informatique.
3. Avec son expérience Jean-Guy souhaite qu'on lui offre un gros salaire.
4. Assurance Lacerte veut avoir un(e) employé(e) doué(e) pour la vente.
5. Cet(te) employé(e) doit être flexible et organisé(e).
6. L'annonce dans le numéro du 26 juillet a beaucoup intéressé Jean-Guy.
7. M. Bagnal peut vérifier les qualifications de Jean-Guy en regardant son CV.
8. M. Bagnal serait très reconnaissant si Jean-Guy voulait bien se présenter vendredi, le 8 août.

2 1. non
2. non
3. oui
4. oui
5. non
6. oui
7. oui
8. non
9. non
10. oui

Game

Jeopardy

To practice recalling vocabulary learned in the second- and third-level books, you may want to play this game with your students. Construct a game board out of cardboard, cloth or similar material. It should be large enough to accommodate five rows of pockets vertically and five rows of pockets horizontally. The five pockets in each vertical row should each contain a question, all in the same category. (This makes for a total of 25 questions representing five different categories.) Above the top row of each set of horizontal pockets, attach (with paper clips or pins) a card labeling each category, for example, **le travail**, **les arts**, **les rapports humains**, **l'école** and **les problèmes de la France contem-** poraine. Next, write questions along a scale of increasing difficulty and place them accordingly in the pockets. For example, you might ask, **Comment dit-on "grateful" en français?** Divide the class into two teams. Have a student from one team choose a category and whichever question from it that he or she wants to try. Then do the same for the other team. When- ever a question is missed, give the next player in line on the opposing team a chance at it. A correct answer increases the team's point total. To make the game more challenging, you might have students spell the correct word rather than just identify it.

C'est à toi!

1. Est-ce que tu conduis? Si oui, est-ce toi qui paies l'assurance?
2. Est-ce que tu regardes les petites annonces dans le journal? Pourquoi ou pourquoi pas?
3. Est-ce que tu as jamais écrit un CV? Si oui, pourquoi?
4. Est-ce que tu travailles? Si oui, depuis combien de temps as-tu ce boulot?
5. Quel est le poste parfait pour toi?
6. En quoi est-ce que tu es doué(e)?
7. Selon toi, quelles sont les qualifications d'un(e) bon(ne) lycéen(ne)?
8. Après tes études au lycée, est-ce que tu veux travailler à plein temps ou continuer tes études à l'université?

Enquête culturelle

Presque 12.000.000 de femmes françaises travaillent aujourd'hui. Ça fait 50 pour cent comparé à 39 pour cent en 1970. Comparez ça à l'attitude changeante du Français moyen: en 1978, seulement 30 pour cent des Français disaient que la femme pouvait travailler si elle le désirait; mais aujourd'hui, 50 pour cent disent la même chose. Pourquoi la Française moyenne cherche-t-elle un travail? Les enquêtes révèlent que la femme veut y trouver son indépendance, elle veut chercher son identité et elle veut aider aux finances de la maison. Il faut aussi considérer les changements des conditions de vie. Aujourd'hui deux femmes avec deux enfants sur trois travaillent. C'est peut-être parce qu'il y a beaucoup de femmes qui n'ont pas de mari, mais le plus important, c'est que les couples ont besoin de deux salaires pour bien vivre. Presque 3.500.000 des femmes au travail ont un poste à temps partiel (moins de 15 heures par semaine). C'est le développement des emplois à temps partiel qui a contribué le plus à l'institution du travail féminin. De toutes les personnes qui travaillent à temps partiel, 90 pour cent sont des femmes. Ce sont surtout les assistantes maternelles et les employées de maison.

> *Conseil des ministres, le 8 octobre*
> **❝** La politique familiale doit faciliter l'activité professionnelle des femmes. **❞**

En France 83 pour cent des Françaises avec un enfant travaillent.

■ **Workbook**
Activity 3

🎧 **Audiocassette/CD**
Activity 3

Answers

3 Answers will vary.

Teacher's Notes

1. Cognates in this reading include **pour cent, comparé, attitude, révèlent, indépendance, identité, finances, considérer, conditions, développement, emplois, contribué, institution, féminin, maternelles, consacrent, apprentis, contraire, disposent, produits, symboles, certain, groupe, social, aspirent, prestigieux, juge, économiste, journaliste, projet, ressources, révolution, électronique, transistor, microprocesseur, télématique, union, télécommunications, annoncent, automatisation, éliminé, industrie, production, travailleurs, manuels, techniques, téléservices, suffisante, communiquer, créativité, qualités, personnelles, déterminer** and **réussite**. 2. In 65 percent of couples, both the man and the woman hold regular jobs. Sixty-seven percent of French men find it normal that the woman in a couple earns more than the man. 3. Women aged 60 and over attribute advances in their lives to: contraception (48%), household appliances (43%), the possibility of entering any field (41%), changes in men's attitudes (35%), legalized abortion (23%), the simplification of divorce (13%), and the development of **l'union libre** (13%). 4. The number of French women working is highest for the 25- to 29-year age group, the majority of whom have not yet had a child.

Seulement 18 pour cent des jeunes entre 18 et 25 ans ont un boulot à plein temps, et cinq pour cent un travail à temps partiel. Les autres sont des étudiants qui consacrent leur temps à étudier, des gens qui apprennent un métier (les apprentis) et des personnes qui font un stage. Mais on ne peut pas dire que les jeunes Français n'ont pas d'argent. Au contraire, ils disposent de 150 francs par semaine. Ils se paient des distractions (cafés, cinémas), des vêtements et de la musique (stéréo, CDs). Les jeunes Français croient qu'il est important d'acheter des produits "symboles" qui indiquent qu'ils sont membres d'un certain groupe social. À quels emplois les jeunes aspirent-ils? Les métiers les plus prestigieux selon les jeunes sont:

- directeur (directrice) d'une compagnie
- juge/avocat(e)
- médecin
- professeur
- ingénieur
- économiste
- journaliste
- chef de projet en ressources humaines

Aspires-tu à une carrière dans la médecine?

JEUNES GENS H/F 18/25 ans environ Job sympa Ambiance cool Formation assurée Contrat salarié **7.000F** (minimum garanti), prime, % Quartier Gambetta M° Pelleport **TÉLÉPHONEZ VITE AU : 40.30.30.30**

Comment le Français moyen dispose-t-il de son salaire?

- transports et communications 16%
- nourriture et boisson 18%
- maison, électricité, chauffage 22%
- vêtements 6%
- articles de maison 7%
- loisirs, spectacles et événements culturels 8%
- services médicaux 10%
- autre 13%

Cooperative Group Practice

"What's My Line?"

You may want your class to play a version of "What's My Line?" to review professions. Put students in small groups of four or five. A volunteer in each group selects a card from a stack that you have prepared listing professions you want to review. The remaining students in the group ask questions that the volunteer answers with **oui** or **non**, for example, **Travailles-tu pour une grande compagnie**? You may want to put a time or question limit on each player's turn. When a student in the group correctly identifies the profession of the volunteer, he or she becomes the next to select a card. To make the game more fun, you may want to include unusual jobs, such as magician, acrobat, carpet cleaner, toll collector, opera singer, lifeguard and zookeeper. Even though students do not know how to express these jobs in French, they will be able to ask adequate questions to discover their identity.

Dans les années 50 une révolution dans le travail a commencé avec l'électronique. Le transistor, le microprocesseur et enfin la télématique (l'union du microprocesseur et des télécommunications) annoncent un nouveau genre de travail. L'automatisation a éliminé beaucoup de boulots dans l'industrie de production. Les travailleurs manuels ont maintenant des emplois dans le service: banquiers (banquières), ingénieurs, serveurs (serveuses) de restaurants, agents de voyage, agents d'assurances, professeurs, policiers (policières), médecins, infirmiers (infirmières). Mais avec tous les boulots techniques et les téléservices, la qualification technique ne va pas être suffisante pour les emplois de demain. Il faut savoir communiquer (surtout dans une autre langue), être prêt(e) à travailler avec les autres, être dynamique et avoir de la créativité. Ces qualités personnelles vont déterminer votre réussite.

Société Domaine Aéronautique recherche :

Ingénieurs Qualité Logiciel   Région Sud-Est
Ingénieurs Qualité Assurance Produits

■ Formation supérieure en informatique avec expérience minimum de cinq ans en développement.
■ Expérience en assurance produits dans les domaines spatial et aéronautique.
■ Connaissance du segment sol et du système de conduite de vols.
■ Connaissance de base en équipements électroniques de satellites.
■ Première expérience en chef de projet, appréciée.
■ Anglais lu, écrit et parlé couramment.
■ Déplacements en France et en Europe possibles.

Envoyer Curriculum-Vitæ, lettre manuscrite, prétentions en précisant la référence 13.450 à : **PRB Communication**, 17 rue Bergère, 75009 PARIS, qui transmettra.

Aujourd'hui en France il y a presque trois millions de Français dans les travaux de service. (Strasbourg)

Répondez aux questions suivantes.

1. Combien de femmes françaises travaillent?
2. Pourquoi la Française moyenne travaille-t-elle?
3. Les femmes qui ont des enfants, travaillent-elles?
4. Pourquoi est-ce que les femmes qui ont un mari veulent travailler?
5. Combien de femmes ont un travail à temps partiel?
6. Est-ce que la majorité des jeunes entre 18 et 25 ans ont un travail?
7. Que font les jeunes qui ne travaillent pas?
8. Qu'achètent les jeunes avec leur argent?
9. Selon les jeunes, quels sont les métiers les plus prestigieux?
10. Quelles vont être les qualifications importantes pour les emplois de demain?

Jean-Luc est apprenti dans une boulangerie.

Answers

4 1. Presque 12.000.000 de femmes françaises travaillent.
2. La Française moyenne veut trouver son indépendance, elle veut chercher son identité et elle veut aider aux finances de la maison.
3. Oui, deux femmes avec deux enfants sur trois travaillent.
4. Les femmes qui ont un mari veulent travailler parce que les couples ont besoin de deux salaires pour bien vivre.
5. Presque 3.500.000 des femmes ont un travail à temps partiel.
6. Non, seulement 18 pour cent des jeunes entre 18 et 25 ans ont un boulot à plein temps, et cinq pour cent un travail à temps partiel.
7. Les jeunes qui ne travaillent pas sont des étudiants, des apprentis et des personnes qui font un stage.
8. Ils se paient des distractions (cafés, cinéma), des vêtements et de la musique (stéréo, CDs).
9. Selon les jeunes, les métiers les plus prestigieux sont directeur (directrice) d'une compagnie, juge/avocat(e), médecin, professeur, ingénieur, économiste, journaliste et chef de projet en ressources humaines.
10. Les qualifications pour les emplois de demain sont de savoir communiquer (surtout dans une autre langue), être prêt(e) à travailler avec les autres, être dynamique et avoir de la créativité.

Teacher's Notes

1. The first revolution in the working world occurred with the invention of the steam engine at the end of the 18th century. The second began with the invention of electricity at the end of the 19th century. 2. **Télétravail** may be the new mode of work in the future. Currently 54 percent of French workers would be willing to work at home if their jobs so permitted. 3. The service industry, the most important and fastest-growing economic sector in France, currently employs 2.9 million people. 4. Forty-nine thousand new jobs were created in management in 1995 alone. All were linked to computer science, production, and research and development.

Workbook
Activity 4

1. The **Structure** section in Unit 4 contains both new and recycled grammatical concepts. 2. Point out to students that the French verbs in the examples are in the present tense, but the English verbs are in the present perfect tense. 3. You may want to explain that the imperfect is used with **depuis** to express how long something had been going on when another event occurred, for example, **Jean-Guy travaillait avec Assurance Canada depuis deux ans quand il a lu l'annonce d'Assurance Lacerte.** *(Jean-Guy had been working at Assurance Canada for two years when he read the Assurance Lacerte advertisement.)* 4. Before a noun or a pronoun plus a verb, use **depuis que**, for example, **Josyane n'a pas vu Claude depuis qu'elle a commencé son nouveau poste.** *(Josyane hasn't seen Claude since she started her new job.)* 5. You might review with students that **il y a**, followed by an expression of time, is used to tell how long ago something happened, for example, **On a embauché Jean-Guy il y a deux ans.** *(They hired Jean-Guy two years ago.)* 6. **Ça fait**, followed by **que** and a verb in the present tense, is used to tell how long ago something happened, for example, **Ça fait deux ans que Jean-Guy travaille ici.** *(Jean-Guy has been working here for two years.)*

---

5 | *Imaginez que vous voulez travailler à temps partiel dans un fast-food français. Remplissez la demande d'emploi (job application) suivante.*

Café OLÉ

Vous avez du temps libre?
Vous cherchez un job sympa, en équipe, près de chez vous ou de votre école?
Vous avez au moins 16 ans?

Alors, rejoignez notre équipe au Café OLÉ aujourd'hui: un job et des horaires "à la carte" vous attendent. C'est très simple. Remplissez cette demande d'emploi, et donnez-la vite au Manager du restaurant.

NOM: TÉL:
PRÉNOM: DATE DE NAISSANCE:
ADRESSE: ÉCOLE:
VILLE: QUALIFICATIONS:
CODE POSTAL: EXPÉRIENCES:

Cochez les cases correspondant aux demi-journées pendant lesquelles vous disposez d'au moins deux heures consécutives de libre.

	lundi	mardi	mercredi	jeudi	vendredi	samedi	dimanche
7h à 11h							
11h à 16h							
16h à 21h							
21h à 1h							

Le Café OLÉ vous attend!

Journal personnel

The electronic revolution is rapidly changing the face of employment. Jobs that were once in high demand are being eliminated, and new jobs are being created in a variety of sectors. In this age of information, what jobs do you think will be most in demand when you are ready to look for full-time employment? In what areas do you think there will be an abundance of new jobs? What jobs will have disappeared? How do you think your education will have prepared you for a job? What classes in high school will have proved to be the most useful to you? After high school how do you plan to use technology to prepare yourself for the world of work?

Structure

Depuis + present tense

Depuis quand (*since when*) plus a verb in the present tense is used to ask when an action began in the past that is still going on in the present. To answer this question, use a present tense verb form, **depuis** (*since*) and an expression of time.

Depuis quand vs. depuis combien de temps

To help students determine whether to choose **depuis quand** or **depuis combien de temps** when asking a question, write a list of time expressions on the board, for example, **1997, le mois d'avril, quatre ans, l'âge de 12 ans, neuf mois, le 28 novembre, deux semaines** and **hier**. Make two columns on the board, one for **depuis quand** and the other for **depuis combien de temps**. Ask students to help you place the time expressions under the correct column and to explain why. Students should tell you that **1997, le mois d'avril, l'âge de 12 ans, le 28 novembre** and **hier** go under the **depuis quand** column because they express "since," or when the action began. Students should tell you that **quatre ans, neuf mois** and **deux semaines** go under the **depuis combien de temps** category because they express "for," or how long the action has been going on. You may want to have students form questions using the time expressions in the two columns.

Depuis quand est-ce que Jean-Guy cherche un nouveau poste? Il regarde les petites annonces depuis le début du mois de juin.

Since when has Jean-Guy been looking for a new job? He's been looking in the want ads since the beginning of the month of June.

Depuis combien de temps (*how long*) plus a verb in the present tense is used to ask how long an action has been going on. To answer this question, use a present tense verb form, **depuis** (*for*) and an expression of time.

Depuis combien de temps cherchez-vous le poste parfait? Je le cherche depuis des mois.

How long have you been looking for the perfect job? I've been looking for months.

"- Avant, le sport préféré de ma femme était très doux. Depuis qu'elle utilise Sega Sport, il est redevenu rugueux et a retrouvé force et vigueur". **Sylvie et Patrick**

Pratique

Quelles sont les professions de ces gens? Depuis combien de temps travaillent-ils? Répondez à ces questions selon les illustrations. Suivez le modèle.

Modèle:

Juliette/5 ans
Juliette est vedette depuis cinq ans.

1. M. Junot/2 semaines

4. M. Minetti/20 ans

2. Claire/5 jours

5. Alain/3 ans

7. M. Brunel/10 ans

3. M. Maurel/32 ans

6. Mlle Renaud/6 mois

8. Mme Chouinard/9 mois

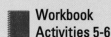

Workbook Activities 5-6

Audiocassette/CD Activity 7

Answers

7 1. Depuis quand Naf Naf vous intéresse?

2. Depuis combien de temps cherchez-vous un nouveau poste?

3. Depuis quand lisez-vous les petites annonces?

4. Depuis quand travaillez-vous aux Galeries Lafayette?

5. Depuis combien de temps y vendez-vous des accessoires?

6. Depuis combien de temps êtes-vous diplômée?

7. Depuis combien de temps êtes-vous bilingue?

8. Depuis quand habitez-vous à Tours?

Teacher's Notes

1. Point out to students that the subjunctive is used when the subjects of the two clauses are different. When the subjects are the same, students can avoid the subjunctive by using an infinitive, for example, **Je préfère travailler à plein temps.** (*I prefer to work full-time.*) 2. You might want to write the "formula" S1 + V1 + **que** + S2 + V2 on the board to illustrate how the two clauses join together to form a subjunctive sentence. 3. Another verb of wish, will or desire that takes the subjunctive is **insister** (*to insist*). **Espérer** (*to hope*), however, takes the indicative, except in a negative or interrogative sentence. 4. Certain verbs of communication, such as **défendre** (*to forbid*), **demander** (*to ask*), **interdire** (*to forbid*), **ordonner** (*to order*) and **permettre** (*to allow*), may take the subjunctive when used to express an indirect request. 5. The command form "Let . . ." is expressed by **Que** followed by the subjunctive. This is an abbreviated form of **permets que** or **permettez que** that comes before only the **je**, **nous**, **il(s)**, **elle(s)** or **on** subjunc-

Modèle:

Je vous attends depuis cinq minutes, Madame Cliquot. Depuis combien de temps m'attendez-vous, Caroline?

Depuis combien de temps est-ce que vous peignez des portraits?

Depuis six mois.

7 Caroline vient de se présenter à une interview avec Mme Cliquot pour un poste à Naf Naf, une boutique de vêtements française. Pour chaque réponse que Caroline a donnée, écrivez la question correspondante que Mme Cliquot lui a posée.

1. Naf Naf m'intéresse depuis l'âge de dix ans.
2. Je cherche un nouveau poste depuis un mois.
3. Je lis les petites annonces depuis le 15 août.
4. Je travaille aux Galeries Lafayette depuis 1998.
5. J'y vends des accessoires depuis neuf mois.
6. Je suis diplômée depuis deux ans.
7. Je suis bilingue depuis sept ans.
8. J'habite à Tours depuis le début du mois de novembre.

The subjunctive after expressions of wish, will or desire

You remember that in French the subjunctive usually comes after **que** in a dependent clause. In the last unit you learned various impersonal expressions that are followed by the subjunctive. Verbs that express wish, will or desire also take the subjunctive. Use the subjunctive after one of these verbs when the wish or desire concerns someone other than the subject.

aimer	*to like, to love*
désirer	*to want*
exiger	*to require*
préférer	*to prefer*
souhaiter	*to wish, to hope*
vouloir	*to want*

J'aime que le temps travaille pour moi.

Je désire que vous fassiez la vaisselle ce soir.

Nous **exigeons** que vous ayez au moins deux années d'expérience.   *We require that you have at least two years of experience.*

Avec mon expérience je **souhaite** qu'on m'**offre** un gros salaire.   *With my experience I hope that they give me a high salary.*

Nous **désirons** aussi que vous soyez fort en informatique.   *We also want you to be strong in computer science.*

tive form, for example, **Qu'il remplisse le formulaire.** (*Let him fill out the form.*)

TPR

Subjunctive or Infinitive?

So that students can distinguish between sentences using the subjunctive and an infinitive, prepare a list of sentences that use either the subjunctive or an infinitive construction, for example, **Maman exige que je fasse la vaisselle** and **Le chef désire embaucher Charles.** Have

students prepare two cards, one with "S" for subjunctive and the other with "I" for infinitive. As you read each sentence, students hold up the "S" card if they hear a sentence with the subjunctive. If they hear a sentence with an infinitive, they hold up the "I" card.

Pratique

Bruno et Julianne sont de nouveaux employés à Quick. Jouez le rôle de M. Abdallah, leur chef. Dites-leur ce que vous voulez qu'ils fassent ou ne fassent pas. Pour chaque phrase, utilisez une expression logique de la liste suivante. Suivez le modèle.

> ne pas dormir derrière le comptoir
> sortir la poubelle
> nettoyer toutes les tables
> ne pas brûler les hamburgers
> dire "Merci" à la clientèle
>
> ne pas étudier au comptoir
> ne pas être en retard
> offrir du café à la clientèle
> ne pas voler d'argent

Modèle:

Je veux que vous ne soyez pas en retard.

1.

2.

3.

4.

5.

6.

7.

8.

En Champagne, la tradition veut qu'on assemble des vins de plusieurs années.

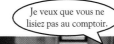
Je veux que vous ne lisiez pas au comptoir.

Cooperative Group Practice

L'ami(e) idéal(e)

To practice using the subjunctive after **aimer, désirer, exiger, préférer, souhaiter** and **vouloir**, put students in small groups of four or five. Make sure that boys and girls are represented in each group. Give each group a stack of note cards that you have prepared listing infinitive expressions that students will comment on to express what they are looking for in the ideal boyfriend or girlfriend, for example, **danser bien, être sensible, être beau/belle, m'offrir des fleurs, me téléphoner chaque jour, aimer rigoler, aller aux matchs sportifs, s'habiller bien, avoir une voiture, être populaire, aimer la musique que j'aime**. The first student forms a sentence using the infinitive on the note card and one of the six verbs that take the subjunctive, for example, **J'aime que mon ami(e) danse bien**. Students take turns forming sentences with the subjunctive until all the note cards have been used. At this point each student summarizes for the group what he or she wants in an ideal partner by making a sentence for each of the verbs. Then have the girls write a paragraph about what the boys are looking for in an ideal girlfriend, and vice versa.

Paired Practice

Les dialogues

To practice forming sentences using an infinitive and the subjunctive, put your students in pairs. One student plays the role of a parent and the other the role of a teenager. Give each pair a situation card that lists two infinitives, for example, **aller au match de basketball/rentrer avant 11h00,** prendre la voiture/mettre ta ceinture de sécurité, inviter des copains/ranger le salon, aller au cinéma/finir tes devoirs, and **faire de la planche à neige/faire attention**. The teenager addresses the parent with an activity that he or she would like to do, for example, **Dis, papa, je voudrais aller au match de basketball ce soir**. The parent responds with the condition that must be met, for example, **Écoute, je veux que tu ailles au match de basketball ce soir, mais j'exige que tu rentres avant 11h00**. After each pair has practiced its dialogue, have all the pairs present theirs to the class. You may want to give students the assignment of listening carefully to each skit and writing down what the parent tells the teenager to do, for example, **Le père de Guy exige qu'il rentre avant 11h00**.

![audio icon] **Audiocassette/CD Activities 9-10**

Answers

9 1. Ma mère veut que je me couche tôt ce soir.

2. Mes parents préfèrent que je prenne le petit déjeuner avant de quitter la maison.

3. Mon frère exige que je sache l'adresse de la compagnie.

4. Mon père désire que j'arrive à l'heure.

5. Mes parents exigent que je remplisse le formulaire de travail.

6. Tout le monde désire que je sois enthousiaste.

7. Ma sœur veut que je réponde sérieusement aux questions.

8. Ma mère souhaite que je remercie le chef du personnel.

10 1. Comment tu trouves le cours de français? Et toi, comment tu trouves le cours de français?

2. Comment tu trouves l'enseignement dans cette école? Et toi, comment tu trouves l'enseignement dans cette école?

3. Comment tu trouves le temps qu'il fait? Et toi, comment tu trouves le temps qu'il fait?

4. Comment tu trouves les émissions à la télé? Et toi, comment tu trouves les émissions à la télé?

5. Comment tu trouves tes parents? Et toi, comment tu trouves tes parents?

6. Comment tu trouves les hommes et les femmes politiques? Et toi, comment tu trouves les hommes et les femmes politiques?

Students' responses to these questions will vary.

Teacher's Note

You might add to the list in Activity 10 and ask each pair to also comment on cocurricular activities at your school, friends, **le directeur** and homework in one of their classes.

Modèle:

ma mère/exiger/s'habiller bien
Ma mère exige que je m'habille bien.

Modèle:

la cantine de l'école
Élève A: Comment tu trouves la cantine de l'école?
Élève B: J'aimerais qu'il y ait plus de choix. Et toi, comment tu trouves la cantine de l'école?
Élève A: J'aimerais qu'on offre plus de salades.

9 *Imaginez que vous êtes Jean-Guy Letourneau. Demain matin vous allez vous présenter à Assurance Lacerte. Dites ce que votre famille veut que vous fassiez pour faire bonne impression.*

1. ma mère/vouloir/se coucher tôt ce soir

2. mes parents/préférer/prendre le petit déjeuner avant de quitter la maison

3. mon frère/exiger/savoir l'adresse de la compagnie

4. mon père/désirer/arriver à l'heure

5. mes parents/exiger/remplir le formulaire de travail

6. tout le monde/désirer/être enthousiaste

7. ma sœur/vouloir/répondre sérieusement aux questions

8. ma mère/souhaiter/remercier le chef du personnel

10 *Avec un(e) partenaire, posez des questions sur comment vous trouvez les personnes et les choses indiquées. Donnez vos opinions en utilisant l'expression* **J'aimerais que**. *Suivez le modèle.*

1. le cours de français

2. l'enseignement dans cette école

3. le temps qu'il fait

4. les émissions à la télé

5. tes parents

6. les hommes et les femmes politiques

Comment tu trouves la nouvelle chanson de Céline Dion?

J'aimerais qu'elle la chante en français.

Cooperative Group Practice

Sentence Completion

To practice forming the subjunctive of regular and irregular verbs after expressions of wish, will or desire, put students in small groups of four or five. Write the following phrases on the board or on an overhead transparency: 1. La compagnie exige que ses employés.... 2. Les élèves de français veulent que le professeur.... 3. Mes amis souhaitent que je.... 4. Maman préfère que nous.... 5. Au travail j'aime que le chef.... 6. L'enfant de cinq ans désire que tu.... Each group writes as many completions as they can think of for each phrase, for example, **La compagnie exige que ses employés (soient bilingues, soient forts dans le service à la clientèle, aient deux ans d'expérience, arrivent à l'heure, suivent des cours**). When each group has finished, you may want to compile a class list of all the sentence completions that the groups came up with.

Communication

Consultez les petites annonces dans un journal français ou américain pour en trouver une qui vous intéresse. (Si vous préférez, vous pouvez inventer une petite annonce intéressante.) Puis copiez la grille suivante, et remplissez-la selon les renseignements de la petite annonce que vous avez choisie. Enfin utilisez la grille pour écrire une petite annonce en français pour ce boulot. (Vous pouvez utiliser votre nom comme chef du personnel.)

nom de la compagnie: _____

chef du personnel: _____

adresse: _____

numéro de téléphone: _____

boulot: _____

responsabilités: _____

qualifications: _____

expérience: _____

éducation: _____

salaire: _____

Échangez la petite annonce que vous venez d'écrire dans l'Activité 11 contre (for) l'annonce d'un(e) partenaire. Puis répondez à cette nouvelle petite annonce en écrivant une lettre au chef du personnel de la compagnie qui offre le boulot. Dites que vous cherchez un boulot et ce que vous voulez dans ce boulot. Mentionnez vos qualifications et votre expérience. Utilisez la lettre de Jean-Guy Letourneau à la page 144 comme modèle.

Oui, je suis diplômée. J'ai fait mes études à l'École Supérieure de Commerce de Lyon.

Avec votre partenaire de l'Activité 12, jouez les rôles du chef du personnel (la personne qui offre le boulot dans l'Activité 12) et du candidat (la personne qui veut être embauchée). Le candidat n'a jamais reçu de réponse à sa lettre. Alors, il décide de téléphoner au chef du personnel. Le candidat dit qu'il cherche un nouveau poste et explique pourquoi il téléphone. Il parle de ses qualifications, de son expérience et de son éducation. Le chef du personnel décide s'il veut inviter le candidat à se présenter ou pas.

 Listening Activity 1

 Quiz *Leçon A*

Teacher's Note

You may want to post the job ads that students make for Activity 11 around the classroom for all to see.

Workbook Activity 7

Advanced Placement

Sur la bonne piste

Writing a Résumé

When you apply for a job, your letter of application should be accompanied by a résumé, or curriculum vitæ. This formal summary introduces you on paper to a prospective employer by giving certain personal information, your background and your experience. It should present these facts in the best possible light so that this potential employer is impressed by your credentials and the care you took to create your résumé, or curriculum vitæ. It should be typed or formatted on a word processor and have a professional appearance. You should present facts clearly and briefly. On your résumé be sure to include:

- your name, address and telephone number
- your objective or goal in seeking a job with this employer, or in this field
- your educational history in reverse chronological order, with the most recent accomplishments listed first
- your work experience in reverse chronological order, with your most recent work experience listed first
- [optional] personal information, such as membership in relevant clubs and organizations, community service, volunteer work, hobbies, etc.
- a list of references whom the employer may contact to get more information about you. Remember to first ask potential references if you may use their names.

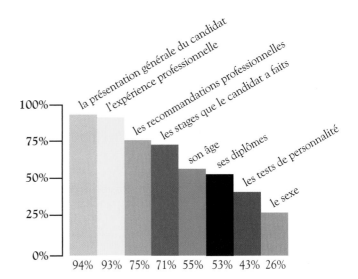

Pourquoi embauchez-vous ce candidat?

Here is a sample résumé written by a French teenager interested in working with young children.

Sandrine CHAUGNOT
12, avenue Saint-Exupéry
94000 Créteil
Tél. 01.49.89.73.00

Née: le 12 mai, 1981 à Troyes

OBJECTIF:	Travailler avec de jeunes enfants chez eux ou à la crèche
FORMATION:	Lycée Descartes, Créteil (en première) Collège Voltaire, Créteil École Sainte-Anne, Créteil

EXPÉRIENCE:

	1997-présent	École des jeunes filles 76, rue Rochambeau Après l'école je jouais à des jeux avec les enfants.
	1996-97	McDonald's 34, place de la Gare Serveuse
	1994-97	M. et Mme François Junot 32, allée de la Toison d'Or J'ai fait du baby-sitting pour leurs deux enfants: un garçon de deux ans et une fille de quatre ans.

LOISIRS:	Football, flûte
À CONTACTER:	Mme Hélène Trélat École des jeunes filles 76, rue Rochambeau, Créteil Tél. 01.49.07.32.82
	M. et Mme François Junot 32, allée de la Toison d'Or, Créteil Tél. 01.49.23.90.87

4 Now think of a summer job that you'd like to have in a French-speaking country. Write your own résumé, stating your objective, background and experience. Follow the format of the sample résumé you have just read.

Teacher's Notes

1. In the U.S. it would be considered unwise and improper to state one's birth date. Sandrine gives her birth date to show her prospective employer that she is old enough to handle a job taking care of children. 2. This is an example of a chronological or historical résumé, which emphasizes work experience. You may want your students to practice writing a functional résumé in addition to or in place of the chronological résumé. In a functional résumé the job seeker emphasizes his or her qualifications and abilities. To write a functional résumé, begin with your name, address, phone number and job objective. Then write four or five paragraphs, each one heading a particular area of expertise or involvement, such as Youth Director, Camp Counselor or Sales Associate. The skills paragraphs should be listed in order of importance; in other words, those skills most similar to the candidate's stated job objective should be listed first. Finally, add a concise chronological listing of employers, job titles and job descriptions with the appropriate dates.

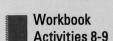

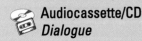

Workbook
Activities 8-9

Audiocassette/CD
Dialogue

Teacher's Notes

1. Communicative functions that are recycled in this lesson are "giving orders," "introducing yourself," "asking for information" and "thanking someone." 2. **Une manifestation** is frequently called **une manif.** 3. Other related terms and expressions include **une caméra de la télévision** (*TV camera*), **se plaindre** (*to complain*) and **une spécialisation** (*specialization*). 4. Lille, located close to the Belgian border, is a model of urban revitalization and renewal. You may want to review with students what they learned about Lille on page 106 in the second level of *C'est à toi!* 5. Demonstrations in France are considered an acceptable means of expressing discontent, usually with regards to a particular national policy. Members of different labor unions, political parties and students are frequent participants. 6. The **SMIC** (**salaire minimum interprofessionnel de croissance**), pronounced [smik], is the index-linked guaranteed minimum wage. It was raised four percent, to 39.43 francs per hour, on July 1, 1997. Before then it was 37.81 francs per hour. The minimum gross pay was adjusted to 6,663.67 francs, and the minimum net pay became 5,239 francs. 7. You might videotape a demonstration on French TV or bring in articles about French demonstrations that have occurred in the past few years. For each demonstration have students identify what the protestors are demonstrating against and the demands they are making. Then ask students to identify complaints that American citizens have with the U.S. government and how they seek to make their causes known.

Leçon B

In this lesson you will be able to:

➤ interview

➤ give opinions

➤ express disagreement

➤ explain a problem

➤ inquire about certainty and uncertainty

➤ express certainty and uncertainty

➤ express intentions

➤ sequence events

Marie-José Tenière, qui est reporter pour TF1, une chaîne de télévision française, va faire un reportage spécial de Lille. Elle va commencer dans un moment. Le bruit qu'on entend vient d'une manifestation. Les rues, qu'on ne peut même pas traverser, sont pleines d'étudiants et de lycéens. Il n'est pas certain que Marie-José puisse s'approcher d'un des manifestants pour lui parler. Attendez, attendez. Ah, voilà. Elle a réussi.

Marie-José: C'est Marie-José Tenière en direct° de Lille. Je parle avec Max Launay, lycéen, qui participe à la manifestation. Je peux vous poser quelques questions?

Max: Ouais, bien sûr.

Marie-José: Max, pourquoi est-ce que les étudiants et les lycéens manifestent° aujourd'hui?

Max: Je ne suis pas sûr° que la raison° soit évidente pour tout le monde.

Marie-José: Croyez-vous que le projet du gouvernement soit une bonne idée?

Max: Non, nous sommes contre° ce projet. Le gouvernement veut créer des emplois° pour les jeunes, mais nous ne pensons pas que ce projet aille assez° loin. Nous, les jeunes, nous comprenons ce qui° se passe. Le problème, c'est qu'il n'y a pas suffisamment° d'emplois pour les jeunes de 18 à 26 ans. Le gouvernement va créer 150.000 emplois. C'est bon. Mais le gouvernement ne veut payer qu'un pourcentage du SMIC.° Et ça, nous ne l'acceptons pas. Je doute que nous acceptions un salaire qui soit inférieur° au salaire minimum. Ce que° le gouvernement n'apprécie pas, c'est qu'un vrai emploi exige un vrai salaire. De plus, on va nous offrir un horaire de travail réduit.

en direct *live*; manifester *participer à une manifestation*; sûr(e) *certain(e)*; une raison *reason*; contre *ne pas être pour*; un emploi *un travail, un boulot*; assez *enough*; ce qui *what*; suffisamment *assez*; le SMIC *minimum wage*; inférieur(e) *moins*; ce que *what*

Marie-José: Et alors, pourquoi êtes-vous ici?

Max: Ben, je vais passer mon bac ES au printemps, et puis, ce que je compte° faire, c'est passer deux années en classes préparatoires aux grandes écoles.° Finalement, je vais essayer de trouver un emploi dans le cadre° administratif. Ce n'est pas vrai que les compagnies fassent le maximum pour embaucher les jeunes. Donc, c'est le gouvernement qui doit les aider. Le taux° de chômage monte pour les jeunes. Ce taux élevé° nous pousse° à faire des études° plus longues. Même si on se spécialise, un emploi n'est pas garanti.

Marie-José: Alors, Max, pensez-vous que le gouvernement fasse attention au message?

Max: Il n'est pas évident que le gouvernement nous écoute. Nous n'avons pas de parti politique. La manifestation, c'est un moyen° de montrer notre mécontentement.°

Marie-José: Ce qui est sûr, c'est que les emplois pour les jeunes restent un problème à résoudre. Alors, Max, merci à vous.

À l'université Mlle Beauvois s'est spécialisée dans la chimie.

Des jeunes Parisiens manifestent contre le racisme.

compter *avoir l'intention de*; **les grandes écoles** *elite, specialized universities*; **le cadre** *sector*; **un taux** *rate*; **élevé(e)** *high*; **pousser** *forcer*; **faire des études** *étudier*; **un moyen** *way*; **le mécontentement** *l'insatisfaction*

Audiocassette/CD Activities 1, 3

Answers

1 1. faux
2. faux
3. vrai
4. vrai
5. faux
6. vrai
7. faux
8. faux
9. faux
10. vrai

2 1. chaîne
2. manifestants
3. en direct
4. contre
5. suffisamment
6. élevé
7. minimum
8. cadre
9. garanti
10. parti

3 Answers will vary.

1 | *Répondez par "vrai" ou "faux" d'après le dialogue.*

1. Marie-José Tenière fait un reportage de Paris.
2. Il n'y a pas beaucoup de monde dans les rues.
3. Max Launay participe à la manifestation.
4. Le projet du gouvernement, c'est de créer des emplois pour les jeunes.
5. Le gouvernement offre de payer le SMIC aux jeunes.
6. Max compte aller à une grande école.
7. Max croit que les compagnies font le maximum pour embaucher les jeunes.
8. Le taux de chômage ne monte pas pour les jeunes de 18 à 26 ans.
9. Si on se spécialise, on est sûr d'avoir un emploi.
10. Pour les jeunes, manifester est un moyen de montrer leur mécontentement.

2 | *Complétez chaque phrase avec l'expression convenable de la liste suivante d'après le dialogue.*

garanti	minimum	parti	chaîne	manifestants
en direct	élevé	cadre	contre	suffisamment

DIMANCHE 31 août
TF1
5.10 Musique. 22238493 5.15 Histoires naturelles. 1936851 5.45 Mésaventures. 1895509 6.10 Intrigues. 2659847 6.40 TF1 infos. 6443122 6.50 Le Disney Club. 57708580

1. TF1 est une... de télévision française.
2. Les... dans les rues font beaucoup de bruit.
3. Marie-José Tenière fait son reportage... des rues de Lille.
4. Max ne pense pas que le projet du gouvernement aille assez loin; il est... ce projet.
5. Il n'y a pas... d'emplois pour les jeunes de 18 à 26 ans.
6. Donc, le taux de chômage de ces jeunes est....
7. Le SMIC, c'est le salaire... qu'on paie.
8. Max espère trouver un emploi dans le... administratif.
9. Mais on ne sait jamais si on va trouver l'emploi qu'on veut parce que l'emploi n'est pas....
10. Les jeunes disent qu'il n'y a pas de... politique qui les écoute.

3 | *C'est à toi!*

1. Est-ce que tu regardes souvent les informations à la télé?
2. Quelle est ta chaîne de télé favorite? Quel reporter préfères-tu?
3. Est-ce que la profession de reporter t'intéresse? Pourquoi ou pourquoi pas?
4. Est-ce que tu as jamais participé à une manifestation? Si oui, contre quoi as-tu manifesté?
5. Est-ce que tu as un boulot? Si oui, reçois-tu le salaire minimum? Crois-tu qu'on te paie suffisamment?
6. Selon toi, est-ce que le gouvernement doit aider les jeunes à trouver un emploi?
7. Après tes études, est-ce que tu voudrais travailler pour une grande compagnie nationale? Pourquoi ou pourquoi pas?
8. Est-ce que tu comptes devenir membre d'un parti politique?

Game

Original Sentences

To practice new vocabulary presented in this lesson, you might want to play this game. Prepare a set of note cards with a new word or term on each one. Then divide the class into two teams. Call the first player from each team to the front of the room. Select the top card from the pile and read aloud the word or term that you want the players to use in a sentence. Both players write a sentence using that word or term. The student who correctly uses the new word or term in a sentence earns a point for his or her team. If both sentences are correct, both teams win a point. When the first two players take their seats, a different player from each team takes a turn. The team with the most points at the end of the allotted time wins.

Depuis longtemps le gouvernement français participe à la direction des conditions de travail. À présent, la semaine officielle de travail est de 39 heures, mais ça n'existe que pour les salariés qui travaillent à plein temps. Certains emplois exigent une semaine plus longue. Les agriculteurs, par exemple, ont la semaine la plus longue à 62 heures de travail pendant que les professeurs à l'école élémentaire ont une semaine de 31,5 heures.

Enquête culturelle

Les gens non-salariés, qui reçoivent un paiement à l'heure, ont une journée de travail plus longue que les salariés. Ils travaillent presque neuf heures par jour comparés aux salariés, qui n'ont qu'une journée longue de sept heures et demie. Ils ont même une semaine plus longue parce qu'ils travaillent six ou sept jours. L'horaire d'une journée de travail varie selon l'activité professionnelle. Dans des bureaux et des magasins, le travail commence entre huit et neuf heures et finit entre 17 et 19 heures. Il y a une courte pause à midi pour le déjeuner. On estime que l'absentéisme au travail est à 11 pour cent du temps de travail théorique.

Les ouvriers du bâtiment *(construction workers)* travaillent 50 heures par semaine.

En France les grands magasins sont fermés pour les jours de fête.

À certains moments de l'année, les longues semaines sont interrompues par des jours de fête, ou jours fériés. Il y a dix jours fériés nationaux en France. Si c'est le jeudi ou le mardi qui est un jour férié, on prolonge le weekend pour faire un "pont" avec un autre jour sans travail, ou jour de congé. L'action du gouvernement permet aux Français 30 jours de vacances (six semaines). C'est vraiment évident au mois d'août, et surtout à Paris où tout semble fermé à la fin de l'été pendant que tout le monde part au bord de la mer ou à la montagne.

Jours de fêtes

Workbook Activity 10

Teacher's Notes

1. Cognates in this reading include **longtemps, direction, conditions, présent, officielle, existe, salariés, agriculteurs, élémentaire, non-salariés, paiement, comparés, varie, activité, professionnelle, pause, estime, absentéisme, pour cent, théorique, interrompues, prolonge, action, permet, population** and **nombre.** 2. In 1997, after a "jobs summit," the French government passed a bill to change the legal working week to 35 hours by January 1, 2000, for companies with more than ten employees. A second bill in 1999 will lay down the precise terms. Optimistic economists expect that this legislation will create 1,400,000 new jobs over five years. Critics of the bill say it will reduce productivity, increase labor costs, put off foreign investors and add to unemployment. 3. Nine out of ten agricultural workers are children of agricultural workers. 4. Eighty-eight percent of French workers are salaried today, as opposed to only 72 percent in 1960. Five and a half million people, or ten percent of the population, work for the government, which places France first among western industrialized nations in the number of government employees. 5. Over fifty percent of the French population eat lunch at home, especially those **en province.** 6. Nearly half the French population do not leave home during July and August for **les grandes vacances.** Of those who leave, 44.8 percent go to the ocean, 24.2 percent go to the countryside and 13.8 percent go to the mountains. Compared to other Europeans, few French people leave the country.

Critical Thinking

Les jours de fête

Put students in pairs or small groups. Tell students that their task is to make a list of the ten national holidays that the French celebrate. To get them started, give each group an American calendar and refer them to the **Mise au point sur... les fêtes dans le monde francophone** in Unit 1 in the second level of *C'est à toi!* By using these resources and reflecting on the role of the Catholic church in French history, students should be able to come up with a complete list: **le 1er janvier (le jour de l'an), Pâques, Pentecôte, le 1er mai (la fête du travail), le 8 mai (l'Armistice 1945), le 14 juillet (la fête nationale), le 15 août (l'Assomption), le 1er novembre (la Toussaint), le 11 novembre (l'Armistice 1918)** and **le 25 décembre (Noël).** Finally, have each pair or group make a calendar highlighting the ten holidays and decorate it to show their understanding of the meaning of each. You may want to post one of the calendars for students to refer to throughout the year.

Workbook Activity 11

Answers

4 1. La semaine officielle de travail en France est de 39 heures.

2. Les professeurs à l'école élémentaire ont une semaine de 31,5 heures.

3. Les non-salariés ont une plus longue journée de travail.

4. Pour les gens qui travaillent dans les bureaux et les magasins, le travail finit entre 17 et 19 heures.

5. Un jour férié est un jour de fête quand il n'y a pas de travail.

6. Il y en a dix en France.

7. Si l'on prolonge une fête avec le weekend, c'est un "pont."

8. Le Français moyen a six semaines de vacances par an.

9. La ville de Paris est déserte en août parce que tout le monde part en vacances au bord de la mer ou à la montagne.

10. Trois millions de Français sont au chômage. Vingt-huit pour cent des jeunes y sont.

Teacher's Notes

1. The relative pronouns **qui** and **que** were introduced on page 220 in the second level of *C'est à toi!* 2. A complex sentence is a sentence that contains one independent clause and one or more subordinate clauses. 3. **Qui** may refer to a person or to a thing. 4. Remind students of the difference between **qui** as a relative pronoun and as an interrogative pronoun. 5. Show your students how each of the model sentences in this section has been formed from two simple ones, for example, **Marie-José Tenière est reporter. Elle s'approche des manifestants.** Then point out the dependent and independent clause in each complex sentence. 6. Show your students that the verb after **qui** is not always in the third person singular. It agrees with **qui**'s antecedent, for example, **C'est moi qui fais le reportage.** 7. You might give your students this hint: Use the relative pronoun **qui** if the next word is a verb.

INFO PLUS LES QUINZE AU CHEVET DU CHÔMAGE

Le chômage continue à être un problème grave pour la France. Trois millions de Français, plus de 12 pour cent de la population, n'ont pas de travail. Le nombre des jeunes de moins de 25 ans qui sont au chômage monte à 28 pour cent.

4 | *Répondez aux questions suivantes.*

1. De combien d'heures est la semaine officielle de travail en France?
2. Qui a une semaine de moins de 35 heures?
3. Qui a une plus longue journée de travail, les salariés ou les non-salariés?
4. À quelle heure le travail finit-il pour les gens qui travaillent dans des bureaux et des magasins?
5. Un jour férié, qu'est-ce que c'est?
6. Combien de jours fériés nationaux y a-t-il en France?
7. Si l'on prolonge une fête avec le weekend, qu'est-ce que c'est?
8. Combien de semaines de vacances a le Français moyen par an?
9. Pourquoi la ville de Paris est-elle déserte en août?
10. Combien de Français sont au chômage? Combien de jeunes?

Journal personnel

To compare what you have just learned about general working conditions in France to those in the U.S., talk to several adults you know who have full-time jobs. How many hours a week do they work? Are they salaried or hourly employees? How many vacation days do they have each year? How many of these days are extended weekends? How much time do they take for lunch? How flexible are their working conditions? Do they have flex-time (variable hours)? What provisions are there for childcare? Compare the answers the adults give you to what you now know about working conditions in France. As you begin to think about full-time employment, what working conditions are the most critical to you? How important are salary, vacations, health and dental insurance, provisions for childcare and flextime?

Structure

The relative pronouns *qui* and *que*

The relative pronouns **qui** and **que** connect two clauses in a complex sentence. The pronouns **qui** and **que** introduce a dependent clause that describes a preceding person or thing, called the antecedent.

Qui (*who, which, that*) is used as the subject of the dependent clause. The verb that follows **qui** agrees with the antecedent.

Marie-José Tenière, qui est reporter, s'approche des manifestants.

Marie-José Tenière, who is a reporter, approaches some demonstrators.

Dans le « Petit Louvre », une collection qui n'oublie aucun grand maître.

give your students this hint: Use the relative pronoun **qui** if the next word is a verb.

TPR

Qui ou que?

Have each student make two simple flash cards, one that says **qui** and another that says **que**. Then say two clauses, for example, **j'ai acheté le CD** and **tu as aimé.** Students hold up the **qui** card if the clauses should be joined by **qui**; they hold up the **que** card if the clauses should be joined by **que**.

Critical Thinking

Relative Pronouns

Put students in pairs. Give each pair a magazine or newspaper in English. Tell students to copy ten sentences that they find that use a relative pronoun. Then ask students to write down if they would use **qui** or **que** if they were to express these sentences in French.

Le projet du gouvernement, qui crée des emplois pour les jeunes, ne va pas assez loin.

The government's project, which creates jobs for young people, doesn't go far enough.

Que (*that, whom, which*) is used as the direct object of the dependent clause.

Le manifestant que nous entendons est un étudiant.

The demonstrator whom we hear is a student.

Le salaire qu'on leur offre est inférieur au salaire minimum.

The salary that they're offering them is less than the minimum salary.

CARTE D'OR
FRUITS QUE J'ADORE

La glace que Claudette prépare est délicieuse. (Périgueux)

When the dependent clause is in the **passé composé**, the past participle of the verb agrees in gender and in number with the antecedent of **que**.

Les emplois qu'ils ont trouvés étaient dans le cadre administratif.

The jobs that they found were in the administrative sector.

C'est "Femme" qu'elle a choisi

Pratique

*Complétez les phrases suivantes avec **qui** ou **que**.*

1. J'ai lu toutes les petites annonces... j'ai trouvées dans le journal.
2. Il y avait beaucoup de postes... semblaient être intéressants.
3. Mais c'était le poste à la Fnac... m'intéressait le plus.
4. Je connais une fille... y travaille.
5. Cette fille,... s'appelle Mélanie, aime bien son boulot.
6. Selon Mélanie, le salaire... on offre est inférieur au salaire minimum.
7. Alors, j'ai téléphoné à la Fnac, et j'ai parlé à M. Dugas, le chef du personnel... embauche tous les nouveaux employés.
8. Selon M. Dugas, j'ai l'expérience et les qualifications... il cherche.
9. Il m'a demandé de me présenter aujourd'hui. Donc, je dois choisir les vêtements... je vais porter.
10. Je dois aussi penser aux questions... M. Dugas va me poser pendant mon rendez-vous.

« J'ai du mal à m'arracher à cette Russie que j'aime et dont j'ai appris la langue dans ma jeunesse. »

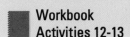

**Workbook
Activities 12-13**

**Audiocassette/CD
Activity 6**

Answers

6 Possible answers:

1. C'est l'argent que le chef donne à l'employé.
2. C'est une personne qui participe à une manifestation.
3. Ce sont des personnes qui ont les mêmes idées politiques.
4. C'est le salaire minimum qui est garanti par le gouvernement.
5. C'est quelque chose qu'on remplit avant de commencer un nouvel emploi.
6. C'est la personne qui embauche les nouveaux employés.
7. C'est une lettre qu'on donne au chef du personnel avec son nom, son adresse, son numéro de téléphone, ses qualifications, son expérience et son éducation.
8. C'est la première chose que vous dites quand vous voyez quelqu'un.

Teacher's Notes

1. You may want to point out to students that in the last three examples, **ce qui** and **ce que** come at the beginning of the sentence to emphasize what follows. **Ce qui** or **ce que** in the dependent clause often comes before **c'est** or **ce sont** in the independent clause. 2. **Ce qui**, as the subject of the dependent clause, is usually followed by the **il/elle** form of the verb and is modified by masculine singular adjectives. 3. **Ce que**, as the direct object of the dependent clause, is usually followed by a subject. 4. **Ce que** becomes **ce qu'** when it precedes a word beginning with a vowel sound. **Ce qui**, however, is invariable. 5. Point out that **ce qui** is pronounced [ski] and **ce que** is pronounced [skə]. 6. Tell students that **qu'est-ce qui** and **qu'est-ce que**, both meaning "what," are used

Modèles:

un(e) étudiant(e)
C'est une personne qui suit des cours à l'université.

le bac
C'est l'examen qu'on passe à la fin de la terminale.

Le Magazine qui passe en revue tout ce qui fait la Mode

castorama
tout ce qu'il vous faut

6 | *Faites des phrases avec* **qui** *ou* **que** *pour identifier les personnes suivantes et pour expliquer les choses suivantes. Suivez les modèles.*

1. un salaire
2. un(e) manifestant(e)
3. un parti
4. le SMIC
5. un formulaire de travail
6. un chef du personnel
7. un CV
8. une salutation

La clientèle, ce sont les personnes qui achètent les produits ou les services d'une compagnie.

The relative pronouns *ce qui* and *ce que*

You just learned that the relative pronouns **qui** and **que** always have a definite antecedent. But if the antecedent is not specific or if it is unknown, put **ce** in front of **qui** or **que** to form **ce qui** or **ce que**.

Ce qui (*what*) is used as the subject of the dependent clause.

Nous comprenons ce qui se passe.	*We understand what is happening.*
Ce qui est sûr, c'est que les emplois pour les jeunes sont un problème.	*What is sure is that jobs for young people are a problem.*

Quand tu fais du shopping, est-ce que tu regardes seulement ce qui est en solde? (Paris)

Ce que (*what*) is used as the direct object of the dependent clause.

Ce que le gouvernement n'apprécie pas, c'est qu'un vrai emploi exige un vrai salaire.	*What the government doesn't appreciate is that a real job requires a real salary.*
Ce que je compte faire, c'est passer deux années en classes préparatoires.	*What I intend to do is spend two years taking preparatory classes.*

to ask questions but not to answer them, for example, *Qu'est-ce qui se passe?* and *Qu'est-ce qu'ils ont fait?* 7. **Ce qui** can be used to answer a question beginning with **qu'est-ce qui**, and **ce que** can be used to answer a question beginning with **qu'est-ce que**, for example, **Je sais ce qui se passe** and **Je sais ce qu'ils ont fait**. 8. To emphasize the indefinite pronoun **ce**, use **c'est** followed by **ce qui** or

ce que, for example, **C'est ce qui est facile** or **C'est ce qu'il sait**. **C'est**, followed by **ce qui** or **ce que**, can also be used to emphasize any noun, for example, **Ce paysage, c'est ce qu'il lui plaît** or **Cet aérogramme, c'est ce qu'elle nous a envoyé**. 9. After a preposition use the relative pronoun **quoi**, for example, **Je ne sais pas (ce) à quoi vous pensez**. **Ce** is usually omitted in this

instance. 10. **Tout ce qui** or **tout ce que** is the equivalent of "everything that" or "all that," for example, **Tout ce que j'achète coûte cher** or **Tout ce qui brille n'est pas or**. 11. You may want your students to write three different lists of things they like (**ce qui me plaît**), things that annoy them (**ce qui m'embête**) and things that worry them (**ce qui m'inquiète**).

Pratique

Dites que vous ne savez pas la réponse à chaque question. Utilisez **ce qui** *ou* **ce que**.

1. Qu'est-ce qui est évident pour tout le monde?
2. Qu'est-ce que le gouvernement va créer?
3. Qu'est-ce qu'on va offrir aux jeunes?
4. Qu'est-ce que les jeunes n'acceptent pas?
5. Qu'est-ce qui pousse les lycéens à faire des études plus longues?
6. Qu'est-ce que Max va essayer de trouver?
7. Qu'est-ce qui n'est pas garanti?
8. Qu'est-ce qui reste un problème à résoudre?

Modèles:

Qu'est-ce que Max compte faire après le bac?
Je ne sais pas ce que Max compte faire après le bac.

Qu'est-ce qui se passe?
Je ne sais pas ce qui se passe.

OÙ TROUVER CE QUE VOUS CHERCHEZ ?

Est-ce que Leïla va faire ses études à la Sorbonne l'année prochaine?

Je ne sais pas ce que Leïla va faire l'année prochaine.

Ce qu'ils veulent, ce qu'ils refusent...

Complétez les phrases suivantes avec **ce qui** *ou* **ce que**.

1. ... est évident pour tout le monde, c'est la raison de cette manifestation.
2. ... le gouvernement va créer, ce sont des emplois pour les jeunes.
3. ... on va offrir aux jeunes, c'est un horaire de travail réduit.
4. ... les jeunes n'acceptent pas, c'est un salaire qui est inférieur au salaire minimum.
5. ... pousse les lycéens à faire des études plus longues, c'est un taux de chômage élevé.
6. ... Max compte faire après le bac, c'est passer deux années en classes préparatoires aux grandes écoles.
7. ... Max va essayer de trouver, c'est un emploi dans le cadre administratif.
8. ... n'est pas garanti, c'est l'emploi.
9. ... reste un problème à résoudre, ce sont les emplois pour les jeunes.

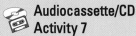

Audiocassette/CD Activity 7

Answers

7 1. Je ne sais pas ce qui est évident pour tout le monde.
2. Je ne sais pas ce que le gouvernement va créer.
3. Je ne sais pas ce qu'on va offrir aux jeunes.
4. Je ne sais pas ce que les jeunes n'acceptent pas.
5. Je ne sais pas ce qui pousse les lycéens à faire des études plus longues.
6. Je ne sais pas ce que Max va essayer de trouver.
7. Je ne sais pas ce qui n'est pas garanti.
8. Je ne sais pas ce qui reste un problème à résoudre.

8 1. Ce qui
2. Ce que
3. Ce qu'
4. Ce que
5. Ce qui
6. Ce que
7. Ce que
8. Ce qui
9. Ce qui

Paired Practice

Exchange Student

To provide practice with sentences using **ce qui**, put students in pairs. Give each student a worksheet with the following questions so he or she can plan what to ask André, a new French exchange student in your school, in an interview for the French class newsletter: 1. Qu'est-ce qui l'intéresse le plus comme passe-temps? 2. Qu'est-ce qu'il aime mieux comme musique? 3. Qu'est-ce qu'il y a d'intéressant à faire dans sa ville en France? 4. Qu'est-ce qui lui plaît aux États-Unis? 5. Qu'est-ce qu'il voudrait faire pendant son séjour aux États-Unis? 6. Qu'est-ce qu'il achète pour sa famille et ses amis en France? Tell the pairs to take turns changing the questions to sentences using **ce qui**, stating what they could ask André, for example, **On pourrait lui demander ce qui l'intéresse le plus comme passe-temps.**

Cooperative Group Practice

C'est ce qu'il faut

To practice using the relative pronoun **ce que**, put students in small groups of four or five. Prepare a set of note cards on which you write tasks that require an appliance, a machine or an object to do, for example, **repasser les chemises, tondre la pelouse, faire sécher le linge, se laver la** figure, **faire la vaisselle, se raser** and **se brosser les dents**. Give each group a similar set of cards. The first student in each group takes the top card and says what is needed to do that task, for example, **Un fer à repasser, c'est ce qu'il faut pour repasser les chemises.** Students take turns until all the note cards in the pile have been used.

Critical Thinking

Ce qui and ce que

Have pairs write six sentences using **ce qui** and **ce que** and copy them on construction paper, leaving off the relative pronouns. Each pair exchanges sentences with those of another pair and explains to them why a subject or direct object is needed in each dependent clause.

Answers

9 1. Qu'est-ce qui te plaît? Et toi, qu'est-ce qui te plaît?

2. Qu'est-ce que tu achètes au centre commercial? Et toi, qu'est-ce que tu achètes au centre commercial?

3. Qu'est-ce que tu aimes manger? Et toi, qu'est-ce que tu aimes manger?

4. Qu'est-ce qui te fait rigoler? Et toi, qu'est-ce qui te fait rigoler?

5. Qu'est-ce qui t'inquiète? Et toi, qu'est-ce qui t'inquiète?

6. Qu'est-ce que tu apprécies? Et toi, qu'est-ce que tu apprécies?

7. Qu'est-ce que tu comptes faire après tes études? Et toi, qu'est-ce que tu comptes faire après tes études?

8. Qu'est-ce qui te pousse à réussir? Et toi, qu'est-ce qui te pousse à réussir?

Students' responses to these questions will vary.

Teacher's Notes

1. When used in the negative, **douter** indicates certainty and takes the indicative, for example, **Le reporter ne doute pas que les manifestants veulent un vrai salaire pour un vrai emploi.**
2. Other expressions that take the subjunctive because they express doubt or uncertainty include **il est douteux, il se peut, il est peu probable, il semble** and **ça m'étonnerait. Il me semble,** however, expresses a positive statement of opinion, so it is followed by the indicative.
3. **Espérer,** like **penser** and **croire,** takes the subjunctive when used in the negative or in the interrogative.
4. **Être sûr(e)** and **être certain(e)** take noun or pronoun subjects, while **être vrai** and **être évident** use the impersonal **il** as the subject. 5. **Il est probable, il est clair** and **il**

Modèles:

t'intéresser

Élève A: Qu'est-ce qui t'intéresse?
Élève B: Ce qui m'intéresse, c'est le théâtre. Et toi, qu'est-ce qui t'intéresse?
Élève A: Ce qui m'intéresse, c'est la musculation.

collectionner

Élève A: Qu'est-ce que tu collectionnes?
Élève B: Ce que je collectionne, ce sont les timbres. Et toi, qu'est-ce que tu collectionnes?
Élève A: Ce que je collectionne, ce sont les CDs de Céline Dion.

Crois-tu que le gouvernement français réponde au mécontentement des étudiants? (Paris)

Pensez-vous que le film puisse vraiment contribuer à une prise de conscience par les spectateurs de la situation politique du Tibet?

9 | *Avec un(e) partenaire, posez des questions en utilisant **qu'est-ce qui** ou **qu'est-ce que**. Puis répondez aux questions en utilisant **ce qui** ou **ce que**.*

1. te plaire
2. acheter au centre commercial
3. aimer manger
4. te faire rigoler
5. t'inquiéter
6. apprécier
7. compter faire après tes études
8. te pousser à réussir

Qu'est-ce que tu envoies au chef du personnel?

Ce que je lui envoie, c'est mon CV avec photo.

MATHURINS
CE QUI ARRIVE ET CE QU'ON ATTEND
JUDITH MAGRE
SABINE HAUDEPIN
SAMUEL LABARTHE
PATRICE KERBRAT
EMMANUEL PATRON
JACQUES CONNORT
PHILIPPE ETESSE
MISE EN SCÈNE
PATRICE KERBRAT
DÉCOR
EDOUARD LAUG
COSTUMES
CHRISTIAN GASC
JEAN-MARIE BESSET
LOCATION 42 65 90 00/01

The subjunctive after expressions of doubt or uncertainty

Another use of the subjunctive is after expressions of doubt or uncertainty. For example, the verb **douter** (*to doubt*) is followed by the subjunctive in the dependent clause.

Je doute que nous acceptions un salaire qui soit inférieur au salaire minimum.	*I doubt we'll accept a salary that is less than the minimum salary.*

When the verbs **penser** and **croire** are used in the negative or in the interrogative, they express doubt and are therefore followed by the subjunctive.

Pensez-vous que le gouvernement fasse attention au message?	*Do you think that the government is paying attention to the message?*
Non, je ne crois pas que le gouvernement nous entende.	*No, I don't believe that the government hears us.*

When expressions of certainty, such as **être sûr(e)**, **être certain(e)**, **être vrai** and **être évident**, are used negatively or interrogatively, they, too, express doubt and are followed by the subjunctive.

Il n'est pas certain que Marie-José puisse s'approcher d'un des manifestants.	*It's not certain that Marie-José can approach one of the demonstrators.*

est probable, il est clair and **il paraît** are additional expressions that takes the subjunctive in the negative or in the interrogative.
6. **Se souvenir** is a verb that takes the subjunctive in the negative or in the interrogative. 7. Certain expressions may be followed by the indicative or the subjunctive, depending on the level of doubt or certainty that the speaker intends. For example, **Il semble que le projet va assez loin** indicates much more certainty than **Il semble que le projet aille assez loin.**

TPR

Expressing Doubt and Certainty

Prepare a list of sentence beginnings, such as **Est-il certain que** and **Tu penses que**, that express doubt or certainty. Have students prepare a card with "S" for subjunctive and one with "I" for indicative. Have students hold up the "S" card if the sentence would be completed with the subjunctive or the "I" card if the sentence would be completed with the indicative.

| Je ne suis pas sûr que la raison soit évidente. | I'm not sure that the reason is obvious. |
| Est-il vrai que les compagnies fassent le maximum? | Is it true that companies are doing the maximum? |

N'est-il pas évident que mes crêpes sont bonnes?

However, when **penser** and **croire**, as well as expressions of certainty, are in the affirmative or in the negative interrogative, they no longer express doubt and are followed by the indicative.

| Ne crois-tu pas que le projet est une bonne idée? | Don't you believe that the project is a good idea? |
| Il est évident que le gouvernement y fait attention. | It's obvious that the government is paying attention (to it). |

The following chart can help you determine the use of the subjunctive and the indicative.

Subjunctive	Indicative
Je doute que....	Je ne doute pas que....
Penses-tu que...?	Je pense que....
Je ne pense pas que....	Ne penses-tu pas que...?
Crois-tu que...?	Je crois que....
Je ne crois pas que....	Ne crois-tu pas que...?
Je ne suis pas sûr(e) que....	Je suis sûr(e) que....
Es-tu sûr(e) que...?	N'es-tu pas sûr(e) que...?
Je ne suis pas certain(e) que....	Je suis certain(e) que....
Es-tu certain(e) que...?	N'es-tu pas certain(e) que...?
Il n'est pas vrai que....	Il est vrai que....
Est-il vrai que...?	N'est-il pas vrai que...?
Il n'est pas évident que....	Il est évident que....
Est-il évident que...?	N'est-il pas évident que...?

Pratique

Les employés d'une compagnie participent à une manifestation. Expliquez pourquoi ces employés ne sont contents ni de la compagnie ni de leur chef, M. Bigot, en disant ce qu'ils ne croient pas. Suivez le modèle.

1. M. Bigot/voir leur mécontentement
2. leurs salaires/être assez élevés
3. la compagnie/leur offrir assez d'assurance
4. leurs emplois/être garantis
5. M. Bigot/comprendre leurs besoins
6. la compagnie/apprécier leur travail
7. la compagnie/faire le maximum pour ses employés
8. M. Bigot/essayer de résoudre tous les problèmes

Modèle:

M. Bigot/embaucher assez de femmes
Les manifestants ne croient pas que
M. Bigot embauche assez de femmes.

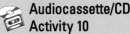

Audiocassette/CD Activity 12

Answers

11 1. comprenne
2. veuille
3. a
4. fasse
5. doit
6. soient
7. aille
8. exige
9. sont
10. fassent

12 1. Penses-tu qu'on puisse trouver un boulot si on se spécialise? Et toi, penses-tu qu'on puisse trouver un boulot si on se spécialise?
2. Penses-tu que l'expérience soit plus importante que l'éducation? Et toi, penses-tu que l'expérience soit plus importante que l'éducation?
3. Penses-tu que les compagnies fassent le maximum pour embaucher les jeunes? Et toi, penses-tu que les compagnies fassent le maximum pour embaucher les jeunes?
4. Penses-tu que le chômage soit un problème très grave? Et toi, penses-tu que le chômage soit un problème très grave?
5. Penses-tu que les salaires des femmes soient moins élevés que les salaires des hommes? Et toi, penses-tu que les salaires des femmes soient moins élevés que les salaires des hommes?
6. Penses-tu que le salaire minimum doive être plus élevé? Et toi, penses-tu que le salaire minimum doive être plus élevé?
Students' responses to these questions will vary.

---

11 *Complétez les phrases avec la forme convenable du verbe entre parenthèses. Attention! Vous pouvez utiliser le subjonctif ou l'indicatif.*

1. Nous doutons que tout le monde... ce qui se passe. (comprendre)
2. Crois-tu que le gouvernement... résoudre le problème du chômage? (vouloir)
3. Il est vrai qu'il n'y... pas suffisamment d'emplois. (avoir)
4. Il n'est pas évident qu'on... le maximum pour aider les jeunes. (faire)
5. Nous sommes sûrs que le gouvernement... aider les compagnies à embaucher plus de jeunes. (devoir)
6. Je ne suis pas certain que tous les jeunes... contre le projet du gouvernement. (être)
7. Les manifestants ne croient pas que ce projet... assez loin. (aller)
8. Est-il évident qu'un vrai emploi... un vrai salaire? (exiger)
9. Je ne doute pas que les manifestants... fatigués. (être)
10. Pensez-vous que les compagnies françaises... attention au message de cette manifestation? (faire)

---

12 *Avec un(e) partenaire, donnez votre opinion sur le monde du travail aux États-Unis. Posez des questions en utilisant* **Penses-tu que...?** *Puis répondez aux questions en utilisant une expression de certitude (***Je pense que***,* **Il est évident que***, etc.) ou une expression de doute (***Je doute que***,* **Il n'est pas vrai que***, etc.).*

1. On peut trouver un boulot si on se spécialise.
2. L'expérience est plus importante que l'éducation.
3. Les compagnies font le maximum pour embaucher les jeunes.
4. Le chômage est un problème très grave.
5. Les salaires des femmes sont moins élevés que les salaires des hommes.
6. Le salaire minimum doit être plus élevé.

Modèle:
Il y a suffisamment d'emplois pour les jeunes.
Élève A: Penses-tu qu'il y ait suffisamment d'emplois pour les jeunes?
Élève B: Non, je ne pense pas qu'il y ait suffisamment d'emplois pour les jeunes. Et toi, penses-tu qu'il y ait suffisamment d'emplois pour les jeunes?
Élève A: Oui, je pense qu'il y a suffisamment d'emplois pour les jeunes.

Communication

*Est-ce qu'il y a des choses dans votre école qui vous semblent injustes? Par exemple, y a-t-il suffisamment de places sur le parking pour les voitures des lycéens? Y a-t-il assez de choix à la cantine de l'école? Y a-t-il suffisamment d'ordinateurs pour tous les lycéens qui en ont besoin? Avec un(e) partenaire, faites une liste de six choses que vous voudriez changer dans votre école. Puis, pour chaque problème que vous avez mentionné, écrivez une phrase qui l'explique. Par exemple, **Nous ne croyons pas qu'il y ait suffisamment de places sur le parking pour les voitures des lycéens.***

Listening Activity 2

Quiz *Leçon B*

Advanced Placement

> Nous ne croyons pas qu'il y ait suffisamment d'ordinateurs pour tous les lycéens qui en ont besoin.

Avec votre partenaire de l'Activité 13, écrivez une lettre au directeur ou à la directrice de votre école où vous décrivez chaque problème que vous avez identifié dans l'Activité 13. Demandez-lui quand vous pouvez vous présenter pour discuter ces problèmes plus en détail. Dites-lui aussi que vous comptez recevoir une réponse à votre lettre. Utilisez la lettre de Jean-Guy Letourneau à la page 144 comme guide.

Avec le/la même partenaire, jouez les rôles d'un(e) des élèves dans l'Activité 14 et du directeur ou de la directrice de l'école. L'élève se présente pour discuter des problèmes qu'il ou elle a identifiés. Après que l'élève a expliqué chaque problème, le directeur ou la directrice décide si on peut le résoudre, et si oui, comment on peut le faire.

Sur la bonne piste

As you prepare to enter the world of work, how will you go about looking for your first job? Where will you look? How will you find an apartment and a car? One resource you can use is the classified ads in the newspaper. As in American papers, French newspapers categorize products and services under different subheadings in **les petites annonces**. When French speakers hunt for jobs, they look in the **Emplois** or **Carrières et emplois** section. To find an apartment, they turn to **Maisons & appartements** or **Immobilier** (*Real Estate*). Cars are advertised in the **Automobiles** section.

Because space is at a premium and customers pay per word to advertise in **les petites annonces**, ads are written in "code," with unnecessary words omitted and common words abbreviated. As you read the ad that follows for an employment opportunity, keep these questions in mind.

1. Who placed the ad?
2. What position is being advertised?
3. Can both men and women apply for this job?
4. Is experience required?
5. How old should the applicant be?
6. Is this a full-time or part-time job?
7. What are the work days for this position?
8. Why is a phone number not listed?
9. In what city is this job located?

> Ch. vendeur (H/F) débutant, pâtiss.
> 18-25a, tps complet lun.-ven., Se prés.
> 6 rue des Halles, 1er.

Teacher's Note

In this **Sur la bonne piste** section, students learn how to decode French newspaper ads about job opportunities, housing and cars.

You can probably guess from the abbreviation **pâtiss.** that a pastry store placed this want ad. **Ch.** stands for **cherche**, so the pastry store is "looking for" a **vendeur.** (Sometimes **rech.** or **recherche** is used instead of **ch.**) **H/F** means that the applicant can be **un homme** or **une femme**, so both sexes may apply. **Débutant** indicates that no experience is necessary; in fact, the employer prefers that the new employee not have any experience and is willing to train him or her. The applicant should be between the ages of 18 and 25, as indicated by **18-25a (ans)**. The abbreviation **tps** stands for **temps**; **temps complet** means that this is a full-time job, with hours on Monday through Friday (**lun.-ven.**), as opposed to **temps partiel** or **mi-temps** (*part-time*). A phone number is not listed because the applicant is requested to present himself or herself in person (**se présenter**) at the store at 6, rue des Halles. This job is located in Paris; **1ᵉʳ** refers to the first of the 20 **arrondissements** into which the city is divided.

Here are some other common abbreviations found in **les petites annonces:**

pr	pour
tljrs	tous les jours
F	francs
km	kilomètres
nf	neuf (nouveau)
ttes	toutes
an.	année

In the three lists that follow, you will find additional abbreviations that will help you understand want ads for jobs, apartments and cars. When looking at the number of rooms in an ad for an apartment, it is important to know that the kitchen and bathroom are usually included even if they are not mentioned separately. For example, if an apartment is advertised as having **3P (3 pièces)**, it means that there is a kitchen and bathroom, as well as the three main rooms: a living room, dining room and bedroom, or a living/dining room and two bedrooms.

Carrières et emplois

JF/JH	jeune fille ou jeune homme
réf.	références
boul.	boulangerie
rens.	renseignements

Maisons & appartements

meub.	meublé (avec table, lit, chaise, etc.)
imm.	immeuble
ch.	chauffage (le contraire de "la climatisation")
ref. nf.	refait à neuf
ét.	étage
asc.	ascenseur
cuis.	cuisine
bns.	salle de bains
chbre	chambre
m	mètres
M	mois

Automobiles

radio K7	radio-cassette
1ᵉ main	première main
à déb.	à débattre (on n'a pas décidé combien va coûter la voiture)
vds	(je) vends
cv	cylindres
ptes.	portes
mét.	métal (couleur)
break	une longue voiture à l'américaine

Maintenant vous allez lire des petites annonces pour des emplois, des appartements et des voitures. Pour vous préparer à les lire, répondez aux questions suivantes.

1. As-tu un emploi? Si oui, comment l'as-tu trouvé? Si tu n'as pas d'emploi, qu'est-ce qui t'intéresse comme boulot?
2. Si tu louais un appartement, est-ce que tu aurais un(e) camarade de chambre? Combien de pièces voudrais-tu? Où voudrais-tu habiter?
3. As-tu une voiture? Selon toi, est-ce que la couleur et l'année d'une voiture sont importantes? Préfères-tu acheter une voiture américaine ou japonaise? Pourquoi?

Lisez les petites annonces suivantes.

Carrières et emplois

1. Ch. JF ou JH, avec réf., pr aller chercher tljrs à l'école deux enfants et s'en occuper de 16h30 à 18h30, merc. de 11h à 18h, en échange d'une chambre aménagée, tout confort, 8ᵉ. Tél. soir: 01.47.11.21.17.

2. Rech. serveur/se 18/26a à mi-tps, souriant(e). Service du midi. Tél. 01.44.68.98.87.

3. Boul. ch. vendeur/se, bonne présentation, réf. exigées, repos lun., mar., se prés. 1 rue Meynadier 75019.

4. Urgent rech. F et H de ménage. Tps complet. Rens. 01.36.68.20.59.

Aidez les gens suivants à trouver un emploi dans les petites annonces. Dites le numéro de l'annonce qui les intéresserait.

1. Francis veut travailler deux ou trois heures par jour. Il est étudiant à la Sorbonne, mais il n'a pas cours entre 11h30 et 15h30.
2. Sandrine désire travailler tous les jours, de 9h00 jusqu'à 17h30.
3. Martine aime faire du baby-sitting. Elle veut quitter la maison de ses parents, mais elle n'a pas assez d'argent pour louer un appartement.
4. Amadou est vendeur dans une boutique le lundi et le mardi. Il faut qu'il trouve un deuxième boulot.

Teacher's Notes

1. You may want students to work in pairs and ask each other the pre-reading questions. 2. You may want your students to work in pairs as they find answers for Activities 17, 18 and 19. 3. Optional activity. To provide additional practice reading the **Emplois** or **Carrières et emplois** section of a francophone newspaper, put students in pairs and give each pair a copy of the want ads section. For each pair, prepare a list of five jobs, for example, secretary, nurse, engineer, salesperson and accountant. (Each pair receives a different list.) Tell each pair to locate the heading under which they find each job listed in the francophone want ads. Then have them find one want ad for each profession that clearly lists the qualifications and experience required. Finally, have them report to the class on their findings for both tasks. 4. Optional activity. You may want to have students write a want ad for a job they are seeking during summer vacation. Students could base their ad on the résumé they wrote in the **Sur la bonne piste** section in **Leçon A**.

Answers

18 1. salon, cuisine, salle de bains, W.-C., meubles
2. salon, chambre, cuisine, salle de bains, W.-C., ascenseur
3. salon, cuisine, salle de bains, W.-C.
4. chambre, cuisine, salle de bains, W.-C., meubles

19 1. 3
2. 1
3. 4
4. 2

Teacher's Notes

1. Optional activity. To provide additional practice reading the real estate section of a francophone newspaper, ask students to find the ideal residence for three possible stages in their life, when they are: A. college students, B. married with two children, and C. retired. To show their comprehension of the ads they select, have students draw a floor plan of the residences.
2. Optional activity. You might ask students to imagine that they are selling their current residence. Have them write an ad for their house, condo or apartment using the abbreviations listed on page 170.
3. Optional activity. It may be interesting for students to discover what foreign vehicles are popular in France. Put students in pairs, and give each pair a copy of the **Automobiles** section of a French newspaper. Have each pair make a list of the foreign vehicles that are advertised. Students could count how many American, Japanese, German, Italian, etc., cars are advertised and prepare a list in order of popularity. (Make sure to point out that this is not an accurate statistical survey.) Then hold a class discussion in which you compare the students' findings in order to discover which countries appear to import the most cars to France.

IMMOBILIER LOCATIONS

Maisons & appartements

1. 6ᵉ, Odéon, studio meub., bel imm., 4.100F + ch. Tél. 01.40.33.72.65.
2. 10ᵉ, République, 2P, ref. nf., 4ᵉ ét., asc., 3.900F Tél. 01.48.33.72.18.
3. 1ᵉʳ, Les Halles, studio, cuis., bns., WC, 7ᵉ ét. sans asc., 2.900F + ch. Tél. 01.43.06.97.17.
4. Chbre meub., cuis., 200m métro, 2.650F/M. Tél. 01.39.88.53.74.

18 Sur une feuille de papier copiez la grille suivante. Indiquez ce que chaque appartement comprend (includes).

	salon	chambre	cuisine	salle de bains	W.-C.	meubles	ascenseur
1.							
2.							
3.							
4.							

AUTOS MOTOS

Automobiles

1. Renault Safrane RXE V6 auto, 93, ttes options, cuir, clim., radio K7, lecteur CD, 1ᵉ main, 60.000F à déb. Tél. 01.45.31.60.11.
2. Vds Peugeot 205 Zénith, an. 93, 5 ptes., 4cv, bleue mét., 91.000km, 23.000F. Tél. 01.42.41.07.62.
3. Vds Volvo break 7 places. 25.000F déb. Tél. 01.42.23.77.85.
4. 35.000F NISSAN MICRA LAGOO MILLESIME An. 1994, 57.000km GARAGE NISSAN BAYARD Té 01.53.17.12.12. Garantie 6 mois

19 Aidez les gens suivants à trouver une voiture dans les petites annonces. Dites le numéro de l'annonce qui les intéresserait.

1. M. Puente a une femme et quatre enfants. Le weekend ils aiment faire des promenades en voiture à la campagne.
2. Evelyne aime écouter ses CDs quand elle conduit. En été elle n'aime pas avoir très chaud en voiture. Elle peut payer 65.000 francs.
3. Laurent cherche une voiture japonaise avec une garantie de plus de trois mois.
4. Mlle Cazette cherche une voiture française qui coûte moins de 25.000 francs.

Dossier fermé

Imagine que tu passes l'été à Paris. À la fin de ton séjour, tu trouves qu'il y a beaucoup de restaurants et de boutiques qui sont fermés. Qu'est-ce qui se passe?

B.   Tout le monde va en vacances au mois d'août.

La majorité des Français prennent leurs six semaines de vacances en juillet et en août. Les familles passent leurs vacances ensemble à faire du camping ou elles vont à leur maison de campagne, au bord de la mer ou à la montagne. Donc, on ferme souvent les boutiques, les restaurants et les cafés à Paris pour donner le mois d'août au personnel qui y travaille. Le résultat est qu'il n'y a presque personne dans certains quartiers de la capitale.

La famille Delhomme passe ses vacances dans sa maison de campagne sur la côte d'Azur.

Teacher's Note

Students might find it interesting to look for a magazine or newspaper want ad for a house or apartment exchange during July or August, the most popular vacation months in France. Students could explain why they selected a certain house or apartment and plan specific activities during their stay, depending on the region. They could also discuss the questions they would ask the house or apartment owner and offer suggestions to the French family of things to do in their area during the summer.

C'est à moi!

Now that you have completed this unit, take a look at what you should be able to do in French. Can you do all of these tasks?

➤ I can write a letter.

➤ I can say what someone is going to do.

➤ I can express what I desire, wish or want.

➤ I can express hope.

➤ I can state my preference.

➤ I can give my opinion by saying what I think.

➤ I can say that I disagree with something.

➤ I can ask about what is certain and uncertain.

➤ I can tell what is certain and uncertain.

➤ I can describe my talents and abilities at work.

➤ I can talk about things sequentially.

➤ I can evaluate my qualifications.

➤ I can request what I would like.

➤ I can explain a problem related to contemporary society.

➤ I can ask for an interview.

➤ I can say that I expect a positive response.

➤ I can express appreciation.

Pour voir si vous avez bien compris la culture francophone, décidez si chaque phrase est vraie ou fausse.

1. L'attitude des Français a changé et maintenant il y a plus de femmes qui travaillent.
2. La Française moyenne travaille parce qu'elle veut trouver son indépendance, et elle veut chercher son identité.
3. En général, les femmes qui ont des enfants à la maison ne prennent pas de boulot.
4. Presque tous les jeunes gens ont un travail à temps partiel.
5. Avec tous les boulots techniques et les téléservices, il n'est pas très important aujourd'hui de savoir communiquer.
6. La durée de la semaine de travail est différente selon l'emploi qu'on a.
7. Selon la tradition française, toutes les personnes qui travaillent ont une pause de deux heures pour le déjeuner.
8. Souvent on peut prolonger une fête au weekend avec un "pont."
9. Les Français ont six semaines de vacances par an.
10. Plus de 25 pour cent des Français sont au chômage.

Answers

1. vraie
2. vraie
3. fausse
4. fausse
5. fausse
6. vraie
7. fausse
8. vraie
9. vraie
10. fausse

Teacher's Notes

1. France has made rapid progress in the field of telecommunications. In 1983 France Télécom generalized public videotex services. Now all of France receives videotex services on over six million Minitel terminals. French videotex software has been licensed for use in many countries, including the U.S. and Japan. In 1984 France launched its first telecommunications satellite, and has since launched direct broadcasting satellites. In preparation for high-definition television, France, along with other European countries, has developed D2-MAC, which will be the transmission standard for the direct broadcasting satellites (TDFs) in the future. 2. Although industrial production has declined in recent years, industry still accounts for approximately 24.7 percent of gross domestic product, or GDP (**produit intérieur brut**), employing an estimated 29 percent of the labor force. French industry is highly concentrated in a few areas, principally the Paris region, the coal-producing areas of the north, the vicinity of the iron ore deposits of Lorraine and around Lyon in the Rhône valley. The government encourages, with tax and other incentives, the decentralization of industry in order to promote the development of less industrialized areas. Recent industrial development is visible in and around certain coastal areas, primarily Marseille, Dunkirk and the lower Seine valley.

Communication orale

Relisez (reread) l'Activité 13 à la page 155 de la Leçon A. Avec le/la même partenaire, jouez les rôles du chef du personnel qui offre le poste et le candidat qui veut être embauché. Le candidat se présente pour une interview avec le chef du personnel. Pendant l'interview le chef du personnel veut savoir:

1. ce que le candidat cherche dans un poste
2. pourquoi il veut ce poste
3. pourquoi il veut être embauché par cette compagnie
4. si le candidat a les qualifications que la compagnie exige
5. s'il a de l'expérience
6. les noms des personnes qui peuvent le recommander

Le candidat répond aux questions. Il demande les heures de travail, le salaire et quand le poste commence.

Pourquoi est-ce que vous voulez être embauchée par cette compagnie?

Je voudrais travailler pour une grande compagnie internationale.

Communication écrite

Après une interview c'est toujours une bonne idée d'écrire une lettre à la personne qui vous a interviewé(e) pour la remercier. Imaginez que vous êtes le candidat qui vient d'être interviewé dans l'activité précédente. Écrivez une lettre au chef du personnel où vous le remerciez de son temps. Dans votre lettre dites-lui aussi que cette compagnie et ce poste vous intéressent toujours. Mentionnez encore (again) vos qualifications et votre expérience. Utilisez la lettre de Jean-Guy Letourneau à la page 144 comme guide.

Communication active

To write a letter, use:

Monsieur,	*Sir,*
Vous trouverez ci-joint mon CV avec photo.	*Enclosed you will find my curriculum vitæ with a picture.*
En attendant de vous voir,	*Waiting to see you,*
Je vous prie d'agréer, Monsieur (ou Madame), mes salutations distinguées.	*Yours truly,*

To express intentions, use:

Ce que je compte faire, c'est passer deux années en classes préparatoires.	*What I intend to do is spend two years taking preparatory classes.*

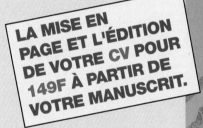

LA MISE EN PAGE ET L'ÉDITION DE VOTRE CV POUR 149F À PARTIR DE VOTRE MANUSCRIT.

Mais écoute, nous désirons que tu sortes avec nous ce soir.

To express desire, use:

Nous désirons que vous soyez fort en informatique.

We want you to be strong in computer science.

To state want, use:

Nous voudrions que vous soyez diplômé(e).

We would like you to have a diploma.

To express hope, use:

Je souhaite qu'on m'offre un gros salaire.

I hope they give me a high salary.

To state a preference, use:

Nous préférons que vous soyez enthousiaste.

We prefer you to be enthusiastic.

To give opinions, use:

Nous sommes contre le projet du gouvernement.

We are against the government's project.

To express disagreement, use:

Et ça, **nous ne l'acceptons pas.**

And we won't accept that.

To inquire about certainty, use:

Pensez-vous que le gouvernement fasse attention au message?

Do you think that the government is paying attention to the message?

Croyez-vous que le projet du gouvernement soit une bonne idée?

Do you believe that the government's project is a good idea?

To express certainty, use:

Ce qui est sûr, c'est que les emplois pour les jeunes restent un problème à résoudre.

What is sure is that jobs for young people remain a problem to be solved.

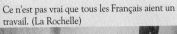

Ce n'est pas vrai que tous les Français aient un travail. (La Rochelle)

To express uncertainty, use:

Il n'est pas certain que Marie-José puisse s'approcher d'un des manifestants.

It's not certain that Marie-José can approach one of the demonstrators.

Nous ne pensons pas que ce projet aille assez loin.

We don't think that this project goes far enough.

Je ne suis pas sûr que la raison soit évidente pour tout le monde.

I'm not sure that the reason is obvious to everybody.

Je doute que nous acceptions un salaire qui soit inférieur au salaire minimum.

I doubt we'll accept a salary that is less than the minimum salary.

Il n'est pas évident que le gouvernement nous écoute.

It's not evident that the government is listening to us.

Ce n'est pas vrai que les compagnies fassent le maximum.

It's not true that companies are doing the maximum.

Listening Activity 3

o describe talents and abilities, use:

Je suis bilingue, diligent et **fort en informatique.**

I'm bilingual, hardworking and strong in computer science.

Organisation internationale recherche

SECRÉTAIRE BILINGUE CONFIRMÉE

Parfaite connaissance TTX et audio. Excellent anglais exigé, bon français important. Salaire mensuel brut de départ 12.247 FF. Écrire en anglais au journal P. A. en précisant sur l'enveloppe la réf. 92570 - 25, avenue Matignon - 75398 Paris Cedex 08 qui transmettra.

o sequence events, use:

Finalement, je vais essayer de trouver un emploi dans le cadre administratif.

Eventually, I'm going to try to find a job in the administrative sector.

o evaluate, use:

Je pense avoir l'expérience et les qualifications que vous cherchez.

I think I have the experience and the qualifications that you're looking for.

J'ai les qualifications qu'on cherche.

I have the qualifications that you're looking for.

o make requests, use:

Remplissez, s'il vous plaît, le formulaire de travail ci-joint.

Please fill out the enclosed work form.

o explain a problem, use:

Le problème, c'est qu'il n'y a pas suffisamment d'emplois.

The problem is that there aren't enough jobs.

J'ai les qualifications que votre compagnie cherche.

«Le problème, c'est que c'était impossible à budgeter.»

o interview, use:

Je peux vous poser quelques questions?

May I ask you some questions?

o express that you expect a positive response, use:

En attendant une réponse favorable,

Waiting for a favorable answer,

o express appreciation, use:

Nous vous serions très reconnaissants de bien vouloir vous présenter vendredi.

We would be very grateful if you would be willing to come on Friday.

Unité 5

Comment se débrouiller en voyage

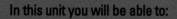

In this unit you will be able to:

➤ write postcards
➤ tell location
➤ tell a story
➤ remember
➤ describe people you remember
➤ indicate knowing and not knowing
➤ identify objects
➤ express likes and dislikes
➤ agree and disagree
➤ give opinions
➤ express dissatisfaction
➤ express complaint
➤ express fear
➤ express regret
➤ admit
➤ express patience
➤ inquire about possibility and impossibility
➤ make requests
➤ express surprise
➤ express happiness
➤ control the volume of a conversation

Tes empreintes ici

Avant de partir en vacances, tu choisis un endroit où tu peux faire toutes les choses que tu voudrais. Tu choisis un hôtel qui offre des chambres comme tu les voudrais. Tu espères passer ton temps en te reposant et en faisant des choses intéressantes sans avoir de problèmes.

Mais est-ce que tu as jamais fait une réservation dans un hôtel, et quand tu es arrivé(e) est-ce qu'il y avait certaines choses que tu ne pouvais pas accepter? Comment est-ce que tu te sentais? Comment est-ce que tu as résolu le problème? As-tu jamais eu d'autres problèmes à résoudre pendant un voyage? Quels problèmes? Qu'as-tu fait pour les résoudre?

As-tu eu des problèmes quand tu es resté(e) dans un hôtel?

Leçon A

In this lesson you will be able to:

➤ express likes and dislikes

➤ agree and disagree

➤ express surprise

➤ give opinions

➤ express fear

➤ inquire about possibility and impossibility

➤ control the volume of a conversation

➤ express dissatisfaction

➤ express regret

➤ make requests

➤ express happiness

➤ tell location

Dossier ouvert

Tu vas passer tes vacances de printemps avec des amis à Saint-Martin dans les Antilles. Tes parents te demandent de leur envoyer des cartes postales de ton voyage. Ils t'offrent des timbres français qu'ils ont achetés pendant leur dernier voyage à Paris et qu'ils n'ont pas encore utilisés. Qu'est-ce que tu en fais?

A. Tu gardes les timbres qu'ils te donnent pour mettre sur les cartes postales que tu vas envoyer de Saint-Martin.
B. Tu dis à tes parents que les timbres français ne sont pas valables à Saint-Martin.
C. Tu laisses les timbres chez toi parce que tu n'en as pas besoin.

- ◆ Situé à 400 mètres de la plage, l'Hôtel Belle Île est parfait pour un groupe d'amis ou une famille. Nous offrons 62 chambres avec grand lit, ventilateur,° climatisation, téléphone, et salle de bains avec douche et sèche-cheveux. En plus° il y a un service de chambre, un ascenseur, la télévision par satellite et un gymnase.
- ◆ La vue panoramique de la mer et du sable° blanc est extra!
- ◆ Le restaurant, Café Fleurs Exotiques, qui donne sur la grande piscine, vous propose une variété de cuisine.
- ◆ Profitez du bureau d'excursions pour faire toutes vos activités préférées.
- ◆ À l'Hôtel Belle Île, on ne s'ennuie° pas!

Y a-t-il un service de chambre et la télévision dans cet hôtel? (Perpignan)

250, av. du Saint, 97150 SAINT-MARTIN
TÉL (590) 62.35.15 FAX (590) 62.25.05

un **ventilateur** *fan;* **en plus** *de plus;* **le sable** *sand;* **s'ennuyer** *to get bored*

■ **Workbook**
Activity 1

 Audiocassette/CD
Brochure

Teacher's Notes

1. From now on, past participles, such as **préférées**, may be used as adjectives. They will not be listed separately in the end vocabulary.
2. Other related terms include **un dessus de lit** (*bedspread*), **monter les valises** (*to bring up the suitcases*), **descendre les valises** (*to bring down the suitcases*), **climatisé** (*air-conditioned*), **un coffre-fort** (*safe*), **un réveil-matin** (*alarm clock*), **une clé** (*key*) and **appeler le garçon d'étage** (*to ring for room service*). For additional hotel-related vocabulary, refer to page 288 in the second-level Annotated Teacher's Edition of *C'est à toi!*

Teacher's Notes

1. You may want to introduce all the forms of the orthographically changing verb **s'ennuyer:** je m'ennuie, tu t'ennuies, il/elle/on s'ennuie, nous nous ennuyons, vous vous ennuyez, ils/elles s'ennuient. 2. **Gars** is pronounced [ga]. 3. Point out that **surprendre** belongs to the **prendre** verb family. 4. **La clim** is a regionalized abbreviation of **la climatisation.** 5. **Ça,** the equivalent of **cela,** is the more informal way of expressing "that" or "it." 6. Here are the forms of the irregular verb **servir:** sers, sers, sert, servons, servez, servent. **Se servir de** will be introduced in Leçon B.

C'est un hôtel où on ne s'ennuie pas, mais où on a des ennuis!°

Pourriez-vous me rendre un service? Je voudrais envoyer un fax.

Bruno: Eh, les gars,° la chambre ne donne pas sur la plage! Ça me surprend° qu'on ne puisse pas voir la mer de ce côté. À ta place,° Antoine, je demanderais une autre chambre. Tu devrais téléphoner à la réception.

Antoine: Chut!° Attends. C'est ce que je suis en train de faire, mais le téléphone est occupé.

Christian: Dis donc, je suis étonné° qu'ils ne mettent° pas la clim° avant l'arrivée de la clientèle. J'ai peur qu'il fasse trop chaud ce soir.

Denis: Tu parles!° J'ai déjà trop chaud. Ça m'embête° que l'ascenseur ne marche° pas. Que je suis fatigué! Je voudrais faire un somme.°

Christian: Et Bruno, toi qui n'arrêtes pas de te peigner, c'est dommage qu'il n'y ait ni sèche-cheveux ni douche dans la salle de bains. Je trouve que le gérant° pourrait faire mieux que ça.

Bruno: Pour ça, je suis bien d'accord.° Antoine, tu as la réception au téléphone?

Antoine: Chut! Oui, ça sonne!°

Denis: Au moins je suis heureux qu'on serve de très bons repas.

Antoine: Allô, Madame, ici c'est la chambre 58. Est-ce que vous pourriez nous rendre un service?° Nous aimerions changer de chambre. Nous voudrions nous installer° au rez-de-chaussée dans une chambre qui donne sur la mer. Est-ce que cela° serait possible?

Madame: Je suis désolée, Monsieur, qu'il n'y ait plus de chambres disponibles° aujourd'hui. Je pourrais vous changer de chambre demain après 14h00. Pouvez-vous vous débrouiller° ce soir?

Antoine: Euh, je crois que oui.° Merci beaucoup, Madame.

---

des ennuis (m.) des problèmes; **un gars** un mec; **surprendre** être surpris(e); **à ta place** *if I w[ere] you*; **Chut!** *Sh!*; **étonné(e)** surpris(e); **mettre** *to turn on*; **la clim** la climatisation; **Tu parles!** *You're not kidding!*; **embêter** *to bother*; **marcher** *to work*; **faire un somme** dormir un peu; **un gérant** *manager*; **être d'accord** *to agree*; **sonner** *to ring*; **rendre un service** aider; **s'installer** déménager; **cela** ça; **disponible** libre; **se débrouiller** *to manage*; **Je crois que oui.** *I think so.*

Répondez aux questions suivantes d'après la brochure et le dialogue.

1. Où est-ce que l'Hôtel Belle Île est situé?
2. Quelle est la spécialité de son restaurant?
3. En quoi est-ce que la chambre 58 ne ressemble pas à la chambre dans la description?
4. Qu'est-ce qui ne marche pas dans cet hôtel?
5. Pour se sentir mieux, qu'est-ce que Denis voudrait faire?
6. Où est-ce que les garçons voudraient s'installer?
7. Pourquoi est-ce que la réceptionniste ne pourrait pas les changer de chambre aujourd'hui?
8. Est-ce qu'Antoine va pouvoir se débrouiller ce soir?

Complétez l'espace blanc avec l'expression convenable de la liste suivante.

gymnase	activités	panoramique	sonne	rendre un service
sert	sable	ennuis	fax	

1. Si on ne téléphone pas à l'Hôtel Belle Île, on peut envoyer un....
2. Si le téléphone est occupé, il ne... pas.
3. On offre des chambres avec une vue... sur la plage de... blanc.
4. Pour la clientèle qui voudrait s'entraîner, il y a un....
5. On profite du bureau d'excursions pour faire toutes ses... préférées.
6. Le gérant est occupé avec tous les... des gens qui ne sont pas contents.
7. Heureusement pour les quatre garçons, on... de bons repas.
8. Madame va leur... demain en les changeant de chambre.

Maman nous sert un bon dîner.

C'est à toi!

1. Où est-ce que tu voudrais aller en vacances? Pourquoi?
2. Est-ce que tu as jamais visité des îles dans la mer des Antilles? Si oui, quelles îles?
3. Quelles sont tes activités préférées?
4. Quels services est-ce que tu demanderais dans un hôtel?
5. Quand il fait chaud, est-ce que tu préfères la clim ou un ventilateur?
6. Si tu étais le/la gérant(e) de l'Hôtel Belle Île, qu'est-ce que tu dirais à Antoine?
7. Quand tu as des ennuis, est-ce que tu peux te débrouiller?
8. Quel(le) ami(e) te rend souvent des services? Qu'est-ce qu'il ou elle fait pour toi?

 Audiocassette/CD Activities 1, 3

Answers

1 Possible answers:

1. L'Hôtel Belle Île est situé à Saint-Martin, à 400 mètres de la plage.
2. Son restaurant offre une variété de cuisine.
3. La chambre 58 n'a pas de télévision, ne donne pas sur la mer, et la salle de bains n'a ni douche ni sèche-cheveux.
4. L'ascenseur ne marche pas dans cet hôtel.
5. Pour se sentir mieux, Denis voudrait faire un somme.
6. Les garçons voudraient s'installer au rez-de-chaussée dans une chambre qui donne sur la mer.
7. La réceptionniste ne peut pas les changer de chambre aujourd'hui parce qu'il n'y en a plus de disponible.
8. Antoine croit que oui.

2 1. fax
2. sonne
3. panoramique, sable
4. gymnase
5. activités
6. ennuis
7. sert
8. rendre un service

3 Answers will vary.

Game

Faites le match

For additional practice reviewing the content of the brochure and the dialogue on pages 181-82, divide the class into two teams. Prepare ten questions about the exposition on construction paper and ten answers on a set of note cards. For example, one match might be: **Comment s'appellent les quatre garçons qui restent à l'Hôtel Belle Île? Ils s'appellent Bruno, Antoine, Christian et Denis.** Tape the questions in random order on the board. Call the first player from each team to the front of the room. Take an answer card and read it to the two players. The player who first removes the matching question from the board wins a point for his or her team. Then the first two players take their seats, and the next two players take their turn. The game continues until there is only one match left to be made. The team with the most points wins.

**Workbook
Activity 3**

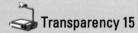

Transparency 15

Teacher's Notes

1. Cognates in this reading include **classifie, Départements d'Outre-Mer, confort, classification, qualité, logement, extérieur, nombre, étoiles, comparez, de luxe, tropical, divisée, partie, hollandaise, secteur, gouverné, différences, administratives, régions, guilder, Indiens, découvert, visiteurs, exploité, quantités, se disputer, Hollande, traité, divisé, peuples, différentes, tourisme, climat, exceptionnel, air, aquatiques, nautique, splendides, touristes, types, scooter, transparente, visibilité, terrain** and **panorama.** 2. **Les Départements d'Outre-Mer (DOM)** are French provinces not located in metropolitan France. The **DOM** include **la Guadeloupe, la Martinique, la Guyane française** and **la Réunion.**

 Enquête culturelle

On classifie les hôtels en France et dans les Départements d'Outre-Mer selon le confort qu'ils offrent à la clientèle. La classification d'hôtels peut vous indiquer les services qu'offre un hôtel (restaurants, piscine, etc.), la qualité du logement et le prix des chambres. À l'extérieur d'un hôtel français, vous pouvez voir un certain nombre d'étoiles (★). Plus il y a d'étoiles, plus l'hôtel est confortable.

L'Hôtel Ducs d'Anjou à Paris a deux étoiles.

CATÉGORIES

Grand luxe et tradition	𝕏𝕏𝕏𝕏𝕏	
Grand confort	𝕏𝕏𝕏𝕏	
Très confortable	𝕏𝕏𝕏	
De bon confort	𝕏𝕏	
Assez confortable	𝕏	
Simple mais convenable		
Dans sa catégorie, hôtel d'équipement moderne		
sans rest. L'hôtel n'a pas de restaurant		
Le restaurant possède des chambres	avec ch.	

Voici la liste de classification qu'on trouve dans le *Guide Michelin Rouge.*

Comparez la description des deux hôtels suivants. Quel hôtel vous semble être un hôtel de luxe?

CHEZ JOSÉPHINE
5 chambres et 1 suite

Hôtel situé sur la plage de Grand Case. Vastes chambres avec salle de bains, climatisation, terrasse sur la mer, cuisine à disposition.

LE DOMAINE
125 chambres et 20 marina suites - niché au fond d'une anse, au bord d'une plage de sable fin de 600 mètres, 60 hectares de jardins et collines verdoyantes.

2 piscines d'eau douce, 2 bars, 4 restaurants, sports aquatiques, accès au centre sportif et au centre de balnéothérapie, tir à l'arc, volleyball, mini golf, galerie marchande, location de voitures. Marina: location de voiliers, bateaux à moteurs, pêche au gros.

Si vous voulez visiter Le Domaine, un hôtel de luxe tropical, il faut que vous alliez à l'île Saint-Martin dans la mer des Antilles. Située à 250 kilomètres de la Guadeloupe, l'île Saint-Martin est divisée en deux. La partie au nord de l'île (Saint-Martin) est française, et la partie au sud de l'île (Sint Maarten) est hollandaise. Le secteur français de l'île Saint-Martin est gouverné par la Guadeloupe, un Département d'Outre-Mer de la France. Il y a des différences administratives entre les deux régions. Par exemple, dans le secteur français on paie avec le franc, mais dans le secteur hollandais, la monnaie, c'est le guilder.

À Philipsburg, la capitale de la partie hollandaise, les maisons montrent l'influence de l'architecture de Hollande. (Saint-Martin)

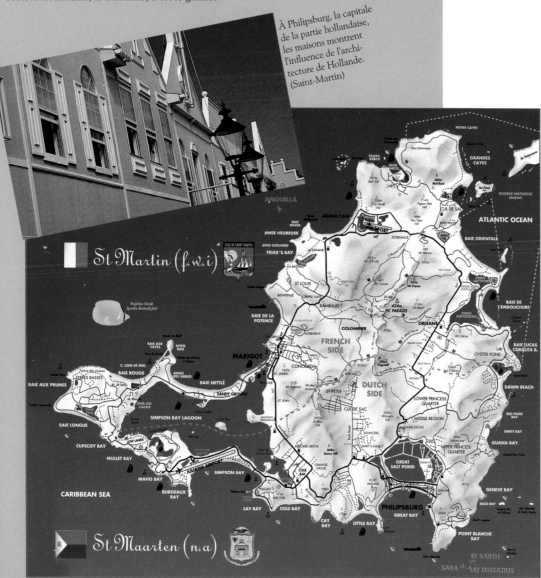

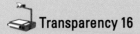

Transparency 16

Teacher's Notes

1. The island of Saint Martin received its name because Columbus landed there on November 11, 1493, the feast day of Saint Martin. The island was settled by the French and the Dutch in the 1640s. For years pirates used the coves and bays of Saint Martin as hiding places. The early sea salt and sugar cane industries died out by the early 20th century. The 1950s brought an economic revival based on tourism, rum distilling and commercial fishing. 2. The population of Saint Martin is composed of the descendants of Dutch or French settlers and African slaves. Half of the popula-tion is Roman Catholic and half Protestant. Over the past 30 years there has been an influx of immigrants from some of the poorer neighboring islands. 3. **Mardi Gras** is celebrated in the streets of Marigot, the capital, and Grand Case, the second largest city. Both sides of the island celebrate Bastille Day. July 21 is Schœlcher Day, in honor of the French parliamen-tarian Victor Schœlcher who fought against slavery. On November 11 residents of both parts of the island celebrate Saint Martin's or Concordia Day. Festivities include parades and ceremonies at the border. 4. The towns on the French side of the island combine West Indian and French charm with open markets that are typically Caribbean, bakeries that are typically French and seaside cafés reminiscent of **la côte d'Azur**. From Paradise Peak, the highest point on the island, you can see the green countryside, coves, turquoise shallows, offshore rocks and islets. 5. U.S. visitors to the French side of the island who do not have a passport need only present a birth certificate or government-autho-rized identification with photo, unless they plan on staying longer than three weeks. 6. U.S. dollars are accepted almost everywhere on the island. 7. Saint Martin is a duty-free island. 8. Crime is on the rise on Saint Martin and tourists are advised against night driving and are cautioned to avoid deserted, isolated beaches. 9. Scuba diving is done from boats as most sites are at some distance from the shore. Snorkeling, parasailing, sailing and deep-sea fishing are also popular aquatic activities.

Les Arawaks étaient les derniers Indiens des Antilles quand Christophe Colomb a découvert Saint-Martin en 1493. Pendant plus d'un siècle, les visiteurs ont exploité cette petite île pour ses grandes quantités de sel. Les Français et les Hollandais ont été les premiers à se disputer l'île, puis les Espagnols et les Anglais ont suivi. Ce n'est qu'en 1648 que la France et la Hollande ont signé un traité qui a divisé l'île. Depuis ce traité, Saint-Martin est la plus petite île du monde où deux peuples de cultures différentes vivent ensemble sans se disputer. Saint-Martin était l'une des premières îles des Antilles à inviter le tourisme, et en est aujourd'hui l'une des plus visitées. Elle a un climat exceptionnel toute l'année avec du soleil pendant 300 jours par an et des températures entre 25°C et 30°C pour l'air comme pour l'eau.

Beaucoup de touristes restent à l'hôtel à Grand Case, la deuxième ville de Saint-Martin.

Saint-Martin offre deux sortes d'activités principales appelées "bleu" et "vert." La catégorie "bleu" est pour les fanas des sports aquatiques. Le tourisme nautique est très populaire à Saint-Martin. Cette île a des plages splendides où les touristes peuvent bien profiter de la mer. Pour passer des vacances formidables à la mer, on vous propose plusieurs types d'excursions. Vous pouvez faire de la plongée sous-marine, de la planche à voile ou du ski nautique. Vous pouvez essayer un scooter des mers. Vous pouvez aussi prendre un bateau et faire une petite excursion à la Martinique. L'eau transparente de la mer des Antilles vous offre une visibilité de 100 pieds sous l'eau.

Il y a 36 belles plages de sable blanc à Saint-Martin.

La catégorie "vert" offre beaucoup d'activités pour les gens qui aiment la nature. Faites une promenade à pied pour découvrir cette belle île, prenez un vélo ou un VTT (vélo tout terrain) ou faites du cheval. Si vous préférez le calme, essayez le golf sur un champ vert. Le tennis est très populaire aussi. Et le footing vous laisse découvrir le magnifique panorama de l'île.

7 BONNES RAISONS DE CHOISIR
SAINT-MARTIN

LES PLAGES: à apprécier dessus dessous...

LA GASTRONOMIE: rendez-vous exceptionnel avec les tables de diverses nationalités...

PARADIS DU SHOPPING HORS TAXES: de la mode italienne à l'électronique japonaise...

LE CLIMAT: destination soleil 300 jours par an...

L'HÔTELLERIE DE QUALITÉ: des grands hôtels aux plus petits...

LA DIVERSITÉ DES ACTIVITÉS SPORTIVES: de la plongée au golf, en passant par les randonnées...

PAYS FRANCOPHONE avec dépaysement créole assuré...

Répondez aux questions suivantes.

1. Qu'est-ce que la classification d'hôtels vous indique?
2. Où est l'île Saint-Martin?
3. Qui contrôle les deux secteurs différents de l'île?
4. Quelles sont les deux monnaies qu'on utilise dans l'île?
5. Qui a découvert Saint-Martin?
6. Pourquoi est-ce que Saint-Martin est l'une des îles les plus visitées des Antilles?
7. Quelles sont les deux sortes d'activités principales à Saint-Martin?
8. Quels sports aquatiques peut-on y faire?
9. Comment est l'eau à Saint-Martin?
10. Quelles activités y a-t-il pour les gens qui aiment la nature?

Paired Practice

L'office du tourisme

Have one student play the role of an employee at the Saint Martin tourist office and the other a tourist who has two requests for information. For example, the tourist might want to know a good beach to go to for windsurfing and a place to go to hear zouk music. Using information obtained from the addresses listed in the teacher's note on this page, the student playing the role of the tourist office employee gives the appropriate information. Other information that the tourist might request includes the name of a hotel, the phone number of the local hospital, banking hours, directions to Fort St. Louis and the name of a local museum.

Answers

4 Possible answers:

1. La classification d'hôtels vous indique les services qu'offre un hôtel, la qualité du logement et le prix des chambres.
2. L'île Saint-Martin est dans la mer des Antilles à 250 kilomètres de la Guadeloupe.
3. La Guadeloupe et la Hollande contrôlent les deux secteurs différents de l'île.
4. On utilise le franc et le guilder à Saint-Martin.
5. Christophe Colomb a découvert Saint-Martin.
6. Saint-Martin est l'une des îles les plus visitées des Antilles parce qu'elle a un climat exceptionnel toute l'année avec beaucoup de soleil.
7. Les deux sortes d'activités principales à Saint-Martin sont appelées "bleu" et "vert."
8. On peut y nager, faire de la plongée sous-marine, de la planche à voile et du ski nautique.
9. L'eau y est aussi chaude que l'air, et l'eau transparente vous permet de voir jusqu'à 100 pieds.
10. Les gens qui aiment la nature peuvent faire une promenade à pied, prendre un vélo ou un VTT et faire du cheval.

Teacher's Note

To obtain tourist information, write to the Saint Martin Tourist Office, Boulevard de France, 97150 Marigot, Saint Martin. Other useful addresses with free information on the island include: Marketing Challenges International, 10 East 21st St., Suite 600, New York, NY 10021 and The Clement-Petrocik Company, 14 E. 60th St., New York, NY 10022.

Workbook Activities 4-5

Answers

5 Answers will vary.

Teacher's Notes

1. If students have little experience with the Internet, they should enter "http://www.hotels + France" to begin their search for a hotel in Activity 5. 2. To vary Activity 5, you might have students look up a hotel in three different cities, or have them find three different price ranges for hotels, i.e., inexpensive, moderate and expensive. 3. The **Structure** section in Unit 5 contains both new and recycled grammatical concepts. 4. The conditional tense was introduced on page 364 in the second level of *C'est à toi!* The conditional tense in sentences with **si** will be reviewed in Unit 7. 5. Point out to students that many verbs with spelling changes in the present tense keep them in the conditional, for example, **j'achèterais, je m'appellerais, j'emmènerais, j'enlèverais, j'essaierais, je me lèverais, je nettoierais, je paierais** and **je pèserais**. 6. Point out that the conditional stem for all verbs ends in **-r**.

Critical Thinking

Expressing "Would"

Write two English sentences on the board, one using "would" in the conditional, the other using "would" in the imperfect, for example, "I would go scuba diving if I had the time" and "When I was young, I would go scuba diving." Then ask students which French tense they would use in each sentence. Students should tell you that they would use the conditional in the first sentence and the imperfect in the second.

Politeness

Ask students how they would make the following sentences more polite when expressing a wish or making a request: 1. Tu peux me rendre un service? 2. Je veux m'installer à la plage. 3. Il faut que vous fassiez attention. 4. Tu dois mettre la clim. Students should say that the verbs would change to **pourrais, voudrais, faudrait** and **devrais**. Then ask students to give the English versions of the new sentences: 1. "Could you help me?" 2. "I would like to move to the beach." 3. "You should be careful." 4. "You ought to turn on the air conditioning." This activity will help students remember that the conditional is used to express politeness.

HÔTEL REGINA
☆☆☆☆
2, place des Pyramides - 75001 Paris
Téléphone : 33 - 01 42 60 31 10
Télex : 670 834 F - Fax : 33 - 01 40 15 95 16

Mississippi
★★★★

LUXE, CALME ET VOLUPTÉ
6 Cottages en bois rouge avec jacuzzi et 13 suites de luxe, de 90 m2, avec jacuzzi privé
terrasse, climatisation, vidéo, Hi-Fi, TV Sony, réfrigérateur américain,
sèche-cheveux, coffre, piste d'hélicoptère, bar et restaurant "Le Mahogany"
au bord de la piscine.

---

5 | *Si vous allez en France, il vous faut un hôtel. Comment en trouver un? Sur Internet tapez (key) "hotels + France" dans votre outil de recherche (search engine) pour trouver des sites d'hôtels en France. Puis choisissez trois de ces hôtels et répondez aux questions suivantes pour chaque hôtel.*

1. Comment s'appelle l'hôtel?
2. Combien d'étoiles l'hôtel a-t-il?
3. Dans quelle ville l'hôtel est-il situé? Quelle en est l'adresse?
4. Quel est son numéro de téléphone?
5. Combien de chambres y a-t-il?
6. Qu'est-ce qu'on peut trouver dans chaque chambre? La clim, la cuisine, le téléphone, la salle de bains, la télévision?
7. Quels services l'hôtel offre-t-il? Garage, parking, piscine, sauna, terrain de golf, terrain de tennis, gymnase, café, restaurant, boutique?
8. Combien coûte la chambre pour une personne? Pour deux personnes?
9. Voudriez-vous passer du temps dans cet hôtel? Pourquoi ou pourquoi pas?

Journal personnel

Have you ever stayed in a hotel? If so, were you pleased with your accommodations and the hotel's services, or did you have a problem? Now assume that you are going on vacation. When you are away from home, how important to you are the amenities that a hotel offers? Which ones are the most essential? Which ones wouldn't you use? Which is more important to you in a hotel, an affordable price or a wide variety of services?

Based on the description of Saint-Martin, it seems that the island is the ideal vacation spot for anyone, no matter his or her interests. Do you agree? Does this part of the francophone world interest you? Would you like to spend your vacation here? If so, why? If you went to Saint-Martin, what would you do on a typical day? What do you think your parents would do?

Structure

Conditional tense

The **conditionnel** (*conditional*) is a tense used to tell what people *would* do or what *would* happen.

Nous **aimerions** changer de chambre.	*We would like to change rooms.*

Je repasserais bien le bac!

To form the conditional of regular **-er** and **-ir** verbs, add to the infinitive the endings of the imperfect tense: **-ais**, **-ais**, **-ait**, **-ions**, **-iez**, **-aient**. For regular **-re** verbs, drop the final **e** from the infinitive before adding the imperfect endings.

Choisirais-tu un hôtel sans restaurant? Cela me **surprendrait**.	*Would you choose a hotel without a restaurant? That would surprise me.*

Some irregular French verbs have an irregular stem in the conditional, but their endings are regular.

Infinitive	Irregular Stem	Conditional
aller	ir-	j'irais
s'asseoir	assiér-	je m'assiérais
avoir	aur-	j'aurais
courir	courr-	je courrais
devoir	devr-	je devrais
envoyer	enverr-	j'enverrais
être	ser-	je serais
faire	fer-	je ferais
falloir	faudr-	il faudrait
mourir	mourr-	je mourrais
pleuvoir	pleuvr-	il pleuvrait
pouvoir	pourr-	je pourrais
recevoir	recevr-	je recevrais
savoir	saur-	je saurais
valoir	vaudr-	il vaudrait
venir	viendr-	je viendrais
voir	verr-	je verrais
vouloir	voudr-	je voudrais

The conditional is often used to make suggestions or to make a request more polite.

À ta place, Antoine, je **demanderais** une autre chambre.	*If I were you, Antoine, I would ask for another room.*
Tu **devrais** téléphoner à la réception. Est-ce que tu **pourrais** le faire maintenant?	*You should call the reception desk. Would you be able to do it now?*

Je voudrais une limonade, s'il vous plaît.

Quelle indication suivrais-tu?

POURRIEZ-VOUS VIVRE UN AMOUR PLATONIQUE?

Ferais-tu de la voile à Saint-Martin?

Audiocassette/CD Activity 6

Answers

6 1. Les passagers s'assiéraient.
2. M. Poux irait au bureau de change.
3. Ma grand-mère prendrait l'ascenseur.
4. Khaled ferait un somme.
5. Sonya et toi, vous changeriez de chambre.
6. Véronique se peignerait.
7. Philippe et moi, nous mettrions la clim.
8. Les Durandeau partiraient.

Teacher's Note

You might lengthen Activity 6 by writing the following supplementary expressions on the board: **avoir faim, avoir besoin d'un plan gratuit, recevoir des amis** and **vouloir être en bonne forme.** Then write a student's name next to each expression and ask the class what those students would do if they were in that situation. Students might answer: **Nicole choisirait des fruits de mer. Jacques irait au syndicat d'initiative. Paul rangerait sa chambre. Caro ferait de la planche à voile.**

Cooperative Group Practice

Forming Sentences

To give students practice forming irregular conditional forms, put them in small groups and have each group make two sets of note cards. On each card in the first set, students write a different subject (a noun or a pronoun). On each card in the second set, students write the infinitive of an irregular verb. Then each student in the group chooses one card from each stack and forms a sentence using the subject, the appropriate conditional form of the irregular verb and an additional word or phrase that is logical, for example, **nous/voir—Nous verrions la vue panoramique.** You may want each group to share a couple of its best sentences with the rest of the class.

Pratique

6 *Dites ce que feraient ces voyageurs dans les situations illustrées. Pour chaque phrase, utilisez une expression logique de la liste suivante. Suivez le modèle.*

changer de chambre	faire un somme
s'asseoir	aller au bureau de change
mettre la clim	demander une chambre avec un grand lit
partir	prendre l'ascenseur
se peigner	

Modèle:

M. et Mme Campeau

M. et Mme Campeau demanderaient une chambre avec un grand lit.

1. les passagers

2. M. Poux

3. ma grand-mère

4. Khaled

5. Sonya et toi, vous

6. Véronique

7. Philippe et moi, nous

8. les Durandeau

Que choisirais-tu?

So that students can practice making hypothetical choices, put them in small groups of four or five. Prepare an overhead transparency listing pairs of hypothetical situations, for example, **travailler pour une compagnie d'assurance ou dans un commissariat; habiter à la campagne ou en ville; regarder des paysages ou des natures mortes; étudier le russe ou le grec; aller au cinéma ou au théâtre; assister à un concert de rock ou à un concert de jazz.** The first student in each group asks the person of his or her choice a question in the conditional, for example, **Travaillerais-tu pour une compagnie d'assurance ou dans un commissariat?** The selected student replies with a complete sentence in the conditional, for example, **Je travaillerais pour une compagnie d'assurance.** Then the second student in the group asks another group member a question. Students continue asking and answering questions until they finish the pairs of choices on the transparency.

Si vous et votre partenaire alliez en vacances à Paris, que feriez-vous? Posez et répondez aux questions. Suivez le modèle.

1. réserver une chambre d'hôtel/chercher une auberge de jeunesse
2. acheter des chèques de voyage/payer avec une carte de crédit
3. prendre le métro/louer une voiture
4. aller au Louvre/visiter le musée Picasso
5. goûter la vraie cuisine française/s'arrêter au Quick
6. manger au café/piqueniquer dans un parc
7. téléphoner à ta famille/envoyer des cartes postales
8. sortir chaque soir/rester dans ta chambre

Modèle:

voyager avec deux valises/choisir un sac à dos

Élève A: Voyagerais-tu avec deux valises, ou choisirais-tu un sac à dos?

Élève B: Je choisirais un sac à dos. Et toi, voyagerais-tu avec deux valises, ou choisirais-tu un sac à dos?

Élève A: Je voyagerais avec deux valises.

Julien et Christelle se reposeraient au Café de Flore. (Paris)

Que diriez-vous DE RECEVOIR chez vous chaque semaine ELLE... FRANCE

Votre amie Clémence vous raconte toujours ses ennuis. Dites-lui ce que vous feriez à sa place. Suivez le modèle.

1. J'ai très froid.
2. Je suis toujours fatiguée.
3. J'ai mal aux dents.
4. Je ne comprends pas les problèmes de maths.
5. J'ai perdu mes notes pour le cours de chimie.
6. Mes vêtements ne me plaisent pas.
7. Je n'ai pas d'argent.
8. Je n'ai pas de boulot.

Paulette m'embête.

À ta place, je ne lui parlerais pas.

Modèle:

Je m'ennuie.
À ta place, je lirais un bon roman.

Paired Practice

Les sketches

So that students can practice forming conditional sentences in a skit, put them in pairs. Give each pair a problem situation, for example: **Tu es tombé(e) en panne sur la route. Tu ne peux pas payer l'addition au restaurant. Tu es au chômage. Tu viens de rater le bac.** Student

A takes the card and makes a phone call to Student B, stating his or her problem. Then Student B offers advice to Student A. Finally, have each pair present its skit to the class. Encourage students to extend their dialogues as far as possible so that they sound realistic, for example: **—Écoute, j'ai un problème. —Qu'est-ce qui s'est passé? —Je suis tombé(e) en panne sur la route. —Où es-tu?**

—Je suis sur le boulevard de la République. —Il y a une station-service sur la rue Victor Hugo. Ce n'est pas loin. À ta place, j'y marcherais. —Merci. —Je t'en prie. —Au revoir. —À bientôt.

🎧 **Audiocassette/CD Activities 7-8**

Answers

7 1. Réserverais-tu une chambre d'hôtel, ou chercherais-tu une auberge de jeunesse? Et toi, réserverais-tu une chambre d'hôtel, ou chercherais-tu une auberge de jeunesse?
2. Achèterais-tu des chèques de voyage, ou paierais-tu avec une carte de crédit? Et toi, achèterais-tu des chèques de voyage, ou paierais-tu avec une carte de crédit?
3. Prendrais-tu le métro, ou louerais-tu une voiture? Et toi, prendrais-tu le métro, ou louerais-tu une voiture?
4. Irais-tu au Louvre, ou visiterais-tu le musée Picasso? Et toi, irais-tu au Louvre, ou visiterais-tu le musée Picasso?
5. Goûterais-tu la vraie cuisine française, ou t'arrêterais-tu au Quick? Et toi, goûterais-tu la vraie cuisine française, ou t'arrêterais-tu au Quick?
6. Mangerais-tu au café, ou piqueniquerais-tu dans un parc? Et toi, mangerais-tu au café, ou piqueniquerais-tu dans un parc?
7. Téléphonerais-tu à ta famille, ou enverrais-tu des cartes postales? Et toi, téléphonerais-tu à ta famille, ou enverrais-tu des cartes postales?
8. Sortirais-tu chaque soir, ou resterais-tu dans ta chambre? Et toi, sortirais-tu chaque soir, ou resterais-tu dans ta chambre?

Students' responses to these questions will vary.

8 Answers will vary.

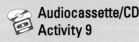
Answers

9 1. Ahmed est fâché que l'ascenseur ne marche pas.
2. Mlle Laurent est triste qu'on ne puisse pas voir la mer.
3. M. Dupont regrette qu'il n'y ait pas de clim.
4. Les Fralin sont contents que l'hôtel serve de très bons repas.
5. Les enfants sont désolés que la piscine soit fermée.
6. Les étudiants sont étonnés qu'une chambre coûte si cher.
7. Pierre est heureux que la salle de bains ait un sèche-cheveux.

Teacher's Notes

1. Other verbs and expressions of emotion include **admirer, approuver, avoir honte, c'est malheureux, craindre, déplorer, étonner, être déçu(e), être embarrassé(e), être ému(e), être enchanté(e), être fier/fière, être flatté(e), être furieux/furieuse, être gêné(e), être navré(e), être ravi(e), être surpris(e), être vexé(e), se réjouir** and **supporter**. 2. Expressions of emotion are also followed by the subjunctive in the negative or interrogative, for example, **Ça ne m'embête pas que tu sois en retard**. 3. You may want to tell students that any verb that suggests some emotion in a particular context may take the subjunctive, for example, **Je ne comprends pas que Marc parte sans me parler**. 4. Remind students that the subjunctive is used when the subjects of the two clauses are different. When they are the same, you avoid the subjunctive by using an infinitive, for example, **Antoine est étonné d'avoir des ennuis à l'hôtel**. 5. You may want to introduce certain conjunctions that also take the subjunctive: **à condition que, à moins que... ne, avant que... ne, bien que, jusqu'à ce que, pour que, pourvu que, quoique** and **sans que**. 6. You may also want students to know that the subjunctive is used with a superlative when an opinion is being expressed, for example, **Saint-Martin, c'est la plus belle île que je connaisse**.

Louis est content que sa chambre soit près de la piscine.

The subjunctive after expressions of emotion

So far you have learned four different uses of the subjunctive. How many of them can you remember? The subjunctive is used in a dependent clause after the expression **il faut que**; after certain impersonal expressions; after expressions of wish, will or desire; and after expressions of doubt or uncertainty. In this lesson you will learn one final use of the subjunctive—after expressions of emotion (for example, happiness, sadness, surprise, fear, anger). Use the subjunctive after one of the following expressions of emotion when the emotion concerns someone other than the subject.

être content(e) que	*to be happy that*
être heureux/heureuse que	*to be happy that*
être triste que	*to be sad that*
être désolé(e) que	*to be sorry that*
être fâché(e) que	*to be angry that*
être étonné(e) que	*to be surprised that*
avoir peur que	*to be afraid that*
regretter que	*to be sorry that*
s'inquiéter que	*to worry that*
Ça me surprend que....	*It surprises me that . . . .*
Ça m'embête que....	*It bothers me that . . . .*
C'est dommage que....	*It's too bad that . . . .*

Ça me surprend qu'on ne puisse pas voir la mer.	*It surprises me that we can't see the sea.*
Je suis étonné qu'ils ne mettent pas la clim.	*I'm surprised that they don't turn on the air conditioning.*
Moi aussi. J'ai peur qu'il fasse trop chaud ce soir.	*Me too. I'm afraid that it's going to be too hot tonight.*
C'est dommage que l'ascenseur ne marche pas.	*It's too bad that the elevator doesn't work.*
Ça m'embête qu'on ait des ennuis dans cet hôtel.	*It bothers me that we have problems in this hotel.*

Pratique

9 *Formez une phrase logique pour chaque illustration qui décrive la réaction de la clientèle de l'hôtel. Choisissez un élément des colonnes A et B pour chaque phrase. Suivez le modèle.*

Modèle:

Françoise a peur que le téléphone soit occupé.

A	B
Françoise a peur	La piscine est fermée.
Ahmed est fâché	Le téléphone est occupé.
Mlle Laurent est triste	La salle de bains a un sèche-cheveux.
M. Dupont regrette	Il n'y a pas de clim.
les Fralin sont contents	L'ascenseur ne marche pas.
les enfants sont désolés	Une chambre coûte si cher.
les étudiants sont étonnés	L'hôtel sert de très bons repas.
Pierre est heureux	On ne peut pas voir la mer.

Critical Thinking

Subjunctive vs. Infinitive

Write two related sentences on the board, one that uses the subjunctive after an expression of emotion and the other that uses an infinitive, for example, **Mes parents sont étonnés que je reçoive un "A" en français** and **Je suis étonné(e) de recevoir un "A" en français**. Ask students why the subjunctive is needed in the first example but not in the second. Students should tell you that in the first sentence the subjects of the two clauses are different. However, in the second sentence the subject is the same. This activity will help students determine when they need to use the subjunctive and when they can use an infinitive instead.

1.

5.

2.

6.

3.

7.

4.

Je suis contente que le téléphone ne soit plus occupé.

Cooperative Group Practice

Forming Sentences

Put students in small groups to practice forming sentences using expressions of emotion followed by the subjunctive. Have each group make three sets of note cards. On each card in the first set, students write an expression of emotion from this lesson. On each card in the second set, students write a subject (a noun or a pronoun), such as **le professeur** or **tu**. On each card in the third set, students write an infinitive expression, such as **être malade aujourd'hui** or **aller à Saint-Martin**. The first student in each group takes the top card from each pile, for example, **s'inquiéter/le professeur/être malade aujourd'hui**, and forms a sentence stating his or her reaction, for example, **Je m'inquiète que le professeur soit malade aujourd'hui**. Students take turns forming sentences until all the cards have been used.

Magazine Pictures

To provide additional practice using the subjunctive after expressions of emotion, put students in small groups of four or five. Each student is responsible for finding a picture from a magazine that he or she can describe using the subjunctive after an expression of emotion. The first student describes his or her picture, for example, **Mme Bouquet est heureuse que sa fille lui téléphone.** Then the second student asks a question about the first student's picture, for example, **Qu'est-ce que sa fille lui dit?** The first student responds, for example, **Sa fille lui dit qu'elle va rendre visite à sa mère le mois prochain.** Have the two students extend their discussion of the picture as far as they can. Then the remaining students in the group take turns describing their pictures and having a conversation with the person on their right.

10 L'hôtel Gobernau à Saint-Martin ne plaît pas du tout à Lucien Darbaud. Complétez la lettre qu'il écrit à l'hôtel en mettant les verbes entre parenthèses à la forme convenable.

Saint-Martin, le 17 mai 1999

Hôtel Gobernau
13, avenue Wilson
Saint-Martin

Monsieur le gérant,

Je regrette que mes amis et moi, nous (devoir) trouver un autre hôtel pour continuer nos vacances ici à Saint-Martin. Votre hôtel ne nous plaît pas du tout. Voici une liste de nos ennuis:

1. Ça nous surprend que l'ascenseur ne (marcher) jamais. Ça nous embête que nous (être) toujours obligés de prendre l'escalier pour monter au quatrième étage.

2. Nous sommes tristes que nos chambres n'(avoir) pas de vue panoramique de la mer. Nous avons réservé deux chambres avec une vue sur la plage!

3. Nous sommes fâchés que vous ne (mettre) pas la climatisation avant 14h00. Nous avons peur qu'il y (faire) toujours trop chaud.

4. Ça nous embête aussi que les portes de nos chambres ne (fermer) pas bien. Nous nous inquiétons que quelqu'un (aller) nous voler!

5. C'est dommage qu'il n'y (avoir) pas de service de chambre dans cet hôtel. Je regrette que mes amis et moi, nous (avoir) toujours besoin de sortir pour manger.

Nous avons essayé de téléphoner à la réception pour vous parler de ces problèmes. Nous sommes étonnés que personne ne nous (répondre). Nous regrettons que vous ne (vouloir) pas nous écouter.

Je vous prie d'agréer, Monsieur, nos salutations distinguées.

Lucien Darbaud

TPR

Uses of the Subjunctive

So that students can differentiate between sentences using the subjunctive after expressions of emotion and sentences using the subjunctive after **il faut que**, impersonal expressions, expressions of wish, will or desire, or expressions of doubt or uncertainty, prepare a list of sentences using the subjunctive in all these categories. Have each student prepare two cards, one with "E" for emotion and one with "O" for other uses of the subjunctive. As you read each sentence, students hold up the "E" card if they hear a sentence using the subjunctive after an expression of emotion. If they hear a sentence using the subjunctive in one of the other categories, they hold up the "O" card.

Imaginez que vous venez d'arriver à l'Hôtel Bon Séjour à Saint-Martin où vous allez passer dix jours. Vous remarquez certaines choses en ce qui concerne l'hôtel. Faites des phrases qui expriment votre réaction. Suivez le modèle.

1. être étonné(e)/Le téléphone est toujours occupé.
2. c'est dommage/L'hôtel n'accepte pas les cartes de crédit.
3. être désolé(e)/Ma chambre est trop petite.
4. être fâché(e)/On ne voit rien de la fenêtre.
5. être content(e)/Le restaurant propose une variété de cuisine.
6. ça m'embête/Le restaurant ferme à 19h00.
7. ça me surprend/On n'offre pas de service de chambre.
8. regretter/On ne peut pas profiter du bureau d'excursions.

Communication

Imaginez que vous êtes le/la gérant(e) d'un nouvel hôtel. Naturellement, vous voulez encourager les touristes à y venir. Vous voulez que tout le monde connaisse les bonnes qualités de votre hôtel. Alors faites une liste de ces qualités. (Par exemple, où votre hôtel est-il situé? Offre-t-il une piscine, un restaurant, un gymnase? Les chambres donnent-elles sur l'océan? Y a-t-il un service de chambre et la télévision par satellite? Y a-t-il un bureau d'excursions?) Puis utilisez toutes ces informations pour dessiner un dépliant pour votre nouvel hôtel. Donnez-lui un nom et un certain nombre d'étoiles (★). Mentionnez aussi le prix des chambres, l'adresse, la ville, le numéro de téléphone et le numéro de fax de votre hôtel.

Avec le/la gérant(e) d'un autre hôtel de l'Activité 12, comparez vos deux hôtels. Posez des questions à votre partenaire, et répondez à ses questions. Par exemple, vous pouvez parler du nombre de chambres, des services et des qualités de vos hôtels. Puis organisez les informations en faisant deux cercles qui se croisent. (Regardez les cercles qui suivent.) Dans le cercle à gauche, faites une liste des qualités uniques de votre hôtel; dans le cercle à droite, faites une liste des qualités uniques de l'hôtel de votre partenaire. Là où les deux cercles se croisent, faites une liste des qualités communes des deux hôtels. Enfin, avec votre partenaire, décrivez vos deux hôtels aux autres élèves en leur montrant vos deux cercles.

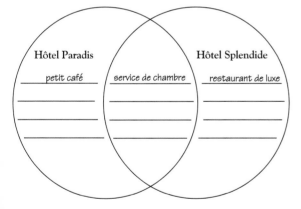

Hôtel Paradis   petit café

service de chambre

Hôtel Splendide   restaurant de luxe

Modèle:

être content(e)/Il y a une grande piscine.
Je suis content(e) qu'il y ait une grande piscine.

Es-tu heureux que le petit déjeuner soit compris?

Offrez-vous la télévision par satellite?

Oui, bien sûr, nous l'offrons.

Answers

11 1. Je suis étonné(e) que le téléphone soit toujours occupé.
2. C'est dommage que l'hôtel n'accepte pas les cartes de crédit.
3. Je suis désolé(e) que ma chambre soit trop petite.
4. Je suis fâché(e) qu'on ne voie rien de la fenêtre.
5. Je suis content(e) que le restaurant propose une variété de cuisine.
6. Ça m'embête que le restaurant ferme à 19h00.
7. Ça me surprend qu'on n'offre pas de service de chambre.
8. Je regrette qu'on ne puisse pas profiter du bureau d'excursions.

Teacher's Note

Students with more artistic ability and/or less writing ability may prefer to design a poster of their hotel rather than a brochure in Activity 12.

Paired Practice

Les bandes dessinées

Take an American comic strip with emotional expressions on the characters' faces and eliminate the words with correction fluid. Put students in pairs and have each pair write a dialogue for the comic strip, using at least one example of the subjunctive after an expression of emotion. Have each pair review the comic strips created by the other pairs in class. Then have students vote on the most creative comic strip.

**Workbook
Activity 8**

**Advanced
Placement**

Teacher's Notes

1. "Telling a Story through Pictures" is a section that has been designed to prepare students for the oral part of the Advanced Placement Exam in French Language, where they are asked to use a sequence of pictures to tell a story. In the AP exam students are often asked to describe a sequence of four to six pictures. This **Sur la bonne piste** section provides two picture stories, one with four frames and one with five frames, to allow for adequate practice. 2. You may want students to practice telling the story sequences first in the present tense, then in the **passé composé**.

Sur la bonne piste

Telling a Story through Pictures

When friends ask you what you did over the weekend, do you often tell a story about something that happened to you, for example, at the shopping mall, a game or a party? Using language to tell a story is something you know how to do naturally in English. But how do you effectively tell a story in French? One way to develop storytelling skills is to practice describing a sequence of pictures. How would you tell a story based on the series of pictures that follows? As you look at them, take a few minutes to consider whom the story is about, where it takes place and what happens. Then tell your story in French to a partner. Each of you can describe two frames of the story. (Before you begin, you may want to review words and expressions relating to train travel found in the second level of *C'est à toi!* on pages 258-59.)

1.
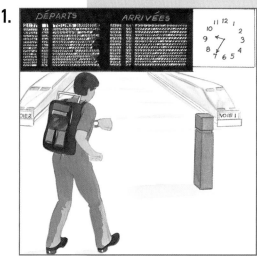

2.
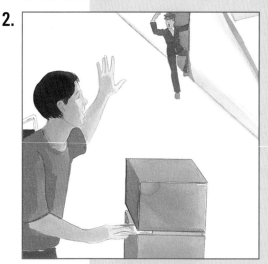

3.

4.

Did you describe the characters, setting and events? These are the three main elements to keep in mind when telling a story based on a sequence of pictures. First, tell whom the story is about. Is the main character in this story a student or an adult? How old is he? What is he wearing? You might even want to give the person a name, such as Julien. To embellish the story, it is important to use your imagination. Why is Julien traveling? Is he going to visit a friend? Is he going on vacation? Look at all the clues. The city of Tours is listed in the arrival and departure information. This might suggest that Julien is going to visit the castles in the Loire Valley. Whenever possible, try to include what you know about francophone culture when telling a story using pictures.

Second, describe the setting. Where does the story take place? In this sequence of pictures, the story moves from the interior of a train station to the interior of a train. As you move from frame to frame, you may need to adjust the setting. Describing the first frame, you might say **Julien arrive à la gare**, but you can add more details, such as **Il regarde le tableau des arrivées et des départs**. In the third frame you might say **Julien monte dans le train**. More specifically, you could add that he's talking to **le contrôleur**. Try to use as many words relating to train travel as you can. For example, can you name the kind of train that Julien is going to take? In some stories, you may be able to include the time, the weather and the season, as well as the obvious location.

Third, describe the events that take place in the story. What do Julien and the other characters do, and in what order? There may be more than one action to describe in each frame. For example, in the first frame Julien looks at his watch as he sees the arrival and departure information. He realizes that he has only two minutes to catch his train. What effect would this information have on him? Would it make him hurry? In describing picture stories you need to make inferences. Sometimes this means describing what happens between two picture frames. Even though you don't actually see Julien hurrying, you can logically say why he would need to hurry, for example, **Julien se dépêche parce que son train va partir dans deux minutes**. What happens after the last frame? You don't see that Julien comes back the next day to catch the right train, but you can arrive at a logical conclusion by revealing this information. Remember to use transition words like **d'abord**, **ensuite**, **puis**, **enfin** and **finalement** as you move from one action to another. Sometimes you may want to use direct dialogue rather than description to tell that certain events are taking place. Instead of saying **Le contrôleur dit à Julien que son billet est pour demain**, you could quote what the inspector says. For example, **Le contrôleur lui dit, "Le problème, c'est que votre billet est pour demain."** Direct dialogue helps to make the story come alive. You may not always discuss the characters, setting and events in that order. It depends on what each picture shows and what you determine is logical to express first, second and third.

Finally, try to relax and enjoy being a storyteller. With practice, you will find that you have a lot to say. Here is how one student told Julien's story based on the sequence of pictures. Compare this story with the one you and your partner told.

> Un lycéen de 17 ans arrive à la gare. Il s'appelle Julien. Il porte un jean, un tee-shirt, des bottes et un sac à dos. Julien va en vacances aujourd'hui. Sa destination est Tours. Julien compte visiter les châteaux

de la Loire… Amboise, Chambord et Chenonceaux. D'abord, Julien regarde le tableau des arrivées et des départs. Son train va partir à 21h37 sur la voie numéro 1. Puis Julien regarde sa montre. Il est 21h35. Mince! Julien se dépêche parce que son train va partir dans deux minutes. Vite, Julien composte son billet. Il voit un contrôleur. Julien lui dit, "Attendez-moi! J'arrive!" Le contrôleur lui répond, "Dépêchez-vous!" Julien monte dans le TGV, mais il n'y a pas de siège pour lui. Il voit un couple âgé, une famille et un homme d'affaires. Julien montre son billet au contrôleur. Le contrôleur lui dit, "Le problème, c'est que votre billet est pour demain." "Ah, d'accord!" dit Julien. Il revient le lendemain, et cette fois, Julien est en avance!

14 | Now tell a story based on the sequence of pictures that follows by describing the characters, setting and events. Remember to use transition words like **d'abord**, **ensuite** and **enfin**, and to use direct dialogue when possible.

le Rocher Percé

**Workbook
Activities 9-10**

Audiocassette/CD
Le Canada, L'avion

Teacher's Notes

1. Communicative functions that are recycled in this lesson are "expressing emotions," "describing past events," "sequencing events," "reporting," "explaining a problem" and "expressing intentions."
2. Other related terms and expressions include **une aérogare** (*airport terminal*), **une piste** (*runway*), **relevez vos tablettes** (*return your trays to their locked position*), **redressez vos sièges** (*return your seats to their upright position*), **aller et retour** (*round-trip*) and **aller simple** (*one-way*).

Leçon B

In this lesson you will be able to:

➤ write postcards

➤ tell location

➤ tell a story

➤ remember

➤ describe people you remember

➤ indicate knowing and not knowing

➤ identify objects

➤ express complaint

➤ admit

➤ express patience

L'été dernier Micheline a fait un voyage° au Canada. Elle a rendu visite à un cousin qui habite à Gaspé dans la province de Québec. Près de Gaspé il y a un parc sauvage,° le Parc de l'Île-Bonaventure-et-du-Rocher-Percé, dont° son cousin lui a souvent parlé. On dit que le rocher° est percé parce qu'il fait un grand arc dans la mer. Son cousin, Mathieu, y est garde forestier.° Micheline a écrit une carte postale à sa meilleure° amie pour lui parler de son arrivée au Canada.

le 25 juin

Chère Isabelle,

Je rêve de ce voyage depuis longtemps, et enfin me voilà au Canada! Tout s'est bien passé° jusqu'à mon arrivée à Dorval. Je faisais la queue au contrôle de sécurité quand je me suis rendu compte° que je n'avais ni mon passeport ni mon sac à dos. J'avais peur de laisser quelque chose dans l'avion. Alors, j'y suis vite retournée. Une hôtesse de l'air et un steward m'ont aidée. La façon dont° ils m'ont traitée était super. Ils ont tout de suite fouillé dans le porte-bagages, tu sais, le truc° au-dessus des sièges. Voilà! On a trouvé le sac à dos, dont° j'avais besoin. Puis j'ai passé la douane. En sortant, j'ai fait la connaissance d'une Canadienne dont° la mère est française. Elle m'a accompagnée à la gare en taxi. J'attends le train pour Gaspé maintenant. À bientôt.

Bisous,°
Micheline

Je n'ai pas mis mon sac à dos dans le porte-bagages.

---

faire un voyage *voyager*; **sauvage** *wildlife*; **dont** *about which*; **un rocher** *rock*; **un garde forestier** *park ranger*; **le/la meilleur(e)** *best*; **se passer** *aller*; **se rendre compte** *to realize*; **la façon dont** *the way in which*; **un truc** *une chose*; **dont** *of which*; **dont** *whose*; **un bisou** *une bise*

🎧 **Audiocassette/CD**
Les cartes postales

Teacher's Notes

1. Tell students to watch out for the different meanings of **dont** in the exposition. 2. Point out to students that **meilleur(e)**, the superlative form of the irregular adjective **bon**, modifies nouns; **mieux** modifies verbs. 3. Students learned **se passer** meaning "to happen" in Unit 2 in the third level of *C'est à toi!* 4. The Montreal International Airport at Dorval is located 14 miles west of downtown Montreal. 5. Explain that **se rendre compte** takes **de** before a noun or pronoun and **que** before a clause. In compound tenses **rendu** cannot agree with the reflexive object pronoun because the latter is always an indirect object. 6. Tell students to use the preposition **de** (not **dans**) before **façon**, i.e., **de quelle façon** (*in which way*) or **de cette façon** (*in that way*). 7. **Porte-bagages** is invariable. 8. Other expressions used to end a postcard include **Amicalement** (*Love*), **Affectueusement** (*Affectionately*) and **Je t'embrasse** (*With love*).

Teacher's Notes

1. The Chaleur is an overnight train that runs between Montreal and Gaspé. It follows the southern coast of the Gaspé Peninsula, along Chaleur Bay, and arrives in Gaspé around noon. 2. Point out that "Mrs. So-and-so" is **Madame une telle.** 3. You may want to introduce the present tense forms of the irregular verb **se plaindre: je me plains, tu te plains, il/elle/on se plaint, nous nous plaignons, vous vous plaignez, ils/elles se plaignent.** Point out that **se plaindre** takes **que** before a clause. 4. Point out that **se tromper** is followed by **de** or **d'** and a noun. 5. Explain that **propre**, meaning "own," precedes the noun; **propre**, meaning "clean," follows the noun. 6. Tell students that **se souvenir** belongs to the **venir** verb family. 7. Students learned **un paysage**, meaning "landscape," in Unit 3 in the third level of *C'est à toi!*

Micheline est bien arrivée à Gaspé, mais pas sans ennuis! Voilà la carte postale qu'elle a écrite à son amie après deux jours chez son cousin.

> le 27 juin
>
> *Chère Isabelle,*
>
> *J'ai pris le Chaleur de Montréal à Gaspé. Pendant que je montais dans le train, j'avais mon billet à la main. Une fois dans la voiture, je ne le regardais plus. Je suis arrivée à mon siège, mais il y avait déjà quelqu'un. Alors, j'ai cherché Monsieur un tel,° le chef de train.° Il était si gentil. Il s'est occupé° de moi avec patience. Il ne s'est plaint° de rien, et il a vérifié le numéro de mon siège. Le problème, c'est que je n'ai pas bien regardé mon billet. C'est pourquoi je me suis trompée° de siège. Enfin, je me suis installée dans mon propre° siège où j'ai passé la nuit.° À midi je suis arrivée à Gaspé. Mon cousin est venu me chercher dans le camion dont il se sert° dans le parc. Aujourd'hui nous avons fait les touristes° et avons parcouru° Gaspé et tout le parc, bien sûr. Je vais toujours me souvenir° de la beauté du paysage.° Demain je vais faire la promenade en bateau dont j'ai tellement° envie. À bientôt.*
>
> *Bisous,*
> *Micheline*

Monsieur un tel *Mr. So-and-so;* **un chef de train** *conductor;* **s'occuper de** *to take care of;* **se plaindre** *to complain;* **se tromper de** *to be mistaken;* **propre** *own;* **une nuit** *pas le jour;* **se servir de** *utiliser;* **faire les touristes** *to act like tourists;* **parcourir** *to travel through;* **se souvenir** *se rappeler;* **un paysage** *une campagne;* **tellement** *so much*

LES BATELIERS DE PERCÉ

✔ Excursions vers le Rocher Percé et l'Île Bonaventure avec arrêt au Parc de l'Île Bonaventure

✔ Navires de 80 à 100 passagers

✔ Information sur le milieu marin par un de nos plongeurs

✔ Stationnement gratuit

Billetterie et stationnement
278, route 132
Percé (Québec) G0C 2L0

Tél.: (418) 782-2974
Téléc.: (418) 782-5660

1 | *Mettez les phrases en ordre chronologique en regardant les deux cartes postales de Micheline. Écrivez "1" pour la première phrase, "2" pour la deuxième phrase, etc.*

1. Une Canadienne a accompagné Micheline à la gare en taxi.
2. Micheline est arrivée à Dorval.
3. Micheline va faire une promenade en bateau.
4. Une hôtesse de l'air et un steward ont aidé Micheline.
5. Micheline a passé la nuit dans le train.
6. Micheline s'est rendu compte qu'elle n'avait pas son sac à dos.
7. Mathieu et Micheline ont parcouru le Parc de l'Île-Bonaventure-et-du-Rocher-Percé.
8. Le chef de train a aidé Micheline à trouver son propre siège.

Critical Thinking

Journal personnel

Ask students to write about the topic of the declining popularity of train travel in the United States. To what do students attribute this decline? What are the advantages and disadvantages of traveling by train? Students might also reflect on what the decline in train travel says about American values. For example, does our support of the automobile industry mean that we value individual freedom more than preserving the environment?

Complétez chaque phrase avec l'expression convenable, selon l'illustration.

Micheline et Mathieu ont parcouru la ville de Gaspé.

1. Mathieu, le cousin de Micheline, est... dans un parc sauvage près de Gaspé.

5. Dans le train,... a vérifié le numéro du siège de Micheline.

2. Gaspé se trouve dans... de Québec.

6. Micheline a passé... dans son propre siège.

3. ... a aidé Micheline à trouver son sac à dos.

7. Mathieu et Micheline... et ont parcouru tout le parc.

4. On l'a trouvé dans....

8. Micheline va toujours... de la beauté du paysage.

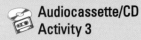
Answers

3 Answers will vary.

Teacher's Notes

1. Cognates in this reading include **spectaculaire, continent, péninsule, gaspésienne, borde, ravagées, couvertes, forêts, golfe, baie, partie, cosmopolite, acadiennes, fondé, expulsées, attraction, touristique, extrême, port, commerce, attaqué, commerciale, dramatique, naturelle, présente, formé, préhistoire, contient, fossiles, nautique, préhistoire, examiner, migrateurs, habitat, tranquille, sanctuaire, danger, extinction, sites, historiques, végétation, variée, observation, observatoires, permettent, différent, aspects, compartiments, face à face, couchette, existent** and **direction**. 2. Cartier landed on the Gaspé Peninsula in 1534. 3. Geographically, the Gaspé Peninsula is among the oldest lands on earth. Most of the area remains unspoiled and timeless, attracting bird watchers, hikers, campers, nature lovers and artists. Fishing villages dot the northeast and east coast of the peninsula, while farmers and lumbermen live around Chaleur Bay. There is also mining of zinc and lead in the area. 4. Chaleur Bay, so named for its relatively warm water, is a sheltered inlet that separates the heart of the Gaspé Peninsula from New Brunswick. 5. Ten thousand Acadians were driven out of Nova Scotia, which French immigrants first began settling in 1604. The Acadians, who were French Catholics, refused to pledge allegiance to England, preferring to preserve their French traditions, culture and language. The 1755 exodus, called **le grand dérangement** (*the "Big Upheaval"*), is the background for Henry

3 | *C'est à toi!*

1. Est-ce que tu es jamais allé(e) dans la province de Québec? Si oui, où?
2. Qu'est-ce que tu rêves de faire depuis longtemps?
3. Est-ce que tu as jamais visité un parc national? Si oui, quelles activités est-ce qu'on y offre?
4. Est-ce que tu as jamais laissé quelque chose d'important dans un avion, un train, un magasin ou à l'école? Si oui, qu'est-ce que tu y as laissé?
5. Est-ce que tu as jamais montré ta ville à un(e) touriste? Si oui, quel est le premier endroit que tu lui as montré?
6. À qui est-ce que tu écris des lettres ou des cartes postales? Écris-tu souvent à cette personne?
7. Est-ce que tu as un(e) meilleur(e) amie(e)? Si oui, comment s'appelle-t-il ou elle?

 ## Enquête culturelle

Pendant son premier voyage au Nouveau Monde pour la France, Jacques Cartier a eu la vue la plus spectaculaire du continent: la côte de la péninsule gaspésienne au Canada. Située au nord-est du Québec, cette péninsule borde l'océan Atlantique avec des côtes rocheuses ravagées par la mer, des groupes d'oiseaux de mer et des montagnes couvertes de forêts. La péninsule est aussi bordée par le golfe du Saint-Laurent au nord-est, le Saint-Laurent au nord et la baie des Chaleurs au sud. Dans la partie sud de la péninsule vivent les Acadiens, les Basques et des Indiens qui donnent à cette partie de la péninsule un riche air cosmopolite.

Douze familles acadiennes ont fondé le village de Bonaventure. Ces familles ont été expulsées de l'Acadie par les Anglais en 1755. Le village est aujourd'hui une attraction touristique.

Découvrez l'Acadie du Québec.
Explorez notre mémoire.
• Musée acadien du Québec à Bonaventure
• Église de Bonaventure
• Fête nationale acadienne (15 août)

Les villages gaspésiens sont pittoresques.

Wadsworth Longfellow's poem "Evangeline." Although most Acadians moved to Louisiana in 1760, some of them resettled in the English colonies of Massachusetts, Virginia and Georgia. Today their descendants are found mainly in Vermont, Maine and New Hampshire. 6. Acadian traditions and heritage are celebrated at Bonaventure's **Musée acadien du Québec**.

Critical Thinking

Journal personnel

Tell students the story of the Acadians' expulsion from their homeland, as explained in the teacher's note on this page. Ask students to explain if the Acadians were treated fairly, in their opinion. Then have them reflect on the difficulties the Acadians must have had in preserving their

language and culture when they left Nova Scotia. Finally, ask students to mention what groups of people in the world are being similarly oppressed today and why.

Le village de Percé, à l'extrême est de la péninsule, était au 17ᵉ siècle un port d'où allaient et venaient les bateaux pour le commerce avec la France. Mais en 1690 les Anglais ont attaqué Percé et ont mis fin à sa vie commerciale. Depuis ce temps-là, Percé est devenu un centre d'attraction touristique de la péninsule, surtout pour son célèbre rocher. Le Rocher Percé se lève de façon dramatique de la mer. Au centre du rocher il y a une arche naturelle qui présente une vue spectaculaire. Long de 438 mètres et haut de 88 mètres, le rocher a été formé sous la mer pendant la préhistoire, et il contient beaucoup de fossiles de la vie nautique de la préhistoire. Il change de couleur lorsque changent la lumière et le temps. Pendant certaines heures de la journée, on peut visiter le rocher à pied pour l'examiner.

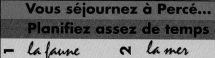

Vous séjournez à Percé...
Planifiez assez de temps

JOUR 1 — la faune
- Centre d'interprétation de la nature.
- Sentiers en montagnes.
- Observation ornithologique.
- Musée - Galeries d'art.

JOUR 3 — le littoral
- Marche au Rocher Percé.
- Pêche (quais/rivières/excursion organisée/étang artificiel).
- Plage d'agates et de jaspes de l'Anse-à-Beaufils.
- À Cap-d'Espoir : plage, phare.

JOUR 2 — la mer
- Croisière vers le Rocher Percé et l'Île Bonaventure (sanctuaire d'oiseaux marins).
- Observation de baleines.
- Plongée sous-marine/planche à voile.

JOUR 4 — l'exploration
- Route panoramique des failles jusqu'à Cannes-de-Roches.
- Coin du Banc : observation ornithologique, cueillette d'agates et jaspes.
- Bridgeville, Barachois, Pointe-Saint-Pierre : observation ornithologique, havres de pêche typiques.
- Saint-Georges-de-Malbaie : rocher «Tête d'Indien», havre de pêche.

À marée haute *(high tide)*, il faut que les touristes prennent un bateau pour s'approcher du Rocher Percé.

Le Parc de l'Île-Bonaventure-et-du-Rocher-Percé, à 800 kilomètres au nord-est de Québec, offre aux oiseaux de mer et aux oiseaux migrateurs un habitat tranquille. Là ils sont préservés en sanctuaire parce que plusieurs sortes de ces oiseaux sont en danger d'extinction. Le parc est ouvert du mois de juin au mois d'octobre. On peut y piqueniquer, faire des promenades, visiter des sites historiques, regarder la végétation variée et faire de l'observation scientifique. C'est un paradis pour les gens qui aiment étudier les oiseaux.

Parc de l'Île-Bonaventure-et-du-Rocher-Percé
4, rue du Quai, C.P. 310 Percé G0C 2L0 (418) 782-2240 ou 782-2721,
Fax. : (418) 782-2241

Teacher's Notes

1. VIA is Canada's national train network. As in the U.S., the ridership of passenger trains in Canada has greatly diminished.
2. Some trains in France have "airplane" seating where all the seats face the same direction.

Si la France a le TGV, l'Amérique du Nord a des trains qui traversent tout le continent avec des voitures "observatoires" qui permettent aux voyageurs d'admirer le paysage du Canada ou des États-Unis.

Le **CANADA.** Découvrez-le en train.

Les trains de France diffèrent des trains de l'Amérique du Nord par quelques aspects. Vous avez déjà appris qu'il faut composter les billets en France. Mais ce n'est pas nécessaire en Amérique du Nord. Lorsque vous avez un billet, vous montez dans le train et vous attendez que le chef de train vienne vérifier votre billet.

Dans beaucoup de trains européens, les voitures sont composées de plusieurs compartiments. Chaque compartiment a six sièges, trois places qui sont face à face avec trois autres dans un très petit espace. Cela permet de vous mettre en groupe d'amis ou de famille pour parler ou jouer aux cartes. Le soir vous pouvez baisser le siège pour en faire un petit lit où vous pouvez dormir. Fermez la fenêtre et la porte et vous avez une petite place pour vous coucher, une "couchette." Les compartiments n'existent pas en Amérique du Nord, où les sièges ressemblent à des places de théâtre où tout le monde regarde dans la même direction. Si vous voulez faire un somme, faites-le dans votre siège.

Dans le TGV Atlantique, choisirais-tu un compartiment ou non?

Répondez aux questions suivantes.

1. Qui a eu la première vue de la péninsule gaspésienne?
2. Où la péninsule gaspésienne est-elle située?
3. Quelle est l'attraction du Parc de l'Île-Bonaventure-et-du-Rocher-Percé?
4. Qu'est-ce qu'il y a au centre du Rocher Percé?
5. Qu'est-ce qui est préservé dans ce parc?
6. Où trouve-t-on les voitures de train "observatoires"?
7. Comment vérifie-t-on le billet de train en Amérique du Nord?
8. Combien de personnes s'asseyent dans le compartiment d'un train européen?
9. Quels sont les avantages d'un compartiment?
10. Comment est-qu'on transforme un compartiment de train en couchette?

Beaucoup de touristes viennent observer les oiseaux de mer et les oiseaux migrateurs au Parc de l'Île-Bonaventure-et-du-Rocher-Percé.

Regardez l'horaire des trains entre Halifax et Montréal. Puis répondez aux questions.

1. Combien de trains par jour font le voyage entre Halifax et Montréal?
2. Quels sont les noms des deux trains qui vont à Matapédia?
3. D'où part chaque train?
4. Si on part de Matapédia à 22h47, à quelle heure arrive-t-on à Montréal?
5. Comment s'appelle le train qui part de Petit Rocher?
6. Peut-on partir de Gaspé le mardi?
7. Si on fait le voyage entre Gaspé et Montréal, y a-t-il des facilités pour dormir dans le train?
8. Combien de temps faut-il pour aller de Québec (Lévis) à Montréal?

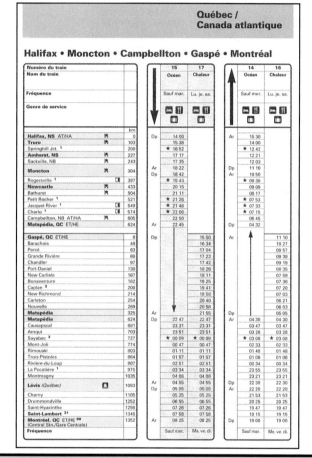

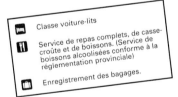

Classe voiture-lits

Service de repas complets, de casse-croûte et de boissons. (Service de boissons alcoolisées conforme à la réglementation provinciale)

Enregistrement des bagages.

Answers

4 1. Jacques Cartier a eu la première vue de la péninsule gaspésienne.
2. La péninsule gaspésienne est située au nord-est du Québec. Elle est bordée par le golfe du Saint-Laurent au nord-est, le Saint-Laurent au nord et la baie des Chaleurs au sud.
3. L'attraction, c'est le Rocher Percé.
4. Au centre du Rocher Percé il y a une arche naturelle.
5. Les oiseaux de mer et les oiseaux migrateurs y sont préservés.
6. On trouve les voitures de train "observatoires" en Amérique du Nord.
7. Le chef de train vient vérifier le billet de train en Amérique du Nord.
8. Six personnes s'asseyent dans le compartiment d'un train européen.
9. Dans un compartiment les personnes sont face à face pour parler ou jouer aux cartes.
10. Pour transformer un compartiment de train en couchette, on baisse le siège pour en faire un petit lit.

5 1. Il n'y a qu'un train qui fait le voyage entre Halifax et Montréal.
2. Les deux trains qui vont à Matapédia sont l'Océan et le Chaleur.
3. L'Océan part de Halifax; le Chaleur part de Gaspé.
4. On arrive à Montréal à 8h25.
5. C'est l'Océan qui part de Petit Rocher.
6. Non, il n'y a pas de train le mardi.
7. Oui, on peut dormir dans le train.
8. Il faut trois heures et vingt minutes pour aller de Québec (Lévis) à Montréal.

Teacher's Notes

1. You may want to tell students that many of the verbs and verbal expressions that are followed by **de** and a noun may also be followed by **de** and an infinitive or a pronoun, for example, **J'ai peur de skier** (*I'm afraid of skiing*) and **Elle se méfie de moi** (*She distrusts me*). 2. Remind students that the expression **avoir peur** may also be followed by **que**, in which case the subjunctive is used in the dependent clause, for example, **J'ai peur qu'il fasse trop chaud ce soir.** (*I'm afraid that it's going to be too hot tonight.*) 3. Point out that when these verbs and verbal expressions are used, **de** has many English translations, such as "of," "about," "with" and "in." Sometimes, however, **de** does not have an English translation, for example, **Le cousin de Micheline se sert de son camion dans le parc.** (*Micheline's cousin uses his truck in the park.*) 4. Other verbs and verbal expressions in French that are followed by **de** and a noun include **avoir honte, discuter, entendre parler, être fier/fière, être satisfait(e), se passer** and **se préoccuper.**

Journal personnel

The beginning of each lesson in this unit describes problems that you might encounter during a trip. Despite careful planning, there always seems to be something unexpected that comes up during any adventure. In **Leçon A** what could Bruno, Antoine, Christian and Denis have done to ensure that their hotel room was satisfactory? What could Micheline have done to avoid the embarrassment of troubling the conductor about her seat on the train? Have you personally experienced any problems during a trip? How can you plan a trip to avoid unpleasant situations such as those encountered by the boys in Saint-Martin or Micheline as she traveled to Gaspé?

Sometimes what seems to be a problem during a trip is simply a cultural misunderstanding. For example, if an American tourist were told that her hotel room in France was on the **deuxième étage**, what mistake would she be making if she walked up to the second floor? Can you think of other types of cultural misunderstandings of this sort that an American might experience while visiting a francophone country? Conversely, what aspects of American culture might confuse a visiting French-speaking tourist?

Structure

Verbs + *de* + nouns

Many verbs and verbal expressions in French are followed by **de** and a noun. Here are some of them.

avoir besoin de	to need
avoir envie de	to want, to feel like
avoir peur de	to be afraid of
être amoureux/amoureuse de	to be in love with
être content(e) de	to be happy about
faire la connaissance de	to meet
se méfier de	to distrust
s'occuper de	to take care of
parler de	to speak/talk about
se plaindre de	to complain about
rêver de	to dream about
se servir de	to use
se souvenir de	to remember
traiter de	to treat
se tromper de	to be mistaken/wrong about

J'AI EU ENVIE D'UNE MAISON CONFORTABLE.

Édouard se sert d'un ordinateur chez lui pour faire ses devoirs.

Si votre copain Frankie vous parle avec émotion des festivals d'Orange ou d'Avignon, pas d'angoisse, c'est La Cinquième.

Cooperative Group Practice

Verbs + *de* + Nouns

So that students can practice identifying the 15 verbs and verbal expressions on this page, put your students into small groups of four or five. Prepare a list of sentences that express a verb or verbal expression from the list on this page without actually using it, for example, **Monique dit au** chef de train qu'elle a froid et qu'elle ne peut pas voir le paysage de son siège. Make copies of the list, and give one to a student in each group that you designate as the leader. When the leader reads a sentence, the first student to call out the expression that would make the sentence more specific, for example, **se plaindre de**, wins a point. After all the sentences have been matched with the correct verb or verbal expression, the leader turns in a list of the students in his or her group and the points that they have earned. Be sure to award points to the leader as well.

Micheline **rêve de ce voyage depuis longtemps.**

Elle **s'est plaint de son siège.**

Mais elle va **se souvenir de la beauté du paysage.**

Micheline has been dreaming about this trip for a long time.

She complained about her seat.

But she is going to remember the beauty of the scenery.

Pratique

Dites ce que font les gens suivants.

1. je/s'occuper

2. M. Delattre/avoir envie

3. Joël et André/être amoureux

4. Mme Leclerc/se plaindre

5. Angélique/avoir besoin

6. Chloé/se méfier

7. Laurent/se servir

8. mes parents/se souvenir

Modèle:

Michèle/rêver
Michèle rêve de la plage.

M. et Mme Roblot parlent des spectacles à Paris cette semaine.

"J'ai surtout des souvenirs d'amours de vacances d'hiver. Je me souviens d'un prof de ski... Un Américain superbe !"

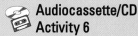 **Audiocassette/CD Activity 6**

Answers

6 Possible answers:

1. Je m'occupe de ma valise.
2. M. Delattre a envie d'un somme.
3. Joël et André sont amoureux de l'hôtesse de l'air.
4. Mme Leclerc se plaint de sa chambre.
5. Angélique a besoin d'un sèche-cheveux.
6. Chloé se méfie du chien.
7. Laurent se sert d'un couteau.
8. Mes parents se souviennent du Rocher Percé.

Cooperative Group Practice

Je me sers de....

To practice forming sentences using **se servir de** followed by a noun, put your students in small groups of four or five. Prepare sets of note cards, writing an activity on each one. Each listed activity, given in the form of an infinitive expression, requires a certain object, for example, **faire de la planche à roulettes, écrire, manger une salade, se brosser les dents, se laver les cheveux, repasser, faire la vaisselle, faire sécher le linge, faire le ménage** and **tondre la pelouse.** Give a set of cards to each group. The first student in each group takes the top card from the stack and forms a sentence saying what he or she is doing, for example, **Je fais de la planche à roulettes.** The student on his or her right asks what the first student uses to do that activity, for example, **De quoi est-ce que tu te sers pour faire de la planche à roulettes?** The first student answers the question, for example, **Je me sers d'une planche à roulettes.** Then the second student takes a card and forms a sentence stating what he or she is doing, beginning the process again. Students take turns in this manner until all the cards are used.

Paired Practice

Answering Questions

To provide additional practice using verbs followed by **de** and a noun, put students in pairs. Prepare a worksheet for Student A and a different worksheet for Student B. Each worksheet lists five infinitives that are followed by **de** and a noun, as well as the tense to be used (in parentheses), for

example, **avoir peur du chien méchant (imparfait).** Student A asks Student B the questions on his or her list, using the correct tense of the indicated verb, for example, **Avais-tu peur du chien méchant?** Student B responds in the negative, supplying a different noun from the one in the question, for example, **Non, j'avais peur de l'examen.** Then Student B forms five questions for Student A, who

changes the noun in each answer. To check students' accuracy, you may want to have them write out their answers.

210

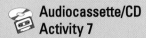

Audiocassette/CD Activity 7

Cooperative Group Practice

Sentence Completion

So that students can practice completing sentences using verbs and verbal expressions followed by **de** and a noun, put them in small groups of four or five. Write the following phrases on the board or on an overhead transparency: 1. Pour faire mes devoirs, j'ai besoin.... 2. En cours je rêve.... 3. Le professeur de français ne se souvient pas.... 4. En été les élèves sont contents.... 5. Le weekend j'ai toujours envie.... 6. À la rentrée j'ai fait la connaissance.... 7. Les mères s'occupent.... 8. À la cantine on a parlé.... 9. Je me suis trompé(e).... Each group writes as many completions as they can think of for each phrase, for example, **Pour faire mes devoirs, j'ai besoin (d'un crayon, d'un cahier, d'un bureau, d'une lampe, d'une gomme, de coca, de musique, d'aide)**. When the groups have finished, you may want to compile a class list of all the sentence completions that they came up with.

Modèle:

Marie-Élise: De quoi as-tu besoin?
Daniel: J'ai besoin d'une nouvelle valise.

La cosmétique a besoin de la nature pour progresser.

Modèle:

Avez-vous fait la connaissance de quelques employés qui vous ont aidé pendant votre séjour?
Oui, nous avons fait la connaissance d'une dame très sympa à la réception qui nous a aidés à changer de chambre le jour après notre arrivée.

ON S'OCCUPE DE TOUT.

7 Imaginez que les élèves dans votre cours de français vont faire un voyage au Québec. Faites une enquête où vous parlez à trois élèves. D'abord copiez la grille suivante. Puis posez à chaque élève les questions indiquées sur ses préparatifs pour le voyage et ses émotions. Enfin notez les réponses dans la grille. Suivez le modèle.

Question	Barbara	Daniel	Babette
avoir besoin		une nouvelle valise	
s'occuper			
avoir peur			
être content(e)			
rêver			

De quoi es-tu content?

Je suis content qu'on serve le dîner pendant le vol.

8 C'est le jour du départ. Bruno, Antoine, Christian et Denis quittent l'Hôtel Belle Île à Saint-Martin. À la réception on leur présente un formulaire de questions sur leur séjour. Relisez leurs expériences dans cet hôtel à la page 182. Puis remplissez ce formulaire pour eux.

1. Vous a-t-on traité d'une façon accueillante? oui ☐ non ☐
2. De quoi aviez-vous besoin dans votre chambre? _____
3. Nous sommes-nous bien occupés de vos besoins? oui ☐ non ☐
4. Pendant votre séjour vous êtes-vous servi de la piscine? oui ☐ non ☐
   Du gymnase? oui ☐ non ☐
5. De quoi allez-vous vous souvenir? _____
6. De quoi allez-vous parler à vos amis? _____
7. De quoi étiez-vous content pendant votre séjour? _____
8. De quoi voulez-vous vous plaindre? _____

The relative pronoun *dont*

You know how to combine two shorter sentences into a longer one by using the relative pronouns **qui** and **que**. The word **dont** is also a relative pronoun, used to connect two clauses in a complex sentence. **Dont** (*of which/whom, about which/whom*) replaces **de** plus a noun and is used with the verbs and verbal expressions that are followed by **de** and a noun that you learned earlier in this lesson.

$$\text{dont} = \text{de} + \text{noun}$$

In the following examples note how **dont** always comes directly after its antecedent to join the sentences in each pair.

Il y a un parc sauvage. Son cousin lui a souvent parlé de ce parc.	*There is a wildlife park. Her cousin often talked to her about this park.*
Il y a un parc sauvage **dont** son cousin lui a souvent parlé.	*There is a wildlife park about which her cousin often talked to her.*
On a trouvé son sac à dos. Elle avait besoin de son sac à dos.	*They found her backpack. She needed her backpack.*
On a trouvé le sac à dos **dont** elle avait besoin.	*They found the backpack that she needed (of which she had need).*

The relative pronoun **dont** means "whose" in sentences where **de** indicates relationship or possession.

J'ai fait la connaissance d'une Canadienne. La mère de la Canadienne est française.	*I met a Canadian woman. The mother of the Canadian woman is French.*
J'ai fait la connaissance d'une Canadienne **dont** la mère est française.	*I met a Canadian woman whose mother is French.*

Dont means "in which" after the expression **la façon**.

La façon **dont** ils m'ont traitée était super.	*The way in which they treated me was great.*

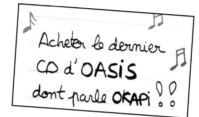

NOUVELLE ELNETT EXTRA-FORTE.

"LE MAINTIEN DONT J'AI BESOIN POUR MES COIFFURES LES PLUS MODE."

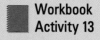
Paired Practice

Forming Sentences with *Dont*

So that students can practice forming sentences with **dont**, put them in pairs. Give Student A a worksheet with the following sentences: 1. Le billet est dans mon sac à dos. 2. Les vacances commencent aujourd'hui. 3. Les passengers sont exigeants. 4. La vue panoramique était super. 5. Le porte-bagages était plein de valises. 6. Voici la carte postale. Give Student B a different worksheet with the following complimentary set of sentences that, when combined with those belonging to Student A, will create new sentences using **dont**: 1. J'ai besoin de mon billet. 2. Anne rêve des vacances depuis longtemps. 3. Le steward s'occupe des passagers. 4. Anne était contente de la vue panoramique. 5. Nous nous sommes servis du porte-bagages. 6. Anne a envie de la carte postale. Tell students to work together to combine the sentences on their separate worksheets. Finally, when all pairs have finished, call on some pairs to read their combined sentences using **dont**.

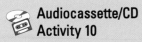

Audiocassette/CD Activity 10

Answers

9 1. La personne dont le chien est très petit s'appelle Mme Lafontaine.
2. La personne dont la femme a soif s'appelle M. Hergy.
3. La personne dont le copain porte des lunettes s'appelle Éric.
4. La personne dont la fille part en voyage s'appelle Mme Charpentier.
5. La personne dont l'enfant dort s'appelle M. Maurel.
6. La personne dont le copain ne se sent pas bien s'appelle Khadim.
7. La personne dont le père lit le journal s'appelle Didier.
8. La personne dont le mari lui a acheté une boisson froide s'appelle Mme Hergy.

10 1. Pendant le voyage en avion, Micheline a perdu le sac à dos dont elle avait besoin.
2. Micheline a fait la connaissance d'une Canadienne dont la mère est française.
3. Voilà le siège de Micheline dont elle s'est plaint.
4. Il y a un parc sauvage près de Gaspé dont le cousin de Micheline lui a souvent parlé.
5. Son cousin a un camion dont il se sert dans le parc.
6. Dans le parc il y a des oiseaux de mer dont Micheline a peur.
7. Demain Micheline va faire la promenade en bateau dont elle a tellement envie.

Pratique

9 | *Dites comment s'appellent les personnes dont on parle.*

Modèle:
Sa mère est triste.
La personne dont la mère est triste s'appelle Christine.

La personne dont le mari travaille dans le train s'appelle Mme Demongeot.

1. Son chien est très petit.
2. Sa femme a soif.
3. Son copain porte des lunettes.
4. Sa fille part en voyage.
5. Son enfant dort.
6. Son copain ne se sent pas bien.
7. Son père lit le journal.
8. Son mari lui a acheté une boisson froide.

10 | *Pour parler du voyage de Micheline à Gaspé, combinez les deux phrases pour en faire une. Utilisez le pronom **dont**.*

Modèle:
Micheline fait un voyage au Canada. Elle rêve de ce voyage depuis longtemps.
Micheline fait un voyage au Canada dont elle rêve depuis longtemps.

1. Pendant le voyage en avion, Micheline a perdu son sac à dos. Elle avait besoin de son sac à dos.
2. Micheline a fait la connaissance d'une Canadienne. La mère de la Canadienne est française.
3. Voilà le siège de Micheline. Elle s'est plaint de ce siège.
4. Il y a un parc sauvage près de Gaspé. Le cousin de Micheline lui a souvent parlé de ce parc.
5. Son cousin a un camion. Il se sert de son camion dans le parc.
6. Dans le parc il y a des oiseaux de mer. Micheline a peur des oiseaux de mer.
7. Demain Micheline va faire une promenade en bateau. Elle a tellement envie de faire cette promenade en bateau.

Cooperative Group Practice

Making *Dont* Personal

So that students can personalize sentences using **dont**, put them in small groups of four or five. Announce a topic that each group should begin with and write it on the board, for example, **une fête dont vous vous souvenez bien.** Students in each group take turns relating a holiday that they remember well and adding a specific detail, for example, **La fête dont je me souviens bien est Noël, 1997. J'ai reçu une stéréo.** After a couple of minutes, change the cue on the board. The next student in line to speak begins with the new cue. Students will get used to switching the topics and picking up where the last student stopped speaking. Other cues that you might use include **un truc dont vous n'avez pas envie, un truc dont vous avez besoin aujourd'hui, un truc dont vous vous servez dans votre chambre, une activité dont vous vous souvenez, un cours dont vous êtes content(e), une personne dont vous avez fait la connaissance cette année** and **une personne dont vous vous méfiez.**

Communication

Imaginez que vous passez 15 jours au Canada avec vos cousins québécois. Écrivez une carte postale à votre meilleur(e) ami(e) pour lui parler de votre séjour. Dites-lui:

1. comment était le voyage au Québec
2. si vous avez eu des ennuis pendant le voyage
3. si vous vous êtes trompé(e) pendant le voyage
4. comment vous trouvez le paysage de la province de Québec
5. si vous vous débrouillez chez vos cousins
6. si vous vous plaignez de quelque chose
7. la façon dont vos cousins vous traitent
8. s'il y a des Québécois intéressants dont vous avez fait la connaissance
9. si vous vous ennuyez ou si vous vous amusez bien
10. les choses dont vous allez toujours vous souvenir

Utilisez la carte postale à la page 202 comme guide.

Avec un(e) partenaire, parlez des derniers voyages que vous avez faits. Souvenez-vous des détails du voyage en disant à votre partenaire:

1. où vous êtes allé(e)
2. pourquoi vous y êtes allé(e)
3. qui vous a accompagné(e)
4. le moyen de transport dont vous vous êtes servi(e)
5. combien de temps vous y êtes resté(e)
6. si tout s'est bien passé ou si vous avez eu des ennuis
7. quelque chose qui vous a surpris(e)
8. quelque chose dont vous étiez content(e)
9. si vous avez fait les touristes
10. si vous voudriez y retourner

Qui t'a accompagnée en Californie?

Mes grands-parents m'y ont accompagnée.

Sur la bonne piste

In this unit you are going to read two scenes from *La cantatrice chauve* (*The Bald Soprano*), a play by Eugène Ionesco. A 20th century French dramatist, Ionesco presents the absurdity and meaninglessness of modern life in his plays. *La cantatrice chauve* has different levels of satire. Satire is humorous writing or speech intended to point out errors, falsehoods, foibles or failings with the intent of reforming human behavior or institutions. One institution that Ionesco satirizes in *La cantatrice chauve* is the melodramatic English theater popular among the British middle class in the 1940s, poking fun at its characters, settings and dialogue. Ionesco also holds up to ridicule the conventions of middle-class life, especially dull, trivial and nonsensical dialogues in everyday conversation. He demonstrates comically that our automatic responses and endless use of clichés prevent real, meaningful communication. In *La cantatrice chauve* what sounds like real conversation is only a series of repetitive and formal sentences used to pass the time in purposeless human interactions. The empty language of the characters reflects their colorless, unemotional, meaningless lives.

Teacher's Note

In *La cantatrice chauve* (1950) Ionesco questions the paralysis of mind and emotions that comes from an unquestioning acceptance of bourgeois values. His other important plays include *Les Chaises* (1952), *Victimes du devoir* (1953), *Amédée ou comment s'en débarrasser* (1954), *Rhinocéros* (1959), *Tueur sans gage* (1959), *Le roi se meurt* (1962), *Le Piéton de l'air* (1963), *La*
Soif et la Faim* (1966) and *Jeux de massacre* (1970). *Les Chaises* is the story of two older people who prepare for the arrival of distinguished visitors. Although the guests are invisible, the stage rapidly fills with chairs to accommodate them. In the end the invisible guests are addressed by a deaf-mute narrator. *Rhinocéros*, with its political message attacking Nazi fascism, recounts Berenger's struggles as he watches the masses around him change into rhinoceroses. When he himself comes down with rhinoceritis, he fights against his desire to become one of the mob, showing himself a hero who is willing to challenge mindless conformity.

 Listening Activity 2

 Quiz *Leçon B*

 Advanced Placement

Teacher's Notes

1. **Sur la bonne piste, Leçon B**, is designed to develop skills that will help students prepare to take the Advanced Placement Exam in French Literature. In this section students read a variety of prose, poetry and drama from different periods, answer content questions and demonstrate their critical understanding of character development, setting, point of view, satire, figures of speech and inference. In this **Sur la bonne piste** section, students learn how to recognize satire and then analyze the satirical elements in two scenes from *La cantatrice chauve*. 2. Eugène Ionesco (1912-94) was a French dramatist, critic and political philosopher born in Romania. He left Romania and his professorship there in 1938 and went to live in France, where he had spent the first 13 years of his life. His work emerged from his embrace of existentialism, the 20th century philosophical school that focused on the essential absurdity of life. His dramas express, imaginatively and tragicomically, the existential belief. Ionesco helped to start and popularize what is known as the theater of the absurd, which presents illogical, absurd and unrealistic scenes, characters, events and juxtapositions in an attempt to convey the essential meaninglessness of human life. For Ionesco, only antireal plays can adequately convey the mechanical nature of modern civilization and the futility of most human endeavor. At the end of his career, Ionesco turned to writing essays, lectures, addresses, literary theories and memoirs. He was elected to the Académie française in 1970.

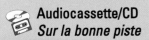

Audiocassette/CD
Sur la bonne piste

Teacher's Notes

1. As a pre-reading activity, students might share any of their own experiences talking to a stranger in a public place. What did they talk about? Did they reveal any personal information about themselves? Why or why not? Did they speak with formal or informal language? Has this type of experience happened to them frequently or infrequently? 2. You might have students read portions of the scenes aloud as a class, then discuss what they think Ionesco might be trying to demonstrate. You might mark your copy of the scenes to coincide with the questions in Activity 14, then ask students the questions progressively as you move through the text.

La cantatrice chauve takes place in the living room of the Smith home. In his stage directions Ionesco describes M. Smith. "... Dans son fauteuil et ses pantoufles anglaises, [M. Smith] fume sa pipe anglaise et lit un journal anglais, près d'un feu anglais. Il a des lunettes anglaises, une petite moustache grise, anglaise." Also in the play are his wife, Mme Smith; another couple, M. and Mme Martin; and the Smiths' maid, Mary. In Scene IV M. and Mme Martin, ostensibly strangers, are sitting in the living room waiting for their dinner hosts M. and Mme Smith to join them. While engaging in trivial conversation, M. and Mme Martin make a series of surprising discoveries about their lives. As you read these two scenes, pay attention to how Ionesco satirizes the insignificant conversation and hollow lives of these two characters, as well as the genre of detective or mystery plays.

13 | *Avant de lire les deux scènes, répondez aux questions suivantes.*

1. Quelles expressions est-ce que tes amis répètent souvent quand ils te parlent? Ces répétitions te semblent-elles normales ou absurdes?
2. As-tu jamais voyagé en train? Si oui, quelle a été ta destination? As-tu parlé aux autres passagers? Si oui, de quoi as-tu parlé?
3. Qu'est-ce que tu dis quand tu crois que tu reconnais quelqu'un?

La cantatrice chauve
Scène IV

(Mme et M. Martin, s'assoient l'un en face de l'autre, sans se parler. Ils se sourient, avec timidité.)

M. Martin: *(le dialogue qui suit doit être dit d'une voix traînante, monotone, un peu chantante, nullement nuancée)* Mes excuses, Madame, mais il me semble, si je ne me trompe, que je vous ai déjà rencontrée quelque part.

Mme Martin: À moi aussi, Monsieur, il me semble que je vous ai déjà rencontré quelque part.

M. Martin: Ne vous aurais-je pas déjà aperçue, Madame, à Manchester, par hasard?

Mme Martin: C'est très possible. Moi, je suis originaire de la ville de Manchester! Mais je ne me souviens pas très bien, Monsieur, je ne pourrais pas dire si je vous y ai aperçu, ou non!

M. Martin: Mon Dieu, comme c'est curieux! Moi aussi je suis originaire de la ville de Manchester, Madame!

Mme Martin: Comme c'est curieux!

M. Martin: Comme c'est curieux!... Seulement, moi, Madame, j'ai quitté la ville de Manchester, il y a cinq semaines, environ.

Mme Martin: Comme c'est curieux! Quelle bizarre coïncidence! Moi aussi, Monsieur, j'ai quitté la ville de Manchester, il y a cinq semaines, environ.

M. Martin: J'ai pris le train d'une demie après huit le matin, qui arrive à Londres à un quart avant cinq, Madame.

Mme Martin: Comme c'est curieux! comme c'est bizarre! et quelle coïncidence! J'ai pris le même train, Monsieur, moi aussi!

Critical Thinking

Journal personnel

Ask students to comment on the following quote by Luigi Pirandello in *Six Characters in Search of an Author:* "Life is full of infinite absurdities, which, strangely enough, do not even need to appear plausible, since they are true." Students should comment on things in their own lives that seem strangely absurd. Ask students to write a paragraph or two about the aspects of human nature and society, habits, traditions and social customs that they find absurd.

M. Martin:	Mon Dieu, comme c'est curieux! peut-être bien alors, Madame, que je vous ai vue dans le train?
Mme Martin:	C'est bien possible, ce n'est pas exclu, c'est plausible et, après tout, pourquoi pas!... Mais je n'en ai aucun souvenir, Monsieur!
M. Martin:	Je voyageais en deuxième classe, Madame. Il n'y a pas de deuxième classe en Angleterre, mais je voyage quand même en deuxième classe.
Mme Martin:	Comme c'est bizarre, que c'est curieux, et quelle coïncidence! Moi aussi, Monsieur, je voyageais en deuxième classe!
M. Martin:	Comme c'est curieux! Nous nous sommes peut-être bien rencontrés en deuxième classe, chère Madame!
Mme Martin:	La chose est bien possible et ce n'est pas du tout exclu. Mais je ne m'en souviens pas très bien, cher Monsieur!
M. Martin:	Ma place était dans le wagon n° 8, sixième compartiment, Madame!
Mme Martin:	Comme c'est curieux! Ma place aussi était dans le wagon n° 8 sixième compartiment, cher Monsieur!
M. Martin:	Comme c'est curieux et quelle coïncidence bizarre! Peut-être nous sommes-nous rencontrés dans le sixième compartiment, chère Madame?
Mme Martin:	C'est bien possible, après tout! Mais je ne m'en souviens pas, cher Monsieur!
M. Martin:	À vrai dire, chère Madame, moi non plus je ne m'en souviens pas, mais il est possible que nous nous soyons aperçus là et si j'y pense bien, la chose me semble même très possible!
Mme Martin:	Oh! vraiment, bien sûr, vraiment, Monsieur!
M. Martin:	Comme c'est curieux!... J'avais la place n° 3, près de la fenêtre, chère Madame.
Mme Martin:	Oh, mon Dieu, comme c'est curieux et comme c'est bizarre, j'avais la place n° 6, près de la fenêtre, en face de vous, cher Monsieur!
M. Martin:	Oh, mon Dieu, comme c'est curieux et quelle coïncidence!... Nous étions donc vis-à-vis, chère Madame! C'est là que nous avons dû nous voir!
Mme Martin:	Comme c'est curieux! C'est possible mais je ne m'en souviens pas, Monsieur!
M. Martin:	À vrai dire, chère Madame, moi non plus je ne m'en souviens pas. Cependant, il est très possible que nous nous soyons vus à cette occasion.
Mme Martin:	C'est vrai, mais je ne m'en suis pas sûre du tout, Monsieur.
M. Martin:	Ce n'était pas vous, chère Madame, la dame qui m'avait prié de mettre sa valise dans le filet et qui ensuite m'a remercié et m'a permis de fumer?
Mme Martin:	Mais si, ça devait être moi, Monsieur! Comme c'est curieux, comme c'est curieux, et quelle coïncidence!
M. Martin:	Comme c'est curieux, comme c'est bizarre, quelle coïncidence! Eh bien alors, alors, nous nous sommes peut-être connus à ce moment-là, Madame?
Mme Martin:	Comme c'est curieux et quelle coïncidence! c'est bien possible, cher Monsieur! Cependant, je ne crois pas m'en souvenir.

Teacher's Notes

1. Point out that the clock strikes at completely random times in this scene and does not seem to be keeping any real time. 2. Have students think back to what they learned about characterization in **Sur la bonne piste** in Unit 3. Ask students if they think M. and Mme Martin are flat or rounded characters. You might ask them the following questions to help them make up their minds: As a reader, do you learn much about M. et Mme Martin, their emotions or the details of their lives? If you overheard their conversation, how would you describe M. and Mme Martin to your friends? Point out that Ionesco made the characters flat and uninteresting in order to critique the shallowness of the middle class. Their repeated phrases and use of formal, polite language indicate that both characters are dull and conventional in their behavior.

M. Martin:	Moi non plus, Madame.... (*Un moment de silence. La pendule sonne 2-1.*)
M. Martin:	Depuis que je suis arrivé à Londres, j'habite rue Bromfield, chère Madame.
Mme Martin:	Comme c'est curieux, comme c'est bizarre! moi aussi, depuis mon arrivée à Londres j'habite rue Bromfield, cher Monsieur.
M. Martin:	Comme c'est curieux, mais alors, mais alors, nous nous sommes peut-être rencontrés rue Bromfield, chère Madame.
Mme Martin:	Comme c'est curieux; comme c'est bizarre! c'est bien possible, après tout! Mais je ne m'en souviens pas, cher Monsieur.
M. Martin:	Je demeure au n° 19, chère Madame.
Mme Martin:	Comme c'est curieux, moi aussi j'habite au n° 19, cher Monsieur.
M. Martin:	Mais alors, mais alors, mais alors, mais alors, mais alors, nous nous sommes peut-être vus dans cette maison, chère Madame?
Mme Martin:	C'est possible, mais je ne m'en souviens pas, cher Monsieur.
M. Martin:	Mon appartement est au cinquième étage, c'est le n° 8, chère Madame.
Mme Martin:	Comme c'est curieux, mon Dieu, comme c'est bizarre! et quelle coïncidence! moi aussi j'habite au cinquième étage, dans l'appartement n° 8, cher Monsieur!
M. Martin:	(*songeur*) Comme c'est curieux, comme c'est curieux, comme c'est curieux et quelle coïncidence! vous savez, dans ma chambre à coucher j'ai un lit. Mon lit est couvert d'un édredon vert. Cette chambre, avec ce lit et son édredon vert, se trouve au fond du corridor entre les water et la bibliothèque, chère Madame!
Mme Martin:	Quelle coïncidence, ah mon Dieu, quelle coïncidence! Ma chambre à coucher a, elle aussi, un lit avec un édredon vert et se trouve au fond du corridor entre les water, cher Monsieur, et la bibliothèque!
M. Martin:	Comme c'est bizarre, curieux, étrange! alors, Madame, nous habitons dans la même chambre et nous dormons dans le même lit, chère Madame. C'est peut-être là que nous nous sommes rencontrés!
Mme Martin:	Comme c'est curieux et quelle coïncidence! C'est bien possible que nous nous y soyons rencontrés, et peut-être même la nuit dernière. Mais je ne m'en souviens pas, cher Monsieur!
M. Martin:	J'ai une petite fille, ma petite fille, elle habite avec moi, chère Madame. Elle a deux ans, elle est blonde, elle a un œil blanc et un œil rouge, elle est très jolie, elle s'appelle Alice, chère Madame.
Mme Martin:	Quelle bizarre coïncidence! moi aussi j'ai une petite fille, elle a deux ans, un œil blanc et un œil rouge, elle est très jolie et s'appelle aussi Alice, cher Monsieur!
M. Martin:	(*même voix traînante, monotone*) Comme c'est curieux et quelle coïncidence! et bizarre! c'est peut-être la même, chère Madame!
Mme Martin:	Comme c'est curieux! c'est bien possible cher Monsieur. (*Un assez long moment de silence... La pendule sonne vingt-neuf fois.*)
M. Martin:	(*après avoir longuement réfléchi, se lève lentement et, sans se presser, se dirige vers Mme Martin qui, surprise par l'air solennel de M. Martin, s'est levée, elle aussi, tout doucement; M. Martin a la même voix rare, monotone, vaguement chantante.*) Alors, chère Madame, je crois qu'il

Mme Martin: n'y a pas de doute, nous nous sommes déjà vus et vous êtes ma propre épouse… Élisabeth, je t'ai retrouvée!

Mme Martin: (*s'approche de M. Martin sans se presser. Ils s'embrassent sans expression. La pendule sonne une fois, très fort. Le coup de la pendule doit être si fort qu'il doit faire sursauter les spectateurs. Les époux Martin ne l'entendent pas.*)

Mme Martin: Donald, c'est toi, darling! (*Ils s'assoient dans le même fauteuil, se tiennent embrassés et s'endorment. La pendule sonne encore plusieurs fois. Mary, sur la pointe des pieds, un doigt sur ses lèvres, entre doucement en scène et s'addresse au public.*)

Scène V

Mary: Élisabeth et Donald sont, maintenant, trop heureux pour pouvoir m'entendre. Je puis donc vous révéler un secret. Élisabeth n'est pas Élisabeth. Donald n'est pas Donald. En voici la preuve: l'enfant dont parle Donald n'est pas la fille d'Élisabeth, ce n'est pas la même personne. La fillette de Donald a un œil blanc et un autre rouge tout comme la fillette d'Élisabeth. Mais tandis que l'enfant de Donald a l'œil blanc à droite et l'œil rouge à gauche, l'enfant d'Élisabeth, lui, a l'œil rouge à droite et le blanc à gauche! Ainsi tout le système d'argumentation de Donald s'écroule en se heurtant à ce dernier obstacle qui anéantit toute sa théorie. Malgré les coïncidences extraordinaires qui semblent être des preuves définitives, Donald et Élisabeth n'étant pas les parents du même enfant ne sont pas Donald et Élisabeth. Il a beau croire qu'il est Donald, elle a beau se croire Élisabeth. Il a beau croire qu'elle est Élisabeth. Elle a beau croire qu'il est Donald: ils se trompent amèrement. Mais qui est le véritable Donald? Quelle est la véritable Élisabeth? Qui donc a intérêt à faire durer cette confusion? Je n'en sais rien. Ne tâchons pas de le savoir. Laissons les choses comme elles sont. (*Elle fait quelques pas vers la porte, puis revient et s'adresse au public.*) Mon vrai nom est Sherlock Holmes. (*Elle sort.*)

Répondez aux questions suivantes.

1. Dans quelle ville est-ce que M. et Mme Martin se sont déjà rencontrés?
2. Quand est-ce qu'ils ont quitté cette ville?
3. Comment M. et Mme Martin ont-ils voyagé à Londres?
4. En quelle classe M. et Mme Martin ont-ils voyagé? Pourquoi est-ce que ce détail est absurde, selon l'information que M. Martin donne sur les trains anglais?
5. Dans quel wagon et dans quel compartiment M. et Mme Martin ont-ils voyagé? Quelles places avaient-ils?
6. Pourquoi est-ce que M. et Mme Martin ne se reconnaissent pas?
7. Comment est-ce que M. Martin a aidé Mme Martin pendant le voyage? Qu'est-ce que Mme Martin lui a permis de faire?

Teacher's Notes

1. Some new words from the play and cognates not in the end vocabulary of *C'est à toi!* are used to ask questions about *La cantatrice chauve* in Activity 14. 2. Ask students to determine what is unusual or absurd about the method M. and Mme Martin use to try to remember each other. Point out that though they use deductive reasoning, M. and Mme Martin arrive at a false conclusion because the chance coincidences that they arrive at would normally be made irrelevant by memory.

Answers

14 Possible answers:

1. M. et Mme Martin se sont déjà rencontrés à Manchester.
2. Ils ont quitté Manchester il y a cinq semaines, environ.
3. Ils ont voyagé à Londres en train.
4. Ils ont voyagé en deuxième classe. C'est absurde parce qu'il n'y a pas de deuxième classe en Angleterre.
5. Ils ont voyagé dans le wagon n° 8, sixième compartiment. M. Martin avait la place n° 3 près de la fenêtre, et Mme Martin avait la place n° 6 en face de lui.
6. Ils ne s'en souviennent pas.
7. M. Martin a aidé Mme Martin en mettant sa valise dans le filet. Mme Martin lui a permis de fumer.
8. Elle est étonnée parce qu'il parle de son appartement à elle—ils habitent tous les deux au n° 19, rue Bromfield, au cinquième étage. Ils ont la même chambre qui se trouve au fond du corridor entre les water et la bibliothèque. Ils ont le même lit avec un édredon vert.
9. L'ultime coïncidence dans la vie de M. et Mme Martin est qu'ils ont une jolie fille blonde qui a deux ans. Elle a un œil blanc et un œil rouge, et elle s'appelle Alice.
10. Quand la pendule sonne 29 fois, elle ne représente pas l'heure vraie.
11. Ils s'assoient dans le même fauteuil, se tiennent embrassés et s'endorment.
12. Nous savons que M. et Mme Martin ne sont pas mari et femme parce qu'ils n'ont pas la même fille. La fille de M. Martin a l'œil blanc à droite et l'œil rouge à gauche, tandis que la fille de Mme Martin a l'œil rouge à droite et l'œil blanc à gauche.

8. Pourquoi est-ce que Mme Martin est étonnée quand M. Martin parle de son appartement?
9. Quelle est l'ultime coïncidence dans la vie de M. et Mme Martin?
10. Quand la pendule sonne, est-ce qu'elle représente l'heure vraie?
11. Que font M. et Mme Martin quand ils concluent qu'ils sont mari et femme?
12. Comment savons-nous que M. et Mme Martin ne sont pas mari et femme?

15 | *Ionesco a suivi un cours de conversation pour apprendre l'anglais, une expérience qui a inspiré la pièce* La cantatrice chauve. *Avec quels deux exemples est-ce qu'il satirise l'expression de l'heure en anglais? Comment diriez-vous l'heure en français?*

16 | *Expliquez comment Ionesco satirise le langage de la bourgeoisie. Par exemple, quelles expressions est-ce que M. et Mme Martin répètent? Est-ce qu'ils les répètent avec émotion? Est-ce qu'ils se parlent formellement? Est-il facile ou difficile de distinguer M. Martin de Mme Martin? Dans quel ton est-ce qu'ils parlent? Comment est-ce que leur manière de parler reflète leur vie bourgeoise?*

17 | *Expliquez comment Ionesco satirise le genre de pièces policières. Quel est le vrai nom de Mary? Souvent dans les pièces policières, un personnage révèle abruptement l'identité d'un autre personnage. Que Mary révèle-t-elle? Suit-elle un procédé logique en déterminant le vrai rapport entre M. et Mme Martin? À votre avis, pourquoi est-ce que ce procédé est absurde?*

Dossier fermé

Tu vas passer tes vacances de printemps avec des amis à Saint-Martin dans les Antilles. Tes parents te demandent de leur envoyer des cartes postales de ton voyage. Ils t'offrent des timbres français qu'ils ont achetés pendant leur dernier voyage à Paris et qu'ils n'ont pas encore utilisés. Qu'est-ce que tu en fais?

    A. Tu gardes les timbres qu'ils te donnent pour mettre sur les cartes postales que tu vas envoyer de Saint-Martin.

Parce que Saint-Martin est gouverné par la Guadeloupe, un Département d'Outre-Mer de la France, la poste à Saint-Martin est la poste française et les timbres que tes parents t'offrent sont valables.

C'est à moi!

Now that you have completed this unit, take a look at what you should be able to do in French. Can you do all of these tasks?

➤ I can write a postcard.

➤ I can tell location.

➤ I can tell a story.

➤ I can remember something.

➤ I can describe people that I remember.

➤ I can say whom I don't know.

➤ I can identify objects.

➤ I can tell what someone likes.

➤ I can agree with someone.

➤ I can give my opinion by saying what I think.

➤ I can say that I'm dissatisfied with something.

➤ I can complain about something.

➤ I can say what I'm afraid of.

➤ I can say what I'm sorry about.

➤ I can admit to something.

➤ I can express patience.

➤ I can ask whether or not something is possible.

➤ I can request what I would like.

➤ I can say what surprises me.

➤ I can say what makes me happy.

➤ I can control the volume of a conversation by telling someone to be quiet.

Pour voir si vous avez bien compris la culture francophone, décidez si chaque phrase est vraie ou fausse.

1. La classification d'hôtels en France est indiquée par le nombre d'étoiles qu'on voit à l'extérieur.
2. Saint-Martin est un Département d'Outre-Mer de la France qui est situé dans la mer des Antilles.
3. L'île Saint-Martin est divisée en deux, et les Espagnols en contrôlent une partie.
4. Beaucoup de touristes visitent Saint-Martin parce que il y fait du soleil toute l'année et les températures sont agréables.

Île
Saint-Martin
Perle de la Caraïbe

Answers

1. vraie
2. fausse
3. fausse
4. vraie
5. fausse
6. fausse
7. fausse
8. vraie
9. fausse
10. vraie

La plongée sous-marine est un sport aquatique très populaire à Saint-Martin.

5. Les fanas des sports aquatiques à Saint-Martin peuvent s'amuser à découvrir l'île en VTT.
6. Le village de Percé et son rocher célèbre se trouvent à l'extrême ouest de la péninsule gaspésienne.
7. Le Rocher Percé est un monument acadien de la région.
8. La péninsule gaspésienne a un sanctuaire pour les oiseaux de mer.
9. Dans les trains américains, comme dans les trains européens, il faut composter le billet avant de monter dans la voiture.
10. Les trains en Amérique du Nord n'ont pas de compartiments comme les trains européens.

Communication orale

Si vous pouviez passer vos vacances n'importe où (anywhere) dans le monde, quel endroit choisiriez-vous? Avec un(e) partenaire, décidez quel endroit vous visiteriez et créez un voyage dont tout le monde rêverait. Copiez la grille suivante. Puis discutez les détails de votre voyage idéal avec votre partenaire, et notez-les dans la grille.

destination	
durée	
moyen de transport	
logement et services	
nourriture	
activités	
attractions	
prix	

Communication écrite

Imaginez que vous travaillez pour une agence de voyages. Le chef veut que vous prépariez un voyage organisé (package tour) pour votre clientèle. Choisissez le voyage dont vous avez discuté dans l'activité précédente. Maintenant créez un dépliant pour ce voyage idéal en utilisant les détails de la grille de l'activité précédente. Développez le dépliant en mentionnant aussi le paysage, les chambres d'hôtel, les repas, etc. (Il vaut mieux que vous vous serviez de beaucoup d'adjectifs.) Après que vous avez fini le dépliant, comparez-le avec le dépliant de votre partenaire de l'activité précédente, qui a préparé un dépliant pour le même voyage.

Communication active

To write postcards, use:

Bisous   Kisses

To tell location, use:

L'hôtel **est situé** à 400 mètres de la plage.
     The hotel is situated 400 meters from the beach.

Mon cousin habite à Gaspé **dans la province de** Québec.
     My cousin lives in Gaspé in the province of Quebec.

La Belle Époque est située à quelques mètres de la Marina Royale. (Saint-Martin)

THÉÂTRE HEBERTOT
CHRISTOPHE MALAVOY
LA VILLE DONT LE PRINCE EST UN ENFANT
HENRY DE MONTHERLANT
avec CLAUDE GIRAUD
mise en scène Pierre BOUTRON
France Inter 43 87 23 23 Télérama

"J'aimerais m'installer à l'étranger, spécialement en Italie ou en France."

To tell a story, use:

Tout s'est bien passé jusqu'à mon arrivée à Dorval. — *Everything went well until my arrival in Dorval.*

To remember, use:

Je vais toujours **me souvenir** de la beauté du paysage. — *I'm going to always remember the beauty of the scenery.*

To describe people you remember, use:

J'ai fait la connaissance d'une Canadienne **dont** la mère est française. — *I met a Canadian woman whose mother is French.*

To indicate not knowing, use:

J'ai cherché **Monsieur un tel**, le chef de train. — *I looked for Mr. So-and-so, the conductor.*

To identify objects, use:

Ils ont tout de suite fouillé dans le porte-bagages, **le truc** au-dessus des sièges. — *They searched right away in the overhead compartment, the thing above the seats.*

To say what someone likes, use:

Nous aimerions changer de chambre. — *We'd like to change rooms.*
Nous voudrions nous installer au rez-de-chaussée. — *We'd like to move to the ground floor.*

To agree, use:

Tu parles! — *You're not kidding!*
Je suis d'accord. — *I agree.*

To give opinions, use:

Je crois que oui. — *I think so.*
Je trouve que le gérant pouvait mieux faire. — *I think that the manager could do better.*

To express dissatisfaction, use:

Ça m'embête que l'ascenseur ne marche pas. — *It bothers me that the elevator doesn't work.*

To complain, use:

Il ne **s'est plaint** de rien. — *He complained about nothing.*

To express fear, use:

J'ai peur qu'il fasse trop chaud ce soir. — *I'm afraid that it's going to be too hot tonight.*

To express regret, use:

C'est dommage qu'il n'y ait ni sèche-cheveux ni douche dans la salle de bains. — *It's too bad that there is neither a hair dryer nor a shower in the bathroom.*
Je suis désolé qu'il ne reste plus de chambres aujourd'hui. — *I'm sorry that there aren't any more rooms today.*

To admit to something, use:

Je me suis trompée de siège. *I was mistaken about the seat.*

To express patience, use:

Il s'est occupé de moi **avec patience.** *He took care of me patiently.*

To inquire about possibility, use:

Est-ce que cela serait possible? *Would that be possible?*

To make requests, use:

Est-ce que vous pourriez nous rendre un service? *Would you be able to help us?*

To express surprise, use:

Ça me surprend qu'on ne puisse pas voir la mer de ce côté. *It surprises me that we can't see the sea from this side.*

Je suis étonné qu'ils ne mettent pas la clim. *I'm surprised that they don't turn on the air conditioning.*

To express happiness, use:

Je suis heureux qu'on serve de très bons repas. *I'm happy that they serve very good meals.*

To control the volume of a conversation, use:

Chut! *Sh!*

Désolée, je me suis trompée de numéro.

Listening Activity 3

Je suis heureuse que tu te débrouilles.

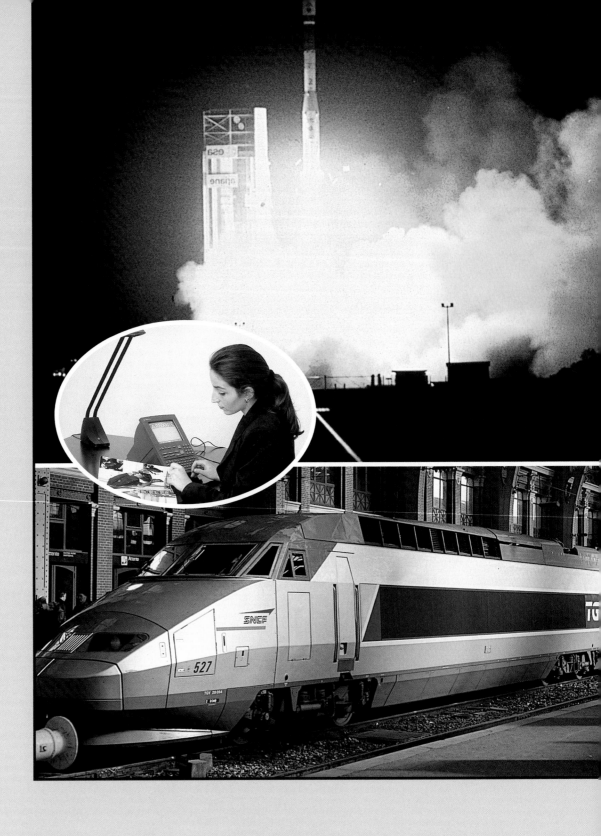

Unité 6

L'avenir: la technologie et l'environnement

In this unit you will be able to:

➤ ask for information

➤ give information

➤ sequence events

➤ list

➤ explain something

➤ give opinions

➤ express enthusiasm

➤ hypothesize

➤ express probability

➤ predict

➤ congratulate and commiserate

➤ express appreciation

➤ forget

➤ make requests

Tes empreintes ici

Dans beaucoup de lycées, les élèves sont obligés de suivre un cours d'informatique pour être diplômés. Est-ce que tu en as déjà suivi un? As-tu un ordinateur chez toi? Si oui, comment est-ce que tu t'en sers?

- Pour chercher des renseignements?
- Pour écrire des exposés?
- Pour parler avec d'autres ados?
- Pour envoyer du courrier?
- Pour jouer à des jeux?
- Pour ton boulot?

Est-ce que tu te sers d'un ordinateur pour préparer des exposés?

Il est certain que tu te sers de ce qu'on a appris de la science des satellites. Par exemple, tu as le choix entre beaucoup de chaînes de télévision, tu sais quel temps il va faire demain et tu peux téléphoner à un endroit très loin de chez toi. Peux-tu penser à d'autres moyens de t'en servir?

Dossier ouvert

Tu es dans un hôtel en France, et tu as besoin de téléphoner à quelqu'un, mais tu ne sais pas son numéro de téléphone. L'hôtel n'a pas d'annuaire (le livre avec les numéros de téléphone), et tu ne connais pas le numéro des "Renseignements." Qu'est-ce que tu fais?

A. Tu demandes à la réception de chercher le numéro de téléphone sur le Minitel.
B. Tu décides d'envoyer un fax.
C. Tu quittes l'hôtel pour chercher la résidence de la personne.

Leçon A

In this lesson you will be able to:

➤ give information

➤ sequence events

➤ list

➤ explain something

➤ give opinions

➤ express probability

➤ predict

Teacher's Notes

1. Communicative functions that are recycled in this lesson are "comparing things," "explaining something," "giving examples," "giving orders" and "expressing astonishment and disbelief." 2. The French telephone directory is called **le Bottin**.

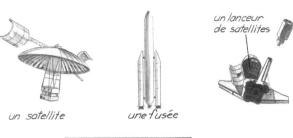

un satellite   une fusée   un lanceur de satellites

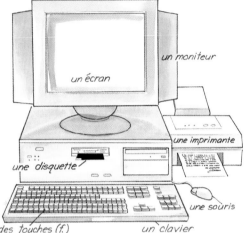

un moniteur
un écran
une imprimante
une disquette
des touches (f.)
une souris
un clavier

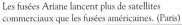

Les fusées Ariane lancent plus de satellites commerciaux que les fusées américaines. (Paris)

La France est un des pays les plus avancés au monde dans le domaine de la technologie. Vous avez déjà entendu parler du° TGV et de l'Eurotunnel, mais il y a deux autres domaines où la France a fait des progrès importants: l'espace et la télématique.°

La France dépense° 300 milliards° de francs par an pour la recherche spatiale. Elle lance° des satellites pour développer sa connaissance° de l'espace. La France est l'un des dix membres de l'Agence spatiale européenne, ou l'ESA, qui a construit la fusée Ariane 5. On lance cette fusée du centre spatial de Kourou en Guyane française. Avec le projet Ariane, l'ESA aura bientôt le plus grand pourcentage sur le marché de lanceurs de satellites commerciaux.

Depuis des années, les Français ont le Minitel, un service télématique. En plus, il y a aujourd'hui des Français qui sont en ligne avec un ordinateur qui permet d'accéder° au web. Pour eux, comme pour tout le monde, c'est très facile. On n'a qu'à cliquer avec la souris pour trouver l'inforoute.° Il est aussi facile d'appuyer° sur les touches du clavier que d'utiliser la souris. Et voilà! Sur l'écran du moniteur on trouve un grand choix d'outils de recherche.° Tout ce qui° se trouve sur le web permet d'accéder à des renseignements. Ensuite, on peut en sauvegarder° sur disquette ou utiliser

---

entendre parler de *to hear about;* **la télématique** *la communication par ordinateur;* **dépenser** *payer;* **un milliard** *billion;* **lancer** *to launch;* **la connaissance** *knowledge;* **accéder** *to access;* **l'inforoute (f.)** *information superhighway;* **appuyer** *to press;* **un outil de recherche** *search engine;* **ce qui** *that;* **sauvegarder** *to save*

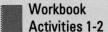

Critical Thinking

Journal personnel

Ask students to write about the pros and cons of the U.S. space program. Are the high costs worthwhile? What do we gain from space exploration and technology? Would the money be better spent on social programs? Ask students to consider these and other relevant questions in their cultural journal.

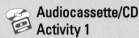

Audiocassette/CD Activity 1

Answers

1 1. fausse
2. vraie
3. fausse
4. vraie
5. vraie
6. fausse
7. vraie
8. fausse

Teacher's Notes

1. The formal name for **l'e-mail** is **le courrier électronique**. 2. Students will want to know that the adjective **branché(e)** means "with it" or "switched on." 3. Four additional Internet addresses that you may want to share with students provide information on the Minitel (http://www.minitel.fr); the French Embassy (http://www.info-france-usa.org); French books, records and videos (http://www.fnac.fr); and Eurostar (http://www.eurostar.com). The Web sites listed were accurate at the time this book was published. However, they may change in the future, and you may need to substitute different addresses from the ones given in the Annotated Teacher's Edition.

Martin envoie un e-mail à son correspondant.

Branchez-vous sur la Mode

ELLE sur Internet
Si votre ordinateur est connecté sur le réseau, accédez à « ELLE on line » en tapant http://www.elle.fr

l'imprimante. Pour envoyer ou recevoir de l'e-mail, on se branche° aussi sur Internet. Et qui n'aime pas s'amuser avec les jeux électroniques?

Internet vous offre de faire des recherches dans toute la France. Par exemple, si vous voulez faire des recherches sur l'Eurotunnel, choisissez deux ou trois outils de recherche, comme http://www.yahoo.fr, http://www.infoseek.com ou http://www.nomade.fr. Ensuite, commencez avec un des outils de recherche dont vous prenez l'adresse. Vous trouverez une liste d'adresses pour l'Eurotunnel. Puis, cliquez sur chaque adresse pour trouver les renseignements que vous cherchez. Voici quelques autres adresses utiles où vous pourrez trouver tout ce qui vous intéresse sur:

la vie des élèves en France	http://www.yahoo.fr/etudiants
la musique	http://www.francevision.com
	http://www.worldmusic.com
l'actualité	http://www.lemonde.fr
les films à Paris	http://www.pariscope.fr
Paris	http://www.paris.org

Finalement, au 21ᵉ siècle on se branchera sur le monde entier. La connaissance scientifique, parmi° d'autres, permettra une vie plus longue et plus riche, et elle sera aussi utile aux gens qu'aux sciences. On n'en reviendra pas!

Le site http://www.paris.org t'informe que le Louvre est fermé le mardi. (Paris)

se brancher *to connect;* **parmi** *among*

1 *D'après ce que vous venez de lire sur la technologie, dites si chaque phrase est vraie ou fausse.*

1. L'espace et la télématique sont deux domaines où la France n'a rien fait dans les dernières années.
2. La France est un membre de l'Agence spatiale européenne.
3. L'ESA aura bientôt le plus grand pourcentage de satellites commerciaux.

4. Les Français ont un service télématique depuis des années.
5. On peut sauvegarder des renseignements sur disquette ou utiliser l'imprimante.
6. Un outil de recherche n'a pas d'adresse.
7. Il est facile pour les élèves américains d'accéder à des renseignements sur, par exemple, la musique française ou les films à Paris.
8. Au 21ᵉ siècle la connaissance scientifique sera moins utile aux gens qu'aux sciences.

3615 TÉLÉ POCHE
Le minitel de Télé Poche à votre service

Complétez chaque phrase avec l'expression convenable de la liste suivante d'après les renseignements que vous venez de lire sur la technologie.

souris	entendu parler	spatiale	progrès
développent	outils de recherche	appuie	dépense
fusée	lance	télématique	

1. Presque tout le monde a... du TGV et de l'Eurotunnel.
2. Dans le domaine de la..., la France a fait beaucoup de....
3. La France... 300 milliards de francs chaque année pour la recherche....
4. Les satellites... la connaissance de l'espace.
5. Ariane 5 est une....
6. On... les fusées de l'ESA en Guyane française.
7. Quand on travaille sur ordinateur, on clique avec la... ou on... sur les touches du clavier.
8. On a un choix d'... pour accéder à des renseignements.

Je clique avec la souris pour trouver l'inforoute.

C'est à toi!

1. Au lycée, pour quel(s) cours est-ce que tu te sers d'un ordinateur? Est-ce que tu t'en sers chaque jour?
2. Est-ce que tu joues aux jeux sur ordinateur? Si oui, quels jeux aimes-tu?
3. Est-ce que tu as un outil de recherche favori?
4. Est-ce que tu envoies des e-mails? Si oui, à qui?
5. Chez toi est-ce que tu as la télévision par satellite?
6. Selon tes parents, sur quoi est-ce que tu dépenses trop d'argent?
7. Est-ce qu'un voyage spatial t'intéresse? Si oui, où voudrais-tu voyager?
8. Comment est-ce que tu vois le 21ᵉ siècle?

Audiocassette/CD Activity 3

Answers

2 1. entendu parler
2. télématique, progrès
3. dépense, spatiale
4. développent
5. fusée
6. lance
7. souris, appuie
8. outils de recherche

3 Answers will vary.

Paired Practice

Crossword Puzzles

After they have completed Activities 1 and 2, have students work in pairs. Instruct each pair to create an original crossword puzzle in French and a separate answer key. You may want to specify a minimum number of horizontal and vertical expressions or give extra credit to the pair whose puzzle contains the most expressions. Ask students to focus on new vocabulary from the exposition and to write their clues in sentence form, for example, **Le Minitel est un service... très populaire en France**. Check each pair's puzzle for accuracy and have students correct any errors. Then have pairs exchange puzzles and solve them.

Workbook Activity 3

Transparency 18

Teacher's Notes

1. Cognates in this reading include **région, technique, économique, système, présent, développé, intérêt, confortable, tunnel, coopération, franco-britannique, construction, abandonner, agence, organiser, applications, combine, aspects, observation, planète, transport, gravité, entreprises, observent, déforestation, effets, conditions, atmosphériques, météorologie, télécommunications, compliqués, internationale, Brésil, équateur, population, minimale, communication, pour cent, différent, spécialement, micro-ordinateur** and **multimédia**. 2. The TGV is one of the world's fastest trains. A newer TGV reaches a speed of about 300 kilometers (185 miles) per hour. When the Paris-Lyon route opened, it cut travel time between the cities to two hours, half as long as before. The Lyon route has been extended to include service to Valence, en route to Marseille. Additional routes served by the TGV connect Paris to Le Mans and Tours to the southwest and Paris to Lille and Calais in the north. The TGV runs on electricity and gets its power from an overhead wire. Besides speed, electric trains have other advantages. They are quieter than other trains and do not produce smoke or exhaust. Engineers are developing faster electric trains called maglev (magnetic levitation) trains. Japanese and German models of these trains test from about 400 to 500 kilometers (250 to 310 miles) per hour. 3. You may want students to use the Internet to plan a trip on the TGV. Have them enter "http://www.sncf.fr/." After selecting "Voyages" on the home page, students click on "Horaires" in order to select the train they want to take. 4. Eurostar is owned by three national railroads: the French

Enquête culturelle

Joker 8 et Joker 30 sont proposés dans tous les TGV Nord Europe.

Le TGV (train à grande vitesse) est le train de service commercial le plus rapide en France. Depuis 1981 ce train traverse chaque jour la région du sud-est de la France à une vitesse de 270 kilomètres à l'heure. La France a connu un succès technique, commercial et économique avec le système du TGV. À présent le système du TGV est très développé et fait de la France le pays qui se sert le plus des lignes à grande vitesse dans le monde. Le TGV entre Paris et Lyon a 350 places pour les passagers. Le train quitte Paris 23 fois par jour, et il part de Lyon pour Paris 23 fois par jour aussi. Ce ne sont pas seulement les Français qui peuvent profiter du TGV. La France a signé un contrat au Texas, et il y a un grand intérêt pour le TGV en Australie, au Canada et à Taiwan.

Dans le TGV Atlantique la deuxième classe est très confortable.

L'Eurostar est un TGV français, anglais et belge. (Paris)

Il y a maintenant un autre TGV français qui devient très populaire. C'est l'Eurostar, le service de trains à grande vitesse entre Paris et Londres. En moins de quatre heures, vous pouvez aller entre ces deux villes en passant par l'Eurotunnel qui va sous la Manche entre la France et l'Angleterre. Pour les Anglais qui voudraient visiter Paris, il y a même des voyages organisés pour visiter le parc d'attractions Disneyland Paris. Beaucoup de Français, d'Anglais et d'autres Européens en profitent parce que c'est confortable, rapide et économique. Les Français et les Anglais ont attendu un tunnel entre leurs deux pays pendant des années. Les premiers dessins pour un tunnel sous la Manche ont été faits en 1751. Mais ce n'est qu'en 1956 qu'on a proposé une coopération franco-britannique pour étudier la possibilité de le construire. En 1974 la construction a commencé des deux côtés de la Manche, mais on a dû abandonner ce projet. On a recommencé la construction en 1985, et enfin, en novembre 1994, l'Eurotunnel s'est ouvert aux premiers trains.

own 50 percent, the British 35 percent and the Belgians 15 percent. Trains traveling from France to England enter the tunnel near Calais at Coquelles, France, and exit near Folkestone, England. The actual time spent in the tunnel is only about half an hour. 5. The Channel Tunnel is also known as the "Chunnel." It serves three types of trains: high-speed passenger trains; shuttle trains for automo-

biles, trucks, buses and their passengers; and freight trains. The tunnel consists of three parallel tubes, two of which are rail tubes. The third is a service tunnel used to supply fresh air and maintenance access to the rail tubes. In case of an emergency, it could also be used to evacuate passengers. The Channel Tunnel was formally opened by England's Queen Elizabeth II and France's President Mitterand on May 6, 1994.

L'Agence spatiale européenne, fondée en 1975 par 14 pays euro-péens, a son siège à Paris. Cette agence cherche à organiser la coopération des pays dans la recherche et la technologie spatiale et à en trouver des applications scientifiques. L'ESA combine la recherche sous plusieurs aspects scientifiques: l'observation de notre planète, la technologie spatiale, le transport spatial, comment lancer les satellites, et les recherches sur la gravité. Mais ce ne sont pas seulement les recherches qui intéressent les pays, c'est aussi les applications de cette technologie spatiale à la vie quotidienne et aux entreprises commerciales des pays. Par exemple, les satellites de l'ESA observent la déforestation et ses effets, pendant que d'autres observent les conditions atmosphériques et le temps. L'ESA lance des satellites commerciaux, surtout pour la météorologie et les télécommunications. Comme la technologie augmente et que les satellites deviennent plus compliqués et plus grands, les fusées Ariane deviennent plus puissantes. La plus puissante, c'est l'Ariane 5 qui a lancé ses premiers satellites en 1997. Arianespace, la compagnie qui vend les lanceurs, connaît une clientèle inter-nationale d'Europe, des États-Unis, du Japon, du Canada et du Brésil. On a choisi de lancer les satellites de Kourou en Guyane française parce que c'est près de l'équateur et de l'océan, le temps est parfait et la population est minimale.

Ariane a lancé le satellite Télécom 2.

Le Minitel est un système de communication télématique parmi les plus modernes du monde. En 1983 on a lancé le service Minitel, service de renseignements par ordinateur branché sur le téléphone. Il y a maintenant 6,5 millions de Minitels dans les maisons françaises. Avec 26 pour cent des familles branchées, la France est le premier pays du monde avec plus de 27.000 services en ligne. On peut réserver des billets pour voyager ou des billets de théâtre par Minitel. On peut aussi envoyer des messages et trouver les numéros de téléphone de tous les Français qui ont le téléphone. Mais il faut payer le temps qu'on utilise, et chaque service a un prix différent.

faire du shopping aux TROIS SUISSES	FF 0,65/min
chercher l'horaire des films au GAUMONT	FF 1,51/min
utiliser le dictionnaire français/anglais	FF 2,30/min
envoyer des fleurs avec INTERFLORA	FF 1,24/min
chercher un code postal	FF 0,65/min
trouver une fête avec ARTS	FF 1,51/min
chercher des renseignements sur le LOUVRE	FF 1,51/min
choisir un cours de langue au BERLITZ	FF 1,51/min
chercher de l'aide pour vos devoirs	FF 0,65/min
chercher un calendrier du golf	FF 1,51/min
envoyer un fax	FF 2,30/min
chercher un appartement avec FNAIM	FF 2,30/min
réserver un billet d'avion avec AIRINFO	FF 2,30/min
chercher les horaires de l'EUROTUNNEL	FF 1,51/min
lire votre horoscope	FF 2,30/min
jouer à un jeu pour enfants NATHAN	FF 1,51/min
chercher les infos générales sur DISNEYLAND	FF 1,51/min

l'officiel des spectacles

3615 OFFi
vous propose son service de

réservations

Théâtres, Concerts, Variétés, Expositions.
Soirées privilège : théâtre + restaurant.

Consultations 1,29 f la minute - Réservations 2,19 f la minute

3615 OFFi SIMPLE ET RAPIDE!

PARIS
RÉGION PARISIENNE

Teacher's Notes

1. **L'Agence spatiale européenne** is known as the European Space Agency (ESA) in English. Its member nations are Belgium, France, Germany, Italy, the Netherlands, the United Kingdom (associated with Australia), Denmark, Spain, Sweden, Switzerland, Ireland, Austria, Norway and Finland. The organization's stated goal is "to provide for and to promote, for exclusively peaceful purposes, cooperation among European States in space research and technology and their space applications, with a view to their being used for scientific purposes and operational space applications systems." Aside from its scientific program, which is directed more towards basic research (studies aimed at widening our knowledge of space, Earth and its environment), ESA's work results in industrial developments and operational products like the launchers of the Ariane family and applications satellites. In 1986, ESA's Giotto space probe studied Halley's comet. The web address for the ESA is http://www.esrin. esa.it/. 2. By the late 1980s Ariane rockets were launching more commercial satellites than U.S. rockets were. Ariane 1 was successfully launched for the first time in 1979. Ariane 2, 3 and 4 all belonged to the same family of launchers. Ariane 5 is designed along completely different lines. Production and marketing for Ariane 5 is handled by Arianespace, a group of European companies.

Teacher's Note

The Minitel, which is owned by France Télécom, has become part of everyday life in France. The telephone company distributed free terminals to provide an electronic phone book to all interested customers. Telephone directory assistance remains the most frequently used service, followed by people looking for prospective dates. Other popular services include banking, real estate, help-wanted ads, home shopping, movie schedules, horoscopes, weather reports and **la messagerie rose**. The Minitel's fastest growth is in professional services, such as financial, legal and scientific databases, that command far higher prices. In 1994 France Télécom introduced a Minitel model capable of reading credit cards. The Minitel does not have memory or any computing capabilities; it is simply a terminal that responds to signals coming from the telephone line. Despite its slowness and inability to perform such functions as transmitting color images or sound, the Minitel has still made the French seven times more likely than Americans to tap into an on-line information service. The web address for the Minitel was given on page 228.

L'ordinateur connaît un certain succès en France, mais il n'y a pas de grand intérêt comme aux États-Unis. Bien sûr, il est important dans tout genre de travail, mais à la maison les gens sont satisfaits du Minitel, et ils n'ont pas besoin de se brancher sur Internet. Les jeux vidéos sont importants pour les jeunes qui aiment utiliser l'ordinateur, spécialement avec le CD-ROM. Vingt pour cent des familles françaises ont un système de micro-ordinateur avec multimédia.

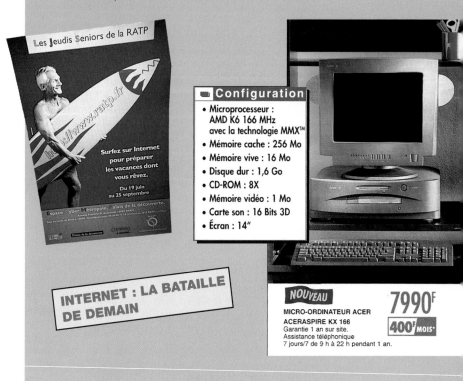

4 | *Répondez aux questions suivantes.*

1. Combien de voyages fait le TGV entre Paris et Lyon chaque jour?
2. Où aux États-Unis est-ce que le TGV va circuler un jour?
3. En combien de temps peut-on aller entre Paris et Londres en Eurostar?
4. Comment est-ce que l'Eurostar passe de l'Angleterre en France?
5. Quand est-ce que les premiers trains sont passés par l'Eurotunnel?
6. Combien de pays participent aux initiatives de l'Agence spatiale européenne?
7. Comment est-ce que l'ESA utilise la technologie spatiale pour la vie quotidienne?

Cross-curricular

Webbing Technology

Have students do additional research on Ariane 5 and the Minitel, perhaps using the Internet. Then have them web the uses for these technologies. Each web should have a center circle with the name of the technology in French and a supporting circle for each use of that technology that they mention. Students with more language ability can write the uses in French; those with more limited ability may write the uses in English.

8. D'où est-ce que l'ESA lance les satellites?
9. Le Minitel, qu'est-ce que c'est?
10. Quel pourcentage de familles françaises ont un système de micro-ordinateur avec multimédia?

L'ESA a lancé Ariane 3 de Kourou en Guyane française.

Journal personnel

In this unit you have been reading about the state of various technologies in France. In many instances France is among the leaders of the industrialized nations in many facets of technology. Can you think of ten technological advances that have taken place in the last 50 years? What role does modern technology play in your daily life? How do the advances in technology in the fields of aerospace, computers, transportation and the environment affect the way you live? How would your life be different if these advances had not taken place?

Structure

Comparative of adjectives

Use the following constructions to compare people and things in French:

plus (*more*)	+	adjective	+	**que** (*than*)
moins (*less*)	+	adjective	+	**que** (*than*)
aussi (*as*)	+	adjective	+	**que** (*as*)

1664. QUATRE CHIFFRES PLUS FORTS QUE TOUS LES MOTS.

Crois-tu qu'un voyage en TGV soit aussi intéressant qu'un voyage en avion?

The adjective being compared agrees in gender and in number with the first noun in the comparison.

La connaissance scientifique sera **aussi utile** aux gens qu'aux sciences.

Scientific knowledge will be as useful to people as to science.

Accéder au web, c'est **plus facile que** jamais.

Accessing the Web is easier than ever.

Le Rasage le Plus Précis et le Plus Confortable au Monde.

Teacher's Notes

1. The **Structure** section in Unit 6 contains both new and recycled grammatical concepts . 2. The comparative of adjectives was presented on page 269 in the first level of *C'est à toi!* and reviewed on page 68 in the second level. 3. Remind students that **que** becomes **qu'** when the word that follows begins with a vowel sound. 4. Students learned the superlative adjective **le meilleur, la meilleure** on page 201 in the third level of *C'est à toi!* You may want to introduce **meilleur(e)** as the irregular comparative of the adjective **bon/bonne**. 5. You might ask several students to stand in front of the class. Then ask the seated students to compare your height to that of the standing students. Students should use the adjective **grand(e)** to make their comparisons, for example, **Robert est moins grand que vous**.

Critical Thinking

Comparative Sentences

Write the following four sentences on the board: **Une fusée est plus chère qu'un ordinateur. Didier est plus grand que toi. Claire est plus déprimée que triste. L'Eurotunnel est plus moderne que je ne pensais.** Next, ask students what can follow **que** in a comparative construction. Students should tell you that **que** can be followed by a noun, a stress pronoun, an adjective or a clause. (You may want to point out that when **que** is followed by a clause, the pleonastic **ne** precedes the verb in formal French.)

TPR

Comparative of Adjectives

Select 12 magazine pictures that lend themselves to making comparisons. Tape them to the board in pairs. Then say sentences that correctly or incorrectly describe the pairs of pictures, for example, **La Renault est moins chère que la Mercedes.** (You may want to point to each picture as you refer to it.) Have students make a "V" card to hold up if the statement that you make is true. Have them make an "F" card to hold up if the statement that you make is false. This activity will help students distinguish between comparisons made with **plus, moins** and **aussi... que.**

Paired Practice

Making Comparisons

Put students in pairs. Ask students to interview their partner based on a list of topics that you write on the board so that students can discover who is more athletic, talkative, older, etc. After interviewing their partner, students take turns saying sentences that compare themselves to their partner, for example, **Tu es plus sportif/sportive que moi.**

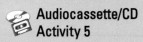

Audiocassette/CD
Activity 5

Answers

5 Possible answers:

1. Une cassette est moins chère qu'un CD.
2. Un satellite est plus moderne qu'un téléphone.
3. La Guyane française est plus exotique que le Canada.
4. La France est aussi avancée que les États-Unis.
5. Les échecs sont aussi amusants que les jeux vidéo.
6. Une souris est aussi importante qu'un clavier.
7. Un bloc-notes est moins scientifique qu'une disquette.
8. Un crayon est aussi utile qu'une imprimante.

Cooperative Group Practice

Le bon vieux temps

So that students can make comparisons between the past and the present, put them in small groups of three. Tell them to play the role of a grandfather or grandmother who is talking about the "good old days" to his or her grandchildren. Write the following list of nouns and adjectives on the board or an overhead transparency: 1. les fêtes/importantes 2. les villes/grandes 3. les gens/accueillants 4. les familles/riches 5. les jeunes gens/diligents 6. les problèmes/sérieux. Each student in the group forms a sentence using the comparative of adjectives for two of the cued responses to tell what life was like when the grandparent was young, for example, **Quand j'étais jeune, les fêtes étaient plus importantes et les villes étaient moins grandes qu'aujourd'hui.**

Pratique

5 | *Comparez les deux objets illustrés en utilisant la forme convenable de l'adjectif indiqué.*

Modèle:

rapide
Une fusée est plus rapide qu'un avion.

Les guichets automatiques sont souvent plus commodes (*convenient*) que les banques.

SUPER CRÈME SOLAIRE VISAGE. PLUS FORTE QUE LE SOLEIL.

1. cher

5. amusant

2. moderne

6. important

3. exotique

7. scientifique

4. avancé

8. utile

Game

Relay Race

So that students can practice making comparisons with adjectives, divide the class into two teams. On the board write a list that provides a framework for sentences that students on each team will form. Each item in the list includes a name, the masculine form of an adjective, a plus, minus, or equal sign (indicating the use of **plus, moins** or **aussi**), and another name, for example, **Jeanne/ généreux +/Éric**. The first player from Team A and Team B goes to the board and writes a comparative sentence based on the first cue, for example, **Jeanne est plus généreuse qu'Éric**. The player from each team races to write the sentence faster than the player from the other team. As soon as the first player returns to his or her seat, the second player from each team goes to the board and writes the second sentence, and so forth, until the list has been completed. The team that finishes with the most correct sentences wins.

Les Français se servent souvent de la négation pour accentuer une idée ou pour être plus polis. Par exemple, on ne dirait pas qu'un homme est pauvre; on dirait qu'il n'est pas riche. C'est la même chose quand on compare deux choses. Avec un(e) partenaire, faites une comparaison entre les deux choses ou personnes indiquées. L'Élève A doit le faire en utilisant **plus**. *L'Élève B doit accentuer la même idée en utilisant* **moins**. *Suivez le modèle.*

1. un centre commercial/une boutique (grand)
2. les films français/les films américains (sérieux)
3. l'intrigue d'un film/sa durée (intéressant)
4. Leonardo DiCaprio/Jack Nicholson (jeune)
5. la chimie/la philosophie (scientifique)
6. Tara Lipinski/Céline Dion (sportif)
7. l'e-mail/la lettre (rapide)
8. le Minitel/Internet (populaire)

Modèle:

la carte de crédit/l'argent liquide (pratique)

Élève A: La carte de crédit est plus pratique que l'argent liquide.

Élève B: Ah oui, l'argent liquide est moins pratique que la carte de crédit.

Les restaurants sont plus chers que les fast-foods.

Ah oui, les fast-foods sont moins chers que les restaurants.

Superlative of adjectives

Use the superlative construction to say that a person or thing has the most of a certain quality compared to all others.

| le/la/les | + | **plus** | + | adjective |

Both the definite article and the adjective agree in gender and in number with the noun they describe. Remember that if an adjective precedes a noun, its superlative form also precedes it. If an adjective follows a noun, so does its superlative form.

L'ESA aura bientôt **le plus grand** pourcentage sur le marché de lanceurs de satellites commerciaux.

The ESA will soon have the largest percentage of the market in commercial satellite launchers.

La France est un des pays **les plus avancés** du monde dans le domaine de la technologie.

France is one of the most advanced countries in the world in the area of technology.

Le Concorde est l'avion commercial le plus rapide du monde.

Workbook Activity 5

Audiocassette/CD Activity 6

Answers

6 1. Un centre commercial est plus grand qu'une boutique.
Ah oui, une boutique est moins grande qu'un centre commercial.

2. Les films français sont plus sérieux que les films américains.
Ah oui, les films américains sont moins sérieux que les films français.

3. L'intrigue d'un film est plus intéressante que sa durée.
Ah oui, la durée d'un film est moins intéressante que son intrigue.

4. Leonardo DiCaprio est plus jeune que Jack Nicholson.
Ah oui, Jack Nicholson est moins jeune que Leonardo DiCaprio.

5. La chimie est plus scientifique que la philosophie.
Ah oui, la philosophie est moins scientifique que la chimie.

6. Tara Lipinski est plus sportive que Céline Dion.
Ah oui, Céline Dion est moins sportive que Tara Lipinski.

7. L'e-mail est plus rapide que la lettre.
Ah oui, la lettre est moins rapide que l'e-mail.

8. Le Minitel est plus populaire qu'Internet.
Ah oui, Internet est moins populaire que le Minitel.

Teacher's Notes

1. The superlative of adjectives was introduced on page 410 in the first level of *C'est à toi!* and reviewed on page 81 in the second level. 2. The preposition **de** and a definite article sometimes follow the superlative to express "in," for example, **C'est la technologie la plus avancée du monde**. 3. You may want to review the adjectives **beau, joli, nouveau, vieux, bon, mauvais, gros, jeune, grand** and **petit**, which precede a noun in the superlative. 4. Superlative comparisons can also be made using **moins**, for example, **Le Minitel est l'ordinateur le moins cher en France**. 5. A superlative construction may be introduced by a possessive adjective, for example, **C'est mon cours le plus intéressant**. 6. Remind students that the superlative of the adjective **bon/bonne** is **le meilleur, la meilleure**, which was introduced in Unit 5. 7. When a relative clause follows the superlative, the verb may be in the subjunctive to imply an opinion, judgment or emotion on the part of the speaker, for example, **C'est l'outil de recherche le plus utile qu'on puisse choisir**.

Pratique

7 Décrivez les choses et les personnes illustrées en utilisant le superlatif et la forme convenable d'un adjectif de la liste suivante. Suivez le modèle.

célèbre	avancé	rapide	populaire
puissant	petit	marrant	vieux

Modèle:

C'est l'ordinateur le plus avancé du monde.

Le plus puissant des plus compacts

1.

5.

2.

6.

3.

7.

4.

---

each team. The first student on the first team answers your first question with a complete sentence, for example, **Ariane est la fusée la plus connue en France**. If the student answers the question correctly, he or she advances to first base, designated by marking a stick figure along the side of the base, and the next player on that team takes a turn. If the student incorrectly answers the sentence,

he or she stays at home plate and the first player from the second team takes a turn. A run is scored after a team gets four correct answers, thus arriving at home plate. The team having the most runs wins. Here are some other questions that you might ask: **Quel ordinateur français est le moins cher? Quelle chanteuse canadienne est la plus populaire? Quel écrivain de romans**

policiers est le plus connu en Europe? Qui était le peintre impressionniste le plus généreux? Quel rocher canadien est le plus célèbre? Quelle est la plus grande ville de France? Quel est le plus vieux musée de Paris? Quel est le quartier le plus moderne de Paris?

Faites une enquête d'opinion avec cinq élèves de votre cours. Copiez d'abord la grille suivante. Puis demandez à chaque élève de vous donner son choix pour chaque catégorie. Enfin écrivez sa réponse dans l'espace blanc convenable.

Catégorie	Luc	Rachel	Denis	Khadim	Nadia
le film/intéressant		*Titanic*			
l'actrice/doué					
le chanteur/populaire					
le tableau/beau					
la profession/exigeant					
le cours/utile					
le professeur/dynamique					
le parc d'attractions/grand					
la voiture/cher					

Modèle:

Karine: À ton avis, quel est le film le plus intéressant?

Rachel: À mon avis, *Titanic* est le film le plus intéressant.

ORIENT BAY
La plus belle des plages de Saint-Martin

À ton avis, quel est le cours le plus utile?

À mon avis, l'informatique est le cours le plus utile.

Future tense

You have already learned to express what you are going to do in the near future by using a present tense form of **aller** before an infinitive.

Je vais accéder au web.   *I'm going to access the Web.*

Another way to talk about events that will happen in the future is to use the future tense, which consists of only one word.

Vous y trouverez les renseignements que vous cherchez.   *You will find there the information that you're looking for.*

The stem of the future tense is the same as that of the conditional tense (the infinitive for **-er** and **-ir** verbs or the infinitive minus **e** for **-re** verbs). The future endings are **-ai**, **-as**, **-a**, **-ons**, **-ez** and **-ont**.

LION
Du 23 juillet au 23 août

Sentiments : Tout va pour le mieux dans le meilleur des mondes. Vous déborderez de charme, ce qui vous donnera un impact incroyable. Mais ce qui vous procurera le plus de joie, c'est qu'on vous trouvera beaux, et qu'on vous le dira.

Cooperative Group Practice

Interview in the Future

To practice regular verbs in the future, write four infinitives or infinitive expressions on the board, for example, **augmenter**, **dépenser**, **entendre parler de** and **construire**. Then have students count off: 1, 2, 3, 4, 1, 2, 3, 4, etc. The first four students form the first group, the second four students form the second group, and so on. The first student in each group asks a question in the future using the first verb, for example, **Comment augmenterez-vous vos connaissances de la technologie cette année?** The other three students in the group answer the question, for example, **J'augmenterai mes connaissances de la technologie cette année en utilisant Internet.** Then the second student interviews the other three students, asking a question that uses the second verb. When each member of the group has asked his or her interview question, ask some students to report the findings of their interviews to the class. Each student says what question he or she asked and reports the answers of the other members of the group.

Workbook Activities 6-7

Answers

8 À ton avis, qui est l'actrice la plus douée?

À ton avis, qui est le chanteur le plus populaire?

À ton avis, quel est le plus beau tableau?

À ton avis, quelle est la profession la plus exigeante?

À ton avis, quel est le cours le plus utile?

À ton avis, qui est le professeur le plus dynamique?

À ton avis, quel est le plus grand parc d'attractions?

À ton avis, quelle est la voiture la plus chère?

Students' responses to these questions will vary.

Teacher's Notes

1. Explain that the near future (**aller** + infinitive) is used to express events that will occur in the immediate future, while **le futur** is used to express events that will take place in the more distant future. There is also a more determined attitude on the part of the speaker using **le futur** that the event will occur, or that he or she is resolved to bring about that event. 2. Many verbs with spelling changes in the present keep them in the future, for example, **j'achèterai, j'emmènerai, j'enlèverai, je m'ennuierai, j'essaierai, je me lèverai, je nettoierai, je paierai** and **je pèserai**. However, for **espérer, préférer** and **répéter**, the é in the last syllable of the stem does not change in the future: **j'espérerai, je préférerai, je répéterai**. For **s'appeler** the final consonant is doubled (**ll**) in all forms, for example, **vous vous appellerez**. 3. You may want to mention some adverbial expressions that can be used with the future tense, for example, **bientôt, demain, dans quatre jours** and **le mois prochain**.

Je regarderai...

LYON

Vous aimerez

<table>
<tr><td colspan="4">trouver</td></tr>
<tr><td>je</td><td>trouverai</td><td>Je trouverai toutes les réponses.</td><td>I'll find all the answers.</td></tr>
<tr><td>tu</td><td>trouveras</td><td>Où trouveras-tu un appartement?</td><td>Where will you find an apartment?</td></tr>
<tr><td>il/elle/on</td><td>trouvera</td><td>On trouvera beaucoup d'outils de recherche.</td><td>You'll find many search engines.</td></tr>
<tr><td>nous</td><td>trouverons</td><td>Qu'est-ce que nous trouverons?</td><td>What will we find?</td></tr>
<tr><td>vous</td><td>trouverez</td><td>Vous trouverez une liste d'adresses.</td><td>You'll find a list of addresses.</td></tr>
<tr><td>ils/elles</td><td>trouveront</td><td>Elles ne trouveront rien.</td><td>They won't find anything.</td></tr>
</table>

On se **branchera** sur le monde entier. — *We will connect to the whole world.*

La connaissance scientifique **permettra** une vie plus longue et plus riche. — *Scientific knowledge will permit a longer and richer life.*

Combien dépensera Julien pour un jean? (La Rochelle)

As in the conditional, some irregular French verbs have an irregular stem in the future, but their endings are regular. (For a list of these verbs and their irregular stems, see page 189.) Note that for all verbs the future stem ends in **-r**.

L'ESA **aura** bientôt le plus grand pourcentage sur le marché de lanceurs satellites commerciaux. — *The ESA will soon have the largest percentage of the market in commercial satellite launchers.*

Vous **pourrez** trouver tout ce qui vous intéresse sur les fusées. — *You will be able to find everything that interests you about rockets.*

Toutes les nouveautés que vous verrez au Mondial

TOTAL

VOUS NE VIENDREZ PLUS CHEZ NOUS PAR HASARD.

Pratique

Complétez chaque phrase au futur en utilisant la forme convenable d'un des verbes de la liste suivante.

chercher	réussir	se brancher	prendre
sauvegarder	attendre	lancer	accéder

1. Nous... l'arrivée de notre nouvel ordinateur.
2. Tout le monde... au web.
3. Avant d'envoyer de l'e-mail, tu... sur Internet.
4. Tes copains et toi, vous... des informations sur disquette.
5. Bien sûr que les élèves..., mais ils devront y mettre un peu plus d'effort.
6. La France... une fusée.
7. Je... des renseignements sur le projet Ariane.
8. ... -vous l'Eurotunnel l'été prochain?

Êtes-vous voyant(e)? Faites des prédictions sur l'avenir en disant si les choses suivantes se passeront ou pas.

1. les États-Unis/faire/des progrès dans le domaine de la technologie
2. tout le monde/pouvoir/accéder à l'inforoute
3. on/envoyer et recevoir/des e-mails tous les jours
4. on/acheter/beaucoup de choses avec l'ordinateur
5. la clientèle/se servir de/l'argent liquide
6. tous les employés/travailler/à la maison
7. les athlètes/demander/un plus grand salaire
8. le gouvernement/résoudre/tous les problèmes du pays
9. tous les Américains/aller/en France
10. il/falloir/parler deux ou trois langues

Modèles:

on/construire/des maisons sous la mer
On construira des maisons sous la mer.

la vie/être/la même
La vie ne sera pas la même.

J'irai goûter ma Normandie...

On éliminera toutes les maladies du monde.

Audiocassette/CD
Activity 11

Answers

11 1. Est-ce que tu auras besoin d'un ordinateur? Et toi, est-ce que tu auras besoin d'un ordinateur?

2. Est-ce que tu te brancheras sur Internet? Et toi, est-ce que tu te brancheras sur Internet?

3. Est-ce que tu feras des recherches en ligne? Et toi, est-ce que tu feras des recherches en ligne?

4. Est-ce que tu choisiras beaucoup d'outils de recherche? Et toi, est-ce que tu choisiras beaucoup d'outils de recherche?

5. Est-ce que tu t'assiéras longtemps devant l'écran? Et toi, est-ce que tu t'assiéras longtemps devant l'écran?

6. Est-ce que tu seras diligent(e) et organisé(e)? Et toi, est-ce que tu seras diligent(e) et organisé(e)?

7. Est-ce que tu te serviras d'un dictionnaire? Et toi, est-ce que tu te serviras d'un dictionnaire?

8. Est-ce que tu sauvegarderas ta dissertation sur disquette? Et toi, est-ce que tu sauvegarderas ta dissertation sur disquette?

Students' responses to these questions will vary.

Modèle:
aller à la bibliothèque
Élève A: Est-ce que tu iras à la bibliothèque?
Élève B: Oui, j'irai à la bibliothèque. Et toi, est-ce que tu iras à la bibliothèque?
Élève A: Non, je n'irai pas à la bibliothèque.

Aujourd'hui à l'école il y a des ordinateurs au labo.

Demain il y aura des ordinateurs dans chaque salle de classe.

---

11 *Avec un(e) partenaire, posez des questions sur ce que vous ferez la prochaine fois que vous devrez écrire une dissertation. Puis répondez aux questions. Suivez le modèle.*

1. avoir besoin d'un ordinateur
2. se brancher sur Internet
3. faire des recherches en ligne
4. choisir beaucoup d'outils de recherche
5. s'asseoir longtemps devant l'écran
6. être diligent(e) et organisé(e)
7. se servir d'un dictionnaire
8. sauvegarder ta dissertation sur disquette

Est-ce que tu utiliseras l'imprimante?

Bien sûr, je l'utiliserai.

Les étudiants feront-ils leur rentrée à Jussieu ?

Communication

12 *Comment sera la vie de demain? Bien sûr qu'il y aura des choses qui seront différentes. Mais y aura-t-il des choses qui ne changeront pas? Avec un(e) partenaire, comparez la vie d'aujourd'hui à la vie de demain. Choisissez un sujet à discuter avec votre partenaire parmi les suivants:*

1. l'école et la vie des élèves
2. la maison et la vie en famille
3. la communication orale et écrite
4. les moyens de transport

D'abord copiez la grille suivante. Puis discutez votre sujet avec votre partenaire. Enfin remplissez la grille avec les idées qui résultent de votre discussion.

la communication orale et écrite	
aujourd'hui	demain
On se sert du téléphone.	*On se servira de l'ordinateur.*

Game

Future Board Game

You might want to create game boards to provide additional practice with regular and irregular verbs in the future. On pieces of poster board or card stock, make a backwards "S" and divide it into even squares. The first square is labeled **Commencez**; the last square is labeled **Gagnez**. The squares in between list the infinitives of regular and irregular verbs. Make sets of cards with pronoun and noun subjects. Put students in smalls groups and give each group a board, a set of cards and a die. The first student in each group rolls the die and advances the number of squares indicated by the roll. Then he or she takes a card from the set and gives a sentence using the subject on the card and the verb on the board. If the student gives a correct sentence, for example, **On recevra**, he or she gets to stay on the square; if the student gives an incorrect sentence, he or she goes back to the beginning of the board. The first student to reach the end of the board wins.

Maintenant, avec votre partenaire, utilisez les idées de votre comparaison entre la vie d'aujourd'hui et la vie de demain pour une présentation orale devant la classe. Essayez de donner six comparaisons.

Écrivez une rédaction qui compare la vie d'aujourd'hui et la vie de demain en la décrivant maintenant et dans l'avenir. Servez-vous des idées de votre grille de l'Activité 12. Faites aussi des observations personnelles sur ces changements. À votre avis, seront-ils bons ou mauvais?

Listening Activity 1

Quiz *Leçon A*

Using Computer Technology

Sur la bonne piste

Today's computer technology can put resources at your fingertips to help you learn more about French and the francophone world. You can use encyclopedias on CD-ROM and search engines on the Internet to help you locate information about francophone-related topics. Tools like spell checkers and grammar checkers can help you become a better writer in French, while corresponding via e-mail can provide additional communicative practice.

If you need background information about a topic, such as the Ariane rocket, start with an encyclopedia on CD-ROM. Perhaps your school's instructional materials center has one, or you may have one at home. Some articles may be accompanied by pictures, sound and film clips. For the most current information on a specific topic, consult the Internet. If you know the Internet address you need, enter it in the field (box) that appears at the top of your screen when your Internet Service Provider (ISP) home page comes up. If you don't have the address, type in key words using the search engine of your choice. Most search engines give you access to articles in more than one language. When you select a French topic, many of the articles that appear will be in French. You may want to try different search engines to find hard-to-locate topics.

Spell checkers and grammar checkers are available in French to help you catch mistakes when you write. Although an English spell checker and grammar checker may be part of your word-processing program, a French spell checker and grammar checker must be installed separately. A French spell checker even tells you when you are missing an accent or have used the wrong one. With a grammar checker, you may be asked to select from a list of writing style levels. If you were writing to a pen pal, you would probably choose the "casual" level, whereas if you were writing a composition for French class, you would probably select the "formal" level. Grammar checkers identify many types of mistakes, such as incorrect words, negation, possessives, plurals, relative clauses, subject-verb agreement, article-noun gender agreement and punctuation. French spell checkers and grammar checkers are useful tools to help you become a better writer.

Practice is the best way to improve your writing skills in French. You may want to correspond by e-mail with another student in your class or with a key pal in a francophone country. To send and receive e-mail, you first need an account with

Teacher's Notes

1. In this unit **Sur la bonne piste, Leçon A**, focuses on using computer technology. Students will learn about resources to help them research topics about francophone culture. 2. You may want to set up e-mail accounts for students so that they can write French e-mail messages to students in another class or school.

Teacher's Notes

1. Some e-mail accounts may not support non-standard characters such as French accent marks.
2. Other word-processing programs may have different ways of making accented letters. 3. To give students practice making accented letters in French, you may want them to do the activity that follows. Tell students that Tim wrote a letter to his pen pal, Élisabeth, on a conventional typewriter. Consequently, he didn't use accent marks. Using either a Windows- or Macintosh-based program, students should rewrite his letter, adding accent marks wherever needed.

Chere Elisabeth,

Ca va? Moi, je vais tres bien. J'ai recu ta derniere lettre. Tu veux que je te rende visite au mois d'aout, mais, tu sais, les billets d'avion coutent beaucoup en cette saison. Donc, ce que je compte faire pendant l'ete, c'est de travailler a la patisserie de ma soeur. Peut-etre que je te verrai pour les vacances d'hiver l'annee prochaine. Reponds-moi vite!

A bientot,
Tim

4. We used the search engine WebCrawler and entered the following headings to find the items in Activity 15: 1. "Les Pages de Paris": select "Magasins & Boutiques," then "Les Grands Magasins" 2. "Les Pages de Paris": select "musées," then "R" for "Musée Auguste Rodin"
3. "l'Afrique": select "Dico Français-Wolof" 4. "Météo France": select "La Météo du Jour"
5. "Marseille France": select "Excite Travel," then "Travel and Tourism" 6. "ESA": select "European Space Agency," then "Launches," then "Ariane 5 Family"
7. "ESA": select "Centres"
8. "Caillebotte": select "Art Masterpieces" 9. "Le Monde": select "Le Monde: Bienvenue"
10. "SNCF": select "SNCF - Les Voyages," then "Horaires, prix, services."

---

an ISP. With your ISP in place and your e-mail software up and running, enter your recipient's Internet address. It is usually a form of his or her name, followed by @ and the name of the server/domain: (.com) for a business, (.org) for an organization, (.edu) for a school, or (.gov) for a governmental agency.

If you use a Windows-based word-processing program, use the numerical keypad on the right side of your keyboard to make letters with accent marks. For example, to key é, hold down the Alt key and press 0233 on the keypad. Here is a brief list of keystroke combinations needed to create other common accented letters:

è	0232	î	0238	û	0251
ê	0234	œ	0156	À	0192
ë	0235	ç	0231	É	0201
â	0226	ù	0249	È	0200
à	0224	ô	0244	Ç	0199

For Macintosh computers, click on the Apple icon and drag it down to "Key Caps." Then go into "Key Caps" and select the font that you want. Hold down the Option key to see the character map. (To see additional letters with accent marks that are not shown on the first character map, hold down the Option and Shift keys.) Make a list of the keystroke combinations that you need. Then exit "Key Caps." To make an accent on a letter, simply hold down the Option key and select the letter where the accent you need can be found. For example, to make ê, hold down the Option key, key i, lift up and key e.

---

15 | To practice using the Internet, find the items that follow. For each one, write the Internet address where you found it.

1. l'adresse des Galeries Lafayette à Paris
2. les heures quand le musée Rodin est ouvert
3. un dictionnaire français-ouolof
4. le temps qu'il fait en France aujourd'hui
5. le nom et l'adresse d'un restaurant à Marseille
6. une photo de l'Ariane 5
7. l'adresse à Paris de l'ESA (Agence spatiale européenne)
8. un tableau de Gustave Caillebotte
9. un article dans un journal français
10. un horaire des trains français

INTERNET
Naviguez sur les meilleurs sites cinéma de l'Internet.

**Workbook
Activity 8**

la pauvreté

une mission humanitaire

Leçon B

In this lesson you will be able to:

➤ ask for information

➤ give information

➤ sequence events

➤ give opinions

➤ express enthusiasm

➤ hypothesize

➤ predict

➤ congratulate and commiserate

➤ express appreciation

➤ forget

➤ make requests

Teacher's Notes

1. Communicative functions that are recycled in this lesson are "describing past events," "thanking someone," "identifying professions," "telling location" and "expressing hope." 2. Point out that the noun **pauvreté** is related to the adjective **pauvre**.

Workbook
Activity 9

Audiocassette/CD
Le journal, Dialogue

Transparencies 3-4

Teacher's Notes

1. Tell students that **une équipe** also describes an athletic team.
2. **Meilleur(e)** is the comparative of the adjective **bon/bonne**. If students question the position of **meilleur** after the noun in the newspaper's title, tell them this is a stylistic choice made to emphasize the adjective. 3. On May 17, 1997, Zaire changed its name to the Democratic Republic of the Congo.
4. Students learned **sauvegarder** as a computer-related word in **Leçon A**. 5. The phrase **a été interdit** is in the passive voice. Explain that in the passive voice, the subject does not perform the action. 6. Other related terms and expressions include **la première page, la une** (*front page*), **une rubrique** (*column*), **l'activisme (m.)** (*activism*), **le Tiers-Monde** (*Third World*), **la qualité de la vie** (*quality of life*), **une espèce en voie d'extinction** (*endangered species*), **l'écologie (f.)** (*ecology*), **un(e) écologiste** (*ecologist*), **un explorateur, une exploratrice** (*explorer*) and **un scaphandrier** (*diver*).

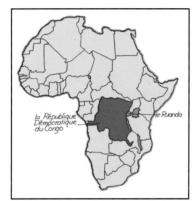

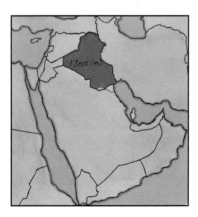

Maryse est chef de son journal du lycée, *Un Monde Meilleur.*° Cet après-midi elle a rendez-vous avec son équipe de reporters. Aussitôt qu'ils seront tous là, ils parleront du prochain numéro dont le sujet sera de sauvegarder la terre.° Voilà, le dernier membre de l'équipe vient d'arriver.

Maryse: Didier, tu parleras de quoi?
Didier: Ben, le titre de l'article sera "La lutte° pour la défense des animaux." Je parlerai de la Fondation Brigitte Bardot. Tu sais, cette actrice célèbre a été la première Française à dénoncer le mauvais traitement des animaux. Grâce° à elle, le commerce de fourrure° de bébés phoques a été interdit. Elle a établi un refuge pour une variété d'animaux en Normandie. Si les animaux sont maltraités,° la fondation viendra les aider. C'est passionnant.°
Maryse: Merci, Dider. Tu me rendras° l'article dès que° tu l'auras, d'accord? Et toi, Philippe, tu choisiras quoi?
Philippe: Tu sais que quand je deviendrai médécin, je travaillerai pour Médecins Sans Frontières.° Alors, je vais décrire les missions humanitaires de ce groupe. Lorsqu'il y aura une guerre, une famine ou de la pauvreté, les médecins viendront aider les gens. Ils ont déjà participé à des missions humanitaires au Ruanda, en Irak et en République Démocratique du Congo.
Maryse: Excellent, Philippe. Rends-moi l'article avant vendredi si tu peux. Et toi, Valérie?
Valérie: Quant à° moi, je parlerai de l'Équipe Cousteau. Je décrirai la lutte pour la protection des mers et des océans. On peut lire les

meilleur(e) *better*; **la terre** *earth*; **une lutte** *fight*; **grâce** *merci*; **la fourrure** *fur*; **maltraité(e)** *mistreated*; **passionnant(e)** *très intéressant(e)*; **rendre** *donner*; **dès que** *aussitôt que*; **une frontière** *border*; **quant à** *as for*

Cross-curricular

Pour une politique engagée

To encourage activism in students, you may want to bring in a guest speaker from a local homeless shelter, an animal shelter, an AIDS organization or the Red Cross. Encourage the guest speaker to provide background information on his or her organization and to enumerate the ways in which students can contribute to it. Then have students creatively express what they learned about the organization from the guest speaker. Students may choose to write a poem or song, make a collage or write a skit to share with the rest of the class.

livres de Jacques-Yves Cousteau si on veut connaître l'histoire de l'océanographie française. Dès qu'on les lira, on appréciera tous ses efforts pour protéger° la mer et les animaux de la mer, son intérêt pour l'éducation avec des films sérieux et amusants, et sa recherche avec les voyages de *La Calypso* et maintenant de *La Calypso II*. C'est l'Équipe Cousteau qui continuera à chercher une stratégie écologique mondiale.°

Maryse: Bon. Bravo à tout le monde! J'espère que notre prochain numéro sera populaire et que les gens deviendront plus engagés° en le lisant. N'oubliez° pas de me rendre vos articles avant vendredi à 16h00.

protéger *to protect*; **mondial(e)** du monde; **engagé(e)** *committed*; **oublier** ne pas se souvenir

---

Corrigez toutes les fautes dans les phrases suivantes d'après le dialogue.

1. Maryse est reporter pour un journal dans sa ville.
2. Le sujet du prochain numéro du journal sera un monde meilleur.
3. C'était Jacques-Yves Cousteau qui a été le premier Français à dénoncer le mauvais traitement des animaux.
4. Si les animaux sont maltraités, Médecins Sans Frontières viendra les aider.
5. Médecins Sans Frontières viendra aider les gens seulement quand il y aura une guerre.
6. La Fondation Brigitte Bardot participe à la lutte pour protéger les mers et les océans.
7. Pour connaître l'histoire de l'océanographie française, on peut lire *La Calypso II*.
8. On oubliera tous les problèmes écologiques en lisant le prochain numéro du journal.

À quelle organisation les expressions suivantes sont-elles associées? D'abord copiez la grille suivante. Puis mettez un ✓ dans le blanc approprié.

	Un Monde Meilleur	la Fondation Brigitte Bardot	Médecins Sans Frontières	l'Équipe Cousteau
1. où il y a de la pauvreté				
2. une stratégie écologique				
3. le prochain numéro				
4. un refuge pour des animaux				
5. contre le commerce de fourrure				
6. des missions humanitaires				
7. une équipe de reporters				
8. l'océanographie				
9. la protection des mers et des océans				
10. le titre de l'article				
11. contre le mauvais traitement des animaux				
12. où il y a une famine				
13. la protection des bébés phoques				

Game

Machine à écrire

You might play this spelling game once students have studied the **Dialogue**. Divide the class into two teams. Then assign a letter of the alphabet and accent marks to individual members of each team. In doing this, be sure each team has members that represent the whole alphabet and all accent marks. (If the class is small, then assign several letters or accent marks to single players.) Start the game by saying a vocabulary word from **Leçon A** or **Leçon B** to one of the teams. This team must spell the word orally. They must do this so fast that they sound like a typewriter; hence, the name of the game. (You may set a time limit for calling out letters, say one or two seconds.) For example, if the word is **passionnant**, the student with the letter **p** calls out that letter in French, and teammates with the appropriate letters complete in turn the spelling of the word. By doing this, the team earns one point. Then the other team gets their turn at a word. Whenever a team fails, its rival gets a chance to spell the same word and win another point.

Teacher's Note

Here are the forms of the orthographically changing verb **protéger**: **protège, protèges, protège, protégeons, protégez, protègent.**

Workbook
Activity 10

 Audiocassette/CD
Activity 3

Answers

3 Answers will vary.

Teacher's Notes

1. Cognates in this reading include **respecter, inspirent, compassion, découvert, limiter, privilégiés, ignorance, désinformation, publiquement, méthodes, organisé, système, humain, création, actions, publications, audiovisuelles, présentations, expérimentations, animales, surpopulation, public, réalisé, souffrent, organisation, internationale, volontaires, populations, politique, économique, religion, indépendants, catastrophe, naturelle, tremblement, Nicaragua, assistance, médicale, Honduras, Liban, camps, réfugiés, Éthiopiens, encouragé, sous-marine, inventeur, exploration, habitants, combiner, reste, secrets, exposé, symphonie, colorée, silence, intégré, archéologue, amateur, caméras, passionné, écologie, planète, explore, aquatique, navigue, invention, Antarctique** and **réserve**. 2. Brigitte Bardot, born in Paris, began her career as a model in the late 1940s. She acted in her first movie in 1952. Her stardom in the U.S. was established with her role in *And... God Created Woman* in 1957. Bardot was considered a sex symbol in the 1950s and 1960s. In 1985 Bardot was recognized as a Chevalier de la Légion d'honneur. 3. Spokesperson for **la protection animale**, Bardot successfully lobbied for the mandatory introduction of stun guns to eliminate all useless suffering of animals in French slaughterhouses. Sales of baby seal fur were abolished in 1977, largely due to her efforts. Other initiatives of the foundation have saved wolves in Mongolia, improved conditions for raising and transporting animals

> J'aimerais travailler dans un refuge pour les animaux.

3 | *C'est à toi!*

1. Est-ce que tu connais les films de Brigitte Bardot? Si oui, quel(s) film(s) as-tu vu(s)?
2. Est-ce que tu porterais quelque chose en fourrure? Pourquoi ou pourquoi pas?
3. Est-ce que tu aimerais travailler dans un refuge pour les animaux? Est-ce qu'il y en a un dans ta ville?
4. Est-ce que tu as vu des films de Jacques-Yves Cousteau? Si oui, quel(s) film(s)?
5. Est-ce que tu as jamais écrit quelque chose pour le journal de ton lycée? Si oui, quoi?
6. Est-ce que tu fais quelque chose pour aider les gens dans ta ville dans la lutte contre la famine? Contre la pauvreté? Si oui, quoi?
7. Est-ce que tu es engagé(e)? Et tes parents?
8. Qu'est-ce que tu penses devenir? Pour qui voudrais-tu travailler?

Enquête culturelle

FONDATION BRIGITTE BARDOT
l'info-journal **N° 20**

S.O.S. FOURRURE :

● Interdiction de l'importation dans les pays de la CEE de fourrures provenant d'animaux piégés;

● Interdiction des pièges à mâchoires.

BRIGITTE BARDOT
L'AMOUR DES BÊTES À TOUT PRIX

Brigitte Bardot, née en 1934, était une vedette du cinéma français où elle a connu un grand succès. Mais elle a quitté l'écran pour s'occuper de la protection des animaux. Bardot croit que tout animal est sensible et qu'on doit respecter les animaux qui inspirent notre compassion. Elle a découvert qu'elle ne pouvait pas limiter son amour à quelques animaux privilégiés, parce que tous les animaux du monde avaient besoin de protection. Les plus grands problèmes que Bardot a trouvés étaient l'ignorance et la désinformation. Elle a dénoncé publiquement les méthodes de traitement des animaux à la boucherie, et elle a organisé un système plus humain. Elle a essayé de sauvegarder les bébés phoques et d'arrêter le commerce de leur fourrure. En 1986 elle a créé la Fondation Brigitte Bardot à Saint-Tropez pour sauvegarder les animaux. Elle a vendu ses bijoux et plusieurs objets d'art pour recevoir l'argent nécessaire pour la création de la fondation. Maintenant la fondation se trouve à Paris d'où elle met en place plusieurs actions importantes: préparer des publications audiovisuelles, donner des conférences, organiser des expositions et faire des présentations aux jeunes.

La fondation a réussi à arrêter des expérimentations animales, à limiter la surpopulation des chiens et des chats, à arrêter le commerce de la fourrure, à dénoncer le commerce des animaux exotiques et à dire au public qu'il ne faut pas manger certains animaux.

Cette boutique de la Fondation Brigitte Bardot se trouve à Saint-Tropez.

destined for slaughter, and helped African countries reduce poaching and ivory sales. 4. In 1988, Bardot moved the foundation's headquarters to Paris. In 1992, the Foundation was recognized as a state-approved organization. 5. The foundation also used to house unwanted dogs and cats. 6. The address for the headquarters of **la Fondation Brigitte Bardot** is 4, rue Franklin, 75116 Paris. To find out more about **la Fondation Brigitte Bardot** on the Internet, enter http://www.fondation brigittebardot.fr/ or "Fondation Brigitte Bardot" using the search engine of your choice.

Bernard Kouchner, médecin français, a réalisé qu'il serait beaucoup plus utile comme médecin dans les pays qui souffrent. Il a donc créé Médecins Sans Frontières, une organisation humanitaire internationale. Ses volontaires cherchent à aider les populations lorsqu'il y a une guerre, une famine ou de la pauvreté. Ni la politique, ni l'économique, ni la religion n'intéresse ces médecins, parce qu'ils restent indépendants. La première mission de cette organisation a été d'aider les gens quand il y avait une catastrophe naturelle, un tremblement de terre, au Nicaragua. Ces volontaires ont tout de suite suivi cette mission avec une autre d'assistance médicale à l'Honduras et une mission de guerre au Liban. Depuis 1971 plus de 20.000 médecins et infirmiers ont aidé plus de 80 pays où la vie est devenue très difficile. Parmi leurs travaux humanitaires, ils ont organisé les camps pour les réfugiés en Asie et en Afrique, ont donné à manger aux Éthiopiens et ont aidé les gens au Ruanda. Il y a quelques années 2.500 volontaires sont allés dans 250 missions dans 65 pays. Les missions humanitaires de ces médecins ont aidé des millions de personnes.

MÉDECINS SANS FRONTIÈRES

Ruanda : trois ans au cœur de la tourmente

Jacques-Yves Cousteau (1910-1997) a encouragé un grand intérêt mondial pour les océans, les mers et la vie sous-marine. Il a été l'inventeur d'un système de plongée qui permet une exploration plus scientifique de ce qu'il y a sous la mer et de tous ses habitants. Cousteau aimait beaucoup le cinéma et la mer. Il a pu combiner les deux avec ses travaux qui ont ouvert au reste du monde les secrets de l'océan. Dans ses livres et ses films, il a exposé la symphonie colorée des animaux et des plantes qui habitent le monde du silence sous-marin. Au début Cousteau travaillait pour le gouvernement français où il a intégré ses travaux sous-marins à son plaisir d'archéologue amateur en tournant des films. Plus tard, avec sa femme et ses enfants, il a aimé descendre sous la mer avec ses caméras. Il a tourné plus de 100 documentaires pour la télévision, ce qui nous a permis de mieux connaître la vie dans les océans. Passionné par son amour pour la mer et son intérêt pour l'écologie, il a créé l'Équipe Cousteau pour sauvegarder la planète et aider à son exploration. Depuis 40 ans l'équipe explore le système aquatique dans son bateau, *La Calypso*. Ce bateau navigue sur tous les océans avec l'idée de protéger l'environnement avec des présentations de films et de livres. Les activités scientifiques de l'Équipe Cousteau ont commencé avec l'invention de "l'aqualung," qui lui permet de plonger sous la mer pour mieux étudier la vie de l'océan. En 1990 l'équipe a lancé une lutte pour sauvegarder l'Antarctique, pour qu'elle ne devienne une réserve naturelle d'étude pour la science.

Diolé et **Cousteau**
Nos amies les baleines
Édition illustrée en couleurs

Les hommes de COUSTEAU

La Calypso par Cousteau, on connaît. Moins l'histoire des hommes qui l'ont suivi cinquante ans sous l'eau. Ce livre leur est, pour une fois, consacré.

Answers

4 Possible answers:

1. Brigitte Bardot était une vedette du cinéma français.
2. La Fondation Brigitte Bardot prépare des publications audiovisuelles, donne des conférences, organise des expositions et fait des présentations aux jeunes.
3. La fondation a réussi à arrêter des expérimentations animales, à limiter la surpopulation des chiens et des chats, à arrêter le commerce de la fourrure, à dénoncer le commerce des animaux exotiques et à dire au public qu'il ne faut pas manger certains animaux.
4. Bernard Kouchner, médecin français, a créé Médecins Sans Frontières.
5. Médecins Sans Frontières va où il y a une guerre, une famine ou de la pauvreté.
6. La première mission humanitaire de cette organisation a été au Nicaragua.
7. Cette organisation a aidé les gens dans plus de 80 pays.
8. Jacques-Yves Cousteau a inventé un système de plongée qui permet une exploration plus scientifique de ce qu'il y a sous la mer et de tous ses habitants.
9. Cousteau a tourné plus de 100 documentaires.
10. L'invention de "l'aqualung" lui permet de plonger sous la mer pour mieux étudier la vie de l'océan.

LE CENTRE DE LA MER

PRÉSENTE
TOUS LES JOURS
à 15h et 16h (sauf le lundi)

UN FILM DE LA SÉRIE :
" L'ODYSSÉE SOUS-MARINE
DE L'ÉQUIPE COUSTEAU "

195, rue Saint-Jacques 75005 PARIS Tel : 46 33 08 61

4 | *Répondez aux questions suivantes.*

1. Que faisait Brigitte Bardot avant son succès avec la protection des animaux?
2. Quelles sont les actions que la Fondation Brigitte Bardot met en place?
3. Qu'est-ce que la fondation a réussi à faire?
4. Qui a créé Médecins Sans Frontières?
5. Où va Médecins Sans Frontières?
6. Où était la première mission humanitaire de cette organisation?
7. Dans combien de pays est-ce que cette organisation a aidé les gens?
8. Qu'est-ce que Jacques-Yves Cousteau a inventé?
9. Combien de documentaires est-ce que Cousteau a tournés?
10. Qu'est-ce que l'invention de "l'aqualung" permet à l'Équipe Cousteau?

5 | *Lisez l'article "Médecins Sans Frontières: C'est qui? C'est quoi?" Puis répondez aux questions après l'article.*

MÉDECINS SANS FRONTIÈRES
C'EST QUI? C'EST QUOI?

"Et moi, est-ce qu'un jour je serai Médecin Sans Frontières?" Voici les réponses à toutes les questions que vous vous posez.

■ **Qui sont les Médecins Sans Frontières?**

Chaque année, 2900 volontaires partent en mission avec Médecins Sans Frontières. Parmi eux, il y a bien sûr le personnel médical: des médecins, des infirmières, des chirurgiens... Mais une partie des volontaires n'appartient pas au corps médical: ce sont les personnes responsables de toutes les questions de matériel (les "logisticiens") et administratives (les "administrateurs"). Il y a en permanence 900 volontaires sur le terrain: on les appelle les "expatriés".

■ **Est-ce qu'à Médecins Sans Frontières on gagne beaucoup d'argent?**

Non. Autant le savoir, on ne s'enrichit pas dans l'action humanitaire. C'est un choix. Celui de vivre une expérience forte en soulageant les souffrances des hommes et des femmes abandonnés à eux-mêmes. Les volontaires perçoivent une indemnité comprise entre 4000 F et 5500 F par mois. Mais durant leur mission, tous les frais sont pris en charge par l'organisation.

■ **Où intervient Médecins Sans Frontières en ce moment?**

Médecins Sans Frontières est présent actuellement dans une soixantaine de pays. Chaque année, de nouvelles missions ouvrent et d'autres se ferment. Médecins Sans Frontières est la plus grande organisation médicale d'urgence. Elle se retrouve ainsi dans des endroits où personne ne va. Son rôle est aussi de témoigner pour alerter l'opinion publique. Tous les ans, elle publie un rapport sur les populations en danger.

■ **Médecins Sans Frontières existe-t-il dans d'autres pays?**

Oui. Médecins Sans Frontières est un mouvement international. Depuis sa création en France en 1971, il s'est développé en Belgique, en Hollande, au Luxembourg, en Espagne et en Suisse. Chacune de ces sections est indépendante mais adhèrent à la même charte.

■ **Comment devient-on membre de Médecins Sans Frontières?**

Pour être un jour recruté comme volontaire, il faut répondre à trois critères:

1. D'abord avoir une bonne compétence professionnelle. Médecins Sans Frontières n'a pas seulement besoin de médecins. Tout le monde a quelque chose à apporter, à condition d'avoir une bonne formation. Les études sont donc essentielles.
2. La maîtrise des langues étrangères est indispensable, en particulier l'anglais.
3. Il faut être très motivé et avoir bon caractère. Dans une mission, on peut vivre à plusieurs dans une petite pièce, se laver tous les matins à l'eau froide et travailler 15 heures par jour. Et tout ça en conservant sa bonne humeur!

■ **Comment aider Médecins Sans Frontières?**

Sur 100 F donnés à Médecins Sans Frontières, 83 F sont utilisés pour les actions sur le terrain, 5 F servent à la gestion de l'association et 12 F sont consacrés à l'information et à la collecte de fonds. Médecins Sans Frontières a besoin d'argent pour poursuivre ses missions. C'est pourquoi, même si tu n'es pas encore médecin, infirmier(ère) ou logisticien, tu peux quand même nous aider. Deviens Ambassadeur Junior de Médecins Sans Frontières et fais connaître à tes parents, tes voisins, tes profs l'opération "1 F par jour". Appelle-nous au (1) 40.21.29.29, pour recevoir ton dossier d'Ambassadeur Junior.

1. Combien de volontaires partent en mission avec Médecins Sans Frontières chaque année?
2. Quels volontaires ne sont pas membres du corps médical?
3. Qui sont les "expatriés"?
4. Combien d'argent est-ce qu'un volontaire reçoit par mois?
5. Dans combien de pays est-ce que Médecins Sans Frontières est présent aujourd'hui?
6. Pourquoi est-ce que Médecins Sans Frontières publie un rapport tous les ans?
7. Dans quels autres pays est-ce que Médecins Sans Frontières s'est développé?
8. À quels trois critères faut-il répondre pour être recruté par Médecins Sans Frontières?
9. Qu'est-ce qu'un ado peut faire pour aider Médecins Sans Frontières?

Journal personnel

In this lesson you have learned about humanitarian actions occurring in some third-world countries. Humanitarian actions can take place in far-off countries, like Rwanda, as well as in your own community. Do problems such as poverty, homelessness, unemployment, hunger, disease, drugs and others exist in your city? Are there local organizations that help people with these problems? What are some additional solutions that you can think of to alleviate these problems? Does your school have any groups that work with these issues? Whom do you know personally that has done something to help people with these problems? What did they accomplish?

Answers

5 Possible answers:

1. Chaque année, 2900 volontaires partent en mission avec Médecins Sans Frontières.
2. Les volontaires qui sont responsables de toutes les questions de matériel et administratives ne sont pas membres du corps médical.
3. Les "expatriés" sont les 900 volontaires en permanence sur le terrain.
4. Un volontaire reçoit entre 4000 F et 5500 F par mois.
5. Médecins Sans Frontières est présent aujourd'hui dans une soixantaine de pays.
6. Médecins Sans Frontières publie un rapport tous les ans pour alerter l'opinion publique sur les populations en danger.
7. Médecins Sans Frontières s'est développé en Belgique, en Hollande, au Luxembourg, en Espagne et en Suisse.
8. Il faut avoir une bonne compétence professionnelle, avoir la maîtrise des langues étrangères, être très motivé et avoir bon caractère.
9. Un ado peut devenir Ambassadeur Junior pour aider Médecins Sans Frontières.

Teacher's Notes

1. **Si** becomes **s'** before **il** and **ils**, but not before **elle**, **elles** or **on** or a word beginning with a vowel sound. 2. Point out that of the three sequences described on this page, the one with **si** and the present along with the future is the most common. 3. The **si** clause is placed at the end of the sentence for emphasis. 4. **Si** meaning "whether" can take any tense.

Critical Thinking

Si Clauses

Write the following sentence on the board: **Si tu m'aides avec mes corvées, je pourrai sortir plus tôt.** Ask students for two ways in which the **si** clause can be expressed in English. Students should tell you that in English, the clause can mean either "if you help me" (present) or "if you will help me" (future). Explain to students that although in English the present or the future may be used, only the present can be used in the **si** clause in French.

Paired Practice

Les conditions

So that students can practice forming the future tense in sentences with **si**, put them in pairs. Prepare a worksheet that asks questions requiring an answer using the future tense and **si** clauses, for example, **Regarderas-tu la télé ce soir?** Tell students to express a condition that must first be met before they will do that activity, for example, **Si je finis mes devoirs, je regarderai la télé ce soir.** Students take turns asking and answering the questions on the worksheet. Here are some other questions that you might ask: **Porteras-tu un imper demain? Iras-tu au cinéma ce weekend? Voyageras-tu cet été? Mettras-tu la clim cet été? Feras-tu des études à l'université plus tard? Iras-tu en France un jour?**

Structure

Future tense in sentences with *si*

To tell what will happen *if* something else happens or *if* some condition contrary to reality is met, use the future tense along with **si** and the present tense. Here is the order of tenses in these sentences with **si**.

si	+	present	future

Didier **parlera** de la Fondation Brigitte Bardot **s'il écrit** un article pour le prochain numéro.

Didier will talk about the Brigitte Bardot Foundation if he writes an article for the next issue.

Si les animaux **sont** maltraités, la fondation **viendra** les aider.

If animals are mistreated, the foundation will come to help them.

With **si** and the present tense, you may also use the present tense or the imperative in the result clause.

si	+	present	present
si	+	present	imperative

On **peut** lire les livres de Cousteau **si** on **veut** connaître l'histoire de l'océanographie.

You can read Cousteau's books if you want to know the history of oceanography.

Rends-moi l'article avant vendredi **si** tu **peux.**

Hand in the article to me before Friday if you can.

Note in the examples above that the phrase with **si** and the present tense can either begin or end the sentence.

Si vous avez une chemise verte, je l'achèterai.

Cooperative Group Practice

Sentence Completion

To practice the future tense in sentences with **si** clauses, put students in small groups of four or five. Give each group a worksheet that you have prepared with six incomplete sentences, for example, **Les ados... s'ils sortent.** Each group writes as many logical completions using the future for each sentence as they can, for example, **Les ados (iront en boîte, mangeront au fast-food, regarderont un match, joueront au foot) s'ils sortent.** Here are five other incomplete sentences that you might use: 1. **Si tu étudies, tu.... 2. Mon meilleur ami... s'il a de l'argent. 3. Si le prof n'arrive pas, nous.... 4. Vous... si vous allez à Paris. 5. Si je deviens engagé(e), je....** After each group finishes, you may want to compile a class list with all the future completions that groups came up with.

Pratique

Qu'est-ce que tout le monde fera si ces conditions existent? Complétez chaque phrase selon l'illustration convenable. Utilisez une expression logique de la liste donnée.

jouer dans la neige	nager
ne plus piqueniquer	jouer au volley
rentrer à la maison	prendre le soleil
faire de la luge	

Modèle:
S'il neige, Chantal et Benoît feront de la luge.

1. S'il fait beau, Caroline....
2. S'il fait beau, Damien et Luc....
3. S'il fait beau, Céline et toi, vous....
4. S'il pleut, Annette et Berthe....
5. S'il pleut, Marc et moi, nous....
6. S'il neige, Nadège et Véro....

Que ferez-vous si...? Avec un(e) partenaire, parlez de ce que vous ferez dans chaque situation. Posez des questions, et puis répondez-y.

1. oublier les devoirs
2. devoir faire des recherches
3. avoir du temps libre
4. être obligé(e) de rester à la maison ce soir
5. ne pas se sentir bien
6. vouloir trouver du boulot

Modèle:
gagner beaucoup d'argent
Élève A: Qu'est-ce que tu feras si tu gagnes beaucoup d'argent?
Élève B: Si je gagne beaucoup d'argent, j'irai en Europe. Et toi, qu'est-ce que tu feras si tu gagnes beaucoup d'argent?
Élève A: Si je gagne beaucoup d'argent, j'achèterai une voiture.

 Audiocassette/CD Activity 7

Answers

6 1. prendra le soleil
2. nageront
3. jouerez au volley
4. rentreront à la maison
5. ne piqueniquerons plus
6. joueront dans la neige

7 1. Qu'est-ce que tu feras si tu oublies les devoirs? Et toi, qu'est-ce que tu feras si tu oublies les devoirs?
2. Qu'est-ce que tu feras si tu dois faire des recherches? Et toi, qu'est-ce que tu feras si tu dois faire des recherches?
3. Qu'est-ce que tu feras si tu as du temps libre? Et toi, qu'est-ce que tu feras si tu as du temps libre?
4. Qu'est-ce que tu feras si tu es obligé(e) de rester à la maison ce soir? Et toi, qu'est-ce que tu feras si tu es obligé(e) de rester à la maison ce soir?
5. Qu'est-ce que tu feras si tu ne te sens pas bien? Et toi, qu'est-ce que tu feras si tu ne te sens pas bien?
6. Qu'est-ce que tu feras si tu veux trouver du boulot? Et toi, qu'est-ce que tu feras si tu veux trouver du boulot?
Students' responses to these questions will vary.

Game

Relay Race

To provide students with additional practice forming the future tense in sentences with **si**, you may want them to play this game. Divide the class into two teams. Prepare a list of 20 questions that require answers using the future tense in sentences with **si**, for example, **Qu'est-ce que tu feras cet été si tu travailles**? Have the first student from each team go to the front of the room and write on the board a complete sentence to answer the question, for example, **Si je travaille cet été, je serai vendeur/vendeuse**. If both students write a correct response, the student who finishes first wins the point for that round. Then have the next two players come to the board and write answers to the second question, and so on. The team with the most points at the end of the game wins.

Workbook Activities 12-13

Answers

8 Possible answers:

1. Si les voyageurs veulent aller rapidement entre Londres et Paris, ils passeront par l'Eurotunnel.
2. Si les touristes veulent aller rapidement entre Lyon et Paris, ils prendront le TGV.
3. Si on veut voir le centre spatial d'où on lance la fusée Ariane, on ira à Kourou.
4. Si on veut trouver l'inforoute, on cliquera avec la souris.
5. Si les élèves veulent faire des recherches, ils accéderont au web.
6. Si on veut aider la défense des animaux, on parlera à la Fondation Brigitte Bardot.
7. Si les médecins veulent participer à des missions humanitaires, ils travailleront pour Médecins Sans Frontières.
8. Si les élèves veulent essayer de sauvegarder la terre, ils écriront des articles pour le journal de leur lycée.

Teacher's Notes

1. A clause with **quand** is placed at the end of the sentence for emphasis. 2. When the verb of the main clause is in the near future or in the imperative and it implies a future event, the future is also used after **quand**, for example, **Quand je serai à Saint-Martin, je vais te téléphoner** and **Quand je serai à Saint-Martin, téléphone-moi!** 3. After the conjunctions **lorsque**, **aussitôt que** and **dès que**, **que** becomes **qu'** before a word that begins with a vowel or a vowel sound. 4. **Tant que** (*as long as*) is another conjunction that takes the future.

Critical Thinking

Clauses with Conjunctions

Write sentences on the board using the conjunctions **lorsque**, **aussitôt que** and **dès que**, for example, **Lorsque je finirai mes études à l'université, je serai comptable. Tu rendras visite à ton correspondant aussitôt que tu arriveras à Paris. Dès que tu liras l'article, tu comprendras la lutte pour la défense des animaux.** Ask students what tense is used in English after each conjunction. Students should tell you that in English these conjunctions take the present tense. This activity will help students remember that these conjunctions take the present in English but the future in French.

Modèle:

On veut étudier l'océanographie.
Si on veut étudier l'océanographie, on lira les livres de Jacques-Yves Cousteau.

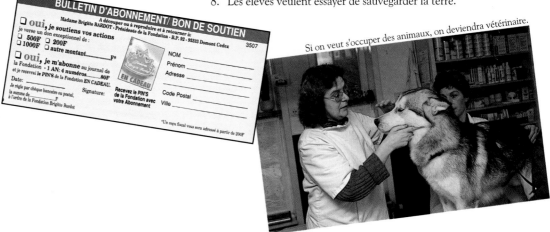

8 | *Que fera-t-on dans chaque situation suivante? Offrez une résolution en écrivant une phrase avec* **si**.

1. Les voyageurs veulent aller rapidement entre Londres et Paris.
2. Les touristes veulent aller rapidement entre Lyon et Paris.
3. On veut voir le centre spatial d'où on lance la fusée Ariane.
4. On veut trouver l'inforoute.
5. Les élèves veulent faire des recherches.
6. On veut aider la défense des animaux.
7. Les médecins veulent participer à des missions humanitaires.
8. Les élèves veulent essayer de sauvegarder la terre.

Si on veut s'occuper des animaux, on deviendra vétérinaire.

Future tense after *quand*

Another use of the future tense is to tell what will happen *when* something else happens in the future. Here is the order of tenses in these sentences with **quand**:

quand + future	future

Quand je deviendrai médecin, je travaillerai pour Médecins Sans Frontières.

When I become a doctor, I will work for Médecins Sans Frontières.

Quand tu seras adulte, que feras-tu comme métier ou profession?

Note that the verb tense after **quand** in the French and English sentences is different. When referring to future events, both French verbs are in the future, whereas the English verb following "when" is in the present tense.

You also use the future tense after the conjunctions **lorsque** (*when*), **aussitôt que** (*as soon as*) and **dès que** (*as soon as*).

Aussitôt qu'ils seront tous là, ils parleront du prochain numéro.	*As soon as they are all there, they will talk about the next issue.*
Tu me rendras l'article dès que tu l'auras?	*Will you hand in the article to me as soon as you have it?*
Lorsqu'il y aura une guerre, les médecins viendront aider les gens.	*When there is a war, the doctors will come to help people.*

Note in the examples above that the phrase with **quand**, **lorsque**, **aussitôt que** or **dès que** can either begin or end the sentence.

Dès que les sandwichs seront prêts, Guillaume les vendra.

Pratique

Formez des phrases logiques pour dire ce qui se passera aussitôt que les personnes suivantes feront certaines choses. Choisissez un élément des colonnes A et B pour chaque phrase. Suivez le modèle.

Modèle:

Aussitôt que les élèves se brancheront, ils seront en ligne.

A	B
les élèves/se brancher	l'envoyer à l'imprimante
nous/recycler	apprécier ses efforts pour protéger la mer
le gouvernement/lancer plus de satellites	en dépenser
Yves/accéder au web	développer sa connaissance de l'espace
les reporters/être tous là	parler du prochain numéro
Élise/finir son article	être en ligne
vous/sauvegarder le document	commencer à sauvegarder la terre
tu/trouver de l'argent	trouver des renseignements utiles
je/lire un livre de Cousteau	le rendre à son chef

Votre partenaire et vous, comment passerez-vous le reste de votre journée? L'Élève A demande à l'Élève B ce qu'il ou elle fera lorsqu'il ou elle sortira du cours de français. L'Élève A continue à poser des questions à l'Élève B fondées sur les réponses qu'il ou elle reçoit. Quand l'Élève B ne peut plus répondre aux questions, il faut changer de rôles. Suivez le modèle.

Modèle:

Élève A: Qu'est-ce que tu feras lorsque tu sortiras du cours de français?

Élève B: Lorsque je sortirai du cours de français, je rentrerai chez moi.

Élève A: Et qu'est-ce que tu feras lorsque tu rentreras chez toi?

Élève B: Lorsque je rentrerai chez moi, je....

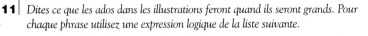

Audiocassette/CD Activity 11

Answers

11 1. Quand Thérèse et sa cousine seront grandes, elles construiront des maisons.

2. Quand mes copains et moi, nous serons grands, nous nourrirons les sans-abri.

3. Quand tu seras grand(e), tu établiras un refuge pour les animaux.

4. Quand Chloé sera grande, elle fera un documentaire sur la vie dans les océans.

5. Quand Serge et toi, vous serez grands, vous travaillerez pour l'environnement.

6. Quand je serai grand(e), je serai médecin.

7. Quand Alain sera grand, il ira en mission humanitaire.

8. Quand tous les ados seront grands, ils deviendront plus engagés.

Paired Practice

La capsule témoin

To provide students with additional practice forming sentences with **quand** and the future, put them in pairs. Tell them that they are preparing a time capsule for students at school to open in the year 2080. Have the pairs make a list of representative items that will show future students what life was like during their high school years. Students should include a book or magazine, a film, a CD and a game. Then have them discuss what the students in 2080 will do when they open the capsule, for example, **Quand les élèves de 2080 ouvriront la capsule témoin, ils liront *People* (ils verront *Titanic*, ils écouteront Tori Amos, ils joueront au MarioKart).** Finally, have each pair make a presentation to the class, with each student describing two of the activities that future students will do when they open the time capsule.

11 Dites ce que les ados dans les illustrations feront quand ils seront grands. Pour chaque phrase utilisez une expression logique de la liste suivante.

Modèle:

Lucien et Abdou
Quand Lucien et Abdou seront grands, ils dénonceront le commerce de fourrure.

Quand vous arrêterez Bond, vous ferez quoi?

Quand Zakia sera grande, elle sera infirmière.

être médecin	aller en mission humanitaire
nourrir les sans-abri	travailler pour l'environnement
construire des maisons	établir un refuge pour les animaux
faire un documentaire sur la vie dans les océans	dénoncer le commerce de fourrure
	devenir plus engagés

1. Thérèse et sa cousine   5. Serge et toi, vous

2. mes copains et moi, nous   6. je

3. tu   7. Alain

4. Chloé   8. tous les ados

Dès que

To provide practice with the conjunction **dès que** and the future tense, put students in pairs. Prepare a worksheet listing infinitive expressions, such as **se lever**, that students will use to inquire about what their partner expects to do as soon as he or she does something else tomorrow morning. Student A uses the first infinitive expression on the worksheet to form a question using **dès que** that Student B answers, for example, **Qu'est-ce que tu feras demain dès que tu te lèveras? Je prendrai une douche dès que je me lèverai.** Then Student B forms a question using the second infinitive expression and Student A answers. Other infinitive expressions that you might include are **prendre le petit déjeuner, se brosser les dents,** **s'habiller, quitter la maison, arriver à l'école, arriver en classe** and **arriver à la cantine.**

Communication

Avec un(e) partenaire, choisissez une mission humanitaire particulière qui vous intéresse. Puis jouez les rôles d'un reporter d'un journal français et d'une personne qui participe à cette mission. Pour faire des recherches avant d'écrire son article sur des missions humanitaires, le reporter doit interviewer la personne engagée pour savoir tous les détails possibles:

- *le nom de la mission*
- *les buts (goals) de cette mission*
- *pourquoi la personne a choisi cette mission*
- *les problèmes qui existent aujourd'hui*
- *ce qui se passera si cette mission ne réussit pas*
- *les progrès qu'on a déjà faits*
- *ce que les gens peuvent faire pour aider*
- *ce qui se passera aussitôt que cette mission réussira*

Il vaut mieux que le reporter prenne des notes pendant qu'il parle à la personne engagée. Après l'interview, changez de rôles, choisissez une autre mission humanitaire et répétez l'activité.

Pourquoi as-tu choisi de lutter pour la défense des animaux?

J'ai lu l'info-journal de la Fondation Brigitte Bardot.

Imaginez que le chef du journal français s'intéresse beaucoup à l'article que vous lui avez proposé sur des missions humanitaires. Avant de publier l'article, le chef exige que vous lui rendiez un petit sommaire de votre interview de l'Activité 12. Écrivez ce sommaire en vous servant de vos notes.

Sur la bonne piste

To appreciate poetry, it is helpful to understand figures of speech and rhyme scheme. Writers create vivid images by using figures of speech, statements that have more than a straightforward, literal meaning. What do the figures of speech in the following two sentences have in common, and how are they different?

> Jennifer is a dancing willow, bending and twisting in the wind.
> Jennifer dances like a willow that bends and twists in the wind.

In the first sentence, Jennifer is described as if she were a willow tree. This is an example of a metaphor, a figure of speech in which one person or thing is described as if it were another. You learned about metaphors in **Unité 8** in the second level of *C'est à toi!* In the second sentence, Jennifer is compared to a willow, but she is not described as if she were the tree itself. This is a simile (**une comparaison**), a figure of speech that makes a comparison using *like* or *as* (**comme** in French). Both metaphors and similes are analyzed by division into two parts, a subject and an object. Jennifer is the subject, and the object is the willow.

Poets and songwriters often use rhyme scheme (**l'agencement des rimes**) to organize their verses. A rhyme scheme is a pattern of end rhymes, words that rhyme at the ends of lines of poetry. The rhyme scheme of a poem is designated by letters, with matching letters signifying matching sounds. Each time a new sound is introduced at the end of a line, a new letter (*a*, *b*, *c*, etc.) is used. Can you figure out the rhyme scheme of Emily Dickinson's poem "The Brain—is wider than the Sky—"? Is it *abba*, *abca* or *abcb*?

Teacher's Notes

1. Before students begin Activity 12, you might encourage them to gather information about their specific humanitarian mission, formulate their ideas, and review or learn the vocabulary they will need for their interviews. You may want to tell the reporters to write out in advance the questions they plan to ask. 2. **Sur la bonne piste, Leçon B**, is designed to develop skills that will help students prepare to take the Advanced Placement Exam in French Literature. In this section, students read a variety of prose, poetry and drama from different periods; answer content questions; and demonstrate their critical understanding of literary techniques, such as character development, setting, point of view, satire, figures of speech and inference. In this **Sur la bonne piste** section, students learn about figures of speech and rhyme scheme.

Cross-curricular

Newspaper Articles

After completing Activities 12 and 13, have students write a newspaper article about the humanitarian mission they learned about. Students can gather additional information on the Internet about **la Fondation Brigitte Bardot, Médecins Sans Frontières, l'Équipe Cousteau**, or any other humanitarian organization that interests them. (See the teacher's notes on pages 246-47 for the Internet addresses of these organizations.) You may want to ask a journalist or the newspaper advisor at your school to give a presentation to your class on tips for writing effective newspaper articles. When the articles are finished, select one for each humanitarian organization that students selected and print them in a class newspaper for all students to read. You may want to call your newspaper *Un Monde Meilleur*.

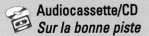

Teacher's Notes

1. Maxime LeForestier, born in Paris in 1949, has been on the French music scene since the 1960s. He began his career singing as a duo with his older sister Catherine. His first album, *Parachutiste*, was released in 1972. His **discographie** includes the titles *Enregistrement Public* (1974), *Maxime LeForestier Chante Brassens* (1979), *Les Rendez-vous Manqués* (1980), *Les Jours Meilleurs* (1984), *Bataclan 1989* and *Passer Ma Route* (1994). In 1996 LeForestier recorded 12 of the songs that Georges Brassens left unedited at his death (*12 Nouvelles de Brassens*). His latest CD is titled *Essentielles* (1997). 2. Before students analyze the lyrics of the song, you may want to play the song for your students. Distribute a copy of the song with blanks for the words that students already know. Then play the song and have students write in the missing words. You might also consider placing the words that will be filled in at the bottom of the page. Then students can cross them off as they fill in the blanks. This activity will give students confidence that they have the vocabulary to understand the song's lyrics. 3. Ask students to find the two examples of the future tense in the song. Point out how the first example, **s'envoleront**, represents an optimistic view of the future, while the second, **arrachera**, suggests a more pessimistic conclusion. Ask students to consider whether LeForestier's viewpoint about the fate of nature in the postindustrial age is essentially optimistic or pessimistic.

The Brain is deeper than the sea—
For—hold them—Blue to Blue—
The one the other will *absorb*—
As Sponges—Buckets—do—

The rhyme scheme of this stanza of Emily Dickinson's poem is *abcb*. "Sea" doesn't rhyme with any of the other end words in the stanza, so the *a* representing this line is not repeated. "Blue" rhymes with "do," so both these lines are described as *b*. "Absorb" is labeled *c* because it is yet another different sound; like *a*, it is not repeated because it has no rhyming match.

As you read "Comme un Arbre," decide what rhyme scheme the French singer Maxime LeForestier uses. Then look for the repeated simile that connects this song-poem about the problems of modern life in the city.

14 *Avant de lire la chanson, répondez aux questions suivantes.*

1. Est-ce que tu habites dans une grande ville? Si oui, aimes-tu y habiter ou pas?
2. Quels problèmes y a-t-il dans les grandes villes?
3. Te sens-tu isolé(e) quand tu es avec des gens que tu ne connais pas?
4. À ton avis, en quoi est-ce qu'une personne ressemble à un arbre?

Comme un Arbre

Comme un arbre dans la ville
Je suis né dans le béton
Coincé entre deux maisons
Sans abri sans domicile
Comme un arbre dans la ville.

Comme un arbre dans la ville
J'ai grandi loin des futaies
Où mes frères des forêts
Ont fondé une famille
Comme un arbre dans la ville.

Entre béton et bitume
Pour pousser je me débats
Mais mes branches volent bas
Si près des autos qui fument
Entre béton et bitume.

Comme un arbre dans la ville
J'ai la fumée des usines
Pour prison, et mes racines
On les recouvre de grilles
Comme un arbre dans la ville.

Comme un arbre dans la ville
J'ai des chansons sur mes feuilles
Qui s'envoleront sous l'œil
De vos fenêtres serviles
Comme un arbre dans la ville.

Entre béton et bitume
On m'arrachera des rues
Pour bâtir où j'ai vécu
Des parkings d'honneur posthume
Entre béton et bitume.

Comme un arbre dans la ville
Ami, fais, après ma mort
Barricades de mon corps
Et du feu de mes brindilles
Comme un arbre dans la ville.

Répondez aux questions suivantes.

1. Quel est l'agencement des rimes de la première strophe (*stanza*)?
2. Quelle est la comparaison qui est répétée, ou à quoi l'habitant (*resident*) de la ville se compare-t-il?
3. L'habitant est-il né dans la ville ou à la campagne?
4. A-t-il une maison?
5. Vit-il avec d'autres membres de sa famille?
6. Dans la troisième strophe, de quoi la ville est-elle composée?
7. Qu'est-ce qui empêche (*prevents*) le développement de l'habitant de la ville, selon la troisième strophe?
8. Dans la quatrième strophe, qu'est-ce qui emprisonne l'habitant de la ville?
9. Que signifie la ligne "J'ai des chansons sur mes feuilles"?
10. Pourquoi arrachera-t-on l'arbre?
11. Dans la dernière strophe, que veut l'habitant de la ville?

La Pollution

Dans tous les pays,
Dans toutes les villes,
Dans toutes les rues,
La pollution!

Dans tous les océans,
Dans toutes les mers,
Dans tous les cours d'eau,
La pollution!

Sur toute la terre,
Dans les airs et dans l'espace
Partout, elle est là,
La pollution!

Mais qui est le responsable
de ce fléau des temps modernes?
C'est encore lui: l'HOMME!

Anthony, 9 ans
École de la Mairie
Algrange, France

Answers

15 Possible answers:

1. L'agencement des rimes de la première strophe est *abbaa*.
2. L'habitant de la ville se compare à un arbre dans la ville.
3. Il est né dans la ville.
4. Non, il n'a pas de maison. C'est un sans-abri.
5. Non, il ne vit pas avec d'autres membres de sa famille.
6. La ville est composée de béton et bitume.
7. La pollution des autos empêche son développement.
8. La fumée des usines et les grilles l'emprisonnent.
9. L'habitant sait fêter la vie.
10. On arrachera l'arbre pour bâtir des parkings.
11. Il veut qu'on se souvienne de lui après sa mort.

Teacher's Note

Some new words used in the song and cognates not found in the end vocabulary of *C'est à toi!* are used to ask questions about "Comme un Arbre" in Activity 15.

Teacher's Notes

1. Optional activity. Put students in small groups. Distribute a collection of famous French poems with rhyme schemes to each group. Have students decipher the rhyme scheme for each poem. Then go over the rhyme schemes so that groups can check their answers. Next, challenge students to find examples of similes and metaphors in the poems and list them on the board. 2. Optional activity. Have students pictorially depict the meaning of the song's theme. Students might draw the urban landscape described in the poem or cut out pictures from magazines and make a collage. 3. Optional activity. Put students in groups of seven. Have each group member memorize one of the stanzas of the song. Then have each group practice reciting the song with books closed. Finally, have one of the groups present the song to the class. 4. You might encourage students to find the lyrics to other LeForestier songs on the Internet. 5. Other **chanteurs engagés** that you might consider introducing to students include Georges Brassens, Serge Reggiani, Michel Berger, Daniel Balavoine, Renaud and Francis Cabrel. 6. Optional activity. Challenge students to find a contemporary **chanson engagée** in English. You might play some of the songs that students bring to class and use them to motivate students before they begin Activity 18. 7. Some students may be interested in putting the poems they write in Activity 18 to music.

16 | *Faites une liste des mots de la chanson qui sont associés à la ville. Puis écrivez un paragraphe où vous décrivez une scène de la ville en utilisant des mots de cette liste.*

17 | *Complétez les comparaisons suivantes en utilisant "comme."*

    1. Je danse....
    2. Mon ami(e) court....
    3. Mon père conduit....
    4. Mon prof de français chante....
    5. Ma chambre est....
    6. Le temps est....

18 | *Écrivez un poème avec une comparaison et l'agencement des rimes* abbaa. *Comme sujet vous pouvez considérer un jardin, une fête, un voyage, la nuit, la mer, l'amitié* (friendship), *la Fondation Brigitte Bardot, Médecins Sans Frontières ou Jacques-Yves Cousteau.*

Dossier fermé

Tu es dans un hôtel en France, et tu as besoin de téléphoner à quelqu'un, mais tu ne sais pas son numéro de téléphone. L'hôtel n'a pas d'annuaire (le livre avec les numéros de téléphone), et tu ne connais pas le numéro des "Renseignements." Qu'est-ce que tu fais?

    A. Tu demandes à la réception de chercher le numéro de téléphone sur le Minitel.

Le Minitel offre une liste alphabétique de tous les Français qui ont le téléphone.

Pourriez-vous chercher un numéro de téléphone sur le Minitel pour moi?

C'est à moi!

Now that you have completed this unit, take a look at what you should be able to do in French. Can you do all of these tasks?

➤ I can ask for and give information about various topics, including what people will do.

➤ I can talk about things sequentially.

➤ I can list things.

➤ I can explain how to do something.

➤ I can give my opinion by saying what I think.

➤ I can express enthusiasm.

➤ I can make an assumption.

➤ I can say what will probably happen.

➤ I can make a prediction.

➤ I can congratulate someone.

➤ I can express appreciation.

➤ I can tell someone not to forget something.

➤ I can request what I would like.

Pour voir si vous avez bien compris la culture francophone, décidez si chaque phrase est vraie ou fausse.

1. La vitesse moyenne du TGV est de 500 kilomètres à l'heure.
2. L'Eurostar est le train qui passe par l'Eurotunnel pour faire le voyage entre Londres et Paris.
3. On a construit l'Eurotunnel très rapidement.
4. L'Agence spatiale européenne lance les satellites de Kourou en Guyane française.
5. Le Minitel est un système d'ordinateurs multimédia qui permet de se brancher sur Internet.
6. La protection des animaux intéresse Brigitte Bardot.
7. La Fondation Brigitte Bardot a eu du succès en arrêtant des expérimentations animales et en limitant la surpopulation des chats et des chiens.
8. Médecins Sans Frontières dépend des gouvernements pour lancer ses missions humanitaires.
9. Le Ruanda est un pays troublé par la guerre et les maladies.
10. Jacques-Yves Cousteau a ouvert les secrets de l'océan à la population qui regarde la télévision.

Answers

1. fausse
2. vraie
3. fausse
4. vraie
5. fausse
6. vraie
7. vraie
8. fausse
9. vraie
10. vraie

Communication orale

À votre avis, quelle est l'avance technologique la plus importante du 20ᵉ siècle? Pour connaître les opinions de vos camarades de classe, faites une enquête. Copiez la grille à la page 260. Puis parlez à trois élèves, et demandez-leur de vous dire leur choix pour l'avance du siècle. Ils peuvent choisir une avance technologique dans le domaine de la vie quotidienne, de la science ou des loisirs.

Demandez-leur aussi de vous expliquer pourquoi ils pensent que cette avance est si importante. Enfin demandez-leur de vous dire comment cette avance a changé la vie des gens. Complétez la grille selon leurs réponses à vos questions.

	l'avance du siècle	pourquoi elle est si importante	comment elle a changé la vie des gens
Justin	le web	La communication quotidienne devient plus facile.	On se sert moins du téléphone. On peut faire du shopping sans quitter la maison.
Caro			
Fred			

Communication écrite

Vous venez de parler des avances technologiques du 20ᵉ siècle et comment elles ont changé la vie des gens. Mais, comme vous le savez bien, le 21ᵉ siècle commence. Essayez de devenir voyant(e) et de prévoir (foresee) quelles avances il y aura dans ce nouveau siècle. Puis écrivez une rédaction où vous décrivez les avances technologiques qu'on fera à l'avenir. Quels en seront les effets dans le domaine de la vie quotidienne, de la science et des loisirs? Comment changeront-elles la vie des gens? Quels problèmes ces avances résoudront-elles? À votre avis, ces avances créeront-elles de nouveaux problèmes?

Communication active

To ask for information use:

Tu parleras de quoi? — *What will you talk about?*
Tu choisiras quoi? — *What will you choose?*

To give information, use:

Je parlerai de la Fondation Brigitte Bardot. — *I will talk about the Brigitte Bardot Foundation.*

Le titre de l'article **sera** "La lutte pour la défense des animaux." — *The title of the article will be "The Fight for the Defense of Animals."*

La France **dépense** 300 milliards de francs par an pour la recherche spatiale. — *France spends 300 billion francs per year for space research.*

Aussitôt que je finirai le journal, je viendrai à table.

To sequence events, use:

En plus, il y a aujourd'hui des Français qui sont en ligne avec un ordinateur qui permet d'accéder au web. — *In addition, today there are French people who are online with a computer that allows them to access the Web.*

Au 21ᵉ siècle on se branchera sur le monde entier. — *In the 21st century we will connect to the whole world.*

Aussitôt qu'ils seront tous là, ils parleront du prochain numéro. — *As soon as they are all there, they will talk about the next issue.*

🎧 **Listening Activity 3**

Tu me rendras l'article **dès que** tu l'auras?	*You will hand in the article to me as soon as you have it?*
Lorsqu'il y aura de la pauvreté, les médecins viendront aider les gens.	*When there is poverty, doctors will come to help people.*

To list, use:

Voici quelques adresses utiles où vous pourrez trouver tout ce qui vous intéresse.	*Here are some useful addresses where you will be able to find everything that interests you.*

On n'a qu'à appuyer sur les touches du clavier pour travailler sur ordinateur.

To explain something, use:

On n'a qu'à cliquer avec la souris pour trouver l'inforoute.	*All you have to do is click on the mouse to find the information superhighway.*

To give opinions, use:

La connaissance scientifique **sera aussi** utile **aux** gens **qu'aux** sciences. **Excellent.**	*Scientific knowledge will be as useful to people as to science. Excellent.*

To express enthusiasm, use:

C'est passionnant. **Excellent.**	*That's exciting. Excellent.*

To hypothesize, use:

Si les animaux **sont** maltraités, la fondation **viendra** les aider.	*If animals are mistreated, the foundation will come to help.*

To express probability, use:

La connaissance scientifique **permettra** une vie plus longue et plus riche.	*Scientific knowledge will permit a longer and richer life.*

To predict, use:

L'ESA **aura** bientôt le plus grand pourcentage sur le marché de lanceurs de satellites commerciaux.	*The ESA will soon have the largest percentage of the market in commercial satellite launchers.*
Quand je deviendrai médecin, je **travaillerai** pour Médecins Sans Frontières.	*When I become a doctor, I will work for Médecins Sans Frontières.*

N'oubliez pas de finir vos devoirs pour demain.

To congratulate someone, use:

Bravo!	*Well done!*

To express appreciation, use:

Grâce à elle, le commerce de fourrure de bébés phoques a été interdit.	*Thanks to her, the fur trade in baby seals has been prohibited.*

To tell someone not to forget, use:

N'oubliez pas de me rendre vos articles avant vendredi à 16h00.	*Don't forget to hand in your articles to me before Friday at 4:00.*

To make requests, use:

Rends-moi l'article avant vendredi **si tu peux.**	*Hand in the article to me before Friday if you can.*

Unité 7

Les Français comme ils sont

In this unit you will be able to:

➤ ask for information

➤ report

➤ state a generalization

➤ explain something

➤ request clarification

➤ clarify

➤ compare

➤ express importance and unimportance

➤ inquire about opinions

➤ ask about preference

➤ state preference

➤ propose solutions

➤ inquire about satisfaction and dissatisfaction

➤ express surprise

➤ agree and disagree

➤ describe character

➤ express compassion

Tes empreintes ici

Est-ce qu'il y a des élèves d'autres pays dans ton école? Si oui, de quels pays viennent-ils? Savez-vous pourquoi ils sont venus aux États-Unis? Est-ce que leurs parents ont un nouvel emploi ici, par exemple? Est-ce que les ados américains acceptent bien ces élèves? Est-ce que les jeunes de ton école sont accueillants? Qu'est-ce que l'école fait pour ces nouveaux élèves? Qu'est-ce que tu fais pour eux?

As-tu jamais visité un pays francophone? Si oui, quel pays? Est-ce que ce pays ressemble aux États-Unis? Comment étaient les gens? Par exemple, étaient-ils très accueillants? Comment décrirais-tu la culture de ce pays?

Connais-tu un élève qui vienne du Sénégal?

Leçon A

In this lesson you will be able to:

➤ ask for information

➤ state a generalization

➤ explain something

➤ compare

➤ request clarification

➤ inquire about opinions

➤ express surprise

➤ inquire about satisfaction and dissatisfaction

➤ propose solutions

Teacher's Note

Communicative functions that are recycled in this lesson are "expressing intentions," "describing past events," "telling location," "making suggestions," "comparing things," "hypothesizing," "giving opinions" and "expressing fear."

Dossier ouvert

Avant ton départ pour la France, ta bonne amie t'a donné de l'argent et t'a demandé de lui acheter un ensemble parisien très chic. Maintenant que tu es à Paris, à quel magasin iras-tu pour acheter cet ensemble?

    A. Tu iras à Mammouth.
    B. Tu iras aux Galeries Lafayette.
    C. Tu iras à Monoprix.

l'Afrique

le Togo

une cité

une HLM

des résidents (m.)

des graffiti (m.)

Non au F.N!

À bas l'école!

Jérôme + Cécile

Claudette + Jacques

un mur

des passants (m.)

 **Workbook
Activity 1**

 Audiocassette/CD
La cité

Transparencies 3-4

Teacher's Notes

1. **Une cité** can also refer to a student hall of residence (**une cité universitaire**). 2. **HLM** is the abbreviation for **habitation à loyer modéré**. As in the United States, public housing developments in France are physically grouped together. However, in some parts of Paris, HLMs are interspersed with private housing developments in an attempt to create a more integrated living environment where no one feels excluded from society. Consequently, in some developments juvenile delinquency is practically nonexistent. There are more than three million HLM units in France. The first HLMs were constructed in 1894 to provide clean and comfortable housing for workers drawn to the cities by industrial jobs. Since 1980 1,300,000 apartments have been built or rehabilitated. In 1996 HLM construction created 20,000 jobs. 3. The feminine form of **un résident** is **une résidente**. 4. **Graffiti** is invariable in the plural. 5. The feminine form of **un passant** is **une passante**. 6. Other related terms include **togolais(e)** (*Togolese*), **un(e) Togolais(e)** (*Togolander*), **un(e) concierge** (*caretaker*), **défavorisé(e)** (*disadvantaged, underprivileged*), **la xénophobie** (*xenophobia*), **xénophobe** (*xenophobic*), **une subvention** (*subsidy*) and **subventionné(e)** (*subsidized*).

**Workbook
Activity 2**

**Audiocassette/CD
Dialogue**

Teacher's Notes

1. You may want to point out that Valérie was one of the reporters for *Un Monde Meilleur* in Unit 6.
2. The noun **immigration (f.)** was introduced in Unit 7 in the second level of *C'est à toi!* 3. **Vue** is a past participle used as an adjective describing the feminine noun **immigration**. Past participles used this way are not listed separately in the end vocabulary. 4. Explain that **T'es** is a colloquial abbreviation of **Tu es**. 5. Point out that the French expression **Vous êtes combien?** asks "How many are you?" instead of "How many of you are there?"
6. By extension, **une HLM** can refer to an entire **cité**, rather than to just one building. 7. Champigny, a city of approximately 80,000 people, is located about nine miles east of Paris on the left bank of the Marne River. Cité Jardins is the oldest of three **cités** located in Champigny. Begun in 1931, its schools and recreation center were added in 1936. 8. The adjective **déprimé(e)** was introduced in Unit 3 in the third level of *C'est à toi!* 9. **La plupart** is followed by **de** plus the definite article.

Valérie est un des reporters d'*Un Monde Meilleur*, le journal de son lycée. Elle va écrire un article au sujet de l'immigration en France vue par un de ses copains. Elle a pris rendez-vous avec Kofi Andjou, un immigré du Togo, dans un café près du lycée. Quelle sera l'opinion de Kofi?

Valérie:	Salut, Kofi! T'es prêt?
Kofi:	Salut, Valérie! Oui, allons-y.
Valérie:	Alors, commençons au début. Depuis combien de temps es-tu en France?
Kofi:	Ben, ma famille et moi, nous sommes ici depuis un an et demi.
Valérie:	Vous êtes combien?
Kofi:	Nous sommes cinq, trois enfants et mes parents.
Valérie:	Pourquoi êtes-vous venus vous installer en France?
Kofi:	Pour plusieurs raisons.
Valérie:	Lesquelles° sont les plus importantes?
Kofi:	Ben, il y a un meilleur choix d'emplois ici et les études universitaires sont plus intéressantes.
Valérie:	Où habitez-vous?
Kofi:	Maintenant nous sommes dans une HLM moderne dont les immeubles sont assez nouveaux. L'année dernière nous habitions une autre HLM.
Valérie:	Ah bon?° Laquelle?
Kofi:	L'HLM Cité Jardins à Champigny.
Valérie:	Ah oui? Je la connais. Comment était l'ambiance de la cité?
Kofi:	C'était plutôt déprimant.°
Valérie:	Comment déprimant?
Kofi:	La plupart° des résidents étaient au chômage.

lesquelles *which ones*; **Ah bon?** *Vraiment?*; **déprimant(e)** *depressing*; **la plupart (de)** *la majorité (de)*

Valérie: D'où venaient les immigrés?

Kofi: Beaucoup de familles d'immigrés, dont les pays d'origine sont les pays maghrébins° et d'autres pays africains, y habitaient.

Valérie: Est-ce que les résidents s'entendaient bien?

Kofi: Les relations entre les résidents étaient tendues.° On appelait° notre HLM un "huit cent huit" car° il y avait 808 apparte-ments. La cité était plutôt comme une cage à lapins. En plus, parce qu'il n'y avait pas beaucoup d'activités pour les jeunes, ils perdaient leur temps° dans la rue. Ils agressaient° les passants et les résidents avec qui ils ne sympathisaient pas.

Valérie: S'il y avait plus d'activités et moins de chômage, est-ce que les relations seraient meilleures?

Kofi: Je crois que oui. À l'HLM où nous habitons maintenant, l'ambiance est différente.

Valérie: Qu'est-ce qu'il y a de différent?

Kofi: Le climat social est différent. Il y a plus de Français parmi les résidents et moins de familles qui touchent° les allocations. Bien sûr, presque toutes les familles touchent les allocations familiales, mais c'est parce qu'elles ont des enfants. Le pour-centage des chômeurs° est moins grand. En plus, c'est plus beau. Il n'y a pas de graffiti sur les murs. Des espaces verts se trouvent partout. Tout est propre.°

Dans la région parisienne, il y a des HLM qui ressemblent aux autres immeubles. (Créteil)

Valérie: Selon toi, à quel avenir° les immigrés peuvent-ils s'attendre?

Kofi: En général, je trouve que les Français acceptent bien les étrangers,° mais il y en a qui ont peur que les immigrés prennent leurs emplois. Ce n'est pas vrai. Les immigrés prennent souvent des emplois très durs dont les autres ne veulent pas.

Valérie: Parmi les immigrés, lesquels ont des ennuis?

Kofi: Aucun groupe n'a plus d'ennuis qu'un autre. La façon dont on traite les gens dépend plus de l'apparence d'une personne que de sa nationalité ou de son pays d'origine.

Valérie: Es-tu optimiste?

Kofi: Naturellement. Si on acceptait que la France est un pays d'immigrés depuis longtemps, on pourrait mieux profiter de la diversité culturelle. De plus, on se rendrait compte que les immigrés sont prêts à travailler et à s'intégrer dans la société française.

Valérie: Merci beaucoup, Kofi. J'espère que nos copains deviendront plus sensibles au côté humain de l'immigration en lisant mon article dans le prochain numéro du journal.

maghrébin(e) du Maghreb (le Maroc, l'Algérie, la Tunisie); **tendu(e)** *strained*; **appeler** *to call*; **car** parce que; **perdre son temps** *to waste one's time*; **agresser** attaquer; **toucher** recevoir; **un chômeur, une chômeuse** une personne au chômage; **propre** *clean*; **l'avenir (m.)** le futur; **un étranger, une étrangère** une personne d'un autre pays

Teacher's Notes

1. You may want to remind students that **le Maghreb** refers to the combined region of Algeria, Morocco and Tunisia. **Le Maghreb** was the subject of the cultural reading beginning on page 231 in the second level of *C'est à toi!* 2. Students learned the singular forms of **s'appeler** in the first level of *C'est à toi!* **S'appeler** also appeared in Unit 4 in the third level. 3. Students learned **toucher**, meaning "to cash," in Unit 11 in the first level of *C'est à toi!* 4. Explain that **l'avenir** refers to the future in time while **le futur** refers to the tense. **Futur(e)** can also be used as an adjective, as in **son futur mari** (*her future husband*). 5. In formal French **avoir peur que** should be followed by the pleonastic **ne** before the subjunctive: **Il y en a qui ont peur que les immigrés ne prennent leurs emplois.** In the dialogue the pleonastic **ne** has been dropped, as it often is in casual conversation. 6. Here are the present tense forms of the orthographically changing verb **s'intégrer**: **je m'intègre, tu t'intègres, il/elle/on s'intègre, nous nous intégrons, vous vous intégrez** and **ils/elles s'intègrent.**

Audiocassette/CD Activity 1

Answers

1 Possible answers:

1. Le prochain article de Valérie est au sujet de l'immigration en France vue par un copain.

2. Valérie a pris rendez-vous avec Kofi Andjou. Il n'est pas français; c'est un immigré du Togo.

3. Les raisons les plus importantes sont la possibilité d'avoir un meilleur choix d'emplois et de faire ses études à l'université.

4. Les pays d'origine des résidents de l'HLM Cité Jardins à Champigny sont les pays maghrébins et d'autres pays africains.

5. On dit que l'HLM Cité Jardins était un "huit cent huit" car il y avait 808 appartements.

6. Il décrit la cité où il habitait comme une cage à lapins.

7. Parce qu'il n'y avait pas beaucoup d'activités pour les jeunes, ils perdaient leur temps dans la rue et agressaient les passants et les résidents avec qui ils ne sympathisaient pas.

8. Là où Kofi habite maintenant, il y a plus de Français parmi les résidents, il y a moins de familles qui touchent les allocations, le pourcentage des chômeurs est moins grand, c'est plus beau et tout est propre.

9. Non, ce n'est pas vrai. Les immigrés prennent souvent des emplois très durs dont les autres ne veulent pas.

10. Les immigrés offrent une diversité culturelle à la société française.

2 1. maghrébins
2. origine
3. étrangers
4. allocations familiales
5. ambiance
6. tendues
7. perd son temps
8. propre
9. Lesquels

---

1 | *Répondez aux questions suivantes d'après le dialogue.*

1. Le prochain article de Valérie, c'est sur quoi?
2. Avec qui est-ce que Valérie a pris rendez-vous? Ce copain de Valérie, est-il français?
3. Pour quelles raisons est-ce que la famille de Kofi a déménagé en France?
4. Quels sont les pays d'origine des résidents de l'HLM Cité Jardins à Champigny?
5. Pourquoi est-ce qu'on dit que l'HLM Cité Jardins était un "huit cent h▶
6. Comment Kofi décrit-il la cité où il habitait?
7. Qu'est-ce que les jeunes y faisaient parce qu'il n'y avait pas beaucoup d'activités pour eux?
8. Comment le climat social est-il différent là où Kofi habite maintenant?
9. Est-ce vrai que les immigrés prennent les emplois des Français?
10. Qu'est-ce que les immigrés offrent à la société française?

---

2 | *Complétez chaque phrase avec l'expression convenable de la liste suivante d'après le dialogue.*

lesquels	maghrébins	étrangers
origine	ambiance	allocations familiales
propre	tendues	perd son temps

Les Aknouch sont une famille maghrébine. (La Rochelle)

1. Les trois pays... sont l'Algérie, le Maroc et la Tunisie.
2. Le Togo, c'est le pays d'... de Kofi.
3. Il y a beaucoup d'... qui ont réussi à s'intégrer dans la société française.
4. S'il y a plus de deux enfants dans une famille, la famille peut toucher d
5. L'... d'une cité est assez déprimante quand il y a beaucoup de résidents au chômage.
6. Si les relations entre les résidents sont difficiles, on peut dire qu'elles son
7. Quand on ne profite pas au maximum de son temps libre, on...
8. Tous les résidents apprécient un immeuble qui est....
9. ... des articles du journal sont les plus intéressants?

Cross-curricular

Cultural Diversity

Have the class make a list of the ethnic groups that live in your community. Tell students to select one of the groups and research it in the instructional materials center or library. Then ask students if they know a representative of each group in your community, and invite these people to be guest speakers. Have students prepare questions in advance to ask the guest speakers about their lives in their native countries, the culture there and their perceptions of American culture and how they learned to adjust to it.

C'est à toi!

1. Vous êtes combien dans ta famille?
2. Quelles sont les nationalités de tes grands-parents?
3. Depuis combien de temps habites-tu dans ta ville?
4. Penses-tu qu'il soit facile ou difficile pour une personne d'un autre pays de s'installer dans la ville où tu habites? Pourquoi?
5. Dans ta ville, où est-ce que tu vois souvent des graffiti?
6. Comment est l'ambiance du quartier où tu habites?
7. De quoi dépend la façon dont tu traites les gens?
8. Si tu devais habiter un autre pays pendant deux ans, quel pays choisirais-tu? Pourquoi?

Enquête culturelle

Le Togo est un petit pays de l'Afrique francophone avec une côte de 56 kilomètres sur l'océan Atlantique. Le climat est tropical et il fait chaud, surtout dans le sud du pays. La France a pris possession du Togo en 1919; il a gagné son indépendance de la France en 1960. L'influence française y est évidente partout. Le français est la langue officielle, et le système d'enseignement ressemble au système français. Le siège du gouvernement est à Lomé. Aujourd'hui la population du pays approche cinq millions d'habitants, mais il n'y a que 50 pour cent des habitants qui savent lire et écrire. L'économie dépend de l'agriculture qui emploie 60 pour cent de la population dans la production de coton, de café et de cacao. Ni la situation politique ni le franc africain n'est solide, donc le pays souffre de problèmes économiques. Quant à l'environnement, le Togo fait face à la déforestation parce qu'on continue à ravager les forêts. Même si le Togo est petit, il connaît les mêmes problèmes que les autres pays africains.

> Je suis togolais. Je parle français et ewé.

L'HLM (habitation à loyer modéré) est, depuis 100 ans, un système d'immeubles qui offre aux ouvriers des appartements confortables à un prix bon marché. Mais la clientèle a changé dans ces dernières années. Parce que le chômage, la pauvreté et le nombre de sans-abri sont en train d'augmenter, le gouvernement offre ces appartements aux personnes qui ne peuvent pas trouver un endroit pour vivre avec leur salaire. Un Français sur quatre habite une HLM. Les HLM représentent 10 pour cent du budget national français et 33 pour cent de toute la construction des immeubles en France. On continue à construire ces immeubles là où on peut trouver de l'espace. Mais l'HLM n'est pas toujours la meilleure solution. Certaines HLM sont mal construites, et les appartements sont trop petits, d'où vient le nom "cage à lapins." Dans la cité on y fait trop de bruit, et on n'y trouve pas toutes les choses dont on a besoin. La population typique d'une cité consiste d' immigrés et de familles avec des enfants. Sarcelles, pas loin de Paris, est une cité où il n'y a ni centre commercial, ni lycée et où il y a peu d'espaces verts. Cela provoque alors d'autres problèmes sociaux là où les relations sont déjà tendues.

Ces HLM se trouvent dans la Cité de l'Ophite à Lourdes.

Teacher's Note

Togo's relationship with Europe began in 1884 when a Togo chief signed a treaty with a representative of the German emperor. Formal German control of Togo began in 1884-85. After World War I the German territory of Togo was divided in two. The western portion became a British mandate, while the eastern part became a French mandate. For ten years, beginning in 1946, the two mandates became trust territories of the United Nations. In 1956 British Togoland became Ghana. French Togoland became the Republic of Togo when the country gained its independence from France. Togo's current president is General Gnassingbé Eyadéma, who has been in power since 1967.

1. Eligibility for **l'allocation logement** depends on a variety of factors, including income, geographic area and the number of persons in the household. For a single person, **l'allocation logement** specifies nine square meters of living space. Two people are entitled to 16 square meters. The maximum living space allowed for a family of eight or more is 70 square meters. 2. Immigrants of Arab heritage are sometimes called **beurs**, which has a negative connotation. 3. In 1995 over 50,000 immigrants entered France. Refugees currently account for 9.1 percent of the country's immigrant population. Twenty-nine percent are joining family members who have already immigrated, while 27 percent are joining French spouses. Twenty-six percent of immigrants are permanent workers. Immigrants tend to speak their native language at home and French outside the home. Three out of four second-generation immigrants speak French to their children. Fifty-two percent of the children of immigrants have to repeat a year of elementary school.

Cross-curricular

Immigration

To compare immigration patterns in the U.S. and France, have students research the following questions: In the U.S., what countries do the greatest number of immigrants come from? How many come from our neighboring countries? Do most immigrants live and work in big cities or in rural areas? What type of work do they do? What percentage of the U.S. population do immigrants comprise? Finally, have students make a chart comparing what they know about immigration in the U.S. and France.

Colonial Roots

Immigration is just one area where France's colonial past continues to impact the present. Focusing on Africa, have students research which countries were former French colonies, when they gained their independence and the relationship they currently have with France, especially economically. What raw materials does France import from former African colonies? What products do the African countries import from France?

Mais il y a d'autres cités qui sont mieux faites. Depuis 1981 on commence à construire des HLM en ville parmi d'autres immeubles où habite une population différente. La ville de Créteil, au sud-est de Paris, en est un bon exemple. Ici les résidents des HLM peuvent s'intégrer à la population du quartier. Tout le monde profite du même centre commercial et des mêmes écoles, et personne ne se sent exclu de la société. Comme résultat, la délinquance juvénile a été presque éliminée. En général, les conditions de vie dans les HLM pourraient être meilleures, mais pour beaucoup de gens, ces conditions sont déjà bien meilleures que d'être sans-abri.

Pour trois enfants, le gouvernement français donne un supplément de 0,73 pour cent en plus de la base des allocations familiales.

Les allocations familiales peuvent bénéficier à tout résident en France, même s'il n'est pas français, s'il a au moins deux enfants qui habitent en France. La famille reçoit une certaine somme d'argent comme base pour l'aider avec la nourriture, les vêtements et le logement. Les enfants doivent avoir moins de 18 ans (20 ans pour les étudiants). Pour chaque enfant on offre de l'argent supplémentaire. Les familles monoparentales peuvent aussi toucher les allocations familiales.

Les immigrés continuent à poser problème en France, surtout parce que l'immigration y reste limitée. Ils représentent huit pour cent de la population française. Trente pour cent des immigrés viennent du Maghreb (le Maroc, l'Algérie et la Tunisie). Ils viennent aussi du Portugal, d'Espagne et d'Italie. Ils vivent principalement dans les villes. Un immigré sur trois habite à Paris, surtout pour des raisons économiques puisqu'ils sont souvent embauchés dans l'industrie. Parce que les immigrés se considèrent souvent "de passage," ils n'ont tendance à acheter ni maisons ni appartements. Il y a beaucoup d'immigrés parmi les ouvriers parce qu'ils sont souvent moins qualifiés que les Français pour les travaux les plus prestigieux. Ils sont particulièrement touchés par le chômage aussi. Voilà pourquoi on voit beaucoup d'immigrés dans les HLM.

Leïla et Fatima, enfants d'immigrés, parlent arabe à la maison et français à l'école.

LES VRAIS CHIFFRES

Quand on parle de l'immigration, il f savoir de quoi on parle.
Il y a actuellement en France :

5 000 000
D'IMMIGRÉS EN SITUATION RÉGULIÈRE

500 000
CLANDESTINS

200 000
ÉTRANGERS QUI S'INSTALLENT EN FRANCE CHAQUE ANNÉE, DONT LA MOITIÉ DE CLANDESTINS

Répondez aux questions suivantes.

1. Où se trouve le Togo?
2. Où voit-on l'influence française au Togo?
3. Quels sont les produits principaux du Togo?
4. À qui loue-t-on les appartements dans les HLM?
5. Quel pourcentage des Français habite les HLM?
6. Quels sont les problèmes des HLM?
7. Qu'est-ce qui permet une meilleure intégration des résidents des HLM?
8. Les gens qui habitent en France mais qui ne sont pas français, peuvent-ils toucher les allocations familiales?
9. Les immigrés représentent quel pourcentage de la population française?
10. D'où vient le plus grand pourcentage des immigrés?

Journal personnel

Due to their different backgrounds, culture and education, people who immigrate to a country often stand out from those who were born there. Some of the country's nationals may complain that the immigrants take away jobs and don't try hard enough to assimilate into the culture of their adopted country.

Do you personally know any immigrants who have moved to your city? If so, talk with them about their reasons for coming to the United States and their plans for the future. Then ask them if they have experienced any prejudice while living here. Finally, ask them to tell you something about the culture of their native country, for example, how they celebrate their national holidays, what religion they practice and what they eat regularly. In their opinion, what advantages are there to living in the United States? What disadvantages are there? Record their observations in your cultural journal.

Do you think you would have difficulty living in a francophone country for an extended period of time? What things about the United States do you think you would miss the most? What things wouldn't you miss at all? Which francophone customs and habits could you adapt to easily? Which ones would be difficult for you to accept?

Structure

Conditional tense in sentences with *si*

Use the conditional tense along with **si** and the imperfect tense to tell what would happen *if* something else happened or *if* some condition contrary to reality were met.

si	+	imperfect	conditional

S'il y avait plus d'activités et moins de chômage, est-ce que les relations **seraient** meilleures? | *If there were more activities and less unemployment, would relations be better?*

Si on acceptait que la France est un pays d'immigrés depuis longtemps, on **pourrait** mieux profiter de la diversité culturelle. | *If we accepted that France has been a country of immigrants for a long time, we would be better able to take advantage of the cultural diversity.*

The phrase with **si** and the imperfect can either begin or end the sentence.

S'il y avait des graffiti aux murs de ton lycée, est-ce que tu y écrirais?

Teacher's Notes

1. The **Structure** section in Unit 7 contains both new and recycled grammatical concepts. 2. The conditional tense in sentences with **si** was introduced on page 419 in the second level of *C'est à toi!* 3. Remind students that **si** becomes **s'** before **il** or **ils**, but not before **elle** or **elles**. 4. The **si** clause may be preceded by **même**, for example, **Je t'appellerais même si je travaillais.** (*I would call you even if I were working.*) 5. The conditional may be preceded by a phrase rather than by a clause with **si**, for example, **À ta place, je ne perdrais pas mon temps.** (*If I were you, I wouldn't waste my time.*)

Paired Practice

Sentence Reconstruction

Put students in pairs. Prepare eight sentences using the conditional with **si** clauses. Cut each sentence in two, making sure that there is only one logical possibility for recombining each sentence, for example, **Si Gérard s'ennuyait à l'hôtel,/il irait au gymnase** and **La cuisine serait propre si tu/faisais la vaisselle.** Place the sixteen sections in an envelope, and give a similar envelope to each pair of students. As each pair finishes recombining the eight sentences, check students' accuracy. You might choose to award a point for each sentence that is correctly recombined.

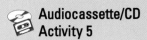

Audiocassette/CD
Activity 5

Answers

5 1. Si Vivianne étudiait, elle réussirait aux examens.

2. Si les élèves ne perdaient pas leur temps, ils termineraient leurs devoirs.

3. Si Édouard rangeait sa chambre, il trouverait son carnet de maths.

4. Si Martin et toi, vous vous serviez du web, vous n'auriez pas besoin d'aller à la bibliothèque.

5. Si je devais aller à un autre lycée, je me sentirais triste.

6. Si les ados suivaient des cours dans une auto-école, ils sauraient conduire.

7. Si tu mangeais à la maison, tu ne dépenserais pas beaucoup d'argent.

6 Possible answers:

Les immigrés s'installeraient en France s'ils avaient un meilleur choix d'emplois.
Kofi et sa famille trouveraient une autre HLM s'ils n'aimaient pas l'ambiance de la cité.
Chaque famille aurait assez d'argent si elle touchait les allocations familiales.
Les jeunes seraient acceptés s'ils n'agressaient pas les passants et les résidents.
Les résidents de l'HLM s'entendraient bien s'ils n'étaient pas au chômage.
L'ambiance de la cité serait meilleure si les relations entre les résidents n'étaient pas tendues.
On pourrait mieux profiter de la diversité culturelle si on acceptait que la France est un pays d'immigrés depuis longtemps.

Pratique

5 *Dites comment la vie des personnes suivantes serait différente si elles faisaient les changements indiqués. Suivez le modèle.*

1. Vivianne ne réussit pas aux examens. (étudier)
2. Les élèves ne terminent pas leurs devoirs. (ne pas perdre leur temps)
3. Édouard ne trouve pas son carnet de maths. (ranger sa chambre)
4. Martin et moi, nous avons besoin d'aller à la bibliothèque. (se servir du web)
5. Tu ne te sens pas triste. (devoir aller à un autre lycée)
6. Les ados ne savent pas conduire. (suivre des cours dans une auto-école)
7. Je dépense beaucoup d'argent. (manger à la maison)

Modèle:

Je ne suis pas en bonne forme. (s'entraîner)
Si tu t'entraînais, tu serais en bonne forme.

Si vous veniez au marché, vous auriez des légumes frais.

«Si j'étais vous, les rayures je les prendrais plutôt verticales.»

Modèle:

Valérie ne pourrait pas écrire son article si Kofi ne lui donnait pas son opinion.

6 *Dites comment seraient les personnes et les choses dans la colonne A si les conditions dans la colonne B existaient. Formez des phrases logiques en choisissant un élément de chaque colonne. Suivez le modèle.*

A	B
Valérie/ne pas pouvoir écrire son article	ils/ne pas aimer l'ambiance de la cité
les immigrés/s'installer en France	ils/ne pas être au chômage
Kofi et sa famille/trouver une autre HLM	ils/avoir un meilleur choix d'emplois
chaque famille/avoir assez d'argent	Kofi/ne pas lui donner son opinion
les jeunes/être acceptés	elle/toucher les allocations familiales
les résidents de l'HLM/s'entendre bien	on/accepter que la France est un pay d'immigrés depuis longtemps
l'ambiance de la cité/être meilleure	les relations entre les résidents/ne pa être tendues
on/pouvoir mieux profiter de la diversité culturelle	ils/ne pas agresser les passants et les résidents

Cooperative Group Practice

Si j'étais....

Put students in small groups of four or five for additional practice with the conditional tense in sentences with **si**. On note cards that you provide, have each student write two problem situations about two different imaginary characters, for example, **Abdou est un nouvel immigré en France. Il ne connaît personne dans son HLM.** Each student puts his or her two note cards into the group pile. The cards are shuffled. Then the first student in each group takes the top card and reads it to the rest of the group. Group members take turns expressing what they would do if they were the character, for example, **Si j'étais Abdou, j'inviterais les ados de mon HLM à une boum.** After each student in the group has expressed a solution to the first problem, the second student takes the second card from the pile and reads it to the rest of the group, and group members begin the process again. Students continue the activity until solutions for each situation card have been expressed.

The interrogative adjective *quel*

The interrogative adjective **quel** asks the question "which" or "what." **Quel** agrees with the noun it describes. **Quel** may precede the noun it describes or come directly before the verb **être**.

	Masculine	Feminine
Singular	quel	quelle
Plural	quels	quelles

Quels immeubles sont assez nouveaux?

Which apartment buildings are quite new?

Quelle sera l'opinion de Kofi?

What will Kofi's opinion be?

Pratique

Valérie va interviewer d'autres ados qui habitent une HLM. Complétez ses questions avec la forme convenable de **quel.**

1. Pour... raisons ta famille a-t-elle décidé de s'installer en France?
2. ... HLM habites-tu?
3. ... sont les pays d'origine des résidents?
4. ... est le plus grand problème des résidents de ton HLM?
5. À... activités les jeunes de ton HLM participent-ils?
6. Selon toi,... est la meilleure HLM?
7. ... groupes d'immigrés ont les plus d'ennuis?
8. ... emplois les immigrés prennent-ils?
9. À ton avis, à... avenir les immigrés peuvent-ils s'attendre?

De quel instrument est-ce que Raoul joue? (Nice)

Imaginez que vous allez passer (to be) à la télé au jeu télévisé Jeopardy. Pour vous préparer, posez une question en utilisant la forme convenable de **quel** *pour chaque phrase qui correspond au dialogue.*

1. C'est *Un Monde Meilleur.*
2. C'est l'immigration en France vue par un copain.
3. C'est le Togo.
4. C'est l'HLM Cité Jardins à Champigny.
5. C'est ce qu'on écrit sur les murs d'une HLM.
6. C'est une HLM moderne dont les immeubles sont assez nouveaux.
7. Ce sont les emplois très durs dont les autres ne veulent pas.

Modèle:

Ce sont le Maroc, l'Algérie et la Tunisie.
Quels sont les trois pays maghrébins?

Quels sont les projets d'Olivier Martinez?

■ **Workbook Activity 5**

 Audiocassette/CD Activity 8

Answers

7 1. quelles
2. Quelle
3. Quels
4. Quel
5. quelles
6. quelle
7. Quels
8. Quels
9. quel

8 Possible answers:

1. Quel est le journal du lycée de Valérie?
2. Quel est le sujet de l'article de Valérie?
3. Quel est le pays d'origine de Kofi?
4. Quelle est l'HLM que Kofi habitait?
5. Quels sont les graffiti?
6. Quelle est l'HLM de Kofi maintenant?
7. Quels sont les emplois que les immigrés prennent souvent?

Teacher's Notes

1. Point out liaison after **quels** and **quelles** when the next word begins with a vowel sound. 2. A preposition may precede **quel**, for example, **Pour quelles raisons travailles-tu?** 3. When **quel** precedes a form of the verb **être**, **quel** agrees with the noun after the verb.

TPR

The Interrogative Adjective *Quel*

So that students can practice selecting the appropriate form of **quel**, prepare a list of questions using all its forms, for example, **Quelle heure est-il? Quel est ton prénom? Quelles émissions aimes-tu regarder? Quels artistes connais-tu?** Have students write the four forms of **quel** on four different sheets of paper. Then tell them to hold up the correct form as you read each question from your list.

Cooperative Group Practice

Interview Questions

To provide additional practice asking questions using **quel**, put students in small groups of four or five. Prepare a set of note cards, writing a profession on each one, for example, **un acteur.** The first student in each group draws a card and identifies his or her profession. The other students in the group think of an interview question using a form of **quel** to ask the first student, for example, **Quel est le nom de votre dernier film?** After each student has asked a question, the second student draws another profession card and the activity begins again.

Answers

9 1. Ah bon? Lesquels?
2. Ah bon? Lesquelles?
3. Ah bon? Lesquelles?
4. Ah bon? Laquelle?
5. Ah bon? Lesquelles?
6. Ah bon? Lequel?
7. Ah bon? Lesquels?
8. Ah bon? Lesquels?

Teacher's Notes

1. Use **de** after **lequel** to express the group you are choosing from, for example, **Lequel de ces restaurants a la meilleure ambiance?** 2. When **lequel** is a preceding direct object, the past participle agrees with it in gender and in number, for example, **Lesquels de ces graffiti as-tu écrits?** 3. **Lequel** contracts with **à** and **de** to form **auquel, duquel,** etc. Point out that in French the preposition never comes at the end of the sentence.

TPR

Lequel

To give students practice selecting the appropriate form of **lequel**, prepare a list of sentences that can logically be followed by a question using **lequel**, for example, **Mahmoud travaillait avec cette technologie.** Read the sentences for the class one at a time. After each sentence, have students hold up a sheet of paper with **lequel, laquelle, lesquels** or **lesquelles** on it to identify which form of the pronoun they would select if asking a question. When students have selected the correct form of **lequel**, say the question that would logically follow the sentence you read so that students can check their answer, for example, **Avec laquelle est-ce que Mahmoud travaillait?**

274

	Masculine	Feminine
Singular	lequel	laquelle
Plural	lesquels	lesquelles

«Parmi la liste suivante d'hommes politiques, avec lequel aimeriez-vous parler?»

Modèle:
J'habite une HLM.
Ah bon? Laquelle?

Paired Practice

Asking Questions

So that students can practice forming questions using **quel** and **lequel**, put them in pairs. Prepare a worksheet listing eight noun/verb combinations, for example, **profession/intéresser.** Student A begins with the first noun/verb combination and forms a question using a form of **quel**, for example,

---

The interrogative pronoun *lequel*

The interrogative pronoun **lequel** asks the question "which one(s)." It is often used to replace the interrogative adjective **quel** plus a noun. **Lequel** consists of two parts: the definite article and **quel**. Both parts agree in gender and in number with the noun they replace.

Quelles raisons sont les plus importantes?	*Which reasons are the most important?*
Lesquelles sont les plus importantes?	*Which (ones) are the most important?*

A form of **lequel** may be the subject or direct object of a sentence or the object of a preposition. **Lequel** can refer to both people and things.

Parmi les immigrés, **lesquels** ont des ennuis?	*Among the immigrants, which ones have problems?*
Il y a beaucoup de familles qui habitent cette HLM. **Laquelle** connais-tu?	*There are a lot of families who live in this HLM. Which one do you know?*
Avec **lequel** de ses copains Valérie a-t-elle pris rendez-vous?	*With which one of her friends did Valérie make an appointment?*

A form of **lequel** may be used as a one-word question.

Nous habitions une autre HLM. Ah bon? **Laquelle?**	*We used to live in another HLM. Really? Which one?*

Pratique

9 | *Katia est très bavarde. Elle dit beaucoup de choses, mais elle ne donne jamais de détails. Pour chaque phrase qu'elle dit, demandez-lui d'être plus précise en utilisant la forme convenable de **lequel**.*

1. Les immeubles de la cité sont assez nouveaux.
2. Il y a beaucoup d'activités pour les jeunes.
3. Ma famille connaît d'autres familles qui habitent ici.
4. Une des familles vient du Togo.
5. Deux filles dans cette famille sont très sympa.
6. Un des enfants dans cette famille perd son temps dans la rue.
7. Quelques résidents ne s'entendent pas bien.
8. Plusieurs groupes d'immigrés ont des ennuis.

Quelle profession t'intéresse? Student B responds, then asks Student A the same question using a form of **lequel**, for example, **Je voudrais être comptable. Laquelle t'intéresse?** After Student A answers, students switch roles and continue with the next combination on the worksheet.

Valérie a d'autres questions à poser aux ados qui habitent une HLM. Complétez ses nouvelles questions avec la forme convenable de **lequel**.

1. Tu avais plusieurs raisons pour t'installer en France. ... était la plus importante?
2. Il y a beaucoup d'HLM. ... as-tu choisie?
3. De tous ces immeubles,... est le plus calme?
4. ... des appartements habites-tu?
5. ... de ces résidents viennent des pays africains?
6. Parmi les groupes d'immigrés,... ont beaucoup d'ennuis?
7. ... des familles touchent les allocations familiales?
8. ... des résidents les jeunes ont-ils agressé?

Faites une enquête sur les préférences de vos camarades de classe. Copiez la grille suivante. Puis, dans chaque catégorie, écrivez deux possibilités. Demandez à trois élèves laquelle de ces deux possibilités ils préfèrent. Écrivez leurs réponses dans les espaces blancs convenables.

Modèle:

Laure: Lequel de ces deux sports préfères-tu, le foot ou le tennis?
Yannick: Je préfère le foot.

		Yannick	Chloé	Khaled
sports	le foot ou le tennis	le foot		
athlètes				
restaurants				
films				
vedettes				
émissions de télé				
chanteurs				
voitures				

Lequel de ces deux chanteurs préfères-tu, Maxime LeForestier ou Alain Bashung?

Je préfère Alain Bashung.

 Audiocassette/CD Activity 11

Answers

10 1. Laquelle
2. Laquelle
3. lequel
4. Lequel
5. Lesquels
6. lesquels
7. Lesquelles
8. Lequel

11 Lequel/laquelle de ces deux athlètes préfères-tu,...?
Lequel de ces deux restaurants préfères-tu,...?
Lequel de ces deux films préfères-tu,...?
Laquelle de ces deux vedettes préfères-tu,...?
Laquelle de ces deux émissions de télé préfères-tu,...?
Lequel de ces deux chanteurs préfères-tu,...?
Laquelle de ces deux voitures préfères-tu,...?
Students' responses to these questions will vary.

Teacher's Note

To extend the survey in Activity 11, you might have students add the following topics: **romans, bandes dessinées, professions, hommes politiques, missions humanitaires** and **loisirs.** You might also ask students to extend their responses when questioned and give reasons for their preferences.

Paired Practice

Les sketches

To provide additional practice with the interrogative pronoun **lequel**, put students in pairs. Prepare a note card for Student A that asks a question intended to find out if a specific activity has been done. This card will be the first line of the pair's skit, for example, **Tu as fait la corvée?**

Student B responds using an appropriate form of **lequel.** Tell students to use their imaginations to extend the conversation as far as they can, for example: —**Tu as fait la corvée? —Laquelle? —La vaisselle. —Non, je n'ai pas eu le temps. —Il faut que tu fasses la vaisselle tout de suite. —D'accord, maman.** Other questions that you might use to start the skits include the

following: **Tu as rempli la fiche? Tu as vu les films? Tu as envoyé le fax? Tu as embauché les immigrés? Tu as lu l'article? Tu as vu l'exposition? Tu as trouvé les magazines?**

**Listening
Activity 1**

**Quiz
*Leçon A***

**Advanced
Placement**

Communication

12 *La France, comme les États-Unis, est un pays d'immigrés depuis longtemps. Il est certain que tous les immigrés ont beaucoup d'ennuis en déménageant dans un nouveau pays. Imaginez que vous êtes un(e) immigré(e) et que vous venez d'arriver en France. Quels obstacles rencontrerez-vous? Faites une liste de questions que vous poseriez si vous alliez dans un centre d'accueil (reception center) pour nouveaux résidents en France. Préparez des questions sur les problèmes de la vie quotidienne, par exemple, le logement (housing), le travail, la nourriture, les allocations familiales, les écoles et la langue.*

13 *Avec un(e) partenaire, comparez les listes de questions que vous avez préparées dans l'Activité 12. Selon les obstacles et les problèmes que vous avez identifiés, discutez comment on pourrait aider les immigrés. Puis, pour chaque obstacle ou problème dans vos listes, proposez une solution. Utilisez la forme d'une proposition, par exemple, "Si les immigrés ne savaient pas la langue et avaient besoin de l'apprendre, on pourrait leur offrir des cours de français." Enfin, présentez les solutions que vous avez discutées à la classe.*

 Sur la bonne piste

Circumlocuting

When new vocabulary words are introduced at the beginning of a lesson in the third level of *C'est à toi!*, glossed definitions are given in French wherever possible. For example, in this unit **un étranger/une étrangère** is defined as **une personne d'un autre pays** and **la plupart** is defined as **la majorité**. You have probably noticed that these French definitions use words you already know or cognates that you can easily understand. When you want to use a specific word or expression but don't know what it is in French, you, too, can use words you already know to get your meaning across. This is called "circumlocution," a term which comes from two Latin words meaning "to talk around." Circumlocution is an important language skill because it widens the scope of what you can talk about in French. You already had some experience circumlocuting on page 164 where you defined some new expressions in French. For example, **le SMIC** is **le salaire minimum garanti par le gouvernement**.

Depending on what you are describing, you may want to give a definition, an example or an explanation. For instance, if you want to talk about a portrait you saw at an art museum but don't know the word for "portrait" in French, you could define it as **un tableau d'une personne**. Or, to communicate a concept such as "car pooling," it might be easier to give an example: **C'est quand ma mère conduit au travail, et elle emmène une autre femme qui lui offre de l'argent.** And finally, if you don't know the French word for an object, such as a can opener, you could explain its use. You might say **C'est quelque chose qui sert à ouvrir les boîtes.** Sometimes it helps to give the shape of the object and tell what it is made of. Here are the words for some shapes and materials that will make your explanations of objects clearer:

carré	square	en métal	made of metal
rond	round	en bois	made of wood
rectangulaire	rectangular	en plastique	made of plastic
triangulaire	triangular	en coton/laine	made of cotton/wool
		en verre	made of glass

How would you describe the shape of a can opener and tell what it is made of? Your listener might understand more easily if you said **C'est quelque chose de rectangulaire en métal qui sert à ouvrir les boîtes**. By practicing circumlocution, you will be able to talk about many more topics in French than you might have thought possible.

Imagine that you are talking with someone in French, but you don't know the expressions for various things. Give a definition, an example or an explanation in French for each expression that follows. Remember to be as specific as possible.

1. a phone book
2. a personal ad
3. a toaster oven
4. a wooden spoon
5. a cuckoo clock
6. a high school yearbook
7. a school bus
8. a ski hat
9. a traffic jam
10. a picture frame
11. talk radio
12. bunk beds

Un(e) manifestant(e), c'est quelqu'un qui participe à une manifestation.

Teacher's Notes

1. To provide additional practice in describing objects, put students in pairs. Hand out an object to each pair. Have each pair explain the function, shape and material of the object. Then have students return the objects and place them on your desk. As each pair explains their object to the class, ask students to write down which of the objects on the desk is being described. Finally, you may want to give the French word for each object. Students may be surprised to learn that some of their explanations closely match the real name of the object. For example, students might describe **un carnet d'adresses** as **un petit carnet rectangulaire en cuir où on met des adresses**. 2. You may want to extend students' circumlocution practice to describing people by giving their approximate age, physical appearance (height; eye color; hair color, texture and length) and clothing. To approximate someone's age, tell students they can use **environ**, for example, **Il a environ 30 ans**. To express height, introduce **mesurer** and give several metric examples, for example, **Il mesure 1 mètre 80**. Tell students that hair can be **raides** (*straight*), **bouclés** (*curly*) or **frisés** (*frizzy*), as well as **courts**, **moyens** or **longs**. To describe clothing more specifically, you may want to introduce **à rayures** (*striped*), **à pois** (*polka dots*) and **à carreaux** (*checked*). So that students can practice their new vocabulary, put them in small groups. Give each student a magazine picture of a person to describe to the group.

Workbook
Activity 8

Audiocassette/CD
Adjectives

Teacher's Notes

1. Communicative functions that are recycled in this lesson are "explaining something," "describing past events," "expressing need and necessity," "stating a preference," "giving opinions," "expressing likes and dislikes" and "giving examples." 2. Point out that **génial(e)** is a synonym for **extra**, which was introduced in Unit 6 in the second level of *C'est à toi!* 3. Tell students that they have already seen the word **journal** in the **Journal personnel** section of each unit. 4. Mention that Philippe was the reporter in Unit 6 who wrote an article for *Un Monde Meilleur* about **Médecins Sans Frontières**. 5. Other related terms and expressions include **faire presser quelqu'un** (*to hurry somebody*), **faire presser les choses** (*to speed things up*), **l'indépendance** (*independence*), **la différence** (*difference*), **différer** (*to differ*) and **la circonspection** (*caution*).

Leçon B

In this lesson you will be able to:

➤ ask about preference

➤ state preference

➤ clarify

➤ report

➤ compare

➤ express importance and unimportance

➤ agree and disagree

➤ describe character

➤ express compassion

Pierre est pressé.

Michèle est indépendante.

Il est génial!

Je suis amoureuse de toi.

Yasmine est ouverte.

Ce foulard est différent.

Fabrice est circonspect.

Philippe aime écrire dans son journal chaque jour.

Philippe adore être reporter pour *Un Monde Meilleur*. Chaque jour il écrit dans son journal. Quelquefois il y trouve des idées pour un article. Regardons ses notes pour savoir ce qu'il a fait cette semaine.

> *lundi*
>
> *Après le cours de philosophie, j'ai rencontré° Émilie, Martin et Anne au Quick. On est de vrais amis, et je peux toujours compter° sur eux. Même si nous n'avons pas les mêmes idées, nous acceptons celles° des autres dans le groupe. Les amis sont si importants pour moi. Cet après-midi j'avais vraiment besoin de rigoler car ma note° de philosophie était mauvaise.*
>
> *Pour prendre un goûter, où peut-on aller? Au Macdo, à Pizza Pino, au Free Time, à Love Burger? Ben, ça dépend. Il faut considérer ce qu'on veut, combien de temps on a et ce qu'on veut dépenser. Aujourd'hui nous étions plus pressés que d'habitude,° alors nous avons choisi le Quick, le fast-food le plus près du lycée. On trouve toujours un bon choix dans ce fast-food-ci.*
>
> *Nous venons tous de familles modernes dans lesquelles les parents travaillent tous les deux. Nos mères n'ont plus le temps de préparer un grand dîner. En France presque 80% des femmes qui ont entre 25 et 49 ans travaillent. Celles qui travaillent ont moins de temps libre mais ont plus de travail à la maison que les femmes américaines, anglaises et canadiennes.*
>
> *Plus les femmes travaillent, plus les repas sont simples et rapides. La famille française d'aujourd'hui dépense moins pour la nourriture qu'avant. C'est parce qu'on dépense plus du budget familial pour le logement.°*

Temps libre des femmes et temps pour le ménage (en heures par semaine)		
	États-Unis	France
Temps libre	33,6	27,7
Ménage	25,8	27,7

Ce qu'une famille dépense pour la nourriture (en %)

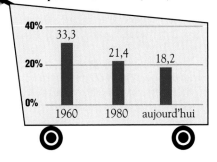

Ce qu'une famille dépense pour le logement (en %)

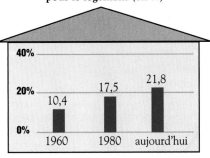

rencontrer *to meet;* **compter** *dépendre;* **celles** *those;* **une note** *grade;* **d'habitude** *usual;*
le logement *housing*

 Workbook Activity 9

 Audiocassette/CD *Journal*

 Transparency 20

Teacher's Notes

1. You may want to say that **rencontrer** is a synonym of **se rejoindre**, which was introduced in Unit 9 in the second level of *C'est à toi!* 2. Point out the two different meanings of **même** in the third sentence of the journal entry. The first **même** means "even"; the second **même** means "same." 3. Students learned **une note**, meaning "note," in Unit 1 in the third level of *C'est à toi!* 4. Introduce the forms of the orthographically changing verb **considérer**: **considère, considères, considère, considérons, considérez, considèrent**. 5. **Lesquelles** in the third paragraph is a relative pronoun, not an interrogative pronoun.

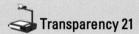

Transparency 21

Teacher's Notes

1. About one in every three marriages in France ends in divorce, but the figure is one in every two marriages in the Paris area. Divorce first became legal in 1792 after the French Revolution. It was banned in 1816 but was reinstated by the Third Republic in 1884. The number of divorces in France has multiplied by four since 1960.
2. Point out that **marier**, when not used reflexively, refers to the action of performing a marriage. 3. Here are the present tense forms of irregular verb **se distraire**: je me distrais, tu te distrais, il/elle/on se distrait, nous nous distrayons, vous vous distrayez and ils/elles se distraient.

une famille nucléaire

des familles monoparentales

Où vont les jeunes quand ils sortent?		
	15-25 ans	plus de 26 ans
cinéma	90	43
discothèque	69	17
concert de rock	42	6
parc d'attractions	37	13
match	36	22
monument national	31	25
musée	27	31
théâtre	17	14

Au bureau de location à la Fnac, Philippe et Martin ont acheté des billets de concert.

mardi

Après quelques ennuis dans le labo de chimie, j'ai rencontré Martin au café du coin° de la rue. Il m'a annoncé que ses parents allaient divorcer. Il a dit que son père passait trop de temps à s'occuper de sa compagnie et que sa mère voudrait réussir dans sa profession d'écrivain. Presque 50% des mariages se terminent en divorce. Dommage que ça soit celui de ses parents! Au revoir la famille nucléaire; bonjour la famille monoparentale! Les gens qui vivent dans une famille non-traditionnelle deviennent plus nombreux. Ceux qui se marient° le font plus tard, à l'âge de 27 ou 28 ans pour les hommes et de 25 ou 26 ans pour les femmes.

Karine et Gérard se sont mariés à l'âge de 27 ans.

mercredi

Quand Émilie, Martin, Anne et moi, nous sommes sortis du lycée, nous sommes allés tout de suite à la Fnac. Émilie et Anne voulaient écouter les nouveaux CDs pendant que Martin et moi, nous sommes allés au bureau de location. J'ai demandé à Martin, "Qu'est-ce que tu voudrais faire le weekend prochain? Assister à un concert? Aller dans une discothèque, au cinéma ou un parc d'attractions?" Il a répondu, "J'aimerais mieux me distraire° à un concert. Voyons ce qu'il y a au Zénith." Donc, pendant que les filles écoutaient de la musique, nous avons acheté des billets pour le concert d'Angélique Kidjo. Ceux que nous avons achetés étaient les plus chers.

un coin *corner*; se marier *l'action de devenir homme et femme*; se distraire *s'amuser*

jeudi

Rien d'important aujourd'hui. Je me suis disputé° avec ma sœur, Laurence. Heureusement, il y a seulement un ou deux enfants dans la plupart des familles françaises. Je trouve qu'une petite sœur est assez!

Il faut étudier ce soir parce que demain j'ai une interro d'anglais.

**Combien d'enfants il y a
dans une famille française**

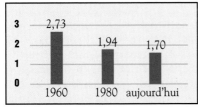

	1960	1980	aujourd'hui
	2,73	1,94	1,70

vendredi

J'ai eu 15 à l'interro. Ben, ouais, celui qui étudie dur réussit. Ce soir j'ai passé des heures au téléphone. C'est génial de pouvoir parler "franglais," avec des mots° d'origine américaine ou anglaise.

J'écoute beaucoup de musique anglaise et américaine. Il y a des groupes francophones qui sont très bons, mais ils sont moins nombreux. Je n'aime pas la loi° qui exige que 40% des chansons qu'une radio passe° entre 6h30 et 22h30 soient en français. Personne ne peut écouter la musique qu'il préfère. C'est une question de liberté de choix. On a le même problème à la télé. Les chaînes sont obligées de diffuser° 60% d'émissions européennes, dont 40% sont des émissions francophones. On ne sait pas s'il faut aimer l'influence culturelle américaine ou pas, mais je la trouve passionnante.

PROGRAMME
Europe 2   Le meilleur de la musique.

se disputer *ne pas être d'accord;* **un mot** *word;* **une loi** *law;* **passer** *to play (on the radio);*
diffuser *to broadcast*

Teacher's Notes

1. You may want to remind the class that French students are graded on a point system, with 20 points being the top score. 2. Laws designed to protect the purity of the French language from **le franglais** exact penalties from organizations funded by the federal government that do not use approved vocabulary. Special terminology committees in areas such as sports, the environment, telecommunications, health and tourism create French equivalents for English words being introduced into the French language.

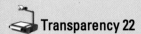
Transparency 22

Teacher's Note

Point out that the comparative form **aussi... que** is used with two adjectives, **independante** and **ouverte**.

```
NAF NAF
CC CRÉTEIL SOLEIL
94000 CRÉTEIL
Boutique N° F944, Caisse    N°  1

01/12/99,18:33 C=R944 V=R944 No=136721
                            PRIX T.T.C
345285176995 CHIENS CO    1    69.00

TOTAL          69.00OFF

DONT TVA    20.60%      11.79 FF
REÇU     ESPÈCES       100.00
RENDU    ESPÈCES       -31.00

MERCI DE VOTRE VISITE ET À BIENTÔT
ÉCHANGE POSSIBLE DANS TOUTES LES
BOUTIQUES NAF NAF AVEC CE TICKET
    TEL : 01 43 99 45 55
```

samedi

Après les cours nous avons fait les magasins. Il y avai
des soldes aux Galeries Lafayette et à Naf Naf. Ce soir
nous avons invité une lycéenne américaine à venir avec nou
au cinéma. Elle s'appelle Shelley (celle qui a les cheveux
roux), et elle passe l'année scolaire dans notre lycée.
Quand Émilie et Anne ont le temps, elles aiment beaucoup
faire les magasins avec Shelley pour pouvoir choisir des
vêtements qui donnent l'air plus américain. Elles ont déjà
acheté des jeans, des chaussures de sport et des pulls de
marque° américaine.

Après le film nous avons pris un coca au café. Shelley
nous a parlé de l'influence française en Amérique. On la
trouve partout: dans les restaurants, les films, les
collections et les expositions de tableaux, le vocabulaire
les vêtements, le rock et même les stylos. Il y a aussi
beaucoup de compagnies françaises qui se trouvent aux
États-Unis. Nous nous amusons avec Shelley qui est toujour
aimable et enthousiaste. Comme nous, elle prend ses cours
au sérieux, et elle est toujours très organisée. Shelley
est aussi indépendante et ouverte qu'Émilie et Anne, mais
elle est différente d'elles aussi parce qu'elle est plus
engagée dans tout ce qui se passe dans son lycée. Par
exemple, elle est membre de l'équipe de foot. Je trouve me
copines françaises un peu plus circonspectes que Shelley,
mais c'est parce que celles-là habitent une grande ville e
leur culture est plus vieille.

Les ados français aiment la sélection de vêtements à Naf Naf.

dimanche

Mes grands-parents sont venus déjeuner chez nous comme
d'habitude. C'est génial, toute la famille ensemble. Après
j'ai dû faire mes devoirs. Quelle longue semaine! Alors, mo
journal, à demain.

une marque *brand*

D'après le journal de Philippe, mettez les événements (events) suivants en ordre chronologique. Écrivez "1" pour la première phrase, "2" pour la deuxième phrase, etc.

1. Philippe a eu 15 à l'interro.
2. Philippe a eu quelques ennuis dans le labo de chimie.
3. Toute la famille était ensemble pour le déjeuner.
4. Émilie, Martin et Anne ont rencontré Philippe chez Quick.
5. Laurence et Philippe se sont disputés.
6. Les copains sont allés au cinéma avec Shelley.
7. Martin et Philippe ont acheté des billets pour un concert.
8. Les quatre amis ont fait du shopping aux Galeries Lafayette.
9. Martin a annoncé que ses parents allaient divorcer.

Lundi, Philippe et ses copains ont choisi le Quick parce qu'ils étaient pressés.

Choisissez l'expression qui complète chaque phrase d'après le journal de Philippe.

1. Quand on est très..., on choisit un fast-food près du lycée.
   a. nombreux   b. pressé   c. circonspect

2. Aujourd'hui une famille française dépense moins pour... qu'avant parce qu'on n'a plus beaucoup de temps pour préparer les repas.
   a. la nourriture   b. le budget familial c. le logement

3. Les parents de Martin allaient....
   a. établir une famille nucléaire
   b. divorcer
   c. se marier

4. Pour..., Martin préfère aller à un concert.
   a. se marier   b. se disputer   c. se distraire

5. Le franglais? Ce sont des... d'origine anglaise ou américaine, comme un fast-food.
   a. mots   b. notes   c. vocabulaire

6. Une radio passe de la musique, mais une chaîne de télévision... des émissions.
   a. annonce   b. considère   c. diffuse

Game

Loto

To practice identifying new vocabulary in this unit, have students make a grid with 16 squares, four in each row. Show a transparency with 16 definitions in French of vocabulary words found in **Leçon A** and **Leçon B**, such as **attaquer**. (You might choose to use the definitions found in the glossed vocabulary or easily recognizable cognates.) Tell students to copy the definitions, placing them at random on their grid. Then orally give the corresponding new French word for each definition, for example, **agresser**. Students mark with an "X" the matching definition on their grid. The student who first covers four squares horizontally, vertically or diagonally calls out "Loto" and gives the new French word for each definition in his or her winning sequence. You may choose to award an extra credit point if the winner can use each word in an original sentence.

LE BOOM
des brasseries

284

Audiocassette/CD
Activity 4

Answers

3 Possible paragraph:

Les Français mangent plus souvent qu'avant dans les fast-foods quand ils sont pressés. La plupart des femmes françaises travaillent, donc, les repas en famille sont plus simples et rapides. On dépense moins du budget familial pour la nourriture et plus pour le logement. Les Français qui vivent dans une famille non-traditionnelle deviennent plus nombreux. La famille monoparentale prend la place de la famille nucléaire.

4 Answers will vary.

7. Émilie et Anne choisissent des vêtements de... américaine.
   a. loi   b. budget   c. marque

8. Shelley est une fille... parce qu'elle participe à beaucoup d'activités dans son lycée.
   a. engagée   b. ouverte   c. non-traditionnelle

Pour ses nouveaux tennis, Karine a choisi une marque américaine.

3 *Écrivez un paragraphe de cinq phrases où vous expliquez ce que vous venez d'apprendre au sujet de la famille française moderne. Parlez des repas, de l'effet sur la vie familiale des parents qui travaillent, du budget familial et de la composition de la famille moderne.*

Quand je sors le weekend, je vais le plus souvent à la discothèque.

4 *C'est à toi!*

1. Est-ce que tu écris dans un journal? Si oui, au sujet de quoi? De tes activités? De tes relations? De tes idées?
2. Est-ce que tu reçois quelquefois de mauvaises notes? Si oui, dans quel(s) cours?
3. Est-ce que tous les membres de ta famille ont la liberté de choisir les émissions qu'ils regardent à la télé?
4. Est-ce que tu te disputes souvent avec les membres de ta famille? Si oui, avec qui?
5. Selon toi, quel est le meilleur âge pour se marier?
6. Quand tu sors le weekend, où vas-tu le plus souvent?
7. Est-ce que tu as les mêmes idées que tes amis? Si non, est-ce que tu acceptes leurs idées?
8. Est-ce que tu connais des Français? Si oui, est-ce qu'ils sont différents des Américains? Comment?

Enquête culturelle

Contrairement à la mentalité et la culture françaises, le fast-food se trouve partout en France. Les Français n'ont pas pu résister à l'invasion des chaînes de restaurants. Il y a les chaînes sandwichs, par exemple, la Brioche Dorée, le Relais H, la Viennoisière et la Pomme de Pain. On peut y manger pour pas cher. Bien sûr, il y a de grandes chaînes de fast-food américaines. On compte plus de 400 Macdo en France, aussi bien que des Burger King, des Domino's, des El Rancho et des Kentucky Fried Chicken. Et la France en a ses imitations : le Quick, Pizza Pino, le Free Time et Love Burger. Les cafétérias sont généralement situées dans des centres commerciaux ou sur les autoroutes. Il y a des Casino Cafétéria, des Flunch et de petits restaurants dans les magasins, comme Monoprix. Les chaînes grill, par exemple, Buffalo Grill, la Courte-Paille et l'Hippopotamus, connaissent beaucoup de succès. Ils offrent des menus complets où on trouve une cuisine plutôt française. Et enfin, il ne faut pas oublier le Hard Rock Café à Paris où se réunissent beaucoup de touristes américains.

Le Free Time ressemble aux fast-foods américains comme le Macdo et Burger King.

NOUVEAU

À bientôt chez Hippo

22, avenue du Général Leclerc, Boulogne
29, rue Berger, Paris 1er
1, boulevard des Capucines, Paris 2ème
1, boulevard Beaumarchais, Paris 4ème
9, rue Lagrange, Paris 5ème
119, boulevard du Montparnasse, Paris 6ème
20, rue Quentin Bauchart, Paris 8ème
6, avenue F.-D. Roosevelt, Paris 8ème
46, avenue de Wagram, Paris 8ème
5/9, boulevard des Batignolles, Paris 8ème
42, avenue des Champs-Elysées, Paris 8ème
27, rue de Dunkerque, Paris 10ème
12, avenue du Maine, Paris 15ème
Aquaboulevard 4, rue Louis Armand, Paris 15ème
14, rue Gérentet, Saint-Etienne
16, avenue Félix Faure, Nice
1 bis, boulevard de Strasbourg, Toulouse

Les déjeuners
d'**HIPPO CLUB**

20, rue
Quentin Bauchart
Paris 8ème

Réservation :
47 20 23 37

Workbook Activity 10

Teacher's Notes

1. Cognates in this reading include **contrairement, mentalité, résister, invasion, chaînes, imitations, cafétérias, généralement, autoroutes, grill, se réunissent, pour cent, reste, modèle, norme, cohabitent, remariage, structure, traditionnelle, insertion, invasion, expressions, acceptable, remplacer, équivalents, suggérés, personnels, sélection, parisiens, classiques, élégant, parfum, observation** and **catalogue**. 2. There are 150 Brioche Dorée restaurants, 130 Relais H restaurants and 80 la Viennoisière restaurants in France. 3. Fast-food dining is known as **la restauration rapide**. 4. Burger King is pulling out of the French market, but McDonald's remains strong in France, with over one million dollars in annual revenue. McDonald's has 42 locations in Paris alone. The McDonald's menu includes **le hamburger, le cheeseburger, le Double Cheeseburger, le Royal Cheese, le Big Mac, le McBacon, le McChicken, le Filet-O-Fish** and **le Happy Meal**. 5. The Hard Rock Café in Paris is located at 14, boulevard Montmartre (9e).

Si la famille française dépense 18,2 pour cent de son budget pour la nourriture et 21,8 pour cent pour le logement, où dépense-t-elle le reste de son argent?

nourriture 18,2%

logement 21,8%

transport et communications 16,2%

vêtements 5,4%

articles de ménage 7,3%

autre 13,2%

loisirs 7,5%

services médicaux et santé 10,4%

En France les familles nucléaires deviennent moins nombreuses.

Le modèle de la famille de deux parents avec des enfants n'est plus la norme. Maintenant en France il y a des couples qui cohabitent sans se marier et qui ont des enfants. Le divorce a augmenté le nombre de familles monoparentales, et dix pour cent des enfants vivent dans ces familles. Le remariage change aussi la structure de la famille traditionnelle. Les enfants peuvent vivre avec d'autres enfants qui viennent d'autres mariages de leurs parents.

un casting franco-américain

Le franglais est l'insertion dans la langue française de mots anglais ou américains. Les jeunes Français le trouvent génial, et ils utilisent souvent des mots du franglais. Le gouvernement français n'aime pas l'invasion de ces expressions, surtout quand il y a une expression française acceptable qui pourrait les remplacer. Si vous êtes avec les jeunes, vous pouvez parler franglais, mais si vous cherchez à faire bonne impression devant les professeurs en France, il vaut mieux utiliser des expressions françaises. Voici une liste de mots franglais et de leurs équivalents français suggérés.

Noir zippé
Veste noire zippée

franglais	français standard
le fast-food	la restauration rapide
le hit-parade	le palmarès
le popcorn	le maïs explosé
le gadget	le truc
le parking	le terrain de stationnement
le stress	la tension
se relaxer	se reposer
le weekend	la fin de semaine
faire du shopping	faire des achats
le zappeur	la télécommande
le walkman	le baladeur
le convenience store	la bazarette
le teleshopping	le téléachat

Partout en France on trouve Monoprix et Prisunic. Ce sont des grands magasins du quartier qui offrent un peu de tout aux meilleurs prix : nourriture, vêtements, articles personnels, articles de ménage et plus. Si vous cherchez un supermarché ou un magasin même plus grand, vous trouverez Carrefour, Mammouth, Auchan et Continent. Ce sont des "grandes surfaces" ou des "hypermarchés." Avec une grande sélection de nourriture, on y vend aussi ce qu'on trouverait dans un Monoprix et des articles de jardin, des jeux, des CDs et des télévisions.

À Mammouth, si vous ne trouvez pas ce que vous cherchez, demandez à la caisse.

INFORMATION CAISSES

Avec Carrefour je positive!

LA VIE AUCHAN. ELLE A QUELQUE CHOSE DE PLUS ÉTONNANT.

Paris compte plusieurs grands magasins très célèbres. Au Bon Marché était le premier grand magasin à ouvrir ses portes sur Paris. Les magasins parisiens les plus populaires sont les Galeries Lafayette et le Printemps, qui offrent des vêtements contemporains et classiques. Les Galeries Lafayette en offrent avec une grande variété de prix dans un magasin à plusieurs étages. C'est le plus grand magasin de Paris. Le Printemps vend de tout dans un magasin aussi élégant que les Galeries Lafayette. C'est un magasin plutôt traditionnel, et la clientèle est généralement plus âgée. Si c'est du parfum que vous cherchez, allez au Printemps où la sélection de parfums est aussi grande qu'un stade de foot. La Samaritaine est plus pratique et vend tout, des poissons rouges aux aspirateurs. À la Samaritaine n'oubliez pas de visiter la tour d'observation au-dessus de leur restaurant d'où vous pouvez voir tout Paris.

GALERIES Lafayette

LE GRAND MAGASIN CAPITALE DE LA MODE

Le Printemps organise des défilés de mode *(fashion shows)* toute l'année.

DEMANDEZ VOTRE CARTE SAMARITAINE, ELLE EST GRATUITE.

Comme aux États-Unis, les Français peuvent aussi faire du shopping par catalogue. La Redoute et les Trois Suisses sont deux magasins qui offrent depuis longtemps des catalogues. On peut même faire sa commande par Minitel.

Teacher's Notes

1. Au Bon Marché, located at 38, rue de Sèvres (7e), has a well-known antiques department. Opened in 1852, the store specializes in linens, tableware and quality furniture. 2. In 1996 Galeries Lafayette celebrated its centennial. The chain operates 30 stores, two of which are in Paris, at 40, boulevard Haussmann (1er) and at the foot of the Tour Maine-Montparnasse (6e). The flagship store on the boulevard Haussmann is listed as a national historic monument. Visited by over 80,000 people each day, its interior is reminiscent of **la Belle Époque**. Galeries Lafayette has also opened stores in New York, Berlin and Peking. Galeries Lafayette's supermarket, which accepts orders by telephone, fax, cable and Minitel, offers home delivery service. 3. Printemps, located at 64, boulevard Haussmann (1er), closely resembles the original Galeries Lafayette store in style and spaciousness. An entire annex is devoted to home furnishings and accessories, but the store is most famous for its perfume department. The men's store, Brummel, is in a separate building. 4. La Samaritaine is located at 19, rue de la Monnaie (1er).

Answers

5 Possible answers:

1. Les fast-foods sont partout en France.
2. La Brioche Dorée, le Relais H, la Viennoisière et la Pomme de Pain sont des chaînes sandwichs en France.
3. Le Quick, Pizza Pino, le Free Time et Love Burger suivent le modèle des chaînes américaines.
4. Le divorce a augmenté le nombre de familles mono-parentales.
5. Le remariage a changé la structure de la famille traditionnelle.
6. Le franglais est l'insertion dans la langue française de mots anglais ou américains.
7. Le gouvernement français n'aime pas l'invasion des expressions américaines.
8. C'est une "grande surface" ou un "hypermarché."
9. Les Galeries Lafayette sont le plus grand magasin de Paris.
10. La Redoute et les Trois Suisses offrent des catalogues.

6 1. au sous-sol
2. au 5e étage
3. au 1er étage, Lafayette Sport
4. au rez-de-chaussée
5. au rez-de-chaussée, Lafayette Sport
6. au 3e étage
7. au 1er étage
8. au rez-de-chaussée
9. au rez-de-chaussée
10. au rez-de-chaussée

5 | *Répondez aux questions suivantes.*

1. Où sont les fast-foods en France?
2. Quelles sont des chaînes sandwichs en France?
3. Quels fast-foods suivent le modèle des chaînes américaines?
4. Qu'est-ce qui a augmenté le nombre de familles monoparentales?
5. Qu'est-ce qui a changé la structure de la famille traditionnelle?
6. Le franglais, qu'est-ce que c'est?
7. Qui n'aime pas l'invasion des expressions américaines?
8. Carrefour, qu'est-ce que c'est?
9. Quel est le plus grand magasin de Paris?
10. Quels magasins offrent des catalogues?

Mammouth est une "grande surface" ou un "hypermarché."

6 | *Les Galeries Lafayette offrent plus de 80.000 marques dans leur magasin, qui est le plus grand de Paris. Regardez le plan du magasin. Puis dites à quel étage on peut trouver les articles suivants.*

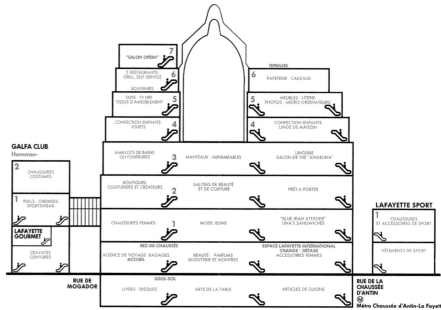

1. un livre sur l'histoire de France
2. une disquette
3. des baskets
4. une valise
5. un sweat
6. des sous-vêtements
7. des vêtements pour ados
8. du mascara
9. un foulard
10. des boucles d'oreilles

Journal personnel

France is filled with American-influenced department stores, super-markets, fast-food restaurants, music, films, brands of clothing and even **franglais**. To what extent do you think that this American "invasion" is a positive force in French life? Why do many French teens readily accept these American influences in their society? Why do you think conservative French people consider this a commercial bombardment into traditional French culture?

On the other hand, in what areas has French culture influenced American life? What American products are advertised with a French "flavor"? What stereotypes about France or French people do these ads reinforce? Make a list of as many French words as you can that are commonly used in English. You might consider the areas of food, fashion and politics.

Structure

Demonstrative adjectives

Demonstrative adjectives point out specific people or things. **Ce**, **cet** and **cette** mean "this" or "that"; **ces** means "these" or "those." Demonstrative adjectives agree with the nouns that follow them.

	Singular		Plural
Masculine before a Consonant Sound	**Masculine before a Vowel Sound**	**Feminine**	
ce coin	cet immigré	**cette** radio	ces notes

Cet après-midi j'avais vraiment besoin de rigoler.	*This afternoon I really needed to laugh.*
Je peux toujours compter sur **ces** amis.	*I can always count on these friends.*

To make a clear distinction between who or what is closer to the speaker and who or what is farther away, add **-ci** after the noun to mean "this" or "these" or **-là** after the noun to mean "that" or "those."

On trouve toujours un bon choix dans ce fast-food**-ci**.	*You always find a good choice at this fast-food restaurant.*
Je dois étudier très dur pour cette interro**-là**.	*I have to study very hard for that test.*

Workbook Activity 11

Teacher's Notes

1. Demonstrative adjectives were introduced on page 249 in the first level of C'*est à toi!* and reviewed on page 67 in the second level. 2. Remind students that there is liaison after **cet** and **ces** when the next word begins with a vowel sound. 3. Tell students that **-ci** stands for **ici** and **-là** stands for **là-bas.**

Paired Practice

Les préférences

Put students in pairs. Give them a worksheet with pairs of pictured items, such as food, clothing, video games and cars. Make one item of each pictured pair smaller so that it looks farther away. The first student in each pair asks his or her partner questions based on the odd-numbered pairs, for example,

Est-ce que tu préfères cette glace-ci ou cette glace-là? The second student responds, for example, **Je préfère cette glace-ci.** Then the second student asks the first student questions based on the even-numbered pairs.

Audiocassette/CD
Activity 7

Answers

7 1. Cette chanson-ci est en anglais.
2. Ces mots-là sont d'origine américaine.
3. Ces groupes-là sont franco-phones.
4. Ces chaînes-ci sont obligées de diffuser beaucoup d'émissions européennes.
5. Cette discothèque-là est populaire parmi les jeunes.
6. Cette marque-ci de chaussures de sport est française.
7. Ces ados-ci sont de bons amis.
8. Cette fille-là est plus engagée dans tout ce qui se passe dans son lycée.

8 1. Comment tu trouves ces bottes? Et toi, comment tu trouves ces bottes?
2. Comment tu trouves ce pull? Et toi, comment tu trouves ce pull?
3. Comment tu trouves cette casquette? Et toi, comment tu trouves cette casquette?
4. Comment tu trouves ces chemises? Et toi, comment tu trouves ces chemises?
5. Comment tu trouves ce tee-shirt? Et toi, comment tu trouves ce tee-shirt?
6. Comment tu trouves cet imperméable? Et toi, comment tu trouves cet imperméable?
Students' responses to these questions will vary.

Pratique

7 *Décrivez les personnes et les choses indiquées en utilisant l'adjectif démonstratif convenable. Suivez les modèles.*

1. la chanson/ici/en anglais
2. les mots/là-bas/d'origine américaine
3. les groupes/là-bas/francophone
4. les chaînes/ici/obligé de diffuser beaucoup d'émissions européennes
5. la discothèque/là-bas/populaire parmi les jeunes
6. marque de chaussures de sport/ici/français
7. les ados/ici/de bons amis
8. la fille/là-bas/plus engagé dans tout ce qui se passe dans son lycée

Modèles:
le cours/ici/plus difficile que les autres
Ce cours-ci est plus difficile que les autres.

la famille/là-bas/monoparental
Cette famille-là est monoparentale.

ATTENTION EXCLU !
Ce mois-ci à la Fnac...

«Ce film-là, je l'ai sous-estimé.»

Pourriez-vous m[...] recommander un h[...]

Cet hôtel-là est moins cher que cet hôtel-ci.

8 *Il y a des soldes à Naf Naf. Avec un(e) partenaire, donnez vos opinions sur les vêtements qui sont en solde. Suivez le modèle.*

Modèle:

299F 199F

Élève A: Comment tu trouves ce jean?
Élève B: Il est assez beau, mais cher. Et toi, comment tu trouves ce jean?
Élève A: Il me semble laid.

299F 149F
1.

Naf Naf
49F 39F
3.

219F 179F
2.

129F 89F
4.

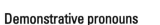

5.   6.

■ **Workbook Activities 12-13**

Demonstrative pronouns

The demonstrative pronoun **celui** points out specific people or things and is often used to replace the demonstrative adjective **ce** plus a noun. The form of **celui** agrees in gender and in number with the noun it replaces. The singular forms mean "this one," "that one" or "the one." The plural forms mean "these," "those" or "the ones."

	Masculine	Feminine
Singular	celui	celle
Plural	ceux	celles

Même si nous n'avons pas les mêmes idées, nous acceptons celles des autres dans le groupe.

Celui qui étudie dur réussit.

Even if we don't have the same ideas, we accept those of the others in the group.

The one who studies hard succeeds.

A demonstrative pronoun is never used alone in a sentence. It is followed by **-ci** or **-là**, **qui** or **que**, or **de**.

Add **-ci** or **-là** after a form of **celui** to indicate a choice, to clarify or to single out. To point out who or what is closer to the speaker (*this one, these*), add **-ci**; to point out who or what is farther away (*that one, those*), add **-là**.

Quels mecs travaillent à la Fnac? Ceux-ci ou ceux-là?

Which guys work at Fnac? These or those?

Je trouve mes copines françaises plus circonspectes que Shelley, mais c'est parce que celles-là habitent une grande ville.

I think my French friends are more reserved than Shelley, but that's because they (those girls) live in a big city.

> chaque mois
> l'histoire et l'actualité du jazz,
> pour ceux qui aiment
> (vraiment) le jazz !

> **Gagnez** votre place de football et celle d'une personne de votre choix pour assister à un match du Tournoi de France.

Et pour visiter les monuments?

Pour celui-ci, allez tout droit, puis tournez à gauche sur l'avenue de la République.

Teacher's Notes

1. **Celui-ci** or **celle-ci** may also mean "the latter." **Celui-là** or **celle-là** may also mean "the former." A form of **celui-ci** always comes before a form of **celui-là** when both occur in the same sentence, for example, **D'où viennent tes copains Shelley et Martin?** (*Where do your friends Shelley and Martin come from?*) **Celui-ci est français, et celle-là est américaine.** (*The latter is French, and the former is American.*) Point out that in English we tend to use the reverse of this phrasing, saying "former" before "latter." 2. When a form of **celui** is used with the relative pronoun **que**, there is agreement between the past participle and the demonstrative pronoun, for example, **Les photos? Celles que nous avons vues étaient jolies.** 3. In formal French a form of **celui-ci** is often used to replace a personal pronoun, for example, **J'ai fait la connaissance de ta camarade de chambre quand celle-ci habitait à Toulon.** 4. A form of **celui de** can also express relationship or origin. It can be followed by an adverb or by a verb.

Paired Practice

Le marché aux puces

Bring to class pairs of some old items, for example, two purses, two skirts, two pairs of tennis shoes, etc. Arrange them on a table so that the similar items are not next to each other. Put students in pairs. One student plays the role of a vendor at a flea market, the other plays the role of a shopper.

The shopper indicates interest in an item, and the vendor asks him or her to specify which one, using a demonstrative pronoun. The vendor gives the price, and the shopper makes a selection. You may want to model the following role-play with a student before pairs begin. —**Je peux voir ces tennis? —Lesquels? Ceux-là? —Non, ceux-ci. —Ils coûtent 25 francs. —Bon. Je les prends.**

On protège toujours ceux que l'on aime.

Modèle:

Philippe est reporter pour ce journal.
Pour celui-ci ou celui-là?

Théâtre Ouvert • Jardin d'hiver
Celle-là
de Daniel Danis • Mise en scène Alain Françon

Add **qui** or **que** after a form of **celui** to identify. Use **celui qui** as the subject and **celui que** as the object.

Les billets pour le concert d'Angélique Kidjo? Ceux que nous avons achetés étaient les plus chers.	*The tickets for the Angélique Kidjo concert? The ones (that) we bought were the most expensive.*
Ceux qui se marient le font plus tard.	*Those who get married do so later.*

Add **de** after a form of **celui** to express possession.

Le mariage qui se termine en divorce? Dommage que ça soit celui de ses parents!	*The marriage that ends in divorce? Too bad it's his parents'!*
Ces notes-ci? Ce sont celles de Philippe.	*These notes? They are Philippe's.*

Pratique

9 | *On vous parle de Philippe, de ses amis et de ce qu'ils ont dit et fait la semaine passée. Mais vous ne comprenez pas exactement de qui ou de quoi on parle, et vous voulez qu'on soit plus précis. Posez des questions avec la forme convenable de* **celui**. *Suivez le modèle.*

1. Philippe accepte ces idées.
2. La note de Philippe dans ce cours n'était pas bonne.
3. Philippe et ses amis trouvent un bon choix dans ces fast-foods.
4. On dit que ce mariage va se terminer en divorce.
5. Les ados ont acheté ces billets.
6. Shelley prend ces cours au sérieux.
7. Shelley est membre de cette équipe.
8. Émilie et Anne préfèrent ces vêtements qui donnent l'air plus américain.
9. Philippe dit que ces compagnies françaises se trouvent aux États-Unis.

Ces passants sont mes professeurs.

Ceux-ci ou ceux-là?

Ces objets perdus, à qui sont-ils (to whom do they belong)?

Marianne   Chloé   Daniel

Nadia

Alex

Philippe

Nora

Hélène

Malick

1. Cette cage-ci?
2. Ces chaussures-ci?
3. Ce CD-ci?
4. Ces chiens-ci?
5. Ces sandwichs-ci?
6. Ce peigne-ci?
7. Ces disquettes-ci?
8. Cette raquette-ci?

Modèle:

Ce carnet-ci?
C'est celui de Philippe.

Avec un(e) partenaire, posez des questions sur vos préférences. Puis répondez aux questions. Suivez le modèle.

1. les tableaux (de Van Gogh/de Monet)
2. la musique (de Céline Dion/de LeAnn Rimes)
3. les livres (de John Grisham/de Jane Austen)
4. les vêtements (de Tommy Hilfiger/de Calvin Klein)
5. la nourriture (qu'on prépare à la maison/qu'on sert au fast-food)
6. les sports (d'été/d'hiver)
7. les voitures (qui viennent du Japon/qui viennent des États-Unis)
8. le climat (du Canada/du Togo)

Modèle:

les films (de Will Smith/de Brad Pitt)

Élève A: Tu préfères les films de Will Smith ou de Brad Pitt?

Élève B: Je préfère ceux de Will Smith. Et toi, tu préfères les films de Will Smith ou de Brad Pitt?

Élève A: Moi aussi, je préfère ceux de Will Smith.

Tu préfères les sculptures de Rodin ou de Claudel?

Je préfère celles de Rodin.

Answers

10 1. C'est celle de Marianne.
2. Ce sont celles de Chloé.
3. C'est celui de Nora.
4. Ce sont ceux de Malick.
5. Ce sont ceux d'Alex.
6. C'est celui de Nadia.
7. Ce sont celles d'Hélène.
8. C'est celle de Daniel.

11 1. Tu préfères les tableaux de Van Gogh ou de Monet? Et toi, tu préfères les tableaux de Van Gogh ou de Monet?
2. Tu préfères la musique de Céline Dion ou de LeAnn Rimes? Et toi, tu préfères la musique de Céline Dion ou de LeAnn Rimes?
3. Tu préfères les livres de John Grisham ou de Jane Austen? Et toi, tu préfères les livres de John Grisham ou de Jane Austen?
4. Tu préfères les vêtements de Tommy Hilfiger ou de Calvin Klein? Et toi, tu préfères les vêtements de Tommy Hilfiger ou de Calvin Klein?
5. Tu préfères la nourriture qu'on prépare à la maison ou qu'on sert au fast-food? Et toi, tu préfères la nourriture qu'on prépare à la maison ou qu'on sert au fast-food?
6. Tu préfères les sports d'été ou d'hiver? Et toi, tu préfères les sports d'été ou d'hiver?
7. Tu préfères les voitures qui viennent du Japon ou qui viennent des États-Unis? Et toi, tu préfères les voitures qui viennent du Japon ou qui viennent des États-Unis?
8. Tu préfères le climat du Canada ou du Togo? Et toi, tu préfères le climat du Canada ou du Togo?
Students' responses to these questions will vary.

Communication

Modèle:

Anne-Marie: Quel est le fast-food
que tu préfères?

Chantal: Celui que je préfère,
c'est Burger King.

Anne-Marie: Ah bon? Pourquoi?

Chantal: Parce qu'on a les
meilleures frites.

12 Faites une enquête pour savoir ce que les élèves dans votre cours de français préfèrent. Copiez la grille suivante. Puis demandez à trois élèves de vous dire le fast-food, le magasin, la musique, les loisirs et le cours qu'ils préfèrent, et pourquoi. Écrivez leurs réponses dans les espaces blancs convenables.

	Chantal	Francis	Élise
fast-food raison	Burger King On a les meilleures frites.		
magasin raison			
musique raison			
loisirs raison			
cours raison			

Quels loisirs préfères-tu?

Je préfère le camping parce que j'aime me distraire à la campagne

13 Et vous, qu'est-ce que vous préférez comme fast-food, magasin, musique, loisirs et cours, et pourquoi? Vos préférences ressemblent-elles à celles des élèves dans votre cours de français? Écrivez un paragraphe où vous comparez vos choix avec ceux des trois élèves dans l'Activité 12. Si vous êtes d'accord avec les choix de ces élèves, comparez vos raisons. Si vous disputez leurs choix, dites pourquoi.

Sur la bonne piste

In this unit you will read an excerpt from *Les petits enfants du siècle*, a novel by Christiane Rochefort about a young girl growing up in **la banlieue de Paris** (*the suburbs of Paris*). As you read, focus on the setting (**le milieu**) of the story. Setting, in its narrowest sense, is the time and place in which a literary work takes place, together with all the details used to create a sense of a particular time and place. The setting does not advance the story's plot. However, it does give a strong sense of the world in which the main character or characters live. Writers create setting by describing such elements as landscape, scenery, buildings, furniture, clothing, weather and season. Do you remember reading an excerpt from *Au revoir, les enfants* in **Unité 3**? The setting of that story, in its narrowest sense, is a Catholic boarding school in France during the Nazi occupation. But we learn more about the setting by focusing on how characters talk and behave. We discover that the students are living in an intensely moral environment where theft cannot go unnoticed or unpunished. The setting of *Au revoir, les enfants* is then also the confrontation between Père Jean and the boys that Joseph, the kitchen worker, traded with. Père Jean uses this opportunity to instruct his pupils about the real meaning of liberty. Père Jean's moral code is contrasted with the code of the secular world, characterized by the black market, where money and the goods it can purchase represent success. This is setting in its broadest sense, a revelation of the general social, political, moral and psychological conditions in which the characters find themselves.

As you read this excerpt from *Les petits enfants du siècle* for the first time, determine its setting in the narrowest sense. Does Josyane live in a house or an apartment? How many rooms does her home have? Does each member of her family have a quiet room to go to, or do they all live on top of each other, scrambling for space? Does Josyane have access to a park in her neighborhood or only to an endless row of tall concrete buildings? What century does the title refer to?

Once you have determined its setting in the narrowest sense, read the story again to define its setting in the broadest sense. What are the general social and psychological conditions that frame Josyane's life? Does Josyane's family belong to the middle class or the working class? Do her parents treat her well, or are they mean to her? Does she have a positive image of herself, or does she have low self-esteem? Why or why not? In response to what incidents does Josyane's character develop? Is she responsible or irresponsible? Do her parents allow her a choice? Based on the social and psychological conditions in Josyane's life, what opportunities do you think she will have in the future? Do you think her adult life will resemble that of her parents?

Avant de lire l'extrait du roman, répondez aux questions suivantes.

1. Où habites-tu? Y es-tu content(e), ou choisirais-tu un autre endroit si c'était possible? Si oui, lequel et pourquoi?
2. Combien d'enfants y a-t-il dans ta famille? Quelles sont les responsabilités de chaque enfant? À quel âge as-tu commencé à faire des corvées à la maison?
3. Est-ce que les rôles de tes parents sont traditionnels ou non-traditionnels? Compterais-tu jouer les mêmes rôles avec ton mari ou ta femme si tu te mariais?

Advanced Placement

Teacher's Notes

1. **Sur la bonne piste, Leçon B**, is designed to develop skills that will help students prepare to take the Advanced Placement Exam in French Literature. In this section students read a variety of prose, poetry and drama from different periods; answer content questions; and demonstrate their critical understanding of literary techniques, such as character development, setting, point of view, satire, figures of speech and inference. In this **Sur la bonne piste** section, students learn about setting in its narrowest and broadest sense. 2. Christiane Rochefort challenged the rosy picture of economic development and social progress by illustrating the negative aspects of France's rapid postwar modernization in *Les petits enfants du siècle* (1961). Considered **un roman réaliste**, *Les petits enfants du siècle* won **le Prix Populiste** in 1962. Rochefort's first novel, *Le repos du guerrier*, caused a scandal with its realistic use of language. Rochefort also wrote *Les stances à Sophie* (1963) and *Une rose pour Morrison* (1966).

Answers

15 1. 6
2. 10
3. 1
4. 2
5. 4
6. 8
7. 9
8. 5
9. 7
10. 3

16 Possible answers:

1. Le milieu de l'histoire est un appartement dans une cité dans la banlieue de Paris.

2. Les parents de Josyane avaient besoin d'argent.

3. On a l'impression que les parents de Josyane n'étaient pas heureux quand elle est née. Ils voulaient de l'argent et des vacances plus qu'un enfant.

4. Cette famille était ouvrière parce que le père travaillait dans une usine et la famille avait besoin d'Allocations Familiales.

5. Josyane dit "Je ne faisais pas les choses comme il faut." Cette attitude vient de ses parents.

6. La mère de Josyane disait à sa fille de se dépêcher de grandir pour qu'elle puisse l'aider un peu.

7. Les parents de Josyane jouaient des rôles traditionnels. Le père travaillait. La mère s'occupait des enfants et de l'appartement. Elle ne travaillait plus à l'usine après la naissance de Chantal.

8. Il y avait cinq enfants dans la famille de Josyane.

9. Josyane achetait le pain, poussait les jumeaux dans leur double landau, le long des blocs, pour qu'ils prennent l'air et surveillait Patrick.

10. Le père de Josyane a donné une gifle à Patrick quand celui-ci a mis un chat dans la machine à laver.

Les petits enfants du siècle

C'était un dimanche au début de l'hiver. Mes parents... étaient heureux, mais ils avaient besoin d'argent. Les Allocations Familiales arriveraient donc au bon moment.

Je naquis... le 2 août. C'était ma date correcte, mais je faisais rater les vacances à mes parents, en les retenant à Paris tout le mois d'août, alors que l'usine, où travaillait mon père, était fermée. Je ne faisais pas les choses comme il faut.

J'étais pourtant en avance pour mon âge: Patrick avait à peine pris ma place dans mon berceau que je me montrais capable, en m'accrochant aux meubles, de quitter la pièce dès qu'il se mettait à pleurer. Au fond je peux bien dire que c'est Patrick qui m'a appris à marcher.

Quand les jumeaux firent leur arrivée à la maison, je m'habillais déjà toute seule et je savais poser sur la table les couverts et le pain, en me mettant sur la pointe des pieds.

—Et dépêche-toi de grandir, disait ma mère, pour que tu puisses m'aider un peu.

Elle était déjà malade quand je la connus. Elle ne pouvait pas aller à l'usine plus d'une semaine de suite. Après la naissance de Chantal, elle s'arrêta complètement.

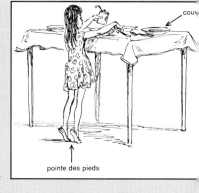

pointe des pieds

À ce moment-là je pouvais déjà rendre pas mal de services, aller acheter le pain, pousser les jumeaux dans leur double landau, le long des blocs, pour qu'ils prennent l'air, et surveiller Patrick, qui était en avance lui aussi, malheureusement. Il n'avait même pas trois ans quand il mit un petit chat dans la machine à laver. Cette fois-là, quand même, papa lui donna une bonne gifle: on n'avait même pas fini de payer la machine.

Je commençais à aller à l'école. Le matin je préparais le déjeuner pour les garçons, je les emmenais à la maternelle, et j'allais à l'école. À midi, on restait à la cantine. J'aimais la cantine, on s'assoit et

gifle

machine à laver

les assiettes arrivent toutes remplies. C'est toujours bon ce qu'il y a dans des assiettes qui arrivent toutes remplies. Les autres filles en général n'aimaient pas la cantine, elles trouvaient que c'était mauvais. Je me demande ce qu'elles avaient à la maison.

Le soir, je ramenais les garçons et je les laissais dans la cour, à jouer avec les autres. Je montais prendre les sous et je redescendais aux commissions. Maman faisait le dîner, papa rentrait et ouvrait la télé, maman et moi nous faisions la vaisselle, et ils allaient se coucher. Moi, je restais dans la cuisine, à faire mes devoirs.

11. Le matin Josyane préparait le déjeuner pour les garçons et elle les emmenait à la maternelle. Le soir elle ramenait les garçons. Elle les laissait jouer dans la cour pendant qu'elle faisait les commissions. Après le dîner elle faisait la vaisselle avec sa mère.

12. Quand elle parle des "assiettes [qui] arrivent toutes remplies," on a l'impression que Josyane mangeait mieux à l'école que chez elle.

13. Le vieil appartement de Josyane était sale avec de l'eau sur le palier. Le nouvel appartement de Josyane était plus grand, avec trois chambres et une cuisine-salle de séjour.

14. Le soir de devoirs représentait un désert de paix où elle entendait le silence.

15. Non, selon Josyane, les devoirs ne servaient à rien.

Maintenant, notre appartement était bien. Avant, on habitait dans le treizième, une sale chambre avec l'eau sur le palier. Quand le quartier avait été démoli, on nous avait mis ici, dans cette Cité. On avait reçu le nombre de pièces auquel nous avions droit selon le nombre d'enfants. Les parents avaient une chambre, les garçons une autre. Moi, je couchais avec les bébés dans la troisième. On avait une salle de bains, où on avait mis la machine à laver, et une cuisine-salle de séjour, où on mangeait. C'est sur la table de la cuisine que je faisais mes devoirs. C'était mon bon moment: quel bonheur quand ils étaient tous couchés, et que je me retrouvais seule dans la nuit et le silence! Le jour, je n'entendais pas le bruit, je ne faisais pas attention; mais le soir j'entendais le silence. Le silence commençait à dix heures: les fenêtres s'éteignaient, les radios se taisaient, les bruits, les voix, et, à dix heures et demie, c'était fini. Plus rien. Le désert. J'étais seule, en paix. Je me suis mise à aimer mes devoirs peu à peu. J'aurais bien passé ma vie à ne faire que des choses qui ne servaient à rien.

Cité

Mettez les événements du roman en ordre chronologique. Écrivez "1" pour la première phrase, "2" pour la deuxième phrase, etc.

1. Chantal est née.
2. Josyane a commencé à aimer ses devoirs.
3. Josyane est née.
4. Josyane a fait rater les vacances à ses parents.
5. Josyane a appris à marcher.
6. Patrick a mis un chat dans la machine à laver.
7. Josyane a commencé à aller à l'école.
8. Les jumeaux sont nés.
9. Josyane a commencé à acheter le pain.
10. Patrick est né.

Répondez aux questions suivantes.

1. Quel est le milieu de l'histoire?
2. De quoi est-ce que les parents de Josyane avaient besoin au début du roman?
3. Avez-vous l'impression que les parents de Josyane étaient heureux quand elle est née? Pourquoi ou pourquoi pas?
4. Cette famille était-elle bourgeoise (*middle class*) ou ouvrière (*working class*)? Comment le savez-vous?
5. Comment est-ce que Josyane se critique dans le deuxième paragraphe? D'où vient cette attitude?

Teacher's Notes

1. Point out that some verbs in this selection, such as **naquis**, **firent** and **donna**, are in the literary past tense, **le passé simple**. You may want to acquaint students with its formation for recognition purposes only.
2. You might want to describe the historical and sociological setting of *Les petits enfants du siècle*. After World War II France enjoyed unparalleled prosperity as it recovered from the devastation of occupation and war. Industrial production increased, and business began to modernize. Employees' incomes increased steadily. The working class became the new consumers as increased spending power made refrigerators, washing machines, cars and televisions more affordable. As more people moved to the city, new housing construction became imperative. Soon old, dilapidated neighborhoods gave rise to suburban **cités**. To increase the birthrate, the government granted tax breaks for each child and made apartment size contingent on family size to encourage families to have more children, a policy known as **la politique nataliste**. Such government incentives encouraged mothers to stay home with their growing families. 3. If students want to finish reading the novel, it is published by EMC/Paradigm in the *Easy Readers* series (Christiane Rochefort *Les petits enfants du siècle*). 4. Some new words used in the novel and cognates not found in the end vocabulary of *C'est à toi!* are used to ask questions about *Les petits enfants du siècle* in Activity 16.

6. Pourquoi la mère de Josyane disait-elle à sa fille de se dépêcher de grandir?
7. Les parents de Josyane jouaient-ils des rôles traditionnels? Pourquoi ou pourquoi pas?
8. Combien d'enfants y avait-il dans la famille de Josyane?
9. Quand Chantal est née, comment est-ce que Josyane aidait sa mère?
10. Comment le père a-t-il discipliné Patrick quand celui-ci a mis un chat dans la machine à laver?
11. Le matin et le soir, que faisait Josyane pour aider sa mère quand Josyane a commencé à aller à l'école?
12. Avez-vous l'impression que Josyane mangeait bien chez elle? Pourquoi ou pourquoi pas?
13. Comment était le vieil appartement de Josyane? Combien de pièces y avait-il dans le nouvel appartement?
14. Que représentait le soir de devoirs pour Josyane?
15. Selon Josyane, les devoirs servaient-ils à quelque chose?

---

17 *Complétez le schéma* (outline) *de l'extrait* (excerpt).

Le titre:

Le milieu:

La période de la vie de Josyane:

Les personnages (*characters*) et une petite description de ce qu'ils font:

---

18 *Indiquez autant de* (as many) *détails que possible pour décrire le milieu dans lequel le roman est situé. On a déjà indiqué un détail pour chaque aspect.*

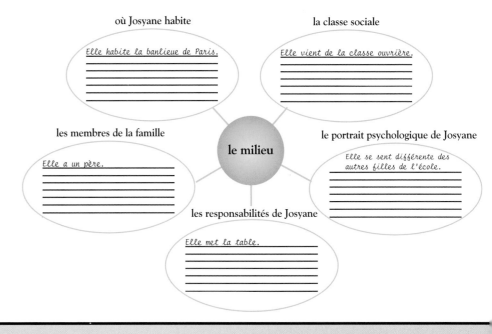

où Josyane habite

Elle habite la banlieue de Paris.

la classe sociale

Elle vient de la classe ouvrière.

les membres de la famille

Elle a un père.

le milieu

le portrait psychologique de Josyane

Elle se sent différente des autres filles de l'école.

les responsabilités de Josyane

Elle met la table.

Écrivez un paragraphe dans lequel vous comparez votre vie à celle de Josyane. Aviez-vous autant de responsabilités qu'elle quand vous étiez petit(e)? Quelles étaient vos responsabilités? Quelles étaient les responsabilités de Josyane? Vos parents jouent-ils des rôles traditionnels ou non-traditionnels? Et les parents de Josyane? Est-ce que votre famille est bourgeoise? Ouvrière? Et la famille de Josyane? Que pensez-vous de vous-même (yourself)? Pourquoi le pensez-vous? Que pense Josyane d'elle-même (herself)? Pourquoi?

Choisissez un endroit réel ou imaginaire pour créer le milieu d'une histoire, par exemple, un café, une pâtisserie, une librairie, un château, une école ou une maison. Commencez avec une description détaillée de l'endroit. Quelles sont les qualités uniques à cet endroit? Y a-t-il des tableaux aux murs ou de la musique? Que voit-on par la fenêtre? Quel temps fait-il? Qu'est-ce qu'on sent (smell)? Ensuite, décrivez les personnages dans cet endroit. Enfin, écrivez un dialogue qui révèle l'aspect social, politique, moral et psychologique dans lequel les personnages se trouvent.

Dossier fermé

Avant ton départ pour la France, ta bonne amie t'a donné de l'argent et t'a demandé de lui acheter un ensemble parisien très chic. Maintenant que tu es à Paris, à quel magasin iras-tu pour acheter cet ensemble?

     B.   Tu iras aux Galeries Lafayette.

On vend des vêtements très chic aux Galeries Lafayette. Mammouth et Monoprix vendent aussi des vêtements, mais pas ceux qui sont vraiment élégants. Si tu veux faire plaisir à ton amie et l'impressionner, achète son ensemble aux Galeries Lafayette.

À Monoprix tu ne trouveras pas d'ensemble élégant.

C'est à moi!

Now that you have completed this unit, take a look at what you should be able to do in French. Can you do all of these tasks?

➤ I can ask for information about various topics, including how long something has been going on.

➤ I can report to someone about something.

➤ I can make a generalization.

➤ I can explain why.

➤ I can ask for and give clarification by pointing out which one(s).

➤ I can compare people and things.

➤ I can say what is unimportant.

➤ I can ask someone's opinion about something.

➤ I can ask about and tell what someone prefers.

➤ I can propose solutions by saying what would happen.

➤ I can ask about someone's dissatisfaction with something.

➤ I can say what surprises me.

➤ I can say that I disagree with someone.

➤ I can describe someone's character traits.

➤ I can express pity.

Pour voir si vous avez bien compris la culture francophone, décidez si chaque phrase est vraie ou fausse.

1. Le Togo est un pays du Maghreb.
2. Les HLM offrent des appartements à tout le monde.
3. Quelquefois on appelle les HLM des "cages à lapins" parce que les appartements sont très petits.
4. En France, si les familles ont au moins deux enfants, elles touchent les allocations familiales.
5. Les immigrés représentent 20 pour cent de la population française.
6. Il y a peu de chaînes de restaurants américaines en France, et elles n'ont pas connu beaucoup de succès.
7. La plupart des enfants français vivent dans des familles monoparentales.
8. Le franglais est bien accepté en France, même par le gouvernement.
9. Carrefour est une "grande surface" où on peut tout acheter.
10. Pour un meilleur choix de parfums, faites du shopping au Printemps.

Answers

1. fausse
2. fausse
3. vraie
4. vraie
5. fausse
6. fausse
7. fausse
8. fausse
9. vraie
10. vraie

Teacher's Notes

1. While French is the official language of Togo, over 40 other languages and dialects are used in daily affairs, including Ewe, Kotokoli, Kabrai, Hausa, Ana and Bassari. 2. Lomé, the largest city as well as the capital of Togo, is located on the western border of the country near Ghana. A bustling seaport, the city is the regional commercial and trade center. 3. Togo suffers from a shortage of schools and qualified teachers. Only about one-fifth of the students who complete elementary school go on to secondary education. Togo's university at Lomé was established in 1965. 4. Other agricultural products, grown mainly for consumption by the population, include corn, rice, manioc, yams, millet and peanuts. In addition to cotton, coffee and cocoa, phosphates are also exported. Togo's economic problems include insufficient export products, periodic droughts and transportation difficulties.

Communication orale

Avec un(e) partenaire, jouez les rôles d'un reporter pour Un Monde Meilleur *et d'un(e) jeune immigré(e). Le reporter interviewe l'immigré(e) pour un article qu'il va écrire au sujet de l'immigration en France vue par un(e) ado. Pendant l'interview le reporter demande à l'immigré(e):*

1. son pays d'origine
2. depuis combien de temps il ou elle est en France
3. pourquoi sa famille est venue s'installer en France
4. si sa famille est monoparentale ou nucléaire
5. si le chef de famille travaille
6. de décrire son logement et son ambiance
7. si la plupart des Français traitent bien l'immigré(e) et sa famille
8. quels problèmes sont les plus sérieux pour les immigrés

Pendant votre conversation, le reporter doit prendre des notes. En finissant l'interview, changez de rôles et répétez l'activité.

Comment est ton logement et son ambiance?

Nous sommes dans une vieille HLM où les résidents s'entendent bien.

Communication écrite

Maintenant, en vous servant de vos notes de l'activité précédente, écrivez l'article pour Un Monde Meilleur *au sujet de l'immigration en France vue par un(e) ado. Après que vous avez discuté les problèmes des immigrés qui sont les plus sérieux, proposez quelques solutions en forme de propositions.*

Communication active

To ask for information, use:

Depuis combien de temps es-tu en France?   *How long have you been in France?*

Vous êtes combien?   *How many of you are there?*

OUVERT
de 8 h 30 à 11 h 30
et
de 12 h 15 à 19 h 30

Vous êtes combien?

Nous sommes trois.

Teacher's Note

Dictation

To provide additional written practice, you might want to give this dictation. Read each sentence twice, once at a natural speed and once more slowly. Have students write what you say. As a group correction activity, either put the paragraph on a transparency in advance or have volunteers write the sentences on the board.

François est un nouveau résident dans une HLM. Laquelle? Celle qui s'appelle Cité Jardins à Champigny. François a déjà deux amis, Pierre et Saïd. Celui-ci est maghrébin, mais celui-là est français. C'est samedi soir et François veut sortir. Saïd lui dit, "Si je ne devais pas travailler ce soir, je sortirais avec toi." Pierre veut aller dans une discothèque. "Cette discothèque-là a une bonne ambiance," dit Pierre quand ils arrivent au coin de la rue. Ils ne perdent pas leur temps. Ils y entrent.

To report, use:

Il m'**a annoncé que** ses parents allaient divorcer.

He announced to me that his parents were going to get divorced.

To state a generalization, use:

La plupart des résidents étaient au chômage.

Most of the residents were unemployed.

To explain something, use:

Pour plusieurs raisons.

For several reasons.

On appelait notre HLM un "huit cent huit" **car** il y avait 808 appartements.

They called our HLM an "808" because there were 808 apartments.

To request clarification, use:

Lesquelles sont les plus importantes?

Which (ones) are the most important?

Parmi les immigrés, **lesquels** ont des ennuis?

Among the immigrants, which ones have problems?

Lesquels vas-tu inviter?

Je vais inviter tous les copains.

To clarify, use:

Même si nous n'avons pas les mêmes idées, nous acceptons **celles** des autres dans le groupe.

Even if we don't have the same ideas, we accept those of the others in the group.

Ceux que nous avons achetés étaient les plus chers.

The ones that we bought were the most expensive.

Celui qui étudie dur réussit.

The one who studies hard succeeds.

Celle qui a les cheveux roux s'appelle Shelley.

The one who has red hair is Shelley.

Ceux qui l'ont déjà fait vous le diront: vous allez faire le voyage de votre vie.

To compare, use:

Il y a **plus de** Français parmi les
résidents.

*There are more French people
among the residents.*

Il y a **moins de** familles qui touchent
les allocations.

*There are fewer families that
get benefits.*

On dépense **plus du** budget familial
pour le logement.

*They spend more of the family
budget for housing.*

Plus les femmes travaillent, **plus** les
repas sont simples et rapides.

*The more women work, the
simpler and faster meals are.*

To express unimportance, use:

Rien d'important aujourd'hui.

Nothing important today.

To inquire about opinions, use:

Quelle sera l'opinion de Kofi?

What will Kofi's opinion be?

Selon toi, à quel avenir les
immigrés peuvent-ils s'attendre?

*According to you, what sort of
future can immigrants expect?*

Es-tu optimiste?

Are you optimistic?

To ask about preference, use:

Qu'est-ce que tu voudrais faire le
weekend prochain?

*What would you like to do next
weekend?*

To state preference, use:

J'aimerais mieux me distraire à
un concert.

*I'd prefer to enjoy myself at a
concert.*

To propose solutions, use:

S'il y avait plus d'activités et moins
de chômage, est-ce que les relations
seraient meilleures?

*If there were more activities and
less unemployment, would
relations be better?*

To inquire about dissatisfaction, use:

Comment déprimant?

How (was it) depressing?

To express surprise, use:

Ah bon?

Really?

To disagree, use:

Je me suis disputé avec ma sœur.

I argued with my sister.

To describe character, use:

Je trouve mes copines françaises **un
peu** plus **circonspectes** que Shelley.

*I think my French friends are a
little more reserved than Shelley.*

To express compassion, use:

Dommage que ça soit celui de
ses parents!

Too bad it's his parents'!

Unité 8

L'histoire de France

In this unit you will be able to:

- ➤ describe past events
- ➤ state factual information
- ➤ use links
- ➤ sequence events
- ➤ explain something
- ➤ express obligation
- ➤ have something done
- ➤ express incapability
- ➤ describe character
- ➤ express criticism
- ➤ state a generalization
- ➤ boast
- ➤ state a preference
- ➤ express appreciation

Tes empreintes ici

Est-ce que l'histoire t'intéresse? As-tu jamais lu des romans d'histoire? Si oui, lesquels? Quels en étaient les héros et les héroïnes? Si tu pouvais faire la connaissance d'un(e) de ces héros ou héroïnes, qui choisirais-tu, et qu'est-ce que tu lui demanderais? Si tu pouvais être une de ces personnes, qui serais-tu? Pourquoi?

Il est intéressant d'imaginer la vie d'avant. Il y a toujours quelque chose dans les siècles passés qui t'intéresse: l'art, la musique, l'histoire politique ou la philosophie, ou peut-être une personne que tu admires pour ses idées ou pour ce qu'elle a fait. Tu trouveras que les gens n'ont pas beaucoup changé au cours de l'histoire du monde.

Aimerais-tu savoir comment vivaient les Français dans le passé? (Ussé)

Leçon A

In this lesson you will be able to:

➤ describe past events

➤ use links

➤ sequence events

➤ explain something

➤ have something done

➤ describe character

➤ state a generalization

➤ boast

➤ express appreciation

Teacher's Note

Communicative functions that are recycled in this lesson are "pointing out something," "describing physical traits," "expressing emotions," "clarifying," "pointing out exceptions" and "comparing things."

Dossier ouvert

Avec un groupe d'élèves de ton école, tu passes 15 jours en France. Pendant votre visite d'une belle cathédrale gothique, le guide vous parle des fenêtres de la cathédrale. Il dit que ces fenêtres, composées de morceaux de verre colorés, ne sont pas connues seulement pour leur beauté. Il dit que dans le passé elles avaient aussi une fonction utile. Qu'est-ce que ces fenêtres faisaient?

A. Elles permettaient aux gens d'entrer dans la cathédrale.
B. Elles permettaient à l'air d'entrer dans la cathédrale.
C. Elles racontaient des histoires de la Bible et des héros et héroïnes français.

Ce sont les événements et les gens qui font l'histoire d'un pays. Quand on étudie le passé,° on voit que les gens se sont occupés des mêmes problèmes que dans le présent. On dit que les temps changent, mais que la nature humaine ne change pas. Pourquoi étudier le passé? Parce que le passé, c'est comme un miroir du présent. Voici des descriptions de quelques personnes importantes qui ont aidé à créer la France.

Vercingétorix (72-46 avant Jésus-Christ)

l'axe chronologique

58 av. J.-C.
Jules César arrive en Gaule

52 av. J.-C.
Vercingétorix est vaincu par César

46 av. J.-C.
Vercingétorix meurt

Au temps des Romains la France s'appelait la Gaule. En ce temps-là les Gaulois° vivaient en tribus indépendantes. Jules César, qui était très ambitieux, voulait faire de la Gaule une province de Rome depuis long-temps. Il contrôlait déjà la plupart de la Gaule, mais il voulait avoir tout le pays pour devenir plus puissant. Un jeune chef qui s'appelait Vercingétorix a réuni les différentes tribus. Il n'avait que 20 ans en 52 avant Jésus-Christ quand ses 80.000 hommes ont rencontré Jules César et son armée à Alésia, près de Dijon. Jules César a réussi à vaincre° Vercingétorix et a déclaré en latin, "*Veni, vidi, vici.*" En français, on dit "Je suis venu, j'ai vu, j'ai vaincu." César a emmené Vercingétorix à Rome où il est resté prisonnier. Après six ans César l'a fait tuer.° Les Français disent que l'an 52 avant Jésus-Christ est le début de leur histoire, et que Vercingétorix est le premier héros français.

le passé le contraire du "présent"; **un(e) Gaulois(e)** une personne qui habitait la Gaule; **vaincre** *to defeat, to conquer;* **tuer** *to kill*

360 apr. J.-C.
Lutèce devient Paris

Teacher's Notes

1. Students learned **occupé(e)**, meaning "busy," in Unit 2 in the second level of *C'est à toi!* and **s'occuper de**, meaning "to take care of," in Unit 2 in the third level. 2. Alésia is the name of a Parisian **métro** stop. 3. The present tense forms of the irregular verb **vaincre** are **vaincs, vaincs, vainc, vainquons, vainquez** and **vainquent**. 4. Vercingétorix had some success fighting the Romans prior to Alésia by engaging in guerilla warfare, raiding Roman supply lines and choosing terrain unfavorable to the Romans for battles. At Alésia Vercingétorix and his warriors fought from a fortress that could not withstand attacks by Caesar's army. After capturing Vercingétorix, Caesar kept him in chains and exhibited him in Rome as part of his Gallic triumph. 5. The Gallic Wars lasted from 58 to 51 B.C. Caesar describes his version of the Gauls' rebellion in the seventh book of *Commentarii de bello gallico*. 6. The following new words appear in the time lines but are not a part of the lesson's active vocabulary: **axe, chronologique, Francs, bataille** and **cathédrale**.

Teacher's Notes

1. You might want to give students background information about the significance of events listed in the time line. In 57 B.C. what are now northern France and Belgium fell to Caesar. Gallic tribes along the Atlantic coast were conquered in 56 B.C., and in 55 B.C. and 54 B.C. Caesar campaigned in Germany and Britain. 2. The uprising led by Vercingétorix was the most serious challenge that Caesar faced in Gaul. Prior to that, Gallic tribes had asked for Caesar's protection against other tribes. 3. When Caesar became emperor, he ruled an empire that extended to the Rhine. Thanks to Caesar, the calendar is divided into 12 months; July is named after him. Caesar was killed as he entered the Senate on March 15, 44 B.C., known as the ides of March.

Charlemagne (742-814)

1. You might want to give students background information about the significance of events listed in the time line. The origins of the Franks are vague and much disputed. They first appeared as settlers along the lower Rhine. From the late third century they expanded into Roman territory in northern Gaul where they rendered military service to the Romans in exchange for status as Roman allies. Due to internal divisions, their expansion was slow and faltering, until Clovis. 2. Under Clovis, Frankish expansion dominated Gaul for 80 years. Probably for political reasons, Clovis was baptized in 496 or 506. A cruel, vicious barbarian, Clovis succeeded in extending his authority from northern France to the Pyrenees. 3. The 17-year kingship of Pépin III served as a preparation for that of his son and successor, Charlemagne. During his reign a large number of wealthy landowners swore fealty to him, and church reform was continued and extended. 4. Aix-la-Chapelle is the French name for the German city of Aachen. 5. The opposite of **Occident** is **Orient** (*East*). 6. It can be argued that the life and reign of Charlemagne belong to the history of Europe and not just that of France. It was the force of his personality that distinguished him from his predecessors and successors. Due to the difficulties involved in ruling a vast empire, Charlemagne made one son, Pépin, king of the Lombards and created a subordinate kingdom of Aquitaine for his son Louis in 781. Charlemagne added the most learned churchmen of the day to his court circle and oversaw the elimination of pagan practices, the proper observance of the Benedictine rule in monasteries, the adoption of standard texts for worship and the adoption of tithing to support churches. In the secular world he succeeded in increasing the number of learning centers, adopting a higher standard of Latin, reforming weights and measures, and introducing a standard, royally

ca. 400
Les Francs arrivent en Gaule

481
Clovis devient roi

486
Paris est la capitale de la France

751
Pépin le Bref devient roi

800
Charlemagne devient empereur

814
Charlemagne meurt

Charlemagne ("Carolus Magnus" en latin ou "Charles le Grand" en français) est né en 742. Son père était Pépin (on l'appelait "Pépin le Bref" parce qu'il était petit) et sa mère était Berthe (on l'appelait "Berthe au grand pied" parce qu'un de ses pieds était plus grand que l'autre). Charlemagne était grand, fort et sportif. Il pouvait lire et parler latin, mais il n'a jamais appris à l'écrire. Charlemagne voulait que tous les hommes sachent lire et écrire. Pour cela il a demandé aux églises d'ouvrir des écoles où on pouvait faire des études gratuites. Il a fait venir les meilleurs professeurs de son temps à son école à Aix-la-Chapelle. Pour préserver la littérature du passé, certains moines° passaient sept heures par jour à copier des livres.

En 800 Charlemagne est devenu empereur d'Occident.° Il a dit qu'il travaillait pour Dieu° en créant un si grand empire. Pour le gouverner il l'a réuni sous les mêmes lois. Il a établi partout le même système monétaire et le même système d'administration. Il a créé des marchés pour améliorer° le commerce et aider les fermiers et les familles. Les progrès en culture, en lois et en administration que Charlemagne a commencés ont pu être appréciés par tous. L'empire de Charlemagne a été le plus grand depuis celui de Jules César. Ses frontières se trouvaient en Italie, en Allemagne et en Espagne. Son fils Louis est devenu empereur en 813, et Charlemagne est mort un an plus tard. Louis a divisé l'empire entre ses trois fils. Leurs empires sont devenus les pays modernes d'Allemagne et de France.

un moine *monk;* **l'Occident (m.)** l'Ouest; **Dieu** *God;* **améliorer** faire mieux

controlled coinage and new judicial procedures. Charlemagne's military successes expanded the borders of his empire. On his death in 814, the entire empire passed to his sole surviving son, Louis. The Carolingian dynasty would never again be as strong.

Guillaume le Conquérant (1027-87)

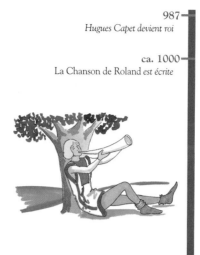

987—
Hugues Capet devient roi

ca. 1000—
La Chanson de Roland est écrite

1066—
*Les Français vainquent les
Anglais à la bataille de Hastings*

Le roi Édouard d'Angleterre a choisi son cousin Guillaume, duc de Normandie, pour être le nouveau roi d'Angleterre. Mais quand Édouard est mort, Harold est devenu roi. En entendant parler de ça, Guillaume s'est fâché. Il était fort, courageux et fier° de ses qualifications, et il pensait qu'il devait être roi. Il a d'abord réuni une armée de 8.000 hommes qui a ensuite traversé la Manche. Enfin Guillaume et son armée sont arrivés à Hastings. Après une lutte difficile, les Français ont vaincu les Anglais. L'armée de Guillaume le Conquérant a été la dernière à vaincre l'Angleterre. C'est pourquoi l'an 1066 est une date importante pour les Anglais et les Français.

Peu après les Anglais ont accepté la langue et la culture des Normands.° Guillaume a gardé les lois d'Édouard pour faire accepter son administration d'une façon plus facile. Ceux qui avaient des terres° ont échangé la loyauté envers° le roi contre° ces terres. Des Normands et des Anglais se sont mariés. Sauf pour la langue, la vie quotidienne n'a pas beaucoup changé. Guillaume a laissé un grand monument, le *Domesday Book*, et il a fait une enquête sur les gens et leurs terres. Mais Guillaume n'a jamais pu utiliser son enquête. Il est tombé° de cheval au cours d'une lutte en France et est mort un mois après en 1087. On voit toujours l'influence de Guillaume, duc de Normandie, dans les lois, le gouvernement, la littérature, la langue et la construction des châteaux et des églises.

1194—

On construit la cathédrale de Chartres

1224—

fier, fière *proud*; un(e) Normand(e) *une personne qui habite la Normandie, une province au nord-ouest de la France*; une terre *land*; envers *à*; contre *pour*; tomber *to fall*

Teacher's Notes

1. You might want to give students background information about the significance of events listed in the time line. Hugues Capet, who ruled from 987 to 996, is responsible for establishing a dynasty that transmitted the crown in the direct maie line for over three hundred years. 2. The cathedral of Chartres was erected on the site of a basilica built by early Christians, which had burned down. Through the cooperation of nobles and peasants alike, it was built in 31 years, a short span of time that gave it an unusual degree of architectural unity. For more background information on the cathedral of Chartres, refer to page 380 in the second-level Annotated Teachers' Edition of *C'est à toi!*

Teacher's Notes

1. The irregular feminine form of the adjective **fier** is **fière**. 2. Point out that **tomber** takes **être** as a helping verb in the **passé composé**. 3. As the closest heir, Guillaume was promised succession to the English throne. Harold agreed to support Guillaume's claim when he was given freedom in 1064 after being shipwrecked on the Norman coast. When Harold received a deathbed endorsement by Edward and the election of the nobles, war was inevitable. Before Guillaume's army set sail, Harold was forced to go to northern England to defeat Norwegian invaders. Guillaume's soldiers arrived on the coast of England before Harold's return. The Battle of Hastings was fought on October 14, 1066, at Senlac, seven miles northwest of Hastings, Sussex. Guillaume actually landed in England on September 28. The armies were roughly equal in size. After the English heavily repulsed the cavalry, Guillaume saved the day by rallying his forces. The battle appeared to be drawn, when toward nightfall Harold was killed and the English forces disintegrated. 4. The advantages that the Norman Conquest conferred on England were numerous. It grafted onto Anglo-Saxon institutions the Normans' superior organization and greater mastery of law. It allowed England to develop wide-reaching foreign influence by keeping the country in closer contact with Europe. In addition, it repressed internal conflict and brought greater security of life and property. Finally, it contributed to the development of Old English into Modern English by lending vocabulary and basic grammar. 5. The *Domesday Book*, considered the most important public record of medieval Europe, lists the property holders in England and the amount of land they held.

Transparency 24

Teacher's Notes

1. You might want to give students background information about the significance of events listed in the time line. The Hundred Years' War refers to a series of conflicts that embroiled France and England intermittently from 1337 to 1453. The remote causes of the conflict were the Norman Conquest of England and the accession to the English throne of Henry Plantagenet, Count of Anjou, as Henry II. Many of the causes of the dispute can be traced to the Treaty of Paris in 1259, which gave a much reduced duchy of Aquitaine to Henry III of England; he was not allowed to govern it without interference from Paris. The economic, social and political effects of the war were profound. It led to a general redistribution of wealth, and it accelerated royal demands for taxation that fostered the development of absolute monarchy in France and of parliamentary government in England. 2. Students learned about the life of Joan of Arc on page 332 in the second level of *C'est à toi!* 3. At the end of the Hundred Years' War, only Calais and the Channel Islands remained of the original extensive Plantagenet holdings in France. 4. Louis VIII, Louis IX's father, reigned for only three years. His territorial additions to France included Auvergne, Poitou and Languedoc. 5. Blanche de Castille was also in charge of her son's education. She played an important role in all his decisions until her death in 1252. 6. Louis IX's first crusade was the Seventh Crusade, which went to Egypt. Once captured, Louis had to pay a high ransom to his captors to secure his release. 7. The singular of **des vitraux** is **un vitrail**. 8. The **Sainte-Chapelle**, introduced on page 402 in the first level of *C'est à toi!*, is a marvel of Gothic architecture. Completed in less than 33 months, it was consecrated in 1248. Stained

1226
Louis IX devient roi

1248
On finit la Sainte-Chapelle

1270
Louis IX meurt

1297
Louis IX devient Saint-Louis

1337
La guerre de Cent Ans commence

1429
Jeanne d'Arc aide le roi Charles VII

1431
Jeanne d'Arc meurt

1453
La guerre de Cent Ans se termine

Louis IX (1214-70)

Louis IX rend la justice à sa cour à Paris.

Louis IX était un roi admiré par les Français. Il est devenu roi en 1226, à l'âge de 12 ans, quand son père, Louis VIII, est mort. Sa mère, Blanche de Castille, a gouverné pour Louis IX parce qu'il était trop jeune. Il est devenu pieux° et courageux. Louis IX était l'ami des gens pauvres parce qu'il faisait attention à leurs besoins. Connu pour son amour de la justice et de la paix,° sa cour se trouvait souvent sous un arbre. Même les autres chefs européens sont venus en France chercher ses conseils.°

Louis IX a participé à deux croisades. Pendant sa première croisade on l'a fait prisonnier. Par conséquent il a été obligé d'acheter sa liberté. Pendant qu'il était roi, Louis IX a fait construire la Sainte-Chapelle à Paris en 1248. Il y a mis des reliques de Jésus-Christ achetées pendant les croisades. Les vitraux° de la Sainte-Chapelle ont des couleurs magnifiques. Ce sont les plus vieux de Paris et parmi les plus beaux du monde. Au cours de sa deuxième croisade, Louis IX est mort de maladie. Les Français l'ont toujours apprécié pour son christianisme et sa justice. En 1297 Louis IX est devenu Saint-Louis.

pieux, pieuse religieux, religieuse; **la paix** le contraire de la "guerre"; **un conseil** une suggestion; **des vitraux (m.)** des fenêtres de morceaux de verre colorés

Il y a 15 belles fenêtres du XIIIᵉ siècle dans la Sainte-Chapelle. (Paris)

glass windows almost 50 feet high are nestled between pencil-like pillars and buttresses which support the weight of the walls and the roof. About half of the windows date from the 13th century. The windows portray more than 1,000 biblical scenes in a kaleidoscope of red, gold, green and blue. There are actually two separate chapels. The somber lower one was used by servants and lower court officials, while the upper one was reserved for the royal family and its courtiers. Damage inflicted during the French Revolution was repaired by Viollet-le-Duc. The **Sainte-Chapelle** was built to house Christ's crown of thorns, obtained from the Venetians in 1239. Other relics include a piece of the cross and a nail from the cross. Today they can all be seen only on Good Friday afternoon, when they are transferred from the chapel to Notre-Dame for public viewing. 9. Louis IX's last crusade, in 1270, was the Eighth Crusade. This time he landed with his army in Tunis. Louis died when a plague broke out.

Mettez les événements suivants en ordre chronologique d'après l'axe chronologique (time line) et les descriptions des Français célèbres. Écrivez "1" pour le premier événement, "2" pour le deuxième événement, etc.

1. Charlemagne a réuni son empire sous les mêmes lois, le même système monétaire et le même système d'administration.
2. Vercingétorix est devenu le premier héros français.
3. Jeanne d'Arc a aidé le roi Charles VII pendant la guerre de Cent Ans.
4. Louis IX a fait construire la Sainte-Chapelle.
5. Jules César est arrivé en Gaule.
6. Les Anglais ont accepté la langue et la culture des Normands.
7. La ville de Paris est devenue la capitale de la France.
8. Les Français ont vaincu les Anglais à Hastings.

> caisse nationale des **monuments historiques** et des **sites** ◇
>
> ## SAINTE CHAPELLE
> entrée
>
> # GRATUIT
> GROUPES SCOLAIRES
>
> VALABLE LE **17/03/1999** **0F**
> VENDU LE 17/03/1999 À 15h15
> CAISSE No 23   0001   952300007734
> ticket à conserver en cas de contrôle

Choisissez l'expression à droite qui décrit les mots à gauche.

1. une tribu
2. un événement
3. la paix
4. les Normands
5. des vitraux
6. la Gaule
7. des moines
8. un conquérant

a. les hommes de l'armée de Guillaume le Conquérant
b. des hommes pieux qui ont copié des livres
c. quelqu'un qui a vaincu d'autres gens
d. des fenêtres de verre qui ont de belles couleurs
e. quand il n'y a pas de guerre
f. le premier nom de la France
g. quelque chose qui se passe
h. un groupe de gens de la même origine gouverné par un chef

C'est à toi!

1. À ton avis, étudier le passé, c'est important? Pourquoi ou pourquoi pas?
2. À ton avis, lequel des hommes que tu viens d'étudier, Vercingétorix, Charlemagne, Guillaume le Conquérant ou Louis IX, a fait le plus pour créer la France moderne? Pourquoi?
3. Si tu pouvais parler à un de ces quatre hommes, à qui parlerais-tu, et qu'est-ce que tu lui demanderais?
4. À ton avis, quelles qualifications le chef d'un pays doit-il avoir?
5. Est-ce que tu penses que la nature humaine change ou pas? Pourquoi?
6. À ton avis, qui est le premier héros américain?
7. Est-ce que tu crois que l'éducation doive être gratuite, même à l'université?
8. Est-ce que tu as envie de voir la Sainte-Chapelle? Pourquoi ou pourquoi pas?

Audiocassette/CD Activity 3

Answers

1 1. 4
2. 2
3. 8
4. 7
5. 1
6. 6
7. 3
8. 5

2 1. h
2. g
3. e
4. a
5. d
6. f
7. b
8. c

3 Answers will vary.

Cross-curricular

Les vitraux

You may want to have students make stained glass windows to illustrate French history. Put students in pairs, and assign each pair an event from the time lines or the exposition in this lesson. Then have pairs draw the event they were assigned on tracing paper and color it using colored markers. To frame their picture, students can use black construction paper. When all the stained glass windows are ready, have students attach them to the windows in chronological order.

Teacher's Notes

1. Cognates in this reading include **exploré, conquis, consacré, conquête, fragmentée, cités, fortifiées, adversaire, populations, groupé, forces, ennemi, batailles, décisives, militaire, volontaires, endurer, attaque, supérieure, helvétiens, popularisées, attraction, général, défendre, biographie, légendaire, poème, épique, actions, héroïques, face, exploits, commandée, passage, sorte, scène, se venger, vaste, nobles, contributions, représentée, cathédrale, période, médiévale, visuelles, gloire, existe, couvre, illustre, mesure, secondaires, documentation, peuple, disputes, lépreux, hospices, fondés, musulmans, expéditions, illustrations** and **religieuses.**
2. Julius Caesar was a soldier, scholar, writer and statesman. He organized the chaos of an outworn government to build one of the greatest ancient empires. 3. Caesar's campaign against the Helvetians opens his memoirs *Commentarii de bello gallico*. 4. In an attempt to drive out Caesar's army, Vercingétorix employed a "scorched earth" policy. 5. Dijon is located 168 miles southeast of Paris and is the seat of government of the Côte d'Or department. It has been the seat of a bishopric since 1731. In 1016 it became the capital of the Dukes of Burgundy, who built up one of the most powerful states in Europe, which included Flanders and parts of Holland. In 1477, after the death of Charles the Bold, the duchy's holdings were broken up. Dijon today has a rich cultural life and a renowned university. The city's great art treasures are housed in the **musée des Beaux-Arts**, located in the **Palais des Ducs**. Although the Dukes of Burgundy held court here, it was in an older building. The **palais** on view today was built mainly in the 17th century to house the parliament. Wealthy parliament members had elegant **hôtels**

Enquête culturelle

On peut toujours voir des monuments romains en France, comme le théâtre d'Arles.

Au temps de Vercingétorix, Jules César avait déjà exploré et conquis une grande partie de l'Europe: l'Helvétie (la Suisse moderne), la Gaule et la Grande Bretagne (l'Angleterre). Avec ses armées romaines, il a rapidement vaincu les grandes tribus et a pris leurs terres pour créer l'empire romain. César a consacré six ans à la conquête de la Gaule. La Gaule était fragmentée en plusieurs cités fortifiées et préservées par de gros murs. Son adversaire principal, Vercingétorix, a pu réunir les populations de ces cités et a groupé toutes ces forces gauloises contre l'ennemi romain. Pendant plus de six mois, ils ont joué au chat et à la souris avant les batailles importantes et décisives. Mais, n'ayant jamais appris la stratégie militaire, cette armée de volontaires n'a pas pu endurer l'attaque de l'armée supérieure de Rome.

Deux des chefs helvétiens et gaulois, dont César a fait la connaissance, étaient Orgétorix et Vercingétorix. Ces noms sont popularisées aujourd'hui dans la bande dessinée *Astérix*. Le héros Astérix est un Gaulois intelligent et courageux. Quand les Français lisent aujourd'hui les aventures d'Astérix et de son ami Obélix, ils se rappellent le début de leur histoire nationale.

Dijon était la capitale de la Bourgogne, une province à l'est de la France. Au 15e siècle, l'influence des ducs de Bourgogne allait de Dijon jusqu'en Belgique. Le Palais des Ducs est toujours un centre d'attraction à Dijon. C'est aujourd'hui à Dijon qu'on prépare la moutarde qui est célèbre partout.

Comme Jules César, Charlemagne était aussi général avant de gouverner la France. On dit que pendant le 8e siècle le héros Roland a aidé Charlemagne à défendre le pays. *La Chanson de Roland*, partie de la biographie légendaire de Charlemagne, est le premier chef-d'œuvre de la littérature française. Elle a été écrite à la fin du 10e siècle, 200 ans après que les héros sont morts. Ce poème épique décrit les actions héroïques de Roland et de son oncle Charlemagne qui étaient courageux face à l'ennemi d'Espagne. Après ses exploits en Espagne, Charlemagne retourne en France et laisse une partie de son armée commandée par Roland à Roncevaux, un passage dans les Pyrénées. Dès que Charlemagne est parti avec la plupart de l'armée, l'ennemi attaque l'armée de Roland et tue presque tous les hommes. Enfin, Roland décide d'appeler

particuliers built in the 17th and 18th centuries. Besides mustard, Dijon is also famous for its **pain d'épices** and local wine trade.
6. The first time Charlemagne waged a campaign against the Moors in Spain, the rear guard of his army was ambushed at Roncevaux in the Pyrenees and all were killed, including, reputedly, his nephew Roland. This historic event inspired the most famous of

all the **chansons de geste**, *La Chanson de Roland*. In the poem Roland is too proud to summon aid until after his friend Oliver and all his men have been killed. Then Roland blows his horn with such force that he bursts his temple and dies. Charlemagne's army then returns and defeats the Saracens. The basic theme of the poem is the epic conflict between ruler and subject. Roland is wrong to set

his pride and fame above the Christian empire. The only manuscript of *La Chanson de Roland* is at Oxford. It is in Anglo-Norman and dates from about 1170. It retains much evidence of its original oral version.

Charlemagne avec son cor, une sorte de trompette. Quand Charlemagne entend le cor, il revient avec son armée. Mais il est déjà trop tard, Roland est mort. En voyant cette scène, Charlemagne décide de se venger et retourne combattre les Espagnols.

L'empire de Charlemagne était si vaste qu'il était difficile à contrôler. Il a donc décidé d'établir sa capitale à Aix-la-Chapelle en Allemagne. Il a fait ouvrir des écoles près de chaque église. Tous les enfants des nobles y étaient des élèves, et parmi eux il y avait Charlemagne, sa femme et ses enfants.

L'histoire de la vie de Charlemagne et de ses contributions à l'histoire française est représentée dans quelques vitraux de la cathédrale de Chartres. Pendant la période médiévale la plupart de la population française ne savait pas lire. Il y avait donc des aides visuelles dont on se servait pour leur apprendre ces histoires de la gloire de la France.

Cette statue de Charlemagne se trouve à Aix-la-Chapelle.

À Bayeux en Normandie, il existe une célèbre tapisserie (un long tapis qui couvre le mur) qu'a fait Mathilde, femme de Guillaume le Conquérant, avec les femmes de la cour. Cette tapisserie illustre la bataille de Hastings avec l'histoire écrite en latin. Elle mesure 70 mètres de long. On l'appelle maintenant la "tapisserie de Bayeux," et on peut la voir dans le musée dans cette ville. C'est comme une bande dessinée médiévale parce qu'il y a 73 scènes représentées en couleurs et expliquées en latin. Au-dessus et en bas, on voit des scènes de la vie quotidienne, des scènes d'animaux, et des scènes de quelques batailles secondaires. Au centre, on voit l'histoire de la bataille de Hastings. Cette documentation artistique pouvait aider les gens de ce temps à comprendre l'histoire.

Dans la tapisserie de Bayeux, il est facile de reconnaître les Anglais; ils ont les cheveux longs et des moustaches.

Teacher's Notes

1. Charlemagne ordered that bishops and abbots of monasteries open free schools in every diocese, and a law was passed that established elementary schools in rural parishes. 2. The Bayeux Tapestry, in reality an embroidery, provides historians with information about the armor, fortifications, ships, costumes and architecture at the time of the Norman Conquest. Details, such as English and Norman hair styles, are so consistent and, where they can be checked against written sources, found to be so accurate, that there is complete confidence in the embroidery as a record of life and manners during the 11th century. The battle scenes on the Bayeux Tapestry are considered to represent an acceptable outline picture of the conflict, revealing a contrast in the tactics of the two armies. Guillaume used archers supported by cavalry, while Harold defended a hill with an infantry phalanx in the Anglo-Scandinavian manner. The embroidery even contains a depiction of Halley's comet, which appeared in April, 1066. The tapestry is housed in the Museum of Queen Matilda in Bayeux.

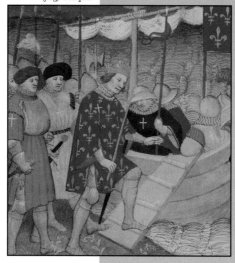

Louis IX part pour les croisades sous le drapeau (*flag*) français.

Louis IX était un roi qui restait près de son peuple. Les hommes venaient le voir pour lui expliquer leurs disputes, puis le roi décidait de leur justice. Il s'occupait des gens malades, des lépreux et des pauvres dans les hospices qu'il avait fondés.

Entre 1096 et 1291, il y a eu huit croisades. C'était des voyages dans la Terre sainte pour délivrer Jérusalem des musulmans. Seulement la première et la troisième croisade ont réussi, mais ces expéditions ont profité aux Français dans le domaine des arts, des sciences, de la littérature et du commerce parce qu'ils pouvaient découvrir des cultures différentes.

Les illustrations des vitraux de la Sainte-Chapelle parlent des histoires religieuses de la Bible en 1 134 scènes.

Pendant la Deuxième Guerre mondiale on a enlevé les vitraux de la Sainte-Chapelle pour les protéger contre les bombes. (Paris)

Les vitraux de Chartres racontent des histoires religieuses et historiques.

4 | *Répondez aux questions suivantes.*

1. Quels pays est-ce que Jules César a conquis?
2. Qu'est-ce que Vercingétorix a réussi à faire?
3. D'où vient le nom d'Astérix?
4. Quel est le produit principal de Dijon?
5. Où peut-on lire l'histoire de Charlemagne et de Roland?
6. Où peut-on voir les scènes de la vie de Charlemagne?
7. Où est racontée l'histoire de la bataille de Hastings?
8. Quelle est la longueur de la tapisserie de Bayeux?
9. Pourquoi est-ce que Louis IX était un roi très populaire?
10. Quelles sont deux aides visuelles qui ont aidé les gens à comprendre l'histoire?

Journal personnel

In this lesson you have read about several of the visual aids used during the Middle Ages to help illiterate people understand and remember history and Bible stories. What visual aids used in fields such as advertising and entertainment do we have in contemporary society that help us understand and remember what we have encountered? Are visual aids used for a different purpose today? Are current aids as effective as those of the past?

Implied in the use of these visual aids is the art of storytelling. Medieval people used visual aids to tell stories about history or religious figures. Is the art of storytelling in our culture as important as it was in the past? Storytelling is still very important in some African countries. For example, **le griot** (*storyteller*) plays an important and powerful role in African society, passing along historical and cultural information and explaining natural phenomena through the telling of legends. Why do you tell stories?

Structure

Expressions with *faire*

As you know, the verb **faire** (*to do, to make*) is one of the most frequently used verbs in French.

Ce sont les événements et les gens qui font l'histoire d'un pays.	*It's events and people that make a country's history.*

Faire is called a "building block" verb because it is used to form so many expressions in French. Some of the most common expressions with **faire** deal with various activities, the weather, shopping and traveling. Here are some examples where **faire** is used in French but a different verb is used in English. How many more can you think of?

Charlemagne a demandé aux églises d'ouvrir des écoles où on pouvait faire des études gratuites.	*Charlemagne asked churches to open schools where people could study free of charge.*
Il faisait froid quand Guillaume le Conquérant et son armée sont arrivés à Hastings.	*It was cold when William the Conqueror and his army arrived in Hastings.*
Louis IX faisait attention aux besoins des gens pauvres.	*Louis IX paid attention to the needs of poor people.*
Pendant la première croisade de Louis IX, on l'a fait prisonnier.	*During Louis IX's first crusade, they took him prisoner.*

> C'est à ce moment-là que tu as commencé à faire de la télé ?

Quand il fait beau, Julien et Aurélie aiment faire de la voile. (La Rochelle)

«X-FILES» FAIT SON CINÉMA !

Audiocassette/CD
Activity 5

Answers

5 1. Nous faisons la connaissance du roi.
2. Nicolas et Francis ne font pas attention.
3. Nadine fait le plein.
4. Mme Piedbœuf et sa fille font les courses.
5. On fait la queue.
6. Tu fais un somme.
7. Vous faites un tour de grande roue.
8. Je fais de la luge.

Paired Practice

Changing Tenses

You might have students practice using **faire** expressions in various tenses. Put students in pairs, and give each pair a note card with a sentence and a tense that they are to change the sentence to, for example, **Claude ferait enregistrer ses bagages (passé composé)**. Student A reads the first sentence to Student B, who identifies the tense being used, for example, conditional, and then changes the sentence to the tense indicated in parentheses, for example, **Claude a fait enregistré ses bagages**. Then tell the pairs to exchange their card for one belonging to another pair, at which point students switch roles. Pairs continue exchanging cards until they have practiced a sentence in the present, **passé composé**, imperfect, conditional and future.

Pratique

Modèle:

Alain

Alain fait ses devoirs.

Combien de personnes font la queue devant cette boulangerie belge? (Antwerp)

5 | *Décrivez chaque illustration en utilisant une des expressions avec **faire** de la liste suivante.*

faire le plein	faire ses devoirs
faire la queue	faire la connaissance du roi
faire les courses	ne pas faire attention
faire un somme	faire un tour de grande roue
faire de la luge	

1.   *nous*

5.   *on*

Nicolas et Francis

2.

6.   *tu*

Nadine

3.

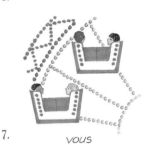

7.   *vous*

Mme Piedbœuf et sa fille

4.

8.   *je*

Game

Les charades

To give students practice reviewing expressions with **faire**, put them in small groups of four or five. Make a stack of note cards for each group on which you write **faire** commands, such as **Fais de la plongée sous-marine**! Give each group a stack of cards. The first student in each group selects a card and silently acts out the listed expression until another student in the group makes a correct identification, for example, **Tu fais de la plongée sous-marine**. The student who accurately identifies the activity selects the next card. Students continue in this fashion until all cards have been used.

Répondez à chaque question au sujet de l'histoire de France en utilisant une expression avec faire. Dans votre réponse utilisez le même temps (tense) que dans la question.

1. Qu'est-ce que Jules César voulait depuis longtemps?
2. Est-ce que César a donné sa liberté à Vercingétorix?
3. Au temps de Charlemagne, est-ce qu'on devait payer ses études?
4. Où Guillaume le Conquérant est-il allé en 1066?
5. Guillaume le Conquérant est-il tombé en faisant du footing?
6. Pourquoi est-ce que les gens pauvres aimaient Louis IX?

> Moi, j'ai fait du saut à l'élastique une fois.

Faire + infinitive

To express the idea of having someone do something or having something done, use a form of the verb **faire** followed by an infinitive. Contrast the following two sentences:

Les Martel construisent une maison.	*The Martels build a house.*
Les Martel font construire une maison.	*The Martels have a house built.*

Who does the actual building of the house in each sentence? In the first example the Martels build the house themselves. However, in the second sentence they have someone else build it for them.

The form of **faire** can be in any tense.

Louis IX a fait construire la Sainte-Chapelle.	*Louis IX had the Sainte-Chapelle built.*
Guillaume a gardé les lois d'Édouard pour faire accepter son administration d'une façon plus facile.	*William kept Édouard's laws in order to have his administration accepted more easily.*

Mme Ollivain fait étudier Guillaume en classe.

> Ici, tout le monde fait croire aux joueurs de la NBA qu'ils sont des surhommes.

> Les 7 «+» qui vous feront choisir Bouygues Telecom

Modèle:

Qu'est-ce qui fait l'histoire d'un pays?
Ce sont les événements et les gens qui font l'histoire d'un pays.

Answers

6 Possible answers:

1. Jules César voulait faire de la Gaule une province de Rome depuis longtemps.
2. Non, César l'a fait prisonnier.
3. Non, au temps de Charlemagne, on pouvait faire des études gratuites.
4. Guillaume le Conquérant a fait un voyage en Angleterre.
5. Non, il est tombé en faisant du cheval.
6. Les gens pauvres aimaient Louis IX parce qu'il faisait attention à leurs besoins.

Teacher's Notes

1. **Faire** + infinitive is also known as **faire causatif**. 2. The infinitive after **faire** can have a subject rather than an object. In the model sentence **la Sainte-Chapelle** is the object. However, in the sentence **Vous ferez venir le prisonnier** (*You'll have the prisoner come*), **le prisonnier** is the subject of **venir**. 3. Object pronouns precede the form of **faire** in their usual order, for example, **Mme Burgat fait envoyer une lettre à sa fille? Oui, elle la lui fait envoyer une lettre.** 4. In a negative command the object pronouns precede the form of **faire**, for example, **Ne les faites pas venir!** 5. To express what someone has done to or for himself or herself, use **faire** + infinitive with an indirect object reflexive pronoun, for example, **Élise s'est fait faire une nouvelle robe.** (*Élise had a new dress made for herself.*) 6. To express who does the action in a causative construction, use **par** or **à** plus a noun or pronoun, for example, **Nous avons fait nettoyer le garage par les enfants.** The **par** or **à** phrase is replaced by an indirect object pronoun, for example, **Nous leur avons fait nettoyer le garage.**

Critical Thinking

Using Faire + Infinitive

Write the infinitive expression **faire tondre la pelouse** on the board. Ask students which verb is conjugated in forming a sentence. Students should tell you that it is **faire**. Then ask students how to ask "Do you have your lawn mowed?" Students should respond **Fais-tu tondre ta pelouse?** This activity will help students see that **faire** is conjugated in the present tense and that the second verb stays in its infinitive form. Remind students they do the same thing with the construction **aller** + infinitive.

Teacher's Note

So that students can differentiate between doing things for themselves and having them done by someone else, have them write three sentences expressing household chores that they normally do, for example, **Je repasse mes vêtements.** Then, beside each sentence, have them write that they are having these chores done by someone else.

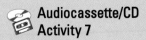
Audiocassette/CD Activity 7

Answers

7 1. Non, ils font peindre leur maison.

2. Non, il fait nettoyer sa chambre.

3. Non, elle prépare le dîner.

4. Non, il fait goûter la soupe.

5. Non, elle nourrit le chien.

6. Non, il éteint la télé.

7. Non, il fait enregistrer ses bagages.

8. Non, ils copient les livres.

When object pronouns are used, they precede the form of **faire.** There is no agreement between the past participle **fait** and a preceding direct object pronoun.

César a fait tuer Vercingétorix? — *Did Caesar have Vercingétorix killed?*

Oui, après six ans il l'a fait tuer. — *Yes, after six years he had him killed.*

Les meilleurs professeurs du temps de Charlemagne? — *The best teachers in Charlemagne's time?*

Il les a fait venir à son école. — *He had them come to his school.*

In an affirmative command, object pronouns are attached with hyphens to the form of **faire.**

Faites-les venir! — *Have them come!*

Pratique

7 *Les personnes indiquées ont-elles fait elles-mêmes (themselves) les actions illustrées? Suivez les modèles.*

Modèles:

Est-ce que M. Gastineau fait construire le garage?
Non, il construit le garage.

Est-ce que M. Gastineau construit le garage?
Non, il fait construire le garage.

1. Est-ce que les Landon peignent leur maison?

2. Est-ce que Laurent nettoie sa chambre?

3. Est-ce que Mme Duteuil fait préparer le dîner?

4. Est-ce qu'Étienne goûte la soupe?

5. Est-ce que Mme Béjart fait nourrir le chien?

6. Est-ce que Damien fait éteind la télé?

7. Est-ce que Jean-Claude enregistre ses bagages?

8. Est-ce que les moines font copier les livres?

BADOIT

L'eau qui fait durer le plaisir

Audiocassette/CD Activities 8-9

Answers

Quand Paulette vous demande si vous avez fait certaines corvées, dites-lui que quelqu'un d'autre (else) les a faites pour vous. Suivez le modèle.

1. Est-ce que tu as mis la table?
2. Est-ce que tu as servi le dîner?
3. Est-ce que tu as fait la vaisselle?
4. Est-ce que tu as rangé ta chambre?
5. Est-ce que tu as changé tes draps?
6. Est-ce que tu as repassé tes chemises?
7. Est-ce que tu as enlevé la poussière?
8. Est-ce que tu as arrosé les plantes?

Modèle:

Est-ce que tu as préparé la salade?
Non, je l'ai fait préparer.

8 1. Non, je l'ai fait mettre.
2. Non, je l'ai fait servir.
3. Non, je l'ai fait faire.
4. Non, je l'ai fait ranger.
5. Non, je les ai fait changer.
6. Non, je les ai fait repasser.
7. Non, je l'ai fait enlever.
8. Non, je les ai fait arroser.

Avec un(e) partenaire, parlez de ce que vos parents vous font faire ou ne pas faire. Posez des questions, et puis répondez-y. Suivez le modèle.

1. téléphoner si tu vas être en retard
2. passer l'aspirateur
3. faire la lessive
4. sortir la poubelle
5. tondre la pelouse
6. payer tes vêtements
7. écrire à tes grands-parents
8. étudier avant de regarder la télé

Modèle:

rentrer avant minuit
Élève A: Tes parents te font rentrer avant minuit?
Élève B: Oui, ils me font rentrer avant minuit. Et toi, tes parents te font rentrer avant minuit?
Élève A: Oui, moi aussi, ils me font rentrer avant minuit.

9 1. Tes parents te font téléphoner si tu vas être en retard? Et toi, tes parents te font téléphoner si tu vas être en retard?
2. Tes parents te font passer l'aspirateur? Et toi, tes parents te font passer l'aspirateur?
3. Tes parents te font faire la lessive? Et toi, tes parents te font faire la lessive?
4. Tes parents te font sortir la poubelle? Et toi, tes parents te font sortir la poubelle?
5. Tes parents te font tondre la pelouse? Et toi, tes parents te font tondre la pelouse?
6. Tes parents te font payer tes vêtements? Et toi, tes parents te font payer tes vêtements?
7. Tes parents te font écrire à tes grands-parents? Et toi, tes parents te font écrire à tes grands-parents?
8. Tes parents te font étudier avant de regarder la télé? Et toi, tes parents te font étudier avant de regarder la télé?
Students' responses to these questions will vary.

Tes parents te font faire le plein quand tu conduis leur voiture?

Non, ils ne me font pas faire le plein.

QUAND ON GAGNE DU TEMPS, ON FAIT GAGNER NOS CLIENTS.

Teacher's Notes

1. Before students begin to write biographies in Activity 12, have them web the information they are going to include. In the center circle they name the person they are going to write about. In the three supporting circles they list the person's character traits, activities and contributions. If students need to be reminded what a web looks like, make an overhead transparency of the web on page 85 in the second level of *C'est à toi!* 2. **Sur la bonne piste, Leçon A**, is designed to develop skills that will help students prepare to take the Advanced Placement Exam in French Language. In this lesson **Sur la bonne piste** develops writing proficiency. Students focus on how to write summaries about literary selections.

Communication

10   *Dans cette leçon vous faites la connaissance de quatre personnes importantes qui ont aidé à créer la France. Qui est-ce qui a aidé à créer notre pays? Pour connaître les opinions de vos camarades de classe, faites une enquête. D'abord copiez la grille suivante. Puis remplissez la première colonne avec les noms de quatre personnes qui, à votre avis, sont les vrais héros ou les vraies héroïnes de l'histoire de notre pays. Ensuite demandez à quatre élèves de vous dire quelle personne de votre liste ils admirent le plus et pourquoi. Complétez la grille avec un ✓ et leurs réponses à vos questions.*

Personne	Daniel	Nora	Cécile	Marc
Abraham Lincoln	✓ *Il voulait la liberté pour tout le monde.*			

11   *Qui est-ce que vous admirez beaucoup? Choisissez une personne de l'histoire de notre pays ou de France, ou quelqu'un qui a influencé votre vie personnelle par ses idées ou par ce qu'il a fait. Puis faites des recherches pour apprendre plus de détails sur la vie de cette personne. Enfin organisez les événements importants de sa vie dans un axe chronologique qui indique les dates qui correspondent à ces événements. Utilisez les axes chronologiques aux pages 307-10 comme guide.*

12   *Écrivez une petite biographie de la personne que vous avez choisie dans l'Activité 11. Décrivez sa personnalité, ce qu'elle a fait et ses contributions à la société. En organisant votre composition, servez-vous de l'axe chronologique que vous avez déjà créé. Utilisez des expressions qui vous aident à lier (link) vos phrases, comme **d'abord**, **ensuite**, **puis**, **après**, **enfin**, **au temps de**, **au cours de**, etc.*

 Sur la bonne piste

Summarizing a Literary Selection

When a friend asks about a movie or TV program you saw, you know how to describe whom it was about and what happened. In this unit you will learn how to write a summary of a poem, story, play or screenplay in French. To write a good summary of a literary selection, it is important to introduce the characters, describe the setting and succinctly highlight the main events. In addition, you should try to relate some of the flavor of the original selection.

When introducing the main characters, think about the relevant facts that the author reveals about them. How old are they? What do they do for a living? Does

the author describe what they look like? The more detail you include, the more the characters will come alive. Some details are more important than others, so you need to be selective. Where does the literary selection take place? In describing the setting, you can include such elements as landscape, scenery, buildings, furniture, clothing, weather and season. If the author spends a lot of time describing an urban setting, for example, this is a clue that the setting is essential to the events of the story and should be mentioned in your summary. To describe the main events, jot down in chronological order every event that takes place in the selection. Then look over your notes, crossing off the minor events and focusing on the main plot of the selection.

Write your summary in the present tense. To tell what happened and to describe how things were prior to the story's main events, use the **passé composé** and the **imparfait**. For example, if you chose to write a summary of *Les petits enfants du siècle* from **Unité 7** and tell about Josyane's life in her new apartment, you would refer to earlier events, such as her birth, in the past tense: "Josyane habite un nouvel appartement dans une HLM. Quand elle est née, ses parents étaient heureux parce qu'ils ont reçu les allocations familiales dont ils avaient besoin."

When writing your summary, be sure to paraphrase, or use your own words. How would you paraphrase the following lines from "Déjeuner du matin" from **Unité 2**? "Il a mis le café/Dans la tasse/Il a mis le lait/Dans la tasse de café/Il a mis le sucre/Dans le café au lait/Avec la petite cuiller/Il a tourné/Il a bu le café au lait." Actually, all the poet says is that the man prepared a cup of **café au lait** and drank it, so you might paraphrase, "Il prépare un café au lait et il le boit." You might also want to quote a particularly vivid line or two that reveal the flavor and style of the selection. As a rule of thumb, try to keep your summary to a quarter of the size of the original text or less.

Now turn to the poem "Déjeuner du matin" on pages 86-87 and read it again, thinking about how you would summarize it by introducing the characters, describing the setting and relating the main events. The poet reveals little about the two characters. All we really know is that they are a man and a woman. Details describing the setting are equally sparse. We know that it is breakfast time. We can infer that there is a table, since the items mentioned would need to be placed on one. We also know that it is raining outside. The events themselves are minor, such as the man drinking a cup of coffee and smoking a cigarette. The main idea is the emotional state of the woman who cries at the end because the man neither looks at nor speaks to her. Here is a possible summary of this poem:

> Un homme et une femme sont à table. C'est l'heure du petit déjeuner. La femme regarde ce que l'homme fait. D'abord, il prépare un café au lait et il le boit. Puis, il allume une cigarette. Ensuite, il met son chapeau et son imperméable parce qu'il pleut. Enfin, il part, et la femme est triste parce qu'il ne lui parle ni la regarde.

Although the summary of "Déjeuner du matin" is not as poetic as the original, it clearly tells whom the poem is about, where it takes place and what happens. You will find it useful to refer to summaries you have written to refresh your memory before class discussions and tests.

Now reread the excerpt from *Au revoir, les enfants* on pages 132-33 of **Unité 3** and write a summary of it. Remember to introduce the characters, describe the setting and relate the main events.

Cooperative Group Practice

Novels in English

To provide additional practice writing summaries of a literary selection, have each student write a summary in French of a novel that they have read in English. Then put students in small groups. Each student reads his or her summary to the rest of the group, who tries to identify the title and the author. Finally each group selects the novel in their group that they think the class will like most and shares that summary with the class.

Paired Practice

Book Jackets

To further acquaint students with French literature, put them in pairs. Assign a famous novel or play to each pair. Students then research the plot of their novel or play in the library. (The *Masterplots* series is a good reference.) Then the pairs write a summary of their literary work on the inside cover of a book jacket they create. On the cover of the book jacket they draw a picture that illustrates the theme of the literary work they have researched. Display all the book jackets for the class to read. You may want to prepare a worksheet that asks questions about the different books and plays displayed so that students will carefully read each book jacket summary.

Novels in English

Voici quelques autres gens importants qui ont aidé à créer la Fran◄

Catherine de Médicis

Louis XVI

Leçon B

In this lesson you will be able to:

➤ describe past events

➤ state factual information

➤ sequence events

➤ express obligation

➤ express incapability

➤ express criticism

➤ state a preference

Le marquis de La Fayette

Georges Haussmann

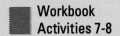

Workbook
Activities 7-8

Audiocassette/CD
Exposition

Catherine de Médicis (1519-89)

À Chenonceaux Catherine de Médicis a fait construire la grande galerie sur cinq arches au-dessus du Cher.

l'axe chronologique

1515 — *François Iᵉʳ devient roi*

1539 — *Le français devient la langue officielle de la France*

1560 — *Charles IX devient roi*

1562 — *Les guerres de Religion commencent*

1572 — *Le massacre de la Saint-Barthélemy a lieu*

1589 — *Henri IV devient roi*

1598 — *L'édit de Nantes annonce la fin des guerres de Religion*

Catherine de Médicis, reine de France, était la femme d'Henri II. C'était une femme intelligente et rusée,° la fille de Laurent II de Médicis de la célèbre famille italienne. Quand son mari, Henri II, et son fils François II sont morts, son fils Charles IX est devenu roi. Charles n'avait que dix ans, donc Catherine a dû gouverner pour lui. Pendant le règne° de Charles IX, Catherine de Médicis jouait un rôle important dans le gouvernement en montrant ses grandes qualifications politiques.

En ce temps-là la France était troublée par des guerres de Religion. Dans ses conseils à ses fils, Catherine a essayé de maintenir la paix entre les protestants et les catholiques, mais elle n'a pas réussi. Une fois, parce qu'elle avait peur pour Charles IX, elle a ordonné le massacre de la Saint-Barthélemy, qui a eu lieu° en 1572. Ce massacre a commencé à Paris et a continué en province.° Presque 30.000 protestants sont morts. Le règne de Charles IX n'a duré° que 14 ans. Quand il est mort en 1574, son frère Henri III, le fils favori de Catherine, est devenu roi. On l'a assassiné en 1589, la même année où sa mère est morte. Les protestants et les catholiques ont beaucoup critiqué Catherine pendant sa vie. Elle était obligée de défendre ses fils, et elle a survécu° à des intrigues politiques très complexes.

rusé(e) *crafty, sly;* un règne *la période pendant qu'un roi ou une reine gouverne;* avoir lieu *se passer;* en province *dans toutes les régions de la France;* durer *to last;* survivre *to survive*

Teacher's Notes

1. Point out that **maintenir** is conjugated like **venir**. 2. Tell students not to confuse **une province** with la Provence. You might write this sentence on the board: **La Provence est une province.** 3. **Défendre** is a regular **-re** verb. 4. **Survivre** belongs to the **vivre** verb family. 5. The Médicis were a family of merchants and bankers who played a critical role in the history of Florence and Tuscany from the 15th century to 1737. In addition, they influenced European politics and arts and letters. 6. In 1533 Catherine de Médicis married the Duke d'Orléans, who in 1547 became Henri II. She was denied domestic happiness due to her husband's infatuation with his mistress, Diane de Poitiers. During the 26 years of her marriage, she played no part in affairs of state, but this changed with Henri's death in 1559. While regent and chief adviser to her incapable sons during their reigns, Catherine sought to preserve the monarchy's power in the mounting chaos of civil war. Despite her responsibility for the St. Bartholomew's Day Massacre, her policies were directed at persuading Catholics and Huguenots to coexist in peace. However, after that event she was distrusted by both religious groups. Catherine was a woman of the Renaissance in her patronage of the arts. She commissioned the Tuileries as one of her building projects.

Teacher's Notes

1. The following new words appear in the time lines but are not a part of the lesson's active vocabulary: **axe, chronologique, officielle, édit, parisien, emprisonnés, défaite, embellissement** and **Franco-allemande.** 2. François I (1494-1547) was engaged in war with Hapsburg emperor Charles V through most of his long reign. As a result of his marriage to Claude de France, Brittany finally came under control of the crown. François I is known as one of the greatest patrons of arts and letters ever to sit on the throne of France. He gave decisive support to the growth in France of new forms of culture. His invitation to Italian artists to work in France resulted in some of their finest works. Students learned about François I on pages 266-67 in the second level of *C'est à toi!* 3. Charles IX (1550-74), frail and of mediocre intelligence, was happy to let his mother, Catherine de Médicis, govern for him. Only in 1572 did he attempt to throw off Catherine's domination. The St. Bartholomew's Day Massacre seems to have broken his spirit, and he subsequently relinquished governing to Catherine again.

Teacher's Notes

1. You might want to give students background information about the significance of events listed in the time line. Louis XIV (1638-1715) ascended the throne at the age of five. His reign was characterized by a quest for order and grandeur. Most of his important work was done in the two decades after 1661, when he determined to rule solely by himself, built an absolute state and enacted many administrative reforms. Afraid of living in Paris after the Fronde, Louis moved to Versailles in 1672. With the nobles constantly around him there, resistance and rebellion from the aristocracy ceased. Determined at all costs to remain visible to his subjects, Louis encouraged the mystique of **le Roi Soleil**. 2. Rich in a history that merges with that of French dramatic literature, **la Comédie-Française** was formed in partnership between Molière's company and those of the Marais Theater and the hôtel de Bourgogne. 3. Students learned about life at the court of Versailles on pages 268-69 in the second level of *C'est à toi!* 4. Louis XV (1715-74), called **le Bien-Aimé**, assumed control of the country in 1723, allowing Cardinal Fleury to govern as first minister. Upon Fleury's death, Louis attempted to act as his own first minister, but he proved unequal to the task. Some historians have blamed his mistresses, especially Pompadour and du Barry, who exercised an important influence on the weak king. 5. You may want to introduce the adjective **autrichien, autrichienne** (*Austrian*). 6. Louis XVI was the last Bourbon king to govern France as an absolute monarch. Early in his reign, he initiated reforms that made him popular with his subjects. Unwittingly, his reinstatement of the **parlements** resurrected the monarchy's most powerful adversaries. Facing bankruptcy in

1788, Louis was forced to summon the Estates General, thereby conceding that the aristocracy would share his power. Louis' lack of decisive leadership at this juncture allowed the national uprising to grow. After **la prise de la Bastille** (*the storming of the Bastille*), Louis publicly showed cooperation with the new regime while working secretly to have it overthrown. Even after he was brought to Paris by an angry mob on October 6, 1789, he refused to accept curtailment of his power. The National Convention deposed Louis, tried him for treason, found him guilty, and ordered him put to death by guillotine. 7. Marie-Antoinette was held prisoner in the **Conciergerie**. Introduced on page 403 in the first level of *C'est à toi!*, it is located on the quai de l'Horloge on the **île de la Cité**. 8. The guillotine was invented by Dr. Joseph Guillotin to carry out the death penalty more efficiently and less painfully. The guillotine was first set up on the **place de Gréve**, then the **place du Carrousel**, and finally the **place de la Concorde**, which was renamed the **place de la Révolution**. The guillotine was last used in 1977.

- **1638**
  Louis XIV est né
- **1643**
  Louis XIV devient roi
- **1670**
  Molière écrit Le Bourgeois gentilhomme
- **1680**
  On établit la Comédie-Française
- **1682**
  La cour déménage à Versailles
- **1715**
  Louis XIV meurt; Louis XV devient roi
- **1756**
  La guerre de Sept Ans a lieu
- **1763**
- **1774**
  Louis XVI devient roi

Louis XVI (1754-93)

47 | **CONCIERGERIE**
1, quai de l'Horloge, 75001 PARIS - ☎ 43 54 30 06 - Fax : 40 51 70 36
Cité - Saint-Michel-Notre Dame, Châtelet-Les Halles - 38
Cet important vestige du palais des Capétiens offre un remarquable témoignage sur l'architecture civile du XIVᵉ siècle avec la salle des Gens d'Armes, la salle des Gardes et les cuisines. La quasi totalité du niveau bas du palais fut transformée en prison au XVᵉ siècle, on peut y visiter les cachots (la cellule de Marie-Antoinette notamment) et découvrir les souvenirs de la Révolution.
OUVERTURE : Hiver 10h-17h - Été 9h30-18h30 - **TARIFS** : 26 F - Réd. : 7 F - 17 F
FERMETURE : 01/01, 01/05, 01/11, 11/11, 25/12
Révolution française

Pendant les derniers mois de sa vie, Marie-Antoinette était prisonnière dans la Conciergerie de Paris.

Quand Louis XVI avait 16 ans et Marie-Antoinette d'Autriche° en avait 15, ils se sont mariés. Quatre ans plus tard ils sont devenus roi et reine. Bientôt ils ont eu des problèmes avec le gouvernement et le peuple français. Louis XVI voulait bien gouverner, mais il préférait la chasse° aux affaires du pays. Louis était timide et trop circonspect dans ce qu'il décidait. En plus, Marie-Antoinette lui donnait de mauvais conseils. Le peuple ne l'aimait pas du tout parce qu'elle n'était pas française et elle dépensait trop d'argent. Le gouvernement avait de graves problèmes politiques, sociaux et monétaires. Trop de gens ne payaient pas d'impôts.° Le pays était pauvre après avoir aidé les Américains pendant la guerre de l'Indépendance américaine, et après avoir dépensé beaucoup d'argent dans des guerres qui n'ont pas réussi. Louis XVI a choisi des hommes honnêtes pour lui donner des conseils, mais, eux aussi, ils n'ont pas pu réussir à lui en faire accepter.

Le 14 juillet 1789, le peuple de Paris a pris la Bastille. C'était le début de la Révolution française. Louis XVI et Marie-Antoinette sont devenus prisonniers à Paris. La violence a continué. Personne n'a pu arrêter la Révolution. Enfin on a guillotiné le roi et la reine, lui en janvier 1793 et elle dix mois plus tard.

l'Autriche (f.) le pays à l'est de la Suisse; **la chasse** *hunting*; **un impôt** *tax*

Le marquis de La Fayette (1757-1834)

Le marquis de La Fayette n'avait que 20 ans quand il est arrivé en Amérique. Il voulait aider le général Washington à vaincre les Anglais. Après avoir accepté de travailler sans salaire, La Fayette est devenu général dans l'armée américaine. Il a participé à beaucoup de batailles et a même passé l'hiver à Valley Forge. Après la guerre de l'Indépendance américaine, La Fayette est rentré en France où il a aidé à négocier la paix et a continué à travailler pour de bonnes relations entre les États-Unis et la France.

Il s'occupait aussi des problèmes de son propre pays. Au début de la Révolution française, il est devenu homme politique et a travaillé dur pour établir une monarchie libérale. La Fayette avait beau° essayer d'arrêter la violence de la Révolution. Mais on ne pouvait pas accepter ses idées, et La Fayette a dû quitter la France. Après être rentré en 1797, il a continué à servir son pays et à maintenir de bonnes relations et le commerce avec les États-Unis.

avoir beau être en vain

1777

La Fayette aide les Américains

1782

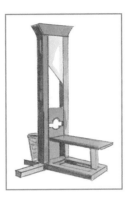

1789

Le peuple parisien prend la Bastille; la Révolution commence

1792

Louis XVI et Marie-Antoinette sont emprisonnés

1793

Louis XVI et Marie-Antoinette sont guillotinés

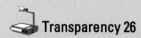
Teacher's Notes

1. You might want to give students background information about the significance of events listed in the time line. Napoléon I (1769-1821), also known as Napoléon Bonaparte, was the greatest military genius of his time and perhaps the greatest general in history. A general at the age of 24, he became first consul of the French republic (1799-1804) and then emperor (1804-14, and again in 1815). He created an empire that covered most of western and central Europe, virtually controlling the continent from 1809 to 1812. He was also an excellent administrator, introducing many useful reforms, including the creation of a strong, efficient central government and the organization of French laws into codes. In 1814 Napoléon abdicated the imperial throne after his defeat at the Battle of the Nations at Leipzig. He was exiled to the island of Elba, but returned during the Hundred Days, only to be resoundingly defeated at Waterloo, Belgium. He spent the rest of his days in exile on the island of St. Helena. His body lies in the Église du Dôme in the **hôtel des Invalides** (see page 405 in the first level of *C'est à toi!*). 2. Napoléon III (1808-73) ruled as emperor of France from 1852-70. He was Napoléon I's nephew, the son of Louis Bonaparte. His public works programs transformed Paris, but failures in foreign policy became his undoing. In 1852, five years after being elected president, Napoléon proclaimed himself emperor. He lost his power when supporters of a new French republic overthrew his empire after France's defeat in the Franco-Prussian War. 3. France was not militarily prepared for the Franco-Prussian War. The Germans easily defeated the French, seized territory in eastern France, and created the new German empire that Otto von Bismarck envisaged. The Franco-Prussian War set the

1804
Napoléon Iᵉʳ devient empereur

1815
Napoléon Iᵉʳ est vaincu à Waterloo

1821
Napoléon Iᵉʳ meurt

1852
Napoléon III devient empereur
1853

Haussmann fait ses projets d'embellissement de la capitale

1869

1870
La guerre Franco-allemande a lieu
1871

Georges Haussmann (1809-91)

La place Charles-de-Gaulle s'appelait la place de l'Étoile jusqu'en 1970 parce que les 12 avenues qui y commencent font penser à une étoile *(star)*. (Paris)

C'est l'ingénieur Georges Haussmann qu'il faut remercier si vous appréciez la beauté de la ville de Paris: les larges° avenues, les quartiers de grands immeubles avec de jolies fleurs aux fenêtres, des jardins et des parcs partout. Si vous faites une promenade le soir, vous saurez pourquoi on appelle Paris "la Ville lumière." C'est parce que presque tous ses monuments sont illuminés. Si vous montez les Champs-Élysées jusqu'à l'arc de triomphe, vous verrez 12 belles avenues qui en sortent. Tout ça, c'est le travail de Georges Haussmann, homme politique engagé, et de ses ingénieurs. Après avoir démoli les plus vieux quartiers de la ville, Haussmann a passé presque 20 ans à transformer la capitale.

large *wide*

stage for World War I by increasing French and German hostility. 4. Point out that **large** is a false cognate. 5. Haussmann was the French administrator responsible for the transformation of Paris from its medieval character to the one that it still largely preserves today. As an urban planner he exerted great influence on city design all over the world. As prefect of the Seine **département**, he undertook large public works projects, approved by Napoléon III. He designed wide, straight, tree-lined avenues through the chaotic mass of small streets, connecting the train terminals and making movement across the city rapid and easy for the first time. The purpose was partly economic, promoting efficient transportation of goods; partly aesthetic, to allow more space and light; and partly military, eliminating the possibility that barricades could be erected. Haussmann also eliminated the foul odors of Paris by creating new systems of water supply and drainage. His other contributions include the creation of **le bois de Boulogne** and **le bois de Vincennes**, the installation of more streetlights and sidewalks, and the demolition of most of the

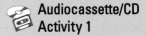
Audiocassette/CD Activity 1

Answers

1 1. faux
2. faux
3. vrai
4. faux
5. vrai
6. vrai
7. faux
8. faux

Répondez par "vrai" ou "faux" d'après les descriptions des Français célèbres.

1. Charles IX a ordonné le massacre de la Saint-Barthélemy.
2. La France était troublée par des guerres de Religion pendant le règne de Louis XVI.
3. Au temps de Louis XVI, la France avait des problèmes sociaux, monétaires et politiques.
4. On a guillotiné Louis XVI et Marie-Antoinette le 14 juillet 1789.

Le peuple de Paris a pris la Bastille le 14 juillet 1789.

5. Le marquis de La Fayette a aidé les Américains pendant la guerre de l'Indépendance américaine.
6. La Fayette a travaillé pour de bonnes relations entre la France et les États-Unis.
7. On appelle Paris "la Ville lumière" parce qu'il y a beaucoup de jolis parcs et de larges avenues.
8. Haussmann a dû démolir tous les monuments de Paris.

private buildings on the **île de la Cité**, which resulted in its current administrative and religious character. Haussmann also built the **Opéra** and the central marketplace known as **les Halles**, which was torn down in the 1960s. Eventually Haussmann's handling of public money under Napoléon III roused criticism and in 1870 he was dismissed.

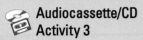

**Audiocassette/CD
Activity 3**

Answers

2 1. conseils
2. complexes
3. chasse
4. Autriche
5. impôts
6. règne
7. bataille
8. large

3 Answers will vary.

2 *Complétez chaque phrase avec le mot convenable d'après les descriptions des Français célèbres.*

impôts	Autriche	large	complexes
bataille	règne	chasse	conseils

1. Catherine de Médicis a donné beaucoup de... à ses fils.
2. Elle a survécu à des intrigues politiques qui étaient très....
3. Louis XVI aimait plus la... que les affaires du pays.
4. Marie-Antoinette n'est pas née en France. Elle est née en....
5. Les... sont l'argent qu'on doit payer au gouvernement.
6. C'était pendant le... de Louis XVI que la Révolution française a commencé.
7. Une grande... a eu lieu à Valley Forge.
8. Les Champs-Élysées sont une... avenue à Paris.

Catherine de Médicis a donné des conseils à son fils Charles IX après qu'il est devenu roi en 1560.

3 *C'est à toi!*

1. Est-ce que tu connais une personne rusée? Si oui, l'admires-tu?
2. Qui te donne des conseils à l'école? À la maison? En suis-tu?
3. Qu'est-ce que tu as beau faire?
4. Est-ce que tu préfères faire du sport ou étudier? Louer des vidéocassettes ou aller au cinéma?
5. Qu'est-ce que tu fais après avoir fini tes devoirs le soir?
6. Qui essaie de maintenir la paix dans ta famille?
7. À ton avis, quelle est la plus belle avenue de ta ville?
8. Est-ce que tu paies des impôts? Selon toi, est-ce que les Américains paient trop d'impôts? Pourquoi ou pourquoi pas?

Quand les rois de France venaient au trône trop jeunes, ils avaient des régentes pour gouverner pour eux. La régente Catherine de Médicis aimait gouverner tellement qu'elle a gardé le contrôle du pays même quand ses fils François II, Charles IX et Henri III étaient rois.

Catherine n'aimait pas les protestants français, qui s'appelaient les Huguenots. Quand leur chef, l'Amiral Coligny, est devenu ami du roi Charles IX, Catherine n'était pas contente. Elle s'inquiétait de l'influence que Coligny aurait sur son fils. Donc, elle a ordonné à Charles de faire tuer Coligny et ses disciples en 1572.

Catherine s'intéressait beaucoup à l'astrologie, à l'occultisme et à la magie. C'est pourquoi elle a fait venir à la cour un certain Michel de Notre-Dame, médecin et astrologue. Après avoir latinisé son nom en Nostradamus, il a commencé à faire des prédictions. En 1555 Nostradamus a écrit un livre, *Centuries astrologiques*, où il a fait plusieurs prédictions. En 1559 le roi Henri II est mort exactement comme avait prédit Nostradamus dans ce livre. Beaucoup de ses autres prédictions sont devenues vraies aussi.

Marie-Antoinette était une autre femme qui a eu une grande influence sur l'histoire de la France sans jamais contrôler le gouvernement. Si le roi Louis XVI était faible, la reine était forte et a beaucoup influencé le roi. Contrairement à la personnalité de son mari, Marie-Antoinette aimait la vie sociale et les fêtes. Parce qu'elle ne faisait attention ni aux traditions de la cour ni à l'étiquette, les Français étaient choqués. On l'a même appelée "cette femme d'Autriche."

Mais Marie-Antoinette n'était pas sensible aux besoins de son peuple. La légende dit que les pauvres ont manifesté parce qu'ils n'avaient pas de pain à manger. Quand Marie-Antoinette a entendu leur demande pour du pain, elle a répondu, "Qu'ils mangent du gâteau!" On n'est pas certain si la reine a vraiment prononcé ces mots, mais si elle l'a bien dit, est-ce qu'elle l'a fait parce qu'elle n'était pas sensible ou parce qu'elle ne comprenait pas la situation?

Enquête culturelle

Henri III, le dernier roi Valois, était le troisième fils d'Henri II et de Catherine de Médicis.

Les Français critiquaient Marie-Antoinette pour les sommes énormes qu'elle dépensait pour ses vêtements.

Teacher's Note

Marie-Antoinette (1755-93) was the daughter of Austrian Emperor Francis I and Empress Maria Theresa. She was married to the dauphin of France to bolster the Austro-French alliance. Her heedless youthful indiscretions and extravagances destroyed her reputation and contributed to negative views of the monarchy by the French people, who held "Madame Deficit" responsible for their own economic distress. During the French Revolution, Marie-Antoinette opposed any reforms that might diminish the power of the monarchy. On October 5 and 6, 1789, the royal family was removed from Versailles to the Tuileries in Paris. In 1791 Marie-Antoinette convinced Louis XVI that the family should flee to the eastern border, but they were apprehended and returned to Paris virtually as prisoners. In 1792, hoping that Austrian forces would crush the revolutionary armies, she betrayed military plans to the enemy. The uprising of August 10, 1792, which led to the imprisonment of the royal family, was caused in part by the general suspicion that the king and queen were guilty of counterrevolutionary intrigue.

Workbook Activity 9

Teacher's Notes

1. Cognates in this reading include **trône, régentes, contrôle, disciples, s'intéressait, astrologie, occultisme, magie, astrologue, latinisé, prédictions, exactement, prédit, influencé, contrairement, traditions, étiquette, choqués, légende, demande, prononcé, situation, ambassadeur, alliance, colonies, respecté, persuader, convaincre, politiquement, profiterait, énorme, proclamé, représentant, colonistes, plans, fédérale, recréer** and **boulevards**.
2. François II (1544-60) was the oldest son of Henri II and Catherine de Médicis. He was the first husband of Mary Stuart, Queen of Scots, whom he married in 1558. In 1559 he became king when his father died in a tournament. As king, François was dominated by his wife's maternal uncles, the Duke de Guise and the Cardinal de Lorraine, who extended a policy of rigorous repression of Calvinist Protestantism. Tension was increasing between the Catholics and the Huguenots when François died.
3. Henri III (1551-89) was the last Valois king of France. He succeeded his brother Charles IX in 1574. Henri was a weak king who was greatly influenced by his mother. Throughout his reign, Henri was caught in the struggle, including warfare, between the Catholics and the Huguenots. Fearing the Huguenot leader, the Duke de Guise, Henri had him assassinated in 1588. The next year Henri himself was assassinated by a religious fanatic. His death made way for the succession of Henri de Navarre. 4. Gaspard de Coligny (1519-72) was the leader of the Huguenots, whom Catherine de Médicis had her son Charles IX kill during the St. Bartholomew's Day Massacre.

Answers

Teacher's Note

In 1776 the Second Continental Congress decided to send a commission to France to seek economic and military assistance. As one of three commissioners, Franklin was immediately engaged in secret negotiations with the French minister of foreign affairs, Charles Gravier, Count de Vergennes, beginning perhaps the most amazing personal success story in the history of diplomacy. In Paris the literary and scientific community greeted him as a hero. Turgot expressed the French idolization of Franklin in a famous epigram, "He seized the lightning from Heaven and the scepter from tyrants." Franklin found his portrait everywhere, on objets d'art from snuffboxes to chamber pots. Wigless, dressed in plain brown clothes and spectacles, he was nicknamed le Bonhomme Richard. His company was sought after by everyone. He frequented the salon of Madame Helvétius and found himself popular among the most fashionable ladies. Working behind the scenes, Franklin sent war supplies across the Atlantic and made friends with influential French officials. Franklin soon discovered that despite French desire to see England defeated, France was too vulnerable to help the American rebels unless chances for success seemed hopeful. In February, 1778, after the American success at Saratoga, the French agreed to sign an alliance. Franklin arranged for French armies and navies to go to North America, supplied American armies with French munitions and outfitted John Paul Jones and the ship Bonhomme Richard. Amazingly, he secured loan after loan from the nearly bankrupt French treasury. Virtually all the outside aid for the American rebels came with Franklin's direct help.

Benjamin Franklin

Au temps de la guerre de l'Indépendance américaine, il y a eu des Français qui sont venus en Amérique et des Américains qui sont allés en France. Le marquis de La Fayette a participé à la Révolution comme général et comme ambassadeur. C'est lui qui est allé en France en ce temps pour créer une alliance entre la France et les colonies américaines. Benjamin Franklin était aussi ambassadeur des colonies en France. Franklin était très populaire et respecté. En 1776 il est allé à la cour de Louis XVI pour le persuader d'aider les colonies dans leur lutte pour l'indépendance. Il a dû convaincre le roi d'accepter que les colonies étaient politiquement indépendantes de l'Angleterre et il a persuadé le roi qu'une alliance entre les deux pays profiterait aux Français. Il a eu un succès énorme. Louis XVI a proclamé que la France était l'amie des colonies américaines et que la France les aiderait. Franklin est devenu le représentant des colonies américaines en France et a négocié la fin de la guerre de l'Indépendance américaine.

Pierre L'Enfant aussi est venu de France pour aider les colonistes avec la guerre de l'Indépendance américaine. Après la guerre, George Washington lui a demandé de faire des plans pour construire la nouvelle capitale fédérale du pays à Washington, D.C. L'Enfant a créé un plan pour la ville avec des avenues qui sortaient d'un centre, comme la ville de Paris. Mais il a dépensé trop d'argent sur ce projet et a dû quitter le poste.

Si L'Enfant a créé la ville de Washington, D.C., selon un plan de Paris, Georges Haussmann a décidé de recréer Paris avec de grands boulevards et de jolies avenues comme ceux de Washington. Lui aussi a dépensé trop d'argent sur ses projets et a dû quitter son poste.

Parce que Charles IX était mineur quand il est devenu roi, Catherine de Médicis gouvernait pour lui.

4 | *Répondez aux questions suivantes.*

1. Une régente, qu'est-ce que c'est?
2. Comment s'appellent les fils de Catherine de Médicis?
3. Qui étaient les Huguenots?
4. Pourquoi Catherine a-t-elle ordonné le massacre de la Saint-Barthélemy?
5. Au 16e siècle qui a fait des prédictions qui sont devenues vraies?
6. Pourquoi Marie-Antoinette avait-elle beaucoup d'influence sur le roi Louis XVI?
7. Selon la légende, quelle phrase célèbre est attribuée à Marie-Antoinette?
8. Quels sont les deux Français qui ont participé à la guerre de l'Indépendance américaine?
9. Pourquoi est-ce que Benjamin Franklin est allé en France?
10. Qu'est-ce que Pierre L'Enfant et Georges Haussmann avaient en commun?

Voici quelques événements importants du 20ᵉ siècle en France. Cherchez dans vos sources (encyclopédies, CD-ROM, Internet ou livres d'histoire) pour écrire l'année où chaque événement a eu lieu.

1. Marie Curie reçoit le Prix Nobel de physique.
2. La France perd 360.000 hommes dans la Bataille de Verdun.
3. Les Américains arrivent à Paris pour délivrer la ville des forces nazies.
4. L'armée vietnamienne conquiert les forces françaises à Diên Biên Phu.
5. Charles de Gaulle devient président de la Cinquième République.
6. Après une longue guerre, l'Algérie gagne son indépendance de la France.
7. Jean-Paul Sartre reçoit le Prix Nobel de littérature et le refuse.
8. Les étudiants parisiens commencent des manifestations violentes.
9. François Mitterand devient le premier président socialiste.
10. Édith Cresson devient Premier ministre.
11. Disneyland Paris ouvre ses portes.

MÉMORIAL-MUSÉE

MÉMORIAL DE VERDUN

DE LA BATAILLE DE

VERDUN
1914   1918
FLEURY-devant-DOUAUMONT

Journal personnel

You have read about several women who have shaped French history without ever having had a position of real power in the government. Has the role of women changed significantly in the course of history? Can you name several women in recent years who have held positions of authority and exerted real power?

So many people have shaped history either by influencing those in power or by doing something extraordinary that changed the way people lived, thought or acted. Name someone in history who did not have a political position, yet played a major role in shaping future generations. What did this person contribute? Can you name some people today who, likewise, do not shape governmental policy but manage to influence people? If so, what have these people accomplished? You may want to consider technological, scientific, artistic and humanitarian contributions.

Structure

Expressions with *avoir*

The verb **avoir** (*to have*) is another frequently used verb in French.

Le gouvernement de Louis XVI **avait** des problèmes politiques et monétaires.	*Louis XVI's government had political and monetary problems.*

Also called a "building block" verb, **avoir** is used in many expressions in French. Some of the most common expressions with **avoir** deal with age, being hot/cold/hungry/thirsty/afraid, or physical ailments. How many more can you think of?

Workbook Activity 10

Answers

5 1. 1903
2. 1916
3. 1944
4. 1954
5. 1958
6. 1962
7. 1964
8. 1968
9. 1981
10. 1991
11. 1992

Teacher's Note

Avoir was introduced on page 95 in the first level of *C'est à toi!* and reviewed on page 34 in the second level and on page 12 in the third level.

Game

Qui suis-je?

So that students can practice identifying historical French figures, place the name of a historical figure on the back of each student. Students circulate around the room asking questions to other students in order to discover their identity, for example, **Est-ce que je vivais au** **17ᵉ siècle?** When all students have discovered who they are, ask them to line up in front of the room in chronological order.

Answers

6 1. avait faim
   2. avait envie d'
   3. avait l'air, avait besoin d'
   4. a eu de la chance
   5. avait soif
   6. avait mal au cœur

ILS AURONT 20 ANS EN L'AN 2000

Les producteurs n'ont pas eu peur?

LA DERNIÈRE EXPOSITION MONDIALE DU SIÈCLE AURA LIEU DANS LA CAPITALE DU PORTUGAL ET DANS L'ESPRIT D'HENRI LE NAVIGATEUR.

Modèle:

Hier c'était l'anniversaire de Guillaume.
Il avait 17 ans.

Quand Louis XVI **avait** 16 ans et Marie-Antoinette en **avait** 15, ils se sont mariés.	When Louis XVI was 16 and Marie-Antoinette was 15, they got married.
Parce que Catherine **avait peur** pour son fils, elle a ordonné le massacre.	Because Catherine was afraid for her son, she ordered the massacre.

Pourquoi M. Denicourt a-t-il mauvaise mine?

Two new expressions with **avoir** are **avoir lieu** (*to take place*) and **avoir beau** plus an infinitive (*to do something in vain*).

Le massacre a eu lieu en 1572.	The massacre took place in 1572.
La Fayette **avait beau** essayer d'arrêter la violence de la Révolution.	La Fayette tried in vain to stop the violence of the Revolution.

Pratique

6 *Racontez l'histoire de la journée de Guillaume selon les illustrations. Utilisez l'expression convenable de la liste suivante pour décrire chaque illustration. Dans votre réponse utilisez le temps convenable du verbe* **avoir**.

avoir de la chance	avoir envie de	avoir mal au cœur
avoir soif	avoir 17 ans	avoir besoin de
avoir l'air	avoir faim	

1. Guillaume....

2. Il... aller au café avec ses amis.

3. Mais, pauvre Guillaume! Il... triste parce qu'il... argent.

5. Guillaume a beaucoup mangé, et il a beaucoup bu parce qu'il....

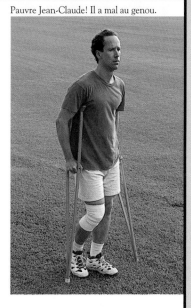

Pauvre Jean-Claude! Il a mal au genou.

 Audiocassette/CD Activity 7

Answers

7 Possible answers:

1. Parce que j'ai peur.
2. Non, j'ai eu beau chercher.
3. Non, je n'ai pas de chance.
4. Parce que j'ai besoin d'argent.
5. Parce qu'il avait chaud.
6. Parce qu'elle a mal à la gorge.
7. Oui, elle a mauvaise mine.
8. Le massacre a eu lieu en 1572.

4. Tout à coup, Guillaume.... Il a trouvé de l'argent!

6. Après avoir mangé, Robert est rentré à la maison tout de suite parce qu'il....

Donnez une réponse logique aux questions suivantes en utilisant une expression avec **avoir** *au temps convenable.*

1. Pourquoi est-ce que tu ne t'approches pas du chien?
2. Tu n'as pas réussi à trouver ton verre de contact?
3. As-tu jamais gagné quelque chose?
4. Pourquoi est-ce que tu as deux boulots?
5. Pourquoi Bruno a-t-il mis la clim?
6. Pourquoi la chanteuse ne peut-elle pas chanter?
7. Tu trouves que Patricia a l'air malade?
8. Quelle est la date du massacre de la Saint-Barthélemy?

Modèle:

Pourquoi est-ce que Camille et sa sœur portent un manteau et des gants?
Parce qu'elles ont froid.

Vous n'en avez pas marre, Isabelle Huppert?

Pourquoi tu ne conduis pas à l'école?

Je n'ai que 17 ans.

Paired Practice

Changing Tenses

You might have students practice using **avoir** expressions in various tenses. Put students in pairs, and give each pair a note card with a sentence and a tense that they are to change the sentence to, for example, **Caro avait de la chance (passé composé)**. Student A reads the first sentence for Student B,

who identifies the tense being used, for example, imperfect, and then changes the sentence to the tense indicated in parentheses, for example, **Caro a eu de la chance**. Then tell the pairs to exchange their card for one belonging to another pair, at which point Student A and Student B switch roles. Pairs continue exchanging cards until they have practiced a sentence in the present, **passé**

composé, imperfect, conditional and future.

**Workbook
Activities 11-12**

**Audiocassette/CD
Activity 8**

Answers

8 Possible answers:

1. Après m'être réveillé(e), je suis sorti(e).
2. Après avoir fait son lit, Suzanne est sortie.
3. Après avoir pris son petit déjeuner, Abdou est sorti.
4. Après s'être brossé les dents, Max est sorti.
5. Après s'être maquillées, Sophie et Annick sont sorties.
6. Après avoir fait le ménage, Chloé et toi, vous êtes sorti(e)s.
7. Après avoir fait la vaisselle, tu es sorti(e).
8. Après avoir fini nos devoirs, Paul et moi, nous sommes sortis.

Teacher's Notes

1. The conjunction **après que** is followed by the indicative, for example, **Une heure après que je suis rentré, elle m'a téléphoné.** 2. Point out that the use of **avoir** or **être** depends on which verb the infinitive takes in the **passé composé.** 3. Note that object pronouns precede the infinitive. 4. In the third example, note the agreement between the past participle **négociée** and the preceding direct object pronoun **l'**, which refers to **la paix.** 5. In the fourth example, note the agreement between the past participle **mariés** and the reflexive pronoun **s'.** The past participle agrees with the reflexive pronoun when that pronoun functions as the direct object. 6. The past infinitive is made negative in one of two ways: the negative may come before the past infinitive, for example, **Après ne pas avoir dormi, j'étais fatigué(e),** or **ne... pas** may surround **avoir** or **être,** for example, **Après n'avoir pas dormi, j'étais fatigué(e).**

Après avoir gagné à la loterie, Chantal a réservé deux billets pour un vol Paris–Fort-de-France.

Past infinitive

To say that one action in the past happened before another one, use the past infinitive. After the preposition **après**, add the helping verb **avoir** or **être** and the past participle of the main verb.

après	+	avoir / être	+	past participle

Après avoir accepté de travailler sans salaire, La Fayette est devenu général.	*After having agreed to work without pay, La Fayette became a general.*
Après être rentré en France, il a continué à servir son pays.	*After having returned to France, he continued to serve his country.*

Agreement of the past participle is the same as in the **passé composé.**

Après l'avoir négociée, La Fayette a travaillé dur pour maintenir la paix entre l'Angleterre et les États-Unis.	*After having negotiated it, La Fayette worked hard to maintain peace between England and the United States.*
Après s'être mariés, Louis XVI et Marie-Antoinette sont devenus roi et reine.	*After having married, Louis XVI and Marie-Antoinette became king and queen.*

Pratique

8 *Dites que les personnes suivantes sont sorties après avoir fait les actions illustrées.*

Modèle:

Après avoir tondu la pelouse, Marcel est sorti.

> Après avoir écumé du côté de la Bastille, Jean-Pierre Robinot a décidé d'aller flâner près des grands boulevards.

1.  *je*

3.  *Abdou*

2.  *Suzanne*

4.  *Max*

Critical Thinking

Choosing a Helping Verb with the Past Infinitive

Write two pairs of sentences using the past infinitive and the **passé composé** on the board, one with **avoir** and one with **être**, for example, **Après s'être habillée, Claire s'est peignée./Claire s'est habillée. Après avoir déjeuné à la cantine, Max a fait ses devoirs à la bibliothèque./Max a déjeuné à la cantine.** Ask students how to determine which helping verb to use when forming sentences with the past infinitive. Students should tell you to use the same helping verb that is used in the **passé composé.**

5. Sophie et Annick

6. Chloé et toi

7. tu

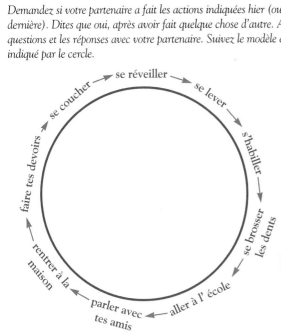

8. Paul et moi

Après s'etre lavé les cheveux, Danielle a demandé le sèche-cheveux à sa sœur.

Demandez si votre partenaire a fait les actions indiquées hier (ou la semaine dernière). Dites que oui, après avoir fait quelque chose d'autre. Alternez les questions et les réponses avec votre partenaire. Suivez le modèle et l'ordre indiqué par le cercle.

Modèle:
Élève A: Est-ce que tu t'es levé(e)?
Élève B: Oui, après m'être réveillé(e), je me suis levé(e).

se réveiller → se lever → s'habiller → se brosser les dents → aller à l'école → parler avec tes amis → rentrer à la maison → faire tes devoirs → se coucher

Est-ce que tu es rentrée à la maison?

Oui, après être allée au cinéma, je suis rentrée à la maison.

Answers

9 Est-ce que tu t'es habillé(e)?
Oui, après m'être levé(e), je me suis habillé(e).
Est-ce que tu t'es brossé les dents?
Oui, après m'être habillé(e), je me suis brossé les dents.
Est-ce que tu es allé(e) à l'école?
Oui, après m'être brossé les dents, je suis allé(e) à l'école.
Est-ce que tu as parlé avec tes amis?
Oui, après être allé(e) à l'école, j'ai parlé avec mes amis.
Est-ce que tu es rentré(e) à la maison?
Oui, après avoir parlé avec mes amis, je suis rentré(e) à la maison.
Est-ce que tu as fait tes devoirs?
Oui, après être rentré(e) à la maison, j'ai fait mes devoirs.
Est-ce que tu t'es couché(e)?
Oui, après avoir fait mes devoirs, je me suis couché(e).

Cooperative Group Practice

How Everyone Felt

To practice forming sentences using the past infinitive, put students in small groups. Give each group a set of note cards that you have prepared listing a noun or pronoun subject, an infinitive expression that will become the past participle and an infinitive expression indicating an emotional reaction, for example, **Marcel/faire la connaissance d'une jolie fille/être heureux**. The first student in each group takes the top card and asks the student on his or her right how the person on the card felt, for example, **Anne, comment se sentait Marcel après avoir fait la connaissance d'une jolie fille?** The questioned student looks at the card that the first student holds out and forms a complete sentence using the past infinitive, for example, **Après avoir fait la connaissance d'une jolie fille, Marcel était heureux.**

Teacher's Note

To provide speaking and listening practice with the past infinitive, you may want to do this activity with your class. Have each student write his or her name on a slip of paper and place it in a bag that you provide. Ask for a student volunteer to come to the front of the classroom. The volunteer selects a name from the bag. Then he or she performs two actions, and the named student describes what the volunteer did, for example, **Après avoir mis une feuille de papier dans la corbeille, tu as pris le manuel sur le bureau du professeur.** Next the named student who gave the sentence goes to the front of the room, and the process begins again. The activity continues until all the name slips have been drawn and each student has given a sentence using the past infinitive and performed two actions.

Answers

10 1. Après avoir emmené Vercingétorix à Rome, César l'a fait tuer.
2. Après avoir entendu la trompette de Roland, Charlemagne est revenu avec son armée.
3. Après être arrivés à Hastings, Guillaume le Conquérant et son armée ont vaincu les Anglais.
4. Après avoir fait construire la Sainte-Chapelle, Louis IX y a mis des reliques de Jésus-Christ.
5. Après avoir lu *Centuries astrologiques* de Nostradamus, Catherine de Médicis l'a fait venir à la cour.
6. Après s'être mariée avec Louis XVI, Marie-Antoinette est devenue reine de France.
7. Après avoir participé à la guerre de l'Indépendance américaine, La Fayette est rentré en France.
8. Après avoir démoli les plus vieux quartiers de Paris, Georges Haussmann les a transformés.

Modèle:

Jules César a réussi à vaincre Vercingétorix. Puis César est retourné à Rome.
Après avoir réussi à vaincre Vercingétorix, Jules César est retourné à Rome.

10 *Combinez chaque groupe de deux phrases en utilisant le passé de l'infinitif. Suivez le modèle.*

1. César a emmené Vercingétorix à Rome. Puis César l'a fait tuer.
2. Charlemagne a entendu la trompette de Roland. Puis Charlemagne est revenu avec son armée.
3. Guillaume le Conquérant et son armée sont arrivés à Hastings. Puis ils ont vaincu les Anglais.
4. Louis IX a fait construire la Sainte-Chapelle. Puis il y a mis des reliques de Jésus-Christ.
5. Catherine de Médicis a lu *Centuries astrologiques* de Nostradamus. Puis elle l'a fait venir à la cour.
6. Marie-Antoinette s'est mariée avec Louis XVI. Puis elle est devenue reine de France.
7. La Fayette a participé à la guerre de l'Indépendance américaine. Puis il est rentré en France.
8. Georges Haussmann a démoli les plus vieux quartiers de Paris. Puis il les a transformés.

Communication

11 *Dans cette leçon vous avez étudié l'histoire de France du 16ᵉ au 19ᵉ siècles. Quant à l'histoire, tout le monde, même ceux qui n'en sont pas fanas, a ses préférences de périodes pour diverses raisons. Pour connaître les opinions de vos camarades de classe, faites une enquête. D'abord copiez la grille suivante. Puis demandez à quatre élèves de vous dire quel siècle et quel personnage de ce siècle les intéressent le plus et de vous dire pourquoi. (Préparez vos propres réponses pour les élèves qui vous intervieweront.) Enfin complétez la grille avec un ✔ et leurs réponses à vos questions.*

Siècle	Amélie	Salim	Anne	Jacques
16ᵉ				
17ᵉ	✔ Louis XIV Je viens de voir le film Man in the Iron Mask, et la vie du Roi Soleil à la cour de Versailles m'intéresse.			
18ᵉ				
19ᵉ				

12 *Maintenant utilisez les réponses de vos camarades de classe (et aussi vos réponses personnelles) pour écrire un paragraphe où vous présentez les résultats de votre enquête dans l'Activité 11. Dites combien d'élèves ont préféré chaque siècle, et indiquez quels personnages ils ont choisis. Puis donnez les raisons de leurs choix.*

Magazine Pictures

Put students in pairs. Display ten magazine pictures that students can describe at the front of the classroom. Tell students to take turns forming logical past infinitive sentences to describe what took place before each pictured activity and then what happened in the picture, for example, **Après avoir mis un short, un tee-shirt et des tennis, Alain a joué au foot.** Then each pair looks for a new picture in a magazine and writes a caption using a past infinitive sentence to describe it. Put the new pictures, numbered, at the front of the room, and write the pairs' captions at random on an overhead transparency. Have each pair match the new captions with the new pictures.

Les dialogues

Put students in pairs to practice using the past infinitive in a dialogue. Tell students to ask what their partner did after finishing chores at home on the weekend. After practicing their dialogues, pairs present them to the class. When the pairs have finished, have each student write sentences using the past infinitive to tell what five of his or her classmates did, for example, **Après avoir fini ses corvées, Julie a vu une exposition au musée.**

Groupez-vous avec quatre autres élèves. Avec vos grilles de l'Activité 11, discutez les résultats de vos enquêtes sur les personnages les plus intéressants de l'histoire de France. Puis préparez une liste de ces personnages selon l'ordre de leur popularité et présentez cette liste à la classe.

Sur la bonne piste

In this unit you are going to develop your research skills and read a scene from a 17th century comedy by Molière, *Le Bourgeois gentilhomme* (*The Would-Be Gentleman*). Some plays, including *Le Bourgeois gentilhomme*, are enriched and more deeply understood by learning about their author and the time period in which they were written. Indeed, Molière's plays can hardly be studied without reference to their historical and social background, so intricately are they connected. After reading the scene, you will pick a topic and do research on it (**Activité 18** on page 342). Knowing some background information about 17th century France and Molière will help you choose a topic that interests you.

Louis XIV, **le Roi Soleil**, believed that he was the "earthly representative of God." He ruled as an absolute monarch from his palace at Versailles. The importance of the court, 20,000 strong, reached its highest point during his reign. An elaborate ritual accompanied the Sun King's most trivial activities, including getting up, going to bed, eating, taking walks and hunting. Under Louis' patronage, the arts, literature and science flourished and various academies were founded. While Louis forced nobles into financial dependence on the crown, he bestowed privileges on the middle class, or bourgeoisie, whom he used to build his centralized bureaucracy. One successful bourgeois who rose to a position of fame and prestige at the court was Molière.

Molière was not only a playwright, but an actor, director and stage manager as well. His aim in writing comedy was simply to entertain. In order to do that Molière said, "Il faut peindre d'après nature." As a keen observer of human nature, Molière created characters who exemplified the best and the worst of the aristocracy and the bourgeoisie of 17th century France. Monsieur Jourdain, the main character in *Le Bourgeois gentilhomme*, is a successful, middle-class businessman who longs to become a nobleman. To attain his goal, he attempts to learn dancing, music, fencing and philosophy from a series of tutors so that he can act and speak like a **gentilhomme**.

Topics you will choose from in **Activité 18** include life at the court of Versailles, the reign of Louis XIV, the rise of the middle class during the 17th century, and the life or plays of Molière. Once you have selected a topic, how do you begin your research? A good place to start is the reference section of your instructional materials center or library, where you can read a general summary of your topic. For example, if you were researching the reign of Louis XIV, you could begin by looking in an encyclopedia first under the heading "France," then under the subheading "History." Or, if you wanted to find information on another of Molière's plays, you could read the plot summary in the drama volume of the *Masterplots* series. (If your instructional materials center or library is computerized, ask if additional reference works are stored on computer.) Next, go to the card catalogue to find books that cover your topic in greater detail. If a certain book interests you, you can look it up under an author card or a title card. Subject cards are filed according to the general

 Listening Activity 2

 Quiz Leçon B

 Advanced Placement

Teacher's Notes

1. **Sur la bonne piste, Leçon B,** is designed to develop skills that will help students prepare to take the Advanced Placement Exam in French Literature. In this section students read a variety of works of prose, poetry and drama from different periods, answer content questions, and demonstrate their critical understanding of literary techniques, such as character development, setting, point of view, satire, figures of speech and inference. In this **Sur la bonne piste** section, students apply research skills to learn background information about Molière's works and time in order to gain a deeper understanding of and appreciation for *Le Bourgeois gentilhomme*. 2. For additional information on life at the court of Versailles during Louis XIV's reign, refer to page 268 in the second-level Annotated Teacher's Edition of *C'est à toi!*. 3. In 1670 Louis XIV ordered a Turkish ballet. Together with the musician Lully, Molière worked out a **comédie-ballet**, *Le Bourgeois gentilhomme,* which was staged at Chambord that October. Molière played the role of M. Jourdain, and Lully was the Grand Mufti. The production cost 49,000 **livres**. For the Court, the comedy was secondary to the dancing, music and the Turkish extravaganza which were the core of the play. Indeed, the *Gazette* of October 18, 1670, called *Le Bourgeois gentilhomme* "un ballet de six entrées accompagné de comédie." 4. The *Masterplots* series provides detailed plot summaries of famous novels and plays, in separate volumes.

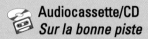

Audiocassette/CD
Sur la bonne piste

Teacher's Notes

1. Molière borrowed from the Italian *commedia dell'arte* a rhetoric of movement and gesture, a choreography of action and language, and a standard repertoire of comic routines. 2. In the 17th century comedy was justified on the grounds that it was socially beneficial, since it exposed human failings to ridicule. With Louis XIV's blessing, Molière thus set himself the task of reforming morals and manners through ridicule. Most of his comic characters are excessive types whose passions are out of balance. We can see many of our own failings in his character portraits. In *Le Bourgeois gentilhomme* Molière's satire is more gentle than in many of his plays, but he takes obvious aim at the sham and hypocrisy of 17th century Paris. He borrowed the stock figure of the parvenu from contemporary 17th century comedy. Yet it is the nobles who come off worst in *Le Bourgeois gentilhomme*. Molière shows his admiration for the fine character of the true bourgeois, Cléonte, and Madame Jourdain's common sense and reliability. 3. You may want to show the French film *Ridicule* to your students to give them an introduction to 18th century court life. Written by Remi Waterhouse and directed by Patrice Leconte, the highly acclaimed film stars Charles Berling, Jean Rochefort and Fanny Ardant.

topic of the book. For example, if you were interested in reading about one of Molière's plays, you could look under "French Literature," then select the sub-heading "17th century."

There may be a computer catalogue that contains the same information as the card catalogue. Simply select the author, title or subject option and key the author's name, the exact title or the general subject heading. Next to the title that you select, you will see a number. Select the number to find the call number to help you locate the book on the shelf. An important feature of the computer catalogue is that it often lets you know whether or not the book has been checked out. Remember that the person who best knows the resources in your instructional materials center or library is the librarian. He or she will be happy to point out additional sources as you research your topic. Finally, you may want to look for information on the Internet. Using a search engine such as those listed on page 228 of **Unité 6**, enter your general subject heading to receive a list of applicable articles.

14 | *Avant de lire la scène suivante du* Bourgeois gentilhomme, *répondez aux questions.*

1. Qu'est-ce que tu regrettes de ton éducation?
2. Quels cours est-ce que tu comptes suivre l'année prochaine? Pourquoi?
3. Quelles sortes de personnes est-ce que tu admires? Est-ce que tu fais quelque chose pour leur ressembler? Par exemple, est-ce que tu imites leurs coiffures (*hairstyles*) ou leurs vêtements?
4. As-tu jamais écrit une lettre d'amour? Si oui, est-ce que quelqu'un t'a aidé(e)?

Le Bourgeois gentilhomme
Acte II, Scène IV

Maître de Philosophie. ....Que voulez-vous apprendre?

Monsieur Jourdain. Tout ce que je pourrai, car j'ai toutes les envies du monde d'être savant; et j'enrage que mon père et ma mère ne m'aient pas fait bien étudier dans toutes les sciences quand j'étais jeune.

Maître de Philosophie. Ce sentiment est raisonnable, *Nam sine doctrina vita est quasi mortis imago.* Vous entendez cela, et vous savez le latin sans doute.

Monsieur Jourdain. Oui, mais faites comme si je ne le savais pas: expliquez-moi ce que cela veut dire.

Maître de Philosophie. Cela veut dire que *Sans la science, la vie est presque une image de la mort.*

Monsieur Jourdain. Ce latin-là a raison.

Maître de Philosophie. N'avez-vous point quelques principes, quelques commencements des sciences?

Monsieur Jourdain. Oh! oui, je sais lire et écrire.

Maître de Philosophie. Par où vous plaît-il que nous commencions? Voulez-vous que je vous apprenne la logique?

Monsieur Jourdain. Qu'est-ce que c'est que cette logique?

Maître de Philosophie. C'est elle qui enseigne les trois opérations de l'esprit.

Cross-curricular

Research Skills

Ask your librarian to conduct a class on library research skills for your students. He or she could explain how to use the card catalogue (traditional or electronic) and the Dewey decimal classification. In addition, he or she can update students on the latest technological services in the instructional materials center or library, as well as where to find relevant reference books such as *Masterplots.*

Monsieur Jourdain.	Qui sont-elles, ces trois opérations de l'esprit?
Maître de Philosophie.	La première, la seconde, et la troisième. La première est de bien concevoir par le moyen des universaux. La seconde, de bien juger par le moyen des catégories; et la troisième, de bien tirer une conséquence par le moyen des figures *Barbara, Celarent, Darii, Ferio, Baralipton,* etc.
Monsieur Jourdain.	Voilà des mots qui sont trop rébarbatifs. Cette logique-là ne me revient point. Apprenons autre chose qui soit plus joli.
Maître de Philosophie.	Voulez-vous apprendre la morale?
Monsieur Jourdain.	La morale?
Maître de Philosophie.	Oui.
Monsieur Jourdain.	Qu'est-ce qu'elle dit cette morale?
Maître de Philosophie.	Elle traite de la félicité, enseigne aux hommes à modérer leurs passions, et....
Monsieur Jourdain.	Non, laissons cela. Je suis bilieux comme tous les diables; et il n'y a morale qui tienne, je me veux mettre en colère tout mon soûl, quand il m'en prend envie.
Maître de Philosophie.	Est-ce la physique que vous voulez apprendre?
Monsieur Jourdain.	Qu'est-ce qu'elle chante cette physique?
Maître de Philosophie.	La physique est celle qui explique les principes des choses naturelles, et les propriétés du corps; qui discourt de la nature des éléments, des métaux, des minéraux, des pierres, des plantes et des animaux, et nous enseigne les causes de tous les météores, l'arc-en-ciel, les feux volants, les comètes, les éclairs, le tonnerre, la foudre, la pluie, la neige, la grêle, les vents et les tourbillons.
Monsieur Jourdain.	Il y a trop de tintamarre là-dedans, trop de brouillamini.
Maître de Philosophie.	Que voulez-vous donc que je vous apprenne?
Monsieur Jourdain.	Apprenez-moi l'orthographe.
Maître de Philosophie.	Très volontiers.
Monsieur Jourdain.	Après vous m'apprendrez l'almanach, pour savoir quand il y a de la lune et quand il n'y en a point.
Maître de Philosophie.	Soit. Pour bien suivre votre pensée et traiter cette matière en philosophe, il faut commencer selon l'ordre des choses, par une exacte connaissance de la nature des lettres, et de la différente manière de les prononcer toutes. Et là-dessus j'ai à vous dire que les lettres sont divisées en voyelles, ainsi dites voyelles parce qu'elles expriment les voix; et en consonnes, ainsi appelées consonnes parce qu'elles sonnent avec les voyelles, et ne font que marquer les diverses articulations des voix. Il y a cinq voyelles ou voix: A, E, I, O, U.
Monsieur Jourdain.	J'entends tout cela.
Maître de Philosophie.	La voix A se forme en ouvrant fort la bouche: A.
Monsieur Jourdain.	A, A. Oui.
Maître de Philosophie.	La voix E se forme en rapprochant la mâchoire d'en bas de celle d'en haut: A, E.
Monsieur Jourdain.	A, E, A, E. Ma foi! oui. Ah! que cela est beau!
Maître de Philosophie.	Et la voix I en rapprochant encore davantage les mâchoires l'une de l'autre, et écartant les deux coins de la bouche vers les oreilles: A, E, I.
Monsieur Jourdain.	A, E, I, I, I, I. Cela est vrai. Vive la science!
Maître de Philosophie.	La voix O se forme en rouvrant les mâchoires en rapprochant les lèvres par les deux coins, le haut et le bas: O.
Monsieur Jourdain.	O, O. Il n'y a rien de plus juste. A, E, I, O, I, O. Cela est admirable! I, O, I, O.

Teacher's Notes

1. Critics contend that Act II, Scene 4, is based on Aristophanes' *Clouds*, where Socrates instructs Strepsiades in philosophy. Just as the dissertation on philosophy degenerates into an absurd grammar lesson in the Aristophanes play, Monsieur Jourdain's instruction in philosophy terminates in a ridiculous study of pronunciation.
2. Two years prior to the production of *Le Bourgois gentilhomme*, the philosopher Cordemoy had published *Discours Physique de la Parole*, which delineated a theory of "grammatical physiology." Molière's spectators were thus in a position to understand and appreciate the playwright's biting satire on the method of pronunciation.

Maître de Philosophie.	L'ouverture de la bouche fait justement comme un petit rond qui représente un O.
Monsieur Jourdain.	O, O, O. Vous avez raison, O. Ah! la belle chose, que de savoir quelque chose!
Maître de Philosophie.	La voix U se forme en rapprochant les dents sans les joindre entièrement, et allongeant les deux lèvres en dehors, les approchant aussi l'une de l'autre sans les joindre tout à fait: U.
Monsieur Jourdain.	U, U. Il n'y a rien de plus véritable: U.
Maître de Philosophie.	Vos deux lèvres s'allongent comme si vous faisiez la moue; d'où vient que si vous la voulez faire à quelqu'un, et vous moquer de lui, vous n sauriez lui dire que: U.
Monsieur Jourdain.	U, U. Cela est vrai. Ah! que n'ai-je étudié plus tôt, pour savoir tout cela?
Maître de Philosophie.	Demain, nous verrons les autres lettres, qui sont les consonnes.
Monsieur Jourdain.	Est-ce qu'il y a des choses aussi curieuses qu'à celles-ci?
Maître de Philosophie.	Sans doute. La consonne D, par exemple, se prononce en donnant d bout de la langue au-dessus des dents d'en haut: DA.
Monsieur Jourdain.	DA, DA. Oui. Ah! les belles choses! les belles choses!
Maître de Philosophie.	L'F en appuyant les dents d'en haut sur la lèvre de dessous: FA.
Monsieur Jourdain.	FA, FA. C'est la vérité. Ah! mon père et ma mère, que je vous veux de mal!
Maître de Philosophie.	Et l'R, en portant le bout de la langue jusqu'au haut du palais, de sor qu'étant frôlée par l'air qui sort avec force, elle lui cède, et revient to jours au même endroit, faisant une manière de tremblement: RRA.
Monsieur Jourdain.	R, R, RA; R, R, R, R, R, RA. Cela est vrai. Ah! l'habile homme que vous êtes! et que j'ai perdu de temps! R, R, R, RA.
Maître de Philosophie.	Je vous expliquerai à fond toutes ces curiosités.
Monsieur Jourdain.	Je vous en prie. Au reste, il faut que je vous fasse une confidence. Je suis amoureux d'une personne de grande qualité, et je souhaiterais qu vous m'aidassiez à lui écrire quelque chose dans un petit billet que je veux laisser tomber à ses pieds.
Maître de Philosophie.	Fort bien.
Monsieur Jourdain.	Cela sera galant, oui.
Maître de Philosophie.	Sans doute. Sont-ce des vers que vous lui voulez écrire?
Monsieur Jourdain.	Non, non, point de vers.
Maître de Philosophie.	Vous ne voulez que de la prose?
Monsieur Jourdain.	Non, je ne veux ni prose ni vers.
Maître de Philosophie.	Il faut bien que ce soit l'un, ou l'autre.
Monsieur Jourdain.	Pourquoi?
Maître de Philosophie.	Par la raison, Monsieur, qu'il n'y a pour s'exprimer que la prose, ou les vers.
Monsieur Jourdain.	Il n'y a que la prose ou les vers?
Maître de Philosophie.	Non, Monsieur: tout ce qui n'est point prose est vers; et tout ce qui n'est point vers est prose.
Monsieur Jourdain.	Et comme l'on parle qu'est-ce que c'est donc que cela?
Maître de Philosophie.	De la prose.
Monsieur Jourdain.	Quoi! quand je dis: "Nicole, apportez-moi mes pantoufles et me donnez mon bonnet de nuit," c'est de la prose?
Maître de Philosophie.	Oui, Monsieur.

Monsieur Jourdain.	Par ma foi! Il y a plus de quarante ans que je dis de la prose sans que j'en susse rien, et je vous suis le plus obligé du monde de m'avoir appris cela. Je voudrais donc lui mettre dans un billet: *Belle Marquise, vos beaux yeux me font mourir d'amour*; mais je voudrais que cela fût mis d'une manière galante, que cela fût tourné gentiment.
Maître de Philosophie.	Mettre que les feux de ses yeux réduisent votre cœur en cendres; que vous souffrez nuit et jour pour elle les violences d'un....
Monsieur Jourdain.	Non, non, non, je ne veux point tout cela; je ne veux que ce que je vous ai dit: *Belle Marquise, vos beaux yeux me font mourir d'amour.*
Maître de Philosophie.	Il faut bien étendre un peu la chose.
Monsieur Jourdain.	Non, vous dis-je, je ne veux que ces seules paroles-là dans le billet, mais tournées à la mode, bien arrangées comme il faut. Je vous prie de me dire un peu, pour voir, les diverses manières dont on les peut mettre.
Maître de Philosophie.	On les peut mettre premièrement comme vous avez dit: *Belle Marquise, vos beaux yeux me font mourir d'amour.* Ou bien: *D'amour mourir me font, belle Marquise, vos beaux yeux.* Ou bien: *Vos yeux beaux d'amour me font, belle Marquise, mourir.* Ou bien: *Mourir vos beaux yeux, belle Marquise, d'amour me font.* Ou bien: *Me font vos yeux beaux mourir, belle Marquise, d'amour.*
Monsieur Jourdain.	Mais de toutes ces façons-là, laquelle est la meilleure?
Maître de Philosophie.	Celle que vous avez dite: *Belle Marquise, vos beaux yeux me font mourir d'amour.*
Monsieur Jourdain.	Cependant je n'ai point étudié, et j'ai fait cela tout du premier coup. Je vous remercie de tout mon cœur, et vous prie de venir demain de bonne heure.
Maître de Philosophie.	Je n'y manquerai pas....

Répondez aux questions suivantes.

1. Avec qui est-ce que M. Jourdain a une leçon?
2. Qu'est-ce que M. Jourdain regrette de son enfance (*childhood*)?
3. Le Maître de Philosophie dit une phrase en latin. Qu'est-ce qu'elle exprime?
4. M. Jourdain a-t-il quelques connaissances des sciences?
5. Quelle est la première matière (*subject*) que le Maître propose?
6. Est-ce que M. Jourdain s'y intéresse? Que veut-il plutôt apprendre?
7. Quelles sont les deux autres matières proposées par le Maître que M. Jourdain rejette?
8. Finalement, qu'est-ce que M. Jourdain veut apprendre?
9. M. Jourdain est-il content d'apprendre les voyelles? Que dit-il au sujet de cette "science"?
10. Selon toi, est-ce que M. Jourdain est un étudiant sérieux? Pourquoi ou pourquoi pas?
11. Qu'est-ce que M. Jourdain va apprendre demain?
12. Pourquoi M. Jourdain demande-t-il de l'aide du Maître?
13. Qu'est-ce que M. Jourdain dit quand il apprend qu'il fait de la prose en parlant?
14. Selon le Maître, laquelle des versions de la lettre de M. Jourdain est la meilleure?
15. Qu'est-ce que tu trouves de comique dans cette scène?

Answers

15 Possible answers:

1. M. Jourdain a une leçon avec le Maître de Philosophie.
2. M. Jourdain regrette que ses parents ne l'aient pas fait bien étudier dans toutes les sciences quand il était jeune.
3. La phrase en latin exprime l'importance de la science.
4. Non, il n'a pas de connaissances des sciences. Il ne sait que lire et écrire.
5. La première matière que le Maître propose est la logique.
6. Non, M. Jourdain ne s'y intéresse pas. Il veut plutôt apprendre autre chose qui soit plus joli.
7. M. Jourdain rejette aussi la morale et la physique.
8. M. Jourdain veut apprendre l'orthographe.
9. Oui, M. Jourdain est content d'apprendre les voyelles. Il dit, "Ah! que cela est beau!" "Vive la science!" "Cela est admirable!", etc.
10. Answers will vary.
11. Demain M. Jourdain va apprendre les consonnes.
12. M. Jourdain demande de l'aide pour écrire son billet d'amour pour la Marquise.
13. Il dit, "Par ma foi! Il y a plus de quarante ans que je dis de la prose sans que j'en susse rien, et je vous suis le plus obligé du monde de m'avoir appris cela."
14. Selon le Maître, la première version, celle de M. Jourdain, est la meilleure.
15. Answers will vary.

Teacher's Note

Some new words used in the play and cognates not found in the end vocabulary of *C'est à toi!* are used to ask questions about *Le Bourgeois gentilhomme* in Activity 15.

16 *Utilisez les encyclopédies et* Masterplots *dans la bibliothèque de votre école pour trouver un article général sur chacun des sujets suivants. Pour chaque sujet écrivez le titre du livre que vous utilisez, le titre de l'article et le sous-titre (subtitle).*

1. l'Empire romaine
2. l'Angleterre normande (après 1066)
3. les croisades
4. l'intrigue de *L'École des femmes* de Molière
5. les châteaux de la Loire
6. les contributions françaises à la guerre de l'Indépendance américaine

17 *Utilisez le fichier* (card catalogue) *dans la bibliothèque de votre école pour trouver un livre sur chacun des six sujets dans l'Activité 16. Pour chaque sujet écrivez le nom de l'auteur* (author), *le titre, la cote* (call number) *et la date de publication.*

18 *Choisissez le sujet qui vous intéresse le plus parmi ceux qui suivent sur l'œuvre* (works) *et le temps de Molière.*

1. la vie à la cour de Versailles
2. le règne de Louis XIV
3. l'importance de la bourgeoisie au 17e siècle
4. la vie de Molière
5. les pièces de Molière

Faites des recherches sur votre sujet en utilisant les encyclopédies, Masterplots, *le fichier et les autres techniques de recherche que vous venez d'apprendre. Puis préparez un plan détaillé* (outline) *de votre sujet. (Utilisez la section "Comment faire un plan détaillé" qui se trouve aux pages 279-81 du deuxième manuel de la série* C'est à toi!*)*

Dossier fermé

Avec un groupe d'élèves de ton école, tu passes 15 jours en France. Pendant votre visite d'une belle cathédrale gothique, le guide vous parle des fenêtres de la cathédrale. Il dit que ces fenêtres, composées de morceaux de verre colorés, ne sont pas connues seulement pour leur beauté. Il dit que dans le passé elles avaient aussi une fonction utile. Qu'est-ce que ces fenêtres faisaient?

C. Elles racontaient des histoires de la Bible et des héros et héroïnes français.

Les gens qui ne pouvaient pas lire se servaient des vitraux des églises pour apprendre les histoires religieuses et celles de la gloire de France. Les vitraux de Chartres, par exemple, racontaient la vie de Charlemagne, et ceux de la Sainte-Chapelle racontaient des histoires de la Bible.

C'est à moi!

Now that you have completed this unit, take a look at what you should be able to do in French. Can you do all of these tasks?

➤ I can talk about what happened in the past.

➤ I can give factual information.

➤ I can use linking expressions to connect narration.

➤ I can talk about things sequentially.

➤ I can explain what something means in another language.

➤ I can say what someone is obliged to do.

➤ I can say that someone has something done.

➤ I can say what someone is incapable of doing.

➤ I can describe someone's character traits.

➤ I can express criticism.

➤ I can make a generalization.

➤ I can boast.

➤ I can state someone's preference.

➤ I can express appreciation.

Pour voir si vous avez bien compris la culture francophone, décidez si chaque phrase est vraie ou fausse.

1. Jules César a vaincu Vercingétorix et les Gaulois.
2. Roland a essayé d'aider Charlemagne quand l'ennemi espagnol a attaqué son armée.
3. Charlemagne voulait établir sa capitale à Paris.
4. La tapisserie et les vitraux ont aidé les gens à comprendre les événements historiques.
5. Le roi Louis IX a participé à toutes les croisades et a réussi à délivrer la Terre sainte.
6. Les trois fils de Catherine de Médicis sont connus comme *Les Trois Mousquetaires*.
7. L'Amiral Coligny a ordonné le massacre de la Saint-Barthélemy.
8. Nostradamus était l'architecte de la cathédrale de Notre-Dame de Paris.
9. Marie-Antoinette plaisait à son peuple, qui l'adorait.
10. Pierre L'Enfant et Georges Haussmann ont travaillé ensemble pour construire un nouveau Paris.

Answers

1. vraie
2. vraie
3. fausse
4. vraie
5. fausse
6. fausse
7. fausse
8. fausse
9. fausse
10. fausse

Communication orale

Avec un(e) partenaire, jouez les rôles de deux personnages historiques que vous venez d'étudier. Imaginez la conversation qui aurait lieu s'ils se rencontraient pour la première fois. Vous pouvez choisir entre ces couples:

- Vercingétorix et Jules César
- Guillaume le Conquérant et Harold
- Catherine de Médicis et Nostradamus
- Louis XVI et Marie-Antoinette
- le marquis de La Fayette et George Washington

Teacher's Note

1. Catherine de Médicis conspired with leading Catholics to assassinate Huguenot leaders and convinced her son, Charles IX, to go along with her plan. The result was the St. Bartholomew's Day Massacre. Coligny, the leader of the Huguenots, was among the first killed when the bells of Saint-Germain-l'Auxerrois began tolling as a signal for the massacre to begin. 2. Nostradamus (1503-66) was born in southern France. His book is a set of prophecies in verse, some of which are open to interpretation. He correctly predicted that Henri II would die when a lance pierced his eye in a tournament. After the death of her husband, Catherine de Médicis had Nostradamus prepare horoscopes for her sons at the château of Blois. Nostradamus also correctly prophesied that Henri de Navarre would become king. 3. On April 13, 1598, the Edict of Nantes granted a broad measure of religious liberty, civil rights and security to Henri IV's Calvinist subjects, the Huguenots.

Pour préparer votre conversation, c'est une bonne idée de faire des recherches pour apprendre plus sur la vie et le caractère de vos personnages. Chaque partenaire doit dire à l'autre comment il le/la trouve et doit donner des raisons spécifiques pour ses sentiments. Avant de commencer votre conversation, vous devez considérer:

- *si votre partenaire et vous, vous vous entendez bien ou mal*
- *si vous aimez ou détestez votre partenaire*
- *si vous êtes d'accord avec ou si vous critiquez les actions de votre partenaire*

Communication écrite

Imaginez que vous êtes l'un des dix personnages qu'on a nommés dans l'activité précédente et que c'est un jour décisif dans votre vie. Écrivez une lettre à quelqu'un que vous connaissez assez bien et décrivez pour lui ce qui vient de se passer. Si vous êtes Catherine de Médicis, par exemple, vous pouvez décrire ce que Nostradamus vient de vous raconter, ou si vous êtes Louis XVI, vous pouvez décrire votre premier jour en prison. Parlez de ce que vous avez fait, en donnant des détails spécifiques de l'événement. Dites aussi qui vous avez vu, en donnant vos impressions de ces personnes. Enfin mentionnez comment vous vous sentez en ce moment.

Communicative active

To describe past events, use:

Après une lutte difficile, **les Français ont vaincu** les Anglais.	*After a difficult fight, the French defeated the English.*
Elle a survécu à des intrigues politiques très complexes.	*She survived some very complicated political intrigues.*

To state factual information, use:

Le massacre de la Saint-Barthélemy **a eu lieu** en 1572.	*The St. Barthélemy Massacre took place in 1572.*

To use links, use:

Au temps des Romains la France s'appelait la Gaule.	*At the time of the Romans, France was called Gaul.*
En ce temps-là les Gaulois vivaient en tribus indépendantes.	*At that time the Gauls lived in independent tribes.*
Au cours de sa deuxième croisade, Louis IX est mort de maladie.	*In the course of his second crusade, Louis IX died of illness.*

To sequence events, use:

Par conséquent il a été obligé d'acheter sa liberté.	*Consequently he had to buy his liberty.*
Après avoir accepté de travailler sans salaire, La Fayette est devenu général.	*After having agreed to work without pay, La Fayette became a general.*

Game

Le pendu

To practice new vocabulary in this unit, you might play "Hangman." The object of *Le pendu* is to spell out words before the figure of a hanged man takes shape. The game calls for some sheer guesswork, but it also reinforces spelling skill. A student at the board writes a set of broken lines corresponding to the number of letters of a word he or she chooses from the unit's vocabulary. One at a time students try to guess the word by calling out letters. The student at the board writes a letter on the appropriate line if a right call is made. For each wrong call, he or she draws elsewhere on the board a line that would become part of a hanged man. Drawing begins with a line-by-line sketch of a gallows. The number of lines needed to form the whole image should be predetermined.

Le bal masqué a eu lieu le 14 février.

Après être rentré, il a continué à servir son pays.

After having returned, he continued to serve his country.

To explain something, use:

En français, on dit "Je suis venu, j'ai vu, j'ai vaincu."

In French it's "I came, I saw, I conquered."

To express obligation, use:

Elle était obligée de défendre ses fils.

She was obliged to defend her sons.

To have something done, use:

Après six ans **César l'a fait tuer.**

After six years Caesar had him killed.

Il a fait venir les meilleurs professeurs de son temps.

He had the best teachers of his time come.

Guillaume a gardé les lois d'Édouard **pour faire accepter** son administration.

William kept Édouard's laws in order to have his administration accepted.

Louis IX a fait construire la Sainte-Chapelle à Paris.

Louis IX had the Sainte-Chapelle built in Paris.

To express incapability, use:

La Fayette **avait beau essayer** d'arrêter la violence de la Révolution.

La Fayette tried in vain to stop the violence of the Revolution.

To describe character, use:

Il était courageux.

He was courageous.

To express criticism, use:

Les protestants et les catholiques **ont** beaucoup **critiqué** Catherine.

Protestants and Catholics criticized Catherine a lot.

To state a generalization, use:

On a dit que les temps changent, mais que la nature humaine ne change pas.

People have said that times change but human nature doesn't.

To boast, use:

César a déclaré, **"Je suis venu, j'ai vu, j'ai vaincu."**

Caesar declared, "I came, I saw, I conquered."

Il était fier de ses qualifications.

He was proud of his qualifications.

To state a preference, use:

Louis XVI **préférait** la chasse **aux** affaires du pays.

Louis XVI preferred hunting to the business of the country.

To express appreciation, use:

Les Français l'ont toujours **apprécié pour** son christianisme et sa justice.

The French have always appreciated him for his Christianity and justice.

Le roi Philippe Auguste a fait construire le Louvre comme une forteresse du 13ᵉ siècle. (Paris)

Guy préférait les jeux vidéo aux émissions télévisées.

Listening Activity 3

Unité 9

L'Afrique francophone

In this unit you will be able to:

➤ write a letter
➤ tell a story
➤ describe past events
➤ sequence events
➤ use links
➤ give information
➤ tell location
➤ ask what something is
➤ identify objects
➤ express ownership
➤ boast
➤ express enthusiasm
➤ compare
➤ remind
➤ express indifference
➤ express disappointment

Leçon A

In this lesson you will be able to:

➤ describe past events

➤ ask what something is

➤ identify objects

➤ tell location

➤ remind

➤ express indifference

➤ express disappointment

➤ express enthusiasm

➤ boast

Tes empreintes ici

As-tu jamais voyagé en Afrique? Si oui, comment l'as-tu trouvée? Si non, voudrais-tu y aller un jour? Quel pays choisirais-tu de visiter? Un pays francophone, peut-être? Penses-tu que la vie quotidienne en Afrique soit très différente de la vie quotidienne ici?

Aimerais-tu connaître la culture africaine? (Sénégal)

Quand un(e) ami(e) te rend visite, quels sont les endroits intéressants que tu aimes lui montrer? Par exemple, tu peux lui montrer:

- le zoo, parce que presque tout le monde aime regarder les éléphants, les singes et les poissons. Quels sont tes animaux favoris?
- un musée, surtout s'il y a une exposition spéciale. Est-ce que les musées d'art, d'histoire ou de la nature t'intéressent? Est-ce qu'il y a un musée célèbre là où tu habites? Lequel?
- un atelier où on crée quelque chose de spécial. Quelquefois on peut y acheter ce qui y est créé. Quelle est la spécialité de ta ville?

Dossier ouvert

Imagine que tu es à Niamey (au Niger), à Abidjan (en Côte-d'Ivoire) ou à Dakar (au Sénégal) en visite touristique. Tous les sites africains et leurs couleurs riches t'impressionnent. Tu vois une femme en jupe et avec un foulard de tête de couleurs vives, et tu veux la prendre en photo. Mais cette femme se fâche. Pourquoi?

A. La femme n'a pas eu le temps de se peigner.
B. Selon la tradition islamique, les Africains n'aiment pas que les touristes les prennent en photo.
C. La femme n'a pas son appareil-photo pour te prendre en photo.

le Niger

le Sahara

Niamey

une case

une concession

un dinosaure

un éléphant

une antilope

un hippopotame

une autruche

une hyène

un lion

un singe

une girafe

Workbook
Activity 1

Audiocassette/CD
Les animaux africains

Transparencies 3-4, 27-28

Teacher's Notes

1. **Niger** is pronounced [niʒer].
2. **Un hippopotame, un éléphant, un lion, un singe** and **une girafe** were introduced in Unit 2 in the second level of *C'est à toi!* 3. Other related terms and expressions include **nigérien, nigérienne** (*Nigerois*), **un Nigérien, une Nigérienne** (*an inhabitant of/from Niger*) and **saharien, saharienne** (*Saharan, tropical*).

Je peux t'emprunter 2.000 francs?

Oui, oui, Je crois que j'ai assez d'argent à te prêter.

Teacher's Notes

1. The **musée national de Niamey**, opened in 1958, is a popular destination for the people of Niger as well as for visiting foreigners. The museum includes several pavilions where the visitor can watch artists and artisans at work, see native animals, stroll through model traditional villages, study the paleontology of the country or sit in the shade in the refreshment area while listening to native storytellers and singers. 2. Point out that **faire partie de** is an idiomatic **faire** expression. 3. The plural of **appareil-photo** is **appareils-photos**. 4. **Gratte-ciel** is invariable. 5. Point out that **malheureusement** belongs to the **heureux** word family.

La girafe avec le gratte-ciel de Niamey derrière montre le contraste entre le passé et le présent au Niger.

Nous sommes samedi. Abdoulaye, un étudiant de l'Université de Niamey, emmène sa nouvelle copine, Salmou, au musée national. Elle était venue faire ses études d'infirmière à Niamey, la capitale du Niger, et ils se sont rencontrés° chez des amis. C'est la première visite de Salmou au musée.

Salmou: Où est le musée, Abdoulaye? Je ne vois qu'un parc.
Abdoulaye: Oui, c'est le parc du musée. Tout ça, c'est le musée national de Niamey.
Salmou: Qu'est-ce qu'il y a alors?
Abdoulaye: Bon, tu vois partout des pavillons d'exposition. Celui des vêtements traditionnels est à droite, celui des instruments de musique est à gauche, et plus loin il y a celui des squelettes de dinosaures du Sahara.
Salmou: Et tous ces enfants qui sont là-bas, qu'est-ce qu'ils regardent?
Abdoulaye: Les hippopotames! Le zoo fait partie du° musée.
Salmou: Il y a aussi des éléphants, n'est-ce pas?
Abdoulaye: Non, mais regarde! Voilà les hyènes, les lions et les singes. Derrière, on trouvera les autruches et les antilopes.
Salmou: Et les girafes?
Abdoulaye: Elles sont de l'autre côté.° Allons voir! Tu as ton appareil-photo?° Ça fera une photo intéressante, les girafes avec un gratte-ciel de Niamey derrière. Ça montrera le contraste entre le passé et le présent.
Salmou: Malheureusement,° j'ai oublié mon appareil-photo. Si j'avai su que c'était si passionnant.... Tiens, qu'est-ce que c'est que° ce pavillon à côté?

se rencontrer faire la connaissance de; **faire partie de** être une partie de; **de l'autre côté** *on the other side*; **un appareil-photo** ce qu'on utilise quand on prend une photo; **un gratte-ciel** *skyscraper*; **malheureusement** *unfortunately*; **Qu'est-ce que c'est que...?** *What is . . .?*

Abdoulaye: Ce sont les villages modèles. On peut voir les concessions des paysans° avec leurs cases en banco.° Même aujourd'hui beaucoup de villages ressemblent toujours à ces villages modèles.

Salmou: Oui, oui, je sais. Dans mon village de Koré Mai Ruwa, tu verras aussi des concessions comme ça. C'est fantastique qu'on puisse voir un peu de notre pays ici. Et les artisans° célèbres dont tu m'as parlé, où sont-ils?

Abdoulaye: Ils se trouvent près de l'entrée du musée. Tu veux voir la maroquinerie?°

Salmou: Des trucs en cuir? Oui, je veux acheter des sandales.

Abdoulaye: Bon alors, allons-y!

Abdoulaye et Salmou vont à l'atelier° des artisans et s'arrêtent devant Garba, un vieil homme qui est en train de travailler.

Salmou: Oh! J'adore ces sandales! Elles sont à° vous, Monsieur?

Garba: Oui, oui. Elles sont à moi.

Abdoulaye: Et ce tapis de Zinder?

Garba: Il est en cuir et en peau° de chèvre. Je n'aime pas me vanter,° mais c'est un travail très fin,° n'est-ce pas? Je suis de Zinder, capitale de la maroquinerie.

Salmou: C'est combien, ces sandales?

Garba: Elles coûtent 3.500 francs, Mademoiselle. Vous faites du...

Salmou: Trente-neuf, Monsieur. Je préfère cette paire-ci.

Garba: Voilà, Mademoiselle. Vous savez, il faut aller à la boutique du musée. Je crois que tout est en solde aujourd'hui.

Salmou: Super! Allons-y, Abdoulaye!

Abdoulaye: Bon, je suis d'accord. Et les autres expositions?

Salmou: Bof!° On verra tout ça un autre jour.

Abdoulaye et Salmou sont dans la boutique du musée.

Vendeuse: Est-ce que les foulards de tête vous intéressent, Mademoiselle? J'en ai de très jolis comme celui-ci en marron et rouge. Il va très bien avec votre pagne.° Et je vous rappelle° que tout est en solde aujourd'hui.

Salmou: Ah oui. Je trouve ces couleurs très jolies. Ce foulard de tête-ci, il fait combien?

Vendeuse: Trois mille francs, Mademoiselle.

Abdoulaye: Attention, hein? Tu as assez d'argent sur toi?

Salmou: Ah! Oh, si seulement j'étais venue avec tout mon argent.... Euh... Abdoulaye, je peux t'emprunter° 2.000 francs?

Abdoulaye: Oui, oui. Je crois que j'ai assez d'argent à te prêter.°

Salmou: Tu es très gentil.

Abdoulaye: Et maintenant je t'invite à prendre un coca au snack-bar du musée.

Beaucoup de Nigériennes portent un foulard de tête.

un paysan, une paysanne une personne qui habite à la campagne; **le banco** *adobe*; **un artisan** *craftsperson*; **la maroquinerie** les objets en cuir; **un atelier** où travaille un artisan; **être à** *to belong to*; **une peau** *skin*; **se vanter** *to boast*; **fin(e)** compliqué(e); **Bof!** Qu'est-ce que je peux dire?; **un pagne** une jupe africaine; **rappeler** *to remind*; **emprunter** *to borrow*; **prêter** *to lend*

Teacher's Notes

1. **Oui, oui** is a common affirmative reply in francophone Africa. 2. Koré Mai Ruwa is a small village southeast of Niamey, between Dosso and Dogon Doutchi. Mai Ruwa means "with water." 3. Point out that **la maroquinerie** comes from the noun **Maroc**. Here it refers to fine leather goods made from animal skins. It can also refer to the business of making fine leather goods or to a store where such goods are purchased. 4. Students learned **un atelier**, meaning "studio," in Unit 3 in the third level of *C'est à toi!* 5. One of Niamey's best artisan cooperatives was established in 1968 at the **musée national de Niamey**. A wide variety of representative crafts from different parts of the country can be found there, such as Djarma blankets, Tuareg jewelry, rugs and fine leather goods from Zinder, brass figurines, camel hair blankets and batik T-shirts. 6. Point out that **être à** is an idiomatic **être** expression. 7. The city of Zinder is located about 900 kilometers east of Niamey. It is known for its decorated adobe houses, large market and leather goods. 8. In Niger and many other African countries, women wear **un foulard de tête**. 9. **Un pagne** is a two-yard length of printed cloth wrapped around the waist as a skirt. 10. Students learned **se rappeler**, meaning "to remember," in Unit 2 in the third level of *C'est à toi!* 11. Prices for crafts purchased in the museum store are fixed and may be higher than in the workshops, where customers are expected to bargain. 12. **Emprunter de l'argent à quelqu'un** means "to borrow money from someone." 13. The currency used in many francophone African countries is the African franc, **le franc CFA (Communauté Financière Africaine)**. Recently, there were slightly more than 600 **francs CFA** to one American dollar.

1 *Choisissez l'expression qui complète chaque phrase d'après le dialogue.*

1. Salmou et Abdoulaye sont....
   a. au musée national de Niamey
   b. à l'Université de Niamey
   c. chez des amis
2. On peut voir tous les pavillons sauf....
   a. le pavillon des vêtements traditionnels
   b. le pavillon des instruments de musique
   c. le pavillon des squelettes d'antilopes
3. La photo des girafes avec un gratte-ciel de Niamey derrière montrerait....
   a. le contraste entre le passé et le présent
   b. le contraste entre Niamey et Koré Mai Ruwa
   c. le zoo et les villages
4. Dans les villages modèles on peut voir des cases dans des....
   a. rues
   b. pavillons
   c. concessions
5. Le tapis de Zinder est en cuir et en....
   a. peau de chèvre
   b. marron et rouge
   c. solde
6. Salmou achète... de Garba.
   a. un tapis
   b. une paire de sandales
   c. des photos de l'atelier des artisans
7. Salmou veut aller à la boutique du musée car....
   a. tout est en solde aujourd'hui
   b. tout est bon marché
   c. elle n'aime pas les pavillons
8. Abdoulaye prête 2.000 francs à Salmou parce qu'elle....
   a. veut lui offrir un foulard de tête
   b. veut plaire à la vendeuse
   c. n'a pas assez d'argent

2 *Vous verrez une page du journal d'Abdoulaye. Il décrit sa journée au musée. Complétez chaque phrase avec l'expression convenable de la liste suivante.*

paire	emprunté	appareil-photo
rappelé	modèles	traditionnels
pavillons	maroquinerie	fait partie
pagne		

Game

Machine à écrire

Divide the class into two teams to practice spelling new vocabulary words introduced in this lesson and any you want to review from previous units. Then assign a letter of the alphabet to individual members of each team. Assign accent marks, too. In doing this, be sure each team has members that represent the whole alphabet and all accent marks. (Depending on the size of the class, you may need to assign more than one letter or accent mark to some students.) Start the game by giving one team a vocabulary word. This team must spell the word orally. They must do this so fast that they sound like a typewriter; hence the name of the game. (You may want to set a time limit for calling out letters.) For example, if the word is **pavillon**, the student with the letter **p** calls out that letter in French, and teammates with the appropriate letters complete in turn the spelling of the word. By doing this, the team earns one point. Then the other team gets its turn at a word. Whenever a team fails to correctly spell a word, its rival gets a chance to spell the same word and win another point.

samedi

Aujourd'hui j'ai emmené Salmou au musée national de Niamey. Je lui ai montré la plupart des... d'exposition, par exemple, celui des vêtements... et le zoo qui... du musée. Elle avait oublié son..., donc elle n'a pas pu prendre de photos. Après avoir visité les villages..., elle avait envie de voir la.... Elle a acheté une... de sandales. Puis nous sommes allés à la boutique du musée où la vendeuse nous a... que tout était en solde. Salmou a choisi un foulard de tête en marron et rouge pour aller avec son.... Elle m'a... 2.000 francs parce qu'elle n'était pas venue avec tout son argent. Après nous avons pris un coca au snack-bar du musée.

Abdoulaye a-t-il montré le pavillon des instruments de musique à Salmou? (Niamey)

C'est à moi!

1. Est-ce que tu voudrais aller en Afrique un jour? Si oui, où irais-tu?
2. Quand tu as des ami(e)s d'une autre ville qui te rendent visite, quels endroits est-ce que tu leur montres?
3. Est-ce que tu aimes aller aux musées? Si oui, lequel préfères-tu?
4. Quels sont tes animaux favoris au zoo?
5. Est-ce que tu aimes prendre des photos? As-tu un appareil-photo?
6. Joues-tu d'un instrument de musique? Si oui, duquel?
7. Est-ce que tu prêtes quelquefois de l'argent à tes ami(e)s?
8. Est-ce que tu empruntes de l'argent à tes ami(e)s? Pourquoi ou pourquoi pas?

Enquête culturelle

Comme plusieurs pays francophones d'Afrique, la république du Niger se trouve dans le désert du Sahara. Le Niger est deux fois plus grand que le Texas. Le fleuve Niger traverse le pays à l'ouest, à l'est du pays on trouve le lac Tchad et le désert est au nord. Le fleuve et le lac donnent de l'eau à ce pays très pauvre qui dépend de l'agriculture pour manger. Comme d'autres pays africains, le Niger connaît les problèmes de déforestation et de désertification. La richesse du pays consiste en sa population animale, mais, malheureusement, la chasse l'a diminuée.

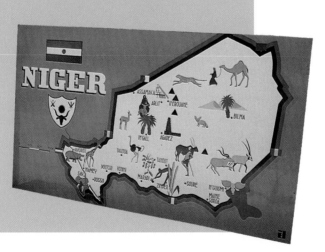

■ Workbook
Activity 3

🎞 Audiocassette/CD
Activity 3

Answers

3 Answers will vary.

Teacher's Notes

1. Cognates in this reading include **république, désert, agriculture, déforestation, désertification, richesse, consiste, population, animale, diminuée, date, colonies, habitants, officielle, islamique, domine, région, pour cent, Nigériens, musulmans, représentation, préhistoire, consacrées, ethnographie, paléontologie, géologie, architecture, traditionnels, objets, poterie, doute, discuter, sauvages, sites, touristiques, gouvernementaux, légendes** and **historiques.** 2. Niger is a landlocked nation that borders Libya, Chad, Nigeria, Benin, Burkina Faso, Mali and Algeria. 3. Nearly 90 percent of the inhabitants of Niger are dependent on agriculture. Peanuts, traditionally the leading cash crop, are no longer economically important, since France withdrew its subsidy. The chief agricultural products are beans, cassava, cotton, hides and skins, livestock, millet, peas, rice and sorghum. 4. Niger is one of the world's top producers of uranium. Natron, phosphate, iron ore, tungsten, salt and tin are also mined. 5. Niger is a developing nation and ranks as one of the world's poorest countries. It has few natural resources. Only three percent of the land is used to grow crops. Droughts periodically devastate Niger's agrarian economy, causing sharp reductions in crop and livestock production. 6. Big game hunting in Niger has been outlawed.

Teacher's Notes

1. Niger was the location of the Songhai Empire, which has been traced back as far as the 7th century. The Hausa city-states of the 10th century developed when immigrants from eastern and northern Africa took control of much of the land along Niger's trade routes. At the beginning of the 19th century, the Fulani rebelled against the Hausa rulers and set up their own kingdom. 2. French occupation of Niger took place in the late 1890s. The Colony of Niger was established in 1922. It became the largest and poorest of the eight colonies that made up French West Africa. Niger gained more control over its internal affairs in 1958, as did other French dependencies. 3. Many buildings in Niamey combine Western and African design. The government of Niger has built low-cost, single-family houses in the capital. Residents of Niamey work primarily in the government, other services, or business. 4. French is widely used in the schools. Most Nigerois speak the language of their ethnic group instead of French. More than 85 percent of the population can understand the Hausa language, which also serves as the language of trade. The language of the Kjerma-Songhai ranks as the second most widely spoken language. Some Nigerois speak Arabic. 5. A small percentage of urban dwellers are Christians. Some Nigerois still practice traditional African religions. 6. Although education in Niger is free, many areas do not have schools. Many students go to Koranic schools. Tent schools serve the nomadic groups in the north. 7. Most of the women of Niger wear long, wrap-around skirts with blouses and sandals. In many areas men wear pants or knee-length shorts with loose shirts or robes. Tuareg men wear turbans with veils. Nomadic tribes who live in the Sahara wear long, loose robes. 8. The major ethnic groups are the Hausa, the Djerma-Songhai and the Kanuri. The Hausa make up about

Je parle haoussa et français.

L'histoire du Niger date de six mille ans. Au début du 20ᵉ siècle, les Français ont établi des colonies au Niger. En 1960 le Niger est devenu indépendant comme plusieurs autres colonies françaises d'Afrique. La capitale du Niger, Niamey, est située sur le fleuve Niger. Elle a une population de 300.000 habitants. C'est le centre d'affaires et de gouvernement. Pour ceux qui font des affaires, il est important de parler français, parce que c'est aussi bien la langue du commerce que la langue officielle. C'est la religion islamique qui domine dans la région, et 80 pour cent des Nigériens sont musulmans.

Le musée national de Niamey est un centre d'éducation pour la population nigérienne. Comme représentation de l'histoire et de la géographie du pays, le musée sert aussi aux touristes. Si la préhistoire vous intéresse, visitez le pavillon de la grande exposition des squelettes des dinosaures qui habitaient la région. Le *Carcharodontosaurus*, un dinosaure plus grand que le *Tyrannosaurus rex*, vivait là il y a 90 millions d'années. D'autres parties du musée sont consacrées à l'ethnographie, la paléontologie, la géologie et l'architecture. Si vous vous arrêtez dans les ateliers des artisans, vous pouvez y admirer leurs articles traditionnels de maroquinerie, des tapis, des objets en argent et en or et aussi de la poterie du pays. Commencez une conversation avec un artisan! Il aimera sans doute vous parler de son travail. Et il est toujours utile de discuter les prix avec l'artisan, parce que vous pourriez trouver des objets d'art à de très bons prix.

N'oubliez pas de prendre votre appareil-photo quand vous visiterez le parc d'animaux sauvages au musée national de Niamey. Il est permis de prendre des photos des animaux et des différents sites touristiques au Niger, mais pas des aéroports ou des centres gouvernementaux. Les gens en Afrique n'aiment pas qu'on les prenne en photo, et c'est toujours une bonne idée de demander d'abord à quelqu'un si vous pouvez prendre sa photo. Et enfin, quand vous aurez faim et soif, allez au snack-bar pour pouvoir sortir au soleil en écoutant des chansons dans la langue nationale ou des légendes historiques.

N'oubliez pas de demander la permission aux Africains avant de les prendre en photo.

half of the country's population. Between one-fourth and one-fifth of the people belong to the Djerma-Songhai group, and only about five percent of the population are Kanuri. All these groups are farmers. The nomadic Fulani and Tuareg together make up about ten percent of the population. During the rainy season, from July to September, they live in the Sahara. In dry months they travel south in search of water and pastureland. 9. A large number of complete, well-preserved dinosaur skeletons were discovered by accident in the Gadoufaoua Desert by two French geologists in the late 1960s. Examples are on display at the **musée national de Niamey**. The skull of a *Carcharodontosaurus* was discovered by Dr. Paul Sereno of the University of Chicago, who estimates the dinosaur's length at 45 feet. 10. Ethnography is the study of human cultures. 11. Paleontology is the study of past geologic periods from fossil remains.

Répondez aux questions suivantes.

1. Où se trouve la république du Niger?
2. Quelles sources d'eau trouve-t-on au Niger?
3. Qu'est-ce qui crée des problèmes pour la population des animaux?
4. Quand est-ce que le Niger est devenu indépendant?
5. Quelle est la langue du commerce au Niger?
6. Quelle est la religion de la plupart des Nigériens?
7. Quels sont les diverses parties du musée national de Niamey?
8. Le *Carcharodontosaurus*, qu'est-ce que c'est?
9. Avant d'acheter quelque chose qu'un artisan a fait, qu'est-ce qu'il est toujours utile de faire?
10. Qu'est-ce qu'on peut photographier au Niger?

Dans le pavillon de paléontologie on apprend les périodes géologiques. (Niamey)

Journal personnel

If you have never visited a certain country or continent, you sometimes have vague notions and stereotypes about what it is like. Before you began to study this lesson, what ideas did you have about life in Africa? What did you think the geography was like? How did you imagine people made a living? In what kinds of buildings did you think they lived and worked? What animals did you think were found there? What kinds of products did you think people made by hand? Where did your ideas of Africa come from? Were they from movies, TV, books, magazines or other sources? How has your picture of Africa changed by learning specific details about life in Niger? Which of your ideas are correct? Which need to be readjusted? What more would you need to know about Niger to be able to say you understand what life is really like there?

Now imagine that Abdoulaye and Salmou have come to the United States to visit you. What images of our country do you think they already have from movies, TV, books, magazines or other sources? Where in the United States would you like to take them to see American geography, animal life, a museum about America's past and authentic American handmade products? What places in your region would you like them to visit in order to expand their understanding of what the United States is really like?

Structure

Expressions with *être*

The verb **être** (*to be*) is another frequently used verb in French.

Tout est en solde aujourd'hui.   *Everything is on sale today.*

Also called a "building block" verb, **être** is used in a number of expressions in French where a different verb is used in English. You have already learned some common expressions with **être** that deal with agreeing with someone, giving the day/date and saying that you are busy doing something.

«JE SUIS ENFIN FIER DE MOI...»

Pour quel genre de métier êtes-vous fait(e)?

Answers

5 1. C'est le dix septembre.
2. Cet homme est en train de travailler une peau de chèvre.
3. Ces sandales, elles sont à vous?
4. Vous êtes de Niamey?
5. Zinder est à 900 kilomètres de Niamey.
6. Oh là là! Il est déjà cinq heures.
7. Bon, je suis d'accord.
8. Ali et Sonia sont en retard.

Bon, je suis d'accord.	Good, I agree.
Nous sommes samedi.	It's Saturday.
Garba est en train de travailler.	Garba is busy working.

To show ownership, use the expression **être à** (*to belong to*). A stress pronoun or a noun follows **être à**.

J'adore ces sandales! Elles sont à vous, Monsieur?	*I love these sandals! Do they belong to you, Sir?*
Oui, oui. Elles sont à moi.	*Yes. They are mine.*

Pratique

5 *Choisissez une phrase de la liste suivante pour accompagner chaque illustration. Puis complétez la phrase avec la forme convenable du verbe **être** au présent.*

Modèle:

Enfin, nous sommes vendredi.

> Bon, je... d'accord.
> Enfin, nous... vendredi.
> Ces sandales, elles... à vous?
> Zinder... à 900 kilomètres de Niamey.
> Cet homme... en train de travailler une peau de chèvre.
> Vous... de Niamey?
> C'... le dix septembre.
> Oh là là! Il... déjà cinq heures.
> Ali et Sonia... en retard.

Ces gens sont de Zinder, au Niger.

Quels sont les prochains films de Russell Crowe (L.A. Confidential)?

1.

3.

2.

4.

Cooperative Group Practice

Identifying Objects

Put students in small groups of four or five. Have each student place an object or a drawing of an object on his or her desk. Designate a leader for each group. The leader asks questions about the ownership of objects in his or her group, for example, **Anne, à qui est la photo?** Anne identifies the owner by using a sentence with **être à**, for example, **La photo est à Michel**. After the leader has asked each student in the group a question, students in the group select a new object or make a new drawing of an object, and a new leader begins a second round of questioning.

5.

6.

7.

8.

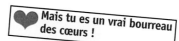

Allons-y!

❤ **Mais tu es un vrai bourreau des cœurs !**

🎧 **Audiocassette/CD Activity 6**

Answers

6 1. À qui est l'appareil-photo?
Il est à Ousmane.
2. À qui sont les photos?
Elles sont à Malick.
3. À qui est le sac à main?
Il est à Saleh.
4. À qui sont les singes?
Ils sont à Assia.
5. À qui sont les sandales?
Elles sont à Amine.
6. À qui est le pagne?
Il est à Yasmine.
7. À qui est le foulard de tête?
Il est à Aya.
8. À qui sont les boissons?
Elles sont à Ahmed.

Avec un(e) partenaire, dites à qui sont les choses suivantes, selon l'illustration. Alternez les questions et les réponses avec votre partenaire. Suivez le modèle.

Modèle:

le portefeuille
Élève A: À qui est le portefeuille?
Élève B: Il est à Mohamed.

1. l'appareil-photo
2. les photos
3. le sac à main
4. les singes
5. les sandales
6. le pagne
7. le foulard de tête
8. les boissons

Paired Practice

Être à and Stress Pronouns

Put students in pairs. Prepare two worksheets for each pair. On one worksheet write a series of eight objects and names or subject pronouns, for example, **la guitare/Bernard** and **la Peugeot/nous**. On the second worksheet copy the same objects but change the names and subject pronouns, for example, **la guitare/Claire** and **la Peugeot/vous**. The student with the first worksheet asks the other student questions about ownership using **être à**, for example, **Est-ce que la guitare est à Bernard** and **Est-ce que la Peugeot est à nous**? The student with the second worksheet gives a negative sentence with a stress pronoun, for example, **Non, elle n'est pas à lui** and **Elle n'est pas à nous**, then provides a sentence indicating the correct ownership, for example, **Elle est à Claire** and **Elle est à vous**. Students switch worksheets and roles after the first four questions.

Teacher's Notes

1. You might want to review the formation of **avoir** and **être** in the imperfect. The imperfect was reviewed on pages 62-63 in the third level of *C'est à toi!* 2. Most short, common adverbs, such as **déjà, beaucoup, bien, enfin, mal, même, peut-être, souvent, toujours, trop, un peu** and **vite**, come before the past participle in the **plus-que-parfait**, just as in the **passé composé**. 3. Agreement between past participles and subjects of verbs conjugated with **être** was reviewed on page 35 in the third level of *C'est à toi!* 4. To review agreement between past participles and preceding direct object pronouns, refer to pages 17 and 31 in the third level of *C'est à toi!* 5. To review agreement between past participles and reflexive pronouns, refer to page 77 in the third level of *C'est à toi!*

Critical Thinking

The Past Perfect in English

Write the sentence **Eve went to Niger** on the board. Then ask students to help you think of several things that Eve *had* done before she left in order to prepare for her trip. For example, students might say that Eve had bought a suitcase and had gone to the bank. Point out the similarity between the past perfect in English and the **plus-que-parfait** in French. Then write two examples of the **plus-que-parfait** using **avoir** and **être**, for example, **Ève avait acheté une valise** and **Ève était allée à la banque**. By looking at these two examples, ask students to tell you how the **plus-que-parfait** is formed. Students should tell you that the helping verb is the imperfect of **avoir** and **être** and the past participle is formed as in the **passé composé**.

Pluperfect tense

The **plus-que-parfait** (*pluperfect* or *past perfect*) is a tense used to tell what had happened in the past before another past action. Like the **passé composé**, the **plus-que-parfait** consists of a helping verb and a past participle. To form the **plus-que-parfait**, use the imperfect tense of the helping verb **avoir** or **être** and the past participle of the main verb. Agreement of the past participle in the **plus-que-parfait** is the same as in the **passé composé**.

> J'ai entendu dire que Val Kilmer avait écrit un recueil de poésies. Est-ce vrai?

	demander	*aller*
j'	avais demandé	étais allé(e)
tu	avais demandé	étais allé(e)
il/elle/on	avait demandé	était allé(e)
nous	avions demandé	étions allé(e)s
vous	aviez demandé	étiez allé(e)(s)(es)
ils/elles	avaient demandé	étaient allé(e)s

Abdoulaye **avait déjà visité** le musée.	*Abdoulaye had already visited the museum.*
Salmou **était venue** faire ses études à Niamey.	*Salmou had come to study in Niamey.*

Guillaume et sa famille avaient fait les touristes à Niamey.

The **plus-que-parfait** is often used to describe a past action that happened before another action in the past. Use the **plus-que-parfait** for the action that is farther back in time and the **passé composé** for the more recent one.

Quand les touristes sont arrivés à l'atelier des artisans, Garba **était** déjà **parti**.	*When the tourists arrived at the workshop of the craftspeople, Garba had already left.*
Salmou a dit qu'elle **avait oublié** son appareil-photo.	*Salmou said that she had forgotten her camera.*

Cooperative Group Practice

Un alibi

Put students in small groups of four or five to give alibis for their whereabouts at M. Montmorency's château when he was killed at 11:00 P.M. in the library. Have students take turns saying where they had been in the château before the murder and where they had last seen the victim, for example, **J'avais flâné dans le jardin. J'avais vu M. Montmorency dans la salle à manger à 8h00.** Then have students play the role of the police inspector and write a report including the details of the testimony of the other group members.

Pratique

Qu'est-ce que vos amis ont dit qu'ils avaient fait pendant les vacances? Répondez selon les illustrations.

1. Marcel et Francis

2. vous

3. Marielle

4. Adja et Sandrine

5. tu

6. Christian

Modèle:

Robert
Robert m'a dit qu'il avait visité le zoo.

Tu m'as dit que tu m'avais acheté un souvenir.

Dites pourquoi tout le monde est arrivé en retard vendredi à l'Université de Niamey.

1. Zakia/ne pas pouvoir trouver ses sandales
2. Abdoulaye et toi, vous/perdre vos sacs à dos
3. Jamila et Myriam/avoir des problèmes en démarrant leur voiture
4. le prof de littérature/oublier ses notes de cours
5. les filles/s'arrêter au kiosque à journaux
6. Mohamed et moi, nous/rencontrer des copains
7. Mahmoud/devoir finir ses devoirs
8. tous les étudiants/ne pas regarder l'heure

Modèle:

Ibrahim/ne pas se lever à l'heure
Ibrahim est arrivé en retard qu'il ne s'était pas levé à l'heure.

"**J**'étais venue à Londres dans l'intention de faire du théâtre."

Audiocassette/CD Activities 7-8

Answers

7 Possible answers:
1. Marcel et Francis m'ont dit qu'ils avaient travaillé dans un fast-food.
2. Vous m'avez dit que vous aviez fait les magasins.
3. Marielle m'a dit qu'elle s'était reposée.
4. Adja et Sandrine m'ont dit qu'elles étaient allées au musée.
5. Tu m'as dit que tu avais tondu la pelouse.
6. Christian m'a dit qu'il avait été malade.

8
1. Zakia est arrivée en retard parce qu'elle n'avait pas pu trouver ses sandales.
2. Abdoulaye et toi, vous êtes arrivés en retard parce que vous aviez perdu vos sacs à dos.
3. Jamila et Myriam sont arrivées en retard parce qu'elles avaient eu des problèmes en démarrant leur voiture.
4. Le prof de littérature est arrivé en retard parce qu'il avait oublié ses notes de cours.
5. Les filles sont arrivées en retard parce qu'elles s'étaient arrêtées au kiosque à journaux.
6. Mohamed et moi, nous sommes arrivés en retard parce que nous avions rencontré des copains.
7. Mahmoud est arrivé en retard parce qu'il avait dû finir ses devoirs.
8. Tous les étudiants sont arrivés en retard parce qu'ils n'avaient pas regardé l'heure.

Paired Practice

Ordering Sentences

To practice using the **passé composé** and the **plus-que-parfait**, put students in pairs. Prepare a set of note cards for each pair with two related activities and a noun or pronoun subject, for example, **visiter le musée national/regarder un plan de Niamey (je)**. The first student in each pair takes a card and reads the two phrases to his or her partner. The partner then changes the phrases into complete sentences and orders them logically using the **plus-que-parfait** followed by the **passé composé**, for example, **J'avais regardé un plan de Niamey. J'ai visité le musée national.** Students take turns until they have made pairs of sentences for each card in the stack.

Answers

9 Possible answers:

1. Salmou était déjà venue faire ses études quand elle a fait la connaissance d'Abdoulaye.
2. Abdoulaye avait déjà étudié longtemps quand il a réussi au bac.
3. Salmou était déjà arrivée à Niamey quand Abdoulaye l'a accompagnée à la fête.
4. Les touristes avaient déjà fait la queue quand le musée a ouvert.
5. Salmou avait déjà acheté un ticket quand elle est entrée dans le musée.
6. Le lion était déjà sorti de sa cage quand Salmou et Abdoulaye l'ont vu.
7. Abdoulaye avait déjà fini son repas quand il a demandé du café.

Teacher's Note

Developing a local brochure, as students do in Activity 11, correlates to the goal of "Communities" in the National Foreign Language Standards.

Game

Sentence Match

Divide the class into two teams. The first two students from the first team come to the front of the room. On a stack of note cards, write sentences in the **passé composé** that explain what happened to someone, for example, **Malick a raté l'examen.** Student A selects a card and writes a sentence in the **plus-que-parfait** that he or she thinks Student B will match as an explanation for that sentence, for example, **Malick n'avait pas étudié.**

Modèle:
Jamila s'approche. Salmou part.
Salmou était déjà partie quand Jamila s'est approchée.

9 | *Dites qu'une chose s'est passée avant une autre en combinant les deux phrases en ordre chronologique. Formez une phrase dans laquelle vous utiliserez le* **passé composé** *et le* **plus-que-parfait**. *Suivez le modèle.*

1. Salmou fait la connaissance d'Abdoulaye. Salmou vient faire ses études.
2. Abdoulaye étudie longtemps. Il réussit au bac.
3. Salmou arrive à Niamey. Abdoulaye l'accompagne à la fête.
4. Les touristes font la queue. Le musée ouvre.
5. Salmou achète un ticket. Elle entre dans le musée.
6. Salmou et Abdoulaye voient le lion. Le lion sort de sa cage.
7. Abdoulaye demande du café. Il finit son repas.

Communication

10 | *Dans le dialogue de cette leçon, Garba dit que Zinder est la capitale de la maroquinerie. Pour quels sites ou monuments ou pour quelles expositions ou choses est-ce que les villes de votre région sont bien connues? D'abord, copiez la grille suivante. Puis, complétez-la avec les noms de cinq villes assez célèbres dans votre région. Pour chaque ville, dites pourquoi elle est bien connue et donnez votre opinion sur son attraction principale. Enfin, interviewez un(e) partenaire, demandez son opinion sur les attractions de vos cinq villes et notez ses réponses.*

	Ville	Pourquoi	Mon opinion	L'opinion de Paul
1.	Bemidji (MN)	sa statue de Paul Bunyan	C'est fantastique!	Bof! Ce n'est qu'une grande statue.
2.				
3.				
4.				
5.				

11 | *Servez-vous de votre grille de l'Activité 10 pour créer un dépliant qui aidera votre région à se vanter de ses sites ou monuments historiques ou de ses expositions ou choses artistiques. Offrez des renseignements sur trois des villes que vous avez choisies dans l'activité précédente. Pour chaque ville que vous décrivez, donnez les détails suivants:*

- le nom de la ville
- où la ville se trouve
- pourquoi la ville est bien connue
- une description de son attraction principale
- l'histoire du site ou monument ou la raison pour laquelle l'exposition ou la chose est célèbre
- si l'on peut y acheter un souvenir spécial
- le tarif ou le prix d'entrée pour visiter l'attraction (s'il y en a un)

Student A returns the card to you. Read the sentence, and ask Student B to give a sentence in the **plus-que-parfait** that explains it. If Student B guesses what Student A wrote, their team earns ten points. If not, Student B gets another turn. If he or she makes an accurate guess on the second try, their team earns five points. If Student B does not guess the correct sentence after two attempts, the other team gets a turn. Teams alternate until all the cards are used. The team with the highest score wins.

Cooperative Group Practice

La photo

Have students bring a photo to class that depicts an activity in which they participated. Each student describes what he or she did in the photo in the **passé composé**, then says two sentences in the **plus-que-parfait** that describe what he or she had done to prepare for that activity, for example, **Samedi après-midi j'ai piqueniqué au zoo. Vendredi j'avais invité Claude. Samedi matin j'avais préparé des sandwichs.**

Comparing and Contrasting

Sur la bonne piste

In this unit you will learn how to compare and contrast. To compare two or more people or things, explain how they are similar. To contrast them, tell how they are different. In order to prepare for writing a comparison–contrast paragraph or composition, you might find it helpful to use one of two graphic organizers: intersecting circles or a comparison frame.

If you use intersecting circles, list features unique to your first subject in the left-hand circle. In the right-hand circle, list features unique to your second subject. Where the circles overlap, list the features that both subjects share. Here is how Caroline prepared intersecting circles for a French assignment to compare and contrast **le musée national de Niamey** with her local science museum.

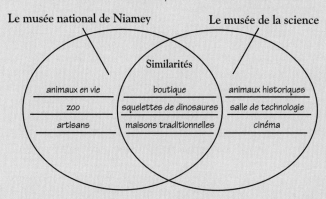

Le musée national de Niamey

Le musée de la science

Similarités

animaux en vie
zoo
artisans

boutique
squelettes de dinosaures
maisons traditionnelles

animaux historiques
salle de technologie
cinéma

If you use a comparison frame, write the two subjects you are comparing at the top. On the left list the categories you are comparing and contrasting. Then fill in the boxes with details. To plan a French composition comparing and contrasting Senegal and Niger, you might use a comparison frame that incorporates the following information:

Catégories	Sujets	
	Le Sénégal	**Le Niger**
géographie	Sahara	Sahara
problèmes de l'environnement	désertification déforestation	désertification déforestation
influence de la colonisation	langue officielle enseignement	langue officielle

By making this comparison frame, you realize that you can make three clear comparisons between Senegal and Niger, but that you need more information in order to contrast them. You also need to find out if the school system in Niger reflects the French educational system, as Senegal's does. Sometimes by making intersecting circles or a comparison frame you find out where you still need to do more research in order to write a thorough comparison–contrast paragraph or composition.

Advanced Placement

Teacher's Notes

1. **Sur la bonne piste, Leçon A,** is designed to develop skills that will help students prepare to take the Advanced Placement Exam in French Language. In this lesson **Sur la bonne piste** develops writing proficiency. Students focus on comparing and contrasting with the help of graphic organizers. 2. By now students may be interested to know that the graphic organizer of two intersecting circles is called a Venn diagram. 3. You may want to review comparisons with your students by telling them that most adjectives and adverbs have three degrees of comparison. It's important to be able to know how to use these forms to compare and contrast. First is the positive, or base, form that appears as the entry word in a dictionary. Second comes the comparative form, and third is the superlative form. The positive form cannot be used to make a comparison. The comparative form shows two people or things being compared. The superlative form compares three or more people or things.

Positive:
Le Louvre est grand.

Abdoulaye explique bien.

Comparative:
Le Louvre est plus grand que le musée Rodin.

Abdoulaye explique mieux que Salmou.

Superlative:
Le Louvre est le plus grand musée de Paris.

Abdoulaye explique le mieux de tous.

4. To further review the comparative and the superlative of adjectives, refer to pages 269 and 410 in the first level of *C'est à toi!* To further review the comparative and superlative of adverbs, refer to pages 373 and 386 in the second-level textbook.

1. Another topic that you might have students compare and contrast is technology in France and the United States. Students could also consider the future of the environment and write an essay outlining what an optimist and a pessimist would say about the future of our planet. 2. Optional activity. Challenge students to find an article in a French magazine or newspaper that compares and contrasts. You might have students make a Venn diagram to compare the points that are compared and contrasted. 3. Optional activity. You might have students give an oral presentation in front of a small group or the class. Students could compare and contrast two friends that they know well or two French paintings with which they are familiar. Have students use visual aids as they talk about the characteristics the friends or the paintings have in common. If they are comparing and contrasting two friends, students could take pictures of the friends engaged in similar and different activities. If they choose to compare and contrast two French paintings, they could bring in reproductions of the paintings and point to them as they discuss the paintings' similarities and differences.

Here are some expressions that you will find useful as you compare and contrast:

ainsi que	as well as
à part	aside from
un(e) autre	another
autrefois	formerly
de nos jours	these days
ceci	this
cela	that
par contre	on the other hand
d'un côté	on one side
de l'autre côté	on the other side
pendant que	while
pourtant	however
mais	but
ne... plus	no longer, not anymore
quant à	as for
non seulement	not only
mais aussi	but also
en plus	in addition

When you finally begin to write your paragraph or composition, choose one of two methods of organization: either compare and contrast the two subjects feature by feature, or first discuss all aspects of one subject and then all of the other. From the first paragraph of Caroline's composition comparing and contrasting **le musée de Niamey** with the science museum in her town, can you tell which method she chose?

Je connais bien le musée de la science de ma ville. Mon grand-père m'y emmenait quand j'étais petite. Quand on y entre, on voit des squelettes de dinosaures. Plus loin, il y a des animaux historiques. Au premier étage on peut entrer dans les maisons traditionnelles des Amérindiens pour apprendre quelque chose sur leur culture. La salle de technologie se trouve aussi au premier étage. Au deuxième étage il y a un cinéma avec un grand écran. J'y ai vu un film sur les îles Galapagos et un autre sur la météorologie. À la fin de nos visites, mon grand-père m'a toujours acheté un petit souvenir de la boutique. On peut y trouver des affiches, des tee-shirts et des livres de sciences.

You can tell that Caroline chose the second method of organization, first discussing all aspects of one subject, then those of the other. In her second paragraph we would read about **le musée de Niamey**.

12 Now try your hand at writing a paragraph comparing and contrasting one of the three topics below. Begin by making intersecting circles or a comparison frame for the topic you choose.

1. la vie en ville/la vie à la campagne
2. deux sports que vous connaissez bien
3. deux films du même genre que vous venez de voir (par exemple, deux comédies

le Mali

le gibier

Ils chassent.

une gazelle

 Workbook
Activity 7

 Audiocassette/CD
La chasse

 Transparencies 3-4, 27-28

Leçon B

In this lesson you will be able to:

➤ write a letter

➤ tell a story

➤ describe past events

➤ sequence events

➤ use links

➤ give information

➤ express ownership

➤ compare

Teacher's Notes

1. Communicative functions that are recycled in this lesson are "telling location," "explaining something," "stating a preference," "giving opinions," "expressing fear" and "expressing need and necessity." 2. The French also use the expression **aller à la chasse** (*to go hunting*). 3. When referring to a person, **gibier** means "prey." 4. Other related terms are **malien, malienne** (*Malian*) and **un Malien, une Malienne** (*an inhabitant of/from Mali*).

**Workbook
Activity 8**

Audiocassette/CD
La lettre

Teacher's Notes

1. Millet is a cereal grass whose grain is used for food in many African countries. 2. **Le bac** was introduced on page 107 in the first level of *C'est à toi!* and mentioned again on page 325 in the second level. 3. Point out that **la réussite** belongs to the same word family as **réussir**. 4. Mopti is one of the principal cities in Mali. 5. Explain that **nouvelles**, meaning "news," is a noun, not to be confused with the adjective, meaning "new." Students might be interested to learn the expression **Pas de nouvelles, bonnes nouvelles!** (*No news is good news!*) 6. Point out that **pluie** comes from the same word family as **pleuvoir** and **plu**. 7. **Pousser** can also be used to express growth in children, for example, **Tu pousses comme un champignon.** (*You're growing well.*) 8. Students learned **projet**, meaning "project," in Unit 4 in the third level of *C'est à toi!* 9. In Mali and many other African countries it was considered valid in the past to arrange marriages between men and women of similar backgrounds for economic reasons.

Cette année Moussa Keita était en terminale, de sorte qu'° il a pu se présenter au bac. Heureusement, il a réussi à l'examen. Après avoir fêté sa réussite° avec ses camarades de classe, Moussa est rentré à Bandiagara, le village où il est né, qui est à 80 kilomètres à l'est de Mopti au Mali. À son arrivée il est allé chercher son grand-père. Il l'a trouvé assis sous un grand baobab dans ses champs de mil en dehors du village. Ils ont parlé très longtemps. La conversation était si intéressante que Moussa avait envie de la décrire à son amie, Yakaré Kouyaté.

> Bandiagara, le 20 juillet
>
> Chère Yakaré,
>
> Un grand "Salut" de la campagne! J'espère que tu vas bien, ainsi que° toute ta famille. J'écris pour t'envoyer de mes nouvelles° et pour recevoir des tiennes.° Ici tout va bien. Les pluies° ont été abondantes, grâce à Dieu. Je travaille dans les champs chaque matin, et le mil pousse° bien.
>
> Quand je suis arrivé, j'ai eu une conversation intéressante avec mon grand-père. Je l'ai informé de mon succès au bac et de mes projets° d'études à l'université. Mon grand-père m'a raconté comment était la vie quand il avait mon âge. D'abord il m'a demandé quand j'allais me marier, car maintenant j'ai 19 ans. À cet âge, lui et mon père, tous les deux, avaient déjà une femme et deux enfants. Je lui ai expliqué que de nos jours,° les étudiants s'intéressent à finir leurs études et qu'ils n'ont pas

de sorte que *so that*; **une réussite** *success*; **ainsi que** *et aussi*; **des nouvelles (f.)** *news*; **les tiens, les tiennes** *yours*; **la pluie** *rain*; **pousser** *to grow*; **un projet** *un plan*; **de nos jours** *aujourd'hui*

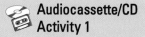

les moyens° de se marier. Je lui ai dit que les jeunes préfèrent se marier pour l'amour, mais mon grand-père pensait que c'était bête. Il a dit que les parents savent mieux choisir les maris et les femmes pour leurs enfants.

Je lui ai demandé combien d'années il avait passées à l'école, et il m'a répondu qu'il n'avait jamais eu l'occasion° d'aller à l'école moderne. Pourtant,° à cette époque-là,° les parents envoyaient presque tous leurs enfants à l'école coranique.° Autrefois,° ils pensaient que l'éducation religieuse était plus importante que l'enseignement en français. Et puis, ils avaient peur que leurs enfants soient pourris° par la grande ville et reviennent au village avec des habitudes européennes. De plus, ils avaient besoin de tous leurs enfants pour travailler aux champs.

Après cela, mon grand-père m'a parlé de ses aventures à la chasse. Au bon vieux temps,° il allait souvent à la chasse avec les autres jeunes hommes du village. Ils chassaient les antilopes et les gazelles. Quant au gibier, il partageait° quelquefois le sien° avec ses amis, et ils partageaient quelquefois le leur° avec lui. Par contre,° aujourd'hui il faut protéger la faune,° et maintenant il est interdit d'aller à la chasse.

Bon, je m'arrête là. J'espère que tes vacances se passent bien. Les miennes° sont trop longues car je ne suis pas avec toi.

À bientôt,

Moussa

---

le moyen *means;* **une occasion** *opportunity;* **pourtant** *however;* **une époque** *le temps;* **coranique** *de la religion islamique;* **autrefois** *au passé;* **pourri(e)** *spoiled;* **au bon vieux temps** *au passé;* **partager** *diviser;* **le sien, la sienne** *his, hers, its, one's;* **le leur, la leur** *theirs;* **par contre** *on the other hand;* **la faune** *les animaux;* **les miens, les miennes** *mine*

Répondez par "vrai" ou "faux" d'après la lettre de Moussa.

1. Moussa a fêté son anniversaire avec ses camarades de classe.
2. Le grand-père de Moussa ne pouvait pas parler avec lui parce qu'il était assis dans un baobab dans ses champs de mil.
3. Le mil pousse bien parce que les pluies ont été abondantes.
4. Moussa et son grand-père ont parlé de la vie de Moussa et de comment la vie de son grand-père était quand il avait le même âge.
5. Selon son grand-père, les parents savent mieux choisir les maris et les femmes pour leurs enfants.
6. Autrefois, les parents pensaient que l'enseignement en français était plus important que l'éducation religieuse.
7. À cette époque-là, les parents avaient peur que leurs enfants prennent des habitudes européennes.
8. Le grand-père de Moussa et ses amis partageaient quelquefois leur gibier.

Moussa et son grand-père ont parlé sous un baobab.

Audiocassette/CD Activity 1

Answers

1 1. faux
2. faux
3. vrai
4. vrai
5. vrai
6. faux
7. vrai
8. vrai

Teacher's Notes

1. Point out that **occasion** is a false cognate. 2. Islam is the principal religion in Mali. The Bambara, Malinke and Voltaic peoples practice traditional African religions. Only about five percent of the population is Christian. 3. When describing food, **pourri(e)** means "rotten." 4. Point out that **la chasse** and **chasser** belong to the same word family. **La chasse** was introduced in Unit 8 in the third level of *C'est à toi!* 5. Point out that **partager** is an orthographically changing verb that follows the pattern of **manger**. Remind students to add an **e** before the **ons** in the **nous** form (**partageons**).

Game

Loto

To practice identifying new vocabulary in this unit, have students make a grid with 16 squares, four in each row. Show a transparency with 16 definitions in French of vocabulary words found in **Leçon A** and **Leçon B**, for example, **les animaux**. (You might choose to use the definitions found in the glossed vocabulary or easily recognizable cognates.) Tell students to copy the definitions, placing them at random on their grid. Then orally give the corresponding new French word for each definition, for example, **la faune**. Students mark with an "X" the matching definition on their grid. The student who first covers four squares horizontally, vertically or diagonally calls out "Loto" and gives the new French word for each square in his or her winning sequence. You may choose to award an extra credit point if the winner can use each word in an original sentence.

Workbook Activity 9

Audiocassette/CD Activity 3

Answers

2 1. nouvelles
   2. Mali
   3. informé
   4. les moyens
   5. l'occasion
   6. chassaient
   7. Par contre
   8. la faune

3 Answers will vary.

Teacher's Notes

1. Cognates in this reading include **république, économie, agriculture, pour cent, cultivée, désert, occupe, vallées, produits, coton, cosmopolite, cohabitent, ethniques, malienne, central, mosquée, islamique, islam, arabe, Arabie Saoudite, population, traditions, basé, intégrées, alcool, modestement, provisions, nomades, fasciner, expression, évoque, existe, imagination, accès, représentante, cause, féminine, princesse, combine, électrique, textes, encouragée, public, instrumentation, impressionnante, erreurs** and **refusons**. 2. Mali is a landlocked nation that borders Algeria, Niger, Burkina Faso, the Ivory Coast, Guinea, Senegal and Mauritania, all former French colonies. 3. The word "Mali" means "where the master resides" and comes from the language of one of the country's former empires, that of the Mandingo people. Mali was called French Sudan until it gained its independence from France in 1960. 4. About 80 percent of the work-force is engaged in agriculture, 19 percent in service industries and one percent in industry and commerce. Women help plant and harvest crops and raise livestock. The leading crops are rice, cassava, corn, millet, sorghum, sugar cane, cotton and peanuts. Most Malian farmers cannot afford agricultural machinery, so they depend on hand tools for almost all their work. Cotton is Mali's chief export, earning about half the country's export income. Other exports include gold, livestock, fish, leather products, meat and peanuts. The production of textiles is the leading manufacturing activity. Most of the country's largest industrial plants were built with foreign aid. Mali's economy has been troubled by sharp drops in world cotton prices and large increases in the cost of imported petroleum and other fuels. 5. **Le Sahara** covers the northern half of the country. The other two major land regions are **le Sahel**, the semidesert in central Mali, and **la zone soudanaise**, the rolling grasslands and forests in the south. In the 1970s and early 1980s, severe droughts led to the deaths of large numbers of people and animals.

---

2 | *Complétez chaque phrase avec l'expression convenable d'après la lettre de Moussa.*

la faune	informé	par contre
les moyens	l'occasion	chassaient
Mali	nouvelles	

1. Moussa a écrit à Yakaré pour lui envoyer de ses....
2. Bandiagara est un village au....
3. Quand Moussa est rentré au village, il a... son grand-père de son succès au bac.
4. De nos jours, les étudiants n'ont pas... de se marier.
5. Son grand-père a dit qu'il n'avait jamais eu... d'assister à l'école moderne.
6. Les jeunes hommes du village... les antilopes et les gazelles.
7. ..., maintenant il est interdit d'aller à la chasse.
8. Aujourd'hui il faut protéger....

M. Vignal envoie de ses nouvelles à son fils.

3 | *C'est à toi!*

1. Est-ce que tu parles souvent avec tes grands-parents? Si oui, de quoi?
2. Combien d'années est-ce que tu as déjà passées à l'école?
3. Est-ce que tu as des projets d'études à l'université? Si oui, qu'est-ce que tu vas y étudier?
4. Est-ce que tes parents ont peur de t'envoyer dans une université dans une grande ville? Si oui, pourquoi?
5. Est-ce que tu comptes te marier? Si oui, quand?
6. Est-ce que tu aimerais vivre dans une société où les parents choisissent les maris et les femmes de leurs enfants? Pourquoi ou pourquoi pas?
7. Est-ce que tu connais quelqu'un qui chasse? Si oui, qu'est-ce qu'il ou elle chasse?
8. Est-ce que tu t'intéresses à la protection des animaux?

 Enquête culturelle

La république du Mali, un autre pays africain, est située entre le Niger et le Sénégal. C'est l'un des pays les plus pauvres du monde. Son économie dépend de l'agriculture, même si seulement 20 pour cent de la terre peut être cultivée. Le désert occupe la plus grande partie du pays, mais il y a aussi des vallées où on peut cultiver des fruits et des légumes. Ces produits, ainsi que le coton et le mil, sont ensuite vendus en Europe.

Bamako est la capitale du Mali. C'est une ville cosmopolite où cohabitent tous les groupes ethniques qui font partie de la culture malienne et où vivent 700.000 personnes. Son marché central, appelé le Marché Rose, est l'un des plus beaux d'Afrique. On peut y acheter des pagnes, des foulards de tête et de la maroquinerie. Sa grande mosquée, l'église islamique, est le centre de la religion principale du pays, l'islam. Le Mali a depuis longtemps des rapports avec le monde arabe. Au 12ᵉ siècle les empereurs du Mali faisaient des voyages religieux, ou pèlerinages, à La Mecque en Arabie Saoudite. C'est cette influence arabe qui reste importante au Mali même aujourd'hui. Maintenant 90 pour cent de la population malienne est islamique et suit les traditions de cette religion. Les écoles coraniques offrent un enseignement religieux basé sur les leçons du *Coran*, le livre religieux de l'islam. Il y a plusieurs traditions islamiques qui sont intégrées dans la vie quotidienne malienne. Par exemple, l'homme peut avoir jusqu'à quatre femmes, l'alcool n'est pas permis, la femme doit s'habiller modestement et les gens n'aiment pas qu'on les prenne en photo.

C'est au puits (*well*) où on se rencontre dans les petits villages maliens.

Le Mali est devenu un centre de commerce quand les caravanes de sel, d'or et d'argent traversaient le désert. Mais, lorsque les Européens ont commencé à faire leur commerce aux ports maritimes, les routes des caravanes ont perdu leur importance, et les oasis sont tombées en déclin. Donc, le Mali est devenu moins important pour l'Afrique. Les caravanes qui traversaient le Sahara s'arrêtaient dans des oasis comme celle de Tombouctou (Timbuktu, en anglais). Elles leur permettaient de prendre de l'eau et d'autres provisions sur la route. La ville de Tombouctou, établie par les nomades au 12ᵉ siècle, continue à fasciner le monde. Dans les pays arabes, une expression populaire évoque une certaine Tombouctou qui n'existe que dans l'imagination, parce que l'accès à la ville est très difficile.

L'une des plus célèbres Maliennes d'aujourd'hui est Oumou Sangaré. Elle est à la fois chanteuse, écrivain, compositeur de musique et représentante de la cause féminine africaine. Dans ses robes de princesse, elle combine le traditionnel avec le non-traditionnel, le vieux avec le moderne, l'Occident avec l'Afrique. Sa musique est accompagnée de guitare électrique et de claviers, aussi bien que de flûtes et de batterie traditionnelles d'Afrique. Ses textes ne traitent pas seulement de problèmes sociaux, mais aussi de la culture de son monde. Cela crée des chansons dont le message est aussi important que l'origine.

Née en 1968 à Bamako, Sangaré a commencé à chanter à un très jeune âge. Sa mère, elle aussi musicienne, l'a encouragée à devenir chanteuse en faisant monter la petite Oumou sur la table pour

Teacher's Notes

1. Bamako lies in the southwest along the Niger River. 2. The Fulani and Toucouleur make up the largest group of Mali's people. The Mandingos form the next largest group. Other groups include the Dogon, Songhai and Voltaic peoples. Caucasians, including Arabs, French, Moors and Tuareg, account for about five percent of Mali's population. 3. The Mali Empire flourished in western Africa from about 1240 to 1500. The cities of the Mali Empire were centers for the caravan trade from beyond the Sahara. The people were successful farmers and herders. Salt was transported in great blocks on the backs of camels across the desert. 4. Timbuktu was founded around the beginning of the 12th century by Tuareg nomads, who came down from the desert for well water during the dry season. From the 13th century on, it was a trade center of the Muslim world, as well as an important spiritual, educational and cultural center. When the city was captured by invaders from Morocco in the late 16th century, it gradually lost its importance. 5. Like other developing African nations, Mali faces major social problems. Most of Mali's adults can neither read nor write, and many of the country's school-age children do not attend school. The average life expectancy is less than 50 years. Approximately one-fifth of the babies born in rural areas die as infants. Malaria is widespread and a chief cause of death among children. Only a few hundred doctors serve the entire population.

Cross-curricular

Geography

Have each student make a map of Mali, labeling the surrounding countries; **le Sahara** in the north; **le Sahel** in the center; **la zone soudanaise** in the south; the rivers **Niger** and **Sénégal**; and the principal cities **Bamako, Kayes, Ségou, Sikasso, Mopti, Gao, Tombouctou** and **Taoudéni**. The next day play a game with the class to practice identifying these geographical features. At the front of the class, display a large unlabeled map of Mali and its surroundings. Then divide the class in half. As one student from each team goes to the map at the same time, name one of these geographical features. The student who locates it first on the map earns one point for his or her team. Continue the game until you have named all the features that you want students to identify. The team with the most points wins the game.

Answers

4 Possible answers:

1. Non, le Mali est l'un des pays les plus pauvres du monde.
2. L'économie du Mali dépend de l'agriculture.
3. La capitale du Mali est Bamako.
4. L'islam est la religion principale du Mali.
5. De nos jours on trouve encore une forte influence arabe au Mali.
6. Selon la tradition islamique, l'homme peut avoir jusqu'à quatre femmes, l'alcool n'est pas permis, la femme doit s'habiller modestement et les gens n'aiment pas qu'on les prenne en photo.
7. Tombouctou est une oasis malienne célèbre.
8. C'est une Malienne qui est chanteuse, écrivain et compositrice de musique.
9. Oumou Sangaré combine la guitare électrique, les claviers, les flûtes et la batterie pour créer sa musique.
10. Ils l'aiment parce qu'elle leur parle du présent de l'Afrique et de leur avenir.

Teacher's Notes

1. Oumou Sangaré's style of music is called "Wassoulou." Her other albums include *Ko sira* (1993) and *Worotan* (1996). Sangaré has appeared in concert all over Europe and North America. 2. *Nervous Conditions*, a novel by Zimbabwe's Tsitsi Dangarembga, describes the roles of four different women in modern Africa.

chanter. Quand elle avait cinq ans, elle a dû chanter au stade de Bamako. Elle avait peur d'ouvrir la bouche, mais sa mère lui a donné un conseil: "Imagine que tu es à la maison, dans la cuisine." Grâce à cela, elle a pu chanter devant un public qui l'a beaucoup appréciée. Plus tard elle a pu voyager partout dans le monde avec le célèbre Ensemble National du Mali. Son premier triomphe a été sa cassette *Moussolou*, qui a su intéresser les jeunes tout en utilisant les instruments traditionnels de son pays. Cela est différent des autres chanteuses africaines, qui préfèrent une instrumentation moderne. Mais c'est Oumou Sangaré qui a combiné les deux genres d'instruments pour mettre ensemble deux genres de musique.

Si la musique d'Oumou Sangaré est impressionnante, le message qu'elle offre est encore plus important. "J'ai compris les erreurs de nos parents...", dit-elle en parlant de son père, qui avait trois femmes. "Nous, les jeunes, nous refusons de continuer à faire ces mêmes erreurs. Un homme ne pourrait-il pas aimer seulement une femme et faire sa vie avec elle? Je crois que c'est ce que beaucoup de jeunes Maliens ont compris en écoutant mes chansons." Les jeunes ne vont pas à ses concerts pour entendre des chansons traditionnelles. Les jeunes Africains veulent qu'on leur parle de leur présent et de leur avenir.

4 | *Répondez aux questions suivantes.*

1. Est-ce que le Mali est un pays assez riche?
2. De quoi dépend l'économie du Mali?
3. Quelle est la capitale du pays?
4. Quelle est la religion principale du Mali?
5. Quelle influence trouve-t-on encore de nos jours au Mali?
6. Quelles sont plusieurs traditions islamiques qu'on observe au Mali?
7. Quelle oasis malienne est devenue célèbre?
8. Qui est Oumou Sangaré?
9. Quels instruments combine-t-elle pour créer sa musique?
10. Pourquoi est-ce que les jeunes Africains aiment Oumou Sangaré?

Les Français ont occupé Tombouctou, une oasis malienne, en 1893.

Utilisez vos différentes sources (encyclopédies, CD-ROM, Internet ou livres d'histoire) pour répondre aux questions suivantes.

1. Combien de kilomètres de côte le Mali a-t-il?
2. Quels pays partagent leurs frontières avec le Mali?
3. Qui est le président du Mali?
4. Quel âge doit-on avoir pour voter au Mali?
5. Quelle langue africaine est-ce que la plupart des Maliens parlent?
6. Combien de personnes au Mali peuvent lire et écrire?
7. Combien d'enfants une Malienne moyenne a-t-elle?
8. Jusqu'à quel âge un Malien moyen peut-il espérer vivre?
9. Quels sont quelques titres des CDs d'Oumou Sangaré?
10. Quel est le style musical d'Oumou Sangaré?

Journal personnel

In this lesson you have read about Oumou Sangaré, a singer who blends her unique style of popular music with an important and uplifting message for her African fans. Many musicians contribute their talents to social and political causes. Do you know of any other French or francophone artists who are socially and politically committed? Do any of your favorite singers or musical groups have a similar commitment to improving social and political conditions and deliver this message musically to their audiences? If so, who are they, and what are the social and political issues that they support?

Structure

Possessive adjectives

Possessive adjectives express ownership or relationship. They agree in gender and in number with the nouns that follow them.

Trente et un pour cent des Maliens peuvent lire et écrire.

	Singular		Plural
	Masculine	Feminine before a Consonant Sound	
my	mon	ma	mes
your	ton	ta	tes
his, her, one's, its	son	sa	ses
our	notre	notre	nos
your	votre	votre	vos
their	leur	leur	leurs

(Masculine "copain", Feminine "famille", Plural "projets")

Miam-miam! C'est notre plat préféré.

Game

Son, sa, ses

Put students in small groups of four or five to practice the possessive adjectives **son**, **sa** and **ses** by playing a card game. Prepare a set of cards for each group. On each card paste the picture of an object and an owner's name. Make sure that each owner has two possessions in the deck of cards. For example, Salmou could own a camera and a pair of sandals. One student in each group shuffles the cards and deals them until none remains. The first player asks another player if he or she has an object belonging to a person represented on one of the first player's cards, for example, **Pierre, as-tu un objet de Salmou?** The interviewed player responds with **Oui** or **Non**. If the answer is **Oui**, the player being interviewed must relinquish the card to the first player. The first player then earns a point if he or she uses the correct possessive adjectives in a sentence, for example, **J'ai son appareil-photo et sa paire de sandales.** If the first player forms an incorrect sentence, the card is returned to its original owner and the second player takes a turn. At the end of the game, when all the pairs of cards have been matched, the player with the most pairs wins.

Answers

5 Possible answers:

1. Il n'y en a pas.
2. L'Algérie, la Côte-d'Ivoire, la Guinée, le Burkina-Faso, la Mauritanie, le Sénégal et le Niger partagent leurs frontières avec le Mali.
3. Le président du Mali est Alpha Oumar Konaré.
4. On doit avoir 21 ans pour voter au Mali.
5. La plupart des Maliens parlent bambara.
6. Trente et un pour cent des Maliens peuvent lire et écrire.
7. Elle a sept enfants.
8. Il peut espérer vivre jusqu'à l'âge de 46 ans.
9. Les titres sont *Moussolou*, *Ko sira* et *Worotan*.
10. Sangaré est représentante de la musique du Wassoulou.

Teacher's Note

Possessive adjectives were introduced on page 128 in the first level of *C'est à toi!* and reviewed on page 8 in the second level.

Audiocassette/CD Activity 6

Answers

6 1. Est-ce que ce pagne est à Salmou?
Oui, c'est son pagne.
2. Est-ce que ces sandales sont à toi?
Oui, ce sont mes sandales.
3. Est-ce que ce foulard de tête est à Mme Yondo?
Oui, c'est son foulard de tête.
4. Est-ce que ces vêtements sont à moi?
Oui, ce sont tes vêtements.
5. Est-ce que ces sacs à dos sont à Abdoulaye et toi?
Oui, ce sont nos sacs à dos.
6. Est-ce que cet appareil-photo est à M. et Mme Ferrié?
Oui, c'est leur appareil-photo.
7. Est-ce que ces photos sont à Céline et moi?
Oui, ce sont vos photos.
8. Est-ce que ce champ de mil est au grand-père de Moussa?
Oui, c'est son champ de mil.

Paired Practice

Ta famille

Put students in pairs. Each student interviews his or her partner about the names of family members, learning the names of the partner's mother, father, sisters and brothers. Then students orally summarize for their partner what they have learned, for example, **Ta mère s'appelle Beth, Ton beau-père s'appelle David, Ta sœur s'appelle Sarah** and **Ton frère s'appelle Mark**.

Mon grand-père m'a parlé de ses aventures à la chasse.	*My grandfather talked to me about his hunting adventures.*

Note that before a feminine singular word beginning with a vowel sound, **ma**, **ta** and **sa** become **mon**, **ton** and **son**, respectively.

Moussa avait envie d'écrire à son amie, Yakaré.	*Moussa wanted to write about it to his friend, Yakaré.*

Pratique

6 *Avec un(e) partenaire, demandez si chaque objet illustré est à la personne indiquée. Puis répondez affirmativement en utilisant un adjectif possessif. Alternez les questions et les réponses avec votre partenaire. Suivez le modèle.*

Modèle:

Garba
Élève A: Est-ce que ce tapis est à Garba?
Élève B: Oui, c'est son tapis.

1. Salmou

5. Abdoulaye et toi

2. toi

6. M. et Mme Ferrié

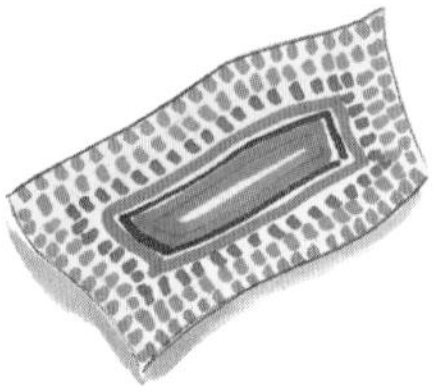

3. Mme Yondo

7. Céline et moi

4. moi

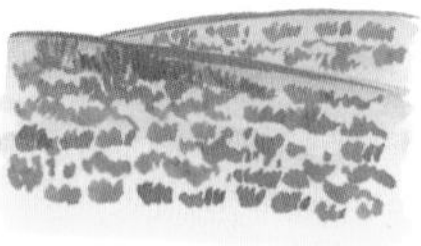

8. le grand-père de Moussa

Teacher's Note

To practice all the possessive adjectives, put students in pairs. Prepare an overhead transparency listing six short sentences followed by nouns, for example, **Je t'emprunte (jean, tennis)**. The first student in each pair completes the sentence by adding the correct possessive adjectives, for example, **Je t'emprunte ton jean et tes tennis**. Students alternate until sentences have been formed for all six items. Here are five other items to include: 1. Vous écrivez (notes, exposé) 2. Je te prête (CD, voiture) 3. Mme Cheval rappelle (mari, enfants) 4. Nous partageons (tarte, sandwichs) 5. Manu et Christelle informent (parents, sœur)

Récrivez (rewrite) les phrases suivantes en utilisant le sujet indiqué. Faites tous les autres changements nécessaires.

1. Abdoulaye et Salmou ont pris leur petit déjeuner chez eux. (tu)
2. Salmou a oublié son argent chez elle. (mes copains)
3. Les artisans ont porté leurs vêtements traditionnels. (ma sœur et moi)
4. Moussa a réussi à son examen. (je)
5. Mon grand-père m'a raconté une de ses aventures. (les hommes du village)
6. J'ai expliqué mes projets à tout le monde. (Moussa)
7. Tu n'as jamais fini tes études. (vous)

Possessive pronouns

A possessive pronoun replaces a noun plus a possessive adjective.

Moussa a réussi à son examen.	*Moussa passed his test.*
Le sien était le 12 juillet, mais	*His was July 12, but Yakaré's test*
l'examen de Yakaré était en juin.	*was in June.*

The possessive pronoun is composed of two words, each of which agrees in gender and in number with the noun it replaces.

	Singular		Plural	
	Masculine	**Feminine**	**Masculine**	**Feminine**
mine	le mien	la mienne	les miens	les miennes
yours	le tien	la tienne	les tiens	les tiennes
his, hers, its, one's	le sien	la sienne	les siens	les siennes
ours	le nôtre	la nôtre	les nôtres	
yours	le vôtre	la vôtre	les vôtres	
theirs	le leur	la leur	les leurs	

Quant au gibier, mon grand-père partageait le sien avec des amis. Les amis de mon grand-père partageaient le leur avec lui.	*As for game, my grandfather shared his with friends. My grandfather's friends shared theirs with him.*
Tes vacances se passent bien? Les miennes sont trop longues.	*Is your vacation going well? Mine is too long.*

When the prepositions **à** and **de** precede a possessive pronoun, the usual combinations result, for example, **au mien, à la mienne, aux miens, aux miennes; du mien, de la mienne, des miens, des miennes.**

J'écris pour t'envoyer de mes nouvelles et pour recevoir des tiennes.	*I'm writing to send you my news and to get yours (news from you).*

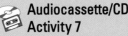

L'ÉTÉ SERA MEURTRIER POUR TOUS LES CHEVEUX. SAUF POUR LES VÔTRES.

Dis, Didier, j'ai oublié mon stylo. Est-ce que je peux t'emprunter le tien?

Oui, je te prête le mien.

Workbook Activities 11-12

Audiocassette/CD Activity 7

Answers

7 1. Tu as pris ton petit déjeuner chez toi.
2. Mes copains ont oublié leur argent chez eux.
3. Ma sœur et moi, nous avons porté nos vêtements traditionnels.
4. J'ai réussi à mon examen.
5. Les hommes du village m'ont raconté une de leurs aventures.
6. Moussa a expliqué ses projets à tout le monde.
7. Vous n'avez jamais fini vos études.

Teacher's Notes

1. Remind students that possessive pronouns, like possessive adjectives, agree with the object possessed, not with the possessor. 2. Point out that the possessive adjectives **notre** and **votre** do not have circumflex accents, whereas **le/la/les nôtre(s)** and **le/la/les vôtre(s)** do. Also mention the difference in pronunciation between **notre** and **le/la/les nôtre(s)** and **votre** and **le/la/les vôtre(s)**. 3. Possessive pronouns may function as subjects, direct objects or objects of a preposition.

Critical Thinking

Possessive Pronouns

Write the following three pairs of sentences on the board: **Mon instrument est nouveau. Le tien est vieux./Salmou porte son nouveau foulard de tête. Assia porte le sien aussi./Nous voyageons avec nos amis. Vous ne voyagez pas avec les vôtres.** Ask students to identify the function of possessive pronouns in the three examples. Students should tell you that, in order, the possessive pronouns function as a subject, a direct object and an object of a preposition. This activity will help students identify when and where they can use possessive pronouns.

Cooperative Group Practice

Ce sont les tiennes!

Put students in small groups, and distribute a picture of an object to each student, for example, **deux glaces** or **un couteau**. Students in each group exchange their picture with that of another student. Then students take turns returning the picture to its rightful owner, saying a sentence using a possessive pronoun, for example, **Ce sont les tiennes!** or **C'est le tien!**

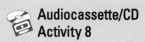

Audiocassette/CD
Activity 8

Answers

8 1. Non, ce n'est pas le sien.
2. Non, ce n'est pas la sienne.
3. Non, ce ne sont pas les leurs.
4. Non, ce ne sont pas les vôtres.
5. Non, ce ne sont pas les tiens.
6. Non, ce n'est pas le leur.
7. Non, ce ne sont pas les miennes.
8. Non, ce n'est pas le mien.
9. Non, ce n'est pas la nôtre.
10. Non, ce n'est pas la tienne.

9 J'espère passer la mienne aussi. Tu vas finir tes devoirs. Et Luc et moi?

Luc et toi, vous allez finir les vôtres aussi. Luc et moi, nous cherchons nos photos. Et Yakaré et Moussa?

Yakaré et Moussa cherchent les leurs aussi. Yakaré et Moussa partagent leur dessert. Et Geneviève et toi?

Geneviève et moi, nous partageons le nôtre aussi. Geneviève et toi, vous perdez votre temps. Et moi?

Tu perds le tien aussi. J'emmène ma sœur au musée. Et Ahmed?

Ahmed emmène la sienne au musée aussi. Ahmed aime ses profs. Et Marianne?

Marianne aime les siens aussi.

Modèle:

Cet appareil-photo est à Abdoulaye?
Non, ce n'est pas le sien.

Modèle:

Élève A: Marianne porte son pagne. Et Carole?
Élève B: Carole porte le sien aussi. Carole espère passer son interro. Et toi?
Élève A: J'espère passer....

☐ **Quand on a un nom comme le sien, il n'est pas facile de se faire un prénom.**

Pratique

8 Répondez négativement aux questions suivantes en utilisant le pronom possessif convenable.

1. Ce tapis de Zinder est à l'artisan?
2. Cette case est à Garba?
3. Ces concessions sont aux paysans?
4. Ces instruments de musique sont à nous?
5. Ces trucs sont à moi?
6. Ce champ de mil est aux Keita?
7. Ces boucles d'oreilles sont à toi?
8. Ce gibier est à toi?
9. Cette voiture est à ta famille et toi?
10. Cette note est à moi?

9 Avec un(e) partenaire, dites ce que font les personnes indiquées. Puis demandez si les personnes qui suivent le font aussi. Dites que oui. Alternez les questions et les réponses avec votre partenaire. Suivez le modèle et l'ordre indiqué par le cercle.

Cooperative Group Practice

Rotating Dialogues

Put students in small groups to practice possessive pronouns. Tell students they are on a trip and staying at a hotel with a friend. Prepare a worksheet with a list of items they were supposed to have packed. The first student in each group turns to the student on his or her right and states that he or she cannot find the first item on the list and asks to borrow the roommate's, for example, **Dis, Tom, je ne peux pas trouver mon rasoir. Est-ce que je peux t'emprunter le tien?** The second student agrees, for example, **Oui, je te prête le mien.** Then the second student plays the role of the borrower, the third student is the lender, and the dialogue begins again. Some other items to include on the list are **mes pantoufles, mon parapluie, mes lunettes de soleil,** and **ma ceinture.**

Dites que tout le monde fait exactement comme Bernadette. Utilisez un pronom possessif, et suivez le modèle.

1. Bernadette se souvient de ses vacances. (Abdou et toi)
2. Bernadette pense beaucoup à ses amies. (Jean et moi)
3. Bernadette écrit une lettre à ses cousins. (toi)
4. Bernadette a besoin de ses bagages. (Cécile et Denis)
5. Bernadette se plaint de sa chambre. (ses parents)
6. Bernadette offre un cadeau à ses parents. (moi)
7. Bernadette se sert souvent de son ordinateur. (Claire)
8. Bernadette s'intéresse à sa recherche. (Sébastien)

Modèle:

Bernadette rend visite à son grand-père. (Laurent)
Et Laurent, il rend visite au sien.

> Bernadette parle de ses projets.

> Et nous, nous parlons des nôtres.

Communication

*Comme la famille de Moussa Keita, chaque famille a ses propres histoires et traditions. Par exemple, peut-être qu'un de vos grands-parents a immigré aux États-Unis d'un autre pays, et qu'il vous a parlé de son arrivée, ses expériences et ses premières impressions de ce pays. Ou il est possible que votre famille fasse quelque chose de spécial pour célébrer une fête, comme Noël ou un anniversaire. Écrivez un paragraphe où vous racontez une des histoires ou traditions de votre famille. Utilisez des expressions comme **d'abord**, **puis**, **ensuite** et **enfin** pour lier vos phrases et des expressions comme **de nos jours**, **à cette époque-là** et **autrefois** pour organiser vos idées et commentaires.*

*Comme on a dit, chaque famille a ses propres histoires et traditions. Pourtant, elles peuvent ressembler à celles d'autres familles, même s'il y a de petites différences. Racontez l'histoire ou la tradition que vous venez de décrire dans l'Activité 11 à deux ou trois élèves dans votre classe, et écoutez pendant qu'ils vous racontent les leurs. Notez les sujets et les détails qui ressemblent aux vôtres et ceux qui sont différents. Utilisez un des diagrammes suggérés (suggested) dans **Sur la bonne piste** à la page 361.*

Maintenant, avec le diagramme que vous avez fait dans l'activité précédente, écrivez une composition où vous comparez et contrastez votre histoire ou tradition de famille avec celle qu'un(e) autre élève vous a racontée.

 Audiocassette/CD
Activity 10

Listening
Activity 2

 Quiz
Leçon B

Answers

10 1. Et Abdou et toi, vous vous souvenez des vôtres.
   2. Et Jean et moi, nous pensons beaucoup aux nôtres.
   3. Et toi, tu écris une lettre aux tiens.
   4. Et Cécile et Denis, ils ont besoin des leurs.
   5. Et ses parents, ils se plaignent de la leur.
   6. Et moi, j'offre un cadeau aux miens.
   7. Et Claire, elle se sert souvent du sien.
   8. Et Sébastien, il s'intéresse à la sienne.

Teacher's Note

Put students in pairs. Prepare a worksheet with sentences using possessive adjectives, for example, **C'est votre appareil-photo.** Students take turns questioning each other and changing the possessive adjectives to possessive pronouns, for example, **C'est le vôtre? Oui, c'est le nôtre.**

Paired Practice

The Peace Corps

Put students in pairs to practice possessive pronouns. Tell students that everyone has volunteered to work in Africa in the Peace Corps. Justin is the first to arrive at the airport on the day of departure. Have students use the correct possessive pronoun to say that everyone is doing the same things as Justin. Prepare a worksheet for Student A with the following sentences: 1. Justin montre son passeport à l'agent. 2. Justin fait enregistrer ses bagages. 3. Justin donne une bise à ses parents. 4. Justin prend une photo de ses amis. 5. Justin montre son billet à l'hôtesse de l'air. 6. Justin met son sac à dos dans le porte-bagages. Prepare another worksheet for Student B, listing a noun or pronoun cue, for example: 1. Carol 2. Kim et Brad 3. tu 4. vous 5. nous 6. je. Student A reads aloud the original sentences, and Student B changes them to include the appropriate form of the indicated possessive pronoun, for example, **Justin montre son passeport à l'agent. Carol lui montre le sien aussi.** After the third sentence, students switch roles.

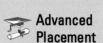

Advanced Placement

1. **Sur la bonne piste, Leçon B**, is designed to develop skills that will help students prepare to take the Advanced Placement Exam in French Literature. In this section students read a variety of prose, poetry and drama from different periods; answer content questions; and demonstrate their critical understanding of literary techniques, such as character development, setting, point of view, satire and figures of speech. In this **Sur la bonne piste** section students learn how to draw cultural inferences.

2. Guillaume Oyônô-Mbia was born in Mvoutessi, the setting for *Trois Prétendants, un Mari*. Like Juliette, he went to boarding school in Cameroon. He continued his postsecondary studies in England at the University of Keele, graduating in 1968. Although perhaps best known for his comedies, such as *Notre fille ne se mariera pas!* (1969) and *His Excellency's Train* (1969), Oyônô-Mbia has also written many short stories. Cautioning the reader or spectator of *Trois Prétendants, un Mari* against seeing him as a champion of women's rights in Africa, Oyônô-Mbia asserts that his motive in writing is primarily to entertain: "Ce n'est qu'en le divertissant réellement qu'on peut espérer amener le public à prendre conscience de certains aspects de notre culture ou de notre vie sociale...." Oyônô-Mbia's greatest hope is that his public "prendrait spontanément part aux chants et aux danses" that fill his plays with local color.

Sur la bonne piste

In Moussa's letter you read about marriage customs in Mali. Now find out if they are similar to those in Cameroon as you read an excerpt from a play by Guillaume Oyônô-Mbia and learn to make cultural inferences. In your daily life you naturally make inferences. For example, if you get to school and realize your French assignment is not in your folder, you infer that you left it at home. Making inferences is like "reading between the lines." To make cultural inferences, use all the information in the reading to form conclusions about the culture of the people and country being described. What societal rules govern the characters' behavior? What do the characters value? How do they act? What do they say? In short stories and novels, the writer sometimes explains cultural facts directly, or the characters reveal them in their speech, thoughts and actions. In plays, clues appear in the set directions and in the characters' dialogue. In *Trois Prétendants, un Mari (Three Suitors, One Husband)*, numerous clues reveal facts about the culture of the people living in rural Cameroon.

In the first scene of Oyônô-Mbia's play, the grandfather, Abessolo, complains about how women are changing in his village. He says to his sons "... vous leur permettez de manger toutes sortes d'animaux tabous.... Je vois les femmes manger même des vipères, des sangliers...." To understand the cultural inference in what he says, look at the chart below. Note that first there is a clue based on the text that summarizes Abessolo's complaint. Next is a cultural inference about life in Cameroon, based on the underlying meaning of the textual clue.

Textual clue	Cultural inference
Abessolo se plaint que les femmes mangent des animaux tabous.	Il y a des animaux tabous au Cameroun, comme des vipères et des sangliers.

Talking to his son Atangana, Abessolo continues to give his "good" advice: "Si je n'avais été là, l'autre jour, tu aurais refusé de prendre les cent mille francs que nous avait versé Ndi, le jeune homme qui veut épouser ma petite-fille Juliette. D'après toi, il fallait attendre pour consulter Juliette elle-même avant d'accepter la dot." Now make your own chart to uncover another cultural inference. What is the textual clue? Explain the situation that Abessolo describes. Based on this situation, what cultural inference can you make about how marriage partners are traditionally determined for young women in Cameroon?

Does your chart look like the one that follows?

Textual clue	Cultural inference
Ndi a donné 100.000 francs comme dot à Atangana parce qu'il veut se marier avec Juliette.	Au Cameroun un prétendant donne une dot au père de la femme qu'il veut épouser.

In *Trois Prétendants, un Mari*, Juliette learns that her father plans to marry her to the suitor who gives him the largest dowry. Juliette has just returned home to Mvoutessi from boarding school and discovers she has two wealthy suitors. However, she is alread

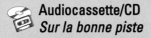

in love with a student who cannot afford to pay her father a dowry. In Act III Juliette talks to her grandmother (Bella), mother (Makrita) and cousin (Matalina) about her future. As you read this scene, look for answers to the questions that follow. They will help you focus on textual clues so that you can make a chart in Activity 16 that will give you cultural insights into life in rural Cameroon.

1. What foods make up part of a typical Cameroonian diet?
2. How has Juliette's father invested in her to make her more valuable as a prospective wife?
3. With the money spent on her education, what could Juliette's father have done for himself instead?
4. According to her mother, what are Juliette's best qualities?
5. How does Matalina think a suitor should demonstrate his love?
6. From whom does Juliette need permission to fall in love and marry?
7. When Juliette marries, what is she expected to do to help her family?

Avant de lire la scène suivante, répondez aux questions.

1. Quand tu as un problème, à qui est-ce que tu parles dans ta famille? Pourquoi?
2. Quand est-ce qu'il faut que tu demandes la permission à tes parents?
3. Est-ce que tu as jamais désobéi à tes parents? Si oui, pourquoi?
4. Si tu te maries un jour, ce sera pour quelles raisons?

Trois Prétendants, un Mari
Acte III

Le soir…. Nous sommes à l'intérieur de la cuisine de Makrita, vaste pièce qu'éclaire un feu de bois au fond, sur lequel bout une marmite…. Makrita et Juliette sont en train de préparer le repas du soir. Au lever du rideau, on voit Bella qui prend des arachides d'une énorme corbeille placée sur une table basse…. Makrita, près du feu, épluche des plantains qu'elle met au fur et à mesure dans la marmite qui bout. Juliette… décortique des arachides, assise sur un petit lit de bambou à gauche de la scène. Makrita est aussi assise sur un lit semblable. Un troisième lit est placé à droite, sur lequel Bella ira s'asseoir plus tard.

Bella: *(ayant rempli son panier)* Maintenant que nous sommes entre femmes, Juliette, il faut que tu m'expliques ton attitude. Pourquoi tu refuses d'épouser le fonctionnaire? Un homme si riche! Tu n'es pas fière d'un tel prétendant?

Juliette: Non, Na' Bella!

Bella: *(qui va s'asseoir)* Non? Tu oses dire non? Comment peux-tu ainsi désobéir à ta famille? Nous nous sommes donnés tant de mal pour t'élever!

Makrita: *(sans s'arrêter d'éplucher les plantains)* Tant de mal, ma fille! Tu ne peux savoir combien c'était difficile à ta grand-mère et à moi de persuader ton père de te donner de l'argent quand tu étais renvoyée de Dibamba pour défaut de pension!

Bella: *(s'asseyant)* Oui! Mon fils était devenu la risée de Mvoutessi! Tous les hommes le trouvaient bête de gaspiller tout l'argent de son cacao sur une fille, au lieu d'épouser d'autres femmes…

Audiocassette/CD
Sur la bonne piste

Teacher's Note

So that students can better understand the setting of *Trois Prétendants, un Mari*, you might choose to provide the following background information on Cameroon. Although Cameroonians speak many tribal dialects, French and English are the country's two official languages. The average literacy rate is 60 percent, and more boys than girls finish school. Eighty percent of students attend elementary school, 26 percent attend high school and only four percent go on to college. More and more young women who live in cities are pursuing an education and getting jobs. About half of the population is Christian, and one-quarter is Muslim; the remainder practice traditional African religions. Even though a Muslim man may have up to four wives, polygamy is decreasing for economic reasons. Traditionally, marriage in Cameroon is considered to be more of a social contract than a love match. The average age at which women marry is 19, but for men it is 27. About two-thirds of the population reside in rural areas, but each year more and more people move to the cities to find jobs.

Makrita:	Ou bien de doter une femme à Oyônô...
Bella:	Une femme à ton frère! Il parle d'épouser une fille sérieuse et très travailleuse aux environs d'Ebolowa.
Juliette:	Et alors...
Makrita:	Et j'ai dit à ton frère: "Ne t'en fais pas pour la dot qu'on te demande de payer pour ta future femme! Ta sœur Juliette est belle et séduisante! De plus, c'est une collégienne! Nous serons riches le jour où un grand monsieur de la ville viendra lui demander la main!"
Bella:	Et c'est justement ce qui s'est passé! Deux prétendants!
Juliette:	Mais je ne veux ni l'un ni l'autre! Je vous l'ai déjà dit!
Makrita:	*(s'arrête un instant)* Quoi? Tu ne veux pas que ton frère, ton propre frère, puisse enfin se marier? Tu ne veux pas que ta mère ait une bru qui l'aide à semer des arachides et du maïs dans ses champs? *(Soupire)* Je crois que tu n'as pas de cœur, Juliette! Tu...

(Matalina entre, portant une assiette posée en équilibre sur la tête. Elle salue les autres joyeusement.)

Matalina:	Mbôlô ô ô?
Les Autres:	Mbôlô ô ô, ah Matalina!
Matalina:	*(allant s'asseoir près de Juliette)* Ma mère t'envoie à manger, Juliette!

(Elle découvre l'assiette.)

Juliette:	*(prenant l'assiette)* Oh... merci!....
Matalina:	... Juliette, comment est-ce qu'une fille peut bien refuser un homme qui l'aime assez pour verser deux cent mille francs de dot pour elle? Il y a des hommes qui n'en auraient pas fait tant, tu sais!
Juliette:	Est-ce que l'argent est une preuve d'amour?
Makrita:	*(couvrant sa marmite)* Bien sûr que oui! Tu ne le savais pas?
Juliette:	Je vous ai dit que mon fiancé n'a pas d'argent, et pourtant je suis sûre qu'il m'aime.
Matalina:	*(sourit, amusée par tant de naïveté)* Sûre! Tu dis que tu es sûre qu'il t'aime? Qu'est-ce qu'il t'a déjà donné?

(Les questions qui suivent sont posées très rapidement.)

Bella:	Combien de robes?
Juliette:	Aucune!
Matalina:	Et tu l'aimes?
Makrita:	Il a une voiture?
Matalina:	Il gagne beaucoup d'argent?
Juliette:	Mais...
Bella:	Est-ce qu'il possède une grande maison?
Matalina:	Il est au Gouvernement?
Bella:	Est-ce qu'il...
Juliette:	*(impatientée)* Rien de tout cela!
Bella:	*(après un temps)* Mais il est d'où, ce jeune homme-là?
Juliette:	Il est d'Ambam!
Les Autres:	*(consternées)* Eé é é é!
Bella:	De si loin? Tu veux donc nous quitter?
Juliette:	*(sourit, malicieuse)* Tu es donc née à Mvoutessi, Na' Bella?
Matalina:	*(avec une pointe de dédain)* Et qu'est-ce que tu lui trouves de si séduisant, à ce garçon?
Juliette:	Rien! Je l'aime!

Bella: (*indignée*) Mais tu es folle, Juliette! Depuis quand est-ce que les filles aiment les gens sans la permission de leur famille? Pourquoi veux-tu nous causer tant de déception? (*Se lève et se dirige vers Juliette*) Je te le répète, mon enfant, il faut que tu nous épouses un grand homme! Il est grand temps que toi aussi tu nous apportes de la nourriture, des boissons, et des richesses de la ville comme Cécilia le fait depuis qu'elle est devenue la maîtresse de cet européen de Mbalmayo! Il est grand temps que notre famille elle aussi devienne respectable!

Juliette: (*amusée*) Respectable? Qu'est-ce que...

Matalina: Écoute, Juliette! Puisque tu ne veux pas te marier, va donc te trouver un grand bureau à Yaoundé, au ministère surtout! (*Ton confidentiel*) On dit que ce n'est pas du tout difficile pour les jolies filles! (*Emballée*) Comme cela, nous viendrons de temps à autre passer quelques mois en ville, comme tout le monde!

Juliette: Pourquoi tu ne vas pas te trouver un grand bureau au ministère, toi, si c'est tellement facile?

(*Matalina se lève, vexée. Elle dit à Bella qui se tenait toujours au centre de la cuisine:*)

Matalina: Je vais rentrer à la maison, Na' Bella! Il fait de plus en plus noir dehors.

Bella: (*la raccompagnant jusqu'à la porte*) Oui, mon enfant.... (*Matalina sort, et Bella se tourne vers Juliette*) Je commence à croire que tu ne vas jamais nous écouter, Juliette!

Juliette: (*essayant de plaider*) Mais c'est vous qui ne me comprenez pas! Je...

Makrita: (*triste et déçue*) Juliette ne sera jamais aussi sage et obéissante que je l'avais toujours espéré! Je suis même sûre qu'une fois mariée à ce grand homme de la ville, elle va souvent l'empêcher de nous donner tout ce que nous exigerons de lui en plus de la dot! (*Commence à ramasser les épluchures de plantains, et à les mettre dans une corbeille à ordures.*) Elle va toujours essayer de limiter les dépenses, au lieu de menacer son mari de divorce chaque fois qu'il refuse de nous donner satisfaction! Je la vois déjà ne servant qu'un petit verre de vin seulement à ses oncles, au lieu d'en donner carrément cinq ou six grandes bouteilles à chacun d'eux!

Bella: (*allant se rasseoir*) Peut-être qu'elle va...

Makrita: (*se redressant*) Je sais comment ces filles d'aujourd'hui traitent les membres de leur famille à Sangmélima! Chaque fois que nous irons lui rendre visite, Juliette va sans doute essayer de se débarrasser de nous après trois semaines seulement, sous prétexte que la nourriture coûte cher en ville!

Juliette: (*éclate d'un rire joyeux*) Ah ah! C'est donc pour cela que tout le monde de ce village tient à me donner au fonctionnaire?....

(*Voix d'hommes dans les coulisses.*)

Bella: Tiens, Juliette! Voilà ton père et ton grand-père qui reviennent de chez le chef! Va vite allumer la grosse lampe à pression avant que mon fils ne commence à rouspéter!

Répondez aux questions suivantes.

1. Que font Bella, Makrita et Juliette dans la cuisine?
2. Selon Bella, comment est-ce que Juliette désobéit à sa famille?
3. Au lieu d'épouser d'autres femmes ou de doter une femme à son fils, comment le père de Juliette a-t-il dépensé l'argent de son cacao?

Teacher's Notes

1. After students have read this excerpt from Act III of *Trois Prétendants, un Mari*, they may want to learn that, at the end of the play, Juliette dupes her father through a ruse involving her suitors' dowries and gets to marry the suitor that she loves. 2. Some new words used in the play and cognates not found in the end vocabulary of *C'est à toi!* are used to ask questions about *Trois prétendants, un Mari* in Activity 15.

Answers

15 Possible answers:

1. Elles préparent le dîner. Bella prend des arachides qu'elle met dans un panier. Makrita épulche des plantains qu'elle met dans la marmite qui bout. Juliette décortique des arachides.
2. Juliette désobéit à sa famille en refusant d'épouser le fonctionnaire riche.
3. Le père de Juliette a payé son éducation.
4. Un grand monsieur viendra demander la main de Juliette parce qu'elle est belle et séduisante et, de plus, elle est collégienne.
5. Juliette a deux prétendants.
6. Une bru aiderait la mère de Juliette à semer des arachides et du maïs dans ses champs.
7. Matalina pense que le fonctionnaire est amoureux de Juliette parce qu'il a versé deux cent mille francs de dot.
8. Selon Matalina, un prétendant devrait offrir des cadeaux à la femme qu'il aime.
9. Matalina, Bella et Makrita pensent que le fiancé de Juliette n'est pas un prétendant sérieux parce qu'il n'offre pas de cadeaux, il n'a pas de voiture, il ne gagne pas beaucoup d'argent, il ne possède pas une grande maison et il n'est pas au Gouvernement.
10. Bella pense que Juliette cause tant de déception parce que Juliette aime son fiancé sans la permission de sa famille.
11. Selon Bella, Juliette doit apporter de la nourriture, des boissons et des richesses de la ville à sa famille.
12. Matalina suggère que Juliette trouve un grand bureau à Yaoundé, au ministère surtout.
13. Juliette devrait servir cinq ou six grandes bouteilles de vin à ses oncles.
14. Non, Juliette ne change pas son attitude à la fin. Elle veut toujours épouser son fiancé pauvre.
15. Answers will vary.

1. Optional activity. Have students interview exchange students to learn about cultural differences in their countries. Tell students to choose one cultural fact or practice and write a paragraph in which that cultural difference is outlined or hinted at. For example, a student who interviewed a Mexican exchange student might write the following: "On the Day of the Dead, Pedro walks to the cemetery with his family. His mother puts flowers on his grandfather's grave. Then she places a blanket on the grass. Pedro opens the basket he carried and places the sandwiches, beverages and apples on separate plates for his parents and brother and sister." Then have each student exchange his or her paragraph with that of another student. Students read the paragraph they received and make a chart, listing a textual clue and a cultural inference that they can make. For example, the student with the paragraph about Pedro might write: (Textual clue) "On the Day of the Dead, Pedro and his family go to the cemetery, put flowers on his grandfather's grave and eat lunch." (Cultural inference) "The Day of the Dead is when Mexican families remember their dead relatives with flowers and picnics at the loved one's grave."

2. Optional activity. Have students write a composition describing the lives of their grandmother, mother and sister (or female cousin). Students can include the educational background, age of marriage, profession and hobbies of all three females. When describing their sister or female cousin's life, students can make predictions based on their present knowledge of that person's choices and dreams for herself. Finally, have students conclude with a commentary on any social changes they see as having taken place in the United States in three generations, based on their examination of the women in their family.

4. Selon sa mère, pourquoi est-ce qu'un grand monsieur viendra demander la main de Juliette?

5. Combien de prétendants Juliette a-t-elle?

6. Comment une bru aiderait-elle la mère de Juliette?

7. Pourquoi Matalina pense-t-elle que le fonctionnaire soit amoureux de Juliette?

8. Selon Matalina, qu'est-ce qu'un prétendant devrait faire pour montrer son amour?

9. Pourquoi est-ce que Matalina, Bella et Makrita pensent que le fiancé de Juliette ne soit pas un prétendant sérieux?

10. Pourquoi Bella pense-t-elle que Juliette cause tant de déception?

11. Selon Bella, quelles sont les obligations familiales de Juliette?

12. Que suggère Matalina puisque Juliette ne veut pas épouser un grand homme?

13. Une fois mariée, qu'est-ce que Juliette devrait servir à ses oncles, selon sa mère?

14. Juliette change-t-elle son attitude à la fin? Que veut-elle finalement?

15. À ton avis, Juliette est-elle courageuse ou obstinée? Pourquoi?

16 | *Faites un schéma comme celui qui se trouve à la page 374. À gauche écrivez cinq descriptions ou citations (quotes) de la pièce qui ont une importance culturelle. À droite écrivez l'inférence culturelle de chaque phrase.*

17 | *Imaginez que Juliette est votre correspondante. Elle vient de vous écrire une lettre où elle a expliqué la culture camerounaise en ce qui concerne le mariage. Écrivez-lui une lettre dans laquelle vous lui expliquez les attitudes américaines sur le mariage. Par exemple, pourquoi est-ce qu'on instruit (educate) les filles aux États-Unis? Comment savez-vous si quelqu'un vous aime? Quelles sont les qualités que vous respectez dans un(e) partenaire? La décision de se marier, est-ce une décision individuelle ou familiale? Quelles sont les obligations familiales d'une femme après son mariage?*

18 | *Avec un(e) partenaire, jouez les rôles de Juliette et de son père. Juliette explique pourquoi elle refuse ses deux prétendants et veut toujours se marier avec l'étudiant pauvre. Son père explique la position de la famille en ce qui concerne son mariage et pourquoi elle doit suivre ses conseils.*

Dossier fermé

Imagine que tu es à Niamey (au Niger), à Abidjan (en Côte-d'Ivoire) ou à Dakar (au Sénégal) en visite touristique. Tous les sites africains et leurs couleurs riches t'impressionnent. Tu vois une femme en jupe et avec un foulard de tête de couleurs vives, et tu veux la prendre en photo. Mais cette femme se fâche. Pourquoi?

    B. Selon la tradition islamique, les Africains n'aiment pas que les touristes les prennent en photo.

Traditionnellement, les Africains n'aiment pas être photographiés sans leur permission.

Cross-curricular

Feminist Themes in Western Literature

Invite an English teacher to speak to your class about a famous piece of literature with feminist themes, for example, *A Doll's House* by Henrik Ibsen. Or ask the teacher to discuss the development of feminist themes in Western literature in the 19th and 20th centuries. After the lecture, encourage students to share their perceptions of female protagonists in novels that they have read in English class or for their own pleasure. Finally, have students discuss what novels with strong female characters they would recommend to a female relative and explain why.

C'est à moi!

Now that you have completed this unit, take a look at what you should be able to do in French. Can you do all of these tasks?

➤ I can write a letter.

➤ I can tell a story.

➤ I can talk about what happened in the past.

➤ I can talk about things sequentially.

➤ I can use linking expressions to connect narration.

➤ I can give information about various topics, including passing tests.

➤ I can tell location.

➤ I can ask what something is.

➤ I can identify objects.

➤ I can say that something belongs to someone.

➤ I can boast.

➤ I can express enthusiasm.

➤ I can compare people and things.

➤ I can remind someone about something.

➤ I can express my indifference about something.

➤ I can say that I'm disappointed.

Pour voir si vous avez bien compris la culture francophone, décidez si chaque phrase est vraie ou fausse.

1. Le Niger était une vieille colonie française.
2. Le Niger et le Mali se trouvent dans le désert du Sahara.
3. Le Niger et le Mali sont parmi les pays les plus riches d'Afrique.
4. La religion principale au Niger et au Mali est l'islam.
5. Selon l'islam, un homme peut avoir jusqu'à quatre femmes.
6. Le Niger et le Mali ont des artisans qui créent des pagnes, des foulards de tête et de la maroquinerie.
7. L'économie du Mali dépend des artisans.
8. Les habitants du Niger et du Mali n'aiment pas qu'on les prenne en photo.
9. Niamey est la capitale du Mali.
10. Oumou Sangaré est une chanteuse malienne qui est très engagée.

Communication orale

Avec un(e) partenaire, parlez d'un voyage ou de vacances dont vous vous souvenez bien. Interviewez votre partenaire pour savoir pourquoi ce voyage ou ces vacances ont été mémorables pour lui ou elle. Aidez votre partenaire à s'en rappeler les détails en lui demandant de vous dire ou de vous décrire:

Answers

1. vraie
2. vraie
3. fausse
4. vraie
5. vraie
6. vraie
7. fausse
8. vraie
9. fausse
10. vraie

- les préparatifs qu'il ou elle avait faits avant son départ
- où il ou elle est allé(e)
- quand il ou elle est parti(e)
- comment il ou elle a voyagé
- s'il ou elle a voyagé avec sa famille ou avec des copains
- la durée du voyage ou des vacances
- si c'était sa première visite à cet endroit
- le temps qu'il faisait là-bas
- ce qu'il ou elle a fait pour s'amuser
- s'il ou elle a visité des sites historiques, des monuments ou des musées
- s'il ou elle a acheté des souvenirs
- s'il ou elle voudrait y retourner un jour et pourquoi

Après l'interview, changez de rôles et répondez aux questions que votre partenaire vous pose.

Communication écrite

*Maintenant écrivez une lettre à un(e) correspondant(e) francophone où vous décrivez le voyage ou les vacances spéciales dont vous vous êtes souvenu(e) dans l'activité précédente. Donnez-lui tous les détails aussi bien que vos impressions générales. Servez-vous des expressions comme **d'abord**, **puis**, **ensuite**, **après cela**, **enfin**, etc., pour lier vos phrases. Si vous voulez, vous pouvez utiliser comme modèle la lettre que Moussa a écrite à Yakaré aux pages 364-65.*

Communication active

Au bon vieux temps, il y avait une fête dans le village tous les étés.

To write a letter, use:

Un grand "Salut" de la campagne!	*A big "Hi" from the country!*
J'écris pour t'envoyer de mes nouvelles et pour recevoir des tiennes.	*I'm writing to send you my news and to get yours (news from you).*
Ici tout va bien.	*Here everything is fine.*
Je m'arrête là.	*I'll quit for now.*

To tell a story, use:

Mon grand-père m'a raconté comment était la vie quand il avait mon âge.	*My grandfather told me how life was when he was my age.*
Au bon vieux temps, il allait souvent à la chasse.	*In the good old days, he often went hunting.*

To describe past events, use:

Elle était venue faire ses études d'infirmière.	*She had come to study nursing.*
Si **j'avais su** que c'était si passionnant....	*If I had known that it was so fascinating . . . .*
Quant au gibier, **il partageait** quelquefois le sien avec ses amis.	*As for game, he sometimes shared his with his friends.*

Listening Activity 3

To sequence events, use:

> **Je lui ai expliqué que de nos jours,** les étudiants s'intéressent à finir leurs études.
>
> *I explained to him that today, students are interested in finishing their studies.*

> **Autrefois,** ils pensaient que l'éducation religieuse était plus importante.
>
> *Formerly, they thought that religious education was more important.*

To use links, use:

> **À cette époque-là,** les parents envoyaient presque tous leurs enfants à l'école coranique.
>
> *At that time, parents sent almost all their children to the Islamic school.*

To give information, use:

> **Je l'ai informé** de mon succès au bac.
>
> *I informed him about my success in the bac.*

To tell location, use:

> Elles sont **de l'autre côté.**
>
> *They are on the other side.*

To ask what something is, use:

> **Qu'est-ce que c'est que** ce pavillon à côté?
>
> *What is this next pavilion?*

To identify objects, use:

> Elles **sont à vous,** Monsieur?
> Oui, oui. Elles **sont à moi.**
>
> *Do they belong to you, Sir?*
> *Yes. They are mine.*

To express ownership, use:

> J'écris pour t'envoyer de mes nouvelles et pour recevoir **des tiennes.**
>
> *I'm writing to send you my news and to get yours (news from you).*

> Quand au gibier, il partageait **le sien** avec ses amis, et ils partageaient **le leur** avec lui.
>
> *As for game, he shared his with his friends, and they shared theirs with him.*

> **Les miennes** sont trop longues.
>
> *Mine are too long.*

To boast, use:

> **Je n'aime pas me vanter, mais** c'est un travail très fin.
>
> *I don't like to boast, but it's very intricate work.*

To express enthusiasm, use:

> **C'est fantastique** qu'on puisse voir un peu de notre pays ici.
>
> *It's fantastic that one can see a little of our country here.*

To compare, use:

> **Par contre,** aujourd'hui il faut protéger la faune.
>
> *On the other hand, today we have to protect animal life.*

To remind, use:

> **Je** vous **rappelle** que tout est en solde aujourd'hui.
>
> *I remind you that everything is on sale today.*

To express indifference, use:

> **Bof!**
>
> *What can I say?*

To express disappointment, use:

> **Malheureusement,** j'ai oublié mon appareil-photo.
>
> *Unfortunately, I forgot my camera.*

Unité 10

On s'adapte

In this unit you will be able to:

- ➤ inquire about health and welfare
- ➤ give information
- ➤ describe past events
- ➤ describe character
- ➤ inquire about capability
- ➤ admit
- ➤ agree and disagree
- ➤ ask for help
- ➤ ask for permission
- ➤ express confirmation
- ➤ ask for a price
- ➤ estimate
- ➤ compare
- ➤ hypothesize
- ➤ express emotions
- ➤ express displeasure
- ➤ express disappointment
- ➤ make suggestions
- ➤ accept and refuse an invitation
- ➤ express gratitude
- ➤ terminate a conversation

Tes empreintes ici

Imagine que tu tombais malade pendant un voyage dans un pays franco-phone et que tu avais besoin d'un médecin. Comment est-ce que tu te débrouillerais? À qui parlerais-tu? Où irais-tu? Quels mots faudrait-il savoir pour expliquer tes problèmes au médecin? Puis après avoir parlé au médecin, il faudrait que tu expliques ce que tu voudrais au pharmacien ou à la pharmacienne. Pourrais-tu le faire?

Que dirais-tu à la pharmacienne si tu tombais malade pendant un voyage en France?

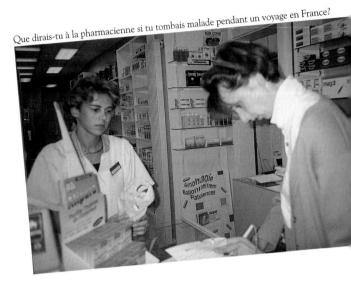

Est-ce que tu as jamais acheté un truc électronique qui ne marchait pas? Si oui, qu'est-ce que tu as fait? Est-ce que tu es retourné(e) au magasin pour t'en plaindre? Est-ce que tu étais satisfait(e) de ce que les employés du magasin ont offert de faire? Pourrais-tu faire la même chose si tu étais dans un pays francophone? Il est important de savoir te préparer le mieux possible pour toutes tes aventures en voyage dans des pays francophones.

Dossier ouvert

Si tu étais en France et tu voyais un accident dans la rue et que quelqu'un avait besoin d'aide médicale, que ferais-tu?

    A. J'essaierais de trouver les parents de la personne malade.
    B. Je ferais le 15 sur un téléphone.
    C. Je téléphonerais au commissariat.

Leçon A

In this lesson you will be able to:

➤ inquire about health and welfare

➤ give information

➤ describe character

➤ inquire about capability

➤ ask for help

➤ express displeasure

➤ agree and disagree

➤ compare

➤ accept and refuse an invitation

➤ express gratitude

➤ terminate a conversation

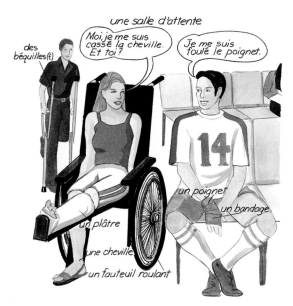

Karine et Mathieu sont des camarades de classe qui habitent le même immeuble à Paris. C'est mercredi, donc ils n'ont pas cours. Karine adore l'histoire. Voilà pourquoi elle est allée à Fontainebleau ce matin. Quant à Mathieu, il trouve le foot passionnant. C'est pourquoi il y jouait avec ses copains. Tous les deux sont maintenant dans la salle d'attente d'un hôpital. Karine et Mathieu sont assis l'un à côté de l'autre.° Elle est dans un fauteuil roulant, sa jambe gauche° élevée.° Il a mal au poignet droit.° Son poignet est entouré° d'un bandage. Karine et Mathieu ne parlent pas de n'importe quel° sujet. Ils parlent de leurs blessures,° naturellement.

l'un(e) à côté de l'autre *next to each other*; **gauche** *left*; **élevé(e)** *pas baissé(e)*; **droit(e)** *right*; **entouré(e)** *wrapped*; **n'importe quel, n'importe quelle** *just any*; **une blessure** *wound*

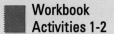

**Workbook
Activities 1-2**

Audiocassette/CD
La salle d'attente, La pharmacie, Dialogue

Transparencies 29-30

Teacher's Notes

1. A synonym for **un bandage** is **un pansement**. 2. Other related terms and expressions include **un comprimé** (*tablet*), **un brancard** (*stretcher*), **un tourniquet** (*tourniquet*), **une canne** (*cane*), **une cassure** (*break*), **une foulure** (*sprain*), **un rayon X** (*X ray*) and **se faire faire une radio** (*to have an X ray*).

Teacher's Notes

1. Point out that **ça fait** plus an expression of time is equivalent to "for," as in **Ça fait une heure** (*For an hour*). **Ça fait** comes only at the beginning of a sentence.
2. **Le SAMU** may be called using a toll-free number that can be dialed from any public phone in France without inserting a **télécarte** or coins. 3. You may want to point out the difference between a hard ball, **une balle**, and an inflated ball, **un ballon**. 4. Students learned **une boîte**, a synonym for **une canette**, in Unit 8 in the first level of *C'est à toi!* 5. **Plusieurs** is used here as an indefinite pronoun, not an indefinite adjective, since the noun **radiographies** is absent. 6. **Un tel** changes to **de tels** in the plural.
7. **Se passer**, another expression for **arriver**, means "to happen" and was presented in Unit 2 in the third level of *C'est à toi!* 8. Remind students that the prefix **re-** in **revoir** means "to do (something) again."
9. Point out that **embêtant** belongs to the same word family as **embêter**, presented in Unit 5 in the third level of *C'est à toi!*

La radiographie montre une jambe cassée.

Karine:	Tu attends depuis combien de temps?
Mathieu:	Je suis ici depuis déjà deux heures.
Karine:	Oh, mon pauvre! Tu es ici depuis plus de temps que moi. Moi, ça fait une heure.
Mathieu:	Qu'as-tu fait?
Karine:	Après avoir passé toute la journée à Fontainebleau, j'étais pressée de rentrer chez moi. Quand je suis descendue du train, je suis tombée. J'avais tellement mal à la cheville, tu ne peux pas imaginer. Je me suis vite rendu compte que je ne pouvais pas me lever. Heureusement, j'ai pu demander à quelqu'un de gentil de venir m'aider. Cette femme est allée téléphoner au SAMU.° Grâce à Dieu, ils sont vite arrivés. Et toi?
Mathieu:	Je jouais au foot avec quelques copains. J'avais le ballon° quand un des gars a essayé de le rattraper.° Il courait si vite que quand il m'a heurté, je suis tombé. Je savais tout de suite que je m'étais fait mal° au poignet. Ma mère m'a emmené à la salle des urgences.° Maintenant elle cherche une canette° de coca pendant que j'attends les résultats de la radiographie.° On t'a déjà fait une radiographie?
Karine:	Oui, plusieurs. Moi aussi, j'attends les résultats. J'ai peur que ma cheville soit cassée.° Après tout, un tel° accident pourrait arriver° à n'importe qui.°
Mathieu:	C'est vrai. Oh, voilà, j'entends mon nom. Je te reverrai° après peut-être....
Karine:	Tiens! On m'appelle aussi maintenant. Alors, à bientôt.

Après une heure Karine et Mathieu se retrouvent° dans la salle d'attente.

Mathieu:	Alors, je vois que tu as un plâtre.
Karine:	Oui, ça va durer deux mois. On a vu sur la radiographie que je m'étais cassé° la cheville. Et toi, tu n'as qu'un bandage?
Mathieu:	Oui. Je l'aurai pour trois ou quatre semaines. Je me suis foulé° le poignet. C'est vraiment quelque chose d'embêtant,° moi qui suis sportif. Pas de chance! Tu n'as pas trop de mal à marcher avec des béquilles?
Karine:	J'aurai autant de° mal au début que la dernière fois. Je me suis déjà cassé l'autre cheville.
Mathieu:	Dis donc, comment vas-tu rentrer chez toi? Ma mère pourrait te conduire, donc tu n'aurais pas besoin d'un taxi.
Karine:	Ça serait très gentil. Je te serais très reconnaissante. Mais d'abord il faut aller à la pharmacie. On m'a donné une ordonnance pour un antibiotique.
Mathieu:	Moi aussi, et j'ai besoin d'une boîte de pastilles et d'aspirine. Oh, voilà ma mère. Allons-y!

le SAMU le service d'assistance médicale d'urgence (*emergency medical service*); **un ballon** (*inflated*) *ball*; **rattraper** *to trap*; **se faire mal** *to hurt oneself*; **une salle des urgences** *emergency room*; **une canette** une boîte; **une radiographie** X *ray*; **cassé(e)** *broken*; **un tel, une telle** *such a*; **arriver** se passer; **n'importe qui** *anyone*; **revoir** *to see again*; **se retrouver** se rencontrer; **se casser** *to break*; **se fouler** *to sprain*; **embêtant(e)** *annoying*; **autant de** *as much*

Répondez aux questions suivantes d'après le dialogue.

1. Qu'est-ce que Karine et Mathieu ont fait mercredi matin puisqu'ils n'avaient pas cours?
2. Où sont-ils maintenant?
3. Depuis combien de temps sont-ils dans la salle d'attente?
4. Qu'a-t-on fait pour aider Karine?
5. Qu'est-ce que Karine et Mathieu attendent dans la salle d'attente?
6. Quelles blessures ont-ils?
7. Pour combien de temps Karine va-t-elle avoir un plâtre?
8. Où vont Karine et Mathieu avant de rentrer chez eux? Pourquoi?

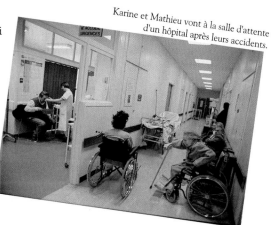

Karine et Mathieu vont à la salle d'attente d'un hôpital après leurs accidents.

Répondez par "vrai" ou "faux" d'après le dialogue. Puis corrigez les fautes dans les phrases qui sont fausses.

1. Karine ne pouvait pas se lever parce qu'elle avait très mal à la cheville.
2. Quelqu'un de méchant a aidé Karine en téléphonant au SAMU.
3. Mathieu est tombé parce qu'il ne sait pas jouer au foot.
4. Karine a peur que sa cheville soit cassée.
5. Mathieu n'a qu'un bandage qu'il doit porter pour trois ou quatre semaines.
6. Mathieu trouve que se fouler le poignet est vraiment quelque chose d'amusant.
7. Karine ne s'est jamais cassé la cheville.
8. Mathieu et Karine vont rentrer à leur immeuble en taxi.

C'est à toi!

1. Qu'est-ce que tu aimes faire quand tu n'as pas cours?
2. Est-ce que tu es membre d'une équipe? Si oui, de quelle équipe?
3. Est-ce que tu as jamais eu mal après un match? Si oui, où as-tu eu mal? Qu'est-ce que tu as fait?
4. Quand tu as une blessure, qu'est-ce que tu fais?
5. Est-ce que tu as eu un accident cette année? Si oui, qu'est-ce qui s'est passé?
6. Est-ce que tu t'es jamais foulé quelque chose? Si oui, quoi? Est-ce que tu t'es jamais cassé quelque chose? Si oui, quoi?
7. Est-ce que tu as jamais été à l'hôpital? Si oui, pour combien de temps?
8. Est-ce que tu aimes regarder les émissions à la télé qui ont lieu dans la salle des urgences d'un hôpital? Si oui, lesquelles?

 Audiocassette/CD Activities 1-3

Answers

1 1. Mercredi matin Karine est allée à Fontainebleau et Mathieu a joué au foot.
2. Ils sont dans la salle d'attente d'un hôpital.
3. Mathieu est dans la salle d'attente depuis deux heures, et Karine y est depuis une heure.
4. Une femme est allée téléphoner au SAMU.
5. Ils attendent les résultats de la radiographie.
6. Karine s'est cassé la cheville, et Mathieu s'est foulé le poignet.
7. Karine va avoir un plâtre pour deux mois.
8. Avant de rentrer chez eux, ils vont à la pharmacie. Tous les deux ont une ordonnance pour un antibiotique, et Mathieu a besoin d'une boîte de pastilles et d'aspirine.

2 1. vrai
2. faux
Quelqu'un de gentil a aidé Karine en téléphonant au SAMU.
3. faux
Mathieu est tombé parce qu'un des garçons a essayé de rattraper le ballon, et ce garçon courait si vite qu'il a heurté Mathieu.
4. vrai
5. vrai
6. faux
Mathieu trouve que se fouler le poignet est vraiment quelque chose d'embêtant.
7. faux
Karine s'est déjà cassé l'autre cheville.
8. faux
La mère de Mathieu va les conduire chez eux.

3 Answers will vary.

Game

L'ordre chronologique

On an overhead transparency write pairs of related sentences that summarize events in the dialogue, for example, **Karine s'est cassé la cheville gauche** and **Elle s'est cassé la cheville droite**. Divide the class into two teams. Call on the first player from Team A to order the first pair of sentences correctly using **d'abord** and **ensuite**, for example, **D'abord, Karine s'est cassé la cheville droite. Ensuite, elle s'est cassé la cheville gauche.** If the student orders the pair of sentences correctly, he or she earns a point for Team A. If not, the first player from Team B takes a turn with the next pair of sentences. When all the pairs of sentences have been ordered, the team with the most points wins.

Teacher's Notes

1. Cognates in this reading include **vaste, forêt, fontaine, confirme, région, style, architecture, façade, réalisation, palais, date, royal, résidence, fréquenté, tranquille, aspect, notable, demi-cercle, adieu, garde, exil, retour, acte, abdication, professionnelle, municipales, Coupe, assistance, médicale, installées, public, chargé, demande, urgente, déterminé, ambulance, assurer, transport, organiser, existence, approprié, extrême, victimes, Samaritain, biblique, qualité, généralement, produits, pharmaceutiques, édifice, croix, directement** and **client**. 2. The forest surrounding Fontainebleau has the same name as the château and the town. French kings, lovers of hunting, often built their castles near woods stocked with game. Artists have been drawn to the forest since the 1840s, when Théodore Rousseau, Jean-François Millet and others determined to paint from nature. They settled in the nearby hamlet of Barbizon, where Rousseau's workshop has been turned into a museum dedicated to the École de Barbizon. 3. There has been a château at Fontainebleau ever since the 12th century, when it was a feudal stronghold. A medieval tower survives, but the present château is the work of François Ier, whose salamander emblem can be seen throughout Fontainebleau. In the Galerie François Ier 14 large paintings pay tribute to the Italian Renaissance and that king's wish to create "a second Rome." The Salle de Bal is a Renaissance ballroom designed by Primaticcio and finished under Henri II, the son of François Ier, whose emblems decorate the walnut-coffered ceiling. In the Chambre de la Reine is a bed made for Marie-Antoinette, who never used it. The silk wall coverings were made in Lyon. The Salle du Trône, formerly the Chambre du Roi, houses Napoléon's grandiose throne.

Enquête culturelle

De ses cinq cours *(courtyards)*, la plus célèbre du château de Fontainebleau s'appelle la Cour du Cheval Blanc.

Fontainebleau est un des châteaux les plus célèbres de France. Au centre d'une vaste et très belle forêt, le château se trouve dans la ville du même nom à 56 kilomètres au sud-est de Paris. Le nom de Fontainebleau vient de "fontaine de belle eau," ce qui confirme la beauté de la région. Le style d'architecture de la façade principale du château montre l'influence de la Renaissance italienne.

Ce château est la réalisation des idées de plusieurs rois. Le palais que nous voyons aujourd'hui date du temps de François Ier, roi de France de 1515 à 1547. Il a fait construire un château royal dans la forêt parce qu'il aimait la chasse et avait besoin d'une résidence près de cet endroit. D'autres rois de France ont souvent fréquenté le château de Fontainebleau et ont passé des mois dans ce lieu tranquille et loin du travail de la cour. L'aspect le plus notable du château est l'escalier de l'entrée qui a la forme d'un demi-cercle. On l'appelle "l'Escalier du Fer à Cheval." C'était ici que l'empereur Napoléon Ier a dit "adieu" à sa garde avant de partir en exil pour l'île d'Elbe en 1814. Bientôt après son retour en France, il a signé son acte d'abdication dans le château.

Tout le monde sait que le sport qui intéresse le plus les Français, c'est le football. Il n'y a pas d'équipes de foot aux lycées, mais on y joue beaucoup en équipes organisées par les Maisons des Jeunes et de la Culture, par les villes ou même entre copains. Toutes les grandes villes ont une équipe professionnelle qui joue contre d'autres équipes municipales. En été les meilleures équipes du monde de foot se présentent aux matchs de la Coupe du Monde de foot. En 1998 la Coupe du Monde a eu lieu en France.

Beaucoup de jeunes footballeurs rêvent de jouer pour une équipe professionnelle un jour.

In the Chambre de Napoléon visitors can see the emperor's small bed. In the Salon de l'Abdication Napoléon wrote his act of abdication in 1814. The number of courtyards indicates the immense size of Fontainebleau. The Cour du Cheval Blanc, once a simple enclosed courtyard, was transformed by François Ier into the main approach to the château. The Escalier du Fer à Cheval, built by Jean Androuet du Cerceau in 1634, was designed to allow carriages to pass beneath the two arches. Outdoors the Jardin de Diane features a bronze fountain of Diana the huntress. The Jardin Anglais, redesigned in the 19th century, is planted with cypress and plantain trees. 4. The **Maisons des Jeunes et de la Culture** were introduced on page 201 in the second level of *C'est à toi!*

En cas d'urgences, les Français font le 15 sur le téléphone pour appeler le SAMU, le service d'assistance médicale d'urgence, dont il y a 105 stations installées en France. C'est un service public chargé de répondre 24 heures sur 24 heures à la demande d'aide médicale urgente. Déterminé à offrir la meilleure réponse possible, le SAMU décide s'il faut un simple conseil médical, un médecin ou une ambulance. Ensuite il peut envoyer une ambulance pour assurer le transport à l'hôpital ou organiser une équipe pour répondre à la demande. L'existence d'un SAMU permet un transport direct à l'hôpital le plus approprié de la région. De plus, le SAMU organise des cours pour mieux préparer les médecins, les infirmières et d'autres personnels médicaux aux besoins d'urgences.

Il est important de savoir que la loi française exige que les personnes qui voient un accident ou un cas de maladie extrême essaient d'aider les victimes. Connue comme "la loi du bon Samaritain" (d'après l'histoire biblique), cette loi cherche à améliorer la qualité de la vie.

Dans ce garage parisien, plusieurs ambulances du SAMU sont disponibles pour répondre à la demande d'aide médicale urgente.

En France quelques magasins ont le nom "drugstore," mais ce n'est pas là qu'il faut aller avec une ordonnance. Au "drugstore" on peut acheter un peu de tout, et généralement on n'y trouve pas de produits pharmaceutiques. Si vous en avez besoin, vous devez chercher une pharmacie. Sur la façade de l'édifice on voit toujours une croix verte et le mot "pharmacie." Les Français se présentent directement au pharmacien ou à la pharmacienne quand ils veulent des conseils sur une maladie qui n'est pas très grave. En France c'est le client ou la cliente, pas le pharmacien ou la pharmacienne, qui doit garder l'ordonnance.

Dans une pharmacie française on peut même trouver des remèdes homéopathiques.

Répondez aux questions suivantes.

1. Où se trouve le château de Fontainebleau?
2. Qui a fait construire le château?
3. Pourquoi les rois de France sont-ils allés à Fontainebleau?
4. Quel sport intéresse le plus les Français?
5. Que fait-on quand on a besoin d'assistance médicale en France?
6. Que décide le SAMU?
7. Qu'est-ce que le SAMU organise pour les personnels médicaux?
8. Qu'est-ce que c'est que "la loi du bon Samaritain"?
9. Est-ce que les Français vont au drugstore quand ils ont besoin de produits pharmaceutiques?
10. En France qui garde l'ordonnance?

Answers

4 1. Le château de Fontainebleau se trouve dans la ville du même nom à 56 kilomètres au sud-est de Paris. Il est au centre d'une vaste et belle forêt.
2. François Ier l'a fait construire.
3. Les rois de France sont allés à Fontainebleau pour la chasse et pour être loin du travail de la cour.
4. C'est le football qui les intéresse le plus.
5. On fait le 15 pour appeler le SAMU quand on a besoin d'assistance médicale en France.
6. Le SAMU décide s'il faut un simple conseil médical, un médecin ou une ambulance.
7. Le SAMU organise des cours pour mieux préparer les médecins, les infirmières et d'autres personnels médicaux aux besoins d'urgences.
8. "La loi du bon Samaritain" exige que les personnes qui voient un accident ou un cas de maladie extrême essaient d'aider les victimes.
9. Non, quand les Français ont besoin de produits pharmaceutiques, ils vont à la pharmacie.
10. En France c'est le client ou la cliente qui garde l'ordonnance.

Teacher's Notes

1. When you call **le SAMU**, the dispatcher takes down details of your problem and then sends out a private ambulance with a driver (about 250-300 francs) or, if necessary, a mobile intensive care unit. For less serious problems, **le SAMU** will dispatch a doctor for a house call (160 francs during the day). If you prefer to be taken to a particular hospital, you should mention this to the ambulance crew, as the usual procedure is to take you to the nearest one. In emergency cases (those requiring intensive care units), billing will be taken care of later. Otherwise, you need to pay in cash at the time you receive assistance. 2. "To witness" is **être témoin de**.

Journal personnel

As you were driving, you saw someone on the pavement next to a crumpled bicycle. The person wasn't moving and obviously needed help. What would you do? Would you keep driving, stop to help the accident victim or phone the police? What would keep you from coming to the victim's aid? If you were the victim, what would you want a passerby to do for you?

You just read about the French law of the good Samaritan that requires a person to help accident victims or those with sudden illnesses. Do you think this law is a good idea? Do you think it's enforceable? Why or why not? Do you think that we should pass a similar law in the United States? Why might some Americans be against passing this law? Do you think their concerns would be justified?

Structure

Expressions of quantity

You have already learned a variety of ways to express quantities of things. These expressions are followed by **de** and a noun:

assez de	*enough*
beaucoup de	*a lot of, many*
combien de	*how much, how many*
moins de	*less*
(un) peu de	*(a) little, few*
plus de	*more*
trop de	*too much, too many*

"Je pense que la peur me bloquait, j'ai mis beaucoup de temps à avoir confiance en moi."

«Je posais trop de questions.»

Tu attends depuis **combien de** temps?	*How long (how much time) have you been waiting?*
Tu es ici depuis **plus de** temps que moi.	*You've been here longer (more time) than I have.*
Tu n'as pas **trop de** mal à marcher avec des béquilles?	*It doesn't hurt too much to walk on crutches?*

To tell "as much" or "as many," use **autant de** before a noun.

J'aurai **autant de** mal au début que la dernière fois.	*It will hurt as much at the beginning as last time.*

Certain nouns also express quantity and are followed by **de**.

une boîte de	*a can of, a box of*
une bouteille de	*a bottle of*
une canette de	*a can of*
un kilo de	*a kilogram of*
un morceau de	*a piece of*
un pot de	*a jar of*
une tasse de	*a cup of*
une tranche de	*a slice of*

J'ai besoin d'une **boîte de** pastilles.   *I need a box of lozenges.*

Est-ce que ce vidéoclub a autant de films que le tien?

J'ai autant de copines que de copains.

Avant la boum

Put students in pairs to practice expressions of quantity. Prepare a picture of a table laden with differing amounts of food items, for example, a small piece of cheese, three cakes, one bottle of lemon-lime soda, two baguettes and a ham, and distribute a copy of the picture to Student A of each pair.

Give Student B of each pair a list of food items to buy for a party. Tell students that they are going to have a party and need to discuss with their partner what items they need to buy to entertain their ten guests adequately. Student B asks Student A if there is enough of each item on the list, for example, **Y a-t-il assez de fromage?** Student A looks at the picture and responds with a sentence using

beaucoup de, (un) peu de or trop de, for example, **Non, il y a seulement un peu de fromage.** When Student B hears the answer, he or she circles the items on the list that still need to be purchased and draws a line through items on the list that do not need to be purchased.

Pratique

La mère de Mathieu vient de faire les courses au supermarché. Dites la quantité qu'elle a achetée des choses illustrées.

Modèle:

Elle a acheté un pot de confiture.

1.

5.

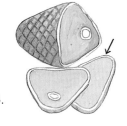

2.

6.

3.

7.

4.

8.

Aurélie et Leïla ont acheté un pot de moutarde et deux bouteilles d'eau minérale. (La Rochelle)

Audiocassette/CD
Activity 5

Answers

5 1. Elle a acheté six canettes de coca.
2. Elle a acheté deux bouteilles d'eau minérale.
3. Elle a acheté deux tranches de jambon.
4. Elle a acheté un pot de moutarde.
5. Elle a acheté un morceau de fromage.
6. Elle a acheté deux kilos de pommes.
7. Elle a acheté une tasse de café.
8. Elle a acheté une boîte de pastilles.

Cooperative Group Practice

Le barbecue

Put students in small groups. Tell students that their task is to prepare a shopping list for a barbecue. Designate a leader, secretary and reporter for each group. The leader asks the group members who wants a certain food item, for example, **Qui veut des hamburgers?** Then he or she determines the quantity of each item that needs to be purchased, for example, **Combien de hamburgers veux-tu manger?** The secretary records the totals. When each group has finished its list, the secretary gives the list to the reporter, who reports to the class on what his or her group needs to purchase, for example, **Il faut que nous achetions trois kilos de hamburger, un pot de moutarde,** **un kilo de fromage, une bouteille de ketchup et dix canettes de coca.**

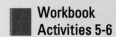

Answers

6 1. Combien de frères as-tu? Et toi, combien de frères as-tu?

2. Combien de cousines as-tu? Et toi, combien de cousines as-tu?

3. Combien de chats as-tu? Et toi, combien de chats as-tu?

4. Combien de cours as-tu? Et toi, combien de cours as-tu?

5. Combien de CDs as-tu? Et toi, combien de CDs as-tu?

6. Combien de casquettes as-tu? Et toi, combien de casquettes as-tu?

Students' responses to these questions and their comparisons will vary.

Teacher's Notes

1. **Aucun(e)... ne (n')** was introduced with other negative expressions in Unit 2 in the third level of *C'est à toi!* 2. **Autre** may be preceded by a definite or an indefinite article. 3. **Certain(e)** takes an indefinite article when the noun that follows it is singular, but it takes no article in its plural form. 4. Point out that **chaque** is always singular. 5. **Même** is preceded by a definite article, for example, **J'ai pris le même antibiotique.** 6. **La plupart de** can be followed by a definite article, a possessive adjective or a demonstrative adjective. 7. **Plusieurs** does not have a feminine form. 8. Remind students that **tout** agrees in gender and in number with the noun it describes, for example, **toutes les bouteilles.** 9. The plural of **un tel, une telle** is **de tels, de telles. Un tel, une telle** does not change after a negative verb, for example, **Je n'ai jamais vu un tel accident.**

Modèle:

sœurs
Élève A: Combien de sœurs as-tu?
Élève B: J'en ai trois. Et toi, combien de sœurs as-tu?
Élève A: J'en ai une.
Élève B: Alors, j'ai plus de sœurs que toi.
Élève A: Et moi, j'en ai moins que toi.

Les Top Boys ont plusieurs projets d'émissions de télé et de disques en route.

RFM Aucune radio ne vous détendra autant.

6 | *Avec un(e) partenaire, posez et répondez aux questions pour déterminer si vous avez plus de, autant de ou moins de ce qu'il ou elle a. Puis comparez vos réponses. Suivez le modèle.*

1. frères
2. cousines
3. chats
4. cours
5. CDs
6. casquettes

> La première fois que je suis sorti avec une fille, j'avais plus de 16 ans.

Indefinite adjectives

Indefinite adjectives describe inexact quantities or types of things. Like other adjectives, indefinite adjectives agree in gender and in number with the nouns they describe. You have already learned these indefinite adjectives:

aucun(e)... ne (n')	*not one, no*
autre	*other*
certain(e)	*certain*
chaque	*each, every*
même	*same*
la plupart de	*most*
plusieurs	*several*
quelques	*some*
tout(e)	*all, every*

J'ai passé toute la journée à Fontainebleau. — *I spent all day at Fontainebleau.*

Je jouais au foot avec quelques copains. — *I was playing soccer with some friends.*

Je me suis déjà cassé l'autre cheville. — *I already broke my other ankle.*

Two new indefinite adjectives are **n'importe quel, n'importe quelle** (*just any*) and **un tel, une telle** (*such a*).

Karine et Mathieu ne parlent pas de n'importe quel sujet. — *Karine and Mathieu aren't talking about just any subject.*

Un tel accident ne pourrait jamais arriver. — *Such an accident could never happen.*

> N'importe quel médecin vous dira la même chose. Ce n'est pas grave.

Paired Practice

Certains/certaines

Put students in pairs to practice the indefinite adjective **certain(e)**. Prepare a worksheet with the following questions and distribute a copy to each pair: 1. Tu as utilisé les outils de recherche? 2. Tu as lu les petites annonces? 3. Tu as écouté les CDs d'Oumou Sangaré? 4. Tu as goûté les plats français? 5. Tu as acheté les magazines au kiosque à journaux? 6. Tu as invité tes camarades de classe à ta boum? 7. Tu as fait les corvées? 8. Tu as vu les expositions? Student A asks Student B the first four questions on the worksheet, and Student B responds using **certains** or **certaines** after **ne... que,** for example, **Je n'ai utilisé que certains outils de recherche.** Then students switch roles, and Student B questions Student A.

Pratique

Regardez ce qui se passe dans la salle des urgences. Puis répondez aux questions en utilisant un des adjectifs de la liste qui suit. Choisissez un adjectif différent pour chaque réponse.

aucun(e)... ne (n')	la plupart de
certain(e)	plusieurs
chaque	quelques
même	tout(e)

Modèle:
Est-ce que tous les fauteuils roulants sont libres?
Non, aucun fauteuil roulant n'est libre.

1. Quelles infirmières sont sérieuses?
2. Est-ce que tous les ados sont avec leurs parents?
3. Est-ce que toutes les filles se sont cassé la jambe?
4. Quel ado marche avec des béquilles?
5. Est-ce que toutes les filles sont dans un fauteuil roulant?
6. Combien de filles ont un plâtre?
7. Quel poignet est-ce que les deux garçons se sont foulé?
8. Combien de filles se sont cassé le bras?

Toute la mode pour faire la fête

- Des scoops vraiment top secrets sur chaque membre de tes BOYS BANDS préférés

★ Je crois savoir qu'un certain **Leonardo DiCaprio** plaît à nombre de lectrices

 Audiocassette/CD Activity 7

Answers

7 Possible answers:
1. Toutes les infirmières sont sérieuses.
2. Non, mais plusieurs ados sont avec leurs parents.
3. Non, quelques filles se sont cassé la jambe.
4. Aucun ado ne marche avec des béquilles.
5. Non, mais la plupart des filles sont dans un fauteuil roulant.
6. Chaque fille a un plâtre.
7. Ils se sont foulé le même poignet.
8. Certaines filles se sont cassé le bras.

Paired Practice

Tous/toutes

Put students in pairs. Prepare a worksheet for each pair listing a series of verbs and nouns, for example, **essayer/les jeux d'adresse au parc d'attractions**. Student A forms questions with **tous** or **toutes** to ask Student B, using the odd-numbered listings, for example, **As-tu essayé tous les jeux d'adresse au parc d'attractions?** Student B answers affirmatively or negatively, for example, **Oui, j'y ai essayé tous les jeux d'adresse** or **Non, je n'y ai pas essayé tous les jeux d'adresse**. Then students switch roles, and Student B forms questions to ask Student A, using the even-numbered listings. Here are other items to include on the worksheet: 1. lire/les articles du journal 2. entendre/les nouvelles du lycée 3. copier/les notes 4. aider/ les immigrés maghrébins 5. voir/les animaux au zoo 6. étudier/les batailles de Napoléon 7. aimer/les chansons de Céline Dion 8. apprécier/les tableaux impressionnistes à l'exposition 9. suivre/les cours de français de ton lycée

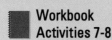

Answers

8 1. Je n'ai jamais vu de tels ballons!

2. Je n'ai jamais vu un tel château!

3. Je n'ai jamais vu un tel accident!

4. Je n'ai jamais vu une telle salle des urgences!

5. Je n'ai jamais vu de telles blessures!

6. Je n'ai jamais vu une telle radiographie!

Teacher's Notes

1. Some other expressions that may be used as indefinite pronouns include **d'autres, l'autre, les un(e)s... les autres, chacun(e), n'importe qui, n'importe quoi, quelques-un(e)s, tel(s), telle(s)** and **certain(e)s.** 2. You may want to put students in pairs to create a short dialogue that incorporates **plusieurs.** For example, in a dialogue about school homework, students might say, **Tu as déjà fait les problèmes de maths? Oui, plusieurs.** Tell students to extend their dialogues to imitate a normal interaction between two people, then have the pairs present their dialogues to the rest of the class.

8 Pour chaque illustration dites que vous n'avez jamais vu une telle chose.

Modèle:

Je n'ai jamais vu de telles fleurs!

1.

2.

3.

M. Mauclair n'a jamais vu un tel festival!

4.

5.

6.

Indefinite pronouns

Indefinite pronouns replace inexact quantities of things or unidentified people. Here are some of the indefinite pronouns that you have already learned:

aucun(e)... ne (n')	*not one*
un(e) autre	*another*
la plupart	*most*
plusieurs	*several*
quelqu'un	*someone, somebody*
quelque chose	*something*
tous les deux	*both*

Tous les deux sont maintenant dans la salle d'attente.	*Both are now in the waiting room.*
On t'a déjà fait une radiographie? Oui, **plusieurs**.	*Have they already taken an X ray? Yes, several.*

To describe **quelqu'un** or **quelque chose**, use the adjective's masculine singular form preceded by **de**.

J'ai pu demander à **quelqu'un** de gentil de venir m'aider.	*I was able to ask someone nice to come and help me.*
C'est vraiment **quelque chose** d'embêtant.	*That's really something annoying.*

Two new indefinite pronouns are **n'importe qui**, meaning "anyone," and **l'un(e)... l'autre**, meaning "(the) one . . . the other."

Karine et Mathieu sont assis **l'un** à côté de **l'autre**.	*Karine and Mathieu are seated next to each other (one next to the other).*
N'importe qui pourra te dire cela.	*Anyone will be able to tell you that.*

Alors, tu invites n'importe qui à ta boum?

Mais non! J'invite seulement nos copains.

Pratique

Jean-Claude a eu un accident quand il jouait au foot. Complétez chacune de ses phrases avec un pronom convenable de la liste suivante. Choisissez un pronom différent pour chaque phrase.

aucun... n'	quelqu'un	une autre
quelque chose	n'importe qui	toutes les deux
la plupart	l'un... l'autre	plusieurs

1. ... des garçons français jouent au foot.
2. ... m'a dit que je suis tombé quand Michel m'a heurté.
3. ... pouvait dire que je m'étais fait mal; c'était très évident.
4. De tous les autres garçons dans notre équipe,... avait de blessures.
5. Il y avait d'autres personnes dans la salle d'attente cet après-midi? Oui,....
6. Oh là là! Je me suis cassé les jambes—...!
7. Des deux médecins qui m'ont aidé, j'ai vu d'abord... qui m'a montré mes radiographies. Puis... m'a donné une ordonnance.
8. Après que le médecin m'a donné une ordonnance, l'infirmière m'a dit qu'elle allait m'en donner....
9. Marcher avec des béquilles, c'est... que je n'ai pas envie de faire.

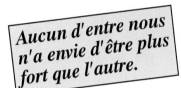

Aucun d'entre nous n'a envie d'être plus fort que l'autre.

IL SE PASSE TOUJOURS QUELQUE CHOSE À AVIGNON

Paired Practice

Tous les deux

Put students in pairs. Prepare a worksheet with eight pairs of sentences about two people in the same location, for example, **Christine est dans un fauteuil roulant. Le poignet de Nadine est entouré d'un bandage.** Student A reads the first four situations to Student B, who identifies the location in a sentence using **tous les deux** and **être**, for example, **Toutes les deux sont dans la salle d'attente.** Then Student A gives the worksheet to Student B, who reads the last four situations to Student A. Tell students to pay attention to the tense used in the pairs of sentences, and to use the same tense when they form their sentences. Here are seven other pairs of sentences to include on the worksheet: 1. M. Guyomard a donné son ordonnance à la pharmacienne. Mme Blondel a acheté de l'aspirine. 2. Salmou regardait les squelettes de dinosaures du Sahara. Abdoulaye visitait le pavillon des vêtements traditionnels du Niger. 3. Solange met son sac à dos dans le porte-bagages. Marie montre son billet à l'hôtesse de l'air. 4. Alex demande l'addition. Claire prend la spé-cialité du jour. 5. Monique a fait un tour de manège. Nicolas est monté dans une auto tamponneuse. 6. Christophe rattrapait le ballon. Adèle regardait le match. 7. Anne parle à la réceptionniste. Denise met ses bagages dans l'ascenseur.

Modèle:

ton professeur de français

Élève A: À mon avis, c'est quelqu'un de sympa.

Élève B: Selon moi, c'est quelqu'un d'intelligent.

C'est quelqu'un d'accueillant.

10 *Avec un(e) partenaire, faites des remarques sur les personnes et les choses suivantes en utilisant* **quelqu'un** *ou* **quelque chose** *et un adjectif convenable.*

1. ton/ta meilleur(e) ami(e)
2. avoir ta propre voiture
3. Christopher Reeve
4. le foot
5. passer trois heures dans une salle d'attente
6. ton/ta dentiste
7. être malade pendant les vacances
8. Leonardo DiCaprio
9. protéger l'environnement
10. voyager en France

Communication

11 *Avec un(e) partenaire, jouez les rôles de deux personnes qui passent la journée à visiter le château et les jardins de Fontainebleau. L'Élève A joue le rôle d'une personne qui vient d'avoir un accident et s'est fait mal. L'Élève B joue le rôle d'une personne qui vient à l'aide de l'Élève A. Pendant votre conversation:*

1. L'Élève A demande à l'Élève B de venir l'aider.
2. L'Élève B offre son aide et demande ce qui s'est passé et ce que l'Élève A a fait.
3. L'Élève A décrit son accident.
4. L'Élève B demande à l'Élève A s'il ou elle a trop de mal à marcher, et l'Élève A lui répond.
5. L'Élève B offre d'aller téléphoner au SAMU.
6. Tous les deux parlent des blessures de l'Élève A en attendant l'arrivée du SAMU.
7. L'Élève A explique pourquoi c'était un accident embêtant.
8. Quand le SAMU arrive, l'Élève A remercie l'Élève B de son aide. L'Élève A dit à l'Élève B qu'il ou elle lui est très reconnaissant(e).
9. L'Élève B dit "Bonne chance!" à l'Élève A.

12 *Écrivez un paragraphe dans lequel vous décrivez un accident que vous avez eu ou une fois où vous êtes tombé(e) malade. Donnez tous les détails sur:*

1. l'accident ou la maladie
2. vos blessures ou vos symptômes, et comment vous vous sentiez
3. qui vous a aidé(e) ou s'est occupé de vous
4. si vous avez dû aller à la salle des urgences, ou si vous avez dû prendre rendez-vous avec le médecin
5. si on vous a fait une radiographie, ou si on vous a donné une ordonnance à faire préparer à la pharmacie
6. si vous vous êtes foulé ou cassé quelque chose
7. si vous aviez un bandage, des béquilles ou un plâtre
8. combien de temps vous avez dû rester au lit, et ce que vous avez fait pour vous amuser

Cooperative Group Practice

Un voyage en France

Put students in small groups. Tell them that Marc is interested in going on the school trip to France, but he could not attend the meeting that took place last night. Prepare a set of questions on note cards that Marc wants to ask the students who attended the meeting. The first student in each group takes a card from the stack and asks the student on his or her right the indicated question, for example, **Jacques et Anne sont venus?** The student on his or her right responds using an indefinite pronoun, for example, **Oui, tous les deux sont venus.** Then the second student in the group takes a card and questions the student on his or her right, and so on. Here are some other questions to include on the cards: 1. Plusieurs élèves sont arrivés en retard? 2. Quelques parents étaient là? 3. La plupart des élèves ont décidé d'aller en France? 4. On a offert des boissons? 5. Notre professeur a parlé au groupe? (Possible answers: 1. Non, aucun n'est arrivé en retard. 2. Oui, plusieurs étaient là. 3. Oui, la plupart ont décidé d'y aller. 4. Oui, quelqu'un en a offert. 5. Non, un autre a parlé au groupe.)

Persuading

Have you ever seen a bumper sticker that really attracted your attention? It probably promoted a cause or person that the driver felt strongly about and cleverly used language to grab your attention. To persuade people, you try to convince them to agree with your opinion and possibly take action. There are five steps to remember when you persuade:

1. Introduce the issue, supplying any background information necessary to help your audience understand it.
2. Present your opinion in a clear, direct statement. For example, to persuade people to support saving the rain forests, you might say, "It's essential to donate to the Rain Forest Action Network in order to preserve the endangered rain forests."
3. Give supporting ideas that appeal to both reason and emotion. To appeal to reason, cite facts, statistics, quotations from experts in the field and examples that can be proven true or false. For example, you might say, "Rain forests are home to half of all the plant and animal species on earth." To appeal to emotion, use words that create strong positive or negative associations, such as "worthy" or "foolish."
4. Gear your argument to your audience, presenting your ideas in a way that will persuade people to accept your opinion. Begin by evaluating your audience as you ask yourself these questions:
   A. What does my audience already know about the issue, and what do they currently think about it?
   B. What types of evidence will most likely sway my audience?
   C. Do I want my audience to change their views and/or to take action?
   If you are trying to get elementary students to agree with your viewpoint on the rain forest, for example, it may be enough to tell them about all the animals and plants that live there. But if your audience is a group of middle-aged business professionals, you may need to be armed with facts. You could say, "Each day 50,000 rain forest acres are lost."
5. Conclude by summarizing your ideas and, if it is your goal, giving a call to action.

Now try your hand at persuading in French, choosing one of the following situations:

1. Write an article for a travel magazine. Encourage your readers to visit a French-speaking location. Remember to introduce your topic, state your opinion, support your position, assess your audience and draw your conclusion.
2. With a partner play the roles of a father and his 17-year-old daughter. The daughter wants her father to buy her a car. The father does not respond to emotional arguments, only to facts and statistics.

Teacher's Notes

1. **Sur la bonne piste, Leçon A,** is designed to develop skills that will help students prepare to take the Advanced Placement Exam in French Language. In this lesson **Sur la bonne piste** develops students' writing and speaking proficiency as they focus on five effective steps to persuade an audience. 2. You may choose to have students do both activities so that they get writing and speaking practice in persuading an audience. You might have the rest of the class vote on the most effective student dialogue presented to convince a father to buy a car for his daughter. 3. Have students make a series of posters for **Fondation Brigitte Bardot, Médecins Sans Frontières** or **l'Équipe Cousteau.** Tell students their goal is to persuade people to donate money to the organization they selected by writing both effective emotional slogans and giving pertinent facts that appeal to reason. Have students use the Internet to find out more about these organizations. 4. Another activity to develop writing proficiency related to persuading an audience is to have students write an article encouraging the reader to view a film of their choice. Students can discuss the quality of the acting and the plot. Before they begin, have students read several film critics' columns. You may want to videotape pairs of students commenting on the same film and show the videotaped film commentaries to the class. 5. Have students write a letter of complaint to the principal of your school, persuading him or her to solve a school problem. 6. To provide additional speaking practice, have pairs of students role-play a student who is trying to persuade a teacher to postpone a test and a teacher who is resistant to the idea.

Cross-curricular

Marketing Strategies

Invite a teacher or business person to speak to students about common advertising strategies used in the media, such as using a celebrity endorsement or personal testimonial to promote a product. Then show students a tape of French commercials and advertisements that you have collected from French magazines. Have students determine the strategy or strategies used for each one. Finally, have pairs of students create an advertisement for a real or imaginary American product that they want French consumers to buy. Point out that students should apply their knowledge of French culture to successfully publicize their product. Videotape the advertisements, and show them to the rest of the class, asking students to identify the publicity strategies used and to rate how successful the advertisements are in their power to persuade consumers to purchase the specific products.

Workbook Activities 9-10

Audiocassette/CD
Le rayon des appareils électroniques, Dialogue

Leçon B

In this lesson you will be able to:

➤ describe past events

➤ ask for permission

➤ express confirmation

➤ admit

➤ ask for a price

➤ estimate

➤ hypothesize

➤ agree and disagree

➤ express emotions

➤ express disappointment

➤ make suggestions

Brian Duffey est un lycéen américain qui passe une semaine à Avignon dans le Midi avec des amis. Brian veut améliorer son français. C'est justement° ce qu'il essayait de faire quand il a acheté un dictionnaire électronique français/anglais à la Fnac. Brian était content de son achat° parce qu'il était en solde. De plus, il avait trouvé un bon de réduction° de 10% dans le journal. Maintenant Brian est frustré parce que son dictionnaire électronique ne marche pas. Il est obligé de le rapporter° au rayon des appareils électroniques. Brian s'approche du comptoir.

Le vendeur: **Oui, Monsieur?**
Brian: **J'ai acheté ce dictionnaire électronique hier mais il ne marche pas. Est-ce que je pourrais l'échanger contre un autre?**
Le vendeur: **Bien sûr, Monsieur, mais je dois voir votre ticket de caisse**

justement *exactement;* un achat *ce qu'on achète;* un bon de réduction *coupon;* rapporter *rendre;* un ticket de caisse *receipt*

Brian:	Oui, je comprends. Je l'ai gardé. Le voilà.
Le vendeur:	Ça vous gêne° si je jette un coup d'œil?°
Brian:	Non, pas du tout.
Le vendeur:	Vous avez bien lu le mode d'emploi?°
Brian:	Oui, mais je dois dire qu'il était un peu compliqué et je n'ai pas bien compris.
Le vendeur:	Laissez-moi° voir.... Vous avez raison.° Il ne marche pas, mais je ne sais pas pourquoi.
Brian:	Dans ce cas qu'est-ce que je peux faire?
Le vendeur:	Bon ben... vous pourriez toujours l'échanger ou le faire réparer, ou je pourrais vous rembourser le prix.
Brian:	Pour le faire réparer il faudrait combien de temps?
Le vendeur:	Environ° dix jours.
Brian:	Pas possible. Je ne suis ici que pour une semaine. J'aurais voulu l'utiliser tout de suite.
Le vendeur:	Alors, c'est à vous de voir.° Tiens! Si° on changeait la pile?
Brian:	Pourquoi pas? J'aurais dû y penser moi-même.°
Le vendeur:	Voyons si j'ai la pile dont vous avez besoin. Oui, voilà. Maintenant essayons de faire marcher cet appareil. Quelle phrase voulez-vous essayer?
Brian:	Cherchez quelque chose de simple, par exemple, "Thank you."
Le vendeur:	Voilà. Vous avez le choix entre plusieurs expressions. Ça marche maintenant. Ce n'était qu'une mauvaise pile.
Brian:	Sans blague!° Si j'avais essayé le dictionnaire électronique avant de quitter le magasin, j'aurais évité° tous ces ennuis. Alors, je vous dois° combien?
Le vendeur:	Rien, Monsieur. Je vous rends ce service gratuitement parce que le dictionnaire est neuf.° J'aurais pu vous éviter tout ce tracas° si c'était moi qui vous avais vendu le dico.° Les clients peuvent toujours essayer les appareils avant de partir.
Brian:	Moi qui étais déçu,° maintenant ça va mieux. Ça me rend° très heureux. Merci mille fois, Monsieur. Au revoir.

gêner embêter; **jeter un coup d'œil** *to take a quick look;* **le mode d'emploi** *instructions;* **laissez-moi** permettez-moi de; **avoir raison** *to be right;* **environ** *about;* **C'est à vous de voir.** *It's up to you.;* **si** *what if;* **moi-même** *myself;* **Sans blague!** *No kidding!;* **éviter** *to avoid;* **devoir** *to owe;* **neuf, neuve** nouveau, nouvelle; **le tracas** *trouble;* **un dico** un dictionnaire; **déçu(e)** *disappointed;* **rendre** faire

---

Mettez ces huit phrases en ordre chronologique d'après le dialogue. Écrivez "1" pour la première phrase, "2" pour la deuxième phrase, etc.

1. Le vendeur change la pile.
2. Brian a trouvé un bon de réduction dans le journal.
3. Brian remercie le vendeur.
4. Brian rapporte le dictionnaire électronique au rayon des appareils électroniques.

Larousse LRE 1100
Le dico à tiroirs.
Définition et correction de plus de 400 000 mots et formes de mots (50 000 noms communs), déclinaisons de mots (masculin-féminin, singulier-pluriel), conjugaison de 6 000 verbes... et de plus, le rappel des 10 dernières recherches effectuées et une fonction hypertexte qui permet de surfer dans le dictionnaire : un mot contenu dans une définition pouvant être lui-même expliqué.
L'avis de la Fnac : un dictionnaire français tout électronique particulièrement riche.
Prix Fnac : 595 F

Teacher's Notes

1. Here are the forms of the orthographically changing verb **jeter**: **jette, jettes, jette, jetons, jetez** and **jettent.** 2. Tell students that **avoir raison** is an idiomatic **avoir** expression. 3. Point out that to express a wish or to make a suggestion, you can use **si + imparfait**, for example, **Si tu me prêtais ta voiture?** (*What if you lent me your car?*) 4. **Devoir**, meaning "to have to," was introduced on page 337 in the first level of *C'est à toi!* 5. **Rien** can be used as a one-word answer to a question. 6. **Neuf** means "brand-new," whereas **nouveau** means "new to you." The irregular feminine form of **neuf** is **neuve.** You may want to introduce the expression **Quoi de neuf?** (*What's new?*) Students may also be interested to learn the response **Rien de neuf.** (*Nothing's new.*) 7. **Dico** is slang for **dictionnaire.** 8. **Déçu(e)** comes from the verb **décevoir** (*to disappoint*) and is a false cognate. 9. **Rendre + adjectif** means "to make" + adjective, for example, **Les nouvelles me rendent heureux/heureuse.** (*The news makes me happy.*) **Rendre,** meaning "to hand in" or "to return," was introduced in Unit 6 in the third level of *C'est à toi!* Students have already learned the expressions **rendre visite (à), rendre un service** and **se rendre compte.**

Game

Original Sentences

To practice new vocabulary introduced in this unit, you might want to have students play this game. Prepare a set of note cards with a new word or expression on each one. Then divide the class into two teams. Call the first player from each team to the front of the room. Select the top card from the pile and read aloud the word or expression that you want the players to use in a sentence. Both players say a sentence using that word or expression. The student who correctly uses the new word or expression in a sentence earns a point for his or her team. If both sentences are correct, both teams win a point. When the first two players take their seats, a different player from each team takes a turn. The team with the most points at the end of the allotted time wins.

Après avoir payé à la caisse, on reçoit un ticket de caisse. (Créteil)

5. Brian a acheté un dictionnaire électronique à la Fnac.

6. Le vendeur cherche une phrase.

7. Brian est frustré parce que le dictionnaire ne marche pas.

8. Brian montre le ticket de caisse au vendeur.

---

2 | *Complétez chaque phrase avec l'expression convenable de la liste suivante d'après le dialogue.*

mode d'emploi	Midi	tracas	jette un coup d'œil
ticket de caisse	frustré	doit	justement

1. Le... est le sud de la France.

2. Améliorer son français, c'est... ce que Brian essayait de faire.

3. Brian n'est pas content de son achat; il est....

4. Pour rapporter quelque chose à la Fnac, il faut que Brian ait le...

5. Quand le vendeur... sur le dictionnaire électronique, il le regarde très vite.

6. Pour savoir faire marcher un appareil, Brian doit lire le...

7. Brian veut savoir s'il... de l'argent au vendeur.

8. Si Brian avait essayé le dictionnaire électronique avant de quitter le magasin, il aurait évité tout ce....

---

3 | *C'est à toi!*

1. Qu'est-ce que tu fais pour mieux parler français?

2. Est-ce que tu as acheté quelque chose qui t'aide quand tu étudies le français? Si oui, quoi?

3. Quand ta famille et toi, vous faites des achats au supermarché, est-ce que vous utilisez quelquefois des bons de réduction?

4. Après avoir acheté quelque chose, pour combien de temps est-ce que tu gardes le ticket de caisse?

5. Après avoir acheté un appareil électronique, est-ce que tu lis toujours le mode d'emploi avant d'utiliser l'appareil?

6. Qu'est-ce que tu fais quand tu ne sais pas faire marcher quelque chose?

7. Est-ce que tu as jamais acheté un appareil électronique qui n'a pas marché? Si oui, qu'est-ce que tu as fait?

8. Si tu rapportes au magasin un appareil qui ne marche pas, préfères-tu qu'on l'échange contre un autre appareil, qu'on le fasse réparer ou qu'on te rembourse?

La région du sud de la France s'appelle fréquemment le Midi. Au sud-est du Midi se trouve une des provinces les plus pittoresques du pays, la Provence. Sa frontière à l'ouest, c'est le Rhône, et à l'est, c'est l'Italie.

Enquête culturelle

Workbook Activity 11

Transparency 31

le Midi
l'Italie
le Rhône
Avignon
la Provence

Une des villes les plus intéressantes de Provence est Avignon. C'est une vieille ville située sur le Rhône. Elle est importante dans l'histoire religieuse du Moyen Âge pour son Palais des Papes, exemple de l'architecture gothique. Au 14ᵉ siècle sept papes (chefs de l'église catholique) ont quitté Rome pour habiter cet édifice, qui était aussi une forteresse. Les papes ont déménagé à Avignon pour être plus indépendants et pour avoir plus d'autorité. En ce temps-là, avec l'arrivée des papes, la ville d'Avignon était une des plus grandes d'Europe. Le Palais des Papes existe toujours à Avignon et sert de site pour un festival d'art dramatique pendant l'été, le Festival d'Avignon. On y présente des pièces de théâtre, des ballets et de la musique classique.

Palais des Papes d'Avignon

Ouvert tous les jours, toute l'année sauf Noël et Jour de l'an.
Renseignements :
Tel : 90 27 50 74
Fax : 90 86 36 12

Ce billet, valable pour une seule visite, n'est ni repris ni échangé. L'usage des appareils photos et des caméras est interdit.

RESA SCO VIS GUID
Prix : 28.00
180399-RSC28 09:30 RES
18-03-99 09:07 CASE01 T: 1 S: 5

RMG Palais des Papes
BP 149 - 84008 Avignon Cédex 01

Cloître de Benoît XII [Photo: Mairie d'Avignon]

Les papes ont habité le Palais des Papes de 1309 à 1376. (Avignon)

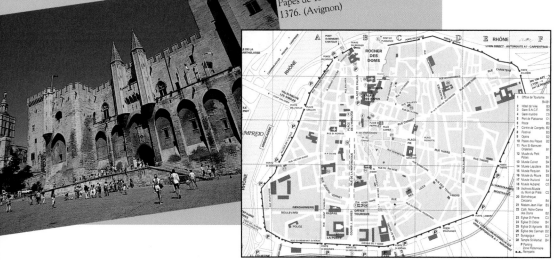

Teacher's Note

Le Palais des Papes was built on the high rocky plateau called **le Rocher des Doms**. Next to the palace are the 12th century Romanesque cathedral **Notre-Dame-des-Doms** and the papal gardens. Built for protection, the palace is a fortress containing two distinct parts: the **Palais Vieux** and the **Palais Neuf**.

Teacher's Notes

1. Cognates in this reading include **région**, **fréquemment**, **pittoresques**, **Palais**, **architecture**, **gothique**, **papes**, **édifice**, **forteresse**, **autorité**, **existe**, **site**, **festival**, **dramatique**, **présente**, **classique**, **épidémie**, **peste**, **mortelle**, **attaquait**, **danse**, **joie**, **image**, **folklorique**, **mélodique** and **macabre**. 2. Students learned about **la Provence** in Unit 3 in the second level of *C'est à toi!* 3. The Rhône is a French and Swiss river. It is the most powerful of all French rivers. 4. Avignon, the capital of the department of Vaucluse, can be reached from Paris by TGV in three hours. A major French tourist center with a population of over 89,500, it is also an important commercial center for grain, leather and wine. The vines that produce the local Côtes du Rhône wine have been cultivated in the area for over 2,000 years. 5. Avignon became a thriving city under the Romans, but it declined during the Germanic invasions of the 5th and 6th centuries. It belonged successively to the kingdoms of Burgundy and Arles and to the counties of Provence and Toulouse. In 1226 Louis VIII destroyed the city for having supported the heretical Albigensians. In 1309 Pope Clement V decided to make Avignon his residence. This period, known as the Babylonian Captivity, made Avignon the center of Western Christendom. When Pope Gregory XI returned to Rome in 1377, Avignon became the residence of the two antipopes Clement VII and Benedict XIII during the Great Schism of the Catholic Church (1378-1417). The papacy held Avignon until 1791, when it was annexed to France.

Answers

4 Possible answers:

1. Le Midi est la partie sud de la France.
2. La Provence est une des provinces les plus pittoresques de France.
3. Le Rhône est sa frontière à l'ouest, et l'Italie est sa frontière à l'est.
4. Avignon se trouve sur le Rhône.
5. Sept papes habitaient à Avignon au 14ᵉ siècle.
6. Avignon était une des plus grandes villes d'Europe au 14ᵉ siècle.
7. La peste tuait les Avignonnais au 14ᵉ siècle.
8. Ils dansaient sur le pont Saint-Bénezet parce qu'ils étaient contents de traverser le fleuve grâce à ce pont et sortir de la ville où il y avait la peste.
9. La chanson évoque les Français qui sont morts à l'époque de la peste.
10. Le Festival d'Avignon a lieu chaque été.

Teacher's Note

Le pont Saint-Bénezet was built because a young shepherd named Bénezet had a vision in which an angel appeared to him, telling him to build a bridge across the Rhône. It took eight years to complete and originally had 22 arches. People danced on an island below the bridge, but over the years, **sous** became **"sur"** le pont d'Avignon.

C'est au Moyen Âge qu'une épidémie de peste, maladie mortelle, attaquait la région. Beaucoup d'Avignonnais sont morts de la peste, mais quelques Avignonnais ont réussi à sortir de la ville en prenant le pont Saint-Bénezet pour traverser le Rhône. Ceux qui ont pu partir d'Avignon et donc se protéger de la peste étaient tellement contents qu'ils ont fêté leur départ de la ville par une danse de joie sur le pont. C'est l'image de cette danse qui a donné la chanson "Sur le pont d'Avignon":

Le pont d'Avignon du 12ᵉ siècle n'a aujourd'hui que quatre de ses 22 arches originales.

> Sur le pont d'Avignon
> L'on y danse, l'on y danse,
> Sur le pont d'Avignon
> L'on y danse tout en rond.

D'un côté cette chanson est une chanson folklorique avec son air simple et mélodique. De l'autre côté c'est une danse macabre qui nous rappelle les Français qui sont morts à l'époque de la peste. La chanson reste pourtant populaire même aujourd'hui parmi les Français et ceux qui apprennent la langue.

4 | *Répondez aux questions suivantes.*

1. Comment s'appelle la partie sud de la France?
2. Qu'est-ce que c'est que la Provence?
3. Quelles sont les frontières de la Provence?
4. Où la ville d'Avignon est-elle située?
5. Qui habitait à Avignon au 14ᵉ siècle?
6. Au 14ᵉ siècle, quelle ville française était une des plus grandes d'Europe?
7. Au 14ᵉ siècle, quelle maladie tuait les Avignonnais?
8. Pourquoi les Avignonnais dansaient-ils sur le pont Saint-Bénezet?
9. Qu'évoque la chanson "Sur le pont d'Avignon"?
10. De nos jours qu'est-ce qui se passe à Avignon chaque été?

Lisez des renseignements d'un dépliant qui décrit des attractions de la ville d'Avignon. Puis répondez aux questions qui suivent.

Avignon, site stratégique dans la vallée du Rhône, doit son origine au Rocher des Doms. Avec la venue des papes au XIVème, la ville devient une seconde Rome. L'art l'enrichira aux XVII et XVIIIèmes, et elle demeurera terre pontificale jusqu'à la révolution.

■ **PALAIS DES PAPES**

place du palais   tél.   90 27 50 74/71
                   fax   90 86 61 21

• du 2/11 au 31/03: 9h – 12h45/14h – 18h
• du 1/04 au 1/11: 9h – 19h (festival 9h – 21h)
• du 5/08 au 30/09: 9h – 20h

Caisses fermées 45 mn avant. Visites guidées toute l'année. Fermé 1/01 et 25/12.

Forteresse gothique du XIVe siècle, où séjournèrent sept papes et deux antipapes. La cour d'honneur abrite le festival depuis 1947.

■ **PONT ST BÉNEZET**

rue Ferruce   tél.   90 85 60 16
tous les jours sauf 25/12, 1/01, 1/05 et 14/07

• du 1/11 au 29/02: 9h – 13h/14h – 17h sauf lundi
• octobre et mars: 9h – 13h/14h – 17h tous les jours
• du 1/04 au 30/09: 9h – 18h30 tous les jours

Le pont d'Avignon fut construit au XIIe siècle, détruit plusieurs fois par les crues du Rhône, il fut reconstruit à plusieurs reprises jusqu'au XVIIe. La chapelle St Nicolas est dédiée au patron des mariniers. Il abrite le musée du costume rhodanien.

■ **MUSÉE LAPIDAIRE**

27, rue de la République   tél.   90 85 75 38

• 10h – 12h/14h – 18h, sauf mardi, 1/01, 1/05, 25/12

Archéologie antique dans une belle chapelle baroque du XVIIe.

■ **MUSÉE THÉODORE AUBANEL**

7 place St Pierre   tél.   90 82 95 54

Musée privé ouvert au public sur rendez-vous. Visites gratuites et commentées.

Fermé J.F., samedi, dimanche et août.

Littérature provençale et histoire de l'imprimerie.

■ **MUSÉE REQUIEN**

67, rue Joseph Vernet   tél.   90 82 43 51

• du mardi au samedi: 9h – 12h/14h – 18h
• gratuit

Histoire naturelle

Le Festival d'Avignon

Créé en 1947 par Jean Vilar, le Festival d'Avignon est devenu le rendez-vous mondial du spectacle vivant. Il se déroule généralement entre le 10 juillet et le 5 août. Festival de création, son programme annuel est établi autour de l'actualité du théâtre, de la danse et de la musique. Il accueille 120 000 spectateurs. Un avant-programme est disponible chaque année à partir du 15 mars, alors que le programme définitif est diffusé dès le 10 mai.

Le Festival off

Il s'est développé à partir de la fin des années 60. Près de 100 lieux, plus de 350 spectacles. Des "jeunes compagnies" venues de toutes les régions de France et du monde entier. La jeune création, très présente dans les rues de la ville, crée l'atmosphère festive unique qu'apprécie un large public de plus en plus nombreux autour de cette centaine de lieux ouverts à l'occasion de cette immense confrontation artistique où sont représentées toutes les disciplines du Spectacle Vivant. (Avant-programme vers le 15 mai)

---

1. Pourquoi est-ce que la ville d'Avignon s'appelle "une seconde Rome"?
2. Si vous visitez le Palais des Papes en juin, à quelle heure y a-t-il des visites guidées?
3. Où le Festival d'Avignon a-t-il lieu?
4. Quelles sont les dates du festival?
5. Combien de personnes assistent au festival chaque année?
6. Comment s'appelle le festival alternatif où jouent les jeunes compagnies théâtrales?
7. Comment s'appelle la petite chapelle qui se trouve sur le pont Saint-Bénezet?
8. Si vous vous intéressez à l'archéologie, quel musée faut-il visiter?
9. Quel musée est fermé pendant les vacances d'août?
10. Quel est le tarif d'entrée au musée d'histoire naturelle?

Answers

5 Possible answers:

1. Avignon s'appelle "une seconde Rome" parce que les papes y ont habité.
2. En juin il y a des visites guidées au Palais des Papes entre 9h00 et 19h00.
3. Le Festival d'Avignon a lieu à la cour d'honneur du Palais des Papes.
4. Le festival se déroule entre le 10 juillet et le 5 août.
5. Il y a 120.000 personnes qui y assistent chaque année.
6. Le Festival off est le festival alternatif.
7. La chapelle Saint-Nicolas est sur le pont Saint-Bénezet.
8. Il faut visiter le Musée Lapidaire.
9. Le Musée Théodore Aubanel est fermé pendant les vacances d'août.
10. L'entrée au musée d'histoire naturelle est gratuite.

Workbook Activities 12-13

Teacher's Notes

1. Briefly review the conditional tense forms of **avoir** and **être**, which were reviewed on page 189 in the third level of *C'est à toi!* 2. Have students name the two compound tenses they have already learned (the **passé composé** and the **plus-que-parfait**). 3. You may want to point out the English equivalents of the past conditional of **devoir**, **pouvoir** and **vouloir**: **Vous auriez dû rapporter votre ticket de caisse.** (*You should have brought back your receipt.*) **Vous auriez pu me rembourser le prix.** (*You could have reimbursed me the price.*) **J'aurais voulu l'échanger.** (*I would have liked to exchange it.*) 4. In the past conditional, the agreement rules for the past participle are the same as in the **passé composé**, for example, **Tu aurais réparé la télé./Tu l'aurais réparée.**

Journal personnel

The song "Sur le pont d'Avignon" recalls the terrible flight of the residents of Avignon from the plague that ravaged their city in the 14th century. Some contemporary songs also commemorate historical events. For example, upon the death of Diana, Princess of Wales, who was inspired to write a song about her? What lyrics of that song do you remember? Why do you think it became so popular? Do you know to whom the singer's original version of "Candle in the Wind" pays tribute? What songs did your parents grow up with that tell about a person, place or historical event? Can you think of any American folk songs or popular songs, similar to "Sur le pont d'Avignon," that make us remember something or someone?

Structure

Past conditional tense

The past conditional (**le conditionnel passé**) is a tense used to tell what would have happened in the past if certain conditions had been met. Like the **passé composé** and the **plus-que-parfait**, the past conditional consists of a helping verb and a past participle. To form the past conditional, use the conditional tense of the helping verb **avoir** or **être** and the past participle of the main verb. Agreement of the past participle in the past conditional is the same as in the **passé composé** and the **plus-que-parfait**.

"J'aurais adoré être jardinier!"

	réparer	*se lever*
je/j'	aurais réparé	me serais levé(e)
tu	aurais réparé	te serais levé(e)
il/elle/on	aurait réparé	se serait levé(e)
nous	aurions réparé	nous serions levé(e)s
vous	auriez réparé	vous seriez levé(e)(s)(es)
ils/elles	auraient réparé	se seraient levé(e)s

J'aurais voulu l'utiliser tout de suite.

I would have wanted to use it right away.

Le client ne **serait** pas **parti** du magasin sans avoir lu le mode d'emploi.

The customer would not have left the store without having read the instructions.

J'aurais voulu vous rejoindre pour un match de tennis. Malheureusement, il pleut.

Game

Past Conditional Toss

On the board write the infinitive of a verb that you want to practice in the past conditional, such as **s'adapter**. Then toss a ball to a student as you call out a subject pronoun, such as **je**. This student says the appropriate past conditional form, for example, **je me serais adapté(e)**, then tosses the ball to another student while calling out a different subject pronoun. After four or five students have played with the first verb, write a new verb on the board. The student holding the ball begins the next round.

Pratique

Dites ce que ces personnes auraient fait si elles avaient voyagé à Avignon avec Brian et ses amis, selon les illustrations et les verbes indiqués.

1. tout le monde/danser

2. les jeunes/visiter

3. Serge et toi, vous/participer

4. Jeanne et Françoise/aller

5. Jacqueline/s'intéresser

6. tu/faire du shopping

7. je/améliorer

8. nous/s'amuser

Modèle:

Jean-Marc et son amie/flâner
Jean-Marc et son amie auraient flâné dans les rues.

Nous nous serions reposés au jardin du Palais des Papes.

Cooperative Group Practice

À Paris

Put students in small groups of four or five. Prepare a set of note cards for each group, writing sentences that express what Chantal did during a recent stay in Paris. The first student reads the top card in the stack, for example, **Je me suis arrêtée au kiosque à journaux**. Then the rest of the members of the group take turns giving a sentence in the past conditional, expressing what they would have done instead, for example, **Je me serais arrêté(e) à la pâtisserie**. When everyone in the group has said a sentence, the second student plays the role of Chantal by reading the second card in the stack, and the process begins again. You might have students record a point for themselves each time they say a correct sentence and record the points at the end of the activity. Here are some other sentences to include on the note cards: 1. Je suis allée au musée Picasso. 2. J'ai déjeuné au fast-food. 3. J'ai fait une promenade dans le bois de Vincennes. 4. J'ai fait du shopping aux Galeries Lafayette. 5. J'ai visité la tour Eiffel. 6. Je suis rentrée à l'hôtel à pied.

Answers

6 Possible answers:

1. Tout le monde aurait dansé sur le pont d'Avignon.
2. Les jeunes auraient visité le Palais des Papes.
3. Serge et toi, vous auriez participé au Festival d'Avignon.
4. Jeanne et Françoise seraient allées au concert de rock.
5. Jacqueline se serait intéressée au ballet.
6. Tu aurais fait du shopping à la Fnac.
7. J'aurais amélioré mon français.
8. Nous nous serions beaucoup amusés.

Paired Practice

À ta place

Put students in pairs. Prepare a set of note cards for each pair expressing situations using infinitives, for example, **arriver à l'école en retard/se lever tard**. Student A forms a sentence in the **passé composé** with **parce que** to express his or her problem situation, for example, **Je suis arrivé(e) à l'école en retard parce que je me suis levé(e) tard**. Student B expresses what he or she would have done in Student A's place, for example, **À ta place, je me serais levé(e) tôt**. Then Student B takes a card and forms a sentence that Student A responds to. Students alternate in this fashion until all the cards have been used. Here are some other situations that you might use: 1. tomber/ne pas faire attention en faisant de la planche à neige 2. ne pas pouvoir acheter le manuel du cours/dépenser trop d'argent dans un restaurant cher 3. rater l'examen/ne pas étudier 4. avoir un accident de voiture/rouler trop vite 5. se fouler la cheville/se dépêcher

Audiocassette/CD Activity 8

Answers

7 Je n'aurais pas quitté un restaurant sans avoir payé l'addition.

Je ne serais pas allé(e) au cinéma sans avoir su quel film on jouait.

Je ne serais pas entré(e) dans un théâtre sans avoir acheté de billet.

Je n'aurais pas choisi un appareil électronique sans l'avoir utilisé.

Je n'aurais pas envoyé une lettre sans y avoir mis des timbres.

Je n'aurais pas acheté une voiture sans l'avoir conduite.

Je ne serais pas parti(e) sans avoir dit "au revoir."

8 1. Aurais-tu vu le pont d'Avignon? Et toi, aurais-tu vu le pont d'Avignon?

2. Serais-tu allé(e) sur la côte d'Azur? Et toi, serais-tu allé(e) sur la côte d'Azur?

3. Aurais-tu passé du temps au bord de la mer? Et toi, aurais-tu passé du temps au bord de la mer?

4. Aurais-tu pris des photos? Et toi, aurais-tu pris des photos?

5. Aurais-tu envoyé des cartes postales à ta famille? Et toi, aurais-tu envoyé des cartes postales à ta famille?

6. Serais-tu resté(e) dans une auberge de jeunesse? Et toi, serais-tu resté(e) dans une auberge de jeunesse?

7. Serais-tu sorti(e) tous les soirs? Et toi, serais-tu sorti(e) tous les soirs?

8. Aurais-tu essayé d'améliorer ton français? Et toi, aurais-tu essayé d'améliorer ton français?

Students' responses to these questions will vary.

Modèle:

Je n'aurais pas mangé dans un restaurant sans avoir regardé le menu.

7 *Dites ce que vous n'auriez pas fait sans avoir fait quelque chose d'autre. Formez huit phrases logiques en utilisant le conditionnel passé. Choisissez un élément des colonnes A et B pour chaque phrase. Suivez le modèle.*

A	B
manger dans un restaurant	sans avoir dit "au revoir"
quitter un restaurant	sans l'avoir utilisé
aller au cinéma	sans avoir regardé le menu
entrer dans un théâtre	sans avoir su quel film on jouait
choisir un appareil électronique	
envoyer une lettre	sans l'avoir conduite
acheter une voiture	sans y avoir mis des timbres
partir	sans avoir payé l'addition
	sans avoir acheté de billet

Aurais-tu choisi un appareil électronique sans l'avoir utilisé? (Créteil)

Modèle:

louer un vélo
Élève A: Aurais-tu loué un vélo?
Élève B: Bien sûr, j'en aurais loué un. Et toi, aurais-tu loué un vélo?
Élève A: Non, je n'en aurais pas loué.

8 *Avec un(e) partenaire, parlez de ce que vous auriez fait ou pas si vous aviez eu l'occasion d'aller dans le Midi avec Brian et ses amis. Suivez le modèle.*

1. voir le pont d'Avignon
2. aller sur la côte d'Azur
3. passer du temps au bord de la mer
4. prendre des photos
5. envoyer des cartes postales à ta famille
6. rester dans une auberge de jeunesse
7. sortir tous les soirs
8. essayer d'améliorer ton français

Sur quoi auriez-vous aimé garder le secret?

Game

Le baseball

On an overhead transparency write a list of sentences using the past conditional and place a new noun or pronoun subject after each one, for example, **Je serais allé(e) dans le Midi. (vous)** Divide the class into two teams, for example, **les tigres** and **les couguars**. Then draw two baseball diamonds on the board, one for each team. The first student on the first team says a sentence using the noun or pronoun subject in parentheses, for example, **Vous seriez allé(e)(s)(es) dans le Midi.** If the student changes the sentence correctly, he or she advances to first base, designated by marking a stick figure along the side of the base, and the next player on that team takes a turn. If the student incorrectly changes the sentence, he or she stays at home plate and the first player from the second team takes a turn. A run is scored after a team gets four correct answers, thus arriving at home plate. The team with the most runs wins.

Past conditional tense in sentences with *si*

Use the past conditional tense along with **si** and the **plus-que-parfait** to tell what would have happened *if* something else had already happened or *if* some condition contrary to reality had been met.

si	+	plus-que-parfait	past conditional

Si j'avais essayé le dictionnaire électronique avant de quitter le magasin, j'**aurais évité** tous ces ennuis.

If I had tried the electronic dictionary before leaving the store, I would have avoided all these problems.

J'**aurais pu** vous éviter tout ce tracas si c'était moi qui vous avais vendu le dico.

I would have been able to save you all this trouble if I had sold you the dictionary.

Note in the examples above that the phrase with **si** and the **plus-que-parfait** can either begin or end the sentence.

Pratique

Dites ce que les personnes suivantes auraient fait si elles avaient eu ce qui est illustré. Suivez le modèle.

1. je/aller à la Fnac

3. Édouard et moi, nous/vouloir l'utiliser tout de suite

2. tu/faire marcher l'appareil électronique

4. Olivier et toi, vous/régler l'affaire

Modèle:

Francine/payer moins
Si Francine avait eu un bon d'achat, elle aurait payé moins.

Si vous étiez allée au Festival d'Avignon, vous vous seriez amusée.

Workbook Activities 14-15

Answers

9 1. Si j'avais eu de l'argent, je serais allé(e) à la Fnac.
2. Si tu avais eu des piles, tu aurais fait marcher l'appareil électronique.
3. Si Édouard et moi, nous avions eu un dictionnaire électronique, nous aurions voulu l'utiliser tout de suite.
4. Si Olivier et toi, vous aviez eu un ticket de caisse, vous auriez réglé l'affaire.
5. Si les ados avaient eu un accident, ils auraient téléphoné au SAMU.
6. Si mon père avait eu des pastilles, il se serait dépêché d'en prendre.
7. Si Nadia avait eu une ordonnance, elle se serait arrêtée à la pharmacie.
8. Si tu avais eu des béquilles, tu aurais pu marcher.

Teacher's Notes

1. You may want to review the other two types of **si** clauses that students have learned to form. The future tense in sentences with **si** was presented in Unit 6. The conditional tense in sentences with **si** was presented in Unit 7. 2. The past conditional occurs only in the result clause. It is never used in the **si** clause. 3. The same tense sequence applies to the expression **même si**, for example, **Même si vous aviez bien lu le mode d'emploi, le dico électronique n'aurait pas marché**. 4. The condition may be expressed by a phrase rather than a **si** clause, for example, **Avec plus d'argent, je serais resté(e) à Saint-Martin pendant un mois**.

Cooperative Group Practice

Sentence Completion

Put students in small groups of four or five. Give each group a worksheet that you have prepared with six incomplete sentences using **si** and the **plus-que-parfait**, for example, **Si je ne m'étais pas cassé la jambe, j'....** Each group writes as many logical completions as they can that use the past conditional, for example, **Si je ne m'étais pas cassé la jambe, j'(aurais joué au foot, aurais fait de la planche à neige, aurais couru, aurais skié)**. Here are five other incomplete sentences that you might use: 1. S'il avait fait beau le weekend dernier, nous.... 2. Si Napoléon avait vécu au temps de César, il.... 3. Si mes camarades de classe étaient allés en France l'été dernier, ils.... 4. Si vous n'aviez pas dépensé tout votre argent, vous.... 5. Si tu avais eu un accident, tu....

Answers

10 Possible answers:

Karine serait arrivée à Fontainebleau à 10h00 si le train était parti à l'heure.

Je me serais fait mal si j'étais tombé(e) en descendant du train.

Tu aurais eu besoin de béquilles si tu t'étais foulé la cheville.

Brian aurait compris le problème s'il avait jeté un coup d'œil.

Nous aurions fait réparer le dictionnaire électronique s'il n'avait pas marché.

Vous auriez échangé votre nouvel appareil si vous aviez gardé le ticket de caisse.

Le vendeur leur aurait remboursé le prix si les clients n'avaient pas été contents de leur achat.

Les clients auraient été très heureux si la vendeuse leur avait rendu un service.

Teacher's Note

Have students complete the following sentences with a logical verb in the past conditional to tell what would have happened to Brian at Fnac. A. Si Brian avait essayé le dico électronique avant de partir de la Fnac, il.... B. Si Brian n'avait pas rapporté son ticket de caisse, le vendeur.... C. Si Brian n'avait pas trouvé de bon de réduction, il.... D. Si le vendeur n'avait pas jeté un coup d'œil sur le dico électronique, Brian....

5. les ados/téléphoner au SAMU

7. Nadia/s'arrêter à la pharmacie

6. mon père/se dépêcher d'en prendre

8. tu/pouvoir marcher

10 *Formez huit phrases logiques qui expliquent ce qui se serait passé s'il y avait eu certaines conditions. Choisissez un élément des colonnes A et B pour chaque phrase. Suivez le modèle.*

Modèle:
Patrick aurait joué au foot s'il avait eu un ballon.

A	B
Patrick/jouer au foot	tu/se fouler la cheville
Karine/arriver à Fontainebleau à 10h00	je/tomber en descendant du train
	il/avoir un ballon
je/se faire mal	les clients/ne pas être contents de leur achat
tu/avoir besoin de béquilles	le train/partir à l'heure
Brian/comprendre le problème	la vendeuse/leur rendre un service
nous/faire réparer le dictionnaire électronique	vous/garder le ticket de caisse
vous/échanger votre nouvel appareil	il/jeter un coup d'œil
le vendeur/leur rembourser le prix	il/ne pas marcher
les clients/être très heureux	

Si Caro avait eu un plâtre, ses amis auraient écrit dessus (*on it*).

Game

Matching Cards

Prepare a note card for each student in class. Write a clause with **si** on one card, and the past conditional on another, for example, **Si j'avais eu mon ordonnance,/je serais allé(e) à la pharmacie.** Mix up the cards, then hand one to each student. Students circulate around the room to find the matching half of their sentence. When all the matches have been found, students return to their seats and one student in each pair reads aloud the entire sentence. You might also take a card if there is an uneven number of students in the class.

Avec un(e) partenaire, posez des questions sur ce que vous auriez fait si les choses indiquées s'étaient passées. Puis répondez aux questions. Suivez le modèle.

1. tu/te réveiller très tard
2. tu/avoir mal à la gorge
3. ta voiture/tomber en panne
4. tu/perdre tes devoirs
5. quelqu'un/te voler ton argent
6. tes parents/ne pas te permettre de sortir
7. tu/gagner mille dollars
8. tu/passer une semaine dans le Midi

Modèle:

tu/te casser le bras

Élève A: Qu'est-ce que tu aurais fait si tu t'étais cassé le bras?

Élève B: Si je m'étais cassé le bras, je serais allé(e) à la salle des urgences. Et toi, qu'est-ce que tu aurais fait si tu t'étais cassé le bras?

Élève A: Si je m'étais cassé le bras, j'aurais téléphoné au SAMU.

Qu'est-ce que vous auriez fait si vous aviez perdu vos chèques de voyage?

Communication

Avec un(e) partenaire, jouez les rôles de deux personnes dans un grand magasin. La première personne joue le rôle d'une vendeuse qui travaille au rayon des appareils électroniques. La deuxième personne joue le rôle d'un client qui y a acheté quelque chose qui ne marche pas. Pendant votre conversation:

1. La vendeuse demande si elle peut aider le client.
2. Le client lui montre ce qu'il a acheté et explique que l'appareil ne marche pas.
3. La vendeuse lui demande s'il a gardé le ticket de caisse.
4. La vendeuse lui demande si elle peut jeter un coup d'œil.
5. La vendeuse confirme qu'il y a un problème.
6. Le client dit pourquoi il est déçu et demande ce qu'il peut faire.
7. La vendeuse offre deux suggestions pour régler l'affaire.
8. Le client choisit la solution qu'il préfère.
9. Le client demande combien il lui doit.
10. La vendeuse lui dit que ce service est gratuit.
11. Le client remercie la vendeuse.

On apprécie tous les vendeurs ou les vendeuses qui nous rendent un service, comme celui de l'Activité 12. Mais avez-vous jamais dû discuter un problème avec un vendeur ou une vendeuse qui était impoli(e) et ne vous a pas aidé(e)? Écrivez un paragraphe dans lequel vous décrivez ce problème, tout ce qui s'est passé pendant votre conversation avec la personne impolie et comment vous vous êtes senti(e) en quittant le magasin. Qu'est-ce que vous auriez fait si vous aviez su tout cela à l'avance? (Si vous n'avez jamais été dans une situation comme celle-ci, vous pouvez en créer une en vous servant de votre imagination.)

Audiocassette/CD
Sur la bonne piste

Advanced Placement

Teacher's Note

In this **Sur la bonne piste** section, students learn how to read instructions in French.

Sur la bonne piste

In this unit you will learn some tips on how to read instructions in French.

- First, make sure the instructions you are reading or following match your purpose. For example, if you are looking at a VCR instruction manual to learn how to record a program, you would look for the section on recording, not for the section on connecting the VCR to your TV.

- Second, think about the kinds of new words that you will need to understand. When reading a VCR manual, for example, you can expect to see some electronic terms with which you are most likely unfamiliar because they belong to a specialized, technical vocabulary. Remember to look for cognates, words that you recognize because they look like English words. Try to spot familiar stems (**racines**) in new words so that you can guess their meaning. For example, in **refroidir**, you see the stem **froid**, so you can guess that the verb means "to cool." But be prepared to use your French/English dictionary to look up key words that are repeated throughout the instructions if you can't figure them out on your own.

- Third, use any illustrations or photos to help you understand each step in the process. Pictures provide clues that make instructions more understandable.

- Finally, visualize each step. If it's clear in your mind what you must do first, second, third, etc., you will understand the directions more easily.

Now apply this strategy as you read the recipe for a French dessert.

---

14 | *Avant de lire la recette* (recipe), *répondez aux questions suivantes.*
1. Est-ce que tu aimes faire la cuisine?
2. Quels plats est-ce que tu sais préparer?
3. La bonne cuisine fait partie de toutes les cultures. Quelle cuisine préfères-tu? Pourquoi?

Gâteau renversé aux poires caramélisées

les ingrédients

           2 ou 3 poires mûres

pour le caramel: 100 g de sucre
           2 cuillerées à soupe d'eau

pour la pâte: 2 œufs
           100 g de sucre en poudre
           125 g de farine
           60 g de beurre
           1/2 sachet de levure chimique

Cross-curricular

Metric Conversions

Ask a math or home economics instructor to give a lesson to your students on how to make metric conversions. Then have students convert the metric measurements in the recipe to our system. Students should end up with these equivalents:

100 g = 2/3 c.

125 g = 1 c.

60 g = 5 Tbsp.

½ sachet = 1/4 tsp.

Finally, have students make the **Gâteau renversé aux poires caramélisées** at home or in the home economics kitchen using these equivalents.

Dans une petite casserole, préparez un caramel blond clair. Mélangez le sucre et l'eau à température élevée jusqu'à ce que le sucre soit fondu, brun clair et transparent.

Puis versez immédiatement le caramel dans un moule. Préparez la pâte. Puis mélangez les œufs avec le sucre en poudre.

Lorsque le mélange est mousseux,

ajoutez la farine et la levure,

puis le beurre fondu. Pelez les poires; coupez-les en fines tranches après avoir enlevé le cœur et les pépins.

Ensuite disposez les tranches en corolle sur le caramel.

F

Versez la pâte sur les poires sans les déplacer,

G

et couvrez les fruits uniformément.

H

Faites cuire à 220°C jusqu'à ce que la pâte soit dorée. Piquez la pâte avec la pointe d'un cou-teau. Si le couteau est taché de pâte quand vous l'enlevez, cuisez le gâteau pendant quelques minutes de plus. Si le couteau est propre, sortez le gâteau du four.

I

Démoulez le gâteau quand il est encore chaud. Couvrez le moule avec une grande assiette. Mettez des gants, tenez le moule et l'assiette ensemble fermement et retournez-les de sorte que le gâteau tombe dans l'assiette.

Laissez refroidir quelques minutes et vous serez prêt à servir.

Teacher's Note

Before students read the recipe, you may want to review the formation of the imperative, which was presented on page 296 in the first level of *C'est à toi!* and reviewed on page 79 in the second level.

Transparency 32

Answers

15 Possible answers:

1. On prépare un gâteau renversé aux poires caramélisées.
2. Deux nouveaux mots qui ressemblent aux mots anglais sont "transparent" et "uniformément."
3. Un nouveau mot qui est facile à comprendre est "cuillerées à soupe." En anglais, c'est "tablespoons."
4. Cinq mots clés dans la recette sont "farine," "levure," "mélanger," "verser" et "moule."
5. On a besoin de poires pour faire ce dessert.
6. Les ingrédients pour le caramel sont 100 g de sucre et deux cuillerées à soupe d'eau.
7. Ensuite on prépare la pâte.
8. On les coupe en fines tranches.
9. On les couvre uniformément.
10. On fait cuire le gâteau à 220°C.
11. Il faut piquer la pâte avec la pointe d'un couteau pour voir si le gâteau est prêt.
12. On couvre le moule avec une assiette, puis on retourne l'assiette et le moule de sorte que le gâteau tombe dans l'assiette.

16 1. 6
2. 10
3. 3
4. 4
5. 8
6. 2
7. 5
8. 9
9. 1
10. 7

17 1. 2
2. 6
3. 5
4. 1
5. 7
6. 4
7. 3

15 Répondez aux questions suivantes.

1. Qu'est-ce qu'on prépare?
2. Quels sont deux nouveaux mots que tu as compris tout de suite parce qu'ils ressemblent aux mots anglais?
3. Quel nouveau mot est facile à comprendre parce que tu reconnais sa racine? Quelle est la définition de ce mot en anglais?
4. Quels sont cinq mots clés (*key*) dans la recette que tu devrais chercher dans ton dictionnaire?
5. De quel fruit a-t-on besoin pour faire ce dessert?
6. Quels sont les ingrédients pour le caramel?
7. Après avoir fait le caramel, qu'est-ce qu'on prépare ensuite?
8. Comment coupe-t-on les poires?
9. Comment couvre-t-on les fruits?
10. À quelle température est-ce qu'on fait cuire le gâteau?
11. Pourquoi faut-il piquer la pâte avec la pointe d'un couteau?
12. Comment démoule-t-on le gâteau?

16 Mettez les instructions suivantes en ordre chronologique d'après la recette. Écrivez "1" pour la première phrase, "2" pour la deuxième phrase, etc.

1. Disposez les tranches en corolle sur le caramel.
2. Laissez refroidir quelques minutes.
3. Ajoutez la farine et la levure.
4. Pelez les poires.
5. Faites cuire à 220°C.
6. Mélangez les œufs avec le sucre en poudre.
7. Enlevez le cœur et les pépins des poires.
8. Piquez la pâte avec la pointe d'un couteau.
9. Préparez le caramel.
10. Couvrez les poires avec la pâte.

17 Voici les instructions pour faire un masque de carnaval. Elles sont accompagnées d'illustrations à la page suivante. Les instructions sont numérotées correctement, mais les illustrations ne sont pas en ordre. D'abord, lisez les instructions en vous servant des mots qui ressemblent aux mots anglais. Puis, cherchez les mots clés que vous ne comprenez pas dans votre dictionnaire. Enfin, mettez les illustrations en ordre chronologique.

Pour faire un masque simple	
Le matériel:	
du carton-pâte (46 cm de haut x 30,5 cm de large)	des marqueurs
un crayon	du ruban adhésif
une agrafeuse	des boutons
des agrafes	des feuilles
des ciseaux	des couleurs
de la ficelle ou un élastique étroit	des plumes

Teacher's Notes

1. Some new words used in the recipe and cognates not found in the end vocabulary of *C'est à toi!* are used in Activities 15 and 16.
2. Optional activity. Have students videotape a cooking lesson. First, tell students to select a favorite recipe and convert the measurements to the metric system. Then, tell them to break down the recipe into easy steps and write a script. Have students practice making their favorite recipe at home and bring in their finished dish. Then videotape each student preparing and mixing the ingredients in class or the home economics kitchen. At the end of their "show," students can pull out the finished dish that they prepared at home to show the class what it should look like. You may want to have a taste test and award first-, second- and third-place ribbons to the winners.
3. Optional activity. Bring to class a **mode d'emploi** that uses infinitives rather than imperatives. Then have students rewrite the instructions for the recipe on pages 410-11 or the mask on page 413 using infinitives.

1. Pliez la feuille de carton-pâte en deux.
2. Pliez la feuille encore une fois pour qu'elle soit divisée en quatre.
3. Dépliez la feuille et tenez-la contre votre visage de sorte que la ligne la plus longue vous coupe le visage en deux verticalement, et la ligne la plus courte vous coupe les yeux horizontalement. Indiquez où sont les yeux avec un crayon. Coupez des trous de 2,54 cm de large, mais faites attention que les trous ne soient pas à plus de 1,9 cm du pli au centre de la feuille.
4. Dépliez la feuille de sorte que vous puissiez voir à travers les trous. Indiquez où sont le nez et la bouche avec un crayon, et découpez des trous avec les ciseaux.
5. En pliant, dépliant et coupant en plusieurs sens, vous pouvez créer la silhouette désirée aux bords du masque. Pour sculpter le masque, vous pouvez couper les bords et les joindre avec des agrafes. Couvrez les agrafes avec du ruban adhésif pour que cela ne vous coupe pas.
6. Faites un trou de chaque côté du masque, à 1,9 cm du bord du masque à côté des yeux. Attachez de la ficelle ou des élastiques étroits pour que le masque tienne sur votre tête.
7. Décorez votre masque comme vous voudrez avec des marqueurs, des boutons, des feuilles, des rubans, des couleurs, des plumes, etc.

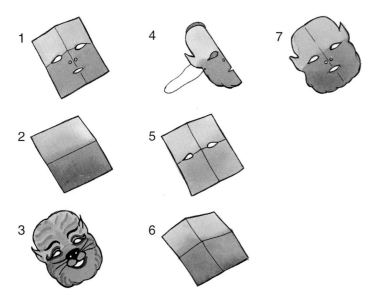

Dossier fermé

Si tu étais en France et tu voyais un accident dans la rue et que quelqu'un avait besoin d'aide médicale, que ferais-tu?

    B.   Je ferais le 15 sur un téléphone.

Le 15 est le numéro de téléphone du SAMU, le service d'assistance médicale d'urgence. Aux États-Unis, tu fais le 911 en cas d'urgences, mais en France c'est le 15 que tu fais.

C'est à moi!

Now that you have completed this unit, take a look at what you should be able to do in French. Can you do all of these tasks?

➤ I can ask about someone's health.
➤ I can give information about various topics, including health.
➤ I can talk about what happened in the past.
➤ I can describe someone's character traits.
➤ I can ask if someone can do something.
➤ I can admit to something.
➤ I can agree with someone.
➤ I can ask someone for help.
➤ I can ask for permission.
➤ I can confirm what someone has said.
➤ I can ask for the price of something.
➤ I can estimate something.
➤ I can compare things.
➤ I can make an assumption.
➤ I can express emotions.
➤ I can say what displeases me.
➤ I can say that I'm disappointed.
➤ I can suggest what people can do.
➤ I can accept an invitation.
➤ I can say that I'm grateful.
➤ I can end a conversation.

Pour voir si vous avez bien compris la culture française, décidez si chaque phrase est vraie ou fausse.

1. Fontainebleau était la résidence des rois quand ils allaient à la chasse.
2. La chasse est le sport le plus populaire parmi les Français.
3. La Coupe du Monde est un grand événement sportif de football.
4. Les Français téléphonent au SAMU quand ils ont besoin d'aide médicale rapide.
5. Les Français sont obligés d'offrir de l'aide quand ils voient un accident.
6. Les Français vont au drugstore quand ils ont besoin de faire préparer une ordonnance.
7. On appelle la région du sud de la France le Midi.
8. La ville d'Avignon se trouve en Provence.
9. Les papes sont allés de Rome à Avignon pour se protéger de la peste.
10. Le Festival d'Avignon a lieu chaque année sur le pont Saint-Bénezet.

Answers

1. vraie
2. fausse
3. vraie
4. vraie
5. vraie
6. fausse
7. vraie
8. vraie
9. fausse
10. fausse

Teacher's Note

1. The severe old part of the **Palais des Papes**, called the **Palais Vieux**, reflects the austere temperament of Pope Benedict XII, while the artistic new palace, or **Palais Neuf**, reflects the cultivated tastes of Pope Clement VI. The most striking feature of the palace is the great hall, which is famous for its acoustics. In the banquet hall lined with Gobelin tapestries, the cardinals gathered to elect a new pope. Clement VI's study, called the Stag Room due to the hunting frescoes and ceramic tiles, is the palace's most lovely room. 2. Avignon's famous summer festival is France's largest. It was founded in 1947 by Gérard Philippe and Jean Vilar.

Communication orale

Avec un(e) partenaire, jouez les rôles de deux personnes dans une pharmacie. La première personne joue le rôle d'une personne qui ne se sent pas du tout bien parce qu'elle a mangé quelque chose de mauvais. La deuxième personne joue le rôle d'un pharmacien ou une pharmacienne. En parlant avec le pharmacien ou la pharmacienne, la personne malade doit:

1. demander si le pharmacien ou la pharmacienne peut faire quelque chose pour l'aider
2. expliquer pourquoi elle ne se sent pas bien
3. dire où elle a mal
4. demander si le pharmacien ou la pharmacienne peut suggérer quelque chose à prendre pour se sentir mieux
5. demander le mode d'emploi du médicament
6. demander le prix du médicament
7. dire qu'elle lui est très reconnaissante
8. lui dire "au revoir"

Pendant la conversation le pharmacien ou la pharmacienne doit répondre logiquement à ce que la personne malade dit.

Communication écrite

Imaginez qu'un(e) de vos ami(e)s francophones vous a invité(e) à passer le weekend à la maison de campagne de sa famille. Malheureusement, vous venez d'avoir un accident, et vous avez des blessures. Écrivez une lettre aux parents de votre ami(e) pour refuser l'invitation. Dans votre lettre, dites:

1. que vous êtes très reconnaissant(e) de leur invitation
2. pourquoi vous devez la refuser
3. que si vous n'aviez pas eu cet accident, vous auriez bien voulu l'accepter
4. ce qui s'est passé
5. où vous avez mal
6. qui vous a aidé(e) et comment
7. que vous êtes très déçu(e) de ne pas accepter leur invitation
8. que vous leur souhaitez un bon weekend

Communication active

To inquire about health and welfare, use:

Qu'as-tu fait?   *What did you do?*

To give information, use:

Je me suis cassé la cheville.   *I broke my ankle.*

Je me suis foulé le poignet.   *I sprained my wrist.*

To describe past events, use:

J'aurais voulu l'utiliser tout de suite.   *I would have wanted to use it right away.*

To describe character, use:

J'ai pu demander à **quelqu'un de** gentil.   *I was able to ask someone nice.*

To inquire about capability, use:

Tu n'as pas trop de mal à marcher avec des béquilles?   *It doesn't hurt too much to walk on crutches?*

To admit, use:

Je dois dire qu'il était un peu compliqué.   *I must say that it was a little complicated.*

To agree with someone, use:

Sans blague!   *No kidding!*

To ask for help, use:

J'ai pu demander à quelqu'un de gentil **de venir m'aider.**   *I was able to ask someone nice to come and help me.*

To ask for permission, use:

Ça vous gêne si je jette un coup d'œil?   *Does it bother you if I take a quick look?*

Laissez-moi voir.   *Let me see.*

To express confirmation, use:

Vous avez raison.   *You're right.*

To ask for a price, use:

Je vous dois combien?   *How much do I owe you?*

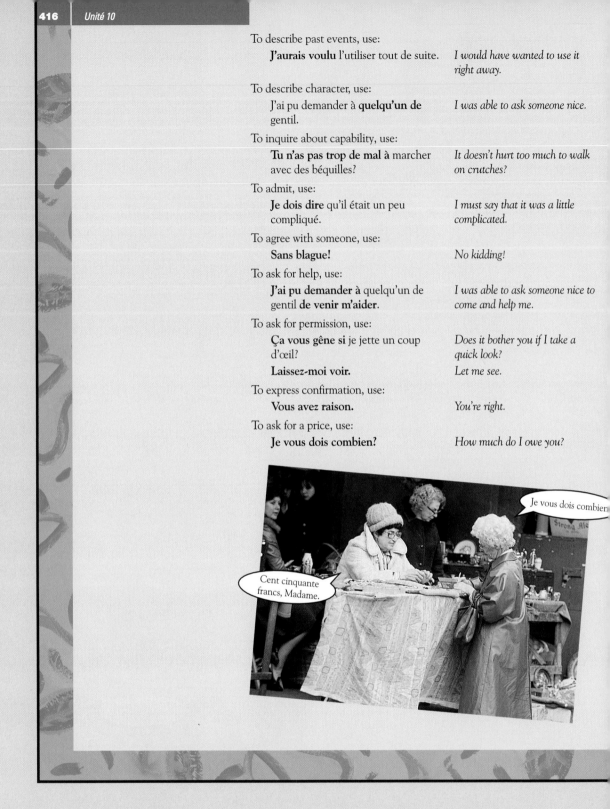

To estimate, use:

Environ dix jours.   *About ten days.*

To compare, use:

J'aurai **autant de** mal au début que la dernière fois.   *It will hurt as much at the beginning as last time.*

To hypothesize, use:

Si j'avais essayé le dictionnaire électronique avant de quitter le magasin, j'**aurais évité** tous ces ennuis.   *If I had tried the electronic dictionary before leaving the store, I would have avoided all these problems.*

To express emotions, use:

Brian est **frustré** parce que son dictionnaire électronique ne marche pas.   *Brian is frustrated because his electronic dictionary doesn't work.*

Ça me rend très heureux.   *That makes me very happy.*

To express displeasure, use:

C'est vraiment quelque chose d'embêtant.   *That's really something annoying.*

To express disappointment, use:

Moi qui étais **déçu**, maintenant ça va mieux.   *I was disappointed, now things are better.*

To make suggestions, use:

Si on changeait la pile?   *What if we changed the battery?*

ET SI VOUS PASSIEZ UN NOËL CRÉOLE ?

To accept an invitation, use:

Ça serait très gentil.   *That would be very nice.*

To express gratitude, use:

Je te serais très reconnaissante.   *I'd be very grateful.*

To terminate a conversation, use:

Je te reverrai.   *I'll see you again.*

À bientôt.   *See you soon.*

Grammar Summary

Subject Pronouns

Singular	Plural
je	nous
tu	vous
il/elle/on	ils/elles

Indefinite Articles

Singular		Plural
Masculine	Feminine	
un	une	des

Definite Articles

Singular			Plural
Before a Consonant Sound		Before a Vowel Sound	
Masculine	Feminine		
le	la	l'	les

À + Definite Articles

Singular			Plural
Before a Consonant Sound		Before a Vowel Sound	
Masculine	Feminine		
au	à la	à l'	aux

De + Definite Articles

Singular			Plural
Before a Consonant Sound		Before a Vowel Sound	
Masculine	Feminine		
du	de la	de l'	des

Partitive Articles

Before a Consonant Sound		Before a Vowel Sound
Masculine	**Feminine**	
du pain	**de la** glace	**de l'**eau

In negative sentences the partitive article becomes *de (d')*.

Expressions of Quantity

combien	how much, how many
assez	enough
beaucoup	a lot of, many
(un) peu	(a) little, few
trop	too much, too many

These expressions are followed by *de (d')* before a noun.

Question Words

combien	how much, how many
comment	what, how
où	where
pourquoi	why
qu'est-ce que	what
quand	when
quel, quelle	what, which
qui	who, whom

Question Formation

1. By a rising tone of voice
   Vous travaillez beaucoup?
2. By beginning with *est-ce que*
   Est-ce que vous travaillez beaucoup?
3. By adding *n'est-ce pas?*
   Vous travaillez beaucoup, n'est-ce pas?
4. By inversion
   Travaillez-vous beaucoup?

Possessive Adjectives

	Singular		Plural
Masculine	**Feminine before a Consonant Sound**	**Feminine before a Vowel Sound**	
mon	ma	mon	mes
ton	ta	ton	tes
son	sa	son	ses
notre	notre	notre	nos
votre	votre	votre	vos
leur	leur	leur	leurs

Demonstrative Adjectives

	Masculine before a Consonant Sound	Masculine before a Vowel Sound	Feminine
Singular	ce	cet	cette
Plural	ces	ces	ces

Indefinite Adjectives

aucun(e)... ne (n')	not one, no
autre	other
certain(e)	certain
chaque	each, every
même	same
la plupart de	most
plusieurs	several
quelques	some
tout(e)	all, every

Quel

	Masculine	Feminine
Singular	quel	quelle
Plural	quels	quelles

Tout

	Masculine	Feminine
Singular	tout	toute
Plural	tous	toutes

Agreement of Adjectives

	Masculine	Feminine
add **e**	Il est bavard.	Elle est bavarde.
no change	Il est suisse.	Elle est suisse.
change **-er** to **-ère**	Il est cher.	Elle est chère.
change **-eux** to **-euse**	Il est paresseux.	Elle est paresseuse.
double consonant + **e**	Il est gros.	Elle est grosse.

Irregular Feminine Adjectives

Masculine		Feminine
Before a Consonant Sound	Before a Vowel Sound	
blanc		blanche
frais		fraîche
long		longue
beau	bel	belle
nouveau	nouvel	nouvelle
vieux	vieil	vieille

Irregular Plural Adjectives

	Singular	Plural
no change	amoureux	amoureux
	bon marché	bon marché
	frais	frais
	heureux	heureux
	marron	marron
	orange	orange
	paresseux	paresseux
	super	super
	sympa	sympa
	vieux	vieux
-eau ➔ **-eaux**	beau	beaux
	nouveau	nouveaux
-al ➔ **-aux**	national	nationaux

Position of Adjectives

Most adjectives usually follow their nouns. But adjectives expressing beauty, age, goodness and size precede their nouns. Some of these preceding adjectives are:

autre	joli
beau	mauvais
bon	nouveau
grand	petit
gros	vieux
jeune	

Comparative of Adjectives

plus	+	adjective	+	**que**
moins	+	adjective	+	**que**
aussi	+	adjective	+	**que**

Superlative of Adjectives

le/la/les	+	**plus**	+	adjective

Irregular Plural Nouns

	Singular	Plural
no change	autobus	autobus
-al ➤ **-aux**	animal	animaux
	journal	journaux
-eau ➤ **-eaux**	bateau	bateaux
-eu ➤ **-eux**	feu	feux
	jeu	jeux

Comparative of Adverbs

plus	+	adverb	+	**que**
moins	+	adverb	+	**que**
aussi	+	adverb	+	**que**

Some adverbs have an irregular comparative form:

Adverb	Comparative
bien (*well*)	**mieux** (*better*)
beaucoup (*a lot, much*)	**plus** (*more*)
peu (*little*)	**moins** (*less*)

Superlative of Adverbs

le	+	plus	+	adverb

To form the superlative of *bien*, *beaucoup* and *peu*, put *le* before these adverbs' irregular comparative forms.

Adverb	Comparative	Superlative
bien	mieux	le mieux
beaucoup	plus	le plus
peu	moins	le moins

Expressions of Quantity

assez de	enough
beaucoup de	a lot of, many
combien de	how much, how many
moins de	less
(un) peu de	(a) little, few
plus de	more
trop de	too much, too many

une boîte de	a can of, a box of
une bouteille de	a bottle of
une canette de	a can of
un kilo de	a kilogram of
un morceau de	a piece of
un pot de	a jar of
une tasse de	a cup of
une tranche de	a slice of

Direct Object Pronouns

	Masculine	Feminine	Before a Vowel Sound
Singular	me te le	me te la	m' t' l'
Plural	nous vous les	nous vous les	nous vous les

Indirect Object Pronouns

	Masculine or Feminine	Before a Vowel Sound
Singular	me te lui	m' t' lui
Plural	nous vous leur	nous vous leur

Order of Double Object Pronouns

subject + $\begin{cases} \text{me} \\ \text{te} \\ \text{nous} \\ \text{vous} \\ \text{se} \end{cases}$ + $\begin{cases} \text{le} \\ \text{la} \\ \text{les} \end{cases}$ + $\begin{cases} \text{lui} \\ \text{leur} \end{cases}$ + y + en + verb

Stress Pronouns

Singular		Plural	
moi	*je*	nous	*nous*
toi	*tu*	vous	*vous*
lui	*il*	eux	*ils*
elle	*elle*	elles	*elles*

Interrogative Pronouns

	Subject	Direct Object	Object of Preposition
People	qui qui est-ce qui	qui qui est-ce que	qui
Things	qu'est-ce qui	que qu'est-ce que	quoi

Lequel

	Masculine	Feminine
Singular	lequel	laquelle
Plural	lesquels	lesquelles

Dont

dont = de + noun

Demonstrative Pronouns

	Masculine	Feminine
Singular	celui	celle
Plural	ceux	celles

Possessive Pronouns

	Singular		Plural	
	Masculine	Feminine	Masculine	Feminine
mine	le mien	la mienne	les miens	les miennes
yours	le tien	la tienne	les tiens	les tiennes
his, hers, its, one's	le sien	la sienne	les siens	les siennes
ours	le nôtre	la nôtre	les nôtres	
your	le vôtre	la vôtre	les vôtres	
theirs	le leur	la leur	les leurs	

Indefinite Pronouns

aucun(e)... ne (n')	not one
un(e) autre	another
la plupart	most
plusieurs	several
quelqu'un	someone, somebody
quelque chose	something
tous les deux	both

Present Tense of Regular Verbs

-er			
parler			
je	parle	nous	parlons
tu	parles	vous	parlez
il/elle/on	parle	ils/elles	parlent

-ir finir			
je	finis	nous	finissons
tu	finis	vous	finissez
il/elle/on	finit	ils/elles	finissent

-re perdre			
je	perds	nous	perdons
tu	perds	vous	perdez
il/elle/on	perd	ils/elles	perdent

Regular Imperatives

-er parler	-ir finir	-re perdre
parle	finis	perds
parlez	finissez	perdez
parlons	finissons	perdons

Present Tense of Reflexive Verbs

se coucher					
je	me	couche	nous	nous	couchons
tu	te	couches	vous	vous	couchez
il/elle/on	se	couche	ils/elles	se	couchent

Imperative of Reflexive Verbs

-er se réveiller
Réveille-toi!
Réveillez-vous!
Réveillons-nous!

Present Tense of Irregular Verbs

accéder			
j'	accède	nous	accédons
tu	accèdes	vous	accédez
il/elle/on	accède	ils/elles	accèdent

conduire			
je	conduis	nous	conduisons
tu	conduis	vous	conduisez
il/elle/on	conduit	ils/elles	conduisent

acheter			
j'	achète	nous	achetons
tu	achètes	vous	achetez
il/elle/on	achète	ils/elles	achètent

connaître			
je	connais	nous	connaissons
tu	connais	vous	connaissez
il/elle/on	connaît	ils/elles	connaissent

aller			
je	vais	nous	allons
tu	vas	vous	allez
il/elle/on	va	ils/elles	vont

construire			
je	construis	nous	construisons
tu	construis	vous	construisez
il/elle/on	construit	ils/elles	construisent

appeler			
j'	appelle	nous	appelons
tu	appelles	vous	appelez
il/elle/on	appelle	ils/elles	appellent

courir			
je	cours	nous	courons
tu	cours	vous	courez
il/elle/on	court	ils/elles	courent

appuyer			
j'	appuie	nous	appuyons
tu	appuies	vous	appuyez
il/elle/on	appuie	ils/elles	appuient

croire			
je	crois	nous	croyons
tu	crois	vous	croyez
il/elle/on	croit	ils/elles	croient

s'asseoir					
je	m'	assieds	nous	nous	asseyons
tu	t'	assieds	vous	vous	asseyez
il/elle/on	s'	assied	ils/elles	s'	asseyent

devoir			
je	dois	nous	devons
tu	dois	vous	devez
il/elle/on	doit	ils/elles	doivent

avoir			
j'	ai	nous	avons
tu	as	vous	avez
il/elle/on	a	ils/elles	ont

dire			
je	dis	nous	disons
tu	dis	vous	dites
il/elle/on	dit	ils/elles	disent

boire			
je	bois	nous	buvons
tu	bois	vous	buvez
il/elle/on	boit	ils/elles	boivent

se distraire					
je	me	distrais	nous	nous	distrayons
tu	te	distrais	vous	vous	distrayez
il/elle/on	se	distrait	ils/elles	se	distraient

dormir		
je dors	nous	dormons
tu dors	vous	dormez
il/elle/on dort	ils/elles	dorment

lire		
je lis	nous	lisons
tu lis	vous	lisez
il/elle/on lit	ils/elles	lisent

écrire		
j' écris	nous	écrivons
tu écris	vous	écrivez
il/elle/on écrit	ils/elles	écrivent

maintenir		
je maintiens	nous	maintenons
tu maintiens	vous	maintenez
il/elle/on maintient	ils/elles	maintiennent

s'ennuyer			
je m' ennuie	nous nous	ennuyons
tu t' ennuies	vous vous	ennuyez
il/elle/on s' ennuie	ils/elles s'	ennuient

mettre		
je mets	nous	mettons
tu mets	vous	mettez
il/elle/on met	ils/elles	mettent

essayer		
j' essaie	nous	essayons
tu essaies	vous	essayez
il/elle/on essaie	ils/elles	essaient

mourir		
je meurs	nous	mourons
tu meurs	vous	mourez
il/elle/on meurt	ils/elles	meurent

être		
je suis	nous	sommes
tu es	vous	êtes
il/elle/on est	ils/elles	sont

naître		
je nais	nous	naissons
tu nais	vous	naissez
il/elle/on naît	ils/elles	naissent

faire		
je fais	nous	faisons
tu fais	vous	faites
il/elle/on fait	ils/elles	font

offrir		
j' offre	nous	offrons
tu offres	vous	offrez
il/elle/on offre	ils/elles	offrent

falloir	
il faut	

ouvrir		
j' ouvre	nous	ouvrons
tu ouvres	vous	ouvrez
il/elle/on ouvre	ils/elles	ouvrent

s'intégrer			
je m' intègre	nous nous	intégrons
tu t' intègres	vous vous	intégrez
il/elle/on s' intègre	ils/elles s'	intègrent

partir		
je pars	nous	partons
tu pars	vous	partez
il/elle/on part	ils/elles	partent

jeter		
je jette	nous	jetons
tu jettes	vous	jetez
il/elle/on jette	ils/elles	jettent

payer			
je	paie	nous	payons
tu	paies	vous	payez
il/elle/on	paie	ils/elles	paient

recevoir			
je	reçois	nous	recevons
tu	reçois	vous	recevez
il/elle/on	reçoit	ils/elles	reçoivent

peindre			
je	peins	nous	peignons
tu	peins	vous	peignez
il/elle/on	peint	ils/elles	peignent

répéter			
je	répète	nous	répétons
tu	répètes	vous	répétez
il/elle/on	répète	ils/elles	répètent

se plaindre					
je	me	plains	nous	nous	plaignons
tu	te	plains	vous	vous	plaignez
il/elle/on	se	plaint	ils/elles	se	plaignent

savoir			
je	sais	nous	savons
tu	sais	vous	savez
il/elle/on	sait	ils/elles	savent

plaire			
je	plais	nous	plaisons
tu	plais	vous	plaisez
il/elle/on	plaît	ils/elles	plaisent

sécher			
je	sèche	nous	séchons
tu	sèches	vous	séchez
il/elle/on	sèche	ils/elles	sèchent

pleuvoir	
il	pleut

se sentir					
je	me	sens	nous	nous	sentons
tu	te	sens	vous	vous	sentez
il/elle/on	se	sent	ils/elles	se	sentent

pouvoir			
je	peux	nous	pouvons
tu	peux	vous	pouvez
il/elle/on	peut	ils/elles	peuvent

servir			
je	sers	nous	servons
tu	sers	vous	servez
il/elle/on	sert	ils/elles	servent

préférer			
je	préfère	nous	préférons
tu	préfères	vous	préférez
il/elle/on	préfère	ils/elles	préfèrent

sortir			
je	sors	nous	sortons
tu	sors	vous	sortez
il/elle/on	sort	ils/elles	sortent

prendre			
je	prends	nous	prenons
tu	prends	vous	prenez
il/elle/on	prend	ils/elles	prennent

suivre			
je	suis	nous	suivons
tu	suis	vous	suivez
il/elle/on	suit	ils/elles	suivent

protéger			
je	protège	nous	protégeons
tu	protèges	vous	protégez
il/elle/on	protège	ils/elles	protègent

se taire					
je	me	tais	nous	nous	taisons
tu	te	tais	vous	vous	taisez
il/elle/on	se	tait	ils/elles	se	taisent

vaincre		
je	vaincs	nous vainquons
tu	vaincs	vous vainquez
il/elle/on	vainc	ils/elles vainquent

valoir		
je	vaux	nous valons
tu	vaux	vous valez
il/elle/on	vaut	ils/elles valent

venir		
je	viens	nous venons
tu	viens	vous venez
il/elle/on	vient	ils/elles viennent

vivre		
je	vis	nous vivons
tu	vis	vous vivez
il/elle/on	vit	ils/elles vivent

voir		
je	vois	nous voyons
tu	vois	vous voyez
il/elle/on	voit	ils/elles voient

vouloir		
je	veux	nous voulons
tu	veux	vous voulez
il/elle/on	veut	ils/elles veulent

Verbs + *à* + Infinitives

aider	commencer	réussir
s'amuser	continuer	
apprendre	inviter	

Verbs + *de* + Infinitives

arrêter	demander	finir
choisir	se dépêcher	offrir
décider	dire	rêver

Verbs + Infinitives

adorer	espérer	savoir
aimer	falloir	sembler
aller	pouvoir	venir
désirer	préférer	vouloir
devoir	regarder	

Verbs + *de* + Nouns

avoir besoin de	to need
avoir envie de	to want, to feel like
avoir peur de	to be afraid of
être amoureux/amoureuse de	to be in love with
être content(e) de	to be happy about
faire la connaissance de	to meet
se méfier de	to distrust
s'occuper de	to take care of
parler de	to speak/talk about
se plaindre de	to complain about
rêver de	to dream about
se servir de	to use
se souvenir de	to remember
traiter de	to treat
se tromper de	to be mistaken/wrong about

Negation in Present Tense

ne... jamais	Je **ne** vois **jamais** Hélène.
ne... pas	Vous **ne** mangez **pas**.
ne... personne	Il **n'**y a **personne** ici.
ne... plus	Tu **ne** fais **plus** de footing?
ne... rien	Nous **ne** faisons **rien**.

Passé Composé with Regular Past Participles

jouer				
j' ai	joué	nous	avons	joué
tu as	joué	vous	avez	joué
il/elle/on a	joué	ils/elles	ont	joué

finir				
j' ai	fini	nous	avons	fini
tu as	fini	vous	avez	fini
il/elle/on a	fini	ils/elles	ont	fini

attendre				
j' ai	attendu	nous	avons	attendu
tu as	attendu	vous	avez	attendu
il/elle/on a	attendu	ils/elles	ont	attendu

Passé Composé with Irregular Past Participles

Infinitive	Past Participle
avoir	eu
boire	bu
conduire	conduit
connaître	connu
courir	couru
croire	cru
devoir	dû
dire	dit
écrire	écrit
être	été
faire	fait
falloir	fallu
lire	lu
mettre	mis
offrir	offert
ouvrir	ouvert
pouvoir	pu
prendre	pris
recevoir	reçu
savoir	su
suivre	suivi
vivre	vécu
voir	vu
vouloir	voulu

Passé Composé with *Être*

aller			sortir		
je	suis	allé	je	suis	sorti
je	suis	allée	je	suis	sortie
tu	es	allé	tu	es	sorti
tu	es	allée	tu	es	sortie
il	est	allé	il	est	sorti
elle	est	allée	elle	est	sortie
on	est	allé	on	est	sorti
nous	sommes	allés	nous	sommes	sortis
nous	sommes	allées	nous	sommes	sorties
vous	êtes	allé	vous	êtes	sorti
vous	êtes	allée	vous	êtes	sortie
vous	êtes	allés	vous	êtes	sortis
vous	êtes	allées	vous	êtes	sorties
ils	sont	allés	ils	sont	sortis
elles	sont	allées	elles	sont	sorties

Some of the verbs that use *être* as the helping verb in the *passé composé* are:

Infinitive	Past Participle
aller	allé
arriver	arrivé
descendre	descendu
devenir	devenu
entrer	entré
monter	monté
mourir	mort
naître	né
partir	parti
rentrer	rentré
rester	resté
retourner	retourné
revenir	revenu
sortir	sorti
tomber	tombé
venir	venu

Passé Composé of Reflexive Verbs

se réveiller			
je	me	suis	réveillé
je	me	suis	réveillée
tu	t'	es	réveillé
tu	t'	es	réveillée
il	s'	est	réveillé
elle	s'	est	réveillée
on	s'	est	réveillé
nous	nous	sommes	réveillés
nous	nous	sommes	réveillées
vous	vous	êtes	réveillé
vous	vous	êtes	réveillée
vous	vous	êtes	réveillés
vous	vous	êtes	réveillées
ils	se	sont	réveillés
elles	se	sont	réveillées

Present Participle

Verb	Present Participle
entrer	**entrant**
aller	**allant**
offrir	**offrant**
sortir	**sortant**
répondre	**répondant**
dire	**disant**

Past Infinitive

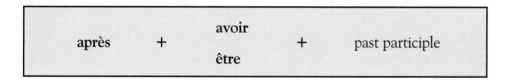

après	+	avoir être	+	past participle

Subjunctive of Regular Verbs

	chanter	choisir	vendre
que je	chante	choisisse	vende
que tu	chantes	choisisses	vendes
qu'il/elle/on	chante	choisisse	vende
que nous	chantions	choisissions	vendions
que vous	chantiez	choisissiez	vendiez
qu'ils/elles	chantent	choisissent	vendent

Subjunctive of Irregular Verbs

	aller	faire	pouvoir	savoir	vouloir
que je (j')	aille	fasse	puisse	sache	veuille
que tu	ailles	fasses	puisses	saches	veuilles
qu'il/elle/on	aille	fasse	puisse	sache	veuille
que nous	allions	fassions	puissions	sachions	voulions
que vous	alliez	fassiez	puissiez	sachiez	vouliez
qu'ils/elles	aillent	fassent	puissent	sachent	veuillent

	boire	croire	devoir	prendre	recevoir
que je	boive	croie	doive	prenne	reçoive
que tu	boives	croies	doives	prennes	reçoives
qu'il/elle/on	boive	croie	doive	prenne	reçoive
que nous	buvions	croyions	devions	prenions	recevions
que vous	buviez	croyiez	deviez	preniez	receviez
qu'ils/elles	boivent	croient	doivent	prennent	reçoivent

	venir	voir	avoir	être
que je (j')	vienne	voie	aie	sois
que tu	viennes	voies	aies	sois
qu'il/elle/on	vienne	voie	ait	soit
que nous	venions	voyions	ayons	soyons
que vous	veniez	voyiez	ayez	soyez
qu'ils/elles	viennent	voient	aient	soient

Subjunctive after Impersonal Expressions

il est nécessaire que	it is necessary that
il est important que	it is important that
il est indispensable que	it is indispensable that
il est essentiel que	it is essential that
il est possible que	it is possible that
il est impossible que	it is impossible that
il vaut mieux que	it is better that
il est bon que	it is good that
il est surprenant que	it is surprising that
il est utile que	it is useful that

Subjunctive after Expressions of Wish, Will or Desire

aimer	to like, to love	*préférer*	to prefer
désirer	to want	*souhaiter*	to wish, to hope
exiger	to require	*vouloir*	to want

Subjunctive after Expressions of Emotion

être content(e) que	to be happy that
être heureux/heureuse que	to be happy that
être triste que	to be sad that
être désolé(e) que	to be sorry that
être fâché(e) que	to be angry that
être étonné(e) que	to be surprised that
avoir peur que	to be afraid that
regretter que	to be sorry that
s'inquiéter que	to worry that
Ça me surprend que....	It surprises me that . . . .
Ça m'embête que....	It bothers me that . . . .
C'est dommage que....	It's too bad that . . . .

Use of the Subjunctive and the Indicative

Subjunctive	Indicative
Je doute que....	Je ne doute pas que....
Penses-tu que...?	Je pense que....
Je ne pense pas que....	Ne penses-tu pas que...?
Crois-tu que...?	Je crois que....
Je ne crois pas que....	Ne crois-tu pas que...?
Je ne suis pas sûr(e) que....	Je suis sûr(e) que....
Es-tu sûr(e) que...?	N'es-tu pas sûr(e) que...?
Je ne suis pas certain(e) que....	Je suis certain(e) que....
Es-tu certain(e) que...?	N'es-tu pas certain(e) que...?
Il n'est pas vrai que....	Il est vrai que....
Est-il vrai que...?	N'est-il pas vrai que...?
Il n'est pas évident que....	Il est évident que....
Est-il évident que...?	N'est-il pas évident que...?

Imperfect Tense

travailler			
je	travaillais	nous	travaillions
tu	travaillais	vous	travailliez
il/elle/on	travaillait	ils/elles	travaillaient

Imperfect Tense of *Être*

être			
j'	étais	nous	étions
tu	étais	vous	étiez
il/elle/on	était	ils/elles	étaient

Conditional Tense of Regular Verbs

jouer			
je	jouerais	nous	jouerions
tu	jouerais	vous	joueriez
il/elle/on	jouerait	ils/elles	joueraient

Conditional Tense of Irregular Verbs

Infinitive	Conditional Stem
aller	ir-
s'asseoir	assiér-
avoir	aur-
courir	courr-
devoir	devr-
envoyer	enverr-
être	ser-
faire	fer-
falloir	faudr-
mourir	mourr-
pleuvoir	pleuvr-
pouvoir	pourr-
recevoir	recevr-
savoir	saur-
valoir	vaudr-
venir	viendr-
voir	verr-
vouloir	voudr-

Conditional Tense with *Si*

si	+	imperfect	conditional

Future Tense of Regular Verbs

trouver			
je	**trouverai**	Je **trouverai** toutes les réponses.	*I'll find all the answers.*
tu	**trouveras**	Où **trouveras**-tu un appartement?	*Where will you find an apartment?*
il/elle/on	**trouvera**	On **trouvera** beaucoup d'outils de recherche.	*You'll find many search engines.*
nous	**trouverons**	Qu'est-ce que nous **trouverons**?	*What will we find?*
vous	**trouverez**	Vous **trouverez** une liste d'adresses.	*You'll find a list of addresses.*
ils/elles	**trouveront**	Elles ne **trouveront** rien.	*They won't find anything.*

Future Tense after Quand

quand	+	future	future

Future Tense with *Si*

si	+	present	future
si	+	present	present
si	+	present	imperative

Pluperfect Tense

	demander	aller
j'	avais demandé	étais allé(e)
tu	avais demandé	étais allé(e)
il/elle/on	avait demandé	était allé(e)
nous	avions demandé	étions allé(e)s
vous	aviez demandé	étiez allé(e)(s)(es)
ils/elles	avaient demandé	étaient allé(e)s

Past Conditional Tense

	réparer	se lever
je/j'	aurais réparé	me serais levé(e)
tu	aurais réparé	te serais levé(e)
il/elle/on	aurait réparé	se serait levé(e)
nous	aurions réparé	nous serions levé(e)s
vous	auriez réparé	vous seriez levé(e)(s)(es)
ils/elles	auraient réparé	se seraient levé(e)s

Past Conditional Tense with *Si*

si	+	**plus-que-parfait**	past conditional

Ordinal Numbers

1er	=	premier	6e =	sixième
2^e	=	deuxième	7e =	septième
3^e	=	troisième	8e =	huitième
4^e	=	quatrième	9e =	neuvième
5^e	=	cinquième	10e =	dixième

Vocabulary
French/English

All words and expressions introduced as active vocabulary in the *C'est à toi!* textbook series appear in this end vocabulary. The number following the meaning of each word or expression indicates the unit in which it appears for the first time in this textbook. If there is more than one meaning for a word or expression and it has appeared in different units, the corresponding unit numbers are listed. Words and expressions that were introduced in the first two levels of *C'est à toi!* do not have a number after them.

A

à to; at; in; *À bientôt.* See you soon.; *à côté (de)* beside, next to; *À demain.* See you tomorrow.; *à droite* to (on) the right; *à gauche* to (on) the left; *à l'heure* on time; *à la fois* all at once; *à la télé* on TV; *à mon avis* in my opinion; *à part* aside from; *à pied* on foot; *à plein temps* full-time 4; *à ta place* if I were you 5; *À tes souhaits!* Bless you!

abondant(e) plentiful 9

une **abréviation** abbreviation 3

accéder to access 6

accélérer to accelerate

un **accent** accent 2

accepter to accept

un **accessoire** accessory

un **accident** accident 10

accompagner to accompany 5

accueillant(e) hospitable, friendly 2

un **achat** purchase 10

acheter to buy

un **acteur, une actrice** actor, actress

actif, active active

une **activité** activity 5

l' **actualité (f.)** current events

s' **adapter** to adapt 10

une **addition** bill, check (at a restaurant)

administratif, administrative administrative 4

une **administration** administration 8

admirer to admire

un(e) **ado** teenager

adorer to love

une **adresse** address

l' **aérobic (m.)** aerobics

un **aérogramme** aerogram (air letter)

un **aéroport** airport

des **affaires (f.)** business 8; *des affaires de toilette (f.)* toiletries

une **affiche** poster

l' **affranchissement (m.)** postage

africain(e) African

l' **Afrique (f.)** Africa

l' **âge (m.)** age; *Tu as quel âge?* How old are you?

âgé(e) old

un **agent** agent; *un agent de police* police officer

une **agrafeuse** stapler 1

agréer to accept 4; *Je vous prie d'agréer, Monsieur (ou Madame), mes salutations distinguées.* yours truly 4

agresser to attack 7

ah oh; *Ah bon?* Really 7

l' **aide (f.)** help

aider to help

aimable nice

aimer to like, to love

ainsi que as well as 9

l' **air (m.)** appearance 2

un **album** album 3

l' **alcoolisme (m.)** alcoholism

l' **algèbre (f.)** algebra 1

l' **Algérie (f.)** Algeria

algérien, algérienne Algerian

l' **Allemagne (f.)** Germany

l' **allemand (m.)** German (language)

allemand(e) German

aller to go; *allons-y* let's go (there)

allô hello (on telephone)

des **allocations (f.)** benefits, allowance 7

allumer to turn on

alors (well) then

une **ambassade** embassy 2

une **ambiance** atmosphere 7

ambitieux, ambitieuse ambitious 8

améliorer to improve 8

une **amende** fine

américain(e) American

l' **Amérique (f.)** America; *l'Amérique du Nord (f.)* North America; *l'Amérique du Sud (f.)* South America

un(e) **ami(e)** friend

l' **amour (m.)** love

amoureux, amoureuse in love

amusant(e) funny, amusing

s' **amuser** to have fun, to have a good time

un **an** year; *J'ai... ans.* I'm . . . years old.

l' **anglais (m.)** English (language)

anglais(e) English

l' **Angleterre (f.)** England

un **animal** animal

une **année** year

un **anniversaire** birthday; *Bon anniversaire!* Happy Birthday!

une **annonce** advertisement 4; *des petites annonces* want ads 4

annoncer to announce 4

un **anorak** ski jacket

un **antibiotique** antibiotic 10

une **antilope** antelope 9

août August

un **appareil** appliance 10; *un appareil-photo* camera 9

une **apparence** appearance 7

un **appartement** apartment

appeler to call 7; *s'appeler* to be named 4

apprécier to appreciate 4

apprendre to learn

s' **approcher (de)** to approach, to come up (to) 2

appuyer to press 6

après after

l' **après-midi (m.)** afternoon

un **arbre** tree

un **arc** arch

une **arcade** arcade 1

une **arche** arch

l' **argent (m.)** money, silver; *l'argent liquide (m.)* cash

une **armée** army

une **armoire** wardrobe

arrêter to stop; *s'arrêter* to stop

une **arrivée** arrival

arriver to arrive; to happen 10

un **arrondissement** district 3

arroser to water

l' **art (m.)** art

un **article** article 6

un **artisan** craftsperson 9

un(e) **artiste** artist

un **ascenseur** elevator

asiatique Asian

l' **Asie (f.)** Asia

un **aspirateur** vacuum cleaner

une **aspirine** aspirin 10

assassiner to assassinate 8

s' **asseoir** to sit down

assez rather, quite; enough 4; *assez de* enough

une **assiette** plate

assis(e) seated

un(e) **assistant(e)** assistant 3

assister à to attend

l' **assurance (f.)** insurance 4

un **atelier** studio 3; workshop 9

un(e) **athlète** athlete

attendre to wait (for); *s'attendre à* to expect 2

une **attente: une salle d'attente** waiting room 10

Attention! Watch out! Be careful!

atterrir to land

au to (the), at (the); in (the); on the; *au moins* at least; *au revoir* good-bye; *Au secours!* Help!; *au-dessus de* above

une **auberge de jeunesse** youth hostel

aucun(e)... ne (n') not one, no 2

aujourd'hui today

aussi also, too; as

aussitôt que as soon as

l' **Australie (f.)** Australia

australien, australienne Australian

autant de as much, as many 10

une **auto (automobile)** car; *une auto tamponneuse* bumper car 1

autobiographique autobiographical 3

un **autobus** (city) bus

une **auto-école** driving school

automatique automatic

l' **automne (m.)** autumn, fall

autre other; *un(e) autre* another

autrefois formerly 9

l' **Autriche (f.)** Austria 8

une **autruche** ostrich 9

aux to (the), at (the), in (the)

avance: en avance early

avancé(e) advanced 6

avant (de) before

avec with

l' **avenir (m.)** future 6

une **aventure** adventure

une **avenue** avenue

un **avion** airplane; *par avion* by air mail

un **avis: à mon avis** in my opinion

un(e) **avocat(e)** lawyer

avoir to have; *avoir beau* (to do something) in vain 8; *avoir besoin de* to need; *avoir bonne/mauvaise mine* to look well/sick; *avoir chaud* to be warm, hot; *avoir de la chance* to be lucky 1; *avoir envie de* to want, to feel like; *avoir faim* to be hungry; *avoir froid* to be cold; *avoir l'air* to look 2; *avoir lieu* to take place 8; *avoir mal (à...)* to hurt, to have a/an ... ache, to have a sore ...; *avoir mal au cœur* to feel nauseous; *avoir peur (de)* to be afraid (of); *avoir quel âge* to be how old; *avoir raison* to be right 10; *avoir soif* to be thirsty; *avoir... ans* to be ... (years old)

avril April

B

le **baby-sitting** baby-sitting

le **bac (baccalauréat)** diploma/exam at end of *lycée*

des **bagages (m.)** luggage, baggage

une **bague** ring

une **baguette** long, thin loaf of bread

une **baignoire** bathtub

un **bain: un peignoir de bain** bathrobe; *une salle de bains* bathroom

baisser to lower
un **bal** dance
un **balcon** balcony
un **ballet** ballet 3
un **ballon** (inflated) ball 10
une **banane** banana
le **banco** adobe 9
un **bandage** bandage 10
une **bande: une bande dessinée**
   comic strip; *une bande*
   originale sound track 3
une **banque** bank
un **banquier, une banquière**
   banker
un **baobab** baobab tree 9
une **barbe** beard
   bas: en bas at the bottom 3
des **bas (m.)** (panty) hose
le **basket (basketball)** basketball
des **baskets (f.)** hightops
une **bataille** battle 8
un **bateau** boat
un **bâton** ski pole
une **batterie** drums
   bavard(e) talkative
   beau, bel, belle beautiful,
   handsome; *avoir beau* (to do
   something) in vain 8
   beaucoup a lot, (very) much;
   beaucoup de a lot of, many
un **beau-frère** stepbrother,
   brother-in-law
un **beau-père** stepfather, father-
   in-law
la **beauté** beauty 5
un **bébé** baby 6
   beige beige
   belge Belgian
la **Belgique** Belgium
une **belle-mère** stepmother,
   mother-in-law
une **belle-sœur** stepsister, sister-in-
   law
   ben well; *bon ben* well then
le **Bénin** Benin 3
une **béquille** crutch 10
un **besoin** need 4; *avoir besoin de*
   to need

bête stupid, dumb
Beurk! Yuk!
le **beurre** butter
une **bibliothèque** library
bien well; really; fine, good;
   bien sûr of course
bientôt soon
Bienvenue! Welcome!
un **bijou** jewel
bilingue bilingual 4
un **billet** ticket; bill (money)
la **biologie** biology
une **bise** kiss
un **bisou** kiss 5
une **blague** joke 10; *Sans blague!*
   No kidding! 10
blanc, blanche white
blessure wound 10
bleu(e) blue
un **bloc-notes** notepad 1
blond(e) blond
un **blouson** jacket (outdoor)
le **bœuf** beef
Bof! What can I say? 9
boire to drink
une **boisson** drink, beverage
une **boîte** dance club; can; box 10;
   une boîte aux lettres mailbox
un **bol** bowl
bon, bonne good; *Ah bon?*
   Really? 7; *Bon anniversaire!*
   Happy Birthday!; *bon ben*
   well then; *bon marché*
   cheap; *Bonne journée!* Have
   a good day!
un **bon de réduction** coupon 10
bonjour hello
bonsoir good evening
le **bord** side, shore; *au bord de la*
   mer at the seashore
une **botte** boot
une **bouche** mouth
un **boucher, une bouchère**
   butcher
une **boucherie** butcher shop
une **boucle d'oreille** earring
une **bouillabaisse** fish soup

un **boulanger, une boulangère**
   baker
une **boulangerie** bakery
un **boulot** job, work
une **boum** party
une **bouteille** bottle
une **boutique** shop, boutique
un **bracelet** bracelet
se **brancher** to connect 6
un **bras** arm
Bravo! Well done! 6
une **brosse: une brosse à cheveux**
   hairbrush; *une brosse à dents*
   toothbrush
se **brosser** to brush
un **bruit** noise
brûler to burn
brun(e) dark (hair), brown
un **budget** budget 7
un **bulletin météo** weather report
un **bureau** desk; office 1; *un*
   bureau de change currency
   exchange; *un bureau de*
   location box office 3
burlesque burlesque, comical
un **bus** (city) bus

C

c'est this is, it's; he is, she is;
   that's; *C'est à vous de voir.*
   It's up to you. 10
ça that, it; *Ça fait....* That's/
   It's . . . .; *Ça fait combien?*
   How much is it/that?; *Ça va?*
   How are things going?; *Ça va*
   bien. Things are going well.
un **cabinet** (doctor or dentist's)
   office
un **cadeau** gift, present
le **cadre** sector 4
un **café** café; coffee; *un café au lait*
   coffee with milk
une **cage** cage 7; *une cage à lapins*
   rabbit hutch 7
un **cahier** notebook
une **caisse** cashier's (desk)
un **caissier, une caissière** cashier
le **calcul** calculus 1

un **calendrier** calendar

calme quiet; calm 2

une **camarade: une camarade de chambre** roommate; *une camarade de classe* classmate

le **camembert** Camembert cheese

le **Cameroun** Cameroon

camerounais(e) Cameroonian

un **camion** truck

la **campagne** country, countryside

le **camping** camping

un **camping** campground

le **Canada** Canada

canadien, canadienne Canadian

un **canapé** couch, sofa

un **canard** duck

une **canette** can 10

un **canoë** canoe

une **cantine** cafeteria

une **capitale** capital

un **capot** hood

car because 7

un **car** tour bus 2

un **carnet** notebook 1

une **carotte** carrot

une **carte** map; card; *une carte de crédit* credit card; *une carte postale* postcard

un **cas** case

une **cascade** waterfall

une **case** hut 9

une **casquette** cap

cassé(e) broken 10

se **casser** to break 10

une **cassette** cassette

un(e) **catholique** Catholic 8

un **CD** CD

ce, cet, cette; ces this, that; these, those; *ce que* what 4; *ce qui* what 4, that 6; *ce sont* they are, these are, those are

une **ceinture** belt; *une ceinture de sécurité* seat belt

cela that 5

célèbre famous

celui, celle; ceux, celles this one, that one, the one; these, those, the ones 7

un **censeur** assistant principal, dean 1

cent (one) hundred

un **centre** center; *un centre commercial* shopping center, mall

des **céréales (f.)** cereal

une **cerise** cherry

certain(e) certain 4

une **chaîne** channel 4

une **chaise** chair

une **chambre** bedroom; room; *une camarade de chambre* roommate

un **champ** field

un **champignon** mushroom

la **chance** luck

un **change: un bureau de change** currency exchange

un **changement** change

changer to change; *changer de vitesse* to shift gears

une **chanson** song

chanter to sing 3

un **chanteur, une chanteuse** singer

un **chapeau** hat

une **chapelle** chapel

chaque each, every

une **charcuterie** delicatessen

un **charcutier, une charcutière** delicatessen owner

chargé(e) full

la **chasse** hunting 8

chasser to hunt 9

un **chat** cat

un **château** castle

chaud(e) warm, hot; *avoir chaud* to be warm, hot

un **chauffeur** driver

une **chaussette** sock

une **chaussure** shoe

un **chef** chef; boss 2; head 4; chief 8; *un chef d'orchestre* conductor 3; *un chef-d'œuvre* masterpiece 3; *un chef de train* conductor 5

un **chemin** path, way

une **chemise** shirt

un **chèque de voyage** traveler's check

cher, chère expensive; dear

chercher to look for; *venir chercher* to pick up, to come and get

un **chercheur, une chercheuse** researcher

un(e) **chéri(e)** darling

un **cheval** horse

des **cheveux (m.)** hair

une **cheville** ankle 10

une **chèvre** goat

chez to the house/home of; at the house/home of; *chez moi* to my house

un **chien** dog

la **chimie** chemistry

la **Chine** China

chinois(e) Chinese

des **chips (m.)** snacks

le **chocolat** chocolate; *un chocolat chaud* hot chocolate

choisir to choose

un **choix** choice

le **chômage** unemployment

un **chômeur, une chômeuse** unemployed person 7

une **chose** thing; *quelque chose* something

le **christianisme** Christianity 8

Chut! Sh! 5

ciao bye

ci-joint enclosed 4

un **cimetière** cemetery

le **cinéma** movies

un **cinéma** movie theater 3

cinq five

cinquante fifty

cinquième fifth

circonspect(e) cautious, reserved 7

la **circulation** traffic

une **cité** housing development 7

un **citron** lemon

une **clarinette** clarinet

une **classe** class

un **clavier** keyboard 6

un(e) **client(e)** customer 10

une **clientèle** customers, clientele 4

un **climat** climate 7

la **climatisation (clim)** air conditioning

un **clip** video clip

cliquer to click 6

un **coca** Coke

un **cochon** pig

un **cœur** heart; *avoir mal au cœur* to feel nauseous

un **coiffeur, une coiffeuse** hairdresser

un **coin** corner 7

un **colis** package

une **collection** collection 3

collectionner to collect

un **collier** necklace

combien how much; *combien de* how much, how many

une **comédie** comedy

une **commande** order

comme like, for; how; as; *comme ci, comme ça* so-so; *comme d'habitude* as usual

commencer to begin

comment what; how; *Comment vas-tu?* How are you?

un(e) **commerçant(e)** shopkeeper

le **commerce** trade 6

commercial(e) commercial 6

un **commissariat** police station 2

une **compagnie** company 4

complet, complète complete, full

complexe complicated 8

compliqué(e) complicated 10

composer to compose 3

un **compositeur, une compositrice** composer 3

composter to stamp

un **composteur** ticket stamping machine

comprendre to understand 1

compris(e) included

un(e) **comptable** accountant

compter to intend 4; to count, to rely 7

un **comptoir** counter

un **concert** concert

une **concession** African housing area 9

un **conducteur, une conductrice** driver

conduire to drive

une **conférence** lecture 1

la **confiture** jam

la **connaissance** knowledge 6

une **connaissance** acquaintance

connaître to know

un(e) **conquérant(e)** conqueror 8

un **conseil** (piece of) advice 8

considérer to consider 7

consommer to use

la **construction** building 8

construire to build 6

une **consultation** séance, session 1

contemporain(e) contemporary

content(e) happy

continuer to continue

un **contraste** contrast 9

un **contrat** contract 4

contre against 4; for 8; *par contre* on the other hand 9

un **contrôle de sécurité** security check

contrôler to control

un **contrôleur, une contrôleuse** inspector

controversé(e) controversial 3

une **conversation** conversation

un **copain, une copine** friend

copier to copy 8

un **coq** rooster; *le coq au vin* chicken cooked in wine

des **coquilles Saint-Jacques au curry (f.)** curried scallops

coranique of the Islamic religion 9

une **corbeille** wastebasket

un **corps** body

un(e) **correspondant(e)** host brother/sister

une **corvée** chore

un **costume** man's suit

une **côte** coast; *la côte d'Azur* Riviera

un **côté** side; *à côté (de)* beside, next to; *de l'autre côté* on the other side 9

la **Côte-d'Ivoire** Ivory Coast

un **cou** neck

se **coucher** to go to bed

une **couleur** color

un **couloir** hall; aisle

un **coup: Donne-moi un coup de main....** Give me a hand . . . .; *jeter un coup d'œil* to take a quick look 10

un **couple** couple

une **cour** court 8

courageux, courageuse courageous

courir to run

le **courrier** mail

un **cours** course, class; *au cours de* in the course of, during

une **course** race

les **courses: faire les courses** to go grocery shopping

court(e) short

le **couscous** couscous

un(e) **cousin(e)** cousin

un **couteau** knife

coûter to cost

un **couvert** table setting

un **crabe** crab

un **crayon** pencil

créer to create 4

une **crème caramel** caramel custard

une **crémerie** dairy store

une **crêpe** crêpe; pancake

une **crevette** shrimp

critiquer to criticize 8

croire to believe, to think; *Je crois que oui.* I think so. 5

une **croisade** crusade 8

un **croisement** intersection

un **croissant** croissant

des **crudités (f.)** raw vegetables

une **cuiller** spoon

le **cuir** leather

une **cuisine** kitchen; cooking

un **cuisinier, une cuisinière** cook

une **cuisinière** stove

la **culture** culture

culturel, culturelle cultural 7

un **CV** curriculum vitae 4

D

d'abord first

d'accord OK; *être d'accord* to agree 5

d'après according to

d'habitude usual 7

une **dame** lady

dans in; on

danser to dance

une **date** date

de (d') of, from; a, an, any; some; in, by; about; *de l'autre côté* on the other side 9; *de nos jours* these days 9; *de plus* furthermore, what's more, more; *de sorte que* so that 9

se **débrouiller** to manage 5

le **début** beginning 2

une **décapotable** convertible

décembre December

décider (de) to decide

une **déclaration** report 2

déclarer to declare

décoller to take off

décrire to describe

déçu(e) disappointed 10

défendre to defend 8

la **défense** defense 6

un **défilé** parade

se **déguiser** to dress up

dehors outside

déjà already

déjeuner to have lunch

le **déjeuner** lunch; *le petit déjeuner* breakfast

délivrer to free

demain tomorrow

demander to ask for; to ask

démarrer to start (up)

déménager to move

demi(e) half; *et demi(e)* thirty (minutes), half past

un **demi-frère** half-brother

une **demi-heure** half an hour

une **demi-sœur** half-sister

démolir to demolish 8

dénoncer to denouce, to expose 6

une **dent** tooth; *une brosse à dents* toothbrush

le **dentifrice** toothpaste

un(e) **dentiste** dentist

un **départ** departure

dépasser to pass, to exceed

se **dépêcher** to hurry

dépendre (de) to depend (on) 7

dépenser to spend 6

déprimant(e) depressing 7

déprimé(e) depressed 2

depuis for, since; *depuis combien de temps* how long; *depuis quand* since when

dernier, dernière last

derrière behind

des some; from (the), of (the); any

dès que as soon as 6

descendre to go down; to get off 3

une **description** description 3

se **déshabiller** to undress

désirer to want; *Vous désirez?* What would you like?

désolé(e) sorry

un **dessert** dessert

le **dessin** drawing; *un dessin animé* cartoon

dessus: au-dessus de above

une **destination** destination

deux two

deuxième second

devant in front of

développer to develop 6

devenir to become

devoir to have to; to owe 10

les **devoirs (m.)** homework

un **dico (dictionnaire)** dictionary

Dieu (m.) God 8

différent(e) different 7

difficile hard, difficult

diffuser to broadcast 7

diligent(e) hardworking

dimanche (m.) Sunday

un **dindon** turkey

le **dîner** dinner, supper

un **dinosaure** dinosaur 9

diplômé(e) possessing a diploma 4

dire to say, to tell

direct(e) direct; *en direct* live 4

un **directeur, une directrice** principal 1

dis say

une **discothèque** discotheque 7

disponible available 5

se **disputer** to argue 7

une **disquette** diskette

une **dissertation** research paper 1

distingué(e) distinguished 4; *Je vous prie d'agréer, Monsieur (ou Madame), mes salutations distinguées.* yours truly 4

une **distraction** entertainment 3

se **distraire** to enjoy oneself, to have a good time 7

une **diversité** diversity 7

diviser to divide 8

un **divorce** divorce 7

divorcer to get divorced 7

dix ten

dix-huit eighteen

dixième tenth

dix-neuf nineteen

dix-sept seventeen

un **docteur** doctor

un **document** document 2

un **documentaire** documentary

un **doigt** finger; *un doigt de pied* toe

un **dollar** dollar

un **domaine** field, area 6

Dommage! Too bad!

donc so, then

donner to give; *donner sur* to overlook; *Donnez-moi....* Give me . . . .

dont of which/whom, about which/whom, whose 5; *la façon dont* the way in which 5

dormir to sleep

un **dortoir** dormitory room (for more than one person)

un **dos** back

la **douane** customs

un **douanier, une douanière** customs agent

doubler to pass (a vehicle)

doucement gradually

une **douche** shower

doué(e) gifted

douter to doubt 4

douze twelve

un **drame** drama

un **drap** sheet

la **drogue** drugs

droit(e) right 10; *à droite* to (on) the right

drôle funny

du from (the), of (the); some, any; in (the)

un **duc** duke 8

dur(e) hard

une **durée** length 3

durer to last 8

dynamique dynamic

E

l' **eau (f.)** water; *l'eau minérale (f.)* mineral water

échanger to exchange

les **échecs (m.)** chess

une **école** school; *les grandes écoles* elite, specialized universities 4

écologique ecological 6

écoute listen

écouter to listen (to); *écouter de la musique* to listen to music

un **écran** screen 6

écrire to write

un **écrivain** writer

l' **éducation (f.)** education

un **effort** effort

effrayé(e) frightened 2

une **église** church

égoïste selfish

Eh! Hey!

électronique electronic 6

un **éléphant** elephant

un(e) **élève** student

élevé(e) high 4; raised 10

elle she, it; her

elles they (f.); them (f.)

l' **e-mail (m.)** e-mail 6

embaucher to hire 4

embêtant(e) annoying 10

embêter to bother 5

une **émission** program

emmener to take (someone) along

un **empereur** emperor 8

un **empire** empire 8

un **emploi** job 4; *un emploi du temps* schedule

un(e) **employé(e)** employee, clerk 2

emprunter (à) to borrow (from) 9

en to (the); on; in; by; as; made of; some, any, of

(about, from) it/them; while, upon 2; *en avance* early; *en bas* at the bottom 3; *en direct* live 4; *en général* in general 3; *en ligne* online 6; *en plus* in addition 5; *en retard* late; *en solde* on sale

enchanté(e) delighted

encore still; *ne (n')... pas encore* not yet

un **endroit** place 2

l' **énergie (f.)** energy

un(e) **enfant** child

enfin finally

engagé(e) committed 6

enlever to remove; *enlever la poussière* to dust

des **ennuis (m.)** problems 5

s' **ennuyer** to get bored, to be bored 5

une **enquête** survey

enregistrer to record 3; *faire enregistrer ses bagages (m.)* to check one's baggage

l' **enseignement (m.)** education 1

ensemble together

un **ensemble** outfit

ensuite next 1

entendre to hear; *entendre parler de* to hear about 6; *s'entendre* to get along 2

enthousiaste enthusiastic 4

entier, entière whole 6

entouré(e) wrapped 10

s' **entraîner** to train, to work out 1

entre between, among

une **entrée** entrance; entrée (course before main dish)

entrer to enter, to come in

une **enveloppe** envelope

envers towards 8

l' **envie (f.): avoir envie de** to want, to feel like

environ about 10

l' **environnement (m.)** environment

envoyer to send

une épaule shoulder

épicé(e) spicy

une époque time 9

l' épouvante (f.) horror

épuisé(e) exhausted 2

une équipe team 6

l' escalade (f.) climbing

une escale stop, stopover

un escalier stairs, staircase

un escargot snail

l' espace (m.) space 6

l' Espagne (f.) Spain

l' espagnol (m.) Spanish (language)

espagnol(e) Spanish

espérer to hope

essayer to try 1

l' essence (f.) gasoline

essentiel, essentielle essential 3

est is

l' est (m.) east

est-ce que? (phrase introducing a question)

et and

établir to establish 6

un étage floor, story

un étang pond

les États-Unis (m.) United States

l' été (m.) summer

éteindre to turn off

étonné(e) surprised 5

un étranger, une étrangère foreigner 7

être to be; *être à* to belong to 9; *être d'accord* to agree 5; *être en train de* (**+ infinitive**) to be busy (doing something); *Nous sommes le* (**+ date**). It's the (+ date).

une étude study

un(e) étudiant(e) student

étudier to study; *Étudions....* Let's study . . . .

euh uhm

l' Europe (f.) Europe

européen, européenne European

eux them (m.)

un événement event 8

évident(e) evident, obvious 4

un évier sink

éviter to avoid 10

un examen test, exam 1

excellent(e) excellent 6

une excursion trip

excusez-moi excuse me

un exemple: par exemple for example

exigeant(e) demanding 2

exiger to require 4

exotique exotic

une expérience experience 4

expliquer to explain 2

un exposé report 1

une exposition exhibit, exhibition

une expression expression 10

extra fantastic, terrific, great

F

une fac (faculté) university

fâché(e) angry 2

se fâcher to get angry 2

facile easy

une façon way 5; *la façon dont* the way in which 5

un facteur, une factrice letter carrier

faible weak

la faim hunger; *J'ai faim.* I'm hungry.

faire to do, to make; *faire attention* to pay attention 2; *faire de l'aérobic (m.)* to do aerobics; *faire de l'escalade (f.)* to go climbing; *faire de la gym (gymnastique)* to do gymnastics; *faire de la luge* to go tobogganing 1; *faire de la musculation* to do body building; *faire de la planche à neige* to go snowboarding 1; *faire de la planche à roulettes* to go skateboarding 1; *faire*
de la planche à voile to go windsurfing; *faire de la plongée sous-marine* to go scuba diving; *faire de la voile* to go sailing; *faire des études* to study 4; *faire du* (**+ number**) to wear size (+ number); *faire du baby-sitting* to baby-sit; *faire du camping* to go camping, to camp; *faire du canoë* to go canoeing; *faire du cheval* to go horse-back riding; *faire du footing* to go running; *faire du karaté* to do karate; *faire du roller* to go in-line skating; *faire du shopping* to go shopping; *faire du ski de fond* to go cross-country skiing 1; *faire du ski nautique* to go waterskiing, to water-ski; *faire du sport* to play sports; *faire du vélo* to go biking; *faire enregistrer ses bagages (m.)* to check one's baggage; *faire la connaissance (de)* to meet; *faire la queue* to stand in line; *faire le plein* to fill up the gas tank; *faire le tour* to take a tour; *faire les courses* to go grocery shopping; *faire les devoirs* to do homework; *faire les magasins* to go shopping; *faire les touristes* to act like tourists 5; *faire partie de* to be a part of 9; *faire prisonnier/prisonnière* to take prisoner 8; *faire sécher le linge* to dry clothes; *faire un somme* to take a nap 5; *faire un stage* to have on-the-job training; *faire un tour* to go for a ride; *faire un tour de grande roue* to go on the Ferris wheel 1; *faire un tour de manège* to go on the merry-go-round 1; *faire un tour de montagnes russes* to go on the roller coaster 1; *faire un voyage* to take a trip 5; *faire une promenade* to go for a ride, to go for a walk; *se faire mal* to hurt oneself 10

fait: Ça fait.... That's/It's . . .
.; *Quel temps fait-il?* What's
the weather like? How's the
weather?; *Il fait beau.* It's
(The weather's) beautiful/
nice.; *Il fait chaud.* It's (The
weather's) hot/warm.; *Il fait
du soleil.* It's sunny.; *Il fait du
vent.* It's windy.; *Il fait frais.*
It's (The weather's) cool.; *Il
fait froid.* It's (The weather's)
cold.; *Il fait mauvais.* It's
(The weather's) bad.

falloir to be necessary, to have
to

familial(e) family 7

une **famille** family

une **famine** famine 6

un(e) **fana** fanatic, buff

fantastique fantastic 9

un **fast-food** fast-food restaurant

fatigant(e) tiring 2

fatigué(e) tired

la **faune** animal life 9

faut: il faut it is necessary,
one has to/must, we/you
have to/must; *il me faut* I
need

un **fauteuil** armchair; *un fauteuil
roulant* wheelchair 10

favorable favorable

favori, favorite favorite

un **fax** fax 5

faxer to fax

une **femme** wife; woman; *une
femme au foyer* housewife;
une femme d'affaires
businesswoman; *une femme
politique* politician

une **fenêtre** window

un **fer à repasser** iron

une **ferme** farm

fermer to close

un **fermier, une fermière** farmer

une **fête** holiday, festival

fêter to celebrate

un **feu** (traffic) light; *un feu
d'artifice* fireworks

une **feuille de papier** sheet of
paper

un **feuilleton** soap opera

un **feutre** felt-tip pen 1

février February

une **fiche: une fiche d'inscription**
registration form 1; *une fiche
de commande* order form

fier, fière proud 8

la **fièvre** fever

une **figure** face

une **fille** girl; daughter

un **film** movie

un **fils** son

la **fin** end 1

fin(e) intricate 9

finalement eventually, in the
end

finir to finish

flâner to stroll

une **fleur** flower

un(e) **fleuriste** florist

un **fleuve** river

flexible flexible 4

une **flûte** flute

une **fois** time; once 1; *à la fois* all
at once

le **fon** Fon (African language) 3

le **fond: au fond de** at the end
of

une **fondation** foundation 6

le **foot (football)** soccer

le **footing** running

une **forme: être en bonne/
mauvaise forme** to be in
good/bad shape

formidable great, terrific

un **formulaire** form 4

fort(e) strong

un **fou, une folle** crazy person 1

fouiller to search, to go
through 2

un **foulard** scarf

se **fouler** to sprain 10

un **four** oven

une **fourchette** fork

la **fourrure** fur 6

frais, fraîche cool, fresh

une **fraise** strawberry

un **franc** franc

le **français** French (language)

français(e) French

la **France** France

franchement frankly

francophone French-speaking

le **franglais** franglais (English
words used in French) 7

un **frère** brother

un **frigo** refrigerator

des **frissons (m.)** chills

des **frites (f.)** French fries

froid(e) cold; *avoir froid* to be
cold

le **fromage** cheese

une **frontière** border, boundary 6

un **fruit** fruit; *des fruits de mer (m.)*
seafood

frustré(e) frustrated 10

une **fusée** rocket 6

G

gagner to win 1

une **galère: Quelle galère!** What
a drag!

une **galerie** hall, gallery; *la galerie
des miroirs déformants* fun
house 1

un **gant** glove; *un gant de toilette*
bath mitt

un **garage** garage

garanti(e) guaranteed 4

un **garçon** boy

un **garde forestier** park ranger 5

garder to keep

une **gare** train station

un **gars** guy 5

un **gâteau** cake

gâter to spoil

gauche left 10; *à gauche* to
(on) the left

la **Gaule** Gaul 8

un(e) **Gaulois(e)** inhabitant of/from Gaul 8

une **gazelle** gazelle 9

gêner to bother 10

un **général** general 8

général(e) general 3

généreux, généreuse generous

génial(e) great, terrific, fantastic 7

un **genou** knee

un **genre** kind, type 3

des **gens (m.)** people

gentil, gentille nice

la **géographie** geography

la **géométrie** geometry 1

un(e) **gérant(e)** manager 5

le **gibier** game 9

une **girafe** giraffe

une **glace** ice cream; mirror; *une glace à la vanille* vanilla ice cream; *une glace au chocolat* chocolate ice cream

le **golf** golf

une **gomme** eraser 1

une **gorge** throat

un **gorille** gorilla

goûter to taste

le **goûter** afternoon snack

un **gouvernement** government 4

gouverner to govern 8

grâce thanks 6

des **graffiti (m.)** graffiti 7

grand(e) tall, big, large; *les grandes écoles* elite, specialized universities 4

une **grand-mère** grandmother

un **grand-parent** grandparent 2

un **grand-père** grandfather

une **grange** barn

un **gratte-ciel** skyscraper 9

gratuit(e) free

gratuitement free 10

grave serious

le **grec** Greek 1

un **grenier** attic

la **grippe** flu

gris(e) gray

gros, grosse big, fat, large

un **groupe** group 5

la **Guadeloupe** Guadeloupe

guadeloupéen, guadeloupéenne inhabitant of/from Guadeloupe

une **guerre** war

un **guichet** ticket window; *un guichet automatique* ATM machine

un **guide** guidebook 3

guillotiner to guillotine 8

une **guitare** guitar

guyanais(e) inhabitant of/from French Guiana

la **Guyane française** French Guiana

la **gym (gymnastique)** gymnastics

un **gymnase** gym 5

H

habillé(e) dressed 2

s' **habiller** to get dressed

habiter to live

une **habitude** habit 9

Haïti (f.) Haiti

haïtien, haïtienne Haitian

un **hamburger** hamburger

des **haricots verts (m.)** green beans

haut(e) tall, high

Hein? Huh? What? 1

un **héros, une héroïne** hero, heroine

l' **heure (f.)** hour, time, o'clock; *à l'heure* on time; *Quelle heure est-il?* What time is it?

heureusement fortunately

heureux, heureuse happy

heurter to hit, to run into 1

hier yesterday

un **hippopotame** hippopotamus

l' **histoire (f.)** history; story

le **hit-parade** the charts

l' **hiver (m.)** winter

une **HLM (habitation à loyer modéré)** public housing 7

un **homme** man; *un homme au foyer* househusband; *un homme d'affaires* businessman; *un homme politique* politician

honnête honest

un **hôpital** hospital 10

un **horaire** schedule, timetable

un **hot-dog** hot dog

un **hôtel** hotel

une **hôtesse de l'air** flight attendant 5

l' **huile (f.)** oil

huit eight

huitième eighth

humain(e) human 2

humanitaire humanitarian 6

un **hyène** hyena 9

I

ici here

une **idée** idea

il he, it

il y a there is, there are; ago; *Il n'y a pas de quoi.* You're welcome.

une **île** island

illuminé(e) illuminated 8

ils they (m.)

imaginer to imagine

un(e) **imbécile** idiot 2

un **immeuble** apartment building

l' **immigration (f.)** immigration

un(e) **immigré(e)** immigrant 7

un **imperméable (imper)** raincoat

important(e) important 2

impossible impossible 3

un **impôt** tax 8

une **impression** impression, feeling 3

impressionniste Impressionist

une **imprimante** printer 6

incroyable unbelievable 2

l' **indépendance (f.)** independence 8

indépendant(e) independent 7

un **indice** rating 3

indiquer to indicate

indispensable indispensable 3

l' **Indochine (f.)** Indochina 3

inférieur(e) less, lower 4

un **infirmier, une infirmière** nurse

une **influence** influence 7

un **informaticien, une informaticienne** computer specialist

des **informations (f.)** news

l' **informatique (f.)** computer science

informer to inform 9

l' **inforoute (f.)** information superhighway 6

un **ingénieur** engineer

s' **inquiéter** to worry

s' **installer** to move 5

un **instrument** instrument 9

s' **intégrer** to become integrated 7

intelligent(e) intelligent

interdit(e) prohibited 3

intéressant(e) interesting

intéresser to interest; *s'intéresser à* to be interested in 9

un **intérêt** interest 6

une **interro (interrogation)** quiz, test

une **intrigue** plot 3

inutile useless 2

inviter to invite

l' **Irak (m.)** Iraq 6

l' **Italie (f.)** Italy

italien, italienne Italian

ivoirien, ivoirienne from the Ivory Coast

J

j' I

jamais ever 1; *ne (n')... jamais* never

une **jambe** leg

le **jambon** ham

janvier January

le **Japon** Japan

japonais(e) Japanese

un **jardin** garden, lawn; park

jaune yellow

le **jazz** jazz

je I

un **jean** (pair of) jeans

jeter un coup d'œil to take a quick look 10

un **jeu** game; *un jeu télévisé* game show; *des jeux d'adresse* games of skill 1; *des jeux vidéo (m.)* video games

jeudi (m.) Thursday

jeune young

un(e) **jeune** young person 3

joli(e) pretty

jouer to play; to act, to play (a part) 3; *jouer au basket* to play basketball; *jouer au foot* to play soccer; *jouer au golf* to play golf; *jouer au tennis* to play tennis; *jouer au volley* to play volleyball; *jouer aux cartes (f.)* to play cards; *jouer aux échecs (m.)* to play chess; *jouer aux jeux vidéo* to play video games

un **jour** day; *de nos jours* these days 9

un **journal** newspaper; journal 7

le **journalisme** journalism

un(e) **journaliste** journalist

une **journée** day; *Bonne journée!* Have a good day!

juillet July

juin June

jumeau, jumelle twin

une **jupe** skirt

le **jus: le jus d'orange** orange juice; *le jus de fruit* fruit juice; *le jus de pamplemousse* grapefruit juice; *le jus de pomme* apple juice; *le jus de raisin* grape juice; *le jus de tomate* tomato juice

jusqu'à up to, until

juste just, only

justement exactly 10

la **justice** justice 8

K

le **karaté** karate

le **ketchup** ketchup

un **kilogramme (kilo)** kilogram

un **kilomètre** kilometer

un **kiosque à journaux** newsstand 3

L

là there, here

là-bas over there

un **labo (laboratoire)** laboratory 1

un **lac** lake

laid(e) unattractive

laisser to leave; *laissez-moi* let me 10

le **lait** milk

une **lampe** lamp

lancer to launch 6

un **lanceur de satellites** satellite launcher 6

une **langue** language 3

un **lapin** rabbit

large wide 8

le **latin** Latin (language)

se **laver** to wash (oneself)

un **lave-vaisselle** dishwasher

le, la, l' the; him, her, it; *le (+ day of the week)* on (+ day of the week); *le (+ number)* on the (+ ordinal number)

une **leçon** lesson

la **lecture** reading 1

un **légume** vegetable

le **lendemain** the next day

lequel, laquelle; lesquels, lesquelles which one; which ones 7

les the; them

la **lessive** laundry

une **lettre** letter; *une boîte aux lettres* mailbox

leur their; to them

le **leur, la leur** theirs 9

se **lever** to get up

une **lèvre** lip; *le rouge à lèvres* lipstick

libéral(e) liberal 8

la **liberté** liberty

une **librairie** bookstore

libre free (not busy)

un **lieu** place 8; *avoir lieu* to take place 8

une **ligne** line 6; *en ligne* online 6

la **limite de vitesse** speed limit

une **limonade** lemon-lime soda

le **linge: faire sécher le linge** to dry clothes

un **lion** lion

liquide: l'argent liquide (m.) cash

lire to read

une **liste** list 1

un **lit** bed; *des lits jumeaux* twin beds; *un grand lit* double bed

la **littérature** literature 1

un **livre** book

une **location: un bureau de location** box office 3

le **logement** housing 7

une **loi** law 7

loin far

les **loisirs (m.)** leisure activities

long, longue long

longtemps (for) a long time 5

lorsque when 3

louer to rent

la **loyauté** loyalty 8

une **luge** toboggan 1

lui to him, to her; him

une **lumière** light

lundi (m.) Monday

des **lunettes (f.)** glasses; *des lunettes de soleil (f.)* sunglasses

une **lutte** fight 6

le **Luxembourg** Luxembourg

luxembourgeois(e) from Luxembourg

un **lycée** high school

un **lycéen, une lycéenne** high school student 1

M

m'appelle: je m'appelle my name is

une **machine à laver** washer

Madagascar (f.) Madagascar

Madame (Mme) Mrs., Ma'am; *Madame une telle* Mrs. So-and-so 5

Mademoiselle (Mlle) Miss

un **magasin** store; *un grand magasin* department store

un **magazine** magazine

maghrébin(e) inhabitant of/from the Maghreb 7

un **magnétoscope** VCR

magnifique magnificent

mai May

un **maillot de bain** swimsuit

une **main** hand

maintenant now

maintenir to maintain 8

une **mairie** town hall

mais but

une **maison** house

mal bad, badly; *avoir mal (à...)* to hurt, to have a/an . . . ache, to have a sore . . .

malade sick

une **maladie** disease, illness

malgache inhabitant of/from Madagascar

malheureusement unfortunately 9

le **Mali** Mali 9

maltraité(e) mistreated 6

maman (f.) Mom

la **Manche** English Channel

un **manège** merry-go-round 1

manger to eat; *manger de la pizza* to eat pizza; *une salle à manger* dining room

un(e) **manifestant(e)** demonstrator 4

une **manifestation** demonstration 4

manifester to demonstrate 4

un **manteau** coat

un **manuel** textbook 1

le **maquillage** makeup

se **maquiller** to put on makeup

un(e) **marchand(e)** merchant

un **marché** market

marcher to walk; to work 5

mardi (m.) Tuesday

un **mari** husband

un **mariage** marriage

un(e) **marié(e)** groom, bride

se **marier** to get married 7

le **Maroc** Morocco

marocain(e) Moroccan

la **maroquinerie** leather goods 9

une **marque** brand 7

un(e) **marquis(e)** marquis, marchioness 8

marrant(e) funny

marre: J'en ai marre! I'm sick of it! I've had it!

marron brown

mars March

martiniquais(e) inhabitant of/from Martinique

la **Martinique** Martinique

le **mascara** mascara

un **massacre** massacre 8

un **match** game, match

les **maths (f.)** math

un **matin** morning; *le matin* in the morning

mauvais(e) bad

le **maximum** maximum 4; *Il faut profiter de la vie au maximum.* We have to live life to the fullest.

la **mayonnaise** mayonnaise

me (to) me; myself

un **mec** guy

méchant(e) mean

le **mécontentement** dissatisfaction 4

un **médecin** doctor

se **méfier de** to distrust 2

meilleur(e) better 6; *le meilleur, la meilleure* best 5

un **melon** melon

un **membre** member

même even; same 3

le **ménage** housework

un **menu** fixed-price meal

une **mer** sea; *au bord de la mer* at the seashore; *des fruits de mer* seafood; *la mer des Antilles* Caribbean Sea; *la mer du Nord* North Sea; *la mer Méditerranée* Mediterranean Sea

merci thanks

mercredi (m.) Wednesday

une **mère** mother

Mesdames ladies

un **message** message

Messieurs-Dames ladies and gentlemen

un **métier** trade, craft

un **mètre** meter 5

un **métro** subway

un **metteur en scène** director

mettre to put (on), to set; to turn on 5

mexicain(e) Mexican

le **Mexique** Mexico

un **micro-onde** microwave

midi noon

le **Midi** the south of France 10

le **mien, la mienne** mine 9

mieux better; *le mieux* the best

mignon, mignonne cute

le **mil** millet 9

mille (one) thousand

un **milliard** billion 6

un **million** million

mince slender; *Mince!* Darn!

la **mine: avoir bonne/mauvaise mine** to look well/sick

minimum minimum 4

un **minivan** minivan

minuit midnight

une **minute** minute

un **miroir** mirror 1

une **mission** mission 6

moche ugly

le **mode d'emploi** instructions 10

modèle model 9

moderne modern

moi me, I

moi-même myself 10

un **moine** monk 8

moins minus; less; *au moins* at least; *moins le quart* quarter to

un **mois** month

un **moment** moment

mon, ma; mes my

Monaco (m.) Monaco

une **monarchie** monarchy 8

le **monde** world; people

mondial(e) world-wide 6

monégasque inhabitant of/from Monaco

monétaire monetary 8

un **moniteur, une monitrice** instructor; monitor 6

la **monnaie** change

monoparental(e) single-parent 7

Monsieur Mr., Sir; *Monsieur un tel* Mr. So-and-so 5

une **montagne** mountain; *des montagnes russes* roller coaster 1

monter to go up; to get on; to get in

une **montre** watch

montrer to show; *Montrez-moi....* Show me . . . .

un **monument** monument

un **morceau** piece

un **mot** word 7

un **mouchoir** handkerchief

une **moule** mussel

mourir to die

une **mousse** mousse; *une mousse au chocolat* chocolate mousse

la **moutarde** mustard

un **mouton** sheep

le **moyen** way 4; means 9

moyen, moyenne medium

un **mur** wall 7

mûr(e) ripe

la **musculation** body building

un **musée** museum

un **musicien, une musicienne** musician

la **musique** music

mystérieux, mystérieuse mysterious

N

n'est-ce pas? isn't that so?

n'importe quel, n'importe quelle just any 10

n'importe qui anyone 10

nager to swim

naître to be born

une **nappe** tablecloth

national(e) national

une **nationalité** nationality

la **nature** nature 3; *une nature morte* still life 3

naturellement naturally

ne (n')... aucun(e) no, not any 2

ne (n')... jamais never

ne (n')... ni... ni... neither . . . nor 2

ne (n')... pas not

ne (n')... pas encore not yet

ne (n')... personne no one, nobody, not anyone

ne (n')... plus no longer, not anymore

ne (n')... que only 2

ne (n')... rien nothing, not anything

nécessaire necessary 3

négocier to negotiate 8

la **neige** snow 1

neiger: Il neige. It's snowing.

nettoyer to clean

neuf nine

neuf, neuve new 10

neuvième ninth

un **nez** nose

ni... ni... ne (n') neither . . . nor 2

le **Niger** Niger 9

noir(e) black

un **nom** name; *un nom de jeune fille* maiden name 2

nombreux, nombreuse numerous 7

non no

non-traditionnel, non-traditionnelle nontraditional 7

le **nord** north

un(e) **Normand(e)** inhabitant of/from Normandy 8

une **note** note 1; grade 7

notre; nos our

le **nôtre, la nôtre** ours 9

nourrir to feed

la **nourriture** food

nous we; us; ourselves; to us

nouveau, nouvel, nouvelle new

des **nouvelles (f.)** news 9

novembre November

nucléaire nuclear

une **nuit** night 5

un **numéro** number; issue 4; *un numéro de téléphone* telephone number

O

un **objet d'art** objet d'art

obligé(e): être obligé(e) de to be obliged to, to have to

une **occasion** opportunity 9

l' **Occident (m.)** West 8

occupé(e) busy

s' **occuper de** to take care of 5; to deal with 8

un **océan** ocean; *l'océan Atlantique (m.)* Atlantic Ocean; *l'océan Indien (m.)* Indian Ocean; *l'océan Pacifique (m.)* Pacific Ocean

l' **océanographie (f.)** oceanography 6

octobre October

un **œil** eye; *jeter un coup d'œil* to take a quick look 10

un **œuf** egg; *des œufs brouillés (m.)* scrambled eggs; *des œufs sur le plat (m.)* fried eggs

offrir to offer, to give

oh oh; *Oh là là!* Wow! Oh no! Oh dear!

un **oignon** onion

un **oiseau** bird

OK OK

une **omelette** omelette

on they, we, one; *On y va?* Shall we go (there)?

un **oncle** uncle

onze eleven

une **opinion** opinion

optimiste optimistic 7

l' **or (m.)** gold

oral(e) oral 1

orange orange

une **orange** orange

un **orchestre** orchestra 3

ordinaire regular (gasoline)

un **ordinateur** computer

une **ordonnance** prescription 10

ordonner to order 8

une **oreille** ear

organisé(e) organized 4

une **origine** origin 7

ou or

où where

ouais yeah

oublier to forget 6

l' **ouest (m.)** west

oui yes

un **ours** bear

un **outil de recherche** search engine 6

ouvert(e) frank 7

un **ouvrier, une ouvrière** (factory) worker

ouvrir to open

P

un **pagne** African skirt 9

le **pain** bread; *le pain grillé* toast; *le pain perdu* French toast

une **paire** pair 9

la **paix** peace 8

un **pamplemousse** grapefruit

une **panne** breakdown; *tomber en panne* to have a (mechanical) breakdown

un **panneau** sign

panoramique panoramic 5

un **pantalon** (pair of) pants

une **pantoufle** slipper

papa (m.) Dad

par per; by; *par avion* by air mail; *par conséquent* consequently 8; *par contre* on the other hand 9; *par exemple* for example

le **paradis** paradise

un **parapluie** umbrella

un **parc** park; *un parc d'attractions* amusement park 1

parce que because

parcourir to travel through, to cover 5

pardon excuse me

un **pare-brise** windshield

un **parent** parent; relative

paresseux, paresseuse lazy

parfait(e) perfect

parier to bet

parler to speak, to talk; *Tu parles!* No way! You're kidding!, You're not kidding! 5

parmi among 6

part: à part aside from

partager to share 9

un **parti** (political) party 4

participer à to take part in 4

une **partie** part 6

partir to leave

partout everywhere 3

pas not; *pas du tout* not at all

un **passager, une passagère** passenger

un(e) **passant(e)** passerby 7

le **passé** past 8

un **passeport** passport

passer to show (a movie); to spend (time); to pass, to go (by); to take (a test) 1; to play (on the radio) 7; *passer à la douane* to go through customs; *passer l'aspirateur (m.)* to vacuum; *se passer* to happen 2, to go 5

un **passe-temps** pastime 1

passionnant(e) exciting, fascinating 6

une **pastèque** watermelon

une **pastille** lozenge 10

le **pâté** pâté

la **patience** patience 5

une **pâtisserie** pastry store

un **pâtissier, une pâtissière** pastry store owner

pauvre poor

la **pauvreté** poverty 6

un **pavillon** pavilion, hall 9

payer to pay 2

un **pays** country

un **paysage** landscape 3; scenery 5

un **paysan, une paysanne** peasant 9

une **peau** skin 9

une **pêche** peach

un **peigne** comb

se **peigner** to comb (one's hair)

un **peignoir de bain** bathrobe

peindre to paint 3

un(e) **peintre** painter 3

une **pelouse** lawn

pendant during; *pendant que* while 2

une **pendule** clock

pénible unpleasant

penser (à) to think (of)

percé pierced 5

perdre to lose; *perdre son temps* to waste one's time 7

un **père** father

se **perfectionner** to improve

permettre to permit, to allow 6

un **permis de conduire** driver's license

une **personnalité** personality

une **personne** person; *ne (n')... personne* no one, nobody, not anyone; *personne ne (n')* nobody, no one 2

le **personnel** personnel, staff 4

peser to weigh

petit(e) short, little, small; *le petit déjeuner* breakfast; *mon petit* son

des **petits pois (m.)** peas

(un) **peu** (a) little; *(un) peu de* (a) little, few

le **peuple** people 8

la **peur: avoir peur (de)** to be afraid (of)

peut-être maybe

une **pharmacie** pharmacy, drugstore 10

un **pharmacien, une pharmacienne** pharmacist

la **philosophie** philosophy

un **phoque** seal

une **photo** photo, picture

une **phrase** phrase, sentence 10

la **physique** physics

un **piano** piano

une **pièce** room; coin; *une pièce (de théâtre)* play 3

un **pied** foot; *à pied* on foot; *un doigt de pied* toe

pieux, pieuse pious 8

une **pile** battery 10

un **pilote** pilot

piqueniquer to have a picnic

une **piscine** swimming pool

une **piste** trail, run, track 1

une **pizza** pizza

un **placard** cupboard

la **place** room, space; *une place (public)* square; place; seat 3; *à ta place* if I were you 5

placé(e) placed, situated

une **plage** beach

se **plaindre** to complain 5

plaire to please 3

un **plaisir** pleasure

plaît: ... me plaît. I like . . . .

un **plan** map

une **planche: une planche à neige** snowboard 1; *une planche à roulettes* skateboard 1; *la planche à voile* windsurfing

une **plante** plant

un **plat** dish; *le plat principal* main course

un **plâtre** cast 10

plein(e) full; *à plein temps* full-time 4; *faire le plein* to fill up the gas tank

pleuvoir: Il pleut. It's raining.

le **plomb** lead

la **plongée sous-marine** scuba diving

plonger to dive

la **pluie** rain 9

la **plupart (de)** most 7

plus more; *de plus* furthermore, what's more, more; *en plus* in addition 5; *le plus* **(+ adverb)** the most (+ adverb); *le/la/les plus* **(+ adjective)** the most (+ adjective); *ne (n')... plus* no longer, not anymore; *plus tard* later

plusieurs several 3

plûtot rather 2

un **pneu** tire

po: les sciences po political science 1

un **poignet** wrist 10

une **poire** pear

les **pois (m.): des petits pois (m.)** peas

un **poisson** fish; *un poisson rouge* goldfish

le **poivre** pepper

poli(e) polite

la **police** police 2

un **policier, une policière** detective

politique political

la **pollution** pollution

une **pomme** apple; *une pomme de terre* potato

un **pompier** firefighter

un(e) **pompiste** gas station attendant

un **pont** bridge

populaire popular 3

le **porc** pork

une **porte** door; gate; *une porte d'embarquement* departure gate; *un porte-bagages* overhead compartment 5

un **portefeuille** billfold, wallet

porter to wear

poser to ask (a question) 2

une **possibilité** possibility

possible possible

un **poste** job, position 4

une **poste** post office

un **postier, une postière** postal worker

un **pot** jar

le **potage** soup

une **poubelle** garbage can

une **poule** hen

un **poulet** chicken

pour for; (in order) to

un **pourcentage** percentage 4

pourquoi why

pourri(e) spoiled 9

pourtant however 9

pousser to push 4; to grow 9

la **poussière** dust; *enlever la poussière* to dust

pouvoir to be able to

pratique practical

préférer to prefer

premier, première first

prendre to take, to have (food or drink); *prendre rendez-vous* to make an appointment

un **prénom** first name

préparatoire preparatory 4

préparer to prepare; *se préparer* to get ready

près (de) near

le **présent** present 8

présenter to introduce; *se présenter* to come, to appear 4

préserver to save, to protect

presque almost

pressé(e) in a hurry 7

prêt(e) ready

prêter to lend 9

prier to beg 4; *Je vous en prie.* You're welcome.; *Je vous prie d'agréer, Monsieur (ou Madame), mes salutations distinguées.* yours truly 4

principal(e) main

le **printemps** spring

un **prisonnier, une prisonnière** prisoner 8

un **prix** price 3

un **problème** problem

prochain(e) next

un(e) **prof** teacher

un **professeur** teacher

une **profession** occupation

profiter de to take advantage of; *Il faut profiter de la vie au maximum.* We have to live life to the fullest.

le **progrès** progress 6

un **projet** project 4; plan 9

une **promenade** ride; walk

proposer to propose 5

propre own 5; clean 7

la **protection** protection 6

protéger to protect 6

un(e) **protestant(e)** Protestant 8

une **province** province 5; *en province* in the provinces 8

puis then

puisque since 2

puissant(e) powerful

un **pull** sweater

un **pyjama** pyjamas

Q

qu'est-ce que what; *Qu'est-ce que c'est?* What is it/this?; *Qu'est-ce que c'est que...?* What is . . . ? 9; *Qu'est-ce que tu as?* What's the matter with you?

qu'est-ce qui what

un **quai** platform

une **qualification** qualification 4

quand when

quant à as for 6

quarante forty

un **quart** quarter; *et quart* fifteen (minutes after), quarter after; *moins le quart* quarter to

un **quartier** quarter, neighborhood

quatorze fourteen

quatre four

quatre-vingt-dix ninety

quatre-vingts eighty

quatrième fourth

que how; than, as, that; which, whom; what; *Que je suis bête!* How dumb I am!; *Que vous êtes gentils!* How nice you are!

le **Québec** Quebec (Province) 4

un(e) **Québécois(e)** inhabitant of/from Quebec

quel, quelle what, which; *Quel, Quelle... !* What (a) . . . !

quelqu'un someone, somebody

quelque chose something

quelquefois sometimes

quelques some

une **question** question 2

la **queue: faire la queue** to stand in line

qui who, whom; which, that; *qui est-ce que* whom; *qui est-ce qui* who

une **quiche** quiche

quinze fifteen

quitter to leave (a person or place)

quoi what; *Il n'y a pas de quoi.* You're welcome.

quotidien, quotidienne daily

R

raconter to tell (about)

une **radio** radio 7

une **radiographie** X ray 10

un **raisin** grape

une **raison** reason 4; *avoir raison* to be right 10

ranger to pick up, to arrange

rapide fast

rapidement rapidly, fast

rappeler to remind 9; *se rappeler* to remember 2

rapporter to bring back 10

des **rapports (m.)** relations, relationship 2

une **raquette** racket

se **raser** to shave

un **rasoir** razor

rassurant(e) reassuring 2

rater to fail 1

rattraper to trap 10

un **rayon** (store) department 10

un **récépissé** receipt 2

la **réception** reception desk

un(e) **réceptionniste** receptionist

recevoir to receive, to get

la **recherche** research 1; *un outil de recherche* search engine 6

recommander to recommend

recommencer to begin again

reconnaissant(e) grateful 4

reconnaître to recognize 3

recycler recycle

la **rédaction** composition 1

une **réduction** reduction 10

réduit(e) reduced 3

un **refuge** shelter 6

regarder to watch; to look (at); *se regarder* to look at oneself

le **reggae** reggae

régler to pay

un **règne** reign 8

regretter to be sorry; to regret 2

une **reine** queen

se **rejoindre** to meet

une **relation** relation(ship) 7

religieux, religieuse religious 9

la **religion** religion 8

une **relique** relic 8

rembourser to reimburse 10

remercier to thank

remplir to fill (out)

rencontrer to meet 7; *se rencontrer* to meet 9

un **rendez-vous** appointment; *prendre rendez-vous* to make an appointment

rendre to hand in, to return 6; *rendre* (**+ adjective**) to make 10; *rendre un service* to help 5; *rendre visite (à)* to visit; *se rendre compte* to realize 5

des **renseignements (m.)** information 3

la **rentrée** first day of school 1

rentrer to come home, to return, to come back

réparer to repair 10

un **repas** meal

repasser to iron

répéter to repeat 2

répondre to answer 2

une **réponse** answer 2

un **reportage** report 4

un **reporter** reporter

se **reposer** to rest 2

la **République Démocratique du Congo** Democratic Republic of the Congo 6

le **R.E.R. (Réseau Express Régional)** express subway to suburbs

une **réservation** reservation

réserver to reserve

un(e) **résident(e)** resident 7

résoudre to solve

une **responsabilité** responsibility 1

ressembler à to look like, to resemble

un **restaurant** restaurant

rester to stay, to remain

un **résultat** result 10

retard: en retard late

retourner to return 5

se **retrouver** to meet 10

réunir to reunite, to bring together 8

réussir to pass (a test), to succeed

une **réussite** success 9

se **réveiller** to wake up

revenir to come back, to return; *Je n'en reviens pas.* I can't get over it. 1

rêver to dream

revoir to see again 10

une **révolution** revolution 8

le **rez-de-chaussée** ground floor

un **rhume** cold

riche rich

rien nothing 10; *ne (n')... rien* nothing, not anything; *rien ne (n')* nothing 2

rigoler to laugh 1; *rigoler comme des fous* to laugh like crazy 1

une **rivière** river

une **robe** dress

un **rocher** rock 5

rocheux, rocheuse rocky

le **rock** rock (music)

un **roi** king

un **rôle** role 3

le **roller** in-line skating

un(e) **Romain(e)** Roman 8

un **roman** novel

rose pink

une **roue** wheel 1; *une grande roue* Ferris wheel 1

rouge red; *le rouge à lèvres* lipstick

roulant(e): un fauteuil roulant wheelchair 10

rouler to drive

une **route** road

roux, rousse red (hair)

le **Ruanda** Rwanda 6

une **rue** street

rusé(e) crafty, sly 8

le **russe** Russian 1

S

s'appelle: elle s'appelle her name is; *il s'appelle* his name is

s'il te plaît please; *s'il vous plaît* please

le **sable** sand 5

un **sac: un sac à dos** backpack; *un sac à main* purse

le **Sahara** Sahara 9

un(e) **saint(e)** saint

une **saison** season

une **salade** salad

un **salaire** salary 4

une **salle: une salle à manger** dining room; *une salle d'attente* waiting room 10; *une salle de bains* bathroom; *une salle de classe* classroom; *une salle de conférences* lecture hall 1; *une salle des urgences* emergency room 10

un **salon** living room

salut hi; good-bye

une **salutation** greeting 4; *Je vous prie d'agréer, Monsieur (ou Madame), mes salutations distinguées.* yours truly 4

samedi (m.) Saturday

le **SAMU (service d'assistance médicale d'urgence)** emergency medical service 10

une **sandale** sandal

un **sandwich** sandwich; *un sandwich au fromage* cheese sandwich; *un sandwich au jambon* ham sandwich

sans without

un(e) **sans-abri** homeless person

la **santé** health

un **satellite** satellite 5

satisfait(e) (de) satisfied (with) 2

la **sauce hollandaise** hollandaise sauce

une **saucisse** sausage

le **saucisson** salami

sauf except

un **saumon** salmon

sauvage wildlife 5

sauvegarder to save 6

savoir to know (how)

le **savon** soap

un **saxophone** saxophone

un **scénario** script 3

un(e) **scénariste** scriptwriter 3

la **science-fiction** science fiction

les **sciences (f.)** science; *les sciences po* political science 1

scientifique scientific

scolaire school

un **sculpteur** sculptor 3

la **sculpture** sculpture

se himself, herself, oneself, themselves

un **sèche-cheveux** hair dryer

un **sèche-linge** dryer

sécher to dry; to skip (a class) 1

le **secours: Au secours!** Help!

un(e) **secrétaire** secretary

la **sécurité: une ceinture de sécurité** seat belt

seize sixteen

un **séjour** family room; stay; *un séjour en famille* family stay

le **sel** salt

selon according to

une **semaine** week

sembler to seem; *Il me semble....* It seems to me ....

le **Sénégal** Senegal

sénégalais(e) Senegalese

un **sens unique** one-way (street)

sensible sensitive

se **sentir** to feel 2

sept seven

septembre September

septième seventh

sérieusement seriously

sérieux, sérieuse serious; *au sérieux* seriously

un **serveur, une serveuse** server

un **service** service 4; *rendre un service* to help 5

une **serviette** napkin; towel

servir to serve 5; *se servir de* to use 5

seulement only

le **shampooing** shampoo

le **shopping** shopping

un **short** (pair of) shorts

si yes (on the contrary); so; if; what if 10

le **SIDA** AIDS

un **siècle** century

un **siège** seat

le **sien, la sienne** his, hers, its, one's 9

un **signe** sign 3

signer to sign

simple simple 7

un **singe** monkey

le **sirop d'érable** maple syrup

situé(e) situated 5

six six

sixième sixth

le **ski: le ski de fond** cross-country skiing 1; *le ski nautique* waterskiing

skier to ski

le **SMIC** minimum wage 4

un **snack-bar** snack bar 9

social(e) social 7

une **société** society 7

une **sœur** sister

la **soif: J'ai soif.** I'm thirsty.

un **soir** evening; *ce soir* tonight; *le soir* in the evening

soixante sixty

soixante-dix seventy

des **soldes** (f.) sale(s)

le **soleil** sun

solide steady

un **somme** nap 5; *faire un somme* to take a nap 5

son, sa; ses his, her, one's, its

sonner to ring 5

une **sorte: de sorte que** so that 9

sortir to go out; *sortir la poubelle* to take out the garbage

un **souhait: À tes souhaits!** Bless you!

souhaiter to wish, to hope 4

la **soupe** soup

souriant(e) smiling 2

une **souris** mouse 6

sous under

un **sous-sol** basement

des **sous-vêtements (m.)** underwear

se **souvenir** to remember 5

souvent often

spatial(e) space 6

spécial(e) special

se **spécialiser** to specialize 4

une **spécialité** specialty

un **spectacle** show 3

un **sport** sport

sportif, sportive athletic

un **squelette** skeleton 9

un **stade** stadium

un **stage** on-the-job training

une **station** station; *une station-service* gas station

une **statue** statue

un **steak** steak; *un steak-frites* steak with French fries

une **stéréo** stereo

un **steward** flight attendant 5

une **stratégie** strategy 6

un **stylo** pen

le **succès** success 3

le **sucre** sugar

le **sud** south

suffisamment enough 4

suisse Swiss

la **Suisse** Switzerland

suivant(e) following, next

suivre to follow, to take (a class)

un **sujet** subject 6; *au sujet de* about 7

super super, terrific, great; premium (gasoline)

superbe superb

un **supermarché** supermarket

un **supplément** extra charge

sur on; in; about; to

sûr(e) sure 4; *bien sûr* of course

surprenant(e) surprising 2

surprendre to surprise 5

une **surprise** surprise

surtout especially

survivre to survive 8

un **sweat** sweatshirt

sympa (sympathique) nice

sympathiser to get along

un **syndicat d'initiative** tourist office

un **synthé (synthétiseur)** synthesizer

un **système** system 8

T

t'appelles: tu t'appelles your name is

un **tabac** tobacco shop

une **table** table

un **tableau** (chalk)board; painting; *le tableau des arrivées et des départs* arrival and departure information

Tahiti (f.) Tahiti

tahitien, tahitienne Tahitian

une **taille** size

un **taille-crayon** pencil sharpener

un **tailleur** woman's suit

se **taire** to be quiet 2

Tant mieux. That's great.

Tant pis. Too bad.

une **tante** aunt

un **tapis** rug

tard late; *plus tard* later

un **tarif** rate, price 3

une **tarte (aux fraises)** (strawberry) pie

une **tartine** slice of buttered bread

une **tasse** cup

un **taux** rate 4

un **taxi** taxi

te to you; yourself; you

la **technologie** technology 6

un **tee-shirt** T-shirt

un **tel, une telle** such a 10

la **télé (télévision)** TV, television; *à la télé* on TV

un **télégramme** telegram

la **télématique** communication by computer 6

un **téléphone** telephone

téléphoner to phone (someone), to make a call

tellement so much 5

une **température** temperature

le **temps** weather; time; *Quel temps fait-il?* What's the weather like? How's the weather?; *à plein temps* full-time 4; *au bon vieux temps* in the good old days 9

tendu(e) strained 7

des **tennis (m.)** tennis shoes

le **tennis** tennis

la **terminale** last year of *lycée*

terminer to finish; *se terminer* to end 4

la **terre** earth 6; land 8; *une pomme de terre* potato

le **terrorisme** terrorism

une **tête** head

le **thé** tea; *le thé au citron* tea with lemon; *le thé au lait* tea with milk

un **théâtre** theater

un **ticket** ticket 1; *un ticket de caisse* receipt 10

le **tien, la tienne** yours 9

Tiens! Hey!

un **tigre** tiger

un **timbre** stamp

timide timid, shy

un **titre** title 6

le **Togo** Togo 7

toi you

les **toilettes (f.)** toilet

une **tomate** tomato

un **tombeau** tomb

tomber to fall 8; *tomber en panne* to have a (mechanical) breakdown

ton, ta; tes your

une **tondeuse** lawn mower

tondre to mow

tôt early

une **touche** key (on keyboard) 6

toucher to cash; to get 7

toujours always; still

un **tour** trip; *le tour* tour

une **tour** tower

un(e) **touriste** tourist 5

une **tournée** tour

tourner to turn; to shoot (a movie) 3

tous all

la **Toussaint** All Saints' Day

tout all, everything; *tout à coup* all of a sudden 2; *tout de suite* right away, right now; *tout droit* straight ahead

tout(e); tous, toutes all, every; *tous les deux* both; *tout le monde* everybody

le **tracas** trouble 10

traditionnel, traditionnelle traditional 9

un **train** train; *être en train de* (+ **infinitive**) to be busy (doing something)

un **traitement** treatment 6

traiter to treat 5

un **trajet** trip

une **tranche** slice

transformer to transform 8

le **travail** work

travailler to work

traverser to cross

treize thirteen

trente thirty

très very

une **tribu** tribe 8

un **triomphe** triumph

triste sad

trois three

troisième third

un **trombone** trombone; paper clip 1

se **tromper (de)** to be mistaken, to be wrong 5

une **trompette** trumpet

trop too; too much; *trop de* too much, too many

troublé(e) disrupted 8

une **trousse** pencil case

trouver to find; to think; *se trouver* to be (located) 3

un **truc** thing 5

tu you

tuer to kill 8

la **Tunisie** Tunisia

tunisien, tunisienne Tunisian

U

un, une one; a, an; *l'un(e)... l'autre* (the) one ... the other 10

universitaire university 7

une **université** university

une **urgence: la salle des urgences** emergency room 10

utile useful 3

utiliser to use

V

les **vacances (f.)** vacation

une **vache** cow

vachement really, very

vaincre to defeat, to conquer 8

la **vaisselle** dishes

valable valid 3

une **valise** suitcase

valoir mieux to be better 3

se **vanter** to boast 9

une **variété** variety 3

un **vase** vase

vaut: il vaut mieux it is better 3

vécu(e) real-life 3

une **vedette** (movie) star 3

la **veille** night before

un **vélo** bicycle, bike

un **vendeur, une vendeuse** salesperson

vendre to sell

vendredi (m.) Friday

venir to come; *venir chercher* to pick up, to come and get; *venir de* (+ **infinitive**) to have just

le **vent** wind

la **vente** sales 4

un **ventilateur** fan 5

un **ventre** stomach

vérifier to check

un **verre** glass; *des verres de contact (m.)* contacts

une **version** version 3

vert(e) green

une **veste** (sport) jacket

des **vêtements (m.)** clothes

un **vétérinaire** veterinarian

une **vidéocassette** videocassette

la **vie** life

le **Vietnam** Vietnam

vietnamien, vietnamienne Vietnamese

vieux, vieil, vieille old; *mon vieux* buddy

vif, vive bright

un **village** village

une **ville** city; *en ville* downtown

le **vin** wine

vingt twenty

la **violence** violence 8

violet, violette purple

un **violon** violin

une **visite** visit; *rendre visite (à)* to visit

visiter to visit (a place)

vite fast, quickly

la **vitesse** speed; *changer de vitesse*

to shift gears; *la limite de vitesse* speed limit

des **vitraux (m.)** stained glass windows 8

vivre to live

le **vocabulaire** vocabulary 7

voici here is/are

une **voie** (train) track

voilà here is/are, there is/are; that's it

la **voile** sailing

voir to see

une **voiture** car; (train) car; *une voiture de sport* sports car

une **voix** voice

un **vol** flight; theft 2

voler to steal (from), to rob 2

le **volley (volleyball)** volleyball

votre; vos your

le **vôtre, la vôtre** yours 9

voudrais would like

vouloir to want; *vouloir bien* to be willing

vous you; to you; yourself, yourselves

un **voyage** trip

voyager to travel

un **voyageur, une voyageuse** traveler

un(e) **voyant(e)** fortuneteller, clairvoyant 1

voyons let's see

vrai(e) true; real

vraiment really

une **vue** view

W

les **W.-C. (m.)** toilet

le **web** Web 6

un **weekend** weekend

Y

y there, (about) it

le **yaourt** yogurt

des **yeux (m.)** eyes

Z

le **Zaïre** Zaire

zaïrois(e) Zairian

un **zèbre** zebra

zéro zero

un **zoo** zoo

Zut! Darn!

Vocabulary
English/French

All words and expressions introduced as active vocabulary in the *C'est à toi!* textbook series appear in this end vocabulary. The number following the meaning of each word or expression indicates the unit in which it appears for the first time in this textbook. If there is more than one meaning for a word or expression and it has appeared in different units, the corresponding unit numbers are listed. Words and expressions that were introduced in the first two levels of *C'est à toi!* do not have a number after them.

A

a un, une; de (d'); *a lot* beaucoup; *a lot of* beaucoup de

abbreviation une abréviation 3

to be **able to** pouvoir

about de (d'); sur; en; au sujet de 7; environ 10; *about them* en; *about which/whom* dont 5; (*about*) *it* y

above au-dessus de

to **accelerate** accélérer

accent un accent 2

to **accept** accepter; agréer 4

to **access** accéder 6

accessory un accessoire

accident un accident 10

to **accompany** accompagner 5

according to d'après; selon

accountant un(e) comptable

ache: to have a/an . . . ache avoir mal (à...)

acquaintance une connaissance

to **act** jouer 3

active actif, active

activities: leisure activities les loisirs (m.)

activity une activité 5

actor un acteur

actress une actrice

to **adapt** s'adapter 10

addition: in addition en plus 5

address une adresse

administration une administration 8

administrative administratif, administrative 4

to **admire** admirer

adobe le banco 9

ads: want ads des petites annonces (f.) 4

advanced avancé(e) 6

advantage: to take advantage of profiter de

adventure une aventure

advertisement une annonce 4

advice (piece of) un conseil 8

aerobics l'aérobic (m.); *to do aerobics* faire de l'aérobic (m.)

aerogram (air letter) un aérogramme

to be **afraid (of)** avoir peur (de)

Africa l'Afrique (f.)

African africain(e); *African housing area* une concession 9; *African skirt* un pagne 9

after après

afternoon l'après-midi (m.)

again: to see again revoir 10

against contre 4

age l'âge (m.)

agent un agent; *customs agent* un douanier, une douanière

ago il y a

to **agree** être d'accord 5

ahead: straight ahead tout droit

AIDS le SIDA

air conditioning la climatisation

air mail: by air mail par avion

airplane un avion

airport un aéroport

aisle un couloir

album un album 3

alcoholism l'alcoolisme (m.)

algebra l'algèbre (f.) 1

Algeria l'Algérie (f.)

Algerian algérien, algérienne

all tout; tous; tout(e), tous, toutes; *all at once* à la fois; *all of a sudden* tout à coup 2; *All Saints' Day* la Toussaint; *not at all* pas du tout

to **allow** permettre 6

allowance des allocations (f.) 7

almost presque

already déjà

also aussi

always toujours

ambitious ambitieux, ambitieuse 8

America l'Amérique (f.); *North America* l'Amérique du Nord (f.); *South America* l'Amérique du Sud (f.)

American américain(e)

among entre; parmi 6

amusement park un parc d'attractions 1

amusing amusant(e)

an un; une; de (d')

and et

angry fâché(e) 2; *to get angry* se fâcher 2

animal un animal; *animal life* la faune 9

ankle une cheville 10

to **announce** annoncer 4

annoying embêtant(e) 10

another un(e) autre

answer une réponse 2

to **answer** répondre 2

antelope une antilope 9

antibiotic un antibiotique 10

any de (d'); des, du; en; *just any* n'importe quel, n'importe quelle 10; *not any* ne (n')... aucun(e) 2

anymore: not anymore ne (n')... plus

anyone n'importe qui 10; *not anyone* ne (n')... personne

anything: not anything ne (n')... rien

apartment un appartement; *apartment building* un immeuble

appearance l'air (m.) 2; une apparence 7

apple une pomme; *apple juice* le jus de pomme

appliance un appareil 10

appointment un rendez-vous; *to make an appointment* prendre rendez-vous

to **appreciate** apprécier 4

to **approach** s'approcher (de) 2

April avril

arcade une arcade 1

arch un arc, une arche

area un domaine 6

to **argue** se disputer 7

arm un bras

armchair un fauteuil

army une armée

to **arrange** ranger

arrival une arrivée; *arrival and departure information* le tableau des arrivées et des départs

to **arrive** arriver

art l'art (m.); *objet d'art* un objet d'art

article un article 6

artist un(e) artiste

as aussi, que; en; comme; *as for* quant à 6; *as many* autant de 10; *as much* autant de 10; *as soon as* aussitôt que; dès que 6; *as usual* comme d'habitude; *as well as* ainsi que 9

Asia l'Asie (f.)

Asian asiatique

aside from à part

to **ask** demander; *to ask (a question)* poser 2; *to ask for* demander

aspirin une aspirine 10

to **assassinate** assassiner 8

assistant un(e) assistant(e) 3; *assistant principal* un censeur 1

at à; *at (the)* au, aux; *at least* au moins; *at the bottom* en bas 3; *at the end of* au fond de; *at the seashore* au bord de la mer

athlete un(e) athlète

athletic sportif, sportive

Atlantic Ocean l'océan Atlantique (m.)

ATM machine un guichet automatique

atmosphere une ambiance 7

to **attack** agresser 7

to **attend** assister à

attendant: flight attendant une hôtesse de l'air 5; *gas station attendant* un(e) pompiste

attention: to pay attention faire attention 2

attic un grenier

August août

aunt une tante

Australia l'Australie (f.)

Australian australien, australienne

Austria l'Autriche (f.) 8

autobiographical autobiographique 3

automatic automatique

autumn l'automne (m.)

available disponible 5

avenue une avenue

to **avoid** éviter 10

B

baby un bébé 6

to **baby-sit** faire du baby-sitting

baby-sitting le baby-sitting

back un dos; *to come back* rentrer, revenir

backpack un sac à dos

bad mal; mauvais(e); *It's bad.* Il fait mauvais.; *Too bad!* Dommage!; Tant pis.

badly mal

baggage des bagages (m.); *to check one's baggage* faire enregistrer ses bagages (m.)

baker un boulanger, une boulangère

bakery une boulangerie

balcony un balcon

ball (inflated) un ballon 10

ballet un ballet 3

banana une banane

bandage un bandage 10

bank une banque

banker un banquier, une banquière

baobab tree un baobab 9

barn une grange

basement un sous-sol

basketball le basket (basket-ball); *to play basketball* jouer au basket

bath mitt un gant de toilette

bathrobe un peignoir de bain

bathroom une salle de bains

bathtub une baignoire

battery une pile 10

battle une bataille 8

to **be** être; *Be careful!* Attention!; *to be (located)* se trouver 3; *to be . . . (years old)* avoir... ans; *to be a part of* faire partie de 9; *to be able to* pouvoir; *to be afraid (of)* avoir peur (de); *to be better* valoir mieux 3; *to be bored* s'ennuyer 5; *to be born* naître; *to be busy (doing something)* être en train de (+ *infinitive*); *to be cold* avoir froid; *to be how old* avoir quel âge; *to be hungry* avoir faim; *to be in good/bad shape* être en bonne/ mauvaise forme; *to be interested in* s'intéresser à 9; *to be (located)* se trouver 3; *to be lucky* avoir de la chance 1; *to be mistaken* se tromper (de) 5; *to be named* s'appeler 4; *to be necessary* falloir; *to be obliged to* être obligé(e) de; *to be quiet* se taire 2; *to be right* avoir raison 10; *to be sorry* regretter; *to be thirsty* avoir soif; *to be warm/hot* avoir chaud; *to be willing* vouloir bien; *to be wrong* se tromper 5

beach une plage

beans: green beans des haricots verts (m.)

bear un ours

beard une barbe

beautiful beau, bel, belle; *It's beautiful.* Il fait beau.

beauty la beauté 5

because parce que; car 7

to **become** devenir; *to become integrated* s'intégrer 7

bed un lit; *double bed* un grand lit; *to go to bed* se coucher; *twin beds* des lits jumeaux

bedroom une chambre

beef le bœuf

before avant (de)

to **beg** prier 4

to **begin** commencer; *to begin again* recommencer

beginning le début 2

behind derrière

beige beige

Belgian belge

Belgium la Belgique

to **believe** croire

to **belong to** être à 9

belt une ceinture; *seat belt* une ceinture de sécurité

benefits des allocations (f.) 7

Benin le Bénin 3

beside à côté (de)

best le meilleur, la meilleure 5; *the best* le mieux

to **bet** parier

better mieux; meilleur(e) 6; *it is better* il vaut mieux 3; *to be better* valoir mieux 3

between entre

beverage une boisson

bicycle un vélo

big grand(e); gros, grosse

bike un vélo

biking: to go biking faire du vélo

bilingual bilingue 4

bill (at a restaurant) une addition; *bill (money)* un billet

billfold un portefeuille

billion un milliard 6

biology la biologie

bird un oiseau

birthday un anniversaire; *Happy Birthday!* Bon anniversaire!

black noir(e)

Bless you! À tes souhaits!

blond blond(e)

blue bleu(e)

board un tableau

to **boast** se vanter 9

boat un bateau

body un corps; *body building* la musculation; *to do body building* faire de la musculation

book un livre

bookstore une librairie

boot une botte

border une frontière 6

to be **bored, to get bored** s'ennuyer 5

to be **born** naître

to **borrow (from)** emprunter (à) 9

boss un chef 2

both tous les deux

to **bother** embêter 5; gêner 10

bottle une bouteille

bottom: at the bottom en bas 3

boundary une frontière 6

boutique une boutique

bowl un bol

box une boîte 10; *box office* un bureau de location 3

boy un garçon

bracelet un bracelet

brand une marque 7

bread le pain; *long, thin loaf of bread* une baguette; *slice of buttered bread* une tartine

to **break** se casser 10

breakdown une panne; *to have a (mechanical) breakdown* tomber en panne

breakfast le petit déjeuner

bride une mariée

bridge un pont

bright vif, vive

to **bring: to bring back** rapporter 10; *to bring together* réunir 8

to **broadcast** diffuser. 7

broken cassé(e) 10

brother un frère; *host brother* un correspondant

brother-in-law un beau-frère

brown brun(e); marron

to **brush** se brosser

buddy mon vieux

budget un budget 7

buff un(e) fana

to **build** construire 6

building la construction 8; *apartment building* un immeuble

bumper car une auto tamponneuse 1

burlesque burlesque

to **burn** brûler

bus: (city) bus un autobus, un bus; *tour bus* un car 2

business des affaires (f.) 8

businessman un homme d'affaires

businesswoman une femme d'affaires

busy occupé(e); *free (not busy)* libre; *to be busy (doing something)* être en train de (+ *infinitive*)

but mais

butcher un boucher, une bouchère; *butcher shop* une boucherie

butter le beurre

to **buy** acheter

by de (d'); en, par; *by air mail* par avion

bye ciao

C

café un café

cafeteria une cantine

cage une cage 7

cake un gâteau

calculus le calcul 1

calendar un calendrier

call: to make a call téléphoner

to **call** appeler 7

calm calme 2

Camembert cheese le camembert

camera un appareil-photo 9

Cameroon le Cameroun

Cameroonian camerounais(e)

to **camp** faire du camping

campground un camping

camping le camping; *to go camping* faire du camping

can une boîte; une canette 10; *garbage can* une poubelle

Canada le Canada

Canadian canadien, canadienne

canoe un canoë

canoeing: to go canoeing faire du canoë

cap une casquette

capital une capitale

car une voiture; une auto (automobile); *bumper car* une auto tamponneuse 1; *(train) car* une voiture; *sports car* une voiture de sport

caramel custard une crème caramel

card une carte; *credit card* une carte de crédit; *to play cards* jouer aux cartes (f.)

care: to take care of s'occuper de 5

careful: Be careful! Attention!

Caribbean Sea la mer des Antilles

carrot une carotte

cartoon un dessin animé

case un cas

cash l'argent liquide (m.)

to **cash** toucher

cashier un caissier, une caissière; *cashier's (desk)* une caisse

cassette une cassette

cast un plâtre 10

castle un château

cat un chat

Catholic un(e) catholique 8

cautious circonspect(e) 7

CD un CD

to **celebrate** fêter

cemetery un cimetière

center un centre; *shopping center* un centre commercial

century un siècle

cereal des céréales (f.)

certain certain(e) 4

chair une chaise

chalkboard un tableau

change la monnaie; un changement

to **change** changer

channel une chaîne 4; *English Channel* la Manche

chapel une chapelle

charge: extra charge un supplément

charts le hit-parade

cheap bon marché

check (at a restaurant) une addition; *security check* un contrôle de sécurité; *traveler's check* un chèque de voyage

to **check** vérifier; *to check one's baggage* faire enregistrer ses bagages (m.)

cheese le fromage; *Camembert cheese* le camembert; *cheese sandwich* un sandwich au fromage

chef un chef

chemistry la chimie

cherry une cerise

chess les échecs (m.); *to play chess* jouer aux échecs (m.)

chicken un poulet; *chicken cooked in wine* le coq au vin

chief un chef 8

child un(e) enfant

chills des frissons (m.)

China la Chine

Chinese chinois(e)

chocolate le chocolat; *chocolate ice cream* une glace au chocolat; *chocolate mousse* une mousse au chocolat; *hot chocolate* un chocolat chaud

choice un choix

to **choose** choisir

chore une corvée

Christianity le christianisme 8

church une église

city une ville

clairvoyant un(e) voyant(e) 1

clarinet une clarinette

class un cours; une classe; *to take (a class)* suivre

classmate une camarade de classe

classroom une salle de classe

clean propre 7

to **clean** nettoyer

cleaner: vacuum cleaner un aspirateur

clerk un(e) employé(e) 2

to **click** cliquer 6

clientele une clientèle 4

climate un climat 7

climbing l'escalade (f.); *to go climbing* faire de l'escalade (f.)

clip: video clip un clip; *paper clip* un trombone 1

clock une pendule

to **close** fermer

clothes des vêtements (m.); *to dry clothes* faire sécher le linge

club: dance club une boîte

coast une côte

coat un manteau

coffee un café; *coffee with milk* un café au lait

coin une pièce

Coke un coca

cold froid(e); *It's cold.* Il fait froid.; *to be cold* avoir froid

cold un rhume

to **collect** collectionner

collection une collection 3

color une couleur

comb un peigne

to **comb (one's hair)** se peigner

to **come** venir; se présenter 4; *to come and get* venir chercher; *to come back* rentrer, revenir; *to come home* rentrer; *to come in* entrer; *to come up (to)* s'approcher (de) 2

comedy une comédie

comic strip une bande dessinée

comical burlesque

commercial commercial(e) 6

committed engagé(e) 6

communication by computer la télématique 6

company une compagnie 4

compartment: overhead compartment un porte-bagages 5

to **complain** se plaindre 5

complete complet, complète

complicated complexe 8; compliqué(e) 10

to **compose** composer 3

composer un compositeur, une compositrice 3

composition la rédaction 1

computer un ordinateur; *communication by computer* la télématique 6; *computer science* l'informatique (f.); *computer specialist* un informaticien, une informaticienne

concert un concert

conductor un chef d'orchestre 3; un chef de train 5

Congo: Democratic Republic of the Congo la République Démocratique du Congo 6

to **connect** se brancher 6

to **conquer** vaincre 8

conqueror un(e) conquérant(e) 8

consequently par conséquent 8

to **consider** considérer 7

contacts des verres de contact (m.)

contemporary contemporain(e)

to **continue** continuer

contract un contrat 4

contrast un contraste 9

to **control** contrôler

controversial controversé(e) 3

conversation une conversation

convertible une décapotable

cook un cuisinier, une cuisinière

cooking la cuisine

cool frais, fraîche; *It's cool.* Il fait frais.

to **copy** copier 8

corner un coin 7

to **cost** coûter

couch un canapé

to **count** compter 7

counter un comptoir

country la campagne; un pays

countryside la campagne

couple un couple

coupon un bon de réduction 10

courageous courageux, courageuse

course un cours; *entrée (course before main dish)* une entrée; *in the course of* au cours de; *main course* le plat principal

court une cour 8

couscous le couscous

cousin un(e) cousin(e)

to **cover** parcourir 5

cow une vache

crab un crabe

craft un métier

craftsperson un artisan 9

crafty rusé(e) 8

crazy: crazy person un fou, une folle 1; *to laugh like crazy* rigoler comme des fous 1

to **create** créer 4

credit card une carte de crédit

crêpe une crêpe

to **criticize** critiquer 8

croissant un croissant

to **cross** traverser

cross-country skiing le ski de fond 1; *to go cross-country skiing* faire du ski de fond 1

crusade une croisade 8

crutch une béquille 10

cultural culturel, culturelle 7

culture la culture

cup une tasse

cupboard un placard

currency exchange un bureau de change

current events l'actualité (f.)

curriculum vitae un CV 4

curried scallops des coquilles Saint-Jacques au curry

custard: caramel custard une crème caramel

customer un(e) client(e) 10

customers une clientèle 4

customs la douane; *customs agent* un douanier, une douanière; *to go through customs* passer à la douane

cute mignon, mignonne

D

Dad papa (m.)

daily quotidien, quotidienne

dairy store une crémerie

dance un bal; *dance club* une boîte

to **dance** danser

dark (hair) brun(e)

darling un(e) chéri(e)

Darn! Zut!; Mince!

date une date

daughter une fille

day un jour; une journée; *Have a good day!* Bonne journée!; *in the good old days* au bon vieux temps 9; *the next day* le lendemain; *these days* de nos jours 9

to **deal with** s'occuper de 8

dean un censeur 1

dear cher, chère

December décembre

to **decide** décider (de)

to **declare** déclarer

to **defeat** vaincre 8

to **defend** défendre 8

defense la défense 6

delicatessen une charcuterie; *delicatessen owner* un charcutier, une charcutière

delighted enchanté(e)

demanding exigeant(e) 2

Democratic Republic of the Congo la République Démocratique du Congo 6

to **demolish** démolir 8

to **demonstrate** manifester 4

demonstration une manifestation 4

demonstrator un(e) manifestant(e) 4

to **denounce** dénoncer 6

dentist un(e) dentiste

department un rayon 10; *department store* un grand magasin

departure un départ; *arrival and departure information* le tableau des arrivées et des départs; *departure gate* une porte d'embarquement

to **depend (on)** dépendre (de) 7

depressed déprimé(e) 2

depressing déprimant(e) 7

to **describe** décrire

description une description 3

desk un bureau; *cashier's (desk)* une caisse; *reception desk* la réception

dessert un dessert

destination une destination

detective un policier, une policière

to **develop** développer 6

dictionary un dictionnaire

to **die** mourir

different différent(e) 7

difficult difficile

dining room une salle à manger

dinner le dîner

dinosaur un dinosaure 9

diploma: diploma at end of lycée le bac (baccalauréat); *possessing a diploma* diplomé(e) 4

direct direct(e)

director un metteur en scène

disappointed déçu(e) 10

discotheque une discothèque 7

disease une maladie

dish un plat

dishes la vaisselle

dishwasher un lave-vaisselle

diskette une disquette

disrupted troublé(e) 8

dissatisfaction le mécontentement 4

distinguished distingué(e) 4

district un arrondissement 3

to **distrust** se méfier de 2

to **dive** plonger

diversity une diversité 7

to **divide** diviser 8

diving: scuba diving la plongée sous-marine; *to go scuba diving* faire de la plongée sous-marine

divorce un divorce 7

divorced: to get divorced divorcer 7

to **do** faire; *(to do something) in vain* avoir beau 8; *to do aerobics* faire de l'aérobic (m.); *to do body building* faire de la musculation; *to do gymnastics* faire de la gym (gymnastique); *to do homework* faire les devoirs; *to do karate* faire du karaté

doctor un médecin; un docteur

document un document 2

documentary un documentaire

dog un chien

dollar un dollar

done: Well done! Bravo! 6

door une porte

dormitory room (for more than one person) un dortoir

double bed un grand lit

to **doubt** douter 4

downtown en ville

drag: What a drag! Quelle galère!

drama un drame

drawing le dessin

to **dream** rêver

dress une robe; *to dress up* se déguiser

dressed habillé(e) 2; *to get dressed* s'habiller

drink une boisson

to **drink** boire

to **drive** conduire; rouler

driver un chauffeur; un conducteur, une conductrice; *driver's license* un permis de conduire

driving school une auto-école

drugs la drogue

drugstore une pharmacie 10

drums une batterie

to **dry** sécher; *to dry clothes* faire sécher le linge

dryer un sèche-linge; *hair dryer* un sèche-cheveux

duck un canard

duke un duc 8

dumb bête; *How dumb I am!* Que je suis bête!

during pendant; au cours de

dust la poussière

to **dust** enlever la poussière

dynamic dynamique

E

each chaque

ear une oreille

early en avance; tôt

earring une boucle d'oreille

earth la terre 6

east l'est (m.)

easy facile

to **eat** manger; *to eat pizza* manger de la pizza

ecological écologique 6

education l'éducation (f.); l'enseignement (m.) 1

effort un effort

egg un œuf; *fried eggs* des œufs sur le plat (m.); *scrambled eggs* des œufs brouillés (m.)

eight huit

eighteen dix-huit

eighth huitième

eighty quatre-vingts

electronic électronique 6

elephant un éléphant

elevator un ascenseur

eleven onze

e-mail l'e-mail (m.) 6

embassy une ambassade 2

emergency: emergency medical service le SAMU (service d'assistance médicale d'urgence) 10; *emergency room* la salle des urgences 10

emperor un empereur 8

empire un empire 8

employee un(e) employé(e) 2

enclosed ci-joint 4

end la fin 1; *at the end of* au fond de; *in the end* finalement

to **end** se terminer 4

energy l'énergie (f.); *nuclear energy* l'énergie nucléaire

engine: search engine un outil de recherche 6

engineer un ingénieur

England l'Angleterre (f.)

English anglais(e); *English (language)* l'anglais (m.); *English Channel* la Manche

to **enjoy (oneself)** se distraire 7

enough assez de; assez, suffisamment 4

to **enter** entrer

entertainment une distraction 3

enthusiastic enthousiaste 4

entrance une entrée

entrée (course before main dish) une entrée

envelope une enveloppe

environment l'environnement (m.)

eraser une gomme 1

especially surtout

essential essentiel, essentielle 3

to **establish** établir 6

Europe l'Europe (f.)

European européen, européenne

even même

evening un soir; *in the evening* le soir

event un événement 8; *current events* l'actualité (f.)

eventually finalement

ever jamais 1

every chaque; tout(e), tous, toutes

everybody tout le monde

everything tout

everywhere partout 3

evident évident(e) 4

exactly justement 10

exam un examen 1; *exam at end of* lycée le bac (baccalauréat)

example: for example par exemple

to **exceed** dépasser

excellent excellent(e) 6

except sauf

exchange: currency exchange un bureau de change

to **exchange** échanger

exciting passionnant(e) 6

excuse me pardon; excusez-moi

exhausted épuisé(e) 2

exhibit, exhibition une exposition

exotic exotique

to **expect** s'attendre à 2

expensive cher, chère

experience une expérience 4

to **explain** expliquer 2

to **expose** dénoncer 6

express subway to suburbs le R.E.R. (Réseau Express Régional)

expression une expression 10

extra charge un supplément

eye un œil; *eyes* des yeux (m.)

F

face une figure

factory worker un ouvrier, une ouvrière

to **fail** rater 1

fall l'automne (m.)

to **fall** tomber 8

family une famille; familial(e) 7; *family room* un séjour; *family stay* un séjour en famille

famine une famine 6

famous célèbre

fan un ventilateur 5

fanatic un(e) fana

fantastic extra; génial(e) 7; fantastique 9

far loin

farm une ferme

farmer un fermier, une fermière

fascinating passionnant(e) 6

fast vite; rapide; rapidement

fast-food restaurant un fast-food

fat gros, grosse

father un père

father-in-law un beau-père

favorable favorable

favorite favori, favorite

fax un fax 5

to **fax** faxer

February février

to **feed** nourrir

to **feel** se sentir 2; *to feel like* avoir envie de; *to feel nauseous* avoir mal au cœur

feeling une impression 3

felt-tip pen un feutre 1

Ferris wheel une grande roue 1; *to go on the Ferris wheel* faire un tour de grande roue 1

festival une fête

fever la fièvre

few (un) peu de

fiction: science fiction la science-fiction

field un champ; un domaine 6

fifteen quinze; *fifteen (minutes after)* et quart

fifth cinquième

fifty cinquante

fight une lutte 6

to **fill (out)** remplir; *to fill up the gas tank* faire le plein

finally enfin

to **find** trouver

fine une amende

fine bien

finger un doigt

to **finish** finir; terminer

firefighter un pompier

fireworks un feu d'artifice

first premier, première; d'abord; *first day of school* la rentrée 1; *first name* un prénom

fish un poisson; *fish soup* une bouillabaisse

five cinq

fixed-price meal un menu

flexible flexible 4

flight un vol; *flight attendant* une hôtesse de l'air, un steward 5

floor un étage; *ground floor* le rez-de-chaussée

florist un(e) fleuriste

flower une fleur

flu la grippe

flute une flûte

to **follow** suivre

following suivant(e)

Fon (African language) le fon 3

food la nourriture

foot un pied; *on foot* à pied

for pour; comme; depuis; contre 8; *(for) a long time* longtemps 5; *as for* quant à 6; *for example* par exemple

foreigner un étranger, une étrangère 7

to **forget** oublier 6

fork une fourchette

form un formulaire 4; *order form* une fiche de commande; *registration form* une fiche d'inscription 1

formerly autrefois 9

fortunately heureusement

fortuneteller un(e) voyant(e) 1

forty quarante

foundation une fondation 6

four quatre

fourteen quatorze

fourth quatrième

franc un franc

France la France; *the south of France* le Midi 10

franglais (English words used in French) le franglais 7

frank ouvert(e) 7

frankly franchement

free gratuit(e); gratuitement 10; *free (not busy)* libre

to **free** délivrer

French français(e); *French (language)* le français; *French fries* des frites (f.); *French toast* le pain perdu; *French-speaking* francophone

French Guiana la Guyane française; *inhabitant of/from French Guiana* guyanais(e)

fresh frais, fraîche

Friday vendredi (m.)

fried eggs des œufs sur le plat (m.)

friend un(e) ami(e); un copain, une copine

friendly accueillant(e) 2

fries: French fries des frites (f.); *steak with French fries* un steak-frites

frightened effrayé(e) 2

from de (d'); *from (the)* des, du; *from it/them* en

front: in front of devant

fruit un fruit; *fruit juice* le jus de fruit

frustrated frustré(e) 10

full chargé(e); plein(e); complet, complète

fullest: We have to live life to the fullest. Il faut profiter de la vie au maximum

full-time à plein temps 4

fun: fun house la galerie des miroirs déformants 1; *to have fun* s'amuser

funny drôle; marrant(e); amusant(e)

fur la fourrure 6

furthermore de plus

future l'avenir (m.) 6

G

gallery une galerie

game un jeu, un match; le gibier 9; *game show* un jeu télévisé; *games of skill* des jeux d'adresse 1; *to play video games* jouer aux jeux vidéo; *video games* des jeux vidéo (m.)

garage un garage

garbage: garbage can une poubelle; *to take out the garbage* sortir la poubelle

garden un jardin

gas station une station-service; *gas station attendant* un(e) pompiste

gas tank: to fill up the gas tank faire le plein

gasoline l'essence (f.); *premium (gasoline)* super; *regular (gasoline)* ordinaire

gate une porte; *departure gate* une porte d'embarquement

Gaul la Gaule 8

gazelle une gazelle 9

gears: to shift gears changer de vitesse

general général(e) 3; un général 8; *in general* en général 3

generous généreux, généreuse

geography la géographie

geometry la géométrie 1

German allemand(e); *German (language)* l'allemand (m.)

Germany l'Allemagne (f.)

to **get** recevoir; toucher 7; *I can't get over it.* Je n'en reviens pas. 1; *to come and get* venir chercher; *to get along* sympathiser; s'entendre 2; *to get angry* se fâcher 2; *to get bored* s'ennuyer 5; *to get divorced* divorcer 7; *to get dressed* s'habiller; *to get in* monter; *to get married* se marier 7; *to get off* descendre 3; *to get on* monter; *to get ready* se préparer; *to get up* se lever

gift un cadeau

gifted doué(e)

giraffe une girafe

girl une fille

to **give** donner; offrir; *Give me . . . .* Donnez-moi....; *Give me a hand . . . .* Donnez-moi un coup de main....

glass un verre

glasses des lunettes (f.)

glove un gant

to **go** aller; se passer 5; *let's go (there)* allons-y; *Shall we go (there)?* On y va?; *to go (by)* passer; *to go biking* faire du vélo; *to go camping* faire du camping; *to go canoeing* faire du canoë; *to go climbing* faire de l'escalade (f.); *to go cross-country skiing* faire du ski de fond 1; *to go down* descendre; *to go for a ride* faire un tour; faire une promenade; *to go for a walk* faire une promenade; *to go grocery shopping* faire les courses; *to go horseback riding* faire du cheval; *to go in-line skating* faire du roller; *to go on the Ferris wheel* faire un tour de grande roue 1; *to go on the merry-go-round* faire un tour de manège 1; *to go on the roller coaster* faire un tour de montagnes russes 1; *to go out* sortir; *to go running* faire du footing; *to go sailing* faire de la voile; *to go scuba diving* faire de la plongée sous-marine; *to go shopping* faire du shopping, faire les magasins; *to go skateboarding* faire de la planche à roulettes 1; *to go snowboarding* faire de la planche à neige 1; *to go through* fouiller 2; *to go through customs* passer à la douane; *to go to bed* se coucher; *to go tobogganing* faire de la luge 1; *to go up* monter; *to go waterskiing* faire du ski nautique; *to go windsurfing* faire de la planche à voile

goat une chèvre

God Dieu (m.) 8

gold l'or (m.)

goldfish un poisson rouge

golf le golf; *to play golf* jouer au golf

good bon, bonne; bien; *good evening* bonsoir; *good-bye* au revoir, salut; *Have a good day!* Bonne journée!; *in the good old days* au bon vieux temps 9

gorilla un gorille

to **govern** gouverner 8

government un gouvernement 4

grade une note 7

gradually doucement

graffiti des graffiti (m.) 7

grandfather un grand-père

grandmother une grand-mère

grandparent un grand-parent 2

grape un raisin; *grape juice* le jus de raisin

grapefruit un pamplemousse; *grapefruit juice* le jus de pamplemousse

grateful reconnaissant(e) 4

gray gris(e)

great super; formidable; extra; génial(e) 7; *That's great.* Tant mieux.

Greek le grec 1

green vert(e); *green beans* des haricots verts (m.)

greeting une salutation 4

groom un marié

ground floor le rez-de-chaussée

group un groupe 5

to **grow** pousser 9

Guadeloupe la Guadeloupe; *inhabitant of/from Guadeloupe* guadeloupéen, guadeloupéenne

guaranteed garanti(e) 4

Guiana: French Guiana la Guyane française; *inhabitant of/from French Guiana* guyanais(e)

guidebook un guide 3

to **guillotine** guillotiner 8

guitar une guitare

guy un mec; un gars 5

gym un gymnase 5

gymnastics la gym, la gymnastique; *to do gymnastics* faire de la gym (gymnastique)

H

habit une habitude 9

hair des cheveux (m.); *hair dryer* un sèche-cheveux; *to comb (one's hair)* se peigner

hairbrush une brosse à cheveux

hairdresser un coiffeur, une coiffeuse

Haiti Haïti (f.)

Haitian haïtien, haïtienne

half demi(e); *half an hour* une demi-heure; *half past* et demi(e)

half-brother un demi-frère

half-sister une demi-sœur

hall un couloir; une galerie; un pavillon 9; *lecture hall* une salle de conférences 1

ham le jambon; *ham sandwich* un sandwich au jambon

hamburger un hamburger

hand une main; *Give me a hand . . . .* Donne-moi un coup de main. . . .; *on the other hand* par contre 9

to **hand in** rendre 6

handkerchief un mouchoir

handsome beau, bel, belle

to **happen** se passer 2; arriver 10

happy content(e), heureux, heureuse; *Happy Birthday!* Bon anniversaire!

hard difficile; dur(e)

hardworking diligent(e)

hat un chapeau

to **have** avoir; *Have a good day!* Bonne journée!; *I've had it!* J'en ai marre!; *one has to, we/you have to* il faut; *to have (food or drink)* prendre; *to have a/an . . . ache, to have a sore . . .* avoir mal; *to have a (mechanical) breakdown* tomber en panne; *to have a good time* s'amuser; se distraire 7; *to have a picnic* piqueniquer; *to have fun* s'amuser; *to have just* venir de (+ infinitive); *to have lunch* déjeuner; *to have on-the-job training* faire un stage; *to have to* devoir, falloir; être obligé(e) de; *We have to live life to the fullest.* Il faut profiter de la vie au maximum.

he il; *he is* c'est

head une tête; un chef 4

health la santé

to **hear** entendre; *to hear about* entendre parler de 6

heart un cœur

hello bonjour; *hello (on telephone)* allô

help l'aide (f.); *Help!* Au secours!

to **help** aider; rendre un service 5

hen une poule

her son, sa; ses; le, la, l'; elle; *her name is* elle s'appelle; *to her* lui

here là; ici; *here is/are* voilà, voici

hero un héros

heroine une héroïne

hers le sien, la sienne 9

herself se

Hey! Eh!, Tiens!

hi salut

high haut(e); élevé(e) 4

high school un lycée; *high school student* un lycéen, une lycéenne 1

hightops des baskets (f.)

him le, la, l'; lui; *to him* lui

himself se

hippopotamus un hippopotame

to **hire** embaucher 4

his son, sa; ses; le sien, la sienne 9; *his name is* il s'appelle

history l'histoire (f.)

to **hit** heurter 1

holiday une fête

hollandaise sauce la sauce hollandaise

home: at/to the home of chez; *to come home* rentrer

homeless person un(e) sans-abri

homework les devoirs (m.); *to do homework* faire les devoirs

honest honnête

hood un capot

to **hope** espérer; souhaiter 4

horror l'épouvante (f.)

horse un cheval

horseback riding: to go horseback riding faire du cheval

hospitable accueillant(e) 2

hospital un hôpital 10

host brother un correspondant; *host sister* une correspondante

hostel: youth hostel une auberge de jeunesse

hot chaud(e); *hot chocolate* un chocolat chaud; *It's hot.* Il fait chaud.; *to be hot* avoir chaud

hot dog un hot-dog

hotel un hôtel

hour l'heure (f.); *half an hour* une demi-heure

house une maison; *at/to the house of* chez; *fun house* la galerie des miroirs déformants 1; *to my house* chez moi

househusband un homme au foyer

housewife une femme au foyer

housework le ménage

housing le logement 7; *African housing area* une concession 9; *housing development* une cité 7; *public housing* une HLM (habitation à loyer modéré) 7

how comment; que; comme; *How are things going?* Ça va?; *How are you?* Comment vas-tu?; *How dumb I am!* Que je suis bête!; *how long* depuis combien de temps; *how many* combien de; *how much* combien, combien de; *How much is it/that?* Ça fait combien?; *How nice you are!* Que vous êtes gentils!; *How old are you?* Tu as quel âge?; *How's the weather?* Quel temps fait-il?

however pourtant 9

Huh? Hein? 1

human humain(e) 2

humanitarian humanitaire 6

hundred: (one) hundred cent

hunger la faim

hungry: I'm hungry. J'ai faim.; *to be hungry* avoir faim

to **hunt** chasser 9

hunting la chasse 8

hurry: in a hurry pressé(e) 7

to **hurry** se dépêcher

to **hurt** avoir mal (à...); *to hurt oneself* se faire mal 10

husband un mari

hut une case 9

hutch: rabbit hutch une cage à lapins 7

hyena un hyène 9

I

I j', je; moi; *I can't get over it.* Je n'en reviens pas. 1; *I need* il me faut; *I think so.* Je crois que oui. 5

ice cream une glace; *chocolate ice cream* une glace au chocolat; *vanilla ice cream* une glace à la vanille

idea une idée

idiot un(e) imbécile 2

if si; *if I were you* à ta place 5; *what if* si 10

illness une maladie

illuminated illuminé(e) 8

to **imagine** imaginer

immigrant un(e) immigré(e) 7

immigration l'immigration (f.)

important important(e) 2

impossible impossible 3

impression une impression 3

Impressionist impressionniste

to **improve** se perfectionner; améliorer 8

in dans; à, en, sur; de (d'); *in (the)* au, aux, du; *in a hurry* pressé(e) 7; *in addition* en plus 5; *in front of* devant; *in general* en général 3; *in my opinion* à mon avis; *in order to* pour; *in the course of* au cours de; *in the end* finalement; *in the evening* le soir; *in the good old days* au bon vieux temps 9; *in the morning* le matin; *in the provinces* en province 8; *(to do something) in vain* avoir beau 8

included compris(e)

independence l'indépendance (f.) 8

independent indépendant(e) 7

Indian Ocean l'océan Indien (m.)

to **indicate** indiquer

indispensable indispensable 3

Indochina l'Indochine (f.) 3

influence une influence 7

to **inform** informer 9

information des renseignements (m.) 3; *arrival and departure information* le tableau des arrivées et des départs; *information superhighway* l'inforoute (f.) 6

inhabitant: inhabitant of/from French Guiana guyanais(e); *inhabitant of/from Gaul* un(e) Gaulois(e) 8; *inhabitant of/from Guadeloupe* guadeloupéen, guadeloupéenne; *inhabitant of/from Madagascar* malgache; *inhabitant of/from Martinique* martiniquais(e); *inhabitant of/from Monaco* monégasque; *inhabitant of/from Normandy* un(e) Normand(e) 8; *inhabitant of/from Quebec* un(e) Québécois(e); *inhabitant of/from the Maghreb* maghrébin(e) 7

in-line skating le roller; *to go in-line skating* faire du roller

inspector un contrôleur, une contrôleuse

instructions le mode d'emploi 10

instructor un moniteur, une monitrice

instrument un instrument 9

insurance l'assurance (f.) 4

integrated: to become integrated s'intégrer 7

intelligent intelligent(e)

to **intend** compter 4

interest un intérêt 6

to **interest** intéresser

interested: to be interested in s'intéresser à 9

interesting intéressant(e)

intersection un croisement

intricate fin(e) 9

to **introduce** présenter

to **invite** inviter

Iraq l'Irak (m.) 6

iron un fer à repasser

to **iron** repasser

is est; *isn't that so?* n'est-ce pas?

Islamic: of the Islamic religion coranique 9

island une île

issue un numéro 4

it elle, il; ça; le, la, l'; y; en; *about it* y; *from it* en; *it is better* il vaut mieux 3; *it is necessary* il faut; *It seems to me . . . .* Il me semble....; *it's* c'est; *It's . . . .* Ça fait....; *It's bad.* Il fait mauvais.; *It's beautiful.* Il fait beau.; *It's cold.* Il fait froid.; *It's cool.* Il fait frais.; *It's hot.* Il fait chaud.; *It's nice.* Il fait beau.; *It's raining.* Il pleut.; *It's snowing.* Il neige.; *It's sunny.* Il fait du soleil.; *It's the (+ date).* Nous sommes le (+ *date*).; *It's up to you.* C'est à vous de voir. 10; *It's warm.* Il fait chaud.; *It's windy.* Il fait du vent.; *of it* en; *that's it* voilà

Italian italien, italienne

Italy l'Italie (f.)

its son, sa; ses; le sien, la sienne 9

Ivory Coast la Côte-d'Ivoire; *from the Ivory Coast* ivoirien, ivoirienne

J

jacket (outdoor) un blouson; *ski jacket* un anorak; *sport jacket* une veste

jam la confiture

January janvier

Japan le Japon

Japanese japonais(e)

jar un pot

jazz le jazz

jeans: (pair of) jeans un jean

jewel un bijou

job un boulot; un emploi, un poste 4; *on-the-job training* un stage

joke une blague 10

journal un journal 7

journalism le journalisme

journalist un(e) journaliste

juice: apple juice le jus de pomme; *fruit juice* le jus de fruit; *grape juice* le jus de raisin; *grapefruit juice* le jus de pamplemousse; *orange juice* le jus d'orange; *tomato juice* le jus de tomate

July juillet

June juin

just juste; *just any* n'importe quel, n'importe quelle 10; *to have just* venir de (+ *infinitive*)

justice la justice 8

K

karate le karaté; *to do karate* faire du karaté

to **keep** garder

ketchup le ketchup

key (on keyboard) une touche 6

keyboard un clavier 6

kidding: No kidding! Sans blague 10; *You're kidding!* Tu parles!; *You're not kidding!* Tu parles! 5

to **kill** tuer 8

kilogram un kilogramme (kilo)

kilometer un kilomètre

kind un genre 3

king un roi

kiss une bise; un bisou 5

kitchen une cuisine

knee un genou

knife un couteau

to **know** connaître; *to know (how)* savoir

knowledge la connaissance 6

L

laboratory un labo (laboratoire) 1

ladies Mesdames; *ladies and gentlemen* Messieurs-Dames

lady une dame

lake un lac

lamp une lampe

land une terre 8

to **land** atterrir

landscape un paysage 3

language une langue 3

large grand(e); gros, grosse

last dernier, dernière; *last year of lycée* la terminale

to **last** durer 8

late en retard; tard

later plus tard

Latin (language) le latin

to **laugh** rigoler 1; *to laugh like crazy* rigoler comme des fous 1

to **launch** lancer 6

launcher: satellite launcher un lanceur de satellites 6

laundry la lessive

law une loi 7

lawn un jardin; une pelouse; *lawn mower* une tondeuse

lawyer un(e) avocat(e)

lazy paresseux, paresseuse

lead le plomb

to **learn** apprendre

least: at least au moins

leather le cuir; *leather goods* la maroquinerie 9

to **leave** partir; laisser; *to leave (a person or place)* quitter

lecture une conférence 1; *lecture hall* une salle de conférences 1

left gauche 10; *to (on) the left* à gauche

leg une jambe

leisure activities les loisirs (m.)

lemon un citron; *tea with lemon* le thé au citron

lemon-lime soda une limonade

to **lend** prêter 9

length une durée 3

less moins; inférieur(e) 4

lesson une leçon

let me laissez-moi 10

letter une lettre; *letter carrier* un facteur, une factrice

liberal libéral(e) 8

liberty la liberté

library une bibliothèque

license: driver's license un permis de conduire

life la vie; *We have to live life to the fullest.* Il faut profiter de la vie au maximum.

light une lumière; *traffic light* un feu

like comme

to **like** aimer; *I like . . . .* . . . me plaît.; *What would you like?* Vous désirez?; *would like* voudrais

limit: speed limit la limite de vitesse

line une ligne 6; *to stand in line* faire la queue

lion un lion

lip une lèvre

lipstick le rouge à lèvres

list une liste 1

to **listen (to)** écouter; *listen* écoute; *to listen to music* écouter de la musique

literature la littérature 1

little petit(e); *a little* (un) peu, (un) peu de

live en direct 4

to **live** habiter; vivre; *We have to live life to the fullest.* Il faut profiter de la vie au maximum.

living room un salon

long long, longue; *(for) a long time* longtemps 5; *how long* depuis combien de temps

longer: no longer ne (n')... plus

look: to take a quick look jeter un coup d'œil 10

to **look** avoir l'air 2; *to look (at)* regarder; *to look at oneself* se regarder; *to look for* chercher; *to look like* ressembler à; *to look well/sick* avoir bonne/mauvaise mine

to **lose** perdre

lot: a lot beaucoup; *a lot of* beaucoup de

love l'amour (m.); *in love* amoureux, amoureuse

to **love** aimer; adorer

lower inférieur(e) 4

to **lower** baisser

loyalty la loyauté 8

lozenge une pastille 10

luck la chance

lucky: to be lucky avoir de la chance 1

luggage des bagages (m.)

lunch le déjeuner; *to have lunch* déjeuner

Luxembourg le Luxembourg; *from Luxembourg* luxembourgeois(e)

M

Ma'am Madame (Mme)

machine: ATM machine un guichet automatique; *ticket stamping machine* un composteur

Madagascar Madagascar (f.); *inhabitant of/from Madagascar* malgache

made of en

magazine un magazine

magnificent magnifique

maiden name un nom de jeune fille 2

mail le courrier

mailbox une boîte aux lettres

main principal(e); *main course* le plat principal

to **maintain** maintenir 8

to **make** faire; rendre (**+ adjective**) 10; *to make a call* téléphoner; *to make an appointment* prendre rendez-vous

makeup le maquillage; *to put on makeup* se maquiller

Mali le Mali 9

mall un centre commercial

man un homme

to **manage** se débrouiller 5

manager un(e) gérant(e) 5

many beaucoup; *as many* autant de 10; *how many* combien de; *too many* trop de

map une carte; un plan

maple syrup le sirop d'érable

March mars

marchioness une marquise 8

market un marché

marquis un marquis 8

marriage un mariage

married: to get married se marier 7

Martinique la Martinique; *inhabitant of/from Martinique* martiniquais(e)

mascara le mascara

massacre un massacre 8

masterpiece un chef-d'œuvre 3

match un match

math les maths (f.)

matter: What's the matter with you? Qu'est-ce que tu as?

maximum le maximum 4

May mai

maybe peut-être

mayonnaise la mayonnaise

me moi; me; *to me* me

meal un repas; *fixed-price meal* un menu

mean méchant(e)

means le moyen 9

medical: emergency medical service le SAMU (service d'assistance médicale d'urgence) 10

Mediterranean Sea la mer Méditerranée

medium moyen, moyenne

to **meet** faire la connaissance (de); se rejoindre; rencontrer 7; se rencontrer 9; se retrouver 10

melon un melon

member un membre

merchant un(e) marchand(e)

merry-go-round un manège 1; *to go on the merry-go-round* faire un tour de manège 1

message un message

meter un mètre 5

Mexican mexicain(e)

Mexico le Mexique

microwave un micro-onde

midnight minuit

milk le lait; *coffee with milk* un café au lait; *tea with milk* le thé au lait

millet le mil 9

million un million

mine le mien, la mienne 9

mineral water l'eau minérale (f.)

minimum minimum 4; *minimum wage* le SMIC 4

minivan un minivan

minus moins

minute une minute

mirror une glace; un miroir 1

Miss Mademoiselle (Mlle)

mission une mission 6

mistaken: to be mistaken se tromper (de) 5

mistreated maltraité(e) 6

mitt: bath mitt un gant de toilette

model modèle 9

modern moderne

Mom maman (f.)

moment un moment

Monaco Monaco (m.); *inhabitant of/from Monaco* monégasque

monarchy une monarchie 8

Monday lundi (m.)

monetary monétaire 8

money l'argent (m.)

monitor un moniteur 6

monk un moine 8

monkey un singe

month un mois

monument un monument

more plus; de plus; *what's more* de plus

morning un matin; *in the morning* le matin

Moroccan marocain(e)

Morocco le Maroc

most la plupart (de) 7; *the most* (**+ adjective**) le/la/les plus (**+ adjective**); *the most* (**+ adverb**) le plus (**+ adverb**)

mother une mère

mother-in-law une belle-mère

mountain une montagne

mouse une souris 6

mousse une mousse; *chocolate mousse* une mousse au chocolat

mouth une bouche

to **move** déménager; s'installer 5

movie un film; *movie theater* un cinéma 3; *movies* le cinéma; *(movie) star* une vedette 3

to **mow** tondre

mower: lawn mower une tondeuse

Mr. Monsieur; *Mr. So-and-so* Monsieur un tel 5

Mrs. Madame (Mme); *Mrs. So-and-so* Madame une telle 5

much: how much combien; combien de; *as much* autant de 10; *How much is it/that?* Ça fait combien?; *so much* tellement 5; *too much* trop de, trop; *very much* beaucoup

museum un musée

mushroom un champignon

music la musique

musician un musicien, une musicienne

mussel une moule

must: one/we/you must il faut

mustard la moutarde

my mon, ma; mes; *my name is* je m'appelle

myself me; moi-même 10

mysterious mystérieux, mystérieuse

N

name un nom; *first name* un prénom; *her name is* elle s'appelle; *his name is* il s'appelle; *maiden name* un nom de jeune fille 2; *my name is* je m'appelle; *your name is* tu t'appelles

named: to be named s'appeler 4

nap un somme 5; *to take a nap* faire un somme 5

napkin une serviette

national national(e)

nationality une nationalité

naturally naturellement

nature la nature 3

nauseous: to feel nauseous avoir mal au cœur

near près (de)

necessary nécessaire 3

to be **necessary** falloir; *it is necessary* il faut

neck un cou

necklace un collier

need un besoin 4

to **need** avoir besoin de; *I need* il me faut

to **negotiate** négocier 8

neighborhood un quartier

neither . . . nor ne (n')... ni... ni..., ni... ni... ne (n') 2

never ne (n')... jamais

new nouveau, nouvel, nouvelle; neuf, neuve 10

news des informations (f.); des nouvelles (f.) 9

newspaper un journal

newsstand un kiosque à journaux 3

next suivant(e); prochain(e); ensuite 1; *next to* à côté (de); *the next day* le lendemain

nice sympa (sympathique); gentil, gentille; aimable; *How nice you are!* Que vous êtes gentils!; *It's nice.* Il fait beau.

Niger le Niger 9

night une nuit 5; *night before* la veille

nine neuf

nineteen dix-neuf

ninety quatre-vingt-dix

ninth neuvième

no non; aucun(e)... ne (n'), ne (n')... aucun(e) 2; *No kidding!* Sans blague 10; *no longer* ne (n')... plus; *no one* ne (n')... personne; personne ne (n') 2; *No way!* Tu parles!

nobody ne (n')... personne; personne ne (n') 2

noise un bruit

nontraditional non-traditionnel, non-traditionnelle 7

noon midi

nor: neither . . . nor ne (n')... ni... ni..., ni... ni... ne (n') 2

Normandy: inhabitant of/from Normandy un(e) Normand(e) 8

north le nord; *North America* l'Amérique du Nord (f.); *North Sea* la mer du Nord

nose un nez

not pas; ne (n')... pas; *not any* ne (n')... aucun(e) 2; *not anymore* ne (n')... plus; *not anyone* ne (n')... personne; *not anything* ne (n')... rien; *not at all* pas du tout; *not one* aucun(e)... ne (n') 2; *not yet* ne (n')... pas encore

note une note 1

notebook un cahier; un carnet 1

notepad un bloc-notes 1

nothing ne (n')... rien; rien ne (n') 2; rien 10

novel un roman

November novembre

now maintenant

nuclear nucléaire; *nuclear energy* l'énergie nucléaire

number un numéro; *telephone number* un numéro de téléphone

numerous nombreux, nombreuse 7

nurse un infirmier, une infirmière

O

o'clock l'heure (f.)

objet d'art un objet d'art

to be **obliged to** être obligé(e) de

obvious évident(e) 4

occupation une profession

ocean un océan; *Atlantic Ocean* l'océan Atlantique (m.); *Indian Ocean* l'océan Indien (m.); *Pacific Ocean* l'océan Pacifique (m.)

oceanography l'océanographie (f.) 6

October octobre

of de (d'); *of (the)* des, du; *of course* bien sûr; *of it/them* en; *of which/whom* dont 5

off: to get off descendre 3

to **offer** offrir

office un bureau 1; *box office* un bureau de location 3; *office (doctor or dentist's)* un cabinet; *tourist office* un syndicat d'initiative

often souvent

oh ah; oh; *Oh no! Oh dear!* Oh là là!

oil l'huile (f.)

OK d'accord; OK

old vieux, vieil, vieille; âgé(e); *How old are you?* Tu as quel âge?; *I'm . . . years old.* J'ai... ans.; *to be . . . (years old)* avoir... ans; *to be how old* avoir quel âge

omelette une omelette

on sur; en; dans; *on (+ day of the week)* le (+ *day of the week*); *on foot* à pied; *on sale* en solde; *on the* au; *on the (+ ordinal number)* le (+ *number*); *on the other hand* par contre 9; *on the other side* de l'autre côté 9; *on time* à l'heure; *on TV* à la télé

once une fois 1; *all at once* à la fois

one un; on; une; *no one* ne (n')... personne; personne ne (n') 2; *(the) one . . . the other* l'un(e)... l'autre 10; *the ones* ceux, celles 7; *this one, that one, the one* celui, celle 7; *which one* lequel, laquelle 7; *which ones* lesquels, lesquelles 7

one's son, sa; ses; le sien, la sienne 9

oneself se; *to enjoy (oneself)* se distraire 7; *to look at oneself* se regarder; *to wash (oneself)* se laver

one-way (street) un sens unique

onion un oignon

online en ligne 6

only juste; seulement; ne (n')... que 2

on-the-job training un stage; *to have on-the-job training* faire un stage

to **open** ouvrir

opinion une opinion; *in my opinion* à mon avis

opportunity une occasion 9

optimistic optimiste 7

or ou

oral oral(e) 1

orange une orange; orange; *orange juice* le jus d'orange

orchestra un orchestre 3

order une commande; *order form* une fiche de commande

to **order** ordonner 8

organized organisé(e) 4

origin une origine 7

ostrich une autruche 9

other autre; *(the) one . . . the other* l'un(e)... l'autre 10

our notre; nos

ours le nôtre, la nôtre 9

ourselves nous

outfit un ensemble

outside dehors

oven un four

over there là-bas

overhead compartment un porte-bagages 5

to **overlook** donner sur

to **owe** devoir 10

own propre 5

owner: pastry store owner un pâtissier, une pâtissière

P

Pacific Ocean l'océan Pacifique (m.)

package un colis

to **paint** peindre 3

painter un(e) peintre 3

painting un tableau

pair une paire 9

pancake une crêpe

panoramic panoramique 5

pants: (pair of) pants un pantalon

panty hose des bas (m.)

paper: paper clip un trombone 1; *research paper* une dissertation 1; *sheet of paper* une feuille de papier

parade un défilé

paradise le paradis

parent un parent

park un jardin; un parc; *amusement park* un parc d'attractions 1; *park ranger* un garde forestier 5

part une partie 6; *to be a part of* faire partie de 9; *to take part in* participer à 4

party une boum; *(political) party* un parti 4

to **pass** passer; dépasser; *to pass (a test)* réussir; *to pass (a vehicle)* doubler

passenger un passager, une passagère

passerby un(e) passant(e) 7

passport un passeport

past le passé 8

pastime un passe-temps 1

pastry store une pâtisserie; *pastry store owner* un pâtissier, une pâtissière

pâté le pâté

path un chemin

patience la patience 5

pavilion un pavillon 9

to **pay** régler; payer 2; *to pay attention* faire attention 2

peace la paix 8

peach une pêche

pear une poire

peas des petits pois (m.)

peasant un paysan, une paysanne 9

pen un stylo; *felt-tip pen* un feutre 1

pencil un crayon; *pencil case* une trousse; *pencil sharpener* un taille-crayon

people le monde; des gens (m.); le peuple 8

pepper le poivre

per par

percentage un pourcentage 4

perfect parfait(e)

to **permit** permettre 6

person une personne; *crazy person* un fou, une folle 1; *homeless person* un(e) sans-abri; *unemployed person* un chômeur, une chômeuse 7; *young person* un(e) jeune 3

personality une personnalité

personnel le personnel 4

pharmacist un pharmacien, une pharmacienne

pharmacy une pharmacie 10

philosophy la philosophie

to **phone (someone)** téléphoner

photo une photo

phrase une phrase 10

physics la physique

piano un piano

to **pick up** ranger; venir chercher

picnic: to have a picnic piqueniquer

picture une photo

pie une tarte; *strawberry pie* une tarte aux fraises

piece un morceau; *(piece of) advice* un conseil 8

pierced percé 5

pig un cochon

pilot un pilote

pink rose

pious pieux, pieuse 8

pizza une pizza; *to eat pizza* manger de la pizza

place une place; un endroit 2; un lieu 8; *to take place* avoir lieu 8

placed placé(e)

plan un projet 9

plant une plante

plate une assiette

platform un quai

play une pièce (de théâtre) 3

to **play** jouer; *to play (a part)* jouer 3; *to play (on the radio)* passer 7; *to play basketball* jouer au basket; *to play cards* jouer aux cartes (f.); *to play chess* jouer aux échecs (m.); *to play golf* jouer au golf; *to play soccer* jouer au foot; *to play sports* faire du sport; *to play tennis* jouer au tennis; *to play video games* jouer aux jeux vidéo; *to play volleyball* jouer au volley

please s'il vous plaît; s'il te plaît

to **please** plaire 3

pleasure un plaisir

plentiful abondant(e) 9

plot une intrigue 3

pole: ski pole un bâton

police la police 2; *police officer* un agent de police; *police station* un commissariat 2

polite poli(e)

political politique; *(political) party* un parti 4; *political science* les sciences po 1

politician un homme politique, une femme politique

pollution la pollution

pond un étang

pool: swimming pool une piscine

poor pauvre

popular populaire 3

pork le porc

position un poste 4

possibility une possibilité

possible possible

post office une poste

postage l'affranchissement (m.)

postal worker un postier, une postière

postcard une carte postale

poster une affiche

potato une pomme de terre

poverty la pauvreté 6

powerful puissant(e)

practical pratique

to **prefer** préférer

premium (gasoline) super

preparatory préparatoire 4

to **prepare** préparer

prescription une ordonnance 10

present un cadeau; le présent 8

to **press** appuyer 6

pretty joli(e)

price un prix, un tarif 3

principal un directeur, une directrice 1; *assistant principal* un censeur 1

printer une imprimante 6

prisoner un prisonnier, une prisonnière 8; *to take prisoner* faire prisonnier/prisonnière 8

problem un problème

problems des ennuis (m.) 5

program une émission

progress le progrès 6

prohibited interdit(e) 3

project un projet 4

to **propose** proposer 5

to **protect** préserver; protéger 6

protection la protection 6

Protestant un(e) protestant(e) 8

proud fier, fière 8

province une province 5; *in the provinces* en province 8

public housing une HLM (habitation à loyer modéré) 7

purchase un achat 10

purple violet, violette

purse un sac à main

to **push** pousser 4

to **put (on)** mettre; *to put on makeup* se maquiller

pyjamas un pyjama

Q

qualification une qualification 4

quarter un quart; un quartier; *quarter after* et quart; *quarter to* moins le quart

Quebec (Province) le Québec 4; *inhabitant of Quebec* un(e) Québécois(e)

queen une reine

question une question 2

quiche une quiche

quickly vite

quiet calme; *to be quiet* se taire 2

quite assez

quiz une interro (interrogation)

R

rabbit un lapin; *rabbit hutch* une cage à lapins 7

race une course

racket une raquette

radio une radio 7; *to play (on the radio)* passer 7

rain la pluie 9

to **rain: It's raining.** Il pleut.

raincoat un imperméable (imper)

raised élevé(e) 10

ranger: park ranger un garde forestier 5

rapidly rapidement

rate un tarif 3; un taux 4

rather assez; plutôt 2

rating un indice 3

raw vegetables des crudités (f.)

razor un rasoir

to **read** lire

reading la lecture 1

ready prêt(e); *to get ready* se préparer

real vrai(e)

to **realize** se rendre compte 5

real-life vécu(e) 3

really bien; vraiment; vachement; *Really?* Ah bon? 7

reason une raison 4

reassuring rassurant(e) 2

receipt un récépissé 2; un ticket de caisse 10

to **receive** recevoir

reception desk la réception

receptionist un(e) réceptionniste

to **recognize** reconnaître 3

to **recommend** recommander

to **record** enregistrer 3

recycle recycler

red rouge; *red (hair)* roux, rousse

reduced réduit(e) 3

reduction une réduction 10

refrigerator un frigo

reggae le reggae

registration form une fiche d'inscription 1

to **regret** regretter 2

regular (gasoline) ordinaire

reign un règne 8

to **reimburse** rembourser 10

relation(ship) une relation 7

relations des rapports (m.) 2

relationship des rapports (m.) 2

relative un parent

relic une relique 8

religion la religion 8

religious religieux, religieuse 9

to **rely** compter 7

to **remain** rester

to **remember** se rappeler 2; se souvenir 5

to **remind** rappeler 9

to **remove** enlever

to **rent** louer

to **repair** réparer 10

to **repeat** répéter 2

report un exposé 1; une déclaration 2; un reportage 4; *weather report* un bulletin météo

reporter un reporter

to **require** exiger 4

research la recherche 1; *research paper* une dissertation 1

researcher un chercheur, une chercheuse

to **resemble** ressembler à

reservation une réservation

to **reserve** réserver

reserved circonspect(e) 7

resident un(e) résident(e) 7

responsibility une responsabilité 1

to **rest** se reposer 2

restaurant un restaurant; *fast-food restaurant* un fast-food

result un résultat 10

to **return** rentrer, revenir; retourner 5; rendre 6

to **reunite** réunir 8

revolution une révolution 8

rich riche

ride une promenade; *to go for a ride* faire un tour; faire une promenade

riding: to go horseback riding faire du cheval

right droit(e) 10; *right away/now* tout de suite; *to be right* avoir raison 10; *to (on) the right* à droite

ring une bague

to **ring** sonner 5

ripe mûr(e)

river un fleuve, une rivière

Riviera la côte d'Azur

road une route

to **rob** voler 2

rock un rocher 5; *rock (music)* le rock

rocket une fusée 6

rocky rocheux, rocheuse

role un rôle 3

roller coaster des montagnes russes 1; *to go on the roller coaster* faire un tour de montagnes russes 1

Roman un(e) Romain(e) 8

room une pièce; la place; une chambre; *dining room* une salle à manger; *dormitory room (for more than one person)* un dortoir; *emergency room* la salle des urgences 10; *family room* un séjour; *living room* un salon; *waiting room* une salle d'attente 10

roommate une camarade de chambre

rooster un coq

rug un tapis

run une piste 1

to **run** courir; *to run into* heurter 1

running le footing; *to go running* faire du footing

Russian le russe 1

Rwanda le Ruanda 6

S

sad triste

Sahara le Sahara 9

sailing la voile; *to go sailing* faire de la voile

saint un(e) saint(e); *All Saints' Day* la Toussaint

salad une salade

salami le saucisson

salary un salaire 4

sale(s) des soldes (f.); *on sale* en solde

sales la vente 4

salesperson un vendeur, une vendeuse

salmon un saumon

salt le sel

same même 3

sand le sable 5

sandal une sandale

sandwich un sandwich; *cheese sandwich* un sandwich au fromage; *ham sandwich* un sandwich au jambon

satellite un satellite 5; *satellite launcher* un lanceur de satellites 6

satisfied (with) satisfait(e) de 2

Saturday samedi (m.)

sauce: hollandaise sauce la sauce hollandaise

sausage une saucisse

to **save** préserver; sauvegarder 6

saxophone un saxophone

to **say** dire; *say* dis; *What can I say?* Bof! 9

scallops: curried scallops des coquilles Saint-Jacques au curry

scarf un foulard

scenery un paysage 5

schedule un emploi du temps; un horaire

school scolaire

school une école; *driving school* une auto-école; *first day of school* la rentrée 1; *high school* un lycée

science les sciences (f.); *political science* les sciences po 1

science fiction la science-fiction

scientific scientifique

scrambled eggs des œufs brouillés (m.)

screen un écran 6

script un scénario 3

scriptwriter un(e) scénariste 3

scuba diving la plongée sous-marine; *to go scuba diving* faire de la plongée sous-marine

sculptor un sculpteur 3

sculpture la sculpture

sea une mer; *Caribbean Sea* la mer des Antilles; *Mediterranean Sea* la mer Méditerranée; *North Sea* la mer du Nord

seafood des fruits de mer (m.)

seal un phoque

séance une consultation 1

search engine un outil de recherche 6

to **search** fouiller 2

seashore: at the seashore au bord de la mer

season une saison

seat un siège; une place 3; *seat belt* une ceinture de sécurité

seated assis(e)

second deuxième

secretary un(e) secrétaire

sector le cadre 4

security check un contrôle de sécurité

to **see** voir; *let's see* voyons; *See you soon.* À bientôt.; *See you tomorrow.* À demain.; *to see again* revoir 10

to **seem** sembler; *It seems to me . . . .* Il me semble....

selfish égoïste

to **sell** vendre

to **send** envoyer

Senegal le Sénégal

Senegalese sénégalais(e)

sensitive sensible

sentence une phrase 10

September septembre

serious sérieux, sérieuse; grave

seriously au sérieux; sérieusement

to **serve** servir 5

server un serveur, une serveuse

service un service 4; *emergency medical service* le SAMU (service d'assistance médicale d'urgence) 10

session une consultation 1

to **set** mettre

setting: table setting un couvert

seven sept

seventeen dix-sept

seventh septième

seventy soixante-dix

several plusieurs 3

Sh! Chut! 5

shampoo le shampooing

shape: to be in good/bad shape être en bonne/ mauvaise forme

to **share** partager 9

sharpener: pencil sharpener un taille-crayon

to **shave** se raser

she elle; *she is* c'est

sheep un mouton

sheet un drap

shelter un refuge 6

to **shift gears** changer de vitesse

shirt une chemise

shoe une chaussure; *tennis shoes* des tennis (m.)

to **shoot (a movie)** tourner 3

shop une boutique

shopkeeper un(e) commerçant(e)

shopping le shopping; *shopping center* un centre commercial; *to go grocery shopping* faire les courses; *to go shopping* faire du shopping, faire les magasins

shore le bord

short court(e), petit(e)

shorts: (pair of) shorts un short

shoulder une épaule

show un spectacle 3; *game show* un jeu télévisé

to **show** montrer; *Show me . . . .* Montrez-moi....; *to show (a movie)* passer

shower une douche

shrimp une crevette

shy timide

sick malade; *I'm sick of it!* J'en ai marre!

side un côté; le bord; *on the other side* de l'autre côté 9

sign un panneau; un signe 3

to **sign** signer

silver l'argent (m.)

simple simple 7

since depuis; puisque 2; *since when* depuis quand

to **sing** chanter 3

singer un chanteur, une chanteuse

single-parent monoparental(e) 7

sink un évier

Sir Monsieur

sister une sœur; *host sister* une correspondante

sister-in-law une belle-sœur

to **sit down** s'asseoir

situated placé(e); situé(e) 5

six six

sixteen seize

sixth sixième

sixty soixante

size une taille

skateboard une planche à roulettes 1

skateboarding: to go skateboarding faire de la planche à roulettes 1

skating: in-line skating le roller; *to go in-line skating* faire du roller

skeleton un squelette 9

ski: ski jacket un anorak; *ski pole* un bâton

to **ski** skier

skill: games of skill des jeux d'adresse 1

skin une peau 9

to **skip (a class)** sécher 1

skirt une jupe; *African skirt* un pagne 9

skyscraper un gratte-ciel 9

to **sleep** dormir

slender mince

slice une tranche; *slice of buttered bread* une tartine

slipper une pantoufle

sly rusé(e) 8

small petit(e)

smiling souriant(e) 2

snack: snack bar un snack-bar 9; *afternoon snack* le goûter

snacks des chips (m.)

snail un escargot

snow la neige 1; *It's snowing.* Il neige.

snowboard une planche à neige 1

snowboarding: to go snowboarding faire de la planche à neige 1

so si; donc; *so-so* comme ci, comme ça; *so much* tellement 5; *so that* de sorte que 9

soap le savon; *soap opera* un feuilleton

soccer le foot (football); *to play soccer* jouer au foot

social social(e) 7

society une société 7

sock une chaussette

soda: lemon-lime soda une limonade

sofa un canapé

to **solve** résoudre

some des; du; de (d'), quelques; en

somebody, someone quelqu'un

something quelque chose

sometimes quelquefois

son un fils; mon petit

song une chanson

soon bientôt; *as soon as* aussitôt que; dès que 6

sore: to have a sore . . . avoir mal (à...)

sorry désolé(e)

to be **sorry** regretter

sound track une bande originale 3

soup la soupe; le potage; *fish soup* une bouillabaisse

south le sud; *South America* l'Amérique du Sud (f.); *the south of France* le Midi 10

space la place; l'espace (m.), spatial(e) 6

Spain l'Espagne (f.)

Spanish espagnol(e); *Spanish (language)* l'espagnol (m.)

to **speak** parler

special spécial(e)

to **specialize** se spécialiser 4

specialty une spécialité

speed la vitesse; *speed limit* la limite de vitesse

to **spend** dépenser 6; *to spend (time)* passer

spicy épicé(e)

to **spoil** gâter

spoiled pourri(e) 9

spoon une cuiller

sport un sport; *sport jacket* une veste; *sports car* une voiture de sport; *to play sports* faire du sport

to **sprain** se fouler 10

spring le printemps

square: public square une place

stadium un stade

staff le personnel 4

stained glass windows des vitraux (m.) 8

staircase, stairs un escalier

stamp un timbre

to **stamp** composter

to **stand in line** faire la queue

stapler une agrafeuse 1

star: (movie) star une vedette 3

to **start (up)** démarrer

station une station; *gas station* une station-service; *gas station attendant* un(e) pompiste; *police station* un commissariat 2; *train station* une gare

statue une statue

stay un séjour; *family stay* un séjour en famille

to **stay** rester

steady solide

steak un steak; *steak with French fries* un steak-frites

to **steal (from)** voler 2

stepbrother un beau-frère

stepfather un beau-père

stepmother une belle-mère

stepsister une belle-sœur

stereo une stéréo

still encore, toujours; *still life* une nature morte 3

stomach un ventre

stop une escale

to **stop** arrêter; s'arrêter

stopover une escale

store un magasin; *department store* un grand magasin

story un étage; une histoire

stove une cuisinière

straight ahead tout droit

strained tendu(e) 7

strategy une stratégie 6

strawberry une fraise; *strawberry pie* une tarte aux fraises

street une rue; *one-way (street)* un sens unique

to **stroll** flâner

strong fort(e)

student un(e) élève, un(e) étudiant(e); *high school student* un lycéen, une lycéenne 1

studio un atelier 3

study une étude

to **study** étudier; faire des études 4; *Let's study . . . .* Étudions....

stupid bête

subject un sujet 6

suburbs: express subway to suburbs le R.E.R. (Réseau Express Régional)

subway un métro; *express subway to suburbs* le R.E.R. (Réseau Express Régional)

to **succeed** réussir

success le succès 3; une réussite 9

such a un tel, une telle 10

sudden: all of a sudden tout à coup 2

sugar le sucre

suit: man's suit un costume; *woman's suit* un tailleur

suitcase une valise

summer l'été (m.)

sun le soleil

Sunday dimanche (m.)

sunglasses des lunettes de soleil (f.)

sunny: It's sunny. Il fait du soleil.

super super

superhighway: information superhighway l'inforoute (f.) 6

superb superbe

supermarket un supermarché

supper le dîner

sure sûr(e) 4

surprise une surprise

to **surprise** surprendre 5

surprised étonné(e) 5

surprising surprenant(e) 2

survey une enquête

to **survive** survivre 8

sweater un pull

sweatshirt un sweat

to **swim** nager

swimming pool une piscine

swimsuit un maillot de bain

Swiss suisse

Switzerland la Suisse

synthesizer un synthé, un synthétiseur

syrup: maple syrup le sirop d'érable

system un système 8

T

table une table; *table setting* un couvert

tablecloth une nappe

Tahiti Tahiti (f.) 10

Tahitian tahitien, tahitienne

to **take** prendre; *to take (a class)* suivre; *to take (a test)* passer 1; *to take a nap* faire un somme 5; *to take a quick look* jeter un coup d'œil 10; *to take a tour* faire le tour; *to take a trip* faire un voyage 5; *to take advantage of* profiter de; *to take (someone) along* emmener; *to take care of* s'occuper de 5; *to take off* décoller; *to take out the garbage* sortir la poubelle; *to take part in* participer à 4; *to take place* avoir lieu 8; *to take prisoner* faire prisonnier/ prisonnière 8

to **talk** parler

talkative bavard(e)

tall grand(e); haut(e)

tank: to fill up the gas tank faire le plein

to **taste** goûter

tax un impôt 8

taxi un taxi

tea le thé; *tea with lemon* le thé au citron; *tea with milk* le thé au lait

teacher un(e) prof, un professeur

team une équipe 6

technology la technologie 6

teenager un(e) ado

telegram un télégramme

telephone un téléphone; *telephone number* un numéro de téléphone

television la télé (télévision)

to **tell** dire; *to tell (about)* raconter

temperature une température

ten dix

tennis le tennis; *tennis shoes* des tennis (m.); *to play tennis* jouer au tennis

tenth dixième

terrific super; formidable; extra; génial(e) 7

terrorism le terrorisme

test une interro (interrogation); un examen 1; *to pass (a test)* réussir; *to take (a test)* passer 1

textbook un manuel 1

than que

to **thank** remercier

thanks merci; grâce 6

that ça; ce, cet, cette, que; qui; cela 5; ce qui 6; *so that* de sorte que 9; *that one* celui, celle 7; *that's* c'est; *That's . . . .* Ça fait....; *That's great.* Tant mieux.; *that's it* voilà

the le, la, l', les; *the one* celui, celle 7; *the ones* ceux, celles 7

theater un théâtre; *movie theater* un cinéma 3

theft un vol 2

their leur

theirs le leur, la leur 9

them les; eux, elles; *about/from them* en; *of them* en; *to them* leur

themselves se

then puis; donc; *(well) then* alors

there là; y; *over there* là-bas; *there is/are* voilà, il y a

these ces; ceux, celles 7; *these are* ce sont; *these days* de nos jours 9

they on; *they (f.)* elles; *they(m.)* ils; *they are* ce sont

thing une chose; un truc 5; *How are things going?* Ça va?; *Things are going well.* Ça va bien.

to **think** croire, trouver; *I think so.* Je crois que oui. 5; *to think (of)* penser (à)

third troisième

thirsty: I'm thirsty. J'ai soif.; *to be thirsty* avoir soif

thirteen treize

thirty trente; *thirty (minutes)* et demi(e)

this ce, cet, cette; *this is* c'est; *this one* celui, celle 7

those ces; ceux, celles 7; *those are* ce sont

thousand: one thousand mille

three trois

throat une gorge

through: to go through fouiller 2

Thursday jeudi (m.)

ticket un billet; un ticket 1; *ticket stamping machine* un composteur; *ticket window* un guichet

tiger un tigre

time l'heure (f.); une fois; le temps; une époque 9; *(for) a long time* longtemps 5; *on time* à l'heure; *to have a good time* s'amuser; se distraire 7; *to waste one's time* perdre son temps 7; *What time is it?* Quelle heure est-il?

timetable un horaire

timid timide

tire un pneu

tired fatigué(e)

tiring fatigant(e) 2

title un titre 6

to à; sur; *in order to* pour; *to (the)* au, aux, en; *to her/him* lui; *to them* leur; *to us* nous

toast le pain grillé; *French toast* le pain perdu

tobacco shop un tabac

toboggan une luge 1

tobogganing: to go tobogganing faire de la luge 1

today aujourd'hui

toe un doigt de pied

together ensemble

Togo le Togo 7

toilet les toilettes (f.), les W.-C. (m.)

toiletries des affaires de toilette (f.)

tomato une tomate; *tomato juice* le jus de tomate

tomb un tombeau

tomorrow demain

tonight ce soir

too aussi; trop; *Too bad!* Dommage!; Tant pis.; *too many* trop de; *too much* trop, trop de

tooth une dent

toothbrush une brosse à dents

toothpaste le dentifrice

tour le tour; une tournée; *to take a tour* faire le tour; *tour bus* un car 2

tourist un(e) touriste 5; *to act like tourists* faire les touristes 5; *tourist office* un syndicat d'initiative

towards envers 8

towel une serviette

tower une tour

town hall une mairie

track une voie; une piste 1; *sound track* une bande originale 3; *train track* une voie

trade un métier; le commerce 6

traditional traditionnel, traditionnelle 9

traffic la circulation; *traffic light* un feu

trail une piste 1

train un train; *(train) car* une voiture; *train station* une gare; *train track* une voie

to **train** s'entraîner 1

training: on-the-job training un stage; *to have on-the-job training* faire un stage

to **transform** transformer 8

to **trap** rattraper 10

to **travel** voyager; *to travel through* parcourir 5

traveler un voyageur, une voyageuse; *traveler's check* un chèque de voyage

to **treat** traiter 5

treatment un traitement 6

tree un arbre; *baobab tree* un baobab 9

tribe une tribu 8

trip un tour; un voyage; une excursion; un trajet; *to take a trip* faire un voyage 5

triumph un triomphe

trombone un trombone

trouble le tracas 10

truck un camion

true vrai(e)

truly: yours truly Je vous prie d'agréer, Monsieur (ou Madame), mes salutations distinguées. 4

trumpet une trompette

to **try** essayer 1

T-shirt un tee-shirt

Tuesday mardi (m.)

Tunisia la Tunisie

Tunisian tunisien, tunisienne

turkey un dindon

to **turn** tourner; *to turn off* éteindre; *to turn on* allumer, mettre 5

TV la télé (télévision); *on TV* à la télé

twelve douze

twenty vingt

twin jumeau, jumelle; *twin beds* des lits jumeaux

two deux

type un genre 3

U

ugly moche

uhm euh

umbrella un parapluie

unattractive laid(e)

unbelievable incroyable 2

uncle un oncle

under sous

to **understand** comprendre 1

underwear des sous-vêtements (m.)

to **undress** se déshabiller

unemployed person un chômeur, une chômeuse 7

unemployment le chômage

unfortunately malheureusement 9

United States les États-Unis (m.)

university une fac (faculté), une université; universitaire 7; *elite, specialized universities* les grandes écoles 4

unpleasant pénible

until, up to jusqu'à

up: It's up to you. C'est à vous de voir. 10

upon en 2

us nous; *to us* nous

to **use** utiliser; consommer; se servir de 5

useful utile 3

useless inutile 2

usual d'habitude 7; *as usual* comme d'habitude

V

vacation les vacances (f.)

to **vacuum** passer l'aspirateur (m.)

vacuum cleaner un aspirateur

vain: (to do something) in vain avoir beau 8

valid valable 3

vanilla ice cream une glace à la vanille

variety une variété 3

vase un vase

VCR un magnétoscope

vegetable un légume; *raw vegetables* des crudités (f.)

version une version 3

very très; vachement; *very much* beaucoup

veterinarian un vétérinaire

video clip un clip

video games des jeux vidéo (m.); *to play video games* jouer aux jeux vidéo

videocassette une vidéocassette

Vietnam le Vietnam

Vietnamese vietnamien, vietnamienne

view une vue

village un village

violence la violence 8

violin un violon

visit une visite

to **visit** rendre visite (à); *to visit (a place)* visiter

vocabulary le vocabulaire 7

voice une voix

volleyball le volley (volley-ball); *to play volleyball* jouer au volley

W

wage: minimum wage le SMIC 4

to **wait (for)** attendre

waiting room une salle d'attente 10

to **wake up** se réveiller

walk une promenade; *to go for a walk* faire une promenade

to **walk** marcher

wall un mur 7

wallet un portefeuille

want ads des petites annonces (f.) 4

to **want** désirer; vouloir; avoir envie de

war une guerre

wardrobe une armoire

warm chaud(e); *It's warm.* Il fait chaud.; *to be warm* avoir chaud

to **wash (oneself)** se laver

washer une machine à laver

to **waste one's time** perdre son temps 7

wastebasket une corbeille

watch une montre

to **watch** regarder; *Watch out!* Attention!

water l'eau (f.); *mineral water* l'eau minérale (f.)

to **water** arroser

waterfall une cascade

watermelon une pastèque

to **water-ski** faire du ski nautique

waterskiing le ski nautique; *to go waterskiing* faire du ski nautique

way un chemin; le moyen 4; une façon 5; *No way!* Tu parles!; *the way in which* la façon dont 5

we nous, on; *We have to live life to the fullest.* Il faut profiter de la vie au maximum.

weak faible

to **wear** porter; *to wear size (+ number)* faire du (+ number)

weather le temps; *The weather's bad.* Il fait mauvais.; *The weather's beautiful/nice.* Il fait beau.; *The weather's cold.* Il fait froid.; *The weather's cool.* Il fait frais.; *The weather's hot/warm.* Il fait chaud.; *weather report* un bulletin météo; *What's the weather like? How's the weather?* Quel temps fait-il?

Web le web 6

Wednesday mercredi (m.)

week une semaine

weekend un weekend

to **weigh** peser

Welcome! Bienvenue!; *You're welcome.* Je vous en prie.; Il n'y a pas de quoi.

well bien; ben; *Well done!* Bravo! 6; *well then* alors, bon ben

were: if I were you à ta place 5

west l'ouest (m.); *West* l'Occident (m.) 8

what comment; qu'est-ce que; quel, quelle; quoi; qu'est-ce qui, que; ce que, ce qui 4; *What?* Hein? 1; *What (a) . . . !* Quel, Quelle...!; *What a drag!* Quelle galère!; *What can I say?* Bof! 9; *what if* si 10; *What is . . .?* Qu'est-ce que c'est que...? 9; *What is it/this?* Qu'est-ce que c'est?; *What time is it?* Quelle heure est-il?; *What would you like?* Vous désirez?; *what's more* de plus; *What's the matter with you?* Qu'est-ce que tu as?; *What's the weather like?* Quel temps fait-il?

wheel une roue 1; *Ferris wheel* une grande roue 1

wheelchair un fauteuil roulant 10

when quand; lorsque 3; *since when* depuis quand

where où

which quel, quelle; que, qui; *about which, of which* dont 5; *the way in which* la façon dont 5; *which one* lequel, laquelle 7; *which ones* lesquels, lesquelles 7

while en, pendant que 2

white blanc, blanche

who qui; qui est-ce qui

whole entier, entière 6

whom qui; que; qui est-ce que; *about whom, of whom* dont 5

whose dont 5

why pourquoi

wide large 8

wife une femme

wildlife sauvage 5

to be **willing** vouloir bien

to **win** gagner 1

wind le vent

window une fenêtre; *ticket window* un guichet

windshield un pare-brise

windsurfing la planche à voile; *to go windsurfing* faire de la planche à voile

windy: It's windy. Il fait du vent.

wine le vin; *chicken cooked in wine* le coq au vin

winter l'hiver (m.)

to **wish** souhaiter 4

with avec

without sans

woman une femme

word un mot 7

work le travail; un boulot

to **work** travailler; marcher 5; *to work out* s'entraîner 1

worker un ouvrier, une ouvrière; *factory worker* un ouvrier, une ouvrière; *postal worker* un postier, une postière

workshop un atelier 9

world le monde

world-wide mondial(e) 6

to **worry** s'inquiéter

would like voudrais

wound une blessure 10

Wow! Oh là là!

wrapped entouré(e) 10

wrist un poignet 10

to **write** écrire

writer un écrivain

wrong: to be wrong se tromper (de) 5

X

X ray une radiographie 10

Y

yeah ouais

year un an; une année; *I'm . . . years old.* J'ai... ans.; *last year of* **lycée** la terminale; *to be . . . (years old)* avoir... ans

yellow jaune

yes oui; *yes (on the contrary)* si

yesterday hier

yet: not yet ne (n')... pas encore

yogurt le yaourt

you tu, vous; toi; te; *if I were you* à ta place 5; *to you* te, vous; *You're kidding!* Tu parles!; *You're not kidding!* Tu parles! 5; *You're welcome.* Je vous en prie.; Il n'y a pas de quoi.

young jeune; *young person* un(e) jeune 3

your ton, ta, tes, votre, vos; *your name is* tu t'appelles

yours le tien, la tienne, le vôtre, la vôtre 9; *yours truly* Je vous prie d'agréer, Monsieur (ou Madame), mes salutations distinguées. 4

yourself te, vous

yourselves vous

youth hostel une auberge de jeunesse

Yuk! Beurk!

Z

Zaire le Zaïre

Zairian zaïrois(e)

zebra un zèbre

zero zéro

zoo un zoo

Grammar Index

Acknowledgments

The following teachers responded to our surveys by offering valuable comments and suggestions in the development of the *C'est à toi!* series:

Sally Ahrens, Camp Hill High School, Camp Hill, PA

Sonia Alcé, Hyde Park High School, Hyde Park, MA

Missie Babb, Isle of Wight Academy, Isle of Wight, VA

Gerald W. Beauchesne, West Springfield High School, West Springfield, MA

Daniel Beniero, Port Sulphur High School, Port Sulphur, LA

Helen H. Bickell, Hilliard High School, Hilliard, OH

Jacqueline Bodi, Exeter Area High School, Exeter, NH

Coy Boé, Glade Junior High School, LaPlace, LA

Joan Bowers, Tamarend Middle School, Warrington, PA

Susan Boyle, Indian Hills Junior High, Clive, IA

Denise H. Brown, Lima Senior High School, Lima, OH

Kristen Carley, St. Joseph's Episcopal School, Boynton Beach, FL

Amber Challifour, Brebeuf Preparatory School, Indianapolis, IN

Augusta D. Clark, Saint Mary's Hall, San Antonio, TX

Colleen Contrada, St. Augustine's, Andover, MA

Elaine Danford, Sidney High School, Sidney, NY

Kelley DeGraaf, Ionia High School, Ionia, MI

Virginia Delaney, Osceola High School, Osceola, WI

Pauline P. Demetri, Cambridge Rindge and Latin, Cambridge, MA

Margaret Schmidt Dess, St. Joseph Middle School, Waukesha, WI

Elizabeth K. Douglas, Ambridge Area High School, Ambridge, PA

Alma A. Dumareille, First International Language Private School, McAllen, TX

Cathy Dunbar, Chino Valley High School, Chino Valley, AZ

Karen Dymit, Hadley Junior High School, Glen Ellyn, IL

Bob Dzama, Parma High School, Parma, OH

Roy Ellefson, North Sanpete High School, Mt. Pleasant, UT

Nancy Farley, Doddridge County High School, West Union, WV

Candyce Fike, Dallas Senior High School, Dallas, TX

Wilma Franko, Brownsville Area High, Brownsville, PA

Kathy A. Ghiata, Alpena High School, Alpena, MI

William B. Gunn, John S. Burke Catholic High School, Goshen, NY

Jane R. Hill, Alton High School, Alton, IL

Lionel Hogu, Hyde Park High School, Hyde Park, MA

Joseph Holland, Rancocas Valley Regional High School, Mt. Holly, NJ

Danette Hopkin, St. Joseph Regional, Port Vue, PA

Darrylin Keenan, Fort Fairfield High School, Fort Fairfield, ME

James Kolmansberger, Pittston Area High School, Yatesville, PA

Jude-Marie LaFrancis, Grayslake High School, Grayslake, IL

Mark C. Lander, Bacon Academy, Colchester, CT

George Lerrigo, Mt. Anthony Union High School, Bennington, VT

Joy Macy, Stilwell Junior High, West Des Moines, IA

William E. Mann, Clay High School, Clay, WV

Phyllis McCauley, Chopticon High School, Morganza, MD

Theresa Michaud, St. Augustine School, Augusta, ME

Muriel Mikulewicz, Trinity High School, Manchester, NH

Shari Miller, Valley High School, West Des Moines, IA

J. Vincent H. Morrissette, Santa Catalina School, Monterey, CA

Jane Much, East Hills Middle School, Bethlehem, PA

Dale Muegenburg, Santa Clara High School, Ventura, CA

Laura A. Peel, Unami Middle School, Chalfont, PA

Nancy Pond, Bement School, Deerfield, MA

Cherry S. Raley, St. Michael's Academy, Austin, TX

Karen S. Rich, St. Philip Catholic Central High School, Battle Creek, MI

Pamela G. Rogers, Tidewater Academy, Wakefield, VA

Lynn Rouse, Brandywine Junior/Senior High School, Granger, IN

John B. Rudder, St. Margaret's School, Tappahannock, VA

Helene Scarcia, Trexler Middle School, Allentown, PA

George P. Shannon, Littlefield Public Schools, Alanson, MI

Russell J. Sloun, Xavier High School, New York, NY

Marcia Smith, Great Mills High School, Great Mills, MD

Stephanie Snook, Crestwood High School, Mantua, OH

Teri S. Summers, Colonial Heights High School, Colonial Heights, VA

Kim Swanson, Swanson School of Languages, Cincinnati, OH

Magdi S. Tadros, Wallace State College, Hanceville, Alabama

Mignon Taylor, White Oak Middle School, Cincinnati, OH

Sandy Thiernau, Rich South High School, Richton Park, IL

Gabrielle Thomas, Judge Memorial Catholic High School, Salt Lake City, UT

Berthe M. Vandenberg, West Ottawa Senior High School, Holland, MI

Rita Cholet White, Visitation Academy, St. Louis, MO

Patricia Young, Greenville High School, Greenville, IL

Jerauld Zahner, Seymour High School, Payson, IL

Gretchen Zick, Thunder Bay Junior High, Alpena, MI

Photo Credits

Cover: Kelly Stribling Sutherland, *First Love*, original acrylic.

Abbreviations: top (t), bottom (b), left (l), right (r), center (c)

Abraham, Bob/The Stock Market: 226

Air France/Documentation Française: 235

ALMASY/Documentation Française: 324

Antoniadis, Leonardo/Documentation Française: 159 (b), 387

Art Institute of Chicago, The, Gustave Caillebotte, French, 1848-1894, Paris Street; Rainy Day, oil on canvas, 1876/77, 212.2 x 276.2 cm, Charles H. and Mary F. S. Worcester Collection, 1964.336: 100 (b)

Art Resource: 327

Barnes, David/The Stock Market: 228 (b)

Bertrand, J./Leo de Wys Inc.: 356 (b)

Bider, Vic/Leo de Wys Inc.: 125

Billings, Henry: vi (t)

Bock, Ed/The Stock Market: 105 (b), 110 (t), 408

Bognar, Tibor/The Stock Market: xii (t)

Boschung, Danilo/Leo de Wys Inc.: 25

Brittany Ferries Photo Library: 180, 181, 182, 192, 193, 195 (t)

Bulloz: 310 (b)

Burgess, Michele: xii (b)

Cavalli, Angelo/Leo de Wys Inc.: 368

Christensen/Sipa Press: 94 (r), 106 (t)

CNES/Documentation Française: 224, 233 (t)

Commission Canadienne du Tourisme: 29 (t)

Communauté urbaine de Québec: 47

d'Angelo, J. J./Eurostar/SNCF-CAV/Documentation Française: 230 (b)

Damm, Fridmar/Leo de Wys Inc.: xiv

Danson, Andrew/Commission Canadienne du Tourisme: 33

de Wys, Leo/IFA/Leo de Wys Inc.: 26, 38 (t), 96, 154, 159 (t)

de Wys, Leo/Sipa/Frilet/Leo de Wys Inc.: 127

de Wys, Leo/Sipa/Fritz/Leo de Wys Inc.: 148

Dewarez, Patrick/Documentation Française: 245, 389 (t)

Disario, Donna/The Stock Market: 137

Documentation Française: 262-63

Downie, G./Visual Contact: 100 (t)

Edgeworth, Anthony/The Stock Market: 345 (t)

Feingersh, Jon/The Stock Market: 79, 102, 103

Flipper, Florent/Unicorn Stock Photos: 7 (t), 166 (b), 113, 277

Fralin, Alfred: 314 (c)

Freda, T./Visual Contact: 178-79

Fried, Robert: iv (b), vi (bl), viii-ix (t), ix (t), xiii (l), 5 (t), 15, 63, 149 (t), 183, 213, 220 (t), 269 (t), 273, 292, 294, 304 (tr), 306, 312, 314 (b), 316, 333 (b), 354 (t), 356 (t), 359, 382-83

Garnett, R./Visual Contact: 205

Gerda, Paul/Leo de Wys Inc.: 252 (b)

Gibson, Keith: 55 (t), 56 (t), 77 (t), 114, 142, 168, 195 (b), 210, 220 (b), 224 (b), 240 (b), 246 (b), 255, 270 (t), 275, 282, 287, 288, 293, 299, 390

Ginies/Sipa Press: 98 (br)

Giraudon/Art Resource: 304 (bl, br), 305 (t), 310 (t), 314 (t), 322 (cr)

Gorbun, Richard/Leo de Wys Inc.: 161 (t)

Greenberg, Jeff/Leo de Wys Inc.: 166 (t), 253, 335 (b)

Simmons, Ben/The Stock Market: 110 (b)

Simson, David: v, vi (br), vii, xiii (r), 2, 5 (b), 6, 7 (l), 8 (b), 9 (b), 10, 11, 12 (t, b), 13 (t, b), 16 (t, c, b), 17, 18, 19, 22, 34, 36, 41, 46, 49 (t), 66 (b), 67, 68, 74 (t), 78, 80 (t, b), 82, 94 (l), 106 (b), 108, 111, 123 (t), 129 (t, b), 130, 139, 164 (t), 169, 191 (b), 201, 223 (t, b), 228 (t), 229, 235 (t), 237, 239, 240 (t), 246 (t), 250, 252 (t), 254, 258, 264, 270 (b), 271, 272, 274, 280 (t, b), 283, 284 (t, b), 285, 286, 289, 290, 291, 301 (t, b), 302, 303, 317, 319, 332, 335 (t), 345 (b), 366, 371, 373, 381 (t, b), 388 (b), 389 (b), 392, 394, 396, 407, 416, 417

Sipa Press: 98 (t)

Société du parc des îles/Office des congrès et du tourisme du grand Montréal: 37

St. Jacques, Pierre/Commission Canadienne du Tourisme: xviii-1, 28 (c, b), 38 (b), 49 (b)

Steedman, Richard/The Stock Market: 105 (t)

Stefan, Claude/MAE/Documentation Française: 116

Sternberg, Will: x (t), 9 (t), 20, 39, 40, 83, 84, 85, 92, 109, 118, 123 (b), 126 (b), 128, 152 (b), 165, 176 (t, b), 189 (b), 238, 260, 261 (b), 268, 315, 370, 372, 391

Stock Market, The: 8 (t)

Straiton, Ken/The Stock Market: 29 (b)

Tauqueur, Siegfried/Leo de Wys Inc.: 107, 126 (t), 191 (t)

Tellus Vision AB: 152 (t), 153, 209, 334, 344, 369 (b), 404

Tremsal, J. M.: 348, 354 (b), 365

Uemura, Masa/Leo de Wys Inc.: iv (t)

Vaillancourt, Sarah: 50-51, 55 (b), 59 (t, b), 63, 73, 76 (t, c), 90, 93, 98 (bl), 101 (t, b), 117, 121 (t, b), 143, 144, 145, 177, 184, 232, 234, 267, 400, 406

van Beek, Bas/Leo de Wys Inc.: 52

Vidler, Steve/Leo de Wys Inc.: 402

Vignal, B./SNCF-CAV/Documentation Française: 212

Additional Credits

Bromhead, Alison and Pat MacLagan, *In France*, EMC Publishing (photo): 313
European Commission (illustrations): 75, 89
Flash Medias (map): 185
Fondation Brigitte Bardot (form): 252
Fondation Brigitte Bardot (newsletter): 246
Fondation Brigitte Bardot (photo): 225
Galeries Lafayette (diagram): 288
Greater Quebec Area Tourism and Convention Bureau (brochure): 29-30
Ionesco, Eugène, *La cantatrice chauve*, Éditions Gallimard, Paris (play): 214-17
L'Officiel des Spectacles, March 19-25, 1997 (film summary): 118
L'Officiel des Spectacles, September 17-23, 1997 (advertisement): 116
L'Officel des Spectacles, September 17-23, 1997 (cover): 114
L'Officiel des Spectacles, September 17-23, 1997 (film summaries): 115-16
L'Officiel des Spectacles, September 17-23, 1997 (theater listings): 117-18
L'Officiel des Spectacles, September 17-23, 1997 (TV page): 104
LeForestier, Catherine and Maxime, "Comme un Arbre," Éditions Coïncidences,
     1973 (song): 256-57
Le Printemps (photo): 287
Malle, Louis, *Au revoir, les enfants*, Éditions Gallimard, Paris (screenplay): 132-33
Médecins Sans Frontières (article): 248
Médecins Sans Frontières (form): 249
Médecins Sans Frontières (photos): 225, 243
Office de tourisme d'Avignon (monument and museum guide): 403
Office de tourisme d'Avignon (map): 401
Office des Congrès et du Tourisme du Grand Montréal (map): 32
Opéra de Paris Garnier (brochure): 95
Oyônô-Mbia, Guillaume, *Trois Prétendants, un Mari*, Éditions CLE, Yaoundé,
     Cameroon: 375-77
Parc des Îles de Montréal (map): 25
Prévert, Jacques, "Déjeuner du matin" in *Paroles*, Éditions Gallimard, Paris
     (poem): 86-87
Prévert, Jacques, "Le Cancre" in *Paroles*, Éditions Gallimard, Paris (poem): 88
RATP ("Carte Orange" and "Paris Visite" card): 60
RATP (R.E.R. map): 58
RATP (brochure): 59
Rochefort, Christiane, *Les petits enfants du siècle* in *Easy Readers* series (a B-Level
     Book), EMC/Paradigm Publishing (novel): 296-97
Sempé, Jean-Jacques and René Goscinny, "La plage, c'est chouette" in *Les
     vacances du petit Nicolas*, Éditions Denoël, Paris (story): 44-45
Tourisme Québec (advertisement): 202
Tourisme Québec (tourist information): 204-5
VIA (timetable): 207

We have attempted to locate owners of copyright materials used in this book. If
an error or omission has occurred, EMC/Paradigm Publishing will acknowledge
the contribution in subsequent printings.